NEURAL NETWORKS FOR INSTRUMENTATION, MEASUREMENT AND RELATED INDUSTRIAL APPLICATIONS

NATO Science Series

A series presenting the results of scientific meetings supported under the NATO Science Programme.

The series is published by IOS Press and Kluwer Academic Publishers in conjunction with the NATO Scientific Affairs Division.

Sub-Series

I.	Life and Behavioural Sciences	IOS Press
II.	Mathematics, Physics and Chemistry	Kluwer Academic Publishers
III.	Computer and Systems Sciences	IOS Press
IV.	Earth and Environmental Sciences	Kluwer Academic Publishers
V.	Science and Technology Policy	IOS Press

The NATO Science Series continues the series of books published formerly as the NATO ASI Series.

The NATO Science Programme offers support for collaboration in civil science between scientists of countries of the Euro-Atlantic Partnership Council. The types of scientific meeting generally supported are "Advanced Study Institutes" and "Advanced Research Workshops", although other types of meeting are supported from time to time. The NATO Science Series collects together the results of these meetings. The meetings are co-organized by scientists from NATO countries and scientists from NATO's Partner countries – countries of the CIS and Central and Eastern Europe.

Advanced Study Institutes are high-level tutorial courses offering in-depth study of latest advances in a field.
Advanced Research Workshops are expert meetings aimed at critical assessment of a field, and identification of directions for future action.

As a consequence of the restructuring of the NATO Science Programme in 1999, the NATO Science Series has been re-organized and there are currently five sub-series as noted above. Please consult the following web sites for information on previous volumes published in the series, as well as details of earlier sub-series:

http://www.nato.int/science
http://www.wkap.nl
http://www.iospress.nl
http://www.wtv-books.de/nato_pco.htm

Series III: Computer and Systems Sciences - Vol. 185 ISSN: 1387-6694

Neural Networks for Instrumentation, Measurement and Related Industrial Applications

Edited by

Sergey Ablameyko

Institute of Engineering Cybernetics,
National Academy of Sciences of Belarus, Belarus

Liviu Goras

Department of Fundamental Electronics,
Technical University of Iasi, Romania

Marco Gori

Department of Information Engineering,
University of Siena, Italy

and

Vincenzo Piuri

Department of Information Technologies,
University of Milan, Italy

IOS Press

Ohmsha

Amsterdam • Berlin • Oxford • Tokyo • Washington, DC

Published in cooperation with NATO Scientific Affairs Division

Proceedings of the NATO Advanced Study Institute on
Neural Networks for Instrumentation, Measurement and Related Industrial Applications
9 – 20 October 2001
Crema, Italy

ISBN 1 58603 303 4 (IOS Press)
ISBN 4 274 90553 5 C3055 (Ohmsha)
Library of Congress Control Number: 2002113599

Publisher
IOS Press
Nieuwe Hemweg 6B
1013 BG Amsterdam
Netherlands
fax: +31 20 620 3419
e-mail: order@iospress.nl

Distributor in the UK and Ireland
IOS Press/Lavis Marketing
73 Lime Walk
Headington
Oxford OX3 7AD
England
fax: +44 1865 75 0079

Distributor in the USA and Canada
IOS Press, Inc.
5795-G Burke Centre Parkway
Burke, VA 22015
USA
fax: +1 703 323 3668
e-mail: iosbooks@iospress.com

Distributor in Germany, Austria and Switzerland
IOS Press/LSL.de
Gerichtsweg 28
D-04103 Leipzig
Germany
fax: +49 341 995 4255

Distributor in Japan
Ohmsha, Ltd.
3-1 Kanda Nishiki-cho
Chiyoda-ku, Tokyo 101-8460
Japan
fax: +81 3 3233 2426

PRINTED IN THE NETHERLANDS

Preface

The aims of this book are to disseminate wider and in-depth theoretical and practical knowledge about neural networks in measurement, instrumentation and related industrial applications, to create a clear consciousness about the effectiveness of these techniques as well as the measurement and instrumentation application problems in industrial environments, to stimulate the theoretical and applied research both in the neural networks and in the industrial sectors, and to promote the practical use of these techniques in the industry.

This book is derived from the exciting and challenging experience of the NATO Advanced Study Institute on Neural Networks for Instrumentation, Measurement, and Related Industrial Applications – NIMIA'2001, held in Crema, Italy, from 9 to 20 October 2001. During this meeting the lecturers and the attendees had the opportunity of learning and discussing the theoretical foundations and the practical use of neural technologies for measurement systems and industrial applications. This book aims to expand the audience of this meeting for wider and more durable benefits.

The editors of this book are very grateful to the lecturers of NIMIA'2001, who greatly contributed to the success of the meeting and to making this book an outstanding starting point for further dissemination of the meeting achievements.

The editors would also like to thank NATO for having generously sponsored NIMIA'2001 and the publication of this book. Special thanks are due to Dr. F. Pedrazzini, the PEST Programme Director, for his highly valuable suggestions and guidance in organizing and running the meeting.

A final thank you to the staff at IOS Press, who made the realization of this book much easier.

The Editors

Sergey ABLAMEYKO
Institute of Engineering Cybernetics, National Academy of Sciences of Belarus
Surganova Str. 6, 220012 Minsk, Belarus

Liviu GORAS
Department of Fundamental of Electronics, Technical University of Iasi
Copou Blvd 11, 6600 Iasi, Romania

Marco GORI
Department of Information Engineering, Universita' degli Studi di Siena
via Roma 56, 53100 Siena, Italy

Vincenzo PIURI
Department of Information Technologies, University of Milan
via Bramante 65, 26013 Crema, Italy

Acknowledgements

The ASI NIMIA'2001 was sponsored by

NATO – North-Atlantic Treaty Organization (Grant No. PST.ASI.977440)

and organized with the technical cooperation of

IEEE I&MS – IEEE Instrumentation and Measurement Society
IEEE NNC – IEEE Neural Network Council,
INNS – International Neural Network Society
ENNS – European Neural Network Society
IAPR TC3 – International Association for Pattern Recognition – Technical Committee on Neural Networks & Computational Intelligence
EUREL – Convention of National Societies of Electrical Engineers of Europe
AEI – Italian Association of Electrical and Electronic Engineers
SIREN – Italian Association for Neural Networks
AI*IA – Italian Association for Artificial Intelligence
UNIMI DTI – University of Milan – Department of Information Technologies

Contents

Neural Networks for Instrumentation, Measurement and Related Industrial Applications
S. Ablameyko et al. (Eds.)
IOS Press, 2003

Chapter 1
Introduction to Neural Networks for Instrumentation, Measurement, and Industrial Applications

Vincenzo PIURI
Department of Information Technologies, University of Milan
via Bramante 65, 26013 Crema, Italy

Sergey ABLAMEYKO
Institute of Engineering Cybernetics, National Academy of Sciences of Belarus
Surganova Str. 6, 220012 Minsk, Belarus

1.1. The scientific and application motivations

Instrumentation and measurement play a relevant role in any industrial applications. Without sensors, transducers, converters, acquisition channels, signal processing, image processing, no measurement system and procedure will exist and, in turn, no industry will actually exist. They are in fact the irreplaceable foundation of any monitoring and automatic control system as well as for any diagnosis and quality assurance.

A deep and wide knowledge about techniques and technologies concerning measurement components and systems becomes more and more necessary to deal with the increasing complexity of nowadays systems: pillars of the modern factories, machinery, and products. This is particularly critical when non-linear complex dynamic behavior is envisioned, when system functionalities, components and interactions are numerous, and when it is difficult to specify completely and accurately the system behavior in a formal way. On this base practitioners can build effective and efficient industrial applications.

In the last decade neural networks have been widely explored as an alternative computational paradigm able to overcome some of the main design problems occurring with the traditional modeling approaches [1-22]. They have been proved effective and suited to specify systems for which an accurate and complete analytical description is difficult to derive or has an unmanageable complexity, while the solution can often be described quite easily by examples. Adaptivity and flexibility as well as system description by examples are of high importance for the theoretical and applied scientific researches. These studies and their applications allow for enhancing the quality of production processes and products both in high-technology industries and in embedded systems for our daily life. Consequently, the impact on the industry competitiveness and the quality of life is high. Besides, they open also new perspective and technological solutions that may increase the application areas and provide new markets and new opportunities of employment.

The experiences performed in the academy as well as in advanced industry largely verified the suitability and -in some cases- the superiority of the neural network approaches. Many practical problems in different industrial, technological, and scientific areas benefit from the extensive use of these technologies to achieve innovative, advanced or better solutions. A number of results concerning the use of neural techniques are known in different applications, encompassing intelligent sensors and acquisition systems, system models, signal processing, image processing, automatic control systems, and diagnosis.

1.2. The scientific and application objective

These results have been presented in many conferences and books, both discussing theoretical aspects and application areas. However, researches and experimental application was usually confined in their own specific theoretical area or application with limited broader perspective through the whole industrial exploitation so as to benefit from possible synergies and analogies about achieved results. And, more important, measurement and metrological issues have not been sufficiently addressed by researchers to assess the solution quality, to allow accurate comparison to traditional methods. Industry needs to rely on solid foundation also for these advanced solutions: this greatly conditions acceptance and use of neural methodologies in the industry.

The 2001 NATO Advanced Study Institute on Neural Networks for Instrumentation, Measurement, and Related Industrial Applications (NIMIA'2001), held in Crema, Italy, on 9-21 October 2001, succeeded in filling the gap in the knowledge of researchers and practitioners, specialized either in industrial areas, or in applications, or in metrological issues, or in neural network methodologies, but without a comprehensive view of the whole set of interdependent issues.

The interdisciplinary view -through theoretical and applied research issues as well as through industrial application issues and requirements- focused on the metrological characterization and prospective of the neural technologies. This was the most relevant and original aspect of NIMIA'2001, never really and in-depth afforded in other meetings, conferences, and academic programs.

The international interest of the scientific and industrial communities in NIMIA'2001 is proved by the technical cooperation of the IEEE Instrumentation and Measurement Society (the worldwide engineering association for instrumentation, measurement, and related industrial applications), as well as the IEEE Neural Network Council, the INNS - International Neural Network Society, and the ENNS - European Neural Network Society (the most re-known and largest international scientific/technological non-profit associations concerned with neural networks). Also the following associations, specialized in scientific or technological areas, gave their technical cooperation: IAPR TC3 - International Association for Pattern Recognition: Technical Committee on Neural Networks & Computational Intelligence, EUREL - Convention of National Societies of Electrical Engineers of Europe, AEI - Italian Association of Electrical and Electronic Engineers: Specialistic Group on Computer Science Technology & Appliances, AIIA - Italian Association for Artificial Intelligence, SIREN - Italian Association for Neural Networks, and UNIMI-DTI - University of Milan: Department of Information Technologies.

This book, authored by the lecturers of NIMIA'2001 and edited by its directors, is one of the immediate follow up of the meeting. The first objective of the book is to consolidate the material presented during the meeting and the results of the discussions with attendees in a comprehensive and hopmogeneous reference. The second goal is to produce a tangible media for wider dissemination of this advanced knowledge and the related achievements:

the aim of the meeting was in fact not limited only to the direct interaction with the attendees, but directed also to bring this knowledge to the attention of a world-wide audience.

1.3. The book organization

Like NIMIA'2001, this book presents the basic issues concerning the neural networks for sensors and measurement systems, for identification in instrumentation and measurement, for instrumentation and measurement dedicated to system and plant control, and for signal and image processing in instrumentation and measurement. The underlying and unifying wire of the presentation is the interdisciplinary and comprehensive point of view of the metrological perspective. Besides, it focus on the use, the benefits, and the problems of neural technologies in instrumentation and measurement for some relevant application areas. This allows for a vertical analysis in the specific industrial area, encompassing different theoretical, technological, and implementation aspects: the specific application areas of instrumentation and measurement based on neural technologies are diagnosis, robotics, laser processing, electrical measurement systems, virtual environments, and medical systems.

Each chapter focuses on a specific topic. Presentation starts from the basic issues, the techniques, the design methodologies, and the application problems. First it tackles the theoretical and practical issues concerning the use of neural networks to enhance quality, characteristics, and performance of the traditional approaches and solutions. Then, it provides an overview of the industrial relevance and impact of the neural techniques by means of a structured presentation of several industrial examples.

The program structure of NIMIA'2001 made it a unique and successful forum for interactive discussion directed to higher dissemination of innovative knowledge, stimulation of interdisciplinary research as well as application, better understanding of the technological opportunities, advancement of the educational consciousness about the relevance of the metrological aspects for applicability to industry, promotion of the practical use of these techniques in the industry, and overall advancement of industry and products. Each and every participant had his own contribution from his specific knowledge to bring to the scientific and practitioner communities for mutual benefit and synergy.

This book aims to extend these benefits to all experts in the neural network areas as well as in metrology and in the industrial applications, for mutual sharing of in-deepth interdisciplinary knowledge and to support further advancements both of the neural disciplines and the industrial application opportunities.

1.4. The book topics

From the NIMIA'2001 experience, this book tackles some of the most relevant areas in the use of neural networks for advanced instrumentation, measurement procedures and related industrial applications.

The first six chapters are dedicated to general issues and methodologies for the use of neural networks in any application area: namely, sensors and measurement systems, system identification, system control, signal processing, and image processing.

The first and basic issue to understand the significance and the usefulness of any quantity observed in a system consists of characterizing that quantity from the metrological point of view. This is the target of Chapter 2. The analysis of sensors, transducers, acquisition systems, analog-to-digital converters, and measurement procedures is in fact required to identify the accuracy of the measured quantity and its relevance for the subsequent use in the applications.

In Chapter 3, neural networks are shown effectively to enhance quality and performance of sensors and measurement systems. In particular, they are proved appropriate to implement sensor linearization, advanced sensors, high-level sensors, sensor fusion, and self-calibration. Design and implementation of systems including sensors and measurement procedures are discussed by tackling all requirements and constraints in a homogeneous framework, encompassing conventional algorithmic approaches and neural components.

In any application the key issue is modeling: Chapter 4 tackles this issue. To solve an application problem we always need to create a model of the envisioned system and figure out a procedure to identify the solution within such a model. In industrial monitoring and control as well as in environmental monitoring, embedded systems, robotics, automotive, avionics and much many other applications, we need to extract a model of the monitored or controlled equipment, system, or environment in order to generate the appropriate actions. The theoretical issues concerning model identification is discussed, as well as the use of conventional techniques. Intrinsic non-linearities of the neural networks make these model families and their ability of static/dynamic configuration an attractive approach to tackle the identification of complex non-linear systems, possibly with dynamic behavior. Neural models, methodologies and techniques are presented to solve this problem and comparisons with other methods are discussed. Some relevant examples point out benefits and drawbacks of neural modeling, especially in industrial environments.

In industrial applications as well as in many systems for the daily life automatic control is a vital part of the system in order to allows for an autonomous and predictable behavior. Many conventional techniques are available in the literature to solve this problem. However, for some complex non-linear cases and for some dynamic systems the conventional solutions are not efficient, accurate, or manageable, while neural networks were proved superior, especially when it is difficult to extract a complete analytical model of the system or when the statistical models are not accurate enough on the whole operating range. Theoretical aspects of neural tracking, direct and inverse control as well as reinforcement learning are discussed in Chapter 5. Some applications are also presented and evaluated to derive some comparative analysis of costs and benefits of neural control with respect to other conventional approaches.

Signal analysis and processing is a relevant area for different applications. In particular, the noise removal is used to enhance the signal quality, signal function approximation is relevant to analyze and understand signals, feature extraction is fundamental to create high-abstraction sensors, and prediction from static and time data series is attractive to foresee the signal behavior. Theoretical issues and some application examples are presented and analyzed in Chapter 6 with specific concern to chaotic time series processing. Comparisons with conventional solutions are also discussed.

Image processing is an important technological area for many industrial and daily-life applications. Noise removal is fundamental to clean the pictures and improve the quality with respect to the visual sensing units. Feature extraction is used to extract high-level information in order to create and capture new knowledge from raw images. Vision systems are useful to guide mobile robotic systems and as driving aids in automotive applications. Character and pattern recognition are useful in a large number of application areas as automatic approaches to perform repetitive recognition tasks in noisy and variable environments (e.g., banking, optical character recognition). Neural networks are shown effective and accurate tools to deal with the low-level image processing operations as well as with the high-level aspects in Chapter 7.

On the basis of these general technologies and methodologies, some specific application areas are then discussed in detail: namely, diagnosis, robotics, industrial laser processing, electrical and dielectrical applications, virtual environments, and medical applications. These cases have particular relevance from the industrial point of view since they constitute the leading edge for many manufacturing processes and are promising solutions for today and future applications.

System diagnosis is a recent application area that largely benefit from the inference and generalization mechanisms provided by the neural networks. Chapter 8 tackles this application area. A non-intrusive approach based on signal and image processing to detect the presence of end-of-production defects and operating-life faults as well as to classify them is highly beneficial for many industrial applications both to enhance the quality of production processes and products, e.g., in avionics, automotive, mechanics, and electronics. The basic issues of using neural networks to create high-level sensors in this application area are shown and evaluated with respect to conventional approaches.

Robotics has many opportunities to make use of neural networks to tackle some major problems concerning sensing and the related applications like control, signal and image processing, vision, motion planning, and multi-agent coordination. Chapter 9 is dedicated to this area. The neural techniques are well suited for the non-linearity of these tasks as well as the need of adaptation to unknown scenarios. The integrated use of these methods also in conjunction with conventional components was discussed and evaluated. Evolutionary and adaptive solutions will make even more attractive the use of robotic systems in industry and in the daily life (domotics and elder/disabled people assistance), especially whenever the operating environment is partially or largely unknown.

Industrial laser processing is an innovative production process for many application fields. The undoubted superior quality of laser cutting, drilling, and welding with respect to conventional processes makes this technology highly appreciated in high-technology industries (e.g., electronics) as well as in mass production (e.g., mechanical industry, automotive). The problems related to real-time control the laser processing and to quality monitoring are discussed in Chapter 10. The use of neural techniques is presented as a highly innovative solution that outperforms other approaches thanks to intrinsic adaptivity and generalization ability.

Electrical and dielectrical applications are one of the fields in which neural technologies were widely and successfully used since some years. Chapter 11 is dedicated to this topic. Electric signal analysis is important to evaluate the quality and the behavior of power supply and, consequently, to monitor and control power plants and distribution networks. Prediction of power load is another application that benefits from neural prediction ability to foresee the expected power needs and act in advance on power generators and distribution. Signal analysis is an innovative aspect of monitoring, control and diagnosis for electric engines and transformers. Observation of partial discharges in dielectrical materials and systems is relevant to guarantee the correct operation of capacitors and insulators. These aspects are widely discussed and compared with conventional approaches in the chapter.

Virtual environments are one of the most recent areas that are becoming important in the industrial and economic scenario. They can be used for simulated reality, e.g., in telecommunication (e.g., videoconferencing), training on complex systems, complex system design (e.g., or robotic systems), electronic commerce, interactive video, entertainment, and remote medical diagnosis and surgery. Adaptivity and generalization ability of neural networks allow for introducing advanced features in these environments and to cope with non-linear aspects, dynamic variations of the operating conditions, and evolving environments. The use of neural networks and their benefits are analyzed and evaluated in Chapter 12.

Medical applications had and will have great expansion by using adaptive solutions based on neural networks. In fact it is relatively easy to collect examples for many of these applications, while it is practically impossible to derive a conventional algorithm having the same efficiency and accuracy. Neural networks are able to analyze biomedical signals, e.g., in electrocardiogram, encephalogram, breath monitoring, and neural system. Feature extraction and prediction by neural networks are relevant tools to monitor and foresee human conditions for advanced health care. Neural image analysis can be used for image reconstruction and enhancement. Prosthesis include neural component to provide a more natural behavior; artificial senses (hearing, vision, odor, taste, tact) can be also exploited in robotics and industrial applications. Diagnostic equipment made impressive advancements especially by using signal and image processing for non-intrusive scanning. These are the main cases considered and discussed in Chapter 13.

1.5. The socio-economical implications

Training researchers and practitioners from several theoretical and application areas on neural networks for measurement, instrumentation and related industrial applications is important since these topics have and will have a major role in developing new theoretical background as well as further scientific advancement and implementation of new practical solutions, encompassing -among many others- embedded systems and intelligent manufacturing systems.

Training of researchers and practitioners is an investment for the advancement of science and industry that will be paid back in the near future by the technological advancement in knowledge, production processes, and products. This will allow in fact to maintain, to expand or even to achieve a leading role in the international scenario. From this training will in particular benefit the less favorite economic areas: coming in contact with the leading experts and the most advanced technologies will be useful for the economic and industrial advancement, for enhancing their worldwide competitiveness, and for creating new job opportunities.

NIMIA'2001 and this book aim to highly contribute to the above goals. NIMIA'2001 had high relevance for training researchers and practitioners since leading scientists and practitioners were gathered from around the world. This allowed the attendees to have wide and in-depth scientific and technical discussions with them for a better understanding of innovative topics and sharing of innovative knowledge. The authors and the editors of this book wish that it can be useful to much more people around the world.

The increasing industrial interest and the possibility of successful industrial application of soft computing technologies for advanced products and enhanced production processes provide a great opportunity to highly trained researchers and practitioners to find a job or enhance their position. A better understanding and knowledge about the book topics will result in better opportunities for developing the industry, for expanding the employment, and for enhancing the employment quality and remuneration. The authors and the editors wish that this book will have therefore a great impact on the career of researchers and practitioners, especially of the young ones.

Continuous education and worldwide dissemination are additional issues that need to be considered in order to enhance and expand the benefits provided by higher training in the topics of this book. NIMIA'2001 was the starting point that allowed for coordinating, homogenizing, and consolidating educational efforts on neural technologies for instrumentation, measurement, and related industrial applications. This book, conference tutorials, e-learning environments, and courses for the industry and in the university will open additional perspectives to researchers and practitioners to stay on the leading edge of science, technology, and applications.

Interactions occurred during NIMIA'2001 and through continuous educational programs derived from this meeting as well as this book have also a relevant social impact. They in fact allowed and will allow for establishing new reciprocal confidence and understanding as well as to know and appreciate new possible partners and to create long lasting friendships and cooperations. All of the above will be useful for positive globalization and link strengthening, as well as to consolidate worldwide relationships and peace through personal friendships, scientific cooperation and industrial joint ventures.

References

[1] R.Hecht-Nielsen, *Neurocomputing*. Reading, MA: Addison-Wesley, 1990.

[2] T.Khanna, *Foundations of Neural Networks*. Reading, MA: Addison-Wesley, 1990.

[3] A.Maren, C.Harston, R.Pap, *Handbook of Neural Computing Applications*. San Diego, CA: Academic Press, 1990.

[4] J.Hertz, A.Krogh, R.G.Palmer, *Introduction to the Theory of Neural Computation*. Redwood City, CA: Addison-Wesley, 1991.

[5] J.A.Anderson, A.Pellionisz, E.Rosenfeld, Eds., *Neurocomputing 2: Directions for Research*. Cambridge, MA: MIT Press, 1990.

[6] E.Gelenbe, Ed., *Neural Networks Advances and Applications, 2*. Amsterdam, The Netherlands: Elsevier Science Publishers, B.V., 1992.

[7] E.Sanchez-Sinencio, C.Lau, *Artificial Neural Networks*. IEEE Press, 1992.

[8] J.M.Zurada, *Introduction to Artificial Neural Systems*. St.Paul, MN: West Publishing Company, 1992.

[9] L. Fausett, *Fundamentals of Neural Networks*. Prentice Hall, Englewood Cliffs, 1994.

[10] S.Haykin, *Neural Networks: A Comprehensive Foundation*. New York: Mcamillan and IEEE Computer Society, 1994.

[11] D.R.Baughmann Y.A.Liu, *Neural Networks in Bioprocessing and Chemical Engineering*. San Diego, CA: Academic, 1995.

[12] C. M. Bishop, *Neural Networks for Pattern Recognition*. Oxford: Clarendon-Press, 1995.

[13] F.U.Dowla, L.L.Rogers, *Solving Problems in Environmental Engineering and Geosciensces with Artificial Neural Networks*. Cambridge, MA: MIT Press, 1995.

[14] M.H.Hassoun, *Fundamentals of Artificial Neural Networks*. Cambridge, MA: MIT Press, 1995.

[15] K.-Y.Siu, V.Roychowdhury, T.Kailath, *Discrete Neural Computation: A Theoretical Foundation*. Englewood Cliffs, NJ: Prentice-Hall, 1995.

[16] B. D. Ripley, *Pattern Recognition and Neural Networks*. Cambridge: Cambridge University Press, 1996.

[17] S. Haykin, *Neural networks: a comprehensive foundation*. New Jersey, USA: Prentice Hall, 1999.

[18] M. Mohammadian, ed., *Computational Intelligence for Modelling, Control and Automation: Intelligent Image Processing, Data Analysis & Information Retrieval*, vol. 56. Amsterdam, The Netherlands: IOS Press, 1999.

[19] E. Oja and S. Kaski, *Kohonen Maps*. Amsterdam: Elsevier, 1999.

[20] E. Micheli-Tzanakou, *Supervised and Unsupervised Pattern Recognition: Feature Extraction and Computational Intelligence*. Boca Raton, FL, USA: CRC Press, 2000.

[21] T. Kohonen, *Self-Organizing Maps*, vol. 30 of *Springer Series in Information Sciences*. Berlin, Heidelberg, New York: Springer, 3 ed., 2001.

[22] J. Kolen and S. Kremer, *A Field Guide to Dynamical Recurrent Networks*. IEEE Press and John Wiley & Sons, Inc., 2001.

Neural Networks for Instrumentation, Measurement and Related Industrial Applications
S. Ablameyko et al. (Eds.)
IOS Press, 2003

Chapter 2
The Fundamentals of Measurement Techniques

Alessandro FERRERO
Department of Electrical Engineering, Politecnico di Milano
piazza L. da Vinci 32, 20133 Milano, Italy

Renzo MARCHESI
Department of Energetics, Politecnico di Milano
piazza L. da Vinci 32, 20133 Milano, Italy

Abstract. The experimental knowledge is the basis of the modern approach to all fields of science and technique, and the measurement activity represents the way this knowledge can be obtained. In this respect the qualification of the measurement results is the most critical point of any experimental approach. This paper provides the very fundamental definitions of the measurement science and covers the methods presently employed to qualify, from the metrological point of view, the result of a measurement. Reference is made to the recommendations presently issued by the International Standard Organizations.

2.1. The measurement concept

The concept of measurement has been deep-rooted in the human culture since the origin of civilization, as it has always represented the basis of the experimental knowledge, the quantitative assessment of goods in commercial transactions, the assertion of a right, and so on. The concept that a measurement result might not be "good" has also been well seated since the beginning, so that we can find the following recommendation in the Bible: "You shall do no unrighteousness in judgment, in measures of length, of weight, or of quantity. Just balances, just weighs, a just ephah, and a just hin shall you have" (Lev, 19, 35-36).

After Galileo Galilei put experimentation at the base of the modern science and showed that it is the only possible starting point for the validation of any scientific theory, the measurement activity has become more and more important. More than one century ago, William Thomson, Lord Kelvin, reinforced this concept by stating: "I often say that when you can measure what you are speaking about, and can express it in numbers, you know something about it; but when you cannot express it in numbers your knowledge about it is of meager and unsatisfactory kind; it may be the beginning of knowledge, but you have scarcely, in your thoughts, advanced to the stage of science, whatever the matter may be. So, therefore, if science is measurement, then without metrology there can be no science".

Under this modern vision of science, the measurement of a physical quantity is generally defined as the quantitative comparison of this same quantity with another one, which is homogeneous with the measured one, and is considered as the measurement unit. In order to perform this quantitative comparison, five agents are needed, as shown in Fig. 1.

- The measurand: it is the quantity to be measured, and it often represents a property of a physical object and is described by a suitable mathematical model.
- The standard: it is the physical realization of the measurement unit.
- The instrument: it is the physical device that performs the comparison.
- The method: the comparison between the measurand and the standard is performed by exploiting some physical phenomena (thermal dilatation, mechanical force between electric charges, and so on); according to the considered phenomenon, different methods can be implemented.
- The operator: he supervises the whole measurement process, operates the measurement devices and reads the instrument.

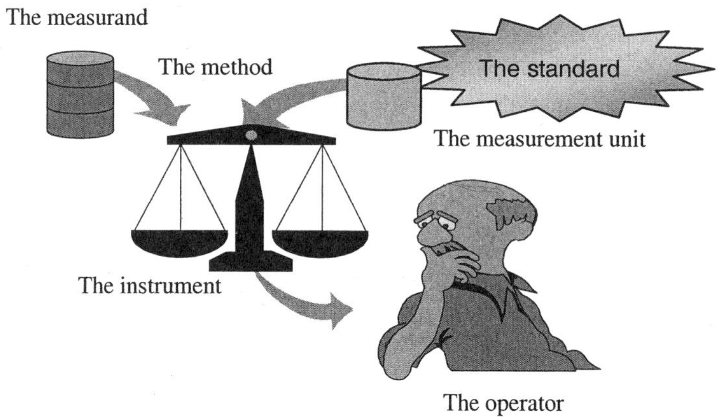

Figure 1: Representation of the measurement process together with the five agents that take part in it.

2.2. A big scientific and technical problem

Even a quick glance to the schematic representation of the measurement process shown in Fig. 1 gives clear evidence that, in practice, all five agents are not ideal. Therefore a basic question comes to the mind: can we "do no unrighteousness in ... measures of length, of weighs, or of quantity"? Can we build "just balances, just weighs, ...", even with the best will in the world? In other, more technically sound words, can we get the true value of the measurand as the result of a measurement?

The answer to this question is, of course, negative, because it can be readily realized that all five agents in Fig. 1 concur to make the measurement result different from the "true" expected value.

As far as the measurand is concerned, it must be taken into account that its knowledge is very often incomplete, and its mathematical model may therefore be incomplete as well. The state of the measurand may be not completely known, and the measurement process itself modifies the measurand state.

The second term of the comparison, the standard, does not realize the measurement unit, but only its good approximation, thus providing an approximate value of the measurement unit itself.

As for the instrument, its behavior is generally different from the ideal one because of its non ideal components, the presence of internally generated noise, the influence of the environmental conditions (temperature, humidity, electromagnetic interference, ...), the possible lack of calibration, its age, and a number of other different reasons still related to the non ideality of the instrument.

Similarly, the measurement method is usually based on the exploitation of a single physical phenomenon, whilst other phenomena may interfere with the considered one, and alter the result of the measurement in such a way that the "true" value cannot be obtained.

At last, the operator is also supposed to contribute in making the result of the measurement different from the expected "true" value because of several reasons, such as, for instance, his insufficient training, an incorrect reading of the instrument indication, an incorrect post processing of the readings, and so on.

The effects of this non-ideal behavior of the agents that take part in the measurement process can be easily experienced by repeating the same measurement procedure a number of times: the results of such measurements always differ from each other, even if the measurement conditions are not changed. Moreover, if the measurement is repeated by another operator, reproducing the same measurement conditions somewhere else, different results are obtained again. If the "true" measurement result is represented as the center of a target, as in Fig. 2, each different result of a measurement is represented as a different shoot, and measurements done by different operators under slightly different conditions can be represented as two different burst patterns on the target.

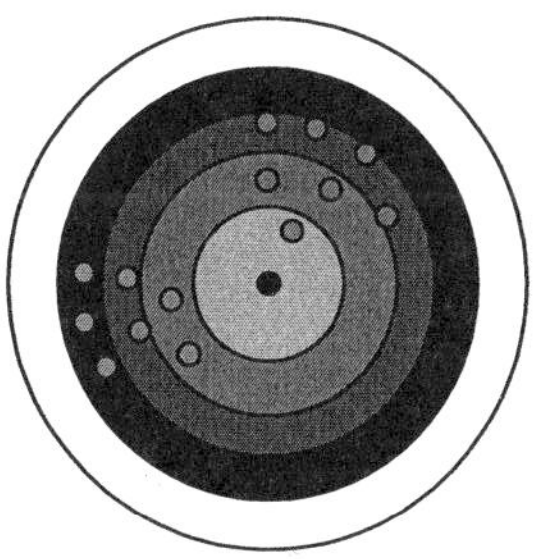

Figure 2: Graphical representation of the dispersion of the results of a measurement.

As a matter of fact, this means that expressing the result of a measurement with a single number (together with the measurement unit) is totally meaningless, because this single number cannot be supposed to represent the measured quantity in a better way than any other result obtained by repeated measurements.

Moreover, since the same result can be barely obtained as the result of a new measurement, there is no way to compare the measurement results, because they are generally always different.

This represents an unacceptable limitation of the measurement practice, since the final aim of any measurement activity is the quantitative comparison: this is not only true when technical and scientific issues are involved, where the results of measurements are compared in order to asses whether a component meets the technical specifications or not, or a theory represents a physical phenomenon in the correct way or not, but also when commercial and legal issue are involved, where quantities and qualities of goods have to be compared, or penalties have to be issued if a tolerance level is passed, and so on.

2.3. The uncertainty concept

The problem outlined in the previous section has been well known since the origin of the measurement practice, and an attempt of solution was provided, in the past, by considering the measurement error as the difference between the actual measured value and the "true" value of the measurand. However this approach is "philosophically" incorrect, since the "true" value cannot be known.

To overcome this further problem, the uncertainty concept has been introduced in the late 80's as a quantifiable attribute of the measurement, able to assess the quality of the measurement process and result. This concept comes from the awareness that when all the known or suspected components of error have been evaluated, and the appropriate corrections have been applied, there still remains an uncertainty about the correctness of the stated results, that is, a doubt about how well the result of the measurement represents the value of the quantity being measured [1].

This concept can be more precisely perceived if three general requirements are considered.

1. The method for evaluating and expressing the uncertainty of the result of a measurement should be universal, that is, it should be applicable to all kinds of measurements and all types of input data used in measurements.
2. The actual quantity used to express the uncertainty should be internally consistent and transferable. The internal consistency means that the uncertainty should be directly derived from the components that contribute to it, as well as independently on how these components are grouped, or on the decomposition of the components into subcomponents. As for transferability, it should be possible to use directly the uncertainty evaluated for one result as a component in evaluating the uncertainty of another measurement in which the first result is used.
3. The method for evaluating and expressing the uncertainty of a measurement should be capable of providing a confidence interval, that is an interval about the measurement result within which the values that could reasonably be attributed to the measurand may be expected to lie with a given level of confidence.

In 1992, the International Organization for Standardization (ISO) provided a well pondered answer to these requirements by issuing the Guide to the Expression of Uncertainty in Measurement [1], where the concept of uncertainty is defined, and operative prescriptions are given on how to estimate the uncertainty of the result of a measurement in agreement with the above requirements. More recently the Guide has been encompassed in several Standards, issued by the International (IEC) and National (UNI-CEI, DIN, AFNOR) Standard Organizations.

2.4. Uncertainty: definitions and methods for its determination

The ISO Guide defines the uncertainty of the result of a measurement as a parameter, associated with the result itself, that characterizes the dispersion of the values that could reasonably be attributed to the measurand.

The adverb "reasonably" is the key point of this definition, because it leaves a large amount of discretionary power to the operator, but it does not exempt him from following some basic guidelines that come from the state of the art of the measurement science.

These guidelines are provided by the ISO Guide itself, which outlines two different ways for expressing the uncertainty.

The first way considers the uncertainty of the result of a measurement as expressed by a standard deviation, or a given multiple of it. This means that the distribution of the possible measurement result is known, or assumptions can be made on it. If, for example, the results of a measurement are supposed to be distributed according to a normal distribution about the mean value $\bar{x}$, as shown in Fig. 3, the uncertainty can be expressed by the distribution standard deviation σ. This means that the probability that a measured value falls within the interval $(\bar{x}-\sigma, \bar{x}+\sigma)$ is the 68.3%. The uncertainty can be also expressed by a multiple 3σ of the standard deviation, so that the probability that a measured value falls within the interval $(\bar{x}-3\sigma, \bar{x}+3\sigma)$ climbs up to the 99.7%. This example shows that the third requirement in the previous section is satisfied, since it is possible to derive a confidence interval, with a given confidence level, from the estimated value of the uncertainty.

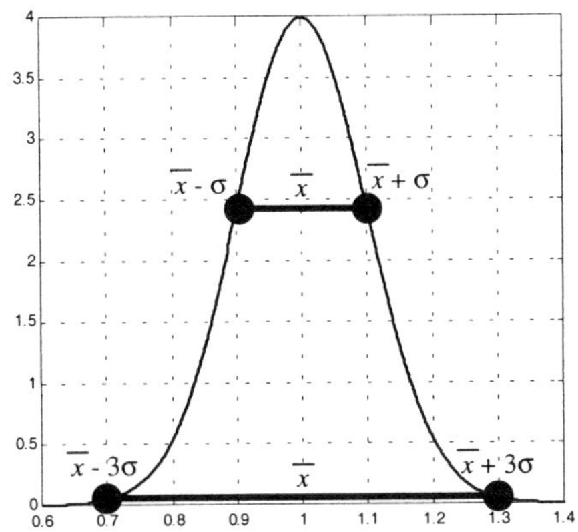

Figure 3: Example of determination of the uncertainty as a standard deviation

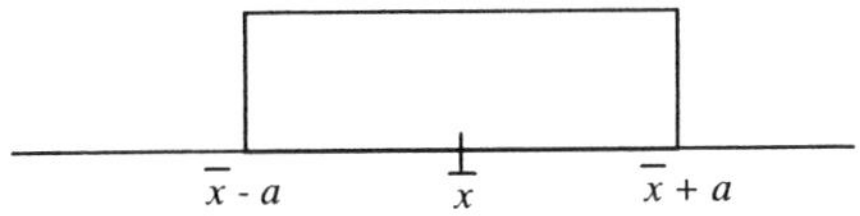

Figure 4: Example of determination of the uncertainty as a confidence interval

The second way considers the uncertainty as a confidence interval about the measured value, as shown in Fig. 4. This method is very often employed to specify the accuracy of a digital multimeter, and the width of the confidence interval is given as $a = z\%$ of reading + $y\%$ of full scale.

When the uncertainty of the measurement result x is expressed as a standard deviation it is called "standard uncertainty" and is written with the notation $u(x)$.

As far as the evaluation of the uncertainty components is concerned, the ISO Guide suggests that some components may be evaluated from the statistical distribution of the results of series of measurements and can be characterized by experimental standard deviations. Of course, this method can be applied whenever a significant number of measurement results can be obtained, by repeating the measurement procedure under the same measurement conditions.

The evaluation of the standard uncertainty by means of the statistical analysis of a series of observations is defined by the ISO Guide as the "type A evaluation".

Other components of uncertainty may be evaluated from assumed probability distributions, where the assumption may be based on experience or other information. These components are also characterized by the standard deviation of the assumed distribution. This method is applied when the measurement procedure cannot be repeated or when the confidence interval about the measurement result is a priori known, i.e. by means of calibration results.

The evaluation of the standard uncertainty by means other than the statistical analysis of a series of observations is defined by the ISO Guide as the "type B evaluation".

When the uncertainty is requested to represent an interval about the result of a measurement within which the values that could reasonably be attributed to the measurand are expected to lie with a given level of confidence, then the expanded uncertainty U is defined as the product of the standard uncertainty $u(x)$ by a suitable integer K that is called coverage factor:

$$U = K \cdot u(x) \tag{1}$$

Of course, the association of a specific level of confidence to the interval defined by the expanded uncertainty requires that explicit or implicit assumptions are made regarding the probability distribution of the measurement results. The level of confidence that may be attributed to this interval can be known only to the extent to which such assumptions may be justified.

All above considerations have been derived for the direct measurement of a single quantity and apply to the results of such a measurement. Quite often, however, the value of a quantity to be measured is obtained from a mathematical computation of the results of other measurements.

According to the second requirement reported in the above section 3, the uncertainty that has to be associated with the result of such a measurement should be obtained from the uncertainty values associated to the single measurement results employed in the evaluation of the measurand. The ISO Guide defines such uncertainty value as the "combined standard uncertainty", that is the "standard uncertainty of the result of a measurement when that result is obtained from the values of a number of other quantities, equal to the positive square root of a sum of terms, being the variances or covariances of these other quantities weighted according to how the measurement result varies with changes in these quantities".

Such a definition can be easily expressed with a mathematical equation when the result y of a measurement depends on N other results x_i, $1 \le i \le N$, of measurements, according to the relationship:

$$y = f(x_1, x_2, \ldots, x_i, \ldots, x_N) \tag{2}$$

Under this assumption, the combined standard uncertainty associated with y is given by:

$$u_c(y) = \sqrt{\sum_{i=1}^{N}\left(\frac{\partial f}{\partial x_i}\right)^2 u^2(x_i) + 2\sum_{i=1}^{N-1}\sum_{j=i+1}^{N}\frac{\partial f}{\partial x_i}\frac{\partial f}{\partial x_j}u(x_i, x_j)}, \tag{3}$$

where $u(x_i)$ is the standard uncertainty associated with the measurement result x_i, and $u(x_i, x_j) = u(x_j, x_i)$ is the estimated covariance of x_i against x_j.

If the degree of correlation between x_i and x_j is expressed in terms of the correlation coefficient:

$$r(x_i, x_j) = \frac{u(x_i, x_j)}{u(x_i)u(x_j)}, \tag{4}$$

where $r(x_i, x_j) = r(x_j, x_i)$, $-1 \le r(x_i, x_j) \le 1$, equation (3) can be slightly changed into:

$$u_c(y) = \sqrt{\sum_{i=1}^{N}\left(\frac{\partial f}{\partial x_i}\right)^2 u^2(x_i) + 2\sum_{i=1}^{N-1}\sum_{j=i+1}^{N}\frac{\partial f}{\partial x_i}\frac{\partial f}{\partial x_j}r(x_i, x_j)u(x_i)u(x_j)}. \tag{5}$$

If the measurement results x_i and x_j are totally uncorrelated, then $r(x_i, x_j) = 0$ and therefore the combined standard uncertainty is given by:

$$u_c(y) = \sqrt{\sum_{i=1}^{N} \left(\frac{\partial f}{\partial x_i} \right)^2 u^2(x_i)} \qquad (6)$$

On the contrary, if the measurement results x_i and x_j are totally correlated, then $r(x_i, x_j) = 1$. The effect of the correlation on the uncertainty estimation can be fully perceived if the following example is considered.

Let us suppose that the electric power consumed by a dc load is measured as $P = VI$, where V is the supply voltage and I is the current flowing through the load. Let us also suppose that V and I are measured by two independent DVMs, the measured value for the voltage is $V = 100$ V, with a standard uncertainty $u(V) = 0.2$ V, and the measured value for the current is $I = 2$ A, with a standard uncertainty $u(I) = 0.01$ A.

Since two independent DVMs have been considered for both voltage and current measurements, the correlation coefficient is $r(V, I) = 0$ and hence equation (6) can be used for the evaluation of the uncertainty associated with the measured value $P = 200$ W for the electric power.

It is:

$$\frac{\partial P}{\partial V} = I, \qquad \frac{\partial P}{\partial I} = V$$

and therefore the combined standard uncertainty provided by (6) is $u_c(P) = 1.08$ W.

Let us now suppose that the same DVM is used for both the voltage and current measurements, and that the uncertainty values associated to the measured values of voltage and current are exactly the same as those estimated for the previous situation. In this case the measurement are totally correlated, since the same instrument has been used. The correlation coefficient is hence $r(V, I) = 1$, equation (5) must be used and therefore the combined standard uncertainty associated with the measured value of P is $u_c(P) = 9.35$ W. The effect of an incorrect estimation of the correlation is quite evident.

2.5. How can the results of different measurements be compared?

One of the most important reasons for introducing the concept of uncertainty in measurement recalled in the previous sections is the need for comparing the results of different measurements of the same quantity. This is a quite critical problem, which is not confined to the technical field, but involves also commercial and legal issues whenever the same quantity has to be evaluated in different places in order to assess, for instance, if the delivered goods meet the specifications provided in the purchase order.

It is quite evident that the uncertainty associated with the different measurement results plays a fundamental role, since it provides confidence intervals within which the value that could be reasonably attributed to the measurand is expected to lie: it can be immediately recognized that the results of two different measurements of the same quantity can be considered as equal if the two confidence intervals defined by their uncertainty values are at least overlapping. Fig. 5 shows this concept.

In this figure the terms "compatible" and "not compatible" are used since they are generally employed instead of "equal" and "different"; in fact, the values of the measurement results can be never considered as equal or different in a strict mathematical sense. However, if the analysis of the measurement uncertainty shows that two results of two different measurements belong to the same confidence interval about the expected value of the measurand, the same results are considered as "compatible".

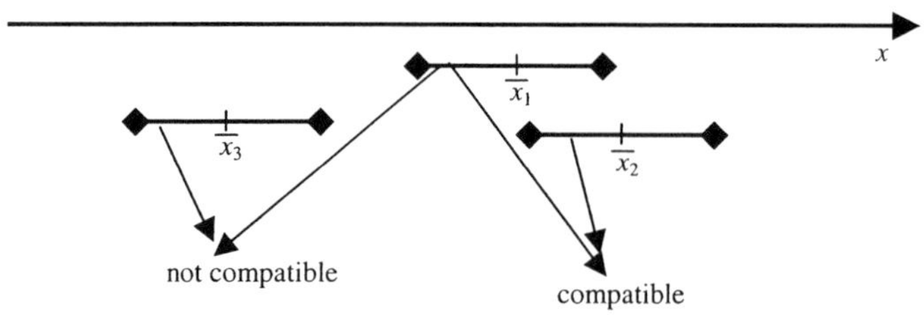

Figure 5: Example of compatible (x_1 and x_2) and non compatible (x_1 and x_3) measurement results, based on the fact that the confidence interval provided by the estimated uncertainty values are (partially) overlapping or not.

The analysis of the confidence intervals based simply on their partial overlapping in order to assess whether two measurements are compatible or not may still lead to ambiguous situations. The most common situation is that of three measurements, x_1, x_2, x_3, with the confidence interval about x_1 partially overlapping the confidence interval about x_2, and this confidence interval partially overlapping the confidence interval about x_3, but in such a way that the interval about x_1 is not overlapping the confidence interval about x_3 at all. This situation shows that x_1 is compatible with x_2, x_2 is compatible with x_3, but x_1 is not compatible with x_3. If x_1 and x_3 are not compared directly, but only through a comparison with x_2, they can be supposed to be compatible, while they are not.

In order to overcome such a problem, a new definition of compatibility is being proposed, that is becoming more and more popular among the calibration laboratories. This definition states that two measurement results x_1 and x_2, associated with the standard uncertainty values $u(x_1)$ and $u(x_2)$ respectively, are considered compatible if:

$$|x_1 - x_2| \le K \cdot \sqrt{u^2(x_1) + u^2(x_2) + 2r(x_1, x_2)u(x_1)u(x_2)}, \tag{7}$$

where $r(x_1, x_2)$ is the correlation factor between x_1 and x_2 and K is the employed coverage factor.

By comparing (7) and (5), it can be readily checked that (7) represents the combined expanded uncertainty associated with $|x_1 - x_2|$. Therefore, the two results are considered compatible when their distance is lower than the combined expanded uncertainty with which this distance can be estimated.

2.6. The role of the standard and the traceability concept

The concepts explained in the previous sections show the meaning of uncertainty in measurement and provide a few guidelines for estimating the uncertainty and compare the results of different measurements. However, one main question appears to be still open: how can be granted that the measurement result, together with the associated uncertainty value, do really characterize "the dispersion of values that could reasonably be attributed to the measurand"?

Indeed, the analysed procedures are mainly statistical computations, based on the assumption that the possible results of the measurement are distributed according to a given probability density function. This assumption is in turn based on experimental evidence or a priori knowledge, but cannot generally grant that the actual value of the measurand lies within the assumed distribution with the given confidence level.

The solution to this problem is found in the correct involvement of the standard in the measurement procedure, as shown in Fig. 1. In fact, if the result of a measurement is compared with the value of the standard, it is possible the state whether the result itself is compatible with actual value of the measurand (that is the actual value lies within the confidence interval provided by the estimated uncertainty) or not, and should hence be discarded.

The procedure that allows to compare the result of a measurement with the value of the standard is called "calibration".

The calibration can be done, of course, by direct comparison with the standard. Though this is the most accurate way to calibrate a measurement device, it is generally expensive and subject to long "waiting lists", due to the low number of standards available. Furthermore, standards are not always available for every measured quantity, and therefore the measurement result must be traced back to the values of the available standards.

An alternate calibration way is the comparison of the measurement result with the one provided by another calibrated measurement device. Of course, since an indirect comparison is performed, the uncertainty that can be assigned to the results provided by a measurement device calibrated in such a way is higher than the one that could be assigned by direct comparison with the value of the standard.

When this indirect calibration is adopted, several steps could be done before finding the direct comparison with the value of the standard: of course, the more the steps are, the higher is the uncertainty value. The property of the result of a measurement to be traced back to a standard, no matter if in a direct or indirect way, is called the "measurement traceability".

The traceability is a strict requirement when the results of different measurements performed on the same quantity with different instruments and methods have to be compared. This is the only way to assess whether the results are actually compatible or not.

The compliance with this requirement has a great importance also from the commercial and legal point of view. In fact, since all national standards are compatible with each other, when the result of a measurement is traced to its national standard, it is also traced to the standards of any other Country whose standard is recognized by the International Standard Organization. This avoids, for instance, the need for doubling the measurement procedures in commercial transactions.

2.7. Conclusions

The very fundamental concepts of the measurement technique have been briefly reported in this paper. The key role played by the uncertainty concept has been emphasized as the only possible way to characterize the result of a measurement and define a confidence interval within which the value that could reasonably be attributed to the measurand is expected to lie.

The guidelines provided by the ISO Guide to the Expression of Uncertainty in Measurement [1] for the estimation of the uncertainty have been shortly recalled and discussed.

Indications on how to take into account the estimated uncertainty values for comparing measurement results have been reported and discussed as well, so that the very fundamentals of the experimental approach to signal and information processing have been covered in the paper.

References

[1] BIPM, IEC, IFCC, ISO, IUPAC, OIML, *Guide to the Expression of Uncertainty in Measurement*, 1993.

Neural Networks for Instrumentation, Measurement and Related Industrial Applications
S. Ablameyko et al. (Eds.)
IOS Press, 2003

Chapter 3
Neural Networks in Intelligent Sensors and Measurement Systems for Industrial Applications

Stefano FERRARI, Vincenzo PIURI
Department of Information Technologies, University of Milan
via Bramante 65, 26013 Crema, Italy

Abstract. This chapter discusses the basic concepts of intelligent instrumentation and measurement systems based on the use of neural networks. The concept of intelligent measurement is introduced as a preliminary step in industrial applications to extract information concerning the monitored or controlled system or plant as well as the surrounding environment. Implementation of intelligent measurement systems encompassing neural components is tackled, by providing a comprehensive approach to optimum system design. Issues and examples concerning the use of neural networks in intelligent sensing and measurement systems are discussed. The main objective is to show the feasibility and the usability of these techniques to implement a wide variety of adaptive sensors as well as to create high-level sensing systems able to extract abstract measures from physical data, with special emphasis on industrial applications.

3.1. Introduction to intelligent measurement systems for industrial applications

The conventional sensors, instrumentation, and measurement systems are based on dedicated components with some tunable parameters which allows for appropriate calibration and, possibly, for some adaptation to the operating conditions. Some flexibility of the physical architecture is provided in virtual instrumentation [1] by adopting a microprocessor-based structure in which the measurement procedure is defined in the algorithms executed by the microprocessors. However, these solutions have a rather limited "intelligence", i.e., a limited ability of extracting knowledge from the real world to define and modify their own behavior. In particular, they are not able to understand and learn the desired behavior from the observation and analysis of sufficient examples of such a behavior; besides, they are not able to dynamically adapt their own behavior to changing operating conditions and requirements.

The use of neural networks as design and implementation technique allows – in several cases of practical interest – for achieving this flexibility and adaptability. Neural networks have in fact been shown effective to tackle several cases in which an algorithmic description of the computation to produce the desired outputs is either difficult to identify or is too complex, while it is rather easy to collect examples of the desired system behavior [2-7]. This is valid also to implement advanced sensors that process basic physical quantities to extract high-level information, possibly mimicking biological systems, to create adaptable and evolvable instrumentation having high accuracy and low uncertainty, and to realize measurement systems that are able to create comprehensive views of the monitored system by intelligent sensor fusion and adaptation [8]. For an introduction to the neural computation, refer to [2-7]: in the sequel of the book, the reader is assumed to be rather familiar with the basic concepts of neural networks.

In Section 3.2 the design issues, technologies and problems are discussed to provide a comprehensive view of the interacting goals and characteristics that need to be carefully balanced for an optimum implementation of an intelligent measurement system. Hardware and software solutions are presented. A comprehensive design methodology is then introduced. In Section 3.3 the practical use of the neural paradigms is discussed in several application cases for intelligent sensors and measurement systems, as a fundamental basis for any industrial applications. Approaches available in the literature are analyzed to show the effectiveness and the efficiency of the neural-based approaches for the given application constraints.

3.2. Design and implementation of neural-based systems for industrial applications

To introduce adaptivity in measurement systems and industrial applications, neural networks were widely experimented, especially when sufficient examples of the expected behavior were available or created at a reasonable cost. A huge number of successful results and cases were reported in the literature, as well as in many other cases neural networks were proved to be not so effective and efficient.

The key for the success with these technologies is the use of a comprehensive and structured design methodology. This methodology should encompass not only the analysis of the desired system behavior, but also the understanding of all application constraints and their incorporation within the overall design process in order to identify the most suited solution in the whole space of the possible ones [9,10]. In particular, ability of strict real-time operation is essential in many industrial applications to deal with the fast evolving application system and environment. Accuracy and uncertainty of the outputs are important in many practical applications, e.g., in monitoring and control systems whenever critical decision must be taken and a smooth behavior of the system is desirable for wearing, economical, or safety reasons; this is the case of many industrial and environmental applications. Economical cost may be critical in mass production applications and when profit margin is rather small. Volume and power consumption may become relevant whenever portability of the application system is vital, e.g., in embedded systems for telecommunication. In several cases, these constraints set conflicting goals for the design process: the final solution needs therefore to balance them in a satisfactory way, possibly according to priorities defined by the designer.

3.2.1 Design of the neural paradigm

Any design methodology has to identify the neural solution that best tackles the specific application problem and satisfies the application constraints. In the literature many neural networks were shown effective in various applications [2-7], ranging from feed-forward multi-layered perceptrons to feed-back networks, from self-organizing maps to radial basis functions, and much many.

The identification of the most suited network is therefore the first complex task for the designer. From an abstract point of view this problem could be tackled by describing the neural computation as a network of processing elements (neurons). Each neuron generates its output by applying a non-linear function to the summation of its inputs. A neuron is connected to all other neurons by weighted links through which its outputs are presented as inputs to the receiving neurons; inputs from the external environment are delivered to all neurons. Memory elements are introduced at the neuron's inputs to allow for memorizing the dynamic behavior of the system. The neural computation is therefore parametric in the number of neurons, the memory elements, the non-linear functions, and the interconnection weights. The neural computation is expected to approximate as best as possible the desired (static or dynamic) behavior described by a set of examples. This view allows for defining a mathematical approach to the identification of the optimum neural computation that solves the envisioned application: the problem could be in fact stated as a functional. The solution of the functional is the best neural computation for the given application problem. Constraints on the system characteristics can be defined so that solution of the functional will be constrained. Unfortunately, this approach is not practically feasible since the optimization space is too huge: the exploration will take an unacceptably long time.

The neural computation needs therefore to be defined in a more efficient way through a sequence of steps that explore the alternatives by exploiting the available knowledge cumulated by researchers and practitioners around the world along the past twenty years. To achieve this goal we start from the desired behavior, as defined by the available examples, and the application constraints (e.g., concerning accuracy, uncertainty, power consumption, economical cost, etc.).

First of all, the most appropriate neural paradigm must be identified among the wide spectrum of neural families proposed in the literature. In particular, the overall topology of the network and the internal structure of the neurons must be selected. In the case different alternatives have been shown effective in cases similar to the envisioned application, all of them should be explored in the subsequent steps to finally achieve the most suited solution. Selection is in fact usually not immediately feasible at this initial design stage since detailed characteristics and constraints need to be taken into account; besides, an accurate evaluation of the performance can be done only when the actual implementation has been selected. For example, feed-forward neural structures can be adopted in all applications in which a mathematical function needs to be approximated or for classification when input-output examples are available. Feedback networks are appropriate for modeling dynamic behaviors, e.g., in control applications, by using a feed-forward structure with a feedback loop which supplies the past history to the network inputs through memory elements. Self-organizing maps are effective for classification when classes are not a-priori defined. The sigmoid function to generate the neuron's output is one of the widely used in theoretical research; in the practice approximated versions outperform the theoretical sigmoid as computation power is concerned.

Second, the most appropriate network model must be chosen within the selected family by defining the structural characteristics of the model. Namely, we need to identify the number of neurons in the network and, in the case of dynamic systems, the length of memory history. Experience can be useful to make these selections. A theoretical framework should consider the complexity of the application problem as defined by the set of examples that characterize the desired behavior. In the literature, some methodological guidelines have been presented to dimension the network [11,12], also by taking into account the quantity and the distribution of examples over the field of the desired behavior. In general, the typical approach is based on tentative cases having different network size and on the analysis of the accuracy achieved in their outputs: from the literature a promising range is foresee, then experiments will lead to subsequent refinements by focusing the attention on the most attracting sub-ranges till the probable optimum structure. Similarly, we should operate to identify the number of memory elements required to hold the system history. It is important to point out that the trial-and-error approach that is used to configure completely the network requires to evaluate the accuracy of the outputs and the other characteristics of the model (e.g., the generalization ability). Consequently, the optimum dimension of the neural network depends on the optimum configuration of the network weights that is achieved at the end of the configuration procedure for the envisioned network structure. To break this loop we need therefore to adopt an iterative approach: we have to complete the configuration by assuming that the network under consideration has the optimum size and, then, go back to evaluate if such network was actually optimum.

The third step consists of configuring the neural network interconnection weights by learning the desired behavior either by a supervised or an unsupervised training procedure. Many techniques were developed in the literature for the different neural models [2-7]. For example, several variations of the back-propagation algorithm were experimented for the feed-forward networks. Extensions for feedback network were also studied. Self-adaptation was proposed for self-organizing maps. Selection of the most suited learning approach can be performed by searching in the best results presented in the literature for the envisioned model family and application. Learning must be configured to take into account the actual characteristics of the implementation that will be adopted. For example, possible approximations of the theoretical non-linear functions, that are adopted to achieve a better implementation (e.g., from the point of view of the circuit complexity and power consumption in the case dedicated hardware solutions, or the computation complexity in the case of software realizations), must be considered also in training to create a consistent solution. Large network errors and even convergence problems in dynamic systems may be in fact induced in the application system during in the operating life by having trained the neural model with ideal conditions and, then, by having applied the approximations. This is the typical case that occurs when training is performed by using a theoretical sigmoid, while a multi-step function is adopted in the real system.

In the fourth step, the training procedure is applied to configure the operational parameters of the network model. Two basic issues must be carefully considered since they greatly affect the quality of the network and, consequently, the accuracy of the outputs: which data should be used for training and how long learning should be continued. In many real applications the examples of the desired behavior are available only in a limited quantity. Often it may be not easy or cheap to collect these examples for different reasons: for example, in some cases running the physical experiments to collect the data may be economically expensive, sometimes there is no personnel available enough to do the tests, in other cases the production cannot be suspended to perform experimental runs, and some operating conditions may be difficult to apply. When a limited set of data is available, it must be split in two parts: one to actually perform training, the second to validate the training result (i.e., the characteristics of the network such as the generalization ability, the robustness, and the accuracy). The validation data should never be used for training in order to have an impartial evaluation; using training data for validation will result in an optimistic – sometimes too much – evaluation of the network abilities. However, the less training data are collected, the lower is the quality of training and the higher is the network error in generating the desired outputs. Some additional guidelines can be found in the literature to deal with these issues and to evaluate the related network accuracy, e.g., see [13]. Duration of training is critical as well. In fact, if learning is too prolonged the network tends to learn the examples too much and to loose the generalization ability. Training should be applied till the network error decreases when test examples are presented: when the error becomes steady, training should be terminated. In the case of periodic or continuous learning, the procedure and the network configuration update must be controlled so as to allow for a high generalization ability and accuracy. By analyzing the neural model and the validation data, we can derive also the confidence that we can have on the computation outputs [14].

More detailed guidelines to create the neural paradigms can be found in the following chapters with specific reference to the envisioned specifications and application areas.

After the previous steps, we obtain a configured neural paradigm that is able to solve the envisioned application problem, possibly with the desired accuracy and uncertainty. It is worth nothing that the configured neural network *is* an algorithm, since it defines exactly sequence of all operations and all operand values required to generate the network outputs from the current input data. When configured, the computation of each neuron is in fact a weighted summation followed by a non-linear function, while the topology of the neural network defines the activation order of the neurons' computation and the data flow. The difference of neural paradigms with conventional algorithmic approaches consists of the fact that the algorithm designer has to define the sequence of operation to solve the application problem, while the neural designer has only to select the computational model and learning identifies the exact sequence of operations from the behavior examples.

In several application cases, neural solutions have been shown superior to algorithmic approaches, when the design and environmental conditions discussed at the beginning of this section apply. In many other cases efficiency and accuracy of algorithms remain outstanding. However, there are several cases in which a suited combination of the characteristics and properties of both of these computational approaches may lead to more advanced solutions. The efficiency of algorithms to tackle specific tasks for which they are known and effective can be in fact merged with the adaptivity and the generalization ability from examples of the neural paradigms. This results in the composite systems [9]. In composite systems the computation is partitioned in algorithmic and neural components to exploit the best features of each of these approaches. From the high-level functional description of the application and the related constraints it is therefore necessary to perform appropriate analysis of the desired behavior to partition the application system and to derive the high-level description of each algorithmic and neural component. Then, learning allows for configuring each neural component so as to create its final algorithmic description. The resulting high-level description of the whole system consists thus of the collection of the algorithmic description of all components, independently from the way in which the designer initially described each of them.

3.2.2 Design of the neural implementation

The second complex task for the designer is now the identification of the most suited solution for implementing the neural computation (or the composite system) that has been reduced to an algorithmic description for the envisioned application and with the given constraints. Several approaches have been presented in the literature, with different performance, cost, power consumption, and accuracy.

Several proposals were made in the literature by using analog hardware (e.g., [15-19]). Analog integrated circuits for neural computation are based on the fundamental laws of electric circuits: the Kirchhoff's and Ohm's laws. According to the Ohm's law, the voltage across an electric dipole is proportional to the current flowing through it. A linear dipole can represent a neural synapses: the voltage across the dipole represents a neuron input and the proportionality constant the related interconnection weight; the current flowing through the dipole is the weighted input. According to the Kirchhoff's current law, the total current entering a circuit node is null (currents exiting the node are accounted as negative terms). If the negative poles of the dipoles associated to a neuron are grounded together, the weighted summation of the neuron's inputs is the total current flowing to the ground. Similar results can be achieved by using other circuit topologies and devices (e.g., operational amplifiers and transistors). The use of analog circuit for neural computation is very effective since computation is performed at a very high speed (i.e., the speed allowed by the propagation and stabilization of the electric signals), the dimension of the circuit is very small, and all neural signals are represented by continuous values (thus allowing for theoretically representing very accurate values). However, there are two main drawbacks that greatly limit the practical usability of this approach. First, the configuration of the neural system is fixed at production time; consequently, the interconnection weights cannot be changed at power up and a specific circuit needs to be fabricated for each application case. Second, fabrication inaccuracies that are typical of any production process make impossible to guarantee a good accuracy of the characteristic parameters of the devices and, consequently, the accuracy of the neural interconnection weights. This approach should be adopted only if the overall network behavior is highly robust with respect to the variation of the network parameters.

Analog hardware with digital weights can be adopted to achieve some configurability of the interconnection weight (e.g., [20,21]). In this case a mixed-mode multiplier computes the input weighting. The multiplier (i.e., the weight) is given in the binary representation. Multiplication is performed in parallel on each multiplier digit by using dedicated circuitries; the analog multiplicand is presented in parallel to each of these single-digit multipliers. Each binary digit of the multiplier controls the flow of the current through the corresponding single-digit multiplier: no current will be generated if the control digit is zero; otherwise a current proportional to the binary weight of the digit is generated. The multiplication result is obtained by adding all currents generated by the single-digit multipliers according to the Kirchhoff's current law. Performance of this approach is still very high and control of the accuracy of characteristic device parameters is limited. Interconnection weights are discretized since they are given in the binary representation; this influences the accuracy of the final outputs. The network dimensions and topology as well as the neuron's operation are fixed at production time, thus limiting the circuit flexibility. The circuit size is larger than the pure analog approach since the mixed-mode multipliers are more complex.

Complete control of the accuracy can be achieved by adopting digital dedicated hardware architectures (e.g., [22-26]): all data are discretized and given in binary representation and all operations are performed digitally. Interconnection weights are configurable, but the network topology and size as well as the neuron's behavior are still fixed at production time. Performance is much lower than in the corresponding analog implementations due to the nature and the realization of the digital operations, but still it is rather high. The circuit complexity becomes relevant and, consequently, the integrated circuit becomes rather large. To limit the size and allow for fabrication, several neural operators often share in time some components, by introducing suited registers and clocking schemes; for example, one digital multiplier can be multiplexed among all interconnection weights of a neuron or the same circuit can compute the operations of several neurons sequentially. These architectures may have a limited circuit complexity for some classes of neural networks, e.g., when the neuron output is a single-digit binary value. The data discretization limits the accuracy, although it is exactly predictable.

The use of configurable digital hardware allows for high configurability (e.g., [27-29]). The typical approach consists of implementing the neural networks on an FPGA: all operations are mapped onto the logic blocks and interconnection paths of the FPGA. The high-level description of the neural operation (e.g., written in C, SystemC, or VHDL languages) is translated into the corresponding FPGA configuration that will be loaded on memory-based architectures or will be used to set the operations and interconnections in fuse-based architectures. Any neural topology and size and any neuron operation can be accommodated in the FPGA, provided that sufficient logic blocks and interconnections are available and that an appropriate operation schedule is adopted. Performance is lower than the dedicated digital architecture since basic neural operations involve more and slower physical components. Accuracy is influenced by the discretized operands.

Programmable digital architectures provide the highest configurability since the neural operations are described in suited programs. Since the computation is known, the accuracy can be evaluated; also in this case accuracy is influenced by the discretized operands.

Neurocomputers were developed to perform the neural computation in an efficient way by preserving the system flexibility (e.g., [30-32]). The behavior of these architectures is similar to the one of a conventional computer: the architecture consists of a memory in which the sequences of specialized operations that describe the neural computation are stored, and processing units that are able to fetch, decode, and execute these sequences stored in the memory. To achieve high performance these architectures make use of dedicated functional units to execute the operations that are the most frequent in the neural computations, and efficient interconnection structures to distribute the neurons' outputs to the receiving neurons. The specialized functional units may be implemented in FPGA to ensure additional flexibility. Any neural network can therefore be implemented by this kind of architectures, provided that the instructions executable by the processing units are able to describe the desired neural behavior.

All of the above solutions suffer from the same problem: the more the architecture is dedicated, the more expensive it becomes since it cannot be mass-produced and reused in a large number of instances and different applications. To overcome this drawback, non-specialized processors should be adopted so that they can be directly purchased on the market as components off the shelf.

In this perspective, digital signal processors (DSP) are an attractive solution that combines reasonably high performance with programmability (e.g., [33-35]). These processors have an architecture that usually includes supports and functional units specialized for the most frequent signal processing operations, e.g., convolution and correlation. Since the weighted summation coincides with these operations, it can be efficiently executed on DSP processors available on the market. The neural computation is obtained by executing dedicated software written for the selected DSP processor. This approach needs anyway to use processors, boards, software development environments, and programming skills that are less available – and thus more expensive – than for the widely-used general-purpose processing architectures.

General-purpose processors are the most flexible computing structures for which many programmers have sufficient knowledge and expertise to produce good programs. Processors for personal computers are among these structures. For these architectures dedicated software can be written in high-level programming languages to perform any neural computation. Performance is lower than in DSP architectures with similar characteristics since the efficient dedicated supports for DSP operations are not available in general-purpose systems. To speed up the performance general-purpose supercomputers can be used, e.g., [36-38].

To reduce the development costs due to the need of experienced programmers and to widen the use of neural computation also among practitioners with limited programming experience, general-purpose architectures with configurable software simulators can be adopted (e.g., [39]). In these software simulators, through a graphical interface, the designer can build the neural paradigm to tackle his application; typically he can select – in a predefined but usually very large set – the desired family of neural networks, the specific network dimension, and the appropriate weight configuration. In some simulators the designer is even allowed for creating his own network model. Performance is usually limited since configurability is obtained by interpreting the neural computation, thus leading to a slow execution. Some of these simulators are however able to produce a compiled version of the neural computation so as to greatly speed it up with respect to the interpreted version.

Dedicated software or neural network simulators are also needed to support learning. In any of these cases the network model adopted for learning must be identical to the one that will be used in the operating life. In particular, great care is necessary in verifying that all network characteristics, the precision of the data representation, the accuracy both of each operation and of the sequences of operations, all data uncertainties are identical in order to guarantee that the learnt behavior coincides with the one shown during the operational life of the neural network.

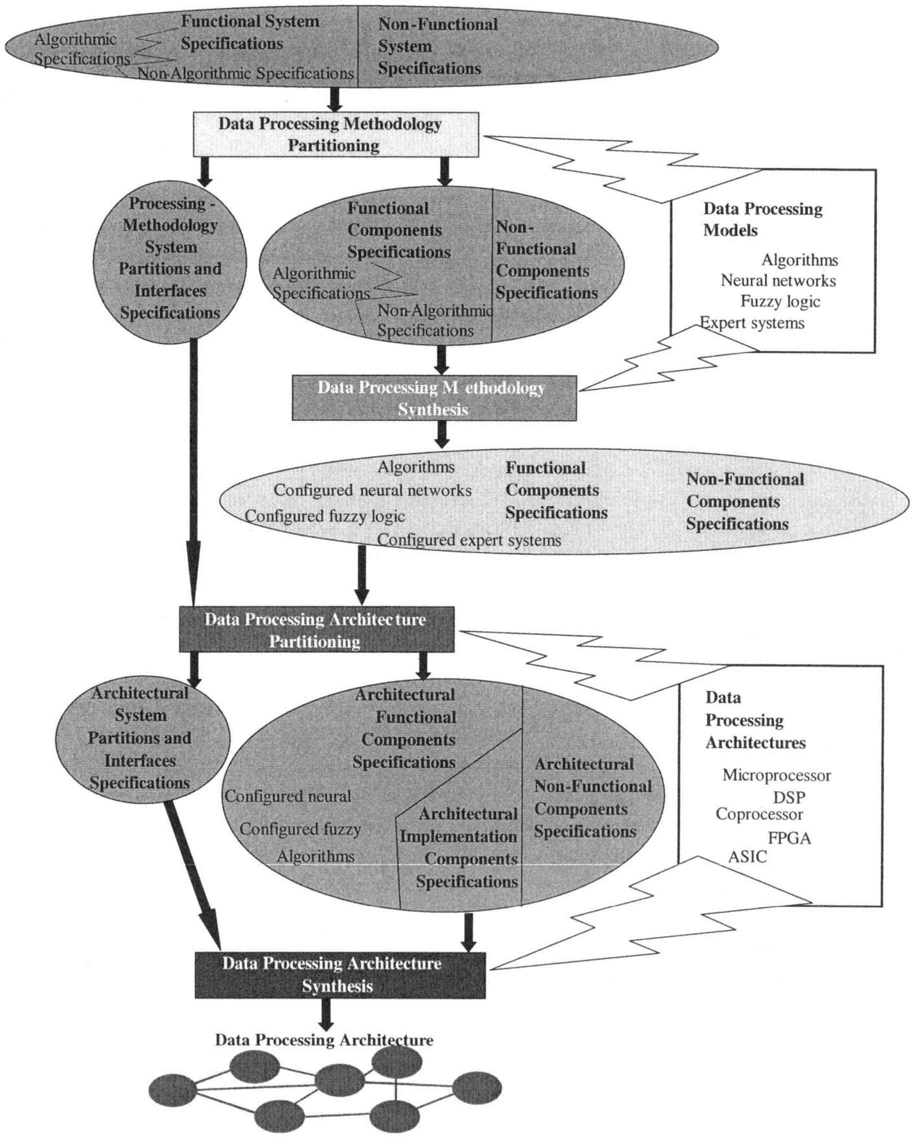

Figure 1: A comprehensive design methodology for composite systems.

3.2.3 A comprehensive design methodology for composite systems

To implement adaptive approaches in measurement systems and industrial applications a compehensive methodology is necessary to specify all issues discussed above at a high abstract level and to synthesize an optimal composite structure, according to a multi-objective optimization function. System-level design techniques (originally proposed for DSP and telecommunication applications based on algorithmic approaches [40]) have been extended (e.g., [9]) to deal also with soft-computing paradigms. This implies to consider two orthogonal perspectives into a homogeneous view with all non-functional and implementation constraints: the algorithmic/soft-computing synthesis and the conventional hardware/software synthesis. The resulting methodology is summarized in Fig. 1.

The first phase of the high-level design methodology consists of the system specification. The functional characteristics define the system behavior. High-level formal specifications are widely used, e.g., by means of the sequencing graphs [41]. For static digital systems, the combinatorial function that generates the expected output for each input is given; in dynamic digital systems, the state diagram relates each pair of input and system state to the output and the next state. Analog models typically describe plants and industrial processes by means of differential equations, often continuous-valued and possibly at the partial derivatives. Data are traditionally represented and processed as crisp values; fuzzy values generalize the data representation when the envisioned characteristic is a deterministic collection of crisp values. Fuzzy rules algorithmically define how the desired outputs must be generated. Expert systems use rules to explore the space of possible solutions. Neural networks are defined by examples by means of the training set: in static networks the input-output pairs for supervised learning or the input set for unsupervised training describe the desired behavior; the evolution of the system state is captured by means of the ordered sequences of the input-output pairs in dynamic networks. To identify the optimum solution for the envisioned application, the design methodology should consider – as early as possible – also all non-functional specifications, e.g., accuracy, uncertainty, performance, real-time operation, throughput, operation complexity, circuit complexity, and power consumption.

The second design phase consists of partitioning the system in components described by different computational paradigms (i.g., into algorithmic and soft computing components), by taking into account also the non-functional constraints. Some algorithmic and soft computing components can be functionally equivalent, even if their expressiveness, completeness, conciseness, and non-functional specifications may be different. The model to be selected is the one that best balances – not necessarily optimizes – the application requirements: the model chosen for a component greatly impacts on the implementation characteristics, e.g., complexity, performance, and power consumption. Computational paradigm partitioning identifies boundaries among components and the related interfaces so that each of these components is efficiently implemented. Natural and evident boundaries are first taken into account as defined by the designer's specifications. Partitioning is then guided by suited quality measurement to split components into simpler subsystems that can be efficiently represented by one model. Aggregation and separation techniques are used to resize components and to group the homogeneous ones in the perspective of the implementation.

The third design phase is the computational paradigm synthesis, which consists of configuring each component and the related interfaces. For algorithmic components the procedure describing the desired computation is derived. For soft computing components the corresponding synthesis is performed. For neural models the learning procedure is applied: this produces the algorithmic description of the network operation. For statistical model, the parameters are identified on the available data by statistic techniques. At the end of the paradigm synthesis, all components are described by algorithms.

The fourth design phase is the hardware/software partitioning that splits the algorithmic specification of the system into components to be implemented in dedicated analog, digital, or mixed hardware devices, in configurable hardware components, or in software programs running on DSP or general-purpose processors. This can be obtained by using one of the many hardware-software co-design techniques proposed in the literature and widely available in commercial CAD tools. Partitioning is guided by the non-functional specifications. It is worth noting that hardware/software partitioning is independent from computational paradigm partitioning. At the end of this phase the processing system architecture and the detailed structure of each component are obtained.

The fifth design phase is the synthesis of the processing architecture. This can be achieved by means of the traditional techniques for system synthesis: programming of the software components and digital/analog synthesis of the hardware devices (e.g., [42]).

3.3. Application of neural techniques for intelligent sensors and measurement systems

Neural techniques were shown effective and efficient in enhancing the characteristics of sensors and measurement systems as well as in industrial applications. In the literature many perspectives were presented to introduce "intelligence" in these systems by means of neural networks:
- sensor enhancement allows for creating devices which are able to physically sense quantities for advanced applications,
- sensor linearization simplifies the use of sensors in measurement systems and applications by providing an idealized view of the sensor,
- sensor fusion merges information from several sensors, possibly of different type, to create new combined measurements,
- sensor diagnosis verifies the correct operation of the sensor and detect the possible presence of errors due to faults,
- virtual sensors indirectly observe quantities for which no specific sensor is available by using information about quantities related to the desired one,
- remote sensing allows for indirectly measuring physical quantities without using a sensor that physically enters in contact with the measurand quantity,
- high-level sensors measure abstract quantities (i.e., not directly related to physical quantities) which are of interest for the applications,
- distributed intelligent sensing systems create a cooperative collection of sensors that provides a comprehensive view of the system under measure,
- calibration allows for correctly relating the measured values performed by sensors and measurement systems to the physical values of the quantities under measurement.

3.3.1 Sensor enhancement

The physical sensing materials have usually complex non-linear behaviors that need to be related to the corresponding values of the measured quantities. In particular, some physical characteristics of the sensing material when operating in physical contact with the measurand quantity vary according to the physical laws that regulate the interaction between the system under measurement and the measurement system. The varying physical quantity of the sensing material that best represent the quantity under measurement is assumed as the output of the sensor: this value is associated to the measurand quantity.

Neural networks can be used to create advanced sensors by suited processing the physical outputs of the sensing materials to extract the measurement of the desired physical quantity, especially when conventional processing techniques have been shown inaccurate or with not sufficient adaptivity. In some cases, neural approaches are also useful to enhance the accuracy of the measurement procedure so as to enhance the quality of the delivered measurements. Among sensors that benefit from neural technologies the literature reports sensors that reproduce the five human senses, as well as sensors for many other environmental and industrial quantities like mechanical quantities (e.g., distance, force, pressure), thermical quantities (e.g., temperature), and chemical quantities (e.g., concentration, presence of substances).

Image sensors are the basic step to reproduce the natural sight. Conventional digital cameras have image sensors, composed by a grid of sensible materials, that are able to capture the light (intensity and color); in each pixel information is transformed into a digital representation. Advanced image sensors mimic the behavior of the natural photoreceptors (the elementary components of the retina) in the human eyes, to allow for capturing images in a more "intelligent" and flexible way [43-45]. Human photoreceptors in fact have self-adaptive abilities to deal with light intensity and color saturation in order to create high-quality images even in the presence of adverse environmental conditions. Besides the image characteristics are represented in an impulsive way for subsequent processing by the brain. The artificial photodetector is obtained by using groups of photodiodes, which are sensible to various wavelengths, and interconnection circuits, that provide lateral connections and information processing among neighboring cells. When the photodetector is hit by light within its sensitivity range, it generate impulses proportional to the light intensity; impulses are then filtered by taking into account the events occurred in time and in the areas nearby. Neural networks are used to implement the non-linear lateral cooperation. This approach may have several benefits, including less saturation, reduced calibration, higher quality, higher accuracy, higher time sensitivity, and less power consumption.

By using either the intelligent photodetectors or conventional cameras with suited post-processing, an artificial retina can be implemented, whose behavior is similar to the human one [46-48], to provide a prosthesis to overcome blindness and severe visual imparities when the optical nerves and the optical brain functions are still in good conditions and operational. At the moment, the complexity of data processing required to generate appropriate signals for the brain is too high to be compacted into a small integrated circuit; besides, power consumption and power supply are still a relevant problem that needs external batteries and frequent recharges. These constraints prevent – nowadays – to realize prosthesis for permanent implantation in the human body instead of the natural retina. However, the feasibility of the approach was demonstrated by using stimulating devices implanted on the optical nerves and a processing system out of the human body: a prototype system was even recently implanted on a patient with interesting – although still low quality – results. The image taken from the image sensor array is transformed into an impulse-based representation suited for stimulating the optical nerves, also by using a neural-based approach. The image representation is then coded and transmitted wireless to the receiver implanted in the human body. Received data are decoded and delivered to the optical nerve stimulators. The image is thus transferred from the artificial eye to the brain for the usual processing and understanding.

At a higher abstraction level, visual sensors analyze an image or a sequence of images to detect and understand the objects contained in the images themselves and, eventually, to observe objects' motion [49-53]. This function mimics the image understanding activity of the natural brain. Objects are identified by extracting characteristic features from the image and by comparing the combinations these features with those of the classes of objects to be recognized: an object is identified when its features are similar to those of one of such classes. Motion is detected and analyzed by observing the variations of the features in the images of the sequence. Neural networks were shown effective for these adaptive tasks, which have many practical applications not only in the medical field, but mainly several industrial and robotics areas whenever image analysis and understanding is important.

Hearing sensor and the artificial cochlea can be realized similarly to the sight aids in order to assist people with severe hearing imparities with adaptive personalized prosthesis [54,55]. Conventional hearing aids increase the volume of any acoustic signal (voice, sounds, noise), possibly by filtering out some frequency bands; in general this approach has limited adaptivity to the patient and deliver too much noise that makes the patient uncomfortable. A neural-based approach can outperform the conventional one for the voice: it can understand the speech and synthesize the voice from the basic phonemes. First a microphone captures the voice; then signal (also neural) processing detects the boundaries between words, extracts the phonemes of each word, and identifies the words possibly by using also a vocabulary. The coded words are then wireless transmitted to the implant in the human body, where they are decoded and used to drive the voice reconstruction by cascading the appropriate phonemes. This signal is used to stimulate the auditory nerve as the natural cochlea does.

Odor sensors and the artificial nose were also successfully experimented by using neural solutions [56-59]. The natural nose identifies odors by detecting the presence and the quantity of chemicals in the air. It has receptors that are sensible to some specific classes of chemicals; the brain merges all olfactory information and classifies the odor on the basis of its experience and its knowledge of objects' smell. In the artificial nose, sensing materials react to the presence of some chemical families, possibly different with those of the natural receptors: these reactions are transduced into electric signals. On the basis of the type of active sensing materials (i.e., the detected family of chemicals) and the amount of their activity, the artificial nose classifies the smelled odor. This system was conceived for automatic odor analysis in industrial applications, e.g., in alimentary factories to identify rotting food or to grade the maturation level. Effectiveness of the neural approach is due to the relevant problem non-linearities and the difficulties to give an algorithmic approach.

Similarly, the natural tongue identifies tastes by analyzing the presence and the quantity of chemicals on the object touched by the tongue (the saliva transports the chemicals from the surface of the tasted object to the papillae). In the artificial tongue [57], sensing materials are used to detect some chemical families that are on the surface of the touched objects, as in the artificial nose. Classification leads to identify the taste of the object according to the kind of tastes to which the sensing materials are reacting and to the knowledge used to configure the classifier. Also the artificial tongue is used to mimic the human counterpart, e.g., in alimentary factory to automatically discriminate different types and mix of foods and beverages. It is worth nothing that artificial nose and tongue are based on the same operating principles: the only difference is how the chemicals are brought to the sensing devices (thorough the air in the nose, by contact or through water in the tongue).

Tactile sensors are important for advanced robotics when robotic hands need to take objects carefully (e.g., delicate, deformable, or slippery objects) or when objects must be tactilely recognized. The natural skin contains an array of tactile sensors that are able to observe the tridimensional field of mechanical force due to gripping an object; from the analysis of the field of mechanical force, the brain is able to recognize the shape of the touched surface by comparing the current one to its knowledge. The artificial tactile sensors reproduce the ability of neurally reconstructing the field of forces from the individual information coming from the sensing units: from the analysis of the field of mechanical force they are able to classify the surface shape, to identify the surface state, and to predict the slippery of the grip [60-63].

By using neural techniques several other advanced sensors were developed to measure mechanical quantities, very well suited for industrial applications. In pressure sensors [64] the neural networks were used to correlate the strongly non-linear output of a barometric cell to the corresponding pressure value, by incorporating the specific characteristics of the cell that vary from one cell to another due to the inaccuracies of the production process. Adaptive distance sensors can be implemented by adopting a sonar- or laser- based system [65,66]. Surface roughness can be deduced by analyzing and intelligent merging several of these measurements taken at a short distance [67]. Velocity and angular velocity can be measured by adaptive analysis of the position of the envisioned object [68,69]. Other quantities reported in the litertaure concern, among the many examples, force [70,71], torque [72,73], and strain [74].

The use of neural networks was proved effective also to implement many other sensors and measurement systems for electromagnetic quantities (e.g., [75]), environmental quantities (e.g., temperature and humidity [76-79]) and chemical and biological quantities (e.g., [80-85]). All these cases have many practical implications, especially in a wide variety of industrial production areas, in the biomedical fields, and in environmental monitoring. The basic goals of the use of neural technologies are the same of the cases presented above: to achieve a better evaluation of the system output, to achieve adaptability of the measurement system, and to describe the desired behavior in an easier way by examples.

3.3.2 Sensor linearization

Linearization of the physical output generated by a sensor is useful for many practical applications in all areas. On the market many cheap sensors become nowadays available: low cost makes them highly desirable to reduce the cost of products and systems. However, these sensors often have non-linear output functions corresponding to linearly changing values of the physical measurand quantity. In these cases the subsequent data processing has to deal with such non-linearity to produce the measured value. For example, thermocouples typically measure the temperature by producing an electric voltage at their outputs; this voltage is non-linearly related to the actual temperature. The temperature value needs to be deduced from a conversion table or function; since the correspondence between the sensor output and the temperature is often quite difficult to be given as a simple function, a look-up table can be adopted. Performing this conversion with the required accuracy a lot of efforts is required either for the possible computational complexity of the complex conversion function or for the large size of the look-up table.

If the sensor output was linear, the conversion will be much easier since it will be a simple multiplication for a constant gain, typical of that sensor. The applications could thus be written in a much simpler way, especially when system control is envisioned.

Unfortunately, the reality cannot be changed to make it ideal. However, it is possible to save the simplified view of a non-linear sensor for the application designers by linearizing the output of the sensor itself, i.e., linearization can be embedded in the sensing system so that non-linearities will remain hidden in it. This will not remove the computational or memory efforts mentioned above since they will remain hidden in the measurement system, but it will allow for a much simpler use of the sensor in the various applications since the non-linear sensor and the linearization procedure will constitute a single system.

Linearization can be pursued by several techniques. As already said, the look-up table is easy to create although may become expensive in terms of memory usage. To save memory at the expenses of computational complexity, a conversion function can be adopted. When only two samples are available, the linear interpolation identifies the straight line that passes through the samples. When some more samples are available, higher accuracy can be achieved by splitting the data set into adjacent intervals and by looking for the broken line that touches all samples. In both cases higher accuracy and smoothness of the interpolation can be obtained by adopting higher-order interpolating functions like quadric functions and polynomials; the drawback is the higher computational complexity when the linearized outputs must be computed. When several examples are available, regression techniques (namely, linear, quadratic, and polynomial regression), possibly in intervals of the sampled quantity, can be used to linearize the output function: the linear, quadratic, or polynomial function that gives the output correspondence is the one that minimizes the average approximation error for the sampled data.

Neural networks are an alternative approach that allows for constructing the output correspondence for the linearized sensor by learning it from examples [86-88]. After learning the neural network computes the function that minimizes the global error on the whole sensor operating range without the need of using different functions for each interval. In sensor linearization the neural network computes therefore the non-linear mapping from the outputs of the physical sensor to the linearized outputs of the ideal sensor. This is a task that is well suited for neural paradigm; in fact multi-layered perceptrons were proved to be universal approximators of non-linear functions, although efficiency is not guaranteed.

The neural approach presents an additional feature: it is able to deal with discretization of the outputs for the digital representation at the same time of linearization. This minimizes the overall error due both to linearization and discretization since the neural network can take both of them into account during the learning phase.

3.3.3 Sensor fusion

Sensors used to observe the status and the behavior of a physical system collect a mass of data that – as a whole – characterizes the system. However, each sensor produces a partial view of the observed system, according to the specific physical quantity it measures. In real applications decisions are usually taken on the basis of the overall system status and behavior, for example to generate the most suited control signals; an individual perspective is in fact often not sufficient to achieve the desired system behavior. The global view needs to be reconstructed by analyzing information from each sensor into a comprehensive perspective. This can be achieved by sensor fusion, i.e., by merging the data produced by each sensor into higher abstraction information to create a single data stream coming from the set of sensors. A wide literature is available about sensor fusion, the related technologies, and applications by using neural-based approaches, e.g., [89-92].

To measure the same physical quantity in a given region of space, more than one sensor (possibly of different type) can be used. This allows for enhancing the confidence in the measurement. In fact the availability of more samples from different sources can be used to better tackle uncertainty and accuracy. The use of different kind of sensors to measure the same physical quantity is useful to enhance the reliability and the confidence in the measured values by exploiting the sensor diversity, at limited costs.

Sensors for different physical quantities of the same physical region are useful to create a comprehensive view of that region by integrating the information provided by each sensor. This kind of integration is specific for each application and group of sensors considered. In general, the availability of multisensorial information allows for depicting a view of the system that averages and amalgamates the individual contributions, thus limiting the dominance of each sensor onto the comprehensive view and, consequently, avoiding polarizations and enhancing the overall quality.

Sensor fusion for data integration can be implemented by means of a single merging procedure that computes all refined and combined outputs depicting the comprehensive view. This is efficient when the interdependencies among the measured quantities are numerous and each of them involves most of the measured quantities. Alternatively, individual merging procedures can be adopted to refine each measurement by taking into account the information provided by the other sensors. This is suited when interdependencies involve a limited number of different physical quantities for each measurement to be refined.

3.3.4 Sensor diagnosis

Various causes (e.g., aging) may lead to measure drifts in sensors. Sensor fusion, e.g., by neural networks and the continuous comparison among the samples taken by various identical sensors about at the same time can be used to early detect this phenomenon and, eventually, to mask its effects by correcting – as much as possible – the wrong measures before recalibrating the drifted sensor itself [93-98]. The correct measure is the one on which most of the sensors agree, within a given tolerance range of values (this interval is due to the uncertainty in the measurement: comparison needs to be considered positive not only if the measured values are identical, but also if their uncertainty intervals overlap). When a sensor is identified as not sufficiently "reliable" due to drifting, its measurements can be ignored and decisions about the subsequent measured values taken only on the basis of the responses of the remaining reliable sensors. This is especially useful when maintenance and recalibration are difficult, or expensive, or even impossible, or cannot be performed too frequently.

Similarly, normal wear and accidents in the operating environment may induce faults into a sensor, i.e., may change the physical structure either of the whole sensor or one or more of its parts. Some of these faults do not affect the normal operation of the sensor, which continues to deliver correct outputs, i.e., to produce measures that coincide with the actual value of the quantity under measurement. Other faults may appear as erroneous values delivered by the sensor, i.e., different from the outputs that such a sensor would have delivered in the absence of the fault. Sensor fusion can be adopted to support various strategies for fault tolerance. First of all, it can be used for sensor error detection. Comparison of the sensors outputs points out the presence of erroneous measurements and, thus, of faulty sensors: an error is detected whenever the compared sensors outputs are different and exceed the intrinsic tolerance due to the measurement uncertainty. The faulty sensor is the one that disagrees from the value delivered by the other sensor. Error correction can be realized by majority voting the sensor outputs (an odd number of sensors is required): the output value – including the tolerance of the measurement uncertainty– on which there is the higher consensus is assumed as the correct value by masking the actual presence of the error. To preserve the detection and correction abilities as much as possible, fault insulation must be applied, by removing the faulty sensor from the active operation (i.e., by ignoring its outputs). It is worth nothing that these abilities are somewhat reduced when a sensor becomes faulty and is insulated since its contribution to the comparisons is now missing. Repair allows for recovering the sensor in the normal operation and for restoring the full fault tolerance abilities.

Different kind of sensors to measure the same physical quantity may enhance the fault tolerance. Different types of sensors will have different wear, or will be subject to different aging mechanisms, or will have different faults and errors. Diversity minimizes the probability that sensors are progressively changing in a similar way about at the same time.

Sensors for different physical quantities of the same physical region can be adopted also to overcome possible drifting or temporary errors in measurements due to local transient events in sensors that have no specific relevance for the observation of the whole system [93,95,97,99,100]. Information produced by a sensor, which are not consistent with the whole picture of the system as created by the other sensors, can be identified as erroneous and, thus, ignored.

Instead of relying on comparison among real data, diagnosis can be also performed by adopting a model-based approach [97,101,102]. A model of the sensor is created by means of system identification techniques (e.g., by using neural models). The model is exploited to predict the expected sensor output from the sensor past outputs without any physical redundancy of the sensor: if the expected output differs too much from the actual one, an error is detected.

3.3.5 Virtual sensors and remote sensing

A real sensor can be used when there are sensing materials and techniques that allow for observing the desired quantity and when this sensor can be placed in the desired location of the system to perform the measurement. In some cases, this is not feasible since direct sensing of the desired physical quantity is not technically viable, or is not convenient for the application, or can be dangerous for the system and operator safety, or is economically expensive.

In some cases, although the desired quantity is difficult to be directly measured, other quantities strictly related to it can be observed more easily. An indirect measurement procedure can thus be created. Sensors are placed in the system (where feasible, appropriate, or convenient) to observe the quantities that can be directly measured. The laws that describe the relationships among the quantities measured by these sensors and with the desired quantity are identified: they can involve mechanical physics, chemistry, optics, electromagnetism, etc. From these laws it is possible to extract a function that gives the indirect measurement of the desired quantity from the values of the directly measured quantities. The sensors for direct measurements and this function constitute a *virtual sensor*. It is virtual since it is not a physically existing sensor to directly observe the desired quantity.

Since neural networks can be widely used as function approximators, they are also effective as data processing tools to merge the values coming from the physical sensors according to the merging function that computes the indirect measurement by applying the relationships among the measured quantities (e.g., [103,104]).

A special case of virtual sensor is when the quantity to be measured is in a location too far from the measuring system. In other cases the quantity to be measured involves a wide region of space and would require a too high number of sensors or an iterative sensing in the whole region, while the desired quantity is only a concise information (e.g., average or total value). In both of these types of cases only an indirect measurement technique is appropriate: in the literature this approach is known as *remote sensing*.

Examples of these measurements taken from satellites encompass the Earth surface parameters (e.g., the canopy temperature, the soil temperature, the canopy water content, and the soil moisture content), the rainfall, the snowfall, the air pollution, the CO emission, the ozone hole, etc. Also in these applications the neural networks proved their effectiveness and – sometimes – their superiority in merging information and extracting concise views [105-109].

3.3.6 High-level sensors

Several applications needs to extract a compact representation of the observed phenomenon or system, by analyzing and combining an often large quantity of data coming from many sensors. This is the case – only to mention very few examples – of production monitoring, product quality assessment, on-line diagnosis of complex systems, human health monitoring, object detection and recognition in vision, motion analysis, pattern and image recognition, decision making, risk prediction, and finance applications.

Only an abstract quantity that concisely characterizes the status and the behavior of the envisioned system is of interest, not the whole mass of sensors data. This quantity does not need to be physical, although it is related to physical quantities. For example, in the product quality monitoring, this concise information is the quality of the product, i.e., the complete integrity of the product or the presence of possible production defects; different classes of quality can be defined and produced object must be analyzed and properly classified.

For these abstract quantities there is obviously no physical sensor to perform direct measurements. However, like in virtual sensors, data collected from real sensors are processed to obtain the measure of the desired abstract quantity (e.g., the quality class in the example above).

Typical processing operations to create high-level sensors are classification and clustering of sensor data. Neural networks have been widely experimented and shown effective as tools to perform these tasks. In the literature many examples and techniques are reported [2-7], according to the presence of a supervisor guidance to create the classes or to the autonomous clustering by similarity. Among the many, some examples available in the literature concerning high-level sensors are [110-112].

3.3.7 Distributed intelligent sensing systems

Measurement systems and related industrial applications are continuously increasing in size and complexity. In particular, they are including many sensors to gather as much information as possible about the status and the evolution of the physical system. In many cases sensors and measurement systems need to be distributed in spaces that can range from a house to a production plant, to a metropolitan to a large geographical area, and even to the whole Earth, in order to collect the desired information and provide a comprehensive view of the whole monitored system. In these cases measurement operations need to be performed in processing architectures, connected in a computer network in order to exchange information and cooperate.

In the literature *networked sensing systems* and *distributed measurement systems* are two models that were proposed for creating these complex measurement systems (e.g., [113-116]). In networked sensing systems, the sensors are connected to a network (either private or public) so that a centralized measurement procedure can request for measurements from sensors and create a comprehensive view of the system by working in a centralized way: only physical sensors are decentralized in the monitored space. In distributed measurement systems the measurement procedure is distributed as well. Data acquisition is performed by a group of cooperating processing systems; each processing unit creates a partial view of the whole system picture by interacting with other units.

A model recently proposed in the field of artificial intelligence is the *perceptive agency* [117]. From a general logical point of view, agents are executors of specific activities, while an agency is a place where agents can meet, interact, and exchange information. Agents can be program running on computers, or hardware architectures dedicated to specific tasks, or robots able to physically interact with the external world. Agents can be fixed or mobile (e.g., mobile software agents able to travel in the computer network, or mobile robots). An agency is a program running on a computer or a computer network to support agent cooperation. A perceptive agency is an agency in which the agents cooperate to perform measurements and monitor the desired system. Differently from distributed measurement systems, in a perceptive agency the components (i.e., the agents) do not know each other in advance: each declares which are its features and cooperation is dynamically built through an interactive agreement process. Such an approach allows – in particular – for high modularity, scalability, fault tolerance, and adaptability.

In all of the distributed architectures mentioned above for the sensing and measurement system, the neural networks can play different relevant roles: they can be used to enhance the individual sensors, to merge multisensor information as virtual sensors, to support adaptive remote sensing, and to create high-level sensors based on distributed information. In summary they can be used to introduce flexibility and adaptability in the distributed sensing and measurement systems, making more "intelligent" these procedure.

3.3.8 Calibration

Calibration [118] is the operation that establish, under given conditions, the relationship between values produced by a sensor or an instrument and the known values of the measurand. In the practice, similarly to sensor linearization, this operation consists in identifying a relationship to convert the physical sensor output into an ideal sensor output. The ideal (although not necessarily linear) description of the sensor behavior is appreciated in the applications to specify the desired behavior on the basis of ideal reference sensors so as to avoid to know the actual details of the specific sensor that has been installed in the system.

Implementation of this conversion relationship may consist either in a look-up table or in a function. As in sensor linearization, the use of a function allows for saving a large amount of memory space. To identify the function global interpolation techniques (e.g., Newton's or Lagrange's interpolation) can be adopted: they compute the polynomial – of a given order – that passes through all calibration samples; coefficients are computed by looking to the whole interval in which the function has to be defined. Local interpolation techniques (e.g., splines) look for the polynomial (of a given order) that passes through the samples contained in small windows (only few samples long) of the whole function codomain. Regression techniques (e.g., least mean squares) looks for functions that approximates the samples, without necessarily passing through them, by minimizing the global approximation error.

Feed-forward neural networks (as universal function approximators) are another regression-type technique that can be effectively used to approximate the desired function described by the sampled calibration data. In several cases neural networks have shown a higher approximation ability, accuracy, robustness, and generalization ability than conventional regression techniques at a similar or mildly higher computational complexity both for static and dynamic calibration (e.g., [119-122]). High generalization ability is highly appreciated in calibration since it allows to achieve the same calibration quality with a smaller number of samples. Conventional regression techniques need to know the maximum order of the polynomial to be used for approximation: neural networks are autonomously able to find the best approximation for the given network dimension.

The sensor fusion ability of neural networks can also be exploited to easier calibrate sensors in which the operating conditions depend from other parameters (e.g., the temperature for a high-accuracy pressure sensor [122]) as well as to calibrate multisensor systems (e.g., [123]).

References

[1] L. Cristaldi, A. Ferrero, and V. Piuri, "Programmable instruments, virtual instruments, and distributed measurement systems: what is really useful, innovative and technically sound?," *IEEE Instrumentation & Measurement Mag.*, vol. 2, pp. 20–27, Sept. 1999.

[2] J. Hertz, A. Krogh, and R. G. Palmer, *An Introduction to the Theory of Neural Computation*. Lecture Notes Volume I, Addison Wesley, 1991.

[3] E. Sinencio-Sanchez and C. Lau, *Artificial Neural Networks: Paradigms, Applications, and Hardware Implementations*. IEEE Press, Dec. 1992.

[4] J. Zurada, *Introduction to Artificial Neural Systems*. St. Paul: West Publishing Company, 1992.

[5] L. Fausett, *Fundamentals of Neural Networks*. Prentice Hall, Englewood Cliffs, 1994.

[6] S. Haykin, *Neural networks: a comprehensive foundation*. New Jersey, USA: Prentice Hall, 1999.

[7] T. Kohonen, *Self-Organizing Maps*, vol. 30 of *Springer Series in Information Sciences*. Berlin, Heidelberg, New York: Springer, 3 ed., 2001.

[8] C. Alippi, A. Ferrero, and V. Piuri, "Artificial intelligence for instruments and measurement applications," *IEEE Instrumentation & Measurement Mag.*, vol. 1, pp. 9–17, June 1998.

[9] C. Alippi, S. Ferrari, V. Piuri, M. Sami, and F. Scotti, "New trends in intelligent systems design for embedded and measurement application," *IEEE Instrumentation & Measurement Mag.*, vol. 2, pp. 36–44, June 1999.

[10] C. Alippi, V. Piuri, and F. Scotti, "Accuracy versus complexity in RBF neural networks," *IEEE Instrumentation & Measurement Mag.*, vol. 4, pp. 32–36, Mar. 2001.

[11] A. Weigend and D. Rumelhart, "The effective dimension of the space of hidden units," in *Proc. IEEE Int. Joint Conf. on Neural Networks, 1991*, vol. 3, pp. 2069–2074, 1991.

[12] C. Alippi, R. Petraccà, and V. Piuri, "Off-line performance maximization in feedforward neural networks by applying virtual neurons and covariance transformations," in *Proc. IEEE Int. Symp. on Circuits and Systems, 1995*, pp. III.2197–III.2200, Apr. 1995.

[13] N. Murata, S. Yoshizawa, and S. Amari, "Network information criteriondetermining the number of hidden units for an artificial neural network model," *IEEE Trans. on Neural Networks*, vol. 5, pp. 865–872, Nov. 1994.

[14] K. Fukunaga, *Introduction to statistical pattern recognition*. New York: Academic Press, 1972.

[15] Y. Ota and B. Wilamowski, "Analog implementation of pulse-coupled neural networks," *IEEE Trans. on Neural Networks*, vol. 10, pp. 539–544, May 1999.

[16] H. Abdelbaki, E. Gelenbe, and S. El-Khamy, "Analog hardware implementation of the random neural network model," in *Proc. IEEE-INNS-ENNS Int. Joint Conf. on Neural Networks, 2000*, pp. 197–201, 2000.

[17] G. Indiveri, "A neuromorphic VLSI device for implementing 2D selective attention systems," *IEEE Trans. on Neural Networks*, vol. 12, pp. 1455–1463, Nov. 2001.

[18] C. Lu, B. Shi, and L. Chen, "Hardware implementation of an on-chip BP learning neural network with programmable neuron characteristics and learning rate adaptation," in *Proc. Int. Joint Conf. on Neural Networks, 2001*, pp. 212–215, 2001.

[19] A. Ö•renci, G. Dundar, and S. Balkir, "Fault-tolerant training of neural networks in the presence of MOS transistor mismatches," *IEEE Trans. on Circuits and Systems II: Analog and Digital Signal Processing*, vol. 48, pp. 272–281, Mar. 2001.

[20] A. Heittmann and U. Ruckert, "Mixed mode VLSI implementation of a neural associative memory," in *Proc. Seventh Int. Conf. on Microelectronics for Neural, Fuzzy and Bio-Inspired Systems, 1999*, pp. 299–306, 1999.

[21] K. Waheed and F. Salam, "A mixed mode self-programming neural system-on-chip for real-time applications," in *Proc. Int. Joint Conf. on Neural Networks, 2001*, vol. 1, pp. 195–200, 2001.

[22] S. Kung, "Tutorial: digital neurocomputing for signal/image processing," in *Proc. 1991 IEEE Workshop Neural Networks for Signal Processing*, pp. 616–644, 1991.

[23] M. Yasunaga, N. Masuda, M. Yagyu, M. Asai, K. Shibata, M. Ooyama, M. Yamada, T. Sakaguchi, and M. Hashimoto, "A self-learning digital neural network using wafer-scale LSI," *IEEE J. of Solid-State Circuits*, vol. 28, pp. 106–114, Feb. 1993.

[24] C. Chin Wang, C. Jung Huang, and Y. Pei Chen, "Design of an innerproduct processor for hardware realization of multi-valued exponential bidirectional associative memory," *IEEE Trans. on Circuits and Systems II: Analog and Digital Signal Processing*, vol. 47, pp. 1271–1278, Nov. 2000.

[25] R. Perfetti and G. Costantini, "Multiplierless digital learning algorithm for cellular neural networks," *IEEE Trans. on Circuits and Systems I: Fundamental Theory and Applications*, vol. 48, pp. 630–635, May 2001.

[26] T. Schoenauer, S. Atasoy, N. Mehrtash, and H. Klar, "NeuroPipe-chip: A digital neuro-processor for spiking neural networks," *IEEE Trans. on Neural Networks*, vol. 13, pp. 205–213, Jan. 2002.

[27] M. Arroyo León, A. Ruiz Castro, and R. Leal Ascencio, "An artificial neural network on a field programmable gate array as a virtual sensor," in *Proc. Third Int. Workshop on Design of Mixed-Mode Integrated Circuits and Applications, 1999*, pp. 114–117, 1999.

[28] G. Frank, G. Hartmann, A. Jahnke, and M. Schäfer, "An accelerator for neural networks with pulse-coded model neurons," *IEEE Trans. on Neural Networks*, vol. 10, pp. 527–538, May 1999.

[29] C.-M. Kim and S. Y. Lee, "A digital chip for robust speech recognition in noisy environment," in *Proc. IEEE Int. Conf. on Acoustics, Speech, and Signal Processing, 2001*, vol. 2, pp. 1089–1092, 2001.

[30] Intel Corp., Santa Clara, CA, *80170NX ETANN, Data Sheet*, 1991.

[31] Y. Sato, K. Shibata, M. Asai, M. Ohki, M. Sugie, T. Sakaguchi, M. Hashimoto, and Y. Kuwabara, "Development of a high-performance general purpose neuro-computer composed of 512 digital neurons," in *Proc. Int. Joint Conf. on Neural Networks, 1993*, vol. 2, pp. 1967–1970, 1993.

[32] U. Ramacher, W. Raab, J. Hachmann, J. Beichter, N. Bruls, M.Wesseling, E. Sicheneder, J. Glass, A. Wurz, and R. Manner, "SYNAPSE-1: a highspeed general purpose parallel neurocomputer system," in *Proc. 9th Int. Parallel Processing Symp., 1995*, pp. 774–781, 1995.

[33] U. Müller, A. Gunzinger, and W. Guggenbühl, "Fast neural net simulation with a DSP processor array," *IEEE Trans. on Neural Networks*, vol. 6, pp. 203–213, Jan. 1995.

[34] M. Murakawa, S. Yoshizawa, I. Kajitani, X. Yao, N. Kajihara, M. Iwata, and T. Higuchi, "The GRD chip: genetic reconfiguration of DSPs for neural network processing," *IEEE Trans. on Computers*, vol. 48, pp. 628–639, June 1999.

[35] V. Cantoni and A. Petrosino, "Neural recognition in a pyramidal structure," *IEEE Trans. on Neural Networks*, vol. 13, pp. 472–480, Mar. 2002.

[36] E. Kerckhoffs, F. Wedman, and E. Frietman, "Speeding up backpropagation training on a hypercube computer," *J. of Neurocomputing*, vol. 4, pp. 43–63, 1992.

[37] M. Kuga, Y. Namiuchi, B. Apduhan, and T. Sueyoshi, "Implementation and performance evaluation of a neural network simulator on highly parallel computer AP-1000," in *Proc. 1993 Int. Conf. on Parallel And Distributed Systems*, pp. 722–726, July 1993.

[38] X. Liu and G. Wilcox, "Benchmarking of the CM-5 and the Cray machines with a very large backpropagation neural network," in *IEEE Int. Conf. on Neural Networks, 1994*, vol. 1, pp. 22–27, 1994.

[39] H. Demuth and M. Beale, *Neural Network Toolbox Users Guide*. The MathWorks, Inc., 7 ed., Mar. 2001.

[40] G. D. Micheli and M. Sami, eds., *Hardware/Software CoDesign*, vol. 310 of *NATO ASI Series*. Kluwer Academic Publishers, 1995.

[41] D. D. Gajski, F. Vahid, S. Narayan, and J. Gong, *Specification and Design of Embedded Systems*. Englewood Cliffs, New Jersey 07632: Prentice Hall, 1994.

[42] Ptolemy – http://ptolemy.eecs.berkeley.edu/

[43] C. Nilson, R. Darling, and R. Pinter, "Shunting neural network photodetector arrays in analog CMOS," *IEEE J. of Solid-State Circuits*, vol. 29, pp. 1291–1296, Oct. 1994.

[44] T. Yagi, Y. Hayashida, and S. Kameda, "An analog VLSI which emulates biological vision," in *Proc. Second Int. Conf. on Knowledge-Based Intelligent Electronic Systems, 1998*, vol. 3, pp. 454–460, 1998.

[45] M. Wilcox and D. Thelen Jr., "A retina with parallel input and pulsed output, extracting high-resolution information," *IEEE Trans. on Neural Networks*, vol. 10, pp. 574–583, May 1999.

[46] M. Becker, R. Eckmiller, and R. Hunermann, "Psychophysical test of a tunable retina encoder for retina implants," in *Proc. Int. Joint Conf. on Neural Networks, 1999*, vol. 1, pp. 192–195, 1999.

[47] W. Liu, K. Vichienchom, M. Clements, S. DeMarco, C. Hughes, E. McGucken, M. Humayun, E. D. Juan, J. Weiland, and R. Greenberg, "A neuro-stimulus chip with telemetry unit for retinal prosthetic device," *IEEE J. of Solid-State Circuits*, vol. 35, pp. 1487–1497, Oct. 2000.

[48] C.-Y. Wu, L.-J. Lin, and K.-H. Huang, "A new light-activated CMOS retinal-pulse generation circuit without external power supply for artificial retinal prostheses," in *The 8th IEEE Int. Conf. on Electronics, Circuits and Systems, 2001*, vol. 2, pp. 619–622, 2001.

[49] S. Watanabe and M. Yoneyama, "An ultrasonic visual sensor for threedimensional object recognition using neural networks," *IEEE Trans. on Robotics and Automation*, vol. 8, pp. 240–249, Apr. 1992.

[50] C.-F. Chiu and C.-Y.Wu, "The design of rotation-invariant pattern recognition using the silicon retina," *IEEE J. of Solid-State Circuits*, vol. 32, pp. 526–534, Apr. 1997.

[51] Z. Lu and B. Shi, "Subpixel resolution binocular visual tracking using analog VLSI vision sensors," *IEEE Trans. on Circuits and Systems II: Analog and Digital Signal Processing*, vol. 47, pp. 1468–1475, Dec. 2000.

[52] N. Goerke, R. Schatten, and R. Eckmiller, "Enhancing active vision by a neural movement predictor," in *Proc. Int. Joint Conf. on Neural Networks, 2001*, vol. 2, pp. 1312–1317, 2001.

[53] G. Foresti and S. Gentili, "A hierarchical classification system for object recognition in underwater environments," *IEEE J. of Oceanic Engineering*, vol. 27, pp. 66–78, Jan. 2002.

[54] M. Leisenberg, "Hearing aids for the profoundly deaf based on neural net speech processing," in *Proc. Int. Conf. on Acoustics, Speech, and Signal Processing, 1995*, vol. 5, pp. 3535–3538, 1995.

[55] C.-H. Chang, G. Anderson, and P. Loizou, "A neural network model for optimizing vowel recognition by cochlear implant listeners," *IEEE Trans. on Neural Systems and Rehabilitation Engineering*, vol. 9, pp. 42–48, Mar. 2001.

[56] C. Di Natale, A. Macagnano, R. Paolesse, E. Tarizzo, A. D'Amico, F. Davide, T. Boschi, M. Faccio, G. Ferri, F. Sinesio, F. Bucarelli, E. Moneta, and G. Quaglia, "A comparison between an electronic nose and human olfaction in a selected case study," in *Proc. Int. Conf. on Solid State Sensors and Actuators, 1997*, vol. 2, pp. 1335–1338, 1997.

[57] P. Wide, F. Winquist, P. Bergsten, and E. Petriu, "The human-based multisensor fusion method for artificial nose and tongue sensor data," *IEEE Trans. on Instrumentation and Measurement*, vol. 47, pp. 1072–1077, Oct. 1998.

[58] R. Dowdeswell and P. Payne, "Odour measurement using conducting polymer gas sensors and an artificial neural network decision system," *Engineering Science and Education Journal*, vol. 8, pp. 129–134, June 1999.

[59] E. Hines, E. Llobet, and J. Gardner, "Electronic noses: a review of signal processing techniques," *IEE Proc. — Circuits, Devices and Systems*, vol. 146, pp. 297–310, Dec. 1999.

[60] G. Canepa, M. Morabito, D. De Rossi, A. Caiti, and T. Parisini, "Shape from touch by a neural net," in *Proc. IEEE Int. Conf. on Robotics and Automation, 1992*, vol. 3, pp. 2075–2080, 1992.

[61] W. McMath, M. Colven, S. Yeung, and E. Petriu, "Tactile pattern recognition using neural networks," in *Proc. Int. Conf. on Industrial Electronics, Control, and Instrumentation, 1993*, vol. 3, pp. 1391–1394, 1993.

[62] A. Caiti, G. Canepa, D. De Rossi, F. Germagnoli, G. Magenes, and T. Parisini, "Towards the realization of an artificial tactile system: fineform discrimination by a tensorial tactile sensor array and neural inversion algorithms," *IEEE Trans. on Systems, Man and Cybernetics*, vol. 25, pp. 933–946, June 1995.

[63] G. Canepa, R. Petrigliano, M. Campanella, and D. D. Rossi, "Detection of incipient object slippage by skin-like sensing and neural network processing," *IEEE Trans. on Systems, Man and Cybernetics, Part B*, vol. 28, pp. 348–356, June 1998.

[64] J. Patra, A. Kot, and G. Panda, "An intelligent pressure sensor using neural networks," *IEEE Trans. on Instrumentation and Measurement*, vol. 49, pp. 829–834, Aug. 2000.

[65] S. Aisawa, K. Noguchi, and T. Matsumoto, "Neural processing-type displacement sensor employing multimode waveguide," *IEEE Photonics Technology Letters*, vol. 3, pp. 394–396, Apr. 1991.

[66] A. Carullo, F. Ferraris, S. Graziani, U. Grimaldi, and M. Parvis, "Ultrasonic distance sensor improvement using a two-level neural-network," *IEEE Trans. on Instrumentation and Measurement*, vol. 45, pp. 677–682, Apr. 1996.

[67] K. Zhang, C. Butler, Q. Yang, and Y. Lu, "A fiber optic sensor for the measurement of surface roughness and displacement using artificial neural networks," *IEEE Trans. on Instrumentation and Measurement*, vol. 46, no. 4, pp. 899–902, 1997.

[68] J. Kramer, R. Sarpeshkar, and C. Koch, "Pulse-based analog VLSI velocity sensors," *IEEE Trans. on Circuits and Systems II: Analog and Digital Signal Processing*, vol. 44, pp. 86–101, Feb. 1997.

[69] G. Brasseur, "Modeling of the front end of a new capacitive finger-type angular-position sensor," *IEEE Trans. on Instrumentation and Measurement*, vol. 50, pp. 111–116, Feb. 2001.

[70] K.-J. Xu and C. Li, "Dynamic decoupling and compensating methods of multi-axis force sensors," *IEEE Trans. on Instrumentation and Measurement*, vol. 49, pp. 935–941, Oct. 2000.

[71] M. H. Choi and W. W. Lee, "A force/moment sensor for intuitive robot teaching application," in *Proc. IEEE Int. Conf. on Robotics and Automation, 2001*, vol. 4, pp. 4011–4016, 2001.

[72] B. Fahimi, G. Suresh, and M. Ehsani, "Torque estimation in switched reluctance motor drive using artificial neural networks," in *Proc. 23rd Int. Conf. on Industrial Electronics, Control and Instrumentation, 1997*, vol. 1, pp. 21–26, 1997.

[73] F. Discenzo, F. Merat, D. Chung, and P. Unsworth, "Low-cost optical neural-net torque transducer," in *IEE Colloquium on Intelligent and Self-Validating Sensors (Ref. No. 1999/160)*, pp. 15/1–15/4, 1999.

[74] W. Bock, E. Porada, and M. Zaremba, "Neural processing-type fiberoptic strain sensor," *IEEE Trans. on Instrumentation and Measurement*, vol. 41, pp. 1062–1066, Dec. 1992.

[75] J. Dias Pereira, O. Postolache, and P. Silva Girão, "A temperature compensated system for magnetic field measurements based on artificial neural networks," *IEEE Trans. on Instrumentation and Measurement*, vol. 47, pp. 494–498, Apr. 1998.

[76] C. Chan, W. Jin, A. Rad, and M. Demokan, "Simultaneous measurement of temperature and strain: an artificial neural network approach," *IEEE Photonics Technology Letters*, vol. 10, pp. 854–856, June 1998.

[77] S.-L. Tsao, J. Wu, and B.-C. Yeh, "High-resolution neural temperature sensor using fiber Bragg gratings," *IEEE J. of Quantum Electronics*, vol. 35, pp. 1590–1596, Nov. 1999.

[78] A. Chatterjee, S. Munshi, M. Dutta, and A. Rakshit, "An artificial neural linearizer for capacitive humidity sensor," in *Proc. 17th IEEE Instrumentation and Measurement Technology Conf., 2000*, vol. 1, pp. 313–317, 2000.

[79] M. Dawson, A. Fung, and M. Manry, "A robust statistical-based estimator for soil moisture retrieval from radar measurements," *IEEE Trans. on Geoscience and Remote Sensing*, vol. 35, pp. 57–67, Jan. 1997.

[80] H.-K. Hong, H. W. Shin, H. S. Park, D. H. Yun, C. H. Kwon, K. Lee, S.-T. Kim, and T. Moriizumi, "Gas identification using oxide semiconductor gas sensor array and neural-network pattern recognition," in *The 8th Int. Conf. on Solid-State Sensors and Actuators, 1995 and Eurosensors IX*, vol. 1, pp. 687–690, 1995.

[81] T. Lu and J. Lerner, "Spectroscopy and hybrid neural network analysis," *Proc. IEEE*, vol. 84, pp. 895 –905, June 1996.

[82] M. Giacomini, C. Ruggiero, S. Bertone, and L. Calegari, "Artificial neural network identification of heterotrophic marine bacteria based on their fatty-acid composition," *IEEE Trans. on Biomedical Engineering*, vol. 44, pp. 1185–1191, Dec. 1997.

[83] A. Pardo, S. Marco, and J. Samitier, "Nonlinear inverse dynamic models of gas sensing systems based on chemical sensor arrays for quantitative measurements," *IEEE Trans. on Instrumentation and Measurement*, vol. 47, pp. 644–651, June 1998.

[84] S. Osowski and K. Brudzewski, "Hybrid neural network for gas analysis measuring system," in *Proc. 16th IEEE Instrumentation and Measurement Technology Conf., 1999*, vol. 1, pp. 440–444, 1999.

[85] T. Sobanski, A. Szczurek, and B. Licznerski, "Application of sensor array and artificial neural network for discrimination and qualification of benzene and ethylbenzene," in *24th Int. Spring Seminar on Electronics Technology: Concurrent Engineering in Electronic Packaging, 2001*, pp. 150–153, 2001.

[86] M. Attari, F. Boudjema, and M. Heniche, "An artificial neural network to linearize a G (tungsten vs. tungsten 26% rhenium) thermocouple characteristic in the range of zero to 2000°C," in *Proc. IEEE Int. Symp. on Industrial Electronics, 1995*, vol. 1, pp. 176–180, 1995.

[87] G. Dempsey, N. Alt, B. Olson, and J. Alig, "Control sensor linearization using a microcontroller-based neural network," in *Proc. IEEE Int. Conf. on Systems, Man, and Cybernetics, 1997*, vol. 4, pp. 3078–3083, 1997.

[88] N. Medrano-Marqués and B. Martín-del-Brío, "Sensor linearization with neural networks," *IEEE Trans. on Industrial Electronics*, vol. 48, pp. 1288–1290, Dec. 2001.

[89] S. Ben-Yacoub, Y. Abdeljaoued, and E. Mayoraz, "Fusion of face and speech data for person identity verification," *IEEE Trans. on Neural Networks*, vol. 10, pp. 1065–1074, Sept. 1999.

[90] A. Filippidis, L. Jain, and N. Martin, "Multisensor data fusion for surface land-mine detection," *IEEE Trans. on Systems, Man and Cybernetics, Part C*, vol. 30, pp. 145–150, Feb. 2000.

[91] Z. Zhang, S. Sun, and F. Zheng, "Image fusion based on median filters and SOFM neural networks: a three-step scheme," *Signal Processing*, vol. 81, pp. 1325–1330, June 2001.

[92] Y. Xia, H. Leung, and E. Bossé, "Neural data fusion algorithms based on a linearly constrained least square method," *IEEE Trans. on Neural Networks*, vol. 13, pp. 320–329, Mar. 2002.

[93] M. Napolitano, G. Silvestri, D. Windon II, J. Casanova, and M. Innocenti, "Sensor validation using hardware-based on-line learning neural networks," *IEEE Trans. on Aerospace and Electronic Systems*, vol. 34, pp. 456–468, Apr. 1998.

[94] O. Postolache, P. Girão, H. Ramos, and J. Dias Pereira, "A temperature sensor fault detector as an artificial neural network application," in *Proc. MELECON 98, 9th Mediterranean Electrotechnical Conf., 1998*, vol. 1, pp. 678–682, 1998.

[95] Y. Liu, Y. Shen, and H. Hu, "A new method for sensor fault detection, isolation and accommodation," in *Proc. 16th IEEE Instrumentation and Measurement Technology Conf., 1999*, vol. 1, pp. 488–492, 1999.

[96] T. Long, E. Hanzevack, and W. Bynum, "Sensor fusion and failure detection using virtual sensors," in *Proc. 1999 American Control Conf.*, vol. 4, pp. 2417 -2421, 1999.

[97] G. Betta and A. Pietrosanto, "Instrument fault detection and isolation: state of the art and new research trends," *IEEE Trans. on Instrumentation and Measurement*, vol. 49, pp. 100–107, Feb. 2000.

[98] A. Sachenko, V. Kochan, V. Turchenko, V. Golovko, J. Savitsky, A. Dunets, and T. Laopoulos, "Sensor errors prediction using neural networks," in *Proc. IEEE-INNS-ENNS Int. Joint Conf. on Neural Networks, 2000*, vol. 4, pp. 441–446, 2000.

[99] H. Jin, C. Chan, H. Zhang, and W. Yeung, "Fault detection of redundant systems based on B-spline neural network," in *Proc. 2000 American Control Conf.*, vol. 2, pp. 1215–1219, 2000.

[100] G. Yen and W. Feng, "Winner take all experts network for sensor validation," in *Proc. 2000 IEEE Int. Conf. on Control Applications, 2000*, pp. 92–97, 2000.

[101] E. Eryurek and B. Upadhyaya, "Sensor validation for power plants using adaptive backpropagation neural network," *IEEE Trans. on Nuclear Science*, vol. 37, pp. 1040–1047, Apr. 1990.

[102] Ş. Naidu, E. Zafiriou, and T. McAvoy, "Use of neural networks for sensor failure detection in a control system," *IEEE Control Systems Mag.*, vol. 10, pp. 49–55, Apr. 1990.

[103] K. Cohen, Y. Hu, W. Tompkins, and J.Webster, "Breath detection using a fuzzy neural network and sensor fusion," in *Proc. Int. Conf. on Acoustics, Speech, and Signal Processing, 1995*, vol. 5, pp. 3491–3494, 1995.

[104] A. Chong, S. Wilcox, and J. Ward, "Prediction of gaseous emissions from a chain grate stoker boiler using neural networks of ARX structure," *IEE Proc. — Science, Measurement and Technology*, vol. 148, pp. 95–102, May 2001.

[105] Y. Ninomiya, "Quantitative estimation of SiO_2 content in igneous rocks using thermal infrared spectra with a neural network approach," *IEEE Trans. on Geoscience and Remote Sensing*, vol. 33, pp. 684–691, May 1995.

[106] D. Tsintikidis, J. Haferman, E. Anagnostou, W. Krajewski, and T. Smith, "A neural network approach to estimating rainfall from spaceborne microwave data," *IEEE Trans. on Geoscience and Remote Sensing*, vol. 35, pp. 1079–1093, Sept. 1997.

[107] P. Chang and L. Li, "Ocean surface wind speed and direction retrievals from the SSM/I," *IEEE Trans. on Geoscience and Remote Sensing*, vol. 36, pp. 1866–1871, Nov. 1998.

[108] Y.-A. Liou, Y. Tzeng, and K. Chen, "A neural-network approach to radiometric sensing of land-surface parameters," *IEEE Trans. on Geoscience and Remote Sensing*, vol. 37, pp. 2718–2724, Nov. 1999.

[109] C. Clerbaux, J. Hadji-Lazaro, S. Payan, C. Camy-Peyret, and G. Mégie, "Retrieval of CO columns from IMG/ADEOS spectra," *IEEE Trans. on Geoscience and Remote Sensing*, vol. 37, pp. 1657–1661, May 1999.

[110] B. Arrue, A. Ollero, and J. M. de Dios, "An intelligent system for false alarm reduction in infrared forest-fire detection," *IEEE Intelligent Systems*, vol. 15, pp. 64–73, May 2000.

[111] T. Chady, M. Enokizono, R. Sikora, T. Todaka, and Y. Tsuchida, "Natural crack recognition using inverse neural model and multi-frequency eddy current method," *IEEE Trans. on Magnetics*, vol. 37, pp. 2797–2799, July 2001.

[112] T. Chady, M. Enokizono, and R. Sikora, "Signal restoration using dynamic neural network model for eddy current nondestructive testing," *IEEE Trans. on Magnetics*, vol. 37, pp. 3737–3740, Sept. 2001.

[113] G. Pottie and W. Kaiser, "Wireless integrated network sensors," *Communications of the ACM*, vol. 43, pp. 51–58, May 2000.

[114] R. Van Dyck and L. Miller, "Distributed sensor processing over an ad hoc wireless network: simulation framework and performance criteria," in *IEEE Military Communications Conf., 2001*, vol. 2, pp. 894–898, 2001.

[115] L. Guibas, "Sensing, tracking and reasoning with relations," *IEEE Signal Processing Mag.*, vol. 19, pp. 73–85, Mar. 2002.

[116] F. Zhao, J. Shin, and J. Reich, "Information-driven dynamic sensor collaboration," *IEEE Signal Processing Mag.*, vol. 19, pp. 61–72, Mar. 2002.

[117] F. Amigoni, A. Brandolini, G. DAntona, R. Ottoboni, and M. Somalvico, "Artificial intelligence in science of measurements and the evolution of the measurements instruments: A perspective conception," in *Proc. 2002 IEEE Int. Symp. on Virtual and Intelligent Measurement Systems*, pp. 26–31, May 2002.

[118] J. Dias Pereira, P. Silva Girão, and O. Postolache, "Fitting transducer characteristics to measured data," *IEEE Instrumentation & Measurement Mag.*, vol. 4, pp. 26–39, Dec. 2001.

[119] W. Bock, E. Porada, M. Beaulieu, and T. Eftimov, "Automatic calibration of a fiber-optic strain sensor using a self-learning system," *IEEE Trans. on Instrumentation and Measurement*, vol. 43, pp. 341–346, Apr. 1994.

[120] P. Kluk and R. Morawski, "Static calibration of transducers using parametrization and neural-network-based approximation," in *Proc. IEEE Instrumentation and Measurement Technology Conf., 1996*, vol. 1, pp. 581–585, June 1996.

[121] D. Massicotte, S. Legendre, and A. Barwicz, "Neural-network-based method of calibration and measurand reconstruction for a high-pressure measuring system," *IEEE Trans. on Instrumentation and Measurement*, vol. 47, pp. 362–370, Apr. 1998.

[122] R. Schultz, "Applications of neural networks for transducer calibration and signal processing of transducer data containing periodic interference," in *Proc. American Control Conf., 1999*, vol. 3, pp. 1661–1662, June 1999.

[123] T.-F. Lu, G. C. Lin, and J. R. He, "Neural-network-based 3D force/torque sensor calibration for robot applications," *Engineering Applications of Artificial Intelligence*, vol. 10, pp. 87–97, Feb. 1997.

Neural Networks for Instrumentation, Measurement and Related Industrial Applications
S. Ablameyko et al. (Eds.)
IOS Press, 2003

Chapter 4
Neural Networks in System Identification

Gábor HORVÁTH
Department of Measurement and Information Systems
Budapest University of Technology and Economics
Magyar tudósok körútja 2, 1521 Budapest, Hungary

Abstract. System identification is an important way of investigating and understanding the world around. Identification is a process of deriving a mathematical model of a predefined part of the world, using observations. There are several different approaches of system identification, and these approaches utilize different forms of knowledge about the system. When only input-output observations are used behavioral or black box model can be constructed. In black box modeling neural networks play an important role. The purpose of this paper is to give an overview of the application of neural networks in system identification. It defines the task of system identification, shows the basic questions and introduces the different approaches can be applied. It deals with the basic neural network architectures, the capability of neural networks and shows the motivations why neural networks are applied in system identification. The paper presents the main steps of neural identification and details the most important special problems, which must be solved when neural networks are used in system modeling. The general statements are illustrated by a real world complex industrial application example, where important practical questions and the strength and weakness of neural identification are also discussed.

4.1. Introduction

System identification is the process of deriving a mathematical model of a system using observed data. Modeling is an essentially important way of exploring, studying and understanding the world around. A model is a formal description of a system, which is a separated part of the world. A model describes certain essential aspects of a system.

In system modeling three main principles have to be considered. These are separation, selection and parsimony.

The world around is a collection of objects, which are in interactions with each other: the operation of one object may have influence on the behavior of others. In modeling we have to separate one part of the world from all the rest. This part is called the system to be modeled. *Separation* means that the boundaries which separate the system from its environment have to be defined

The second key principle is *selection*. Selection means that in modeling only some essential aspects of a system are considered. There are many different interactions between the parts of a system and between the system and its environment. However, in a modeling task all interactions cannot be considered. Some types of interactions have to be taken into account while others must be neglected. The selection of the aspects to be considered depends on the final goal of modeling. Some aspects are important and must be represented in one case, while entirely different aspects are to be represented in another case, even if the system is the same. This means that a model is always imperfect, it is a simplified representation of a system, it only approximates a system. This approximation may be better, more accurate in certain aspects and less accurate in others. Because of this simplification, to work with models is always easier than to work with real systems. However, it also means that the validity of the results obtained using a model of a system is always limited.

The third principle is *parsimony*. In model building many different models can be built using the same observations and all these models can be consistent with the observed data. Some guiding principle has to be used to select one model from the possible ones. Parsimony means that in modeling it is always desirable to use as simple model as possible. Parsimony principle is formulated as the Occam's razor: *The most likely hypothesis is the simplest one that is consistent with all observations.* Or in other words: *The simpler of two theories, two models (when both are consistent with the observed data) is to be preferred.*

4.2. The main steps of modeling

In every modeling task the following main steps can be distinguished:
- collection of prior information,
- selection of model set, model structure,
- experiment design and data collection,
- model parameter estimation,
- model validation.

The role of these steps in the whole identification process is depicted in Figure 1.

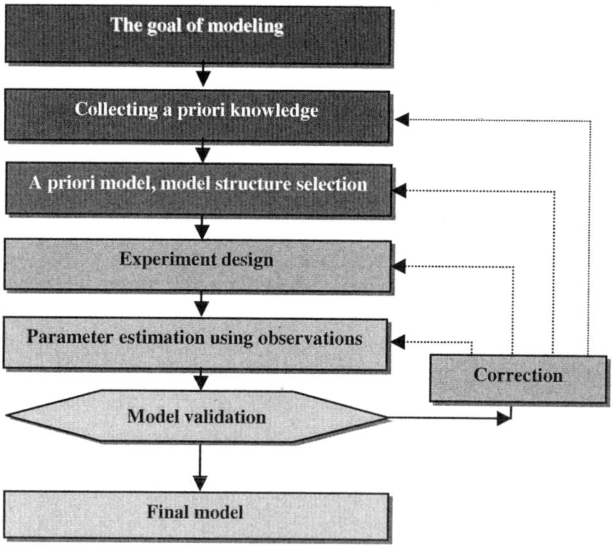

Figure 1: System identification as an iterative process.

In system identification many different approaches can be applied depending on the prior information available, the goal of modeling, what part of the world has to be modeled and what aspects are to be considered, etc.

Model set selection means that the relation between inputs and outputs of a system is formulated in a general mathematical form. This mathematical form defines the structure of the model and defines a set of parameters, the values of which have to be determined during the identification process.

Model classes can be categorized in different ways depending on the aspects taken into consideration.

Based on the *system characteristics* we can distinguish between

- static or dynamic,
- deterministic or stochastic,
- continuous-time or discrete-time,
- lumped parameter or distributed parameter,
- linear or non-linear,
- time invariant or time variant, etc.

models.

All these differentiations are important for the further steps of the whole identification process.

Independently from the previous aspect we can build *parametric* or *nonparametric* models.

In parametric models a definite model structure is selected and only a limited number of parameters must be estimated using observations. In many cases there are some physical insight about the system, we know what important parts of the system can be distinguished, how these parts are connected, etc, so we know the structure of the model. In these cases physical models can be built. Physical models are typical parametric models, where the structure of the model is determined using physical insight.

In nonparametric models there is no definite model structure and the system's behavior is described by the response of the system for special excitation signal. Nonparametric models can be built if we have less knowledge about the system. Typical nonparametric description of a system is the impulse response or the frequency characteristics.

4.2.1 Model set selection

Model set selection is basically determined by the available information. The more information is available the better model can be constructed and the more similarity will be between the system and its model. Based on *prior information* we can speak about white box, grey box or black box models.

When both the structure and the parameters of the model are completely known – complete physical knowledge is available - we have a white box model. White box models can be constructed from the prior information without the need of any observations.

When the model construction is based only on observed data, we speak about input-output or behavioral model. An input-output model is often called empirical or *black box* model as the system to be modeled is considered as a black box, which is characterized with its input-output behavior without any detailed information about its structure. In black box modeling the model structure does not reflect the structure of the physical system, thus the elements of the model structure have no physical meaning. Instead, such model structure has to be chosen that is flexible enough to represent a large class of systems.

Of course the white box and the black box models represent extremes. Models actually employed usually lie somewhere in between. In most of the identification tasks we have certain physical information, however this is not complete (incomplete theoretical knowledge). We can construct a model, the structure of which is selected using available physical insight, so the structure of the model will correspond to that of the physical system. The parameters of the model, however, are not known or only partly known, and they must be estimated from observed data. The model will be fitted empirically using observations. Physical modeling is a typical example of grey-box modeling. The more complete the physical insight the "lighter" grey box model can be obtained and vice verse. The "darkness" of model depends on the missing and known information as shown in Figure 2.

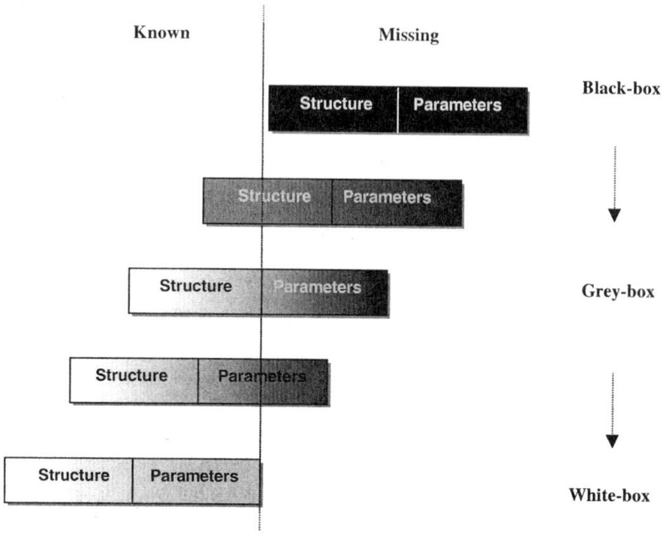

Figure 2: Model categories based on prior information.

The approach used in modeling depends not only on prior information, but the complexity of the modeling procedure and the goal of modeling as well. As building black box models may be much simpler than physical modeling, it is used not only when the lack of physical insight does not let us build physical models, but also in such cases when we have enough physical knowledge, but it is too complex, there are mathematical difficulties, the cost of building physical models is too high, etc.

In black box modeling – contrary to physical ones – the model structure is not determined entirely by selecting the model class. We have to determine the size of the structure, the number of model parameters (e.g., in a polynomial model class the maximum order of the polynomial, etc.). To determine the proper size of the model and the numerical values of the parameters additional information about the system have to be used. This additional information can be obtained from observations. For collecting observations we have to design experiments, to design input signals, and measure the output signals as responses for these input ones.

4.2.2 Experiment design

Experiment design has an important role of getting relevant observations. In the step of experiment design the circumstances of input–output data collection is determined, the excitation signals are designed. The construction of excitation signal depends on the prior knowledge about the system. For example, different excitation signals have to be used to identify a linear and a non-linear system; the excitation depends on whether the system is static or dynamic, deterministic or stochastic, etc. In non-linear system identification the selection of excitation signal depends on the required validity range of the model. Different excitations can be used if model validity is required only for the neighborhood of an operating point or if such model is needed that reflects some important aspects of the system in many different operating points, etc.

In general we have to select input signals that will excite the system in such a way that the input–output data can be observed during the experiment carry enough knowledge about the system. In system identification it is often required to design new and significantly modified experiments during the identification process, where the knowledge collected from the previous experiments are utilized.

In many cases experiment design means to determine what signals can be measured at all, so this step depends largely on the practical identification task. In some identification problems there is no possibility to design excitation, we can only measure the input and output data available in normal operating conditions. This situation may happen when experiment design would be too expensive or when the system to be modeled is an autonomous one, which operates without explicit input signals, etc.

The general and special questions of experiment design are beyond the scope of this paper, interested readers can consult relevant books, e.g. [1,2].

4.2.3 Model parameter estimation

Model set selection means that the relation between inputs and outputs of a system is formulated in a general mathematical form. This mathematical form defines the structure of the model and defines a set of parameters, the values of which have to be determined during the further steps of the identification process. In the sequel we assume that the system implements an $f: R^N \rightarrow R$ mapping, however the scalar output is used only for simplicity. This mapping is represented by a set of input-output measurement data $\{\mathbf{x}(i), y(i)\}_{i=1}^{P}$.

The relation between the input and output measurement data can be described as

$$y(i) = f(\mathbf{x}(i)) + n(i) \tag{1}$$

where $n(i)$ is the observation noise.

This system will be modeled by a general model structure. The mapping of the model $\hat{f}$ will approximate in some sense the mapping of the system.

$$y_M(i) = \hat{f}(\mathbf{x}(i), \mathbf{\Theta}) \tag{2}$$

The model also implements an $R^N \rightarrow R$ mapping; y_M is the output of the model and $\mathbf{\Theta}$ is the parameter vector of the model structure.

Having selected a parametrized model class, the parameters of the model have to be determined. There are well-developed methods, which give estimates for the numerical values of the parameters. These parameter estimation methods utilize different types of knowledge available about the system to be modeled. We may have prior information about the nature of the parameters to be determined (e.g., we may have physical knowledge about the possible range of certain parameters, we may have information if some parameters are deterministic ones or can be considered as random variables with known probability distribution, etc.), but the essential part of the knowledge used for parameter estimation is a set of measurement data, a set of observations $\{\mathbf{x}(i), y(i)\}_{i=1}^{P}$ about the system.

Parameter estimation is a way of adjusting the model parameters for fitting the observations according to some criterion function. The parameter estimation process is shown in Figure 3.

Depending on the criterion function (which also may depend on the prior information about our system) we can speak about least square (LS) estimation, weighted least square (WLS) estimation, maximum likelihood (ML) estimation or Bayes estimation.

A criterion function is a measure of the quality of the model, it is a function of the error between the model output y_M and the system output y:

$$C(\mathbf{\Theta}) = C\left(y - y_M\left(\mathbf{\Theta}, Z^P\right)\right) \tag{3}$$

where Z^P denotes the set of measured data pairs

$$Z^P = \{\mathbf{x}(i), y(i)\}_{i=1}^{P} \tag{4}$$

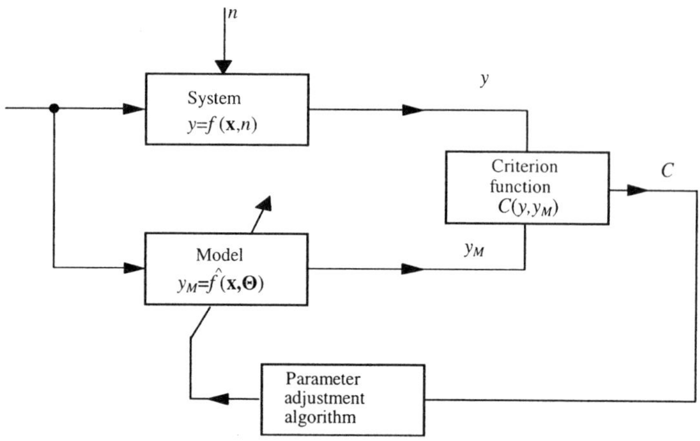

Figure 3: The parameter estimation process.

If both model structure and model size are fixed, model parameters have to be estimated. In parameter estimation the selection of criterion function mainly depends on the prior information. The most common measure of discrepancy is the sum of squared error,

$$C(\mathbf{\Theta}) = \frac{1}{2}\boldsymbol{\varepsilon}(\mathbf{\Theta})^T\boldsymbol{\varepsilon}(\mathbf{\Theta}) = \frac{1}{2}\sum_{i=1}^{P}(\varepsilon(i))^2 = \frac{1}{2}\sum_{i=1}^{P}(y(i) - y_M(i))^2 \tag{5}$$

or the average of the squared error between the model outputs and the observations, which is often called empirical risk:

$$C_{emp}(\mathbf{\Theta}) = \frac{1}{P}\sum_{i=1}^{P}(y(i) - y_M(i))^2 \tag{6}$$

i.e., usually quadratic criterion functions are used.

Quadratic criterion function can always be applied, because it requires only the observed input – output data of the system and the output data of the model for the known input data. The parameter estimate based on this quadratic criterion function is the least square estimate:

$$\mathbf{\Theta}_{LS} = \arg\min_{\mathbf{\Theta}} C(\mathbf{\Theta}) \tag{7}$$

The observations are noisy measurements, so if something is known about the statistical properties of the measurement noise some statistical estimation can be applied. One of the most common statistical estimations is maximum likelihood (ML) estimation, when we select the estimate, which makes the given observations most probable.

$$\mathbf{\Theta}_{ML} = \arg\max_{\mathbf{\Theta}} f(\mathbf{y}_P|\mathbf{x}_P,\mathbf{\Theta}) \tag{8}$$

where $f(\mathbf{y}_P|\mathbf{x}_P,\mathbf{\Theta})$ denotes the conditional probability density function of the observations. The maximum likelihood estimate is illustrated in Figure 4.

If the parameter to be estimated is a random variable and if its probability density function is known, we can apply Bayes estimation. Although Bayes estimation has certain optimality property, it is rarely applied because it requires more prior information than ML or LS estimations.

There is no place to discuss the classical estimation methods in detail. There are many excellent books and papers dealing with the classical system identification methods; they give detailed discussion of parameter estimation methods as well, especially for linear dynamic systems, see e.g. [1-7].

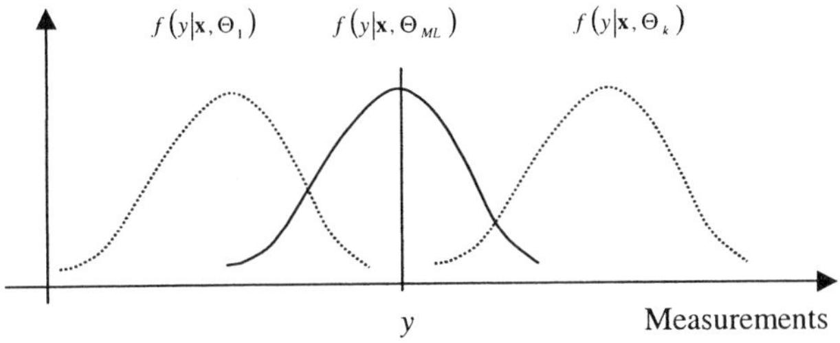

Figure 4: Maximum likelihood estimation.

4.2.4 Model validation

The final step of system identification is the *validation* of the model. For validation a proper criterion as a fitness of the model must be used. The choice of this criterion is extremely important as it determines a measure of the quality of the model. From the result of the validation we can decide whether or not the model is good enough for our purpose. If not, an iterative cycle of structure selection (model class and model size selection), experiment design, parameter estimation and model evaluation must be repeated until a suitable representation is found; so system identification is an iterative process.

4.3. Black box model structures

When we have no prior information about the system to build physical model, black box modeling approach can be used. In black box modeling a general model structure must be selected, which is flexible enough to build models for a wide range of different systems. In this paper we assume that the input – output mapping of the system to be modeled can be described by a continuous function $y=f(\mathbf{x})$. However, as the function is unknown we try to build a model solely on observations about the system's behavior. In a practical black box modeling problem we can observe noisy measurements, where the relation between the measured input and output data can be described again as before:

$$y(i) = f(\mathbf{x}(i)) + n(i) \tag{9}$$

From this point of view black box identification is similar to the general identification case, except that there is no other knowledge about the system than the observations:

$$Z^P = \left\{\mathbf{x}^{(i)}, y^{(i)}\right\}_{i=1}^{P} \tag{10}$$

A black box model will give a relationship between the observed inputs and outputs. The mapping of the model can be described as $y_M(i) = \hat{f}(\mathbf{x}(i),\boldsymbol{\Theta})$, i=1,2,...P, where $\boldsymbol{\Theta}$ is the parameter vector of the model.

There are several different forms of this relationship, however, a general form can be described as a weighted sum of given basis functions $\{G_j(.)\}_{j=1}^{M}$:

$$y_M(k) = \sum_{j=1}^{M} \alpha_j G_j(\mathbf{x}(k)) \tag{11}$$

where the parameter vector is defined as $\boldsymbol{\Theta} = [\alpha_1 \alpha_2 \ldots \alpha_n]^T$.

There are many possible basis function sets, which can be applied successfully in system identification (nonlinear function approximation). For example, we can form polynomial functions, when the mapping of the system is approximated by a polynomial, or we can use complex exponentials, which means, that the mapping of the system is approximated by a Fourier series. But Taylor expansion, wavelets or Volterra series can also be applied. Among the black box structures neural networks play an important role.

The selection between the possibilities usually based on prior information about the system, or on some general (theoretical or practical) advantages or drawbacks of the different black box architectures.

Having selected a basis function set two problems must be solved: (i) how many basis functions are required in this representation, and (ii) how the parameters of the model can be estimated. The first question belongs to the model selection problem, the selection of the size of the model, while the second question is a parameter estimation problem.

The answers to these questions can be divided into two groups. There are general solutions, which are valid for all black box modeling approaches, and there are special results which apply only for a given black box architecture. The general answers are related mainly to the model size problem, while for the parameter estimation task different methods have been developed for the different black box architectures. Most of these methods are discussed in detail in the basic literature of system identification, here only such methods will be presented that are directly related to neural modeling.

The next sections give an overview of neural networks, presents the most important neural architectures and the most important features of the neural paradigm, it shows why neural networks are important in system modeling. The special problems, difficulties in neural modeling and possible solutions to avoid these difficulties will also be discussed.

4.4. Neural networks

Neural networks are distributed information processing systems made up of a great number of highly interconnected identical or similar simple processing units, which are doing local processing, and are arranged in ordered topology. An important feature of these networks is their adaptive nature, which means that its knowledge is acquired from its environment through an adaptive process called learning. The construction of neural networks uses this iterative process instead of applying the conventional construction steps (e.g., programming) of a computing device. The roots of neural networks are in neurobiology; most of the neural network architectures mimic biological neural networks, however in engineering applications this neurobiological origin has only a limited importance and limited effects.

In neural networks several slightly different elementary neurons are used, however, the neural networks used for system modeling usually apply two basic processing elements. The first one is the perceptron and the second is the basis function neuron.

The *perceptron* is a nonlinear model of a neuron. This simple neural model consists of two basic parts: a linear combiner and a nonlinear activation function. The linear combiner computes the scalar product of the input vector **x** of the neuron and a parameter vector (weight vector) **w**:

$$s = \sum_{i=0}^{N} w_i x_i = \mathbf{w}^T \mathbf{x} \tag{12}$$

Every element of the weight vector determines the strength of the connection from the corresponding input. As x_0=1, w_0 serves as a bias value. The bias has the effect of increasing or decreasing the input signal level of the activation function depending on its sign. The nonlinear activation function is applied for the output of the linear combiner. It is responsible for the nonlinear behavior of the neuron model. The mapping of the elementary neuron is:

$$y=g(s)=g(\mathbf{w}^T\mathbf{x}) \tag{13}$$

where $g(.)$ denotes a the nonlinear activation function. In most cases the activation function is a monotonously increasing smooth squashing function, as it limits the permissible amplitude range of the output to some final value. The typical activation functions belong to the family of the sigmoidal functions. The most common elements of this family are the logistic function, $y=\mathrm{sgm}(s)=\dfrac{1}{1+e^{-s}}$ and the hyperbolic tangent function, $y=\tanh(s)=\dfrac{1-e^{-2s}}{1+e^{-2s}}$.

A *basis function neuron* receives simultaneously all components of the N-dimensional real-valued input vector $\mathbf{x}$, then applies a nonlinear basis function on it. The mapping of a basis function neuron usually depends on one or more parameters. The general form of this mapping is given by:

$$y=g(\mathbf{x})=g\|\mathbf{x}-\mathbf{c}\| \tag{14}$$

where $g(.)$ is a nonlinear basis function and $\mathbf{c}$ is a parameter of the basis function. Typical basis functions are the radially symmetric functions, like a Gaussian function, where $\mathbf{c}$ is a centre parameter. In Gaussian basis functions there is another parameter, the width •, as a Gaussian function is given by:

$$g_i(\mathbf{x})=\exp\left[-\|\mathbf{x}-\mathbf{c}_i\|^2/2\sigma_i^2\right] \tag{15}$$

Both neuron types can be used in many, different neural architectures. Here only such architectures will be discussed which can be used for system modeling.

For constructing a neural network first its architecture must be selected, than the free parameters of the architecture must be determined. To select the architecture we must determine what type and how many elementary neurons are to be used and how they should be organized into a certain - usually regular – structure. The values of the free parameters can be determined using the networks' adaptive nature, their learning capability.

System identification usually means identification of dynamic systems, so when dealing with neural architectures the emphasis will be on dynamic neural networks. However, as dynamic networks are based on static ones, first a short overview of the basic static neural architectures will be given.

For presenting the most important dynamic neural structures two different approaches will be followed. We will begin with the classical dynamic neural architectures, then a general approach will be shown, where the nonlinear dynamic mapping is represented as a nonlinear function of a regressor vector. Using this approach, which has been introduced in linear dynamic system identification, we can define important basic nonlinear dynamic model classes.

4.5. Static neural network architectures

The most common neural architecture is the multi-layer perceptron (MLP). An MLP is a feed-forward network built up of perceptron-type neurons, arranged in layers. An MLP has an input layer, one or more hidden layers and an output layer. In Figure 5 a single hidden layer multi-input – multi-output MLP is shown. An MLP is a fully connected network, which means that every node (neuron) in each layer of the network is connected to every other neuron in the adjacent forward layer. The k-th output of a single hidden layer MLP can be written as:

$$y_k = g\left(\sum_{j=0}^{N_2} w_{kj}^{(2)} g\left(\sum_{i=0}^{N_1} w_{ji}^{(1)} x_i\right)\right) \tag{16}$$

Here $w_{kj}^{(l)}$ denotes a weight of the MLP, which belongs to the k-th neuron in layer l and which is connected to the j-th neuron's output of the previous layer. The $g(.)$-s in Eq. (16) stand for the activation functions. In the figure $\mathbf{w}^{(l)}$ contains all weights of layer l.

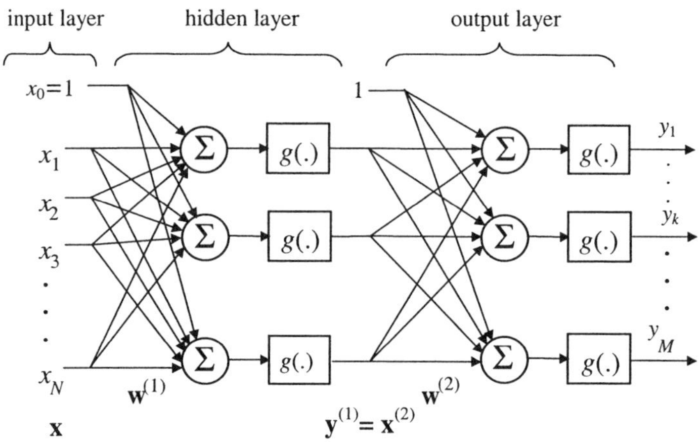

Figure 5: A multi-layer perceptron with one hidden layer.

Perhaps the most important question arising about MLPs is its computational or modeling capability. Concerning this question the main result is that a one hidden-layer feed-forward MLP with sufficient number of hidden processing elements of sigmoidal type, and a single linear output neuron is capable of approximating any continuous function $f: R^N \rightarrow R$ to any desired accuracy.

There are several slightly different mathematical results formulating the universal approximation capability, the most important of which were developed by Hornik [8], Cybenko [9], Funahashi [10], Leshno et al. [11], etc. Here only the result of Cybenko will be cited:

Let g be any continuous sigmoid-type function, then give any continuous real-valued function f on $[0,1]^N$ or any other compact subset of R^N and $\varepsilon > 0$, there exist vectors $\mathbf{w}^{(1)}$ and $\mathbf{w}^{(2)}$, and a parametrized function $\hat{f}(\mathbf{x}, \mathbf{w}^{(1)}, \mathbf{w}^{(2)})$: $[0,1]^N \bullet R$ such that

$$\left| f(\mathbf{x}) - \hat{f}(\mathbf{x}, \mathbf{w}^{(1)}, \mathbf{w}^{(2)}) \right| < \varepsilon \quad \text{for all } \mathbf{x} \in [0,1]^N \tag{17}$$

where

$$\hat{f}(\mathbf{x}, \mathbf{w}^{(1)}, \mathbf{w}^{(2)}) = \sum_{j=1}^{M} w_j^{(2)} g\left(\mathbf{x}^T \mathbf{w}_j^{(1)}\right) = \sum_{j=1}^{M} w_j^{(2)} g\left(\sum_{i=0}^{N} x_i w_{ij}^{(1)}\right) \tag{18}$$

In Eq. (18) $\mathbf{w}^{(1)} = \left[\mathbf{w}_1^{(1)}, \mathbf{w}_2^{(1)}, \ldots, \mathbf{w}_M^{(1)}\right]$ is the weight vector of the first computing layer (what is usually called hidden layer), where $\mathbf{w}_j^{(1)} \in R^{N+1}$ $j=1,2,\ldots M$, is the weight vector of the j-th hidden neuron, $x_0=1$ as defined earlier and $\mathbf{w}^{(2)} = \left[w_1^{(2)}, w_2^{(2)}, \dots, w_M^{(2)}\right]$ is the weight vector of the linear output layer.

This theorem states, that for getting an MLP with universal approximation property only the hidden neurons must be nonlinear, the output neuron may be a simple linear combiner. Moreover it states that one hidden layer is enough. In spite of this result in practical applications two or more hidden layers are often used, as an MLP with more hidden layers may have certain advantages. Such advantage may be, that the total number of neurons is less using more hidden layers or the training of the network, the estimation of its parameters may be easier.

An MLP with one hidden layer can be represented as a weighted sum of some nonlinear basis functions. The general architecture of these networks is depicted in Figure 6.

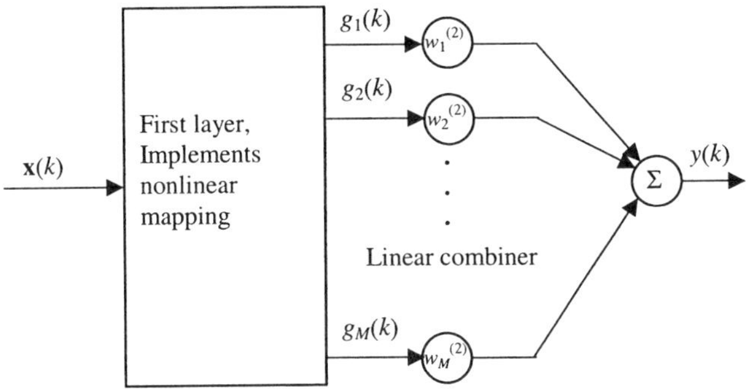

Figure 6: General network with nonlinear hidden layer and linear output layer.

The network has two computing layers: the first one is responsible for an $R^N \rightarrow R^M$ nonlinear mapping, which results in an intermediate vector $\mathbf{g}(k) = [g_1(k), g_2(k), \dots, g_M(k)]^T$. The elements of this intermediate vector are the responses of the basis functions. The output of the mapping is then taken to be a linear combination of the basis functions.

In an MLP the basis functions are parametrized sigmoidal functions where the parameters are the weight values of the hidden layer. So a single hidden layer MLP has two parameter sets: $\mathbf{w}^{(1)}$ consists of all weights of the hidden layer and $\mathbf{w}^{(2)}$ is formed from the weights of the output linear combiner.

There are several further neural network architectures, which also implement weighted sum of basis functions, but where these basis functions are not sigmoidal ones.

When radial basis functions are used the *Radial Basis Function* (RBF) neural network is obtained, but the *Cerebellar Model Articulation Controller* (CMAC) [12] and the *Functional Link Network* (FLN) [13] or the *Polynomial Neural Network* (PNN) [14], etc. are also elements of the two-computing-layer networks, where nonlinear mapping is implemented only in the first (hidden) layer.

Perhaps the most important member of this family and the second most popular network architecture behind MLP is RBF. In an RBF network all neurons of the first computing layer simultaneously receive the N-dimensional real-valued input vector $\mathbf{x}$, so this layer consists of basis function neurons. The outputs of these neurons are not calculated using the weighted-sum/sigmoidal activation mechanism as in an MLP. The output of each hidden basis function neuron is obtained by calculating the "closeness" of the input $\mathbf{x}$ to an N-dimensional parameter vector $\mathbf{c}_j$ associated to the j-th hidden unit. The response of the j-th hidden element is given by:

$$g_j(\mathbf{x}) = g\left(\left\|\mathbf{x} - \mathbf{c}_j\right\|\right) \tag{19}$$

Typical radial basis functions are the Gaussian functions of Eq. (15) where the $\mathbf{c}_i$ vectors are properly selected centres and the σ_i values are the width parameters of the basis functions. The centres are all different for the different hidden neurons, the width parameters may be different, but often a common width parameter σ is used for all basis functions. A Gaussian function is a local basis function where its locality is determined by the width parameter.

The RBF networks – similarly to the MLPs – are also universal approximators [15], where the degree of accuracy can be controlled by three parameters: the number of basis functions used, their location (the centre parameters) and their width. Because of the similar modeling capabilities of MLPs and RBFs, they are alternative neural architectures in black box system identification.

Besides their similarities these two architectures differ from each other in several aspects. These differences - although do not influence their essential modeling capability - may be important from practical point of view. One architecture may require smaller number of nodes and parameters than the other; there may be significant differences between the learning speed of the two architectures, etc. However, all these differences can be considered as technical ones; their detailed discussion is beyond the scope of this paper. Interested readers can consult some excellent books, e.g. [16,17].

CMAC is also a feed-forward network with similar capability. It uses hidden units with local basis functions of predefined-positions. In the simplest case, in binary CMAC [12] - finite support rectangular basis functions are used, but higher-order CMACs can also be defined, when higher order basic splines are applied as local basis functions [17]. The modeling capability of a CMAC is slightly inferior to that of an MLP [18,19] (a binary CMAC implements a piecewise linear mapping, and only higher order CMACs can implement continuous input-output mapping), but it has significant implementation advantages especially when embedded hardware solutions are required [20].

4.6. Dynamic neural architectures

The basic neural network architectures presented in the previous section all implement static nonlinear mapping between their inputs and output,

$$y_M(k) = f(\mathbf{x}(k)) \tag{20}$$

that is the output at a discrete time step k depends only on the input at the same time instant. Static networks can be applied for static nonlinear system modeling.

In black box system identification, however, the really important task is to build models for dynamic systems. In dynamic systems the output at a given time instant depends not only on its current inputs, but on the previous behavior of the system. Dynamic systems are systems with memory.

4.6.1 Extensions to dynamic neural architectures

There are several ways to form dynamic neural networks using static neurons, however in all ways we use storage elements and/or apply feedback. Both approaches can result in several different dynamic neural network architectures.

Storage elements can be used in different parts of a static network. For example, some storage modules can be associated with each neuron, with the inputs or with any intermediate nodes of a static network. As an example a feed-forward dynamic network can be constructed from a static multi-input – single-output network (e.g., from an MLP or RBF) if a tapped delay line is added as shown in Figure 7. This means that the static network is extended by an embedded memory, which stores the past values of the inputs.

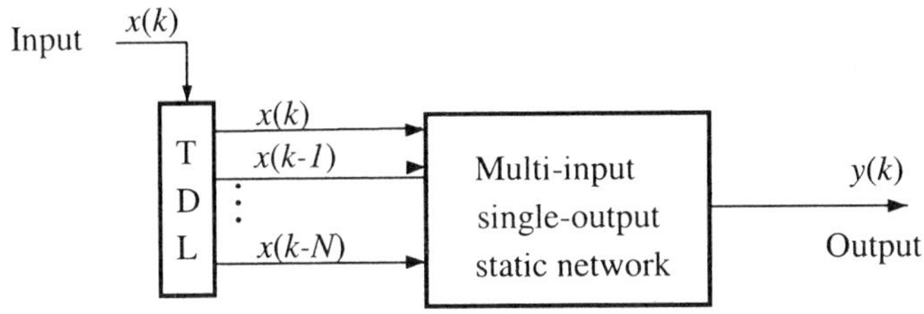

Figure 7. Feed-forward dynamic neural network architecture.

Tapped delay lines can be used not only in the input signal path, but at the intermediate nodes of the network or in the output signal path.

A feed-forward dynamic neural architecture can also be obtained if tapped delay lines are applied for the inputs of all neurons, that is all weights of a static network are replaced by linear filters. If finite impulse response (FIR) filters are used, the resulted dynamic architecture is the FIR-MLP, which is shown in Figure 8.

The output of the i-th neuron in layer l is given as:

$$y_i^{(l)}(k) = g\left(\sum_j z_{ij}^{(l)}(k) = \right) = g\left(\sum_j \mathbf{w}_{ij}^{(l)T} \mathbf{x}_j^{(l)}(k)\right) \tag{21}$$

where $\mathbf{w}_{ij}^{(l)} = \left[w_{ij,0}^{(l)}, w_{ij,1}^{(l)}, \ldots, w_{ij,M_i^{(l)}}^{(l)}\right]^T$ is the j-th filter coefficient vector of node i in layer l, the elements of which are associated with the corresponding taps of the FIR filter. The input vector of this filter is formed from the delayed outputs of the j-th neuron of the previous layer:

$$\mathbf{y}_j^{(l-1)}(k) = \mathbf{x}_j^{(l)}(k) = \left[x_j^{(l)}(k), x_j^{(l)}(k-1), \ldots, x_j^{(l)}\left(k - M_i^{(l)}\right)\right]^T \tag{22}$$

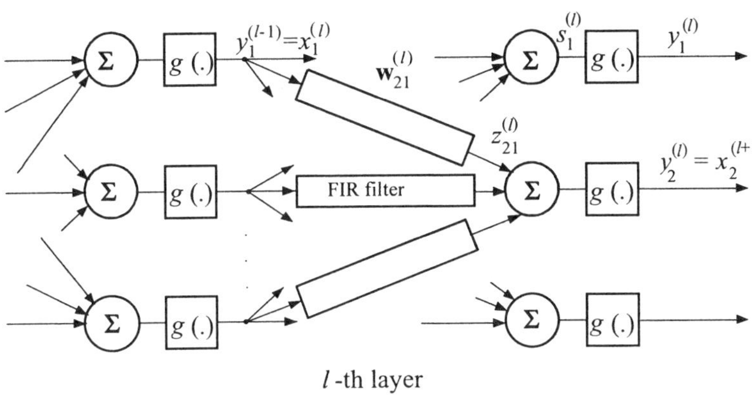

Figure 8. FIR-MLP feed-forward neural network architecture.

If the tapped delay line is used in the output signal path, a feedback architecture can be constructed, where the inputs or some of the inputs of a feed-forward network consist of delayed outputs of the network. The resulted network is a recurrent one. A possible architecture where tapped delay lines are used both in the input and in the output signal paths is shown in Figure. 9.

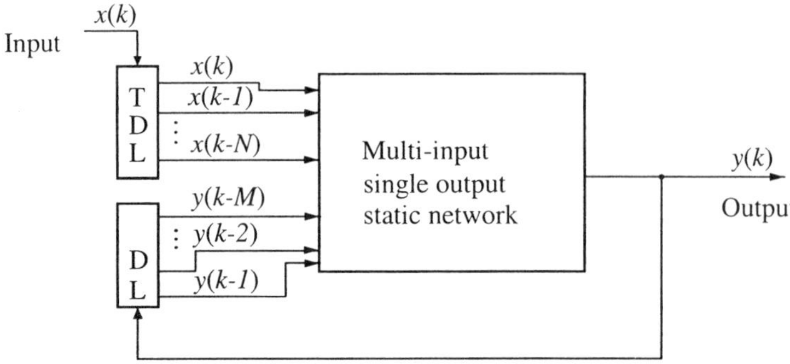

Figure 9: A dynamic neural architecture with feedback.

These dynamic neural networks are general dynamic nonlinear modeling architectures as they are based on static networks with universal approximation property. In these architectures dynamics is introduced into the network using past values of the system inputs, of the intermediate signals and/or of the outputs.

The structure in Figure 9 applies global feedback from the output to the input. However, dynamic behavior can also be obtained if local feedback is used. In this case not the network's output but the output of one or more neuron(s) are applied as inputs of either the same or different neurons. Some possibilities are shown in Figure 10. Such typical dynamic neural architectures are the Jordan and the Elman network [21].

A further possibility to construct dynamic neural network is to combine static neural networks and dynamic linear networks. Within this approach both feed-forward and feedback architectures can be defined as proposed by Narendra [22]. In Figure 11 some combined architectures are shown. In the figure N stands for static neural networks, while $H(z)$ denotes linear dynamic systems.

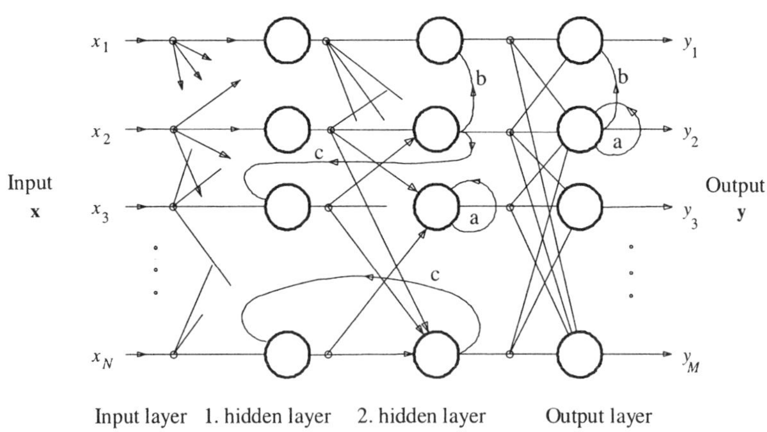

Figure 10: Dynamic neural architecture with local feedback.

The model of Figure 11 a.) is also known as Hammerstein model, while the model of b.) as Hammerstein-Wiener model [2]. Similarly to the Hammerstein model a Wiener model can be constructed where the order of the static nonlinear part and the dynamic linear part is changed over. Also there is a model structure called Wiener – Hammerstein model, which is similar to model b.) except that a static nonlinear system is placed between two linear dynamic ones.

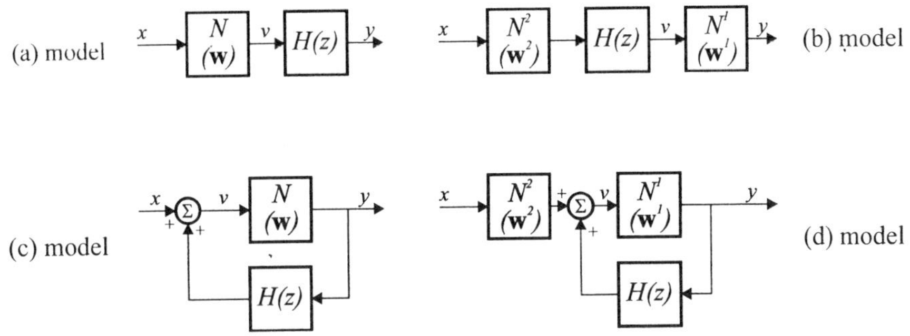

Figure 11: Combined dynamic neural architectures.

4.6.2 General dynamic model structures

Previously many different dynamic neural network architectures were presented. In nonlinear system identification, however, a much more general approach can be followed. In this approach – similarly to the building of linear dynamic black box models – general nonlinear model structures can be formed.

In these dynamic model structures a regressor vector is used, and the output of the model is described as a parametrized function of this regressor vector [23]:

$$y_M(k) = f(\Theta, \varphi(k)) \tag{23}$$

where Θ is the parameter vector and $\varphi(k)$ denotes the regressor vector.

The regressor can be formed from past inputs, past system outputs, past model outputs etc. according to the model structure selected. The following regressors can be defined:

When only the past inputs are used the regressor is formed as:

$$\varphi(k) = [x(k-1), x(k-2), \ldots, x(k-N)] \tag{24}$$

Based on this regressor a feed-forward nonlinear model structure can be constructed. This model - similarly to its linear counterpart - is called an NFIR model. An NFIR model does not contain feedback so it cannot be unstable using any parameter vector. This is the simplest case of regressor-based architectures.

If both past inputs and system outputs are used in the regressor

$$\varphi(k) = [x(k-1), x(k-2), \ldots, x(k-N), y(k-1), y(k-2), \ldots, y(k-P)] \tag{25}$$

the NARX model can be constructed. This model is often called series-parallel model [22], as it uses a feedback, however this feedback comes from the system's - and not the from the model's output, let us avoid forming a really recurrent model architecture.

The regressor can be formed from the past inputs and past model outputs

$$\varphi(k) = [x(k-1), x(k-2), \ldots, x(k-N), y_M(k-1), y_M(k-2), \ldots, y_M(k-P)] \tag{26}$$

The corresponding structure is the NOE model. In a NOE model there is a feedback from model output to its input, so this is a recurrent network. Sometimes NOE model is called as parallel model [22]. Because of its recurrent architecture serious instability problem may arise, which cannot be easily handled.

In the NARMAX model the past inputs, the past system outputs and the past model outputs are all used. Usually the past model outputs are used to compute the past values of the difference between the outputs of the system and the model,

$$\varepsilon(k-i) = y(k-i) - y_M(k-i), \quad i = 1, 2, \ldots, L \tag{27}$$

so the regressor is as follows:

$$\varphi(k)=[x(k-1),\ldots,x(k-N),y(k-1),\ldots,y(k-P),\varepsilon(k-1),\ldots,\varepsilon(k-L)] \tag{28}$$

The regressor for the NBJ models is formed from past inputs, past model outputs and the past values of two different errors, ε and ε_x. Here ε is defined as before, while ε_x is

$$\varepsilon_x(k-i)=y(k-i)-y_{Mx}(k-i),\ i=1,2,\ldots,K \tag{29}$$

In this equation $y_{Mx}(k-i)$ is the model output when only the past inputs are used. The corresponding regressor is

$$\varphi(k)=[x(k-1),\ldots,x(k-N),y_M(k-1),\ldots,y_M(k-P),\varepsilon(k-1),\ldots,\varepsilon(k-L),\varepsilon_x(k-1),\ldots,\varepsilon_x(k-K)] \tag{30}$$

Although the definitions of these general model classes are different from the definition of the classical dynamic neural architectures, those structures can be classified according to these general classes. For example, an FIR-MLP is an NFIR network, but the combined models a) and b) in Figure 11 also belong to the NFIR model class, while the neural structure of Figure 9 is a typical NOE model.

The selection of the proper model class for a given identification problem is not an easy task. Prior information about the problem may help in the selection, although these model classes are considered as general black box architectures and black box approach is usually used if no prior information is available.

The general principle of parsimony can also help to select among the several possible model classes. As formulated by the Occam's razor we always have to select the simplest model, which is consistent with the observations. This means that we should start with linear models and only if the modeling accuracy is not good enough we can go further to the more complex NFIR, NARX, NOE, etc., model structures.

The selection of model structure is only the first step of the neural model construction, further important steps are required: to determine the model size and the model parameters. All these steps need the validation of the model, so model class and model size selection as well as the model parameter estimation cannot be done independently from model validation. The question of model size selection will be discussed in the section of model validation, some basic question of parameter estimation – the learning – are the subject of the next section.

4.7. Model parameter estimation, neural network training

In neural networks the estimation of parameters, the determination of the numerical values of the weights is called learning. As it was mentioned, learning is an iterative process, when the weight values of the network are adjusted step by step until we can achieve the best fit between observed data and the model. The learning rules of neural networks can be categorized as *supervised learning*, which is also referred to as learning with a teacher and *unsupervised learning*. In both cases the learning process utilizes the knowledge available in observation data, what is called training data.

4.7.1 Training of static networks

Neural networks used for system modeling are trained with supervised training. In this case the weights of a neural network are modified by applying a set of labeled training samples $Z^P=\{\mathbf{x}^i,y^i\}_{i=1}^P$. Each training sample consists of a unique input $\mathbf{x}(i)$ and a corresponding desired output $y(i)$. During training every samples are applied to the network: a training sample is selected usually at random from the training set, the input is given to the network and the corresponding response of the network is calculated, then this response, the output of a network is compared to the corresponding desired output. For evaluating the network response, a criterion function is defined which is a function of the difference between the network's output and the desired output.

$$\varepsilon(i) = y(\mathbf{x}(i)) - y_M(\mathbf{x}(i), \mathbf{\Theta}) \tag{31}$$

The network output (and the modeling error too) depends on the network parameters, $\mathbf{\Theta}$. Here $\mathbf{\Theta}$ consists of all weights of a neural network. Usually a quadratic criterion function is used: the most common measure of discrepancy for neural networks is the squared error

$$C(\boldsymbol{\varepsilon}) = \frac{1}{2}\boldsymbol{\varepsilon}^T\boldsymbol{\varepsilon} = \frac{1}{2}\sum_{i=1}^{P}(\varepsilon(i))^2 \tag{32}$$

so the supervised learning process is an LS estimation process.

The figure of merit can be defined in a more complex way. In addition to the standard quadratic error performance measure, a second term can be added.

$$C_c = C(\boldsymbol{\varepsilon}) + \lambda C_r, \tag{33}$$

where $C(\boldsymbol{\varepsilon})$ is the standard criterion function, C_r is a so called *regularization* term and λ is the regularization parameter, which represents the relative importance of the second term. This approach is based on the regularization theory developed by Tikhonov [24]. The regularization term usually adds some constraint to the optimization process. The constraint may reflect some prior knowledge (e.g., smoothness) about the function approximated by the network, can represent a complexity penalty term, or in some cases it is used to improve the statistical stability of the learning process.

When regularization is used for complexity reduction the regularization term can be defined as the sum of all weights of the network:

$$C_r = \|\mathbf{w}\|^2 = \sum_i w_i^2 \tag{34}$$

Using this term in the criterion function the minimization procedure will force some of the weights of the network to take values close to zero, while permitting other weights to retain their relatively large values. The learning procedure using this penalty term is called *weight-decay procedure.* This is a parametric form of regularization as the regularization term depends on the parameters of the network.

There are other forms of regularization, like

$$C_r(\mathbf{w}) = C(\mathbf{w}) + \lambda\Phi(\hat{f}(x)) \tag{35}$$

where $\Phi(\hat{f}(x))$ is some measure of smoothness. This latter is a typical form of nonparametric reularization. Regularization can often lead to significantly improved network performance.

The performance measure is a function of the network parameters; the optimal weights values of the network are reached when the criterion function has a minimum value. For neural networks used for function approximation the criterion function is a continuous function of the parameter vector, thus it can be interpreted as a continuous error surface in the weight space. From this point of view network training is nothing else than a minimum seeking process, where we are looking for a minimum point of the error surface in the weight space.

The error surface depends on the definition of the criterion function and the neural network architecture. For networks having trainable weights only in the linear output layer (e.g., networks with architecture shown in Figure 6) and if the sum of squares error is used as criterion, the error surface will be a quadratic function of the weight vector; the error surface will have a general multidimensional parabolic form. In these networks the first layer is responsible for the nonlinear mapping, but this nonlinear mapping has no adjustable parameters. These networks implement nonlinear but *linear-in-the-parameter* mappings. Typical networks with quadratic error surface is an RBF network if the centre and width parameters are fixed, and a CMAC network where there is no trainable parameter in the first nonlinear layer.

The consequence of the parabolic error surface is that there will be a single minimum, which can be located using rather simple ways. For a quadratic error surface analytic solution can be obtained, however even for such cases usually iterative algorithms, e.g., gradient search methods are used. In gradient-based learning algorithms first the gradient of the error surface at a given weight vector should be determined, then the weight vector is modified in the direction of the negative gradient:

$$\mathbf{w}(k+1)=\mathbf{w}(k)-\mu\nabla(k) \tag{36}$$

Here $\nabla(k)$ is the gradient of the error surface at the k-th iteration, μ is a parameter called learning rate, which determines the size of the step done in the direction of the negative gradient.

Eq. (36) is a general form of the gradient algorithm. For networks with one trainable layer the gradient can be computed directly, however for networks with more than one trainable layer the gradient calculation needs to propagate the error back, as the criterion function gives errors only at the outputs. Such networks, like MLPs require this error back propagation process. The result is the *error backpropagation learning algorithm*, which calculates the gradients using the chain rule of derivative calculus. Because of the need of propagating the error back to the hidden layers, the training of a multi-layer network may be rather computation intensive.

Moreover, the error function for networks with more than one trainable layer may be highly nonlinear and there may exist many minima in the error surface. These networks – like MLPs – implement nonlinear mappings, which are at least partly *nonlinear-in-the-parameter* mappings. Among minima there may be one or more for which the value of the error is the smallest, this is (these are) the global minimum (minima); all the other minimum points are called local minima. For nonlinear-in-the-parameter error surfaces we cannot find general closed form solutions. Instead iterative – usually gradient based – methods are used. Although an iterative, gradient-based algorithm does not guarantee that the global minimum will be reached, the learning rules applied for nonlinear-in-the-parameter neural networks usually are also gradient based algorithms.

A more general gradient-based learning rule can be written as:

$$\mathbf{w}(k+1)=\mathbf{w}(k)+\mu\mathbf{Q}(-\nabla(k)) \tag{37}$$

where $\mathbf{Q}$ is a matrix, which modifies the search direction and which usually reflects some knowledge about the error surface.

Several different gradient rules can be derived from this general one if we specify $\mathbf{Q}$. If $\mathbf{Q}=\mathbf{I}$ the identity matrix, we can get the steepest descent algorithm (Eq. 36). With $\mathbf{Q}=\mathbf{H}^{-1}$ and $\mu=1/2$ the Newton algorithm is obtained, where $\mathbf{H}^{-1}$ is the inverse of the Hessian of the criterion function. The Hessian matrix is defined by

$$\mathbf{H}=\nabla\nabla C(\varepsilon)=\left[\frac{\partial^2 C}{\partial w_i \partial w_j}\right] \tag{38}$$

From the general form of the gradient learning rule the Levenberg-Marquardt rule [16] can also be obtained. In this case an approximation of the Hessian is applied to reduce the computational complexity. The different gradient-based algorithms can reach the minimum using less learning iterations, however, one iteration requires more complex computations than the simple steepest descent method.

4.7.2 Training of dynamic networks

The learning rules discussed so far can be applied for static neural networks. For training dynamic networks some additional problems must be solved. Dynamic networks are sequential networks, which means that they implement nonlinear mapping between input- and output data sequences. So the training samples of input–output data pairs of static networks are replaced by input–output data sequences and the goal of the training is to reduce a squared error derived from the elements of the corresponding error sequences. If $\varepsilon(k)$ is the output error of a dynamic network at discrete time step k, the squared total error can be defined as:

$$\varepsilon_{total} = \sum_{k=1}^{K} \varepsilon^2(k) \tag{39}$$

where K denotes the length of the sequence.

Dynamic networks have memory, and this needs significant modification of the training algorithms. The basic training rules for dynamic systems are also gradient-based algorithms. A common feature of these learning rules is, that - instead of modifying the weights in every step when a new sample is used (as it is usually done in static networks) - the weights are modified only after a whole training sequence were applied to the network. This will let the network be unchanged during a whole training data sequence is applied. The most important family of learning rules appropriate for dynamic networks is called *dynamic backpropagation*.

For training dynamic networks different versions of the dynamic backpropagation have been developed [22]. For feed-forward networks a possible approach is to unfold the network in time. This strategy first removes all time delays in the network by expanding it into an equivalent static network. However, the resulted static network will be much larger, moreover several weights of the extended static network represent actually the same weights, which must be updated in an equivalent way. For feed-forward networks unfolding in time is effective only if tapped delay lines are short. A more efficient learning for such NFIR network as an FIR-MLP (shown in Figure 8) is the temporal backpropagation [25].

For recurrent networks two different approaches are applied most often. The first one uses also unfolding in time, which means that a recurrent dynamic network is transformed into a corresponding feed-forward static one. This transformation maps the neurons with their states at every time step into a new layer, where the number of resulting layers is equal to the length of the unfolding time interval. In the unfolded network all weights of the original recurrent network are repeated in every layer. The resulted static network can be trained by standard backpropagation rule, except that these weights are physically identical and should be modified by the same value in one training step. The unfolding-in-time approach is called backpropagation through time (BPTT) [26].

BPTT can be explained most easily in an example. Figure 12 a.) shows a simple recurrent network with only two neurons. Suppose that a four-length input sequence is used, the corresponding unfolded feed-forward static network is shown in Figure 12 b.). The two networks are equivalent for these four steps, however, we have to care that the weight with the same indexes are identical, they exist only ones, although several copies of the weight are drawn in the unfolded version. Unfolding-in-time is a rather simple way of handling recurrent networks, however it is effective only if the time interval is small.

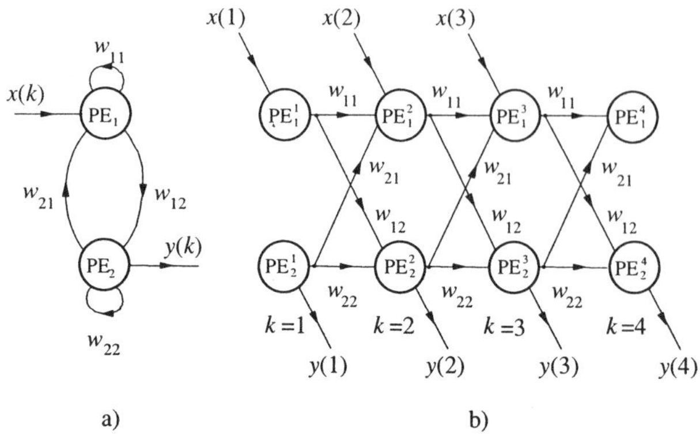

Figure 12: Unfolding-in-time for a simple recurrent network
a) original recurrent network, b) unfolded static feed-forward network

Another method to train a recurrent network is the real-time recurrent learning (RTRL), where the evolution of the gradient over time steps can be written in recursive form [27]. In RTRL the weights are modified in every time steps. This violates the requirement of updating the weights only after a whole training sequence was applied, however, it was found that updating the weights after each time step works well as long as the learning rate μ is kept sufficiently small. Sufficiently small learning rate means that the time scale of the weight changes is much smaller then the time scale of the network operation. Real time recurrent learning avoids the need for allocating memory proportional to the maximum sequence length and leads to rather simple implementations.

During training all training data are usually used many times. The number of training cycles may be quite large, and it is important to find when to stop training. To determine the optimal stopping time the performance of the network must be checked, the network must be validated. So validation helps not only to determine the proper complexity of the network as was indicated before, it is also used to decide whether we have to stop training at a given training cycle.

4.8. Model validation

The goal of the application of neural networks in system identification is to build a black box model of a system using training data. However, this goal is not reached if the model represents the system only at the training points, we need to build an accurate model of the system in the whole operating range of interest. An important feature of a model is that it can approximate well the behavior of a system not only at the training points, but in the whole operating range. This feature is called *generalization.* A neural network without any generalization can only memorize the training points, so it works as a simple lookup table.

Validation is used to estimate the performance of the model, to check its generalization capability. Validation serves several sub-goals. There are validation methods to check if model complexity was selected properly, and there are validation methods what can be used in the learning phase. However, these two sub-goals cannot be reached separately. Usually only a trained model can be validated, which means, that the adequacy of the selected model class and model size can be determined only after model parameters are also determined.

A model of proper complexity is used if both the model class (NFIR, NARX, ... etc.) and the model size (model order, the number of free parameters) are chosen appropriately. A proper model class can be selected either using prior knowledge about the system, or -

according to the principle of parsimony - we have to select as simple model class as possible. For model size selection there are general validation methods used in linear or nonlinear system identification and there are special ones developed for neural networks. To check if the network is trained well, several different validation methods are used. Among them there are methods, which are used for both purposes: to check model complexity and check model parameters.

It is well known, that the more complex model is used the better approximation can be reached at the training points. The reason is that increasing the number of the parameters the degree of freedom will be increased, which means that we can adjust the model parameters to fit the training data more. However, reducing the training error does not reduce necessarily the error at different points obtained from the same problem, but not used in training, so reducing the training error does not mean to get better generalization. For checking the generalization capability of the model we need a set of test data from the same problem, a test set, which is not used in training. Using different data sets for constructing a model and for validating it is an important principle. The validation method based on this principle is called *cross-validation* and it has a distinguished role in neural modeling. The effect of model complexity on the performance of the model can be followed in Figure 13.

It shows the training and test errors versus model complexity. The performance is measured as usual, e.g., they are the sum of the squared errors at all training-points and at all test-points, respectively. It can be seen that as model complexity increases first both the training and the test errors decrease. This behavior can be found until we reach a given complexity. From this point the lowering of the training error goes on, while test error is getting larger. A model of optimal complexity, a model with the best generalization property is obtained at the minimum point of the test error.

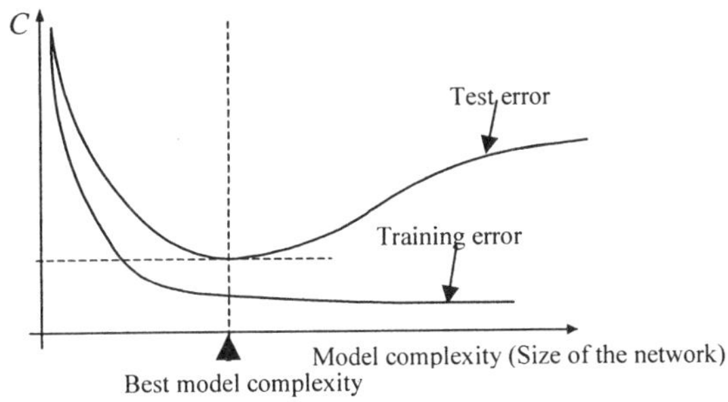

Figure 13. Training and test error versus model complexity

The question of optimal model complexity can be discussed from another point of view. This is the *bias-variance trade-off*. The significance of bias-variance trade-off can be shown if the modeling error is decomposed into a bias and a variance term. As it was defined by Eq. (5), the modeling error is the sum of the squared errors or the average of the squared error

$$MSE_{emp}(\boldsymbol{\Theta}) = \frac{1}{P}\sum_{k=1}^{P}(\varepsilon(k))^2 = \frac{1}{P}\sum_{k=1}^{P}(y(k) - y_M(k))^2 \tag{40}$$

where $\varepsilon(k)$ can be written in a more general form

$$\varepsilon(k) = y(k) - y_M(\boldsymbol{\varphi}(k), \boldsymbol{\Theta}) \tag{41}$$

This error definition is valid for all model structures: if $\boldsymbol{\varphi}(k) = \mathbf{x}(k)$ we will have a static model and if $\boldsymbol{\varphi}(k)$ is one of the regressors defined in section 6, it refers to the error of a dynamic network.

Now, consider the limit in which the number of training data samples goes to infinity, the average of the squared error approximates the mean square error, the expected value of the squared error, where expectation is taken over the whole data set.

$$MSE(\Theta) = E\left\{\left(y - y_M(\Theta)\right)^2\right\} \tag{42}$$

This expression can be decomposed as:

$$MSE(\Theta) = E\left\{\left(y - y_M(\Theta)\right)^2\right\} = E\left\{\left(y_M(\Theta) - E\{y_M(\Theta)\}\right)^2\right\} + \left(y - E\{y_M(\Theta)\}\right)^2 \tag{43}$$

Here the first term is the variance and the second one is the squared bias.

$$MSE\left(y_M(\Theta)\right) = \mathrm{var}\left(y_M(\Theta)\right) + \mathrm{bias}^2\left(y_M(\Theta)\right) \tag{44}$$

The size of the model, the model order will have an effect on the bias-variance trade-off. A small model with fewer than enough free parameters will not have enough complexity to represent the variability of the system's mapping, the bias will generally be high, while the variance is small. A model with too many parameters can fit all training data perfectly, even if they are noisy. In this case the bias term vanishes or at least decreases, but the variance will be significant. (Figure 14.)

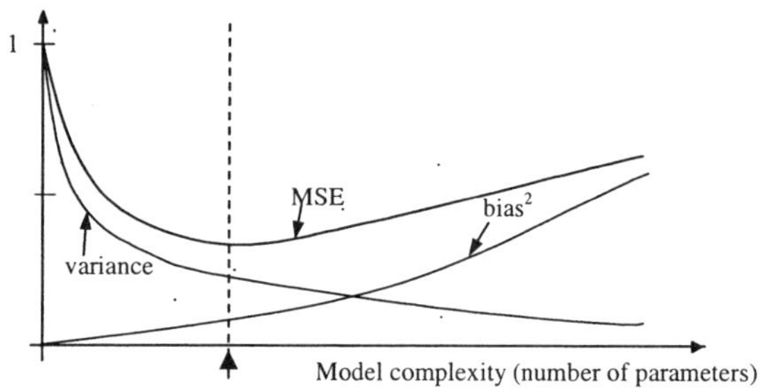

Figure 14: Illustration to the bias-variance trade-off.

In static neural models the model complexity can be adjusted by the number of the hidden neurons. In dynamic models, however this question is more complex. First a proper size of the selected model class must be determined, e.g., for an NFIR architecture we have to select the length of the tapped delay line, or for a NARX or a NARMAX model the lengths of the corresponding tapped delay lines, etc., then the number of hidden neurons which implement the nonlinear mapping have to be determined. Moreover, it can be shown that the selection of the proper model complexity cannot be done independently from the number of available training data samples. There must be some balance between model complexity and the number of training data. The less training points are used, the less knowledge is available from the system and the less free parameters can be used to get a model of good generalization. Of course model complexity must reflect the complexity of the system, more complex systems need more data, which allows building more complex models: models with more parameters.

The question of model complexity versus number of training points and model performance (generalization capability) has been studied from different points of view. One early result for static neural networks gives an upper bound of MSE as a function of the smoothness of the mapping to be approximated, the complexity of the network and the number of training points [28].

$$MSE \le O\left(\frac{C_f^2}{M}\right) + O\left(\frac{MN}{P}\log P\right) \tag{45}$$

where C_f is a measure of smoothness or regularity of the function f, M is the number of hidden neurons, and N is the size of the dimension of the input data.

Another approach is used by the *statistical learning theory* [29] where an upper bound on the generalization error can be derived. For regression problems MSE bounded with probability of at least (1-η) as:

$$\dot{MSE}(\mathbf{\Theta}) \leq \frac{MSE_{\mathrm{emp}}(\mathbf{\Theta})}{1 - c\sqrt{v(h)}} \tag{46}$$

Here

$$v(h) = v\left(\frac{P}{h}, \frac{-\ln\eta}{P}\right) \tag{47}$$

where h is the VC-dimension. VC-dimension is a characteristic parameter of the function set used in the approximation. For the validity of Eq. (46) we need that the probability of observing large values of the error is small [30]. It can be proved that models with good generalization property can be obtained only if h is finite [29]. The generalization bound of Eq. (46) is particularly important for model selection, since it provides an upper limit for complexity for a given sample size P and confidence level η.

4.8.1 Model order selection for dynamic networks

For dynamic systems modeling proper model order selection is especially important. As the correct model order is often not known a priori it makes sense to postulate several different model orders. Based on these, some criterion can be computed that indicated which model order to choose. One intuitive approach would be to construct models of increasing order until the computed squared error reaches a minimum. However as it was shown previously the training error decreases monotonically with increasing model order. Thus, the training error alone might not be sufficient to indicate when to terminate the search for the proper model complexity; model complexity must be penalized to avoid using too complex model structures.

Based on this approach several general criteria were proposed. The most important ones are the Akaike Information Criteria (AIC) [31] and the Minimum Description Length (MDL) [32], which were developed for linear system modeling. Recently for MLPs a network information criterion (NIC) was proposed by Amari [33], which was derived from AIC. The common feature of these criteria is that they have two terms: the first one depends on the approximation error for the training data (i.e. the empirical error), while the second is a penalty term. This penalty grows with the number of free parameters. Thus, if the model is too simple it will give a large value for the criterion because the residual training error is large, while a too complex model will have a large value for the criterion because the complexity term is large.

The methods based on the different criteria need to build and analyze different models, so these methods are rather computation intensive ones and their applicability is questionable in practical cases. Recently a new heuristic method was proposed for identifying the orders of input-output models for unknown nonlinear dynamic systems [34]. This approach is based on the continuity property of the nonlinear functions, which represent input-output mappings of continuous dynamic systems. The interesting and attractive feature of this approach is that it solely depends on the training data. The model orders can be determined using the following index:

$$q^{(N)} = \left(\prod_{k=1}^{p} \sqrt{N}\, q^{(N)}(k)\right)^{1/p} \tag{48}$$

where $q^{(N)}(k)$ is the k-th largest *Lipschitz quotient* among all $q_{ij}^{(N)}$ ($i \neq j$; $i, j = 1, 2, \dots, P$) N is the number of input variables and p is a positive number: usually $0.01P$ -$0.02P$. Here the q_{ij} Lipschitz quotient is defined as:

$$q_{ij} = \frac{|y(i) - y(j)|}{|\mathbf{x}(i) - \mathbf{x}(j)|} \tag{49}$$

where the $\{\mathbf{x}(i), y(i)\}$ i=1, 2, … , P pairs are the measured input-output data samples from which the nonlinear function $f(.)$ have to be reconstructed. This index has the property that $q^{(N+1)}$ is very close to $q^{(N)}$, while $q^{(N-1)}$ is much larger than $q^{(N)}$ if N is the optimal number of the input variables, so a typical curve of $q^{(N)}$ versus N has a definite point (N_0) where the decreasing tendency stops and $q^{(N)}$enters a saturated range. For an NFIR model N_0 is the optimal number of input order. Figure 15 (a) shows a typical curve for $q^{(N)}$.

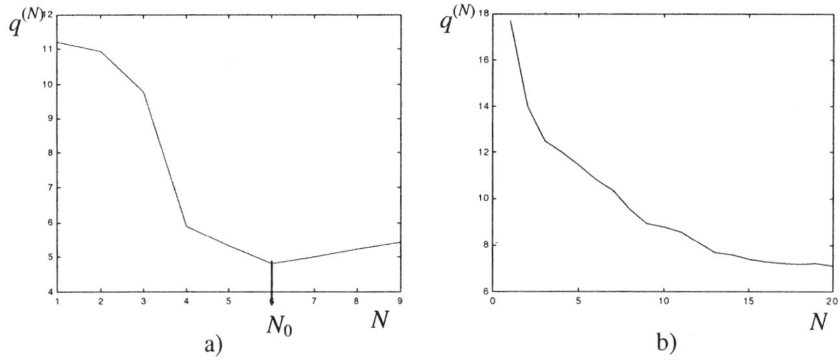

Figure 15: Typical curves of Lipschitz indexes
(a) for noiseless data or data with low noise level, (b) for data with high noise level.

The Lipschitz index can be applied not only for NFIR structures but also for NARX model classes, where two, the order of the feed-forward and the feedback paths must be determined. For NARX model class

$$y_M(k) = f(\varphi(k)) = f[x(k-1), x(k-2), \dots, x(k-M), y(k-1), y(k-2), \dots, y(k-L)] \tag{50}$$

the following strategy can be used. The Lipschitz index $q^{(N)} = q^{(L+M)}$ should be computed for different model orders, where L denotes the feedback and M the feed-forward order values. Starting with N=1, where only $y(k$-1) is used as input $q^{(1+0)}$ can be computed. Then let N = 2, where the both $x(k$-1) and $y(k$-1) are used as inputs and $q^{(1+1)}$ can be computed. For N=3 the third input of the dynamic networks will be $y(k$-2) and $q^{(2+1)}$ will be computed. This strategy can be followed increasing step by step the feedback and the feed-forward orders. If at a given L and M one can observe that $q^{(L+M)}$ is much smaller than $q^{(L-1+M)}$or $q^{(L+M-1)}$, but is very close to $q^{(L+1+M)}$ or $q^{(L+M+1)}$, we reached the appropriate order values.

The most important advantage of this method is that it can give an estimate of the model order without building and validating different complexity models, so it is a much more efficient way of order estimation then the criteria based approaches. However, there is a significant weakness of the Lipschitz method: it is highly sensitive to observation noise. Using noisy data for model construction - depending on the noise level - we can often get a typical curve for the Lipschitz index as shown in Figure 15 (b). The most important feature of this figure is that there is no definite break point.

4.8.2 Cross-validation

Modeling error can be used in another way for model validation. This technique is called cross-validation. In *cross-validation* – as it was mentioned before - the available data set is separated into two parts, a training set and a test set. The basic idea of cross-validation is that one part of the available data set is used for model construction and another part for validation. Cross-validation is a standard tool in statistics [35] and can be used both at the model structure selection and at parameter estimation. Here its role in the training process will be presented.

The previous validation techniques for selecting the proper model structure and size are rather complex, computation intensive methods. This is the most important reason why they are applied only rarely in practical neural model construction. The most common practical way of selecting the size of a neural network is the trial and error approach. First a network structure is selected, then the parameters are trained. Cross-validation is used to decide whether or not the performance of the trained network is good enough. Cross-validation, however, is used for another purpose too.

As it was mentioned in the previous section to determine the stopping time of training is rather difficult as a network with quite large number of free parameters can learn the training data almost perfectly. The more training cycles are applied the smaller error can be achieved on the training set. However, small training error does not guarantee good generalization. Generalization capability can be measured using a set of test data consists of samples never seen during training.

Figure 16 shows two learning curves, the learning curves of the training and the test data. It shows, that usually the training error is smaller than the test error, and both curves decrease monotonically with the number of training iterations till a point, from where the learning curve for the test set starts to increase. The phenomenon when the decrease of the training error is going on, while the test error starts to increase is called overlearning or overfitting. In this case the network will memorize the training points more and more while at the test points the network's response is getting worse, we get a network with poor generalization. Overlearning can be avoided if training is stopped at the minimum point of the test learning curve. This is called *early stopping* and it is an effective way to improve the generalization of the network even if its size is larger than required.

For cross-validation we need a training set and a test set of known examples. However there is a question which must be answered: in what ratio, the data points should be divided into training and testing sets in order to obtain the optimum performance. Using statistical theory a definite answer can be given to this question [36]. When the number of network parameters M is large, the best strategy is to use almost all available known examples in the training set and only $\frac{1}{\sqrt{2M}}$ examples in the testing set, e.g., when $M = 100$, this means that only 7% of the training data points are to be used in the test set to determine the point for early stopping. These results were confirmed by large-scale simulations. The results show that when $P > 30M$ cross-validation is not necessary, because the generalization error becomes worse by using test data to obtain adequate stopping time. However, for $P < 30M$, i.e. the number of the known examples is relatively small compared to the number of network parameters, overtraining occurs and using cross-validation and early stopping improves generalization.

Cross-validation can be used not only for finding the optimal stopping point, but to estimate the generalization error of the network too. In network validation several versions of cross-validation are used. A version called one-leave-out cross-validation is used, especially if the number of known data is small.

The one-leave-out cross-validation is an efficient way of using the examples available. Here we divide the set of examples into two sets as it was proposed before, but only one example will be omitted from the training set and this point will be used for testing. The process will be repeated P times, every time a different example is omitted for testing. Such a procedure allows us to use a high proportion of the available data (all but one) to train the network, while also making use of all data points in evaluating the cross-validation error. The disadvantage of this method is that it requires the training process to be repeated P times.

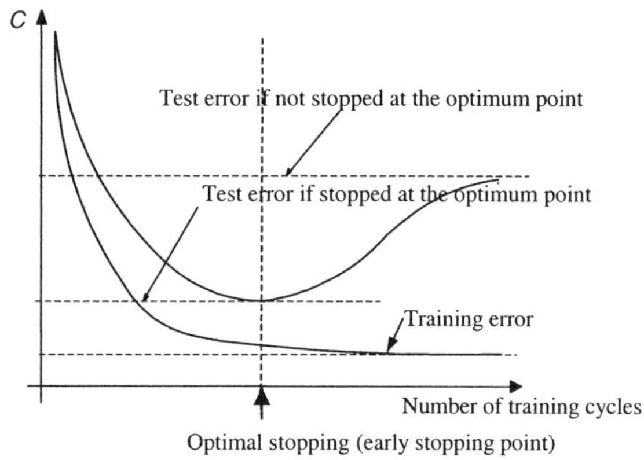

Figure 16: Learning curves for the training and the test data.

4.9. Why neural networks?

In the previous sections we have presented some results, which show that neural networks are general black box structures, so they can be used in black box system identifications. However, using neural networks in system modeling is only one approach among the many available possible ones. There are other black box architectures, and all these architectures can be used to approximate nonlinear mappings of static or dynamic systems, to model nonlinear static or dynamic systems. Moreover, using any of these architectures the steps of model construction are also similar: we have to select a general model structure, a model class, then we have to concretize this model by determining the model size and the model parameters. In all cases the whole process of model building is based on observations and - if any - on prior information.

However, among all these black box architectures neural networks are far the most popular ones. The reasons – at least partly – come from the roots of neural networks: from their neurobiological origin, their ability to learn from examples and from the extremely good problem solving capability of "biological systems", which can be mimicked by artificial neural networks. The historical roots, however, would not be enough for this long time popularity. The real reasons come from the practical advantages of neural modeling.

The application of neural networks has many practical advantages. Among them one can find their relatively simple architecture, their universal approximation capability, etc., but there is an especially important feature of neural networks, mainly MLPs and MLP based dynamic architectures. These networks are not very sensitive to the proper selection of their size; similar performance can be obtained using rather different-size neural models.

In black box modeling to determine the proper size of a model structure is usually a hard task, and choosing improper size often leads to poor models. A too small model is not able to approximate a complex system well enough, a too large model with many free parameters, however, may be very prone to overfitting. These general statements are more or less valid for all modeling approaches, among them for neural networks. MLPs, however, using backpropagation learning rule have a special feature. They may be biased towards implementing smooth interpolation between the training points, which means that they may have rather limited proneness to overfitting.

The effect of this bias is that even using overly complex neural model, overfitting can be avoided. Backpropagation can result in the underutilization of network resources, mainly at the beginning phase of learning, and this can be definitely observed on the training curves. As it was shown in Figure 16 overlearning can be avoided using early stopping. This behavior of MPLs with backpropagation is justified by extensive experimental studies (e.g., [37]), and by explicit analysis, which shows that neural modeling is often ill conditioned, the efficient number of parameters is much less than the nominal number of the network parameters [38,39].

During learning a network can be forced to reduce the number of efficient parameters using regularization, as it was discussed in section 7. However, for MLPs with backpropagation training an implicit regularization, a regularization effect without using an explicit regularization term can be observed. The resulted smooth mapping is an advantageous feature of neural identification as long as the systems to be modeled are continuous ones. Although this implicit regularization cannot be found in other neural networks, similar properties can be obtained easily using some form of explicit regularization, so some inductive bias that is characterized as smooth interpolation between training points can be found not only in MLPs with backpropagation learning, but in RBF or even in CMAC networks.

4.10. Modeling of a complex industrial process using neural networks: special difficulties and solutions (case study)

In industry many complex modeling problems can be found where exact or even approximate theoretical/mathematical relationship between input and output cannot be formulated. The reasons behind this can be the unsatisfactory knowledge we have about the basic underlying physical behavior, chemical reactions, etc., or the high complexity of the input-output relationship. At the same time there is a possibility to collect observations from the system, we can measure input and output data, so an experimental black box model based on the observations can be constructed.

In the previous sections of this paper many general questions of black box modeling and neural networks were discussed. In this section some practical questions will be addressed through a real-world complex industrial modeling example: modeling of a Linz-Donawitz (LD) steel converter.

4.10.1 LD steel-making

Steel-making with an LD converter is a complex physico-chemical process where many parameters have influences on the quality of the resulted steel [40,41]. The complexity of the whole process and the fact that there are many effects that cannot be taken into consideration make this task difficult. The main features of the process are the followings: a large (~150-ton) converter is filled with waste iron (~30 tons), molten pig iron (~ 110 tons) and many additives, then this fluid compound is blasted through with pure oxygen to oxidize the unwanted contamination (e.g., silicon, most of the carbon, etc.).

At the end of the oxygen blowing the quality of the steel is tested and its temperature is measured. If the main quality parameters and the temperature at the end of the steel-making process are within the acceptable and rather narrow range, the whole process is finished and the slag and the steel is tapped off for further processing.

The quality of the steel is influenced by many parameters, however the amount of oxygen used during blasting is the main parameter that can be controlled to obtain predetermined quality steel. From the point of view of steel-making parameters mean the main features, measurement data of components of the input compounds e.g., mass, temperature and the quality parameters of the pig iron and the waste iron, the mass and some quality parameters of all additives, as well as the amount of oxygen used during the blasting process, etc. It is an important and rather hard task to create a reliable predictor for determining the necessary amount of oxygen. To give a reliable prediction we have to know the relation between the input and the output parameters of the steel-making process, therefore we have to build a model of the steel converter. The inputs of the model are formed by all available observations can be obtained from a charge. The outputs are the most important quality parameters of the steel produced, namely its temperature and the carbon content at the end of the blasting.

To present all details of such a complex modeling task is well beyond the possibilities of this paper, so the goal of this section is not to go into the details, instead to point out that besides the basic tasks of system identification mentioned in the previous sections there are important additional ones which cannot be neglected.

A large part of these additional tasks are related to the database construction.

4.10.2 Data base construction for black box identification

In black box modeling the primary knowledge that can be used for model building is a collection of input–output data. So the first task of modeling is to build a proper data base. One serious problem in real-world tasks is that in many cases the number of available data is limited and rather small.

In steel-making the data base can be built only from measurements and observations done during the regular everyday operation of the converter. Steel-making is a typical example where there is no possibility to design special excitation signals and to design experiments for data collection.

Steel production with an LD-converter is organized in campaigns. During one campaign the production is contiguous and in one campaign about 3000 charges of steel is produced. This means that the maximum number of known examples is limited and it cannot be increased. Moreover, the data base collected in one campaign contains typical and special cases, where the data of special cases cannot be used for modeling because of technological reasons. The ratio of special-to-all cases is rather high, it is around 25-30%. The only possibility to increase the size of the data base is to collect data from more campaigns, however, from campaign to campaign the physical parameters of the steel converter are changing significantly and this changing must be followed by the model as well, so one should take care when and how to use the extended data set.

In forming a proper database the further problems have to be considered:

- the problem of dimensionality,
- the problem of uneven distribution of data,
- the problem of noisy and imprecise data,
- the problem of missing data,
- the effects of the correlation between consecutive data.

The problem of dimensionality if often referred to as the curse of dimension. For neural modeling we need representative data, which cover the whole input space. This means that – depending on the dimension of the input space – a rather large number of training and test patterns is required. If N-dimensional inputs are used and if each input component can take R different values in their validity range the number of all possible input data samples is R^N, so it grows exponentially with the dimensionality of the input space. This means that dimension reduction is an important step, especially when the number of training samples cannot be increased arbitrarily. To reduce dimension the following two main approaches can be used:

- Applying some mathematical data compression algorithms, like independent component analysis (ICA), principal component analysis (PCA) or factor analysis. The basic thought behind this approach is that the components of the input data vectors are usually correlated, so without significantly reducing their "information content" less new components can be formed from the original ones.
- By analyzing the raw data and using domain knowledge, the rank of importance of the data components can be estimated and the less important components can be omitted.

In some cases the two approaches can be combined: first – using domain knowledge – we can select the most important input parameters, then on the selected data mathematical data compression algorithms can be applied. In the steel-making problem both methods were considered for reducing the dimension of the observed data, however, the reduction based on domain knowledge proved to be more useful. Instead of using all recorded data, only some 20 most important input components of the original ~50-component data records were used during the training.

The importance of the components was determined using detailed analysis of the data and by the results of some preliminary trained networks. These trained networks were used to determine the sensitivity of the model output to the input components. It turned out that there are some components that have very limited effect on the results, so they could be omitted without significant degradation in the performance of the model. The extensive discussions with skilled personnel of the steel factory about the role of the input components have helped us also to select the most important ones.

As a result three major groups were formed. The first group contained measurement data of clearly high importance, such as mass and temperature values, the waiting time between the finishing of a charge and the start of the next one (this waiting time has an effect on the temperature of the converter before filling it with the new workload). The second group contained clearly negligible data, while the third group contained data of questionable importance. The third group was tested by building several neural models based on the same records of the initial data base, but where the input components of the records were different.

Comparing the performances of the trained networks and analyzing the sensitivity of the model outputs to the different input components the most relevant ones were selected. After 5-10 experiments we could reduce the input parameters from the starting 50 to about 20.

Another common feature of industrial problems is that the input data *are typically not uniformly distributed* over their possible ranges. This means that there may have some clusters, and within these clusters quite a lot and representing data points are available, while there may be other parts of the input space from where only a few examples can be collected. For operating modes from where many data can be collected, appropriate models can be constructed, while in underrepresented operating modes the available data are not enough to build proper black box models.

A further problem is that due to the industrial environment the *registered data are frequently inaccurate and unreliable*. Some of the parameters are measured values (e.g., temperature of pig iron), others are estimated values (e.g., the ratio of the different components of the waste iron), where the acceptable ranges of the values are quite large. It is also typical that some measurements are missing from a record. The precision of the values is rather different even in the case of measured data. If wrong or suspicious data are found, or in case of missing data there are two possibilities: either the data can be corrected, or the whole record is cancelled. Correction is preferred, because of the mentioned dimensionality problem. The large dimensionality and the limited number of data examples makes it very important to save as many patterns as possible.

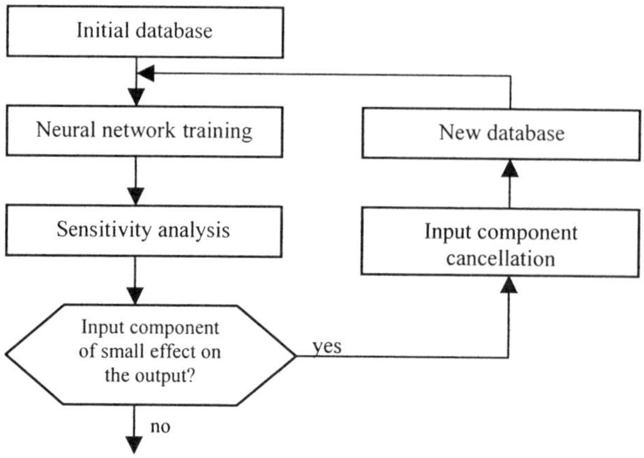

Figure 17: The iterative process of database construction.

Handling of noisy data is a general problem of black box modeling. The methods developed for this problem need some additional information (at least some statistical properties of the measurement noise) and using this additional information a more robust model can be built. Such method is the Errors In Variable (EIV) approach, but Support Vector Machines (SVMs) can also take the noise level into consideration.

The Errors In Variables training method was introduced to reduce the negative effects of measurement noise [42]. The idea behind the method is that knowing some properties of the additive noise, the training process can be modified to compensate the error effects. In EIV approach, instead of the standard quadratic criterion function, a new weighted quadratic criterion function is used, where the weights are the reciprocal values of the variances of the corresponding measurement noise:

$$C_{EIV} = \frac{1}{N} \cdot \sum_{i=1}^{N} \left[\frac{(y(i) - y_M(\boldsymbol{\Theta}, \mathbf{x}^*(i)))^2}{\sigma_{y,i}^2} + \frac{(\mathbf{x}(i) - \mathbf{x}^*(i))}{\sigma_{x,i}^2} \right] \tag{51}$$

In this expression $\{y(i), \mathbf{x}(i)\}$ $i=1, 2, \ldots, P$ denote the measured noisy input-output training examples, $\mathbf{x}^*(i)$ denote the noiseless and naturally not known inputs (during the EIV method estimates of these inputs are also determined), $\sigma_{x,i}^2$ and $\sigma_{y,i}^2$ are the variances of the input and output noise, respectively. The classical LS estimation results in biased estimates of the model parameters, if the input data are noisy. The most attractive feature of the EIV approach is, that it can reduce this bias. This property can be proved if it is applied for training neural networks [43]. The drawback of EIV is its larger computational complexity and the fact that using EIV criterion function the learning process is very prone to overfitting. This latter effect, however, can be avoided using early stopping.

Support Vector Machines are also applies a criterion function that can take the measurement noise into consideration. The criterion function used in SVM is the ε-insensitive function given by Eq. (52).

$$C_{\varepsilon} = \begin{cases} 0 & \text{for} \quad |y - y_M| < \varepsilon \\ |y - y_M| - \varepsilon & \text{otherwise} \end{cases} \tag{52}$$

Using SVMs, the steps of the neural network constructions are rather different from those of the classical neural network approach. An interesting feature of Support Vector Machines is that the size of the model, the model complexity is determined "automatically" while a network of good generalization can be obtained. Another essential difference between the construction of classical neural networks and SVMs is that no training is used in the classical sense, instead the weights of the networks are determined by a quadratic optimization process. The main disadvantage of SVMs is that this quadratic optimization is a rather time and memory consuming method. For details see e.g. [29].

An important feature of the data base is whether or not the *consecutive records are correlated.* This question is closely related to the model class selection, namely if a static or a dynamic model is to be used, and if dynamic one what regressor should be preferred.

4.10.3 Model class selection

Using the principle of parsimony first static and linear models were used. However, using this simple approach the results were far from satisfactory, more complex model class had to be selected. For model class selection prior physical information has great importance. From physical insight it is almost evident that for this industrial process an adequate model can be achieved only if a dynamic model class is chosen. Using this approach it must be taken into consideration that the output quality parameters of a charge depend not only on the current input parameters, but the current state of the converter (e.g., the end temperature of the steel in one charge will have significant effect on the next charge; there is significant difference between the situations when the starting temperature of the empty converter is around the environment temperature of 0-30 °C or it is around 1000 °C. Surely an LD converter is a system with memory.)

A rather simple but useful way to check if static or dynamic model should be chosen is a simple correlation test. Strong correlation between the data records of consecutive charges is an indication that the system has "memory" and dynamic model must be built. This more sophisticated modeling approach can result in more accurate models than pure static ones, as the production of the consecutive charges is not handled as independent elements of a series of similar events.

Using NARX and NARMAX classes the performance of the model can be increased. For dynamic models, however the model order should also be chosen. In this converter modeling task Lipschitz index was used for finding approximate values of model orders. The results show that a NARX model with orders of (3,3) seems to be the best, where the two order parameters refer to the input and the system output orders (see Eq. (29)). However, because of the noisy measurement data, definite break-point on the Lipschitz curve cannot be found. The brake-point can be sharpened using a combined EIV and Lipschitz method [44], when EIV is used for reducing the effects of measurement noise. Another possibility is to use cross-validation for different-order models around the order obtained from the Lipschitz method.

4.10.4 Modular networks

The experiences gained from this industrial modeling task showed, that using a single neural model satisfactory result cannot be obtained. There may be many different reasons behind this experience. One reason can be found in the special characteristics of the data base. As it was mentioned the known examples can be categorized into at least two groups: typical and special ones. The operation of the converter is different in these two cases, and these differences should be reflected by different models. The solution is to use a modular architecture, which contains more models. The selection of the appropriate one is based on the operating mode. The information about the operating mode of the converter can be obtained from some measurement data or some additional information (e.g., it is known that we are at the beginning, in the middle or near the end of a campaign, there may have some information, that the blowing process is greatly different from the standard one, the goal parameters are rather special which occurs rarely, etc.).

This type of modular architecture consists of such models from which one and only one is used in a given case. Other modular architectures can also be constructed where different neural models are cooperating. Instead of using a single neural model an ensemble of models can be used.

There are heuristic and mathematical motivations that justify the use ensemble of networks. According to the heuristic explanation combining several different networks can often improve the performance, however, only if the models implemented by the elements of an ensemble are different.

The advantage of using an ensemble of neural networks can also be justified by a simple mathematical analysis [45]. Let us consider the task of modeling a system's mapping f: $R^N \bullet R$. We assume that we can obtain only noisy samples of this mapping and assume that an ensemble of T independent neural models is available. We define a modular architecture using the ensemble of models and the final output of the ensemble is given by a weighted average as:

$$\bar{y}(\mathbf{x},\boldsymbol{\alpha}) = \sum_{j=0}^{T} \alpha_j y_{M\,j}(\mathbf{x}) \tag{53}$$

where y_{Mj} is the output of the j-th model. We can define two quality measures, the ambiguity and the squared error for every members of the ensemble and for the whole ensemble. The ambiguity of a single member of the ensemble is

$$a_j(\mathbf{x}) = \left[y_{M\,j}(\mathbf{x}) - \bar{y}(\mathbf{x},\alpha)\right]^2 \tag{54}$$

and the ensemble ambiguity is

$$\bar{a}(\mathbf{x},\boldsymbol{\alpha}) = \sum_{j=0}^{T} \alpha_j a_j(\mathbf{x}) \tag{55}$$

This quantifies the disagreement among the models on input **x.** Similarly the quadratic error of model j and the whole ensemble are defined as follows

$$\varepsilon_j(\mathbf{x}) = \left[y(\mathbf{x}) - y_{M\,i}(\mathbf{x})\right]^2 \tag{56}$$

and

$$\varepsilon(\mathbf{x}) = \left[y(\mathbf{x}) - \bar{y}(\mathbf{x},\boldsymbol{\alpha})\right]^2 \tag{57}$$

It can be shown easily that the ensemble quadratic error can be written as:

$$\varepsilon(\mathbf{x}) = \bar{\varepsilon}(\mathbf{x},\boldsymbol{\alpha}) - \bar{a}(\mathbf{x},\boldsymbol{\alpha}) \tag{58}$$

if $\sum_{j=1}^{T} \alpha_j = 1$. In Eq. (58) $\bar{\boldsymbol{\varepsilon}}(\mathbf{x},\boldsymbol{\alpha}) = \sum_{j=0}^{T} \alpha_j \boldsymbol{\varepsilon}_j(\mathbf{x})$ is the weighted error and $\bar{a}(\mathbf{x},\boldsymbol{\alpha})$ is the weighted ambiguity of the models as defined by Eq. (55). Eq. (58) shows that the ensemble quadratic error on **x** can be expressed as the difference between the weighted error and the weighted ambiguity. Taking expectations according to the input distribution we can get the average ensemble generalization error

$$\varepsilon = \bar{\varepsilon} - \bar{a} \tag{59}$$

where ε denotes the expected value of $\varepsilon(\mathbf{x})$ and $\bar{a}$ the expected value of $\bar{a}(\mathbf{x})$. This expression shows that for getting small ensemble generalization error we need accurate and diverse individual models, i.e. they must be as accuratè as possible while they must disagree.

The weights of the individual networks in the ensemble can be estimated from the training example too. There are different ways of this estimation: one of the possibilities is to use a *mixture of experts* (MOE) architecture [46], where the α_j weights as well as the weights of the neural networks are estimated using a joint training process and where the results of training are the maximum likelihood estimates of the needed values. The values of the α_j weights depend on the inputs of the models and they are implemented as outputs of an auxiliary network called gating network.

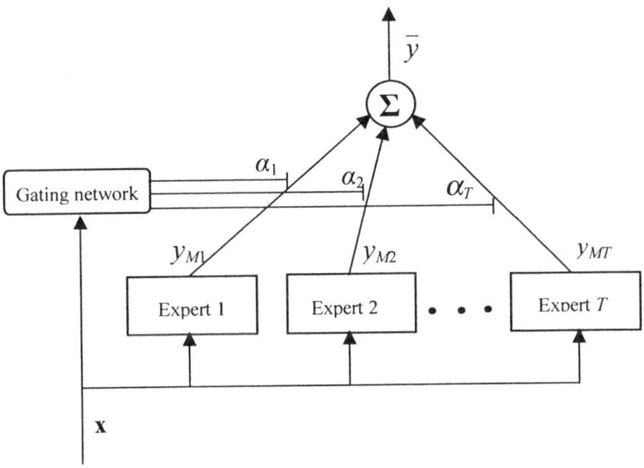

Figure 18: The mixture of experts architecture.

4.10.5 Hybrid models

MOE is a general architecture, where different approaches can be used for implementing the individual experts. Any expert may be a neural model, but any other adaptive or fixed model - like an exact mathematical model, a fuzzy model, a rule based expert system, etc. - can be used as an expert.

The modular philosophy was applied in the steel-making converter modeling task. An important advantage of the modular architecture is, that it can integrate different forms of knowledge available about the physical system, so it is a hybrid-neural modeling system.

In a real-world system identification task usually there is certain prior information, physical knowledge, even if it is not enough to build physical models. To utilize all available knowledge in an efficient way has great importance. The implemented architecture is shown in Figure 19 [47].

The system has three layers. The first (input) layer is an expert system and it is responsible for data preprocessing, data filtering, data correction, filling the gaps in the data base, etc. It is also responsible to find inconsistency of the data, and to find - if any - clusters of the data that can be handled by different means, different approaches. The input expert system has to decide how to handle the current data record, if it is a standard case or it has to be treated specially. It decides according to the given rules of the current model, which neural network or other model must be used. It also can correct some of the data according to the knowledge about measurement noise or measurement device errors. It records this decision also in the knowledge base to be used by the later experts to calculate correction terms and to integrate the results.

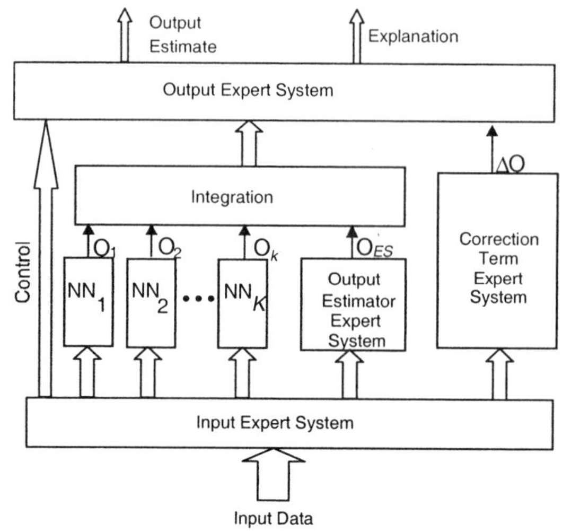

Figure 19: The hybrid-neural modeling system.

The second layer contains the direct modeling devices. It is formed from different neural models that can work with the data belonging to different clusters. In some cases such models cannot be used alone, it may happen that they should be used just together with certain correction terms that modify the result of a neural model. The system makes it possible to build any other modeling device (e.g., mathematical models or expert systems) into this layer in addition to the neural models. However, at present neither mathematical models, nor expert systems can compete with neural ones. So far only such mathematical models could be formed that gave reliable prediction in a small neighborhood of some special working points. These models can be used in the validation of the neural models, or in the explanation generation (see below).

The third or output layer is the decision-maker of the whole modeling system. It has two main tasks: to validate the results, and to make the final prediction using some direct information from the first layer. This layer also uses symbolic rules. It validates the result of the second layer and makes a decision if the result can be accepted at all. This decision-making is based on different information: for example, some direct information from the input layer, or the information obtained from more than one experts of the second layer. As an example for the first case it may happen that the input data are so special that there is no valid model for them in the second layer. Although it is a rare situation, this must be detected by the input expert system and the whole system must be able to give some valid answer even in such cases. This answer informs the staff that in this special case the whole system cannot give reliable output, they must determine it using any other (e.g., conventional) method. In the second case validation is based on the results of more than one expert modules of the second layer. Using these results the output expert system will form the final answer, which may be some combination of the results of more experts or a corrected value of a given expert. The correction term can be determined using the results of other expert modules (e.g., other neural networks), or a separated expert system, the role of which is to determine correction terms directly for the special cases.

A further important task of the output layer is the *explanation generation* what is also based on built-in expert knowledge. As neural networks themselves form black-box models, they cannot generate explanation of the result automatically. However, the acceptance of such results by an industrial community is rather questionable even if this result is quite good. The purpose of explanation generation is to increase the acceptance of the results of the modeling system.

4.11. Conclusions

The purpose of this paper was to give an overview about system identification and to show the important role of neural networks in this field. It was shown that neural networks are general black box modeling devices, which have many attractive features: they are universal approximators, they have the capability of adaptation, fault tolerance, robustness, etc. For system modeling several different static and dynamic neural architectures can be constructed, so neural architectures are flexible enough for a rather large class of identification tasks. The construction of neural models - as they are black box architectures - is mainly based on measurement data observed about the system. This is why one of the most important parts of black box modeling is the collection of as much relevant data as possible, which cover the whole operating range of interest. As it was shown in the example of LD converter modeling, the construction of data base needs to solve many additional problems; to handle noisy data, missing data, unreliable data, to separate the whole data base into training set and test set, etc. All these problems need proper preprocessing, the importance of which cannot be overemphasized.

Moreover, according to the experiences obtained from real-world modeling tasks, prior information and any additional knowledge to the observation has great importance. Prior information helps us to select proper model structure, to design excitation signal if it is possible to use excitation signals at all, to determine the operating range where valid model should be obtained, etc. An important implication obtained from complex real-world identification problems is that using only one approach, one paradigm usually cannot results in satisfactory model. Combining different paradigms, however can join the advantages of the different approaches, can utilize different representations of knowledge, and can help to understand the result obtained. This latter is especially important in neural modeling, because neural models cannot give explanation of the model, and without explanation, the lack of physical meaning may reduce the acceptance of the black box models even if their behavior is rather close to that of the system.

References

[1] L. Ljung, System Identification - Theory for the User. Prentice-Hall, N.J. 2nd edition, 1999.

[2] J. Schoukens and R. Pintelon, System Identification. A Frequency Domain Approach, IEEE Press, New York, 2001.

[3] T. Söderström and P. Stoica, System Indentification, Prentice Hall, Enhlewood Cliffs, NJ. 1989.

[4] P. Eykhoff, System Identification, Parameter and State Estimation, Wiley, New York, 1974.

[5] A. P. Sage and J. L. Melsa, Estimation Theory with Application to Communications and Control, McGraw-Hill, New York, 1971.

[6] H. L. Van Trees, Detection Estimation and Modulation Theory, Part I. Wiley, New York, 1968.

[7] G. C. Goodwin and R. L. Payne, Dynamic System Identification, Academic Press, New York, 1977.

[8] K. Hornik, M. Stinchcombe and H. White, Multilayer Feed-forward Networks are Universal Approximators", Neural Networks Vol. 2. 1989. pp. 359-366.

[9] G. Cybenko, Approximation by Superposition of Sigmoidal Functions, Mathematical Control Signals Systems, Vol. 2. pp. 303-314, 1989.

[10] K. I. Funahashi, On the Approximate Realization of Continuous Mappings by Neural Networks", Neural Networks, Vol. 2. No. 3. pp. 1989. 183-192.

[11] M. Leshno, V. Y. Lin, A. Pinkus and S. Schocken, Multilayer Feed-forward Networks With a Nonpolynomial Activation Function Can Approximate Any Function, Neural Networks, Vol. 6. 1993. pp. 861-67

[12] J. S. Albus, A New Approach to Manipulator Control: The Cerebellar Model Articulation Controller (CMAC), Transaction of the ASME, Sep. 1975. pp. 220-227.

[13] Y. H. Pao, Adaptive Pattern Recognition and Neural Networks, Addison-Wesley, Reading, Mass., 1989, pp. 197-222.

[14] D. F. Specht, Polynomial Neural Networks, Neural Networks, Vol.3. No. 1 pp. 1990. pp. 109-118,

[15] J. Park and I. W. Sandberg, Approximation and Radial-Basis-Function Networks, Neural Computation, Vol 5. No. 2. 1993. pp. 305-316.

[16] S. Haykin, Neural Networks. A comprehensive foundation, Second Edition, Prentice Hall, N. J.1999.

[17] M. H. Hassoun, Fundamentals of Artificial Neural Networks, MIT Press, Cambridge, MA. 1995.
[18] M. Brown and C.Harris, Neurofuzzy Adaptive Modelling and Control, Prentice Hall, New York, 1994.
[19] G. Horváth and T. Szabó, CMAC Neural Network with Improved Generalization Property for System Modelling, Proc. of the IEEE Instrumenation and Measurement Conference, Anchorage, 2002.
[20] T. Szabó and G. Horváth, CMAC and its Extensions for Efficient System Modelling and Diagnosis, Intnl. Journal of Applied Mathematics and Computer Science, Vol. 9. No. 3, pp.571-598, 1999.
[21] J. Hertz, A. Krogh and R. G. Palmer, Introduction to the Theory of Neural Computation, Addison-Wesley Publishing Co. 1991.
[22] K. S. Narendra and K. Pathasarathy, Identification and Control of Dynamical Systems Using Neural Networks, IEEE Trans. Neural Networks, Vol. 1. 1990. pp.
[23] J. Sjöberg, Q. Zhang, L. Ljung, A. Benveniste, B. Delyon, P.-Y. Glorennec, H. Hjalmarsson and A. Juditsky: "Non-linear black-box modeling in system identification: a unified overview", Automatica, 31:1691-1724, 1995.
[24] A.N. Tikhonov, V.Y. Arsenin, Solutions of Ill-posed Problems, Washington, DC: W.H. Winston, 1997
[25] E. A. Wan, Temporal Backpropagation for FIR Neural Networks, Proc. of the 1990 IJCNN, Vol. I. pp. 575-580.
[26] D. E. Rumelhart, G. E. Hinton and R. J. Williams, Learning Internal Representations by Error Propagation, in Rumelhart, D.E. - McClelland, J.L. (Eds.) Parallel Distributed Processing: Explorations in the Microstructure of Cognition, 1. MIT Press. pp. 318-362. 1986.
[27] R. J. Williams and D. Zipser, A Learning Algorithm for Continually Running Fully Recurrent Neural Networks, Neural Computation, Vol. 1. 1989. pp. 270-280.
[28] A. R. Barron, Universal Approximation Bounds for Superposition of Sigmoidal Functions, IEEE Trans. on Information Theory, Vol. 39. No. 3. 1993. pp. 930-945.
[29] V. N. Vapnik, Statistical Learning Theory, Wiley, New York, 1998.
[30] V.Cherkassky, F.Mulier, Learning from Data, Concepts, Theory and Methods, Wiley, New York, 1998
[31] H. Akaike, Information Theory and an Extension of the Maximum Likelihood Principle, Second Intnl. Symposium on Information Theory, Akadémiai Kiadó, Budapest, pp. 267-281. 1972.
[32] J. Rissanen, Modelling by Shortest Data Description, Automatica, Vol. 14. pp. 465-471, 1978.
[33] N. Murata, S. Yoshizawa and Shun-Ichi Amari, Network Information Criterion - Determining the Number of Hidden Units for an Artificial Neural Network Model, IEEE Trans. on Neural Networks, Vol. 5. No. 6. Pp. 865-871.
[34] X. He and H. Asada, A New Method for Identifying Orders of Input-Output Models for Nonlinear Dynamic Systems, Proc. of the American Control Conference, 1993. San Francisco, CA. USA. pp. 2520-2523.
[35] M. Stone, Cross-Validatory Choice and Assesment of Statistical Predictions, Journal of Royal Statistical Society. Se. B. Vol. 36. pp. 111-147.
[36] S. Amari, N. Murata, K.-R. Müller, M. Finke and, H. Yang, Asymptotic Statistical Theory of Ovetraining and Cross-Validation, IEEE Trans. on Neural Networks, Vol. 8. No. 5. pp. 985-998, 1997.
[37] S. Lawrence, C. Lee Giles and Ah Chung Tsoi, What Size Neural Network Gives Optimal Generalization? Convergence Properties of Backpropagation, Technical Report, UMIACS-TR-96-22 and CS-TR-3617, Institute for Advanced Computer Studies, University of Maryland, 1996. p. 33.
[38] S. Saarinen, B. Bramley and G. Cybenko, Ill-conditioning in Neural Network Training Problems, SIAM Journal for Scientific and Statistical Computing, 1991.
[39] L. Ljung and J. Sjöberg, A System Identification Perspective on Neural Networks, 1992.
[40] B. Pataki, G. Horváth, Gy. Strausz, and Zs. Talata, Inverse Neural Modeling of a Linz-Donawitz Steel Converter, e & i Elektrotechnik und Informationstechnik, Vol. 117. No. 1. 2000. pp. 13-17.
[41] G. Horváth, B. Pataki and Gy. Strausz, Black box Modeling of a Complex Industrial Process, Proc. of the 1999 IEEE Conference and Workshop on Engineering of Computer Based Systems, Nashville, TN, USA. 1999. pp. 60-66.
[42] M. Deistler, Linear Dynamic Errors-in-Variables Models, Journal of Applied Probability, Vol. 23. pp. 23-39, 1986.
[43] J. Van Gorp, J. Schoukens and R. Pintelon, Learning Neural Networks with Noisy Inputs Using the Errors-In-Variables Approach, IEEE Trans. on Neural Networks, Vol. 11. No.2 . pp. 402-414. 2000.
[44] G. Horváth, L. Sragner and T. Laczó, Impoved Model Order Estimation by Combining Errors-in-Variables and Lipschitz Methods, a forthcoming paper
[45] P. Sollich and A. Krogh, Learning with Ensembles: How over-fitting can be useful, In Advances in Neural Information Processing Systems 8. D. S. Touretzky, M. C. Mozer and M. E. Hasselmo, eds, MIT Press, pp. 190-196, 1996.
[46] R. A. Jacobs, M. I. Jordan, S. J. Nowlan and G. E. Hinton, Adaptive Mixture of Local Experts, Neural Computation Vol. 3. No.1 pp. 79-87.1991.
[47] P. Berényi, G. Horváth, B. Pataki and Gy. Strausz, Hybrid-Neural Modeling of a Complex Industrial Process, Proc. of the IEEE Instrumentation and Measurement Technology Conference, Vol. III. pp.1424-1429. 2001.

Neural Networks for Instrumentation, Measurement and Related Industrial Applications
S. Ablameyko et al. (Eds.)
IOS Press, 2003

Chapter 5
Neural Techniques in Control

Andrzej PACUT
Institute of Control and Computation Engineering, Warsaw University of Technology
Nowowiejska 15/19, 00–663 Warsaw, Poland

Abstract. Ideas that come to controls from neural networks extend the existing control methodology beyond the classical standards. We discuss such neural techniques developed in various branches of classical control. We first introduce some approximation properties of neural networks important for dynamic systems, and identification techniques based on dynamic backpropagation, showing on examples how to calculate gradients in complex dynamic structures. We then discuss the input-output representations of nonlinear dynamic systems and their neural approximators. We then demonstrate usefulness of neural networks in well established control techniques that are used to solve stabilization tasks, tracking problems, and optimal control problems for nonlinear systems, and in particular, for nonlinear unknown systems.

5.1. Neural control

The subject of this chapter lays in the intersection of controls and neural networks. Neural network methods play here an auxiliary role with respect to the methodology rooted in control theory. Control theory and practice, developed broadly for linear systems with known parameters, meet their obstacles when it comes to linear systems with unknown (and possibly varying) parameters, and nonlinear systems. While very deep and elegant theoretical methods are developed in these areas, they are not easily transformed to implementations, often due to only existential results and/or complex relations necessary to be solved. Neural networks seem to overcome these problems, serving as a general way to approximate various nonlinear static and dynamic relations. Neural networks are thus being builded into the control systems as approximators; such systems may be called the *neural control* systems. We yet stress that this expressions may not be just: the overall methodology, structure, and inside sense of such neural control systems comes from control theory and the neural networks are only supplemental.

Applications of neural networks as elements of control systems bear new control-theoretical problems, related to the influence of local approximation errors to the global performance of such systems. While, initially, only simulations supported the ideas, presently more and more theoretical results prove the soundness of neural approximations in control systems. The initial reservation among control practitioners, caused by no theoretical performance guarantees for neural control systems, may now be overcome and the control practice may reach for new territories.

In this chapter we would like to show how neural network can extend the control methodology beyond the standard areas. We hope to interest control people with various ideas coming from neural networks that have been applied in control. It is also directed to control practitioners who may want to extent their tools. It may be also useful to neural network specialists, to show neural network needs of control theory. To facilitate reading, we also outline some control background beyond the linear control that may be less known to non-specialists.

This chapter by no means presents all the neural network methods that have been applied with success in controls; we certainly missed many interesting and important ideas. Number of paper in this area goes into several hundreds a year. The presented topics surely reflect personal interests of this author, which may not always be related to the importance of the material. We also decided to restrict the discussion to discrete-time continuous-values problems. We yet hope to show the wealth of new ideas that come to controls from neural networks.

Control methods that employ neural networks are as old as the neural network themselves. In fact, at the very early stage of neural networks development, some well known adaptive control techniques were relabeled as neural network techniques. Thanks to the intensive research over many years, both in control and in neural networks, some ideas proved their usefulness and were supported and refined theoretically, while some other were shown to be too optimistic and sometimes without merits. At present, it is clear that *the* property of neural networks employed in control is their ability to approximate arbitrary function with arbitrary accuracy. Probably as important is the existence of simple methods to calculate necessary gradients in control and identification algorithms, related to the gradient backpropagation. Finally, very important yet less developed, are control structures influenced by biological control structures. Contemporary neural control structures typically use well proven control techniques with neural networks used as approximators of structural elements that are unknown or to complex to be used without approximations. Neural approximation of structural elements of control schemes are also used even if the exact solutions are known, but a simple though approximate solution is preferred. Consequently, all classical branches of control developed "neural techniques". There also exist new control schemes that were developed under a direct influence of neural modeling, with control schemes shaped by the existing biological control systems. At present, neural control area is still evolving, proving or disproving the usefulness of the plethora of existing techniques.

Notation. We use standard mathematical notation, so we introduce here only some specific matters that may cause misunderstanding. All vectors are assumed to be column. We use calligraphic letters to denote sets (with some exceptions like $\mathbb{R}$ that stands for real numbers), bold letters for matrices and vectors, and italic letters for their elements and other scalars. Time variable is used in parentheses, and lower indexes are used to denote elements or vectors or matrices. We denote the time delay operator by q^{-1}, and the n-step delay by q^{-n}. We introduce the *tapped-delay line* operator $\mathbf{q}^{-n}$, namely a column vector that consists of the identity and $n-1$ consecutive delays, i.e.

$$\mathbf{q}^{-n}x(k) = \begin{bmatrix} x(k) & x(k-1) & \cdots & x(k-n+1) \end{bmatrix}^T \tag{1}$$

A function of several variables $\mathbf{f} : \mathbb{R}^n \mapsto \mathbb{R}^m$ will have its values referred to as $\mathbf{f}(\mathbf{x})$ or $f(x_1, \ldots, x_n)$. If the function is scalar-valued ($m = 1$), its gradient is assumed to be a column vector and will be denoted by $f_{\mathbf{x}}$

$$f_{\mathbf{x}} = [\frac{\partial f}{\partial x_1} \quad \cdots \quad \frac{\partial f}{\partial x_n}]^T \tag{2}$$

For a vector-valued function $\mathbf{f} : \mathbb{R}^n \mapsto \mathbb{R}^m$, by $\mathbf{f}_{\mathbf{x}}$ we denote its Jacobian, i.e. a $m \times n$ matrix whose rows are equal to transposed gradients of the function components $f_1, \cdots, f_m$, namely

$$\mathbf{f}_{\mathbf{x}} = \frac{\partial \mathbf{f}}{\partial \mathbf{x}} = \left\{ \frac{\partial f_i}{\partial x_j} \right\}_{\substack{i=1,\dots,m \\ j=1,\dots,n}} \tag{3}$$

By $\mathbf{0}$ we denote a zero vector, and by $\mathbf{O}$ a zero-element matrix, regardless of their dimensions (always clear form the context).

In figures, we use single lines for scalar signals, and double lines for vector signals. A double line may split into single lines (usually at the input to a functional box) to illustrate the behavior of signal components, and reversely, single lines can be grouped into a double line (usually at the output from a functional box) to form a vector signal. This enables for "zooming" into a transformation of components of a vector signal.

Roadmap. In Sec. 5.2 we first shortly introduce neural networks with the assumption that the reader is familiar with this topic. We deal only with feedforward networks, and construct dynamical neural systems only through delays in the signal transmissions. We typically do not discuss the internal structure of neural networks but rather treat the network as a whole. In the next subsection we introduce the basic nonlinear systems used in this Chapter. We then discuss approximation abilities of networks, important for dynamic systems, and point out a relation between neural approximations and the curse of dimensionality, extremely important in many control problems.

In Sec. 5.3 we discuss the difference between the chain rule and backpropagation, and show a simple way to derive the backpropagation formulas. Gradient backpropagation can surely be derived from the chain rule, but this method the very basic simplicity of backpropagation. Gradient calculation in complex systems is very substantial in neural approximations used in control systems. We also give examples of application of the presented method.

Section 5.4 is devoted to models of dynamical systems used in control. The very basic problem here is the input-output representation of dynamical systems and the ability of neural networks to approximate such dynamic representations. We discuss local NARX representations, global representations, affine in control approximations, disturbance modeling, and the notion of relative degree.

Next four sections discuss particular neural techniques in controls. We had a problem with a categorization of the cases discussed (by a type of control task, by a control technique used, by neural methodology involved). Even if a categorization is decided, there are always elements of another categorization that are important enough to be discussed separately. We decided to discuss separately stabilization, tracking, optimal control, and reinforcement control. In Sec. 5.5 we discuss the use of neural methods in stabilization, in particular in feedback linearization, Lyapunov method, and in a dead-beat controller method. In Sec. 5.6 we discuss applications of neural networks to tracking, in particular in model reference control, internal model control, general tracking control, and linearization methods. Next section 5.7 is devoted to "neural" optimal control, and in particular to finite horizon problems, predictive control, and dual control. Finally, in Sec. 5.8, we discuss reinforcement control, namely the heuristic dynamic programming with backpropagated critic and dual heuristic programming.

5.2. Neural approximations

5.2.1. Neural networks

The neural networks have already been introduced and many issues were discussed in earlier chapters of this book. We restrict our introduction only to notational issues. In this chapter we will treat the neural network as a vector function of vector variable

$$\mathbf{y} = \mathbf{N}(\mathbf{u}), \qquad \mathbf{u} \in \mathbb{R}^q, \quad \mathbf{y} \in \mathbb{R}^p \tag{4}$$

whose internal structure has a layer form, namely $\mathbf{N} = \boldsymbol{\eta}^{(K)} \cdots \boldsymbol{\eta}^{(2)}\boldsymbol{\eta}^{(1)}$ such that each layer's output is the next layer's input. Consequently, only the last K-th layer sends its output to the outside world (the output layer), and the remaining layers' outputs are internal signals (the hidden layers). Moreover, we always assume that each layer can be presented as a given function $\boldsymbol{\gamma}$ of an affine transformation of its input, namely

$$\eta(\mathbf{u}) = \gamma(\mathbf{W}\mathbf{u} + \mathbf{b}) = \begin{bmatrix} \gamma_1(\mathbf{w}_1^T\mathbf{u} + b_1) \\ \vdots \\ \gamma_p(\mathbf{w}_p^T\mathbf{u} + b_p) \end{bmatrix} \tag{5}$$

where $\mathbf{W}$ is called the weight matrix, $\mathbf{b}$ is the bias vector, and γ_i are the activation functions (we did not indexed the layer, its input and output for better readability). Due to this special form of $\boldsymbol{\gamma}$, the transformation in each layer can be separated into elements $\gamma_i(\mathbf{w}_i^T\mathbf{u} + b_i)$ called the neurons, where $\mathbf{w}_i$ are neurons' weights. We finally add that the vector of biases is customarily treated as the "zero" column of the weight matrix, with the simultaneous extension of the input vector with 'zero'-th element equal to one. While this introduction is quite concise, the reader is referred to the earlier chapters for more thorough exposition. By building-in such *static networks* into dynamic systems we will create *dynamic networks.*

A special type of static network that we use most has only two layers: the linear output layer of weights $\mathbf{V}$ and and the (only) hidden layer of weights $\mathbf{W}$ and biases $\mathbf{b}$, whose activation functions γ are identical (Fig. 1). The family $\mathcal{N}[\gamma]$ of such networks

$$\mathcal{N}[\gamma] = \{\mathbf{N} : \mathbf{N}(\mathbf{u}) = \mathbf{V}\,\gamma(\mathbf{W}\,\mathbf{u} + \mathbf{b})\} \tag{6}$$

is the basic function approximation tool. Networks of this class will be typically used in control systems discussed in this chapter.

5.2.2. Nonlinear systems

Our main object of interest are nonlinear time-invariant multiple-input multiple-output (MIMO) deterministic plants $\mathbb{S} = (\mathbf{f}, \mathbf{h})$ of the form (Fig. 2)

$$\begin{aligned} \mathbf{x}(k+1) &= \mathbf{f}(\mathbf{x}(k), \mathbf{u}(k)) \\ \mathbf{y}(k) &= \mathbf{h}(\mathbf{x}(k)) \end{aligned} \tag{7}$$

where $\mathbf{x}(k) \in \mathbb{R}^n$ is the state vector, $\mathbf{u}(k) \in \mathbb{R}^q$ denotes the plant input, and $\mathbf{y}(k) \in \mathbb{R}^p$ is the plant output. We typically assume that the origin is a stationary point, i.e. $\mathbf{f}(\mathbf{0}, \mathbf{0}) = \mathbf{0}$, $\mathbf{h}(\mathbf{0}) = \mathbf{0}$. For convenience we often take $p = q$, and often specialize to single-input single-output (SISO) plants, i.e. to $p = 1$. In the context of dynamical systems, neural networks are typically used as *filters* that may undergo a continual training with examples presented in ordered way, as opposed to traditional network training with a finite number of examples presented repetitively in an arbitrary order. One may differentiate between networks' use as *adaptive filters* that undergo a continual training with examples continuously fed to the

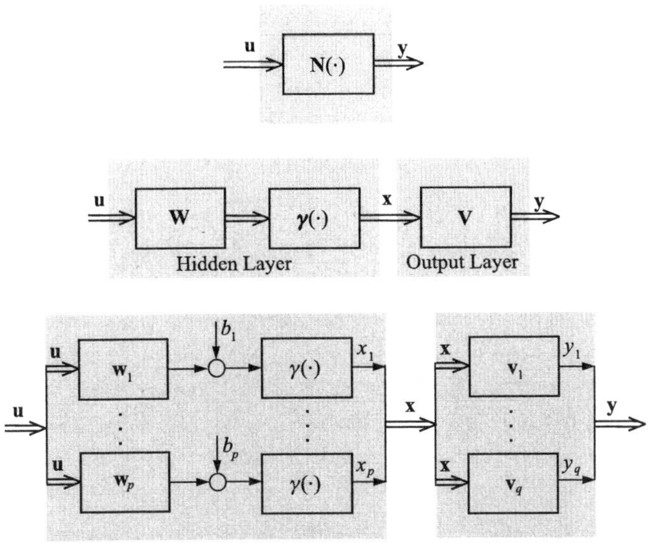

Figure 1: Zooming into a one-hidden layer network of $\mathcal{N}[\gamma]$ class. The network as a function (top); layer structure shown (middle); neurons shown (bottom).

filter and forming a possible infinite sequence, or their use as *non-adaptive filters*, when the training stops at some point and the filter works non-adaptively afterwards. Recurrent networks are treated in control as dynamic systems fed with data, rather than as traditional associated memories.

5.2.3. Approximation problem

Approximation abilities of neural networks are discussed elsewhere in this book, and here we only stress certain properties important for dynamic systems. We say that a family of functions $\widehat{\mathcal{F}}$ has the *universal approximation property* (UAP) for a class of functions $\mathcal{F}$ if for any function $f \in \mathcal{F}$ and any desired accuracy ε there exists a function $\widehat{f} \in \widehat{\mathcal{F}}$ such that

$$d(f, \widehat{f}) \leq \varepsilon \tag{8}$$

where d is a chosen distance between functions. It is known that $\widehat{\mathcal{F}} = \mathcal{N}[\gamma]$ has the UAP for various classes of functions $\mathcal{F}$ provided the activation function γ satisfies certain conditions [11, 14, 20, 18, 48, 19]. Probably the strongest results in this area have been obtained by Leshno, Lin, Pinkus, and Schocken [32] who proved that $\mathcal{N}[\gamma]$ has the UAP for continuous functions over any compact set $\mathcal{U}$, for the distance $d(f, \widehat{f}) = \sup_{\mathbf{u}\in\mathcal{U}} |f(\mathbf{u}) - \widehat{f}(\mathbf{u})|$, *provided γ is not a polynomial.* Similarly, $\mathcal{N}(\gamma)$ has the UAP for functions integrable with k-th power, with $d(f, \widehat{f}) = \left(\int_{\mathcal{U}} |f(\mathbf{u}) - \widehat{f}(\mathbf{u})|^p \, d\mathbf{u}\right)^{1/p}$. The distance can be also extended

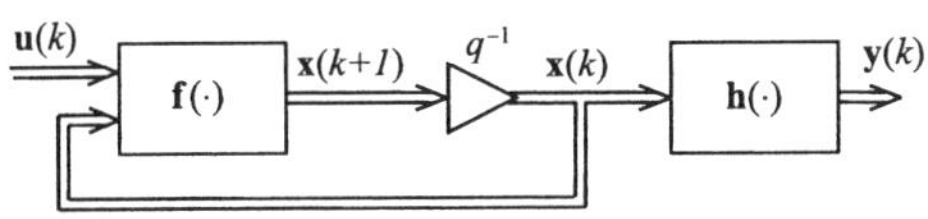

Figure 2: General structure of a nonlinear plant.

to $d(f,\widehat{f}) = \left(\mathcal{E}|f - \widehat{f}|^p\right)^{1/p}$, where $\mathcal{E}$ is the expected value and f are random variables. The condition of being non-polynomial is certainly satisfied by continuous *sigmoids*, i.e. functions γ for which $\gamma(u) \underset{u\to-\infty}{\longrightarrow} = 0$, $\gamma(u) \underset{u\to\infty}{\longrightarrow} = 1$, including the most popular logistic sigmoid activation function

$$\gamma(z) = \frac{1}{1+\exp(-a\,z)} \tag{9}$$

It is important in many control applications that the approximation is performed for a function together with its derivatives. For any nonnegative integer-value vector $\mathbf{k} = [k_1,\ldots,k_q]^T$, denote by $D^{\mathbf{k}}f$ the derivative

$$D^{\mathbf{k}}f(\mathbf{u}) = \frac{\partial^{|\mathbf{k}|}}{\partial u_1^{k_1}\ldots\partial u_q^{k_q}} \tag{10}$$

where $|\mathbf{k}| = \sum_i k_i$ is the derivative order. Additionally, let $D^{\mathbf{0}}f = f$. A m-times continuously differentiable functions on a set $\mathcal{U}$ is *rapidly decreasing*, if for all $|\mathbf{k}| \leq m$

$$|u_1|^{k_1}\cdots|u_q|^{k_q}D^{\mathbf{k}}f(\mathbf{u}) \underset{\max_i|u_i|\to\infty}{\longrightarrow} 0 \tag{11}$$

The measure of approximation accuracy in the form

$$d(f,\widehat{f}) = \max_{|\mathbf{k}|\leq m}\sup_{\mathbf{u}\in\mathcal{U}}|D^{\mathbf{k}}(f(\mathbf{u}) - \widehat{f}(\mathbf{u}))| \tag{12}$$

takes into account discrepancies between the function and its model, as well as between the function and the model derivatives up to a certain order. It is proven by Hornik, Stinchcombe, and White [21] that for any rapidly decreasing function f, any compact set $\mathcal{U}$, and the approximation accuracy (12), the networks $\mathcal{N}[\gamma]$ have the UAP provided γ is ℓ-finite, i.e. it is ℓ-times continuously differentiable, and $0 < \int_{\mathbb{R}}\gamma^{(\ell)}(z)\,dz < \infty$. The logistic sigmoid function (9) is ℓ-finite for any $\ell > 0$, and Gaussian activation functions used in RBF networks are ℓ-finite for any $\ell \geq 0$. Note that polynomials and sinusoidal functions *are not* ℓ-finite for any ℓ.

5.2.4. Approximation of sequences

Control applications require that, to be able to approximate (discrete) dynamic systems, the approximation theorems are extended from function approximation to approximation of sequences of functions. A discrete dynamic system has *approximately finite-memory* if for an arbitrary ε there exists a window of integer length $T > 0$ such that for all t, and all inputs $\mathbf{u} = \{\mathbf{u}(k),\, k \geq 0\}$, one has

$$|y(k) - y_{t,T}(t)| < \varepsilon \tag{13}$$

where $\{y(k),\, k \geq 0\}$ is the output to $\mathbf{u}$, and $\{y_{t,T}(k),\, k \geq 0\}$ is the output to the *windowed input* $\{\mathbf{u}_{t,T}(k), k \geq 0\}$ defined as

$$\mathbf{u}_{t,T}(k) = \begin{cases}\mathbf{u}(k) & \text{for } t-T < k \leq t\\ 0 & \text{otherwise}\end{cases} \tag{14}$$

It is proved by Sandberg [51] that for causal time invariant approximately finite-memory single-output systems, the approximating networks $\mathcal{N}[\gamma]$ have UAP, namely for an arbitrary $\varepsilon > 0$

$$\sup_{k\in\mathbb{R}}|y(k) - \widehat{y}(k)| < \varepsilon \tag{15}$$

uniformly for all inputs $\mathbf{u}$. The network input is equal to $\mathbf{q}^{-T}\mathbf{u}(t)$, i.e. it consists of the current and delayed system inputs. Sandberg's method can be used to generalize function approximation results to discrete dynamic systems.

5.2.5. No curse of dimensionality ?

The famous result of Barron [3] gives an upper bound on the size of the hidden layer that does not depend on the dimension of the input space, thus showing lack of the "curse of dimensionality" for neural approximators. More precisely, consider one-hidden layer networks $\mathcal{N}[\gamma]$ where γ is a bounded continuous sigmoid. Suppose that a function $f : \mathbb{R}^q \mapsto \mathbb{R}$ is to be approximated for $\|\mathbf{u}\| \le r$. Define the approximation error $d(f, \widehat{f})$ by

$$d(f, \widehat{f}) = (\mathcal{E}|f - \widehat{f}|^2)^{1/2} \tag{16}$$

assuming that the distribution of $\mathbf{u}$ is concentrated over $\|\mathbf{u}\| \le r$ i.e. $P\{\|\mathbf{u}\| \le r\} = 1$. Denote by $\bar{f}(\omega) = \int \exp(j\,\omega^T\mathbf{u})\, f(\mathbf{u})\, d\mathbf{u}$, $\omega \in \mathbb{R}^q$, the (q-dimensional) Fourier transform of f. The integral

$$C_f = \int \|\omega\|^2\, |\bar{f}(\omega)|\, d\omega \tag{17}$$

can be regarded as a function complexity index. Barron's theorem [3] states that if the complexity index C_f of the approximated function f is finite then there exists a $\mathcal{N}[\gamma]$ network with n hidden neurons such that the approximation error is bounded by

$$\varepsilon \le \frac{2\,r\,C_f}{\sqrt{n}} \tag{18}$$

In other words, for an approximation error bounded by ε_0, the number of hidden neurons

$$n \le \frac{4\,r^2\,C_f^2}{\varepsilon_0^2} \tag{19}$$

does not depend on the input dimension q. This result shows a computational advantage of neural networks over other approximations like polynomial approximations, splines, etc., for which the required number of parameters grows exponentially with the input space dimension. Barron's result does not yet solves fully the dimensionality issue for neural networks, since the bound (19) depends on the function complexity index C_f that may depend on q. This problem, extremely important for control applications, is still under intensive research.

5.3. Gradient algebra

Gradient backpropagation is probably *the* buzzword of neural networks. It has in fact two different meanings: it is (A) a method of gradient calculation, as introduced by Werbos [59, 62], and – even more commonly – (B) a gradient method of network's weights adjustment, with gradients calculated with the use of backpropagation (meaning A) [50]. Here we will discuss the backpropagation in its first meaning.

5.3.1. Layered systems of functions

To show the difference between the chain rule and backpropagation, consider first a composite function of a single variable x_0 presented in the form of a layered family of functions, namely

$$\begin{aligned} x_1 &= f_1(x_0) \\ &\dots \\ x_k &= f_k(x_{k-1}) \\ &\dots \\ x_n &= f_n(x_{n-1}) \end{aligned} \tag{20}$$

with the appropriate relations between function domains, whose typical example is the multilayer perceptron. Denote $f'_k = \dfrac{df_k}{dx_{k-1}}$, for $i = 1, \dots, n$, and $x'_{k|\ell} = \dfrac{dx_k}{dx_\ell}$ for $x_0, \dots x_{\ell-1}$ fixed, $\ell < k$. The derivative

$$\frac{dx_n}{dx_0} = f'_n(x_{n-1})\, f'_{n-1}(x_{n-2}) \, \dots \, f'_2(x_1)\, f'_1(x_0) \tag{21}$$

can be calculated recursively in many ways, the most important being the *chain rule* algorithm and the *backpropagation* algorithm. Let us first apply a "right-to-left grouping" of terms in (21), namely

$$x'_{n|0} = \frac{dx_n}{dx_0} = f'_n(x_{n-1})\, \underbrace{f'_{n-1}(x_{n-2}) \, \dots \, \underbrace{f'_2(x_1)\, \underbrace{f'_1(x_0)}_{x'_{1|0}}}_{x'_{2|0}}}_{x'_{n-1|0}} \tag{22}$$

The resulting algorithm can be written in the form

$$\begin{aligned} x'_{0|0} &= 1 \\ x'_{k|0} &= f'_k(x_{k-1})\, x'_{k-1|0} \\ x_k &= f_k(x_{k-1}) \qquad k = 1, \dots, n \end{aligned} \tag{23}$$

and is commonly termed the chain rule and also may be called the *forward-propagation*. If a "left-to-right grouping" of terms is applied to (21), namely

$$x'_{n|0} = \frac{dx_n}{dx_0} = \underbrace{\underbrace{\underbrace{f'_n(x_{n-1})}_{x'_{n|n-1}}\, f'_{n-1}(x_{n-2})}_{x'_{n|n-2}} \, \dots \, f'_2(x_1)}_{x'_{n|1}}\, f'_1(x_0) \tag{24}$$

we obtain the backpropagation algorithm

$$\begin{aligned} x'_{n|n} &= 1 \\ x'_{n|\ell} &= x'_{n|\ell+1}\, f'_{\ell+1}(x_\ell), \qquad \ell = n-1, \dots, 0 \end{aligned} \tag{25}$$

In the above formulas we omitted, identical for both algorithms, calculations of values of the variables. An apparent difference between the two algorithms consists in the *order of calculations*. More important though are *intermediate derivatives* calculated by both algorithms. In the chain rule, we calculate derivatives of intermediate variables x_i *with respect to the same independent variable* x_0, to end up with the derivative of x_n. On the other hand, the backpropagation formula consists in calculating derivatives *of the same variable* x_n with respect to intermediate variables x_j, to end up with the derivative with respect to x_0.

The above observations enable to formulate the basic generic principles behind the chain rule and the backpropagation. For any two variables $u = x_k$, $z = x_\ell$, $\ell < k$, the chain rule can

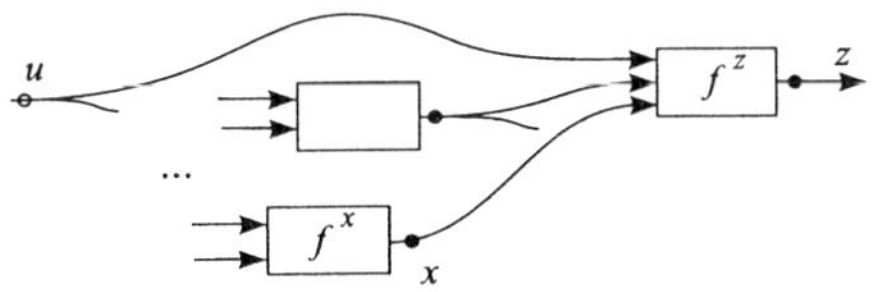

Figure 3: Chain rule for ordered systems. The summation in (26) extends over all variables x *that directly influence* z (i.e., the arguments of f^z). The derivatives are calculated for different variables x (filled dots) with respect to the same variable u (the open dot).

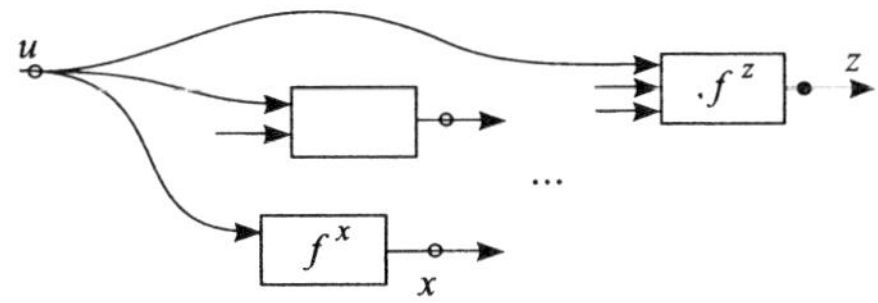

Figure 4: Backpropagation for ordered systems. The summation in (27) extends over all terms x that *are directly influenced* by u (i.e., all functions whose one of the arguments is u). The derivatives are calculated for the same variable y (the filled dot) with respect to different variables x (open dots).

be compactly written as

$$\frac{dz}{du} = \frac{\partial f^z}{\partial u} + \sum_x \frac{\partial f^z}{\partial x}\frac{dx}{du} \tag{26}$$

where by $f^z = f_\ell$ we denoted the function that defines z, and the sum extends over all variables x *that directly influence* z through f^z (i.e., the arguments of f^z), Fig. 3. On the other hand, for the same two variables $u = x_k$, $z = x_\ell$, $\ell < k$, the backpropagation formula has the form

$$\frac{dz}{du} = \frac{\partial f^z}{\partial u} + \sum_x \frac{dz}{dx}\frac{\partial f^x}{\partial u} \tag{27}$$

where f^x denotes the function that defines x, and the summation extends over all terms x that *are directly influenced* by u (i.e., all functions whose one of the arguments is u), Fig. 4. The above two formulas show the essence of the differences between the two algorithms. While for the chain rule one needs derivatives with respect to all variables that *influence* a given intermediate variable, the backpropagation calls for derivatives of all variables that *are influenced* by the present variable. Knowing this, derivation of the gradient for even complicated neural networks is almost trivial. In the matrix form, both methods differ in the order of matrix multiplication [44].

5.3.2. *Gradient calculations in nonlinear dynamic systems*

Suppose that for a dynamic plant (7) both $\mathbf{f}$ and $\mathbf{g}$ are approximated by neural networks, $\widehat{\mathbf{f}}$ and $\widehat{\mathbf{h}}$, respectively, namely

$$\begin{aligned} \mathbf{x}(k+1) &= \widehat{\mathbf{f}}(\mathbf{x}(k), \mathbf{u}(k);\ \mathbf{w}) \\ \mathbf{y}(k) &= \widehat{\mathbf{h}}(\mathbf{x}(k);\ \mathbf{v}) \end{aligned} \tag{28}$$

where $\mathbf{w}$ and $\mathbf{v}$ denote the weight vectors of both networks. Assume that the networks must minimize the cost $J = \sum_{k=1}^{N} \|\mathbf{y}(k) - \mathbf{y}^0(k)\|$ of the discrepancy between the model output $\mathbf{y}$ and the desired output $\mathbf{y}^0$. We show how the chain rule and the backpropagation work for this systems. To avoid cluttering of formulas we often skip the intermediate arguments of functions, e.g., we write $\widehat{\mathbf{f}}(k)$ instead of $\widehat{\mathbf{f}}(\mathbf{x}(k), \mathbf{u}(k);\ \mathbf{w})$.

We first calculate the derivative $\dfrac{dJ}{dv}$ (Fig. 5), where v is any element of $\mathbf{v}$. Since v influences all output coordinates at every moment k, we have

$$\frac{dJ}{dv} = \sum_{k=1}^{N}\sum_{j=1}^{p} \frac{dJ}{dy_j(k)}\frac{\partial \widehat{h}_j(k)}{\partial v} \tag{29}$$

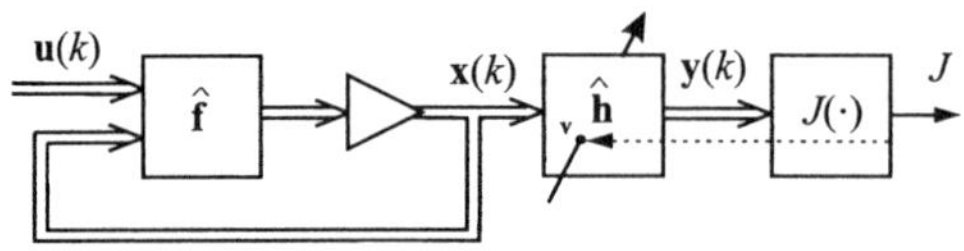

Figure 5: Backpropagation to the weights of the $\widehat{\mathbf{h}}$ network

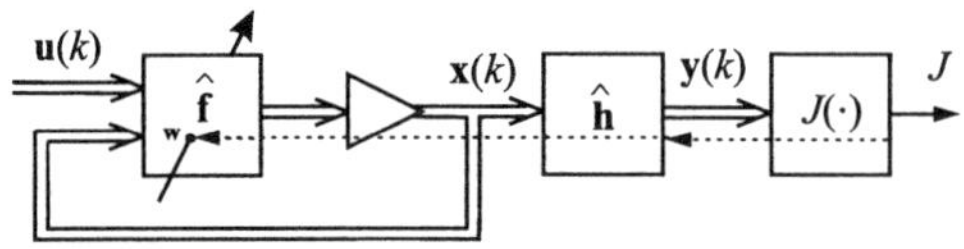

Figure 6: Backpropagation to the weights of the $\widehat{\mathbf{f}}$ network

where N is the number of data points. In turn, every output coordinate $y(k)$ directly influences the cost index, hence

$$\frac{dJ}{dy_i(k)} = y_i(k) - y_i^0(k) \tag{30}$$

Consequently, by (29, 30)

$$\frac{dJ}{dv} = \sum_{k=1}^{N}\sum_{j=1}^{n}(y_i(k) - y_i^0(k))\,\frac{\partial \widehat{h}_j(k)}{\partial v} \tag{31}$$

The derivatives $\dfrac{\partial \widehat{h}_j(k)}{\partial v}$ can themselves be calculated with the use of backpropagation once the structure of the $\widehat{\mathbf{h}}$ network is known. To calculate $\dfrac{dJ}{dw}$, where w is any element of $\mathbf{w}$ (Fig. 6), we notice first that w influences all state coordinates at every moment k. Consequently

$$\frac{dJ}{dw} = \sum_{k=1}^{N}\sum_{j=1}^{n}\frac{dJ}{dx_j(k)}\,\frac{\partial \widehat{f}_j(k)}{\partial w} \tag{32}$$

where the partial derivative can itself be calculated with the use of backpropagation once the structure of the network $\widehat{\mathbf{f}}$ is known. Since every coordinate $x_i(k)$ of the state vector influences every coordinate of the present output vector $y_j(k)$ through the observation equation, and every coordinate of the state at the next moment (except at the last moment) through the state equation, we have

$$\begin{aligned}
\frac{dJ}{dx_i(k)} &= \sum_{j=1}^{p}\frac{dJ}{dy_j(k)}\,\frac{\partial \widehat{h}_j(k)}{\partial x_i(k)} + \sum_{j=1}^{n}\frac{dJ}{dx_j(k+1)}\,\frac{\partial \widehat{f}_j(k)}{\partial x_i(k)} \quad \text{for } k < N \\
\frac{dJ}{dx_i(N)} &= \sum_{j=1}^{p}\frac{dJ}{dy_j(N)}\,\frac{\partial \widehat{h}_j(N)}{\partial x_i(N)}
\end{aligned} \tag{33}$$

where the partial derivatives again can be calculated by *backpropagating through the network* once the structures of the networks $\widehat{\mathbf{f}}$ and $\widehat{\mathbf{h}}$ are known. Finally, every output coordinate directly influences the cost index, hence

$$\frac{dJ}{dy_i(k)} = y_i(k) - y_i^0(k) \tag{34}$$

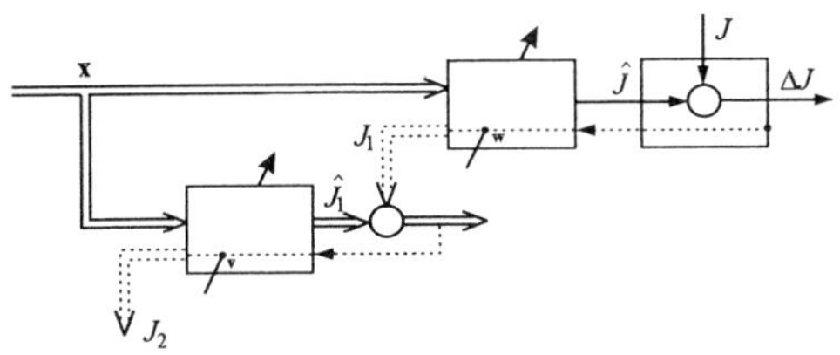

Figure 7: Using two networks to approximate second derivatives.

Introducing the sensitivity gradient $J_{\mathbf{x}}(k) = \left[\frac{dJ}{dx_1(k)} \cdots \frac{dJ}{dx_n(k)}\right]^T$ we may rewrite the backpropagation equations for both networks in a form of linear recurrent equations with time reversed, namely

$$\begin{aligned} J_{\mathbf{x}}(k) &= \widehat{\mathbf{f}}_{\mathbf{x}}(k)^T J_{\mathbf{x}}(k+1) + \widehat{\mathbf{h}}_{\mathbf{x}}(k)^T(\mathbf{y}(k) - \mathbf{y}^0(k)) \\ J_{\mathbf{w}}(k) &= J_{\mathbf{w}}(k+1) + \widehat{\mathbf{f}}_{\mathbf{w}}(k)^T J_{\mathbf{x}}(k) \\ J_{\mathbf{v}}(k) &= J_{\mathbf{v}}(k+1) + \widehat{\mathbf{h}}_{\mathbf{v}}(k)^T(\mathbf{y}(k) - \mathbf{y}^0(k)) \end{aligned} \tag{35}$$

for $k = N, \ldots, 1$, with the initial conditions

$$J_{\mathbf{x}}(N+1) = \mathbf{0}, \qquad J_{\mathbf{w}}(N+1) = \mathbf{0}, \qquad J_{\mathbf{v}}(N+1) = \mathbf{0} \tag{36}$$

and with $\frac{dJ}{dw}$ and $\frac{dJ}{dv}$ as the elements of vectors $J_{\mathbf{w}}(1)$, $J_{\mathbf{v}}(1)$, respectively.

For comparison, we calculate the derivatives for the weights of the $\widehat{\mathbf{f}}$ network by feedforward-propagation. Since J directly depends on all the output variables at all time moments, we have

$$\frac{dJ}{dw} = \sum_{k=1}^{N} \sum_{j=1}^{n} \frac{\partial J}{\partial y_j(k)} \frac{dy_j(k)}{dw} \tag{37}$$

Since any output depends only on all the state variables at the same moment, we obtain

$$\frac{dy_i(k)}{dw} = \sum_{j=1}^{p} \frac{\partial \widehat{h}_i(k)}{\partial x_j(k)} \frac{dx_j(k)}{dw} \tag{38}$$

Finally, since the state depends on the weights directly and through the previous value of all state variables, we have

$$\frac{dx_i(k)}{dw} = \frac{\partial f_i(k)}{\partial w} + \sum_{j=1}^{n} \frac{\partial \widehat{f_i}(k)}{\partial x_j(k-1)} \frac{dx_j(k-1)}{dw} \tag{39}$$

5.3.3. *Second derivatives*

Calculation of second derivatives, required in some algorithms (e.g. DHP, Sec. 5.8.2), is more complex, with or without backpropagation. We recall a little know way to approximate second derivatives with the use of two networks due to Werbos [63]. The first (single output) network approximates a function J and the backpropagation is used to calculate the gradients J_1 which in turn serve as the desired values to the second network, Fig. 7. The second network, trained with the desired derivatives, approximates the gradient $\widehat{J_1}$ and the backpropagation through the second network calculates the second derivatives J_2.

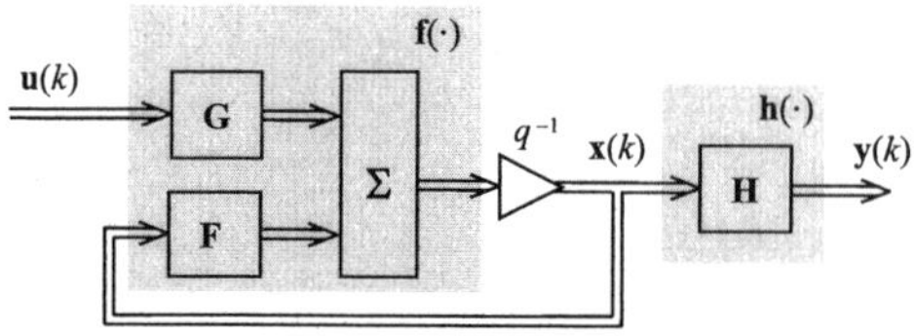

Figure 8: General structure of the linear plant.

5.4. Neural modeling of dynamical systems

5.4.1. Local NARX representation

To introduce input-output (i-o) representations of nonlinear plants, we follow the approach of Levin and Narendra [33, 38]. We first consider well known i-o representations of linear time-invariant plants, extend this representation to nonlinear plants through a linearization, and connect these results to the local and global i-o representations for nonlinear systems.

ARX representation for linear systems. To bring up some very well known results for linear plants, we first consider a linear time-invariant plant $\mathbb{L}(\mathbf{F},\mathbf{G},\mathbf{H})$ (Fig. 8), namely

$$\begin{aligned} \mathbf{x}(k+1) &= \mathbf{F}\,\mathbf{x}(k) + \mathbf{G}\,\mathbf{u}(k) \\ \mathbf{y}(k) &= \mathbf{H}\,\mathbf{x}(k) \end{aligned} \tag{40}$$

where **F**, **G**, and **H** are matrices of appropriate dimensions. The first question we shortly discuss is whether the plant is *observable*, i.e. its state can be recovered from a finite number of input and output values. Since the present and future outputs $\mathbf{y}(k+i)$, $i \geq 0$, are linear combinations of future inputs $\mathbf{u}(k+i)$, $i > 0$, and the present state $\mathbf{x}(k)$, namely

$$\begin{aligned} \mathbf{y}(k) &= \mathbf{H}\,\mathbf{x}(k) \\ \mathbf{y}(k+1) &= \mathbf{HF}\,\mathbf{x}(k) + \mathbf{HG}\,\mathbf{u}(k) \\ &\;\;\vdots \\ \mathbf{y}(k+n-1) &= \mathbf{HF}^{n-1}\,\mathbf{x}(k) + \sum_{j=1}^{n-1} \mathbf{HF}^{j-1}\mathbf{G}\,\mathbf{u}(k+n-1-j) \end{aligned} \tag{41}$$

hence the state $\mathbf{x}(k)$ can be recovered from a finite number of future inputs and outputs once the *observability matrix* W_o defined as

$$W_o = \begin{bmatrix} \mathbf{H} \\ \mathbf{HF} \\ \vdots \\ \mathbf{HF}^{n-1} \end{bmatrix} \in \mathbb{R}^{np\times n} \tag{42}$$

has full column rank, i.e. $\mathrm{r}(W_o) = n$. Moreover, the state $\mathbf{x}(k)$ depends linearly on the *future* inputs and outputs in (41), namely

$$\mathbf{x}(k) = \boldsymbol{\phi}(\mathbf{q}^{-n}\mathbf{y}(k+n-1),\ \mathbf{q}^{-n+1}\mathbf{u}(k+n-2)) \tag{43}$$

where $\boldsymbol{\phi}$ is a linear function resulting from solving (41). Observability enables to eliminate the state from the plant equations (40). Indeed, replacing the state with (43) in the formula

$$\mathbf{y}(k+n) = \mathbf{HF}^{n}\,\mathbf{x}(k) + \sum_{j=1}^{n} \mathbf{HF}^{j-1}\mathbf{G}\,\mathbf{u}(k+n-j) \tag{44}$$

one may present the output as a linear combination of delayed outputs and inputs, namely

$$\mathbf{y}(k+n) = \psi(\mathbf{q}^{-n}\mathbf{y}(k+n-1),\ \mathbf{q}^{-n}\mathbf{u}(k+n-1)) \tag{45}$$

where ψ is a linear function. Consequently, every linear observable plant admits the *ARX representation* of order at most n, namely

$$\mathbf{y}(k+1) = \sum_{i=1}^{n} \mathbf{A}_i\,\mathbf{y}(k-i+1) + \sum_{i=1}^{n} \mathbf{B}_i\,\mathbf{u}(k-i+1) \tag{46}$$

where $\mathbf{A}_i$ and $\mathbf{B}_i$ are matrices. Using the TDL operators (1)

$$\mathbf{q}^{-n}\mathbf{y}(k) = \begin{bmatrix} \mathbf{y}(k) \\ \cdots \\ \mathbf{y}(k-n+1) \end{bmatrix}, \qquad \mathbf{q}^{-n}\mathbf{u}(k) = \begin{bmatrix} \mathbf{u}(k) \\ \cdots \\ \mathbf{u}(k-n+1) \end{bmatrix}, \tag{47}$$

and setting $\mathbf{A} = \begin{bmatrix}\mathbf{A}_1 & \ldots & \mathbf{A}_n\end{bmatrix}$, $\mathbf{B} = \begin{bmatrix}\mathbf{B}_1 & \ldots & \mathbf{B}_n\end{bmatrix}$, we can present the ARX representation (46) in the form

$$\mathbf{y}(k+1) = \mathbf{A}\,\mathbf{q}^{-n}\mathbf{y}(k) + \mathbf{B}\,\mathbf{q}^{-n}\mathbf{u}(k) \tag{48}$$

Alternatively, introduction of two linear non-anticipative operators

$$\begin{aligned} \mathcal{A}(q^{-1}) &= \sum_{i=1}^{n} \mathbf{A}_i\, q^{-i+1} = \mathbf{A}\,\mathbf{q}^{-n} \\ \mathcal{B}(q^{-1}) &= \sum_{i=1}^{n} \mathbf{B}_i\, q^{-i+1} = \mathbf{B}\,\mathbf{q}^{-n} \end{aligned} \tag{49}$$

enables to present (46) in the form

$$\mathbf{y}(k+1) = \mathcal{A}(q^{-1})\,\mathbf{y}(k) + \mathcal{B}(q^{-1})\,\mathbf{u}(k) \tag{50}$$

For SISO systems, $\mathbf{A}$ and $\mathbf{B}$ become vectors $\mathbf{a}$ and $\mathbf{b}$, and we can rewrite the ARX representation (48) as (Fig. 9)

$$y(k+1) = \mathbf{a}^T\mathbf{q}^{-n}y(k) + \mathbf{b}^T\mathbf{q}^{-n}u(k) \tag{51}$$

ARX representation for linearized systems. ARX representation can be specified *locally* also for nonlinear plants by the linearization around the origin. Consider the nonlinear

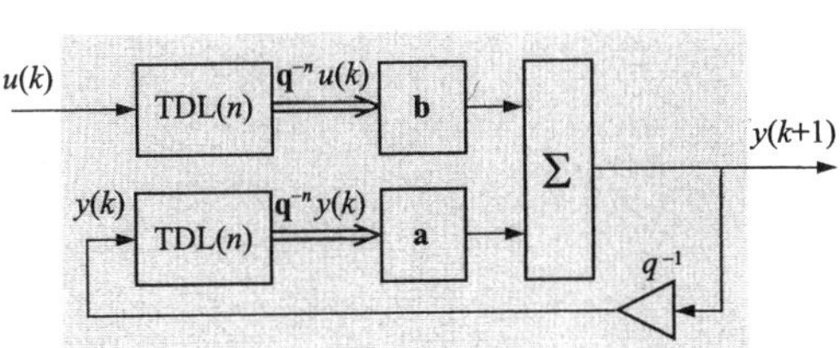

Figure 9: ARX representation for linear observable plants.

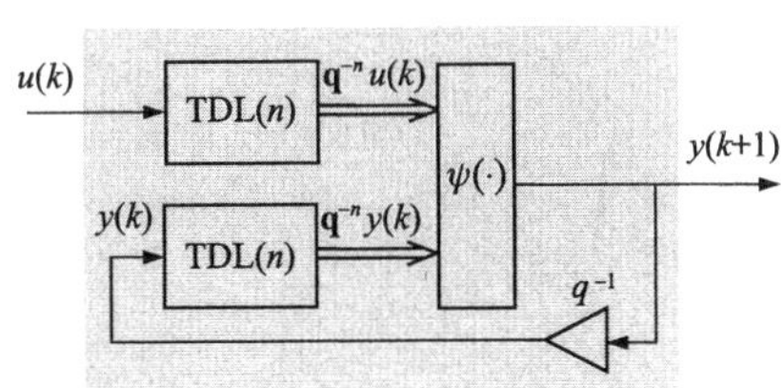

Figure 10: NARX representation for nonlinear locally observable plants. Note that the multiplications by constants and summation in the ARX representation (Fig. 9) have been replaced by a nonlinear function.

time-invariant multiple-input multiple-output (MIMO) deterministic plants $\mathbb{S} = (\mathbf{f}, \mathbf{h})$, (7)

$$\begin{aligned} \mathbf{x}(k+1) &= \mathbf{f}(\mathbf{x}(k), \mathbf{u}(k)) \\ \mathbf{y}(k) &= \mathbf{h}(\mathbf{x}(k)) \end{aligned} \tag{52}$$

and to admit the plant linearization around the origin assume that $\mathbf{f}$ and $\mathbf{h}$ are continuously twice differentiable and have stationary points at the origin, i.e. $\mathbf{f}(\mathbf{0}, \mathbf{0}) = \mathbf{0}$, $\mathbf{h}(\mathbf{0}) = \mathbf{0}$. The *linearized plant* $\mathbb{S}_L = (\mathbf{F}, \mathbf{G}, \mathbf{H})$ has a form (40) where

$$\mathbf{F} = \frac{\partial \mathbf{f}(\mathbf{x}, \mathbf{u})}{\partial \mathbf{x}}\bigg|_{(\mathbf{0},\mathbf{0})}, \qquad \mathbf{G} = \frac{\partial \mathbf{f}(\mathbf{x}, \mathbf{u})}{\partial \mathbf{u}}\bigg|_{(\mathbf{0},\mathbf{0})}, \qquad \mathbf{H} = \frac{\partial \mathbf{h}(\mathbf{x})}{\partial \mathbf{x}}\bigg|_{\mathbf{0}} \tag{53}$$

Practically, such linearized representation is valid only close to the origin and certainly does not carry nonlinear properties of the plant.

NARX representation. Consider now the nonlinear plant (7). Similarly to the linear case, one may express the present and future outputs $\mathbf{y}(k+i)$, $i \geq 0$, as functions of future inputs $\mathbf{u}(k+i)$, $i > 0$, and the present state $\mathbf{x}(k)$, namely

$$\begin{aligned} \mathbf{y}(k) &= \mathbf{h}(\mathbf{x}(k)) \\ \mathbf{y}(k+1) &= \mathbf{h}(\mathbf{f}(\mathbf{x}(k), \mathbf{u}(k))) = \mathbf{h}^{(1)}(\mathbf{x}(k), \mathbf{u}(k)) \\ \mathbf{y}(k+2) &= \mathbf{h}(\mathbf{f}(\mathbf{x}(k+1), \mathbf{u}(k+1))) = \mathbf{h}^{(2)}(\mathbf{x}(k), \mathbf{u}(k), \mathbf{u}(k+1)) \\ &\dots \\ \mathbf{y}(k+n-1) &= \mathbf{h}^{(n-1)}(\mathbf{x}(k), \mathbf{q}^{n-1}\mathbf{u}(k+n-2)) \end{aligned} \tag{54}$$

If the linearized object is observable then *locally around the origin* the state $\mathbf{x}(k)$ of the *nonlinear plant* can be recovered from a finite number of future inputs and outputs in (54),

$$\mathbf{x}(k) = \boldsymbol{\phi}(\mathbf{q}^{-n}\mathbf{y}(k+n-1), \mathbf{q}^{-n+1}\mathbf{u}(k+n-2)) \tag{55}$$

hence, as in the linear case, the output can be expressed by the delayed inputs and outputs

$$\mathbf{y}(k+n) = \boldsymbol{\psi}(\mathbf{q}^{-n}\mathbf{y}(k+n-1), \mathbf{q}^{-n}\mathbf{u}(k+n-1)) \tag{56}$$

but, unlike in the linear case (43,45), neither ϕ nor ψ are linear. Consequently, *locally around the origin*, the nonlinear system admits the NARX (for: Nonlinear ARX) representation, namely, Fig. 10

$$\mathbf{y}(k+1) = \boldsymbol{\psi}(\mathbf{q}^{-n}\mathbf{y}(k), \mathbf{q}^{-n}\mathbf{u}(k)) \tag{57}$$

The nonlinear function can be approximated by a neural network $\widehat{\psi}$ (Fig. 11), namely

$$\mathbf{y}(k+1) = \widehat{\boldsymbol{\psi}}(\mathbf{q}^{-n}\mathbf{y}(k), \mathbf{q}^{-n}\mathbf{u}(k); \mathbf{w}) \tag{58}$$

where $\mathbf{w}$ denotes the weight vector of the network. Note that while $\widehat{\psi}$ can approximate ψ in an arbitrary region, ψ approximates the nonlinear object only locally around the origin, hence the neural approximation remains local.

5.4.2. *Global representations*

Global representations of nonlinear dynamic systems are, in general, unknown. It was proven by Aeyels [2] for *autonomous observable* objects that $2n+1$ values of the output are sufficient to recover the state. Levin and Narendra [34] proved that if the plant state and observation functions $\mathbf{f}$, $\mathbf{g}$ are smooth and the *state function* $\mathbf{f}$ *is invertible with respect to the state* $\mathbf{x}(k)$ then again $2n+1$ past values of inputs and outputs are sufficient to recover the state. Practically,

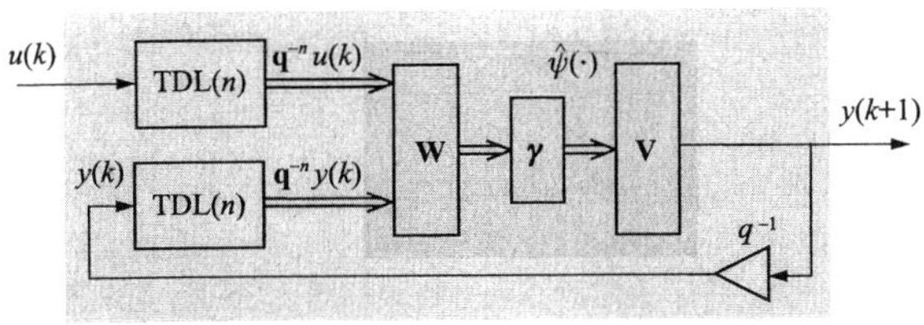

Figure 11: NARX representation, with nonlinear function ψ modeled by a neural network $\widehat{\psi}$. Note that an arbitrary nonlinear function ψ (Fig. 10) has been replaced by a linearly transformed activation function of an affinely transformed argument.

the state invertibility assumption is not stringent for discrete-time plants, since sampling of continuous-time models leads to state invertible discrete-time models.

If the order n of the plant is unknown, one must anyway consider NARX models of sufficiently high orders m.

5.4.3. *Affine-in-control representations*

Several useful approximate representations can be derived from NARX; we discuss only the SISO objects to simplify the notation. By Taylor expansion of ψ around $(\mathbf{q}^{-n}y(k), \mathbf{0})$ one obtains an approximate representation affine in the present and past inputs, namely

$$y(k+1) = \psi_0(\mathbf{q}^{-n}y(k)) + \sum_{i=1}^{n} \psi_i(\mathbf{q}^{-n}y(k))\, u(k-i+1) \tag{59}$$

which can be realized as a scalar product of the delayed plant outputs extended with a constant, and the output of a $n+1$-output neural network $\widehat{\psi}$, namely (Fig. 12)

$$y(k+1) = \widehat{\psi}(\mathbf{q}^{-n}y(k);\, \mathbf{w}) \cdot \begin{bmatrix} 1 \\ \mathbf{q}^{-n}u(k) \end{bmatrix} \tag{60}$$

where $\mathbf{w}$ denotes the weights of the network, and $\cdot$ denotes scalar multiplication of vectors, namely $a \cdot b = a^T b$.

Similarly, by Taylor expansion around $(\mathbf{q}^{-n}y(k), 0, \mathbf{q}^{-n+1}u(k-1))$, one obtains another approximate representation, affine in the present input yet nonlinear in past inputs, namely

$$y(k+1) = \psi_0(\mathbf{q}^{-n}y(k),\, \mathbf{q}^{-n+1}u(k-1)) + \psi_1(\mathbf{q}^{-n}y(k),\, \mathbf{q}^{-n+1}u(k-1))\, u(k) \tag{61}$$

which can be realized with a 2-output neural network $\widehat{\psi}$ (Fig. 13), namely

$$y(k+1) = \widehat{\psi}(\mathbf{q}^{-n}y(k),\, \mathbf{q}^{-n+1}u(k-1);\, \mathbf{w}) \cdot \begin{bmatrix} 1 \\ u(k) \end{bmatrix} \tag{62}$$

5.4.4. *Deterministic modeling of disturbances*

Consider a nonlinear time-invariant plant $\mathbb{S}^{\mathbf{x}} = (\mathbf{f}, \mathbf{h})$

$$\begin{aligned} \mathbf{x}(k+1) &= \mathbf{f}(\mathbf{x}(k), \mathbf{u}(k), \mathbf{v}(k)) \\ \mathbf{y}(k) &= \mathbf{h}(\mathbf{x}(k)) \end{aligned} \tag{63}$$

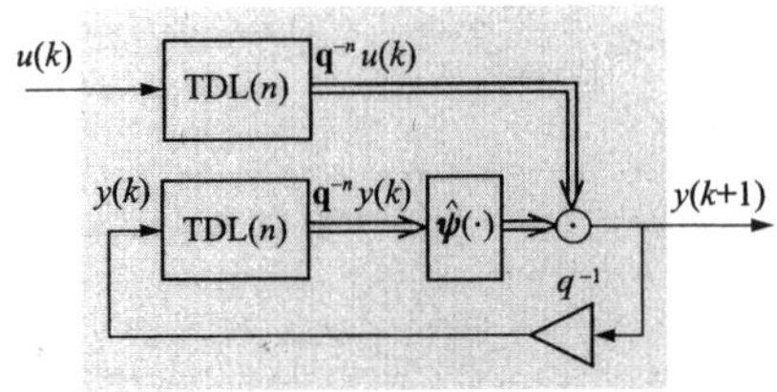

Figure 12: Approximate network representation of nonlinear SISO plants, with the output being an affine function of all inputs. The inputs have been extended with a constant input, and ⊙ denotes the scalar multiplication.

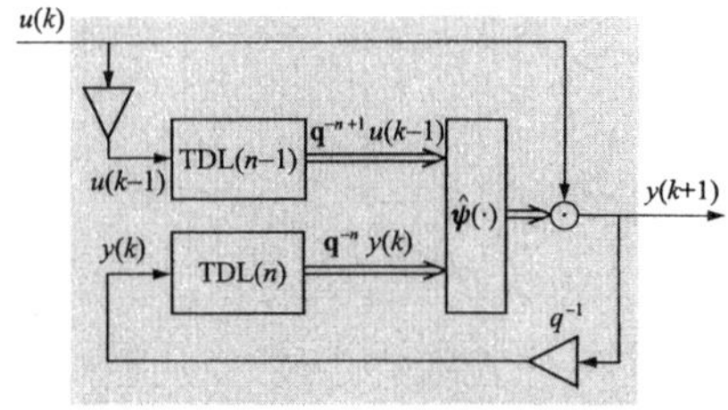

Figure 13: Approximate network representation of nonlinear SISO plants, with the output being an affine function of the recent input.

with disturbances $\mathbf{v} \in \mathbb{R}^s$ represented as the output of a *unmodeled dynamics* $\mathbb{S}^v = (\mathbf{f}^v, \mathbf{h}^v)$, namely

$$\begin{aligned} \mathbf{e}(k+1) &= \mathbf{f}^v(\mathbf{e}(k)) \\ \mathbf{v}(k) &= \mathbf{h}^v(\mathbf{e}(k)) \end{aligned} \tag{64}$$

where $\mathbf{e}$ is the state of the unmodeled dynamics. Assume that both models allow for linearization, and denote the linearized systems by $\mathbb{S}_L^{\mathbf{x}} = (\mathbf{F}, \mathbf{G}, \mathbf{G}^v, \mathbf{H})$, where $\mathbf{G}^v = \left.\dfrac{\partial \mathbf{f}(\mathbf{x}, \mathbf{u}, \mathbf{v})}{\partial \mathbf{v}}\right|_{(\mathbf{0},\mathbf{0},\mathbf{0})}$, and $\mathbb{S}_L^v = (\mathbf{F}^v, \mathbf{O}, \mathbf{H}^v)$, with an obvious extension of previous notation. Consequently, linearization of the entire plant $\mathbb{S} = (\mathbb{S}^{\mathbf{x}}; \mathbb{S}^v)$ leads to $\mathbb{S}_L = (\mathbf{F}^0, \mathbf{G}^0, \mathbf{H}^0)$ where

$$\mathbf{F}^0 = \begin{bmatrix} \mathbf{F} & \mathbf{G}^v\mathbf{H}^v \\ \mathbf{0} & \mathbf{F}^v \end{bmatrix}, \qquad \mathbf{G}^0 = \begin{bmatrix} \mathbf{G} \\ \mathbf{0} \end{bmatrix}, \qquad \mathbf{H}^0 = \begin{bmatrix} \mathbf{H} & \mathbf{0} \end{bmatrix} \tag{65}$$

Assume that both $\mathbb{S}_L^{\mathbf{x}}$ and $\mathbb{S}_L^v$ are observable. It can be proven [37] that the entire linearized plant $\mathbb{S}_L$ is observable if all eigenvalues of the linearized noise dynamics are different from the zeros of the noise-output transfer function, and then $\mathbb{S}_L$ admits representation ARX$(n + s, n + s)$. Consequently, by the same argument as before, the nonlinear object with unmodeled dynamics admits locally representation NARX$(n + s)$. Since *practically* little is known about the unmodeled dynamics, the necessary order of NARX model must be increased until the required accuracy has been achieved.

Various modifications of NARX structures are possible if the disturbances are modeled by stochastic processes [35]. Since mostly deterministic control aspects are discussed in this chapter, we do not discuss this subject due to lack of space.

5.4.5. *Relative degree and alternative NARX models*

Recall that for the linear SISO system $\mathbb{L}(\mathbf{F}, \mathbf{G}, \mathbf{H})$ (40) we have (44)

$$y(k+n) = \mathbf{H}\mathbf{F}^n\,\mathbf{x}(k) + \sum_{j=1}^{n} M_j\,u(k+n-j) \tag{66}$$

where $M_j = \mathbf{H}\mathbf{F}^{j-1}\mathbf{G} \in \mathbb{R}$. The *relative degree* rd$(\mathbb{L})$ is defined as the delay in the input–output transmission, namely the d that satisfies

$$M_1 = \ldots = M_{d-1} = 0 \quad \text{and} \quad M_d \neq 0$$

If $\mathrm{rd}(\mathbb{L}) = d$ then

$$y(k+d) = \mathbf{H}\mathbf{F}^{d}\,\mathbf{x}(k) + \mathbf{H}\mathbf{F}^{d-1}\mathbf{G}\,u(k)$$

This allows for the following *ARX predictor* representation of the linear system

$$y(k+d) = \sum_{j=1}^{n} \bar{a}_j\, y(k-j+1) + \sum_{j=1}^{n} \bar{b}_j\, u(k-j+1) \tag{67}$$

where $\bar{a}_j$, $\bar{b}_j$ are in general different from a_j, b_j.

For nonlinear systems, it is convenient to consider a local notion of the relative degree. Define for a SISO plant

$$\nu_k(\mathbf{x}, u) = \frac{\partial h(\bar{\mathbf{f}}^{k-1}(\mathbf{f}(\mathbf{x}, u)))}{\partial u}$$

where we denoted $\bar{\mathbf{f}}^{(1)}(\mathbf{x}) = \mathbf{f}(\mathbf{x}, 0)$, and $\bar{\mathbf{f}}^{(k)}(\mathbf{x}) = \mathbf{f}(\bar{\mathbf{f}}^{(k-1)}(\mathbf{x}), 0)$. The *local relative degree* (LRD) is equal to d

$$\mathrm{lrd}(\mathbb{S}) = d \tag{68}$$

if for all $(\mathbf{x}, u)$ in some $\mathcal{D} \ni (\mathbf{0}, 0)$

$$\nu_1(\mathbf{x}, u) = \ldots = \nu_{d-1}(\mathbf{x}, u) = 0, \quad \nu_d(\mathbf{x}, u) \neq 0 \tag{69}$$

Similarly, $\mathrm{LRD}(\mathbb{S}) = \infty$ if for all $(\mathbf{x}, u)$ in some $\mathcal{D} \ni (\mathbf{0}, 0)$

$$\nu_k(\mathbf{x}, u) = 0, \quad \text{for all } k \geq 0 \tag{70}$$

In all other cases we say that the local relative degree is *not well defined.* In other words, $\mathrm{lrd}(\mathbb{S})$ is not well defined if for some k and some $\mathcal{D} \ni (\mathbf{0}, 0)$

$$\nu_k(\mathbf{0}, 0) = 0 \quad \nu_k(\mathbf{x}, u) \neq 0 \quad \text{for } (\mathbf{x}, u) \in \mathcal{D} - (\mathbf{0}, 0) \tag{71}$$

Since for linear systems $\nu_k(\mathbf{0}, 0) = M_k$ then *if the local relative degree is well defined*, then $\mathrm{lrd}(\mathbb{S}) = \mathrm{rd}(\mathbb{S}_L)$. Consequently, for SISO systems with well-defined local relative degree d, one can employ a predictor NARX representation in the form (Fig. 14)

$$y(k+d) = \bar{\psi}(\mathbf{q}^{-n} y(k),\, \mathbf{q}^{-n} u(k)) \tag{72}$$

Similar representation can be provided for nonlinear MIMO systems.

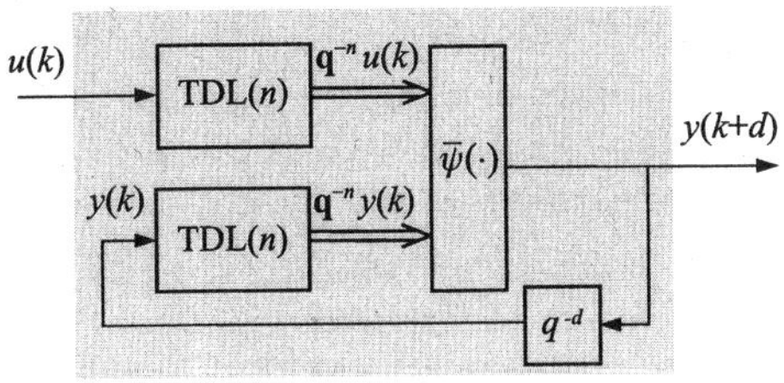

Figure 14: NARX model in the predictor form. The structure is identical to the one shown in Fig. 10, except that the single delay has been replaced by the d-unit delay.

5.5. Stabilization

The basic problem of regulation consists in stabilization of the plant around a fixed operating point. Stabilization is also a first step in various other control tasks. While the problem is solved theoretically for linear plants, nonlinear plants lack constructive solutions. We first recall some basic issues related to stabilization, and then present several approaches to the stabilization task for nonlinear plants that use neural approximators. The first method employs the feedback linearization which makes it possible to employ linear methods to stabilize a nonlinear system. The second approach also employs the linearization principle, but instead of finding the linearizing transformation, a nonlinear feedback law is designed to approximate the Lyapunov function. The last presented approach employs the controllability properties of nonlinear systems to form a nonlinear dead-beat controller that stabilize the nonlinear system in a finite number of steps. Yet another approach to nonlinear system stabilization is presented in [67].

While all the discussed approaches were theoretically known before, they became practically implementable due to neural network approximations.

5.5.1. Preliminaries

Controllability. A plant is called *controllable* in C if every initial state in C can be transformed to any final state in C in a finite number of steps.

For *linear time-invariant controllable systems* (40) this transformation can be done in n steps. It is easy to verify the following equation relating the state with past inputs and states *in linear systems* (40)

$$\mathbf{x}(k+n) = \mathbf{F}^n \mathbf{x}(k) + \sum_{j=1}^{n} \mathbf{F}^{j-1} \mathbf{G}\, \mathbf{u}(k+n-j) \tag{73}$$

hence the linear plant is controllable if and only if the *controllability matrix*

$$\mathbf{W}_c = [\mathbf{G} \;\; \mathbf{FG} \;\; \cdots \;\; \mathbf{F}^{n-1}\mathbf{G}] \tag{74}$$

has full row rank, i.e. rank$(\mathbf{W}_c) = n$. This also shows that any two states can be transformed one into the other in n steps.

For nonlinear systems the notion of *local controllability* is useful (see, e.g. [54, 33]), where we require that for every neighborhood $\mathcal{V}$ of the origin there exists a neighborhood $\mathcal{W}$ of the origin such that every initial state in $\mathcal{W}$ can be transformed to any final state in $\mathcal{W}$ in a finite number of steps without leaving $\mathcal{V}$.

Stability. Consider now an equilibrium $\mathbf{x}_e$: $\mathbf{f}(\mathbf{x}_e, \mathbf{0}) = \mathbf{0}$ and assume that $\mathbf{x}_e = \mathbf{0}$ (If the equilibrium is not at the origin, the coordinates can always be shifted to the equilibrium). The equilibrium is *stable* if for any neighborhood of the origin $\mathcal{V}$ there exists a neighborhood of the origin $\mathcal{W}$ such that if $\mathbf{x}_0 \in \mathcal{W}$ then $\mathbf{x}(k) \in \mathcal{V}$ for all $k > 0$, and *asymptotically stable* if, additionally, $\lim_{k\to\infty} \mathbf{x}(k) = \mathbf{0}$. The equilibrium is finite-stable if the limit is achieved in a finite number of steps. If $\mathcal{W}$ consists of the whole state space, the origin is stable *globally*.

If $\mathbf{f}$ is Lipschitz continuous in a neighborhood of the equilibrium, and the system is asymptotically stable, then the stability property is valid also for systems with bounded disturbances

$$\mathbf{x}(k+1) = \mathbf{f}(\mathbf{x}(k)) + \nu(k) \tag{75}$$

More precisely, the equilibrium is *stable under perturbances* if for any neighborhood of the origin $\mathcal{V}$ there exist a neighborhood of the origin $\mathcal{W}$ such that if $\mathbf{x}_0 \in \mathcal{W}$ and $\nu(k) \in \mathcal{W}$ for all $k > 0$ then $\mathbf{x}(k) \in \mathcal{V}$ for all $k > 0$.

Recall that a function V is *positive definite* in a neighborhood $\mathcal{W}$ of the origin if it is positive in $\mathcal{W}\backslash\mathbf{0}$ and equal to zero at $\mathbf{0}$. A continuous function $V : \mathbb{R}^n \mapsto \mathbb{R}$ is called a *Lyapunov function* for an autonomous system $\mathbf{x}(k+1) = \mathbf{f}(\mathbf{x}(k))$ if in some neighborhood $\mathcal{W}$ of the origin it is positive definite and

$$\Delta V(\mathbf{x}) = V(\mathbf{f}(\mathbf{x})) - V(\mathbf{x}) \leq 0 \tag{76}$$

for all $\mathbf{x} \in \mathcal{W}$. If there exists a Lyapunov function then the equilibrium is stable. If, additionally, $-\Delta V$ is positive definite, the origin is asymptotically stable.

Stabilizability. If there exists a feedback function $\mathbf{g}$ such that the equilibrium point of the closed loop system is asymptotically stable then the system is said to be *stabilizable* (around the equilibrium). It is known (see, e.g. [54]) that if a *linear time-invariant* plant is controllable then it is stabilizable by a linear state feedback$\mathbf{u}(k) = \mathbf{K}\,\mathbf{x}(k)$ or a linear output feedback $\mathbf{u}(k) = \mathbf{K}\,\mathbf{y}(k)$. In fact, the eigenvalues of the state transition matrix $\mathbf{F} + \mathbf{GK}$, or $\mathbf{F} + \mathbf{GKH}$, must just lie inside the unit circle. Since this matrix cam always be made nilpotent, the closed-loop system can be lead to the origin in a finite number (n) steps (dead beat control).

This property has its local extension to nonlinear systems. Namely, if the *linearized system* is controllable then the nonlinear system is *locally controllable* and there exists a linear state feedback that makes the closed loop system locally asymptotically stable (see, e.g. [54]). Moreover, there exists a neighborhood of the origin such that a continuous feedback

$$\mathbf{u}(k) = \mathbf{g}(\mathbf{x}(k)) \tag{77}$$

moves the state to the origin in at most n steps. It is also proven [33] that if C is the set controllable to the origin, then there exists a control law that makes C finitely stable with respect to the origin; the control law in this case is yet not necessarily continuous.

5.5.2. *Stabilization through feedback linearization*

A nonlinear plant (7) is *feedback linearizable* if there exists a transformation $(\boldsymbol{\phi}, \boldsymbol{\mu})$ of the state and input to a new state $\bar{\mathbf{x}}$ and input $\bar{\mathbf{u}}$, namely

$$\begin{aligned} \bar{\mathbf{x}} &= \boldsymbol{\phi}(\mathbf{x}) \\ \mathbf{u} &= \boldsymbol{\mu}(\mathbf{x}, \bar{\mathbf{u}}) \end{aligned} \tag{78}$$

with $\boldsymbol{\phi}$ invertible and continuously differentiable, such that the transformed system is linear. If such the transformation exists only in a neighborhood of $\mathbf{x} = \mathbf{0}, \mathbf{u} = \mathbf{0}$, the system is *locally feedback linearizable* at the origin. While the conditions for existence of such transformations are well known [27, 31], they are difficult to verify and not constructive. Levin and Narendra [33] propose to use neural models of $\boldsymbol{\phi}$ and $\boldsymbol{\mu}$. The networks $\widehat{\boldsymbol{\phi}}, \widehat{\boldsymbol{\mu}}$

$$\begin{aligned} \bar{\mathbf{x}} &= \widehat{\boldsymbol{\phi}}(\mathbf{x}; \mathbf{v}) \\ \mathbf{u} &= \widehat{\boldsymbol{\mu}}(\mathbf{x}, \bar{\mathbf{u}}; \mathbf{w}) \end{aligned} \tag{79}$$

where $\mathbf{w}$, $\mathbf{v}$ denote the weight vectors, are trained to make the output of the transformed system follow a desired linear system

$$\mathbf{x}^0(k+1) = \mathbf{F}^0\,\mathbf{x}^0(k) + \mathbf{G}^0\,\bar{\mathbf{u}}(k) \tag{80}$$

which may take any convenient form. In particular, we may assume

$$\mathbf{F}^0 = \begin{bmatrix} \mathbf{0} & \mathbf{I} \\ 0 & \mathbf{0}^T \end{bmatrix} \qquad \mathbf{G}^0 = \begin{bmatrix} \mathbf{0} \\ 1 \end{bmatrix} \tag{81}$$

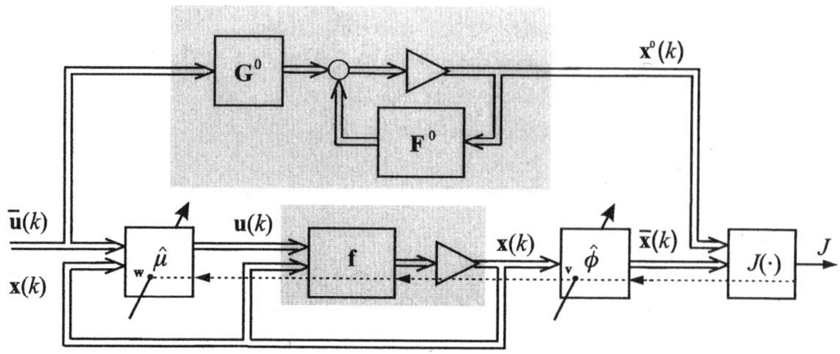

Figure 15: Gradient calculation in feedback linearization networks.

(canonical controllable form). It is shown in [33] that if $\mathbf{f}$ is feedback linearizable and is approximated by its neural model $\widehat{\mathbf{f}}$ with a precision ϵ uniformly over a set of interest $\mathcal{D}$

$$\sup_{\mathbf{x},\mathbf{u}\in\mathcal{D}} \|\mathbf{f}(\mathbf{x},\mathbf{u}) - \widehat{\mathbf{f}}(\mathbf{x},\mathbf{u})\| \le \epsilon_1 \tag{82}$$

then the model $\widehat{\mathbf{f}}$ is approximately feedback linearizable, namely the difference between the outputs of the transformed model and the desired linear system is arbitrarily small uniformly in $\mathcal{D}$

$$\sup_{\mathbf{x},\mathbf{u}\in\mathcal{D}} \|(\mathbf{F}^0\,\bar{\mathbf{x}} + \mathbf{G}^0\,\bar{\mathbf{u}}) - \boldsymbol{\phi}(\widehat{\mathbf{f}}(\mathbf{x},\mathbf{u}))\| \le \epsilon_2 \tag{83}$$

with $\bar{\mathbf{x}}$ and $\mathbf{u}$ given by (78). Consequently, the origin is stable under perturbations, and the neural model will converge in n steps to a ball $\mathcal{B}$ of arbitrarily small radius and centered at the origin, provided ϵ_1 and ϵ_2 are sufficiently small. The local feedback linearizability of the unknown plant can yet be verified only indirectly: without this property the learning procedure is not convergent.

The resulting system is shown in Fig. 15. Let the training error be given by $J = \frac{1}{2}\sum_{k=1}^{N}\|\boldsymbol{\varepsilon}(k)\|^2$ where $\boldsymbol{\varepsilon}(k) = \bar{\mathbf{x}}(k) - \mathbf{x}^0(k)$ denotes the difference between the actual output $\bar{\mathbf{x}}$ and the desired output $\mathbf{x}^0$. We briefly discuss the way the necessary gradients are calculated, and to avoid cluttering of formulas we skip the symbols of all inner functions, for instance we write $\dfrac{\partial f_i(k)}{\partial x_j}$ for $\dfrac{\partial f_i(\mathbf{x}(k),\mathbf{u}(k))}{\partial x_j(k)}$.

Calculation of the cost derivative with respect to any weight v of the $\widehat{\boldsymbol{\phi}}$ network is very simple, namely

$$\frac{dJ}{dv} = \sum_{k=1}^{N}\sum_{j=1}^{n} \varepsilon_j(k)\,\frac{\partial\widehat{\phi}_j(k)}{\partial v} \tag{84}$$

where $\dfrac{\partial\widehat{\phi}_j(k)}{\partial v} = \dfrac{\partial\widehat{\phi}_j(\mathbf{x}(t);\,\mathbf{v})}{\partial v}$ can be calculated by the standard use of backpropagation for the $\widehat{\boldsymbol{\phi}}$ network.

Calculation of the derivative of the cost J with respect to any weight w of the $\widehat{\mu}$ network is more complicated since it involves the gradient propagation for dynamic systems. Either forward-propagation or backpropagation can be used, but we derive here only the backpropagation equations. Using the rule (27) and following the examples of Sec. 5.3.2 we obtain

$$
\begin{aligned}
\frac{dJ}{d\bar{x}_i(k)} &= \varepsilon_i(k) \\
\frac{dJ}{dx_i(k)} &= \sum_j \frac{dJ}{d\bar{x}_j(k)} \frac{\partial \widehat{\phi}_j(k)}{\partial x_i} + \sum_j \frac{dJ}{dx_j(k+1)} \frac{\partial f_j(k)}{\partial x_i} + \sum_j \frac{dJ}{du_j(k)} \frac{\partial \widehat{\mu}_j(k)}{\partial x_i} \\
\frac{dJ}{du_i(k)} &= \sum_j \frac{dJ}{dx_j(k+1)} \frac{\partial f_j(k)}{\partial u_i} \\
\frac{dJ}{dw} &= \sum_k \sum_j \frac{dJ}{du_j(k)} \frac{\partial \widehat{\mu}_j(k)}{\partial w}
\end{aligned}
\tag{85}
$$

Introducing the gradient $J_{\mathbf{x}}(k) = \left\{\frac{dJ}{dx_i(k)}\right\}_{i=1,\dots,n}$, and Jacobian matrices $\widehat{\boldsymbol{\mu}}_{\mathbf{w}}(k)$, $\mathbf{f}_{\mathbf{u}}(k)$, and $\widehat{\boldsymbol{\phi}}_{\mathbf{x}}$, we may rewrite (85) for the weight vector $\mathbf{w}$, in a form of a time-varying linear system driven *in the reverse time* by the output residual $\boldsymbol{\varepsilon}(k)$, namely

$$
\begin{aligned}
J_{\mathbf{w}}(k) &= J_{\mathbf{w}}(k+1) + \widehat{\boldsymbol{\mu}}_{\mathbf{w}}(k)^T \mathbf{f}_{\mathbf{u}}(k)^T J_{\mathbf{x}}(k+1) \\
J_{\mathbf{x}}(k) &= \widehat{\mathbf{F}}^T(k)\, J_{\mathbf{x}}(k+1) + \widehat{\boldsymbol{\phi}}_{\mathbf{x}}^T(k)\, \boldsymbol{\varepsilon}(k)
\end{aligned}
\tag{86}
$$

where

$$
\widehat{\mathbf{F}}(k) = \mathbf{f}_{\mathbf{x}}(k) + \mathbf{f}_{\mathbf{u}}(k)\widehat{\boldsymbol{\mu}}_{\mathbf{x}}(k), \tag{87}
$$

with the initial conditions $J_{\mathbf{w}}(N+1) = \mathbf{0}$, $J_{\mathbf{x}}(N+1) = \mathbf{0}$. The desired gradient $\frac{dJ}{d\mathbf{w}}$ is accumulated in $J_{\mathbf{w}}(k)$ so that $\frac{dJ}{dw} = J_w(1)$. The matrix $\widehat{\boldsymbol{\mu}}_{\mathbf{w}}$ can be calculated by (static) backpropagation. If the nonlinear system is not known then it may be identified off-line by another neural network.

The fact that a *linear feedback* is designed here for the *linearized system* makes this approach valid only in a close vicinity of the equilibrium. Other neural approaches to feedback linearization are presented in [16].

5.5.3. *Stabilization through Lyapunov function adjustment*

Consider a nonlinear plant $\mathbb{S}$ whose linearized version $\mathbb{S}_L = (\mathbf{F}, \mathbf{G}, \mathbf{H})$ is controllable. It can thus be stabilized by a linear static controller $\mathbf{u} = -\mathbf{K}\,\mathbf{y}$. By the linearization principle (Sontag [54, p.170]), the one-step increment of the Lyapunov function $V = \mathbf{x}^T\mathbf{P}\,\mathbf{x}$ for the nonlinear system can approximate function $-\mathbf{x}^T\,\mathbf{Q}\,\mathbf{x}$ in a certain neighborhood C of the origin for any desired positive-definite matrix $\mathbf{Q}$.

These properties were employed in the construction of a locally stabilizing feedback for known nonlinear plants, proposed by Yu and Annaswamy [67]. The method consists of setting up a neural model of the controller for which the Lyapunov function increment is smaller than a desired increment (Fig. 16). One first selects a positive-definite matrix $\mathbf{Q}$ and a feedback matrix $\mathbf{K}$ that makes $\mathbf{F} - \mathbf{G}\,\mathbf{K}\,\mathbf{H}$ asymptotically stable. The Lyapunov function corresponding to the selected $\mathbf{Q}$ can be obtained by solving for a positive-definite $\mathbf{P}$ the discrete-time Lyapunov equation for the closed-loop system

$$
(\mathbf{F} - \mathbf{G}\,\mathbf{K}\,\mathbf{H})^T\,\mathbf{P}\,(\mathbf{F} - \mathbf{G}\,\mathbf{K}\,\mathbf{H}) - \mathbf{P} = -\mathbf{Q} \tag{88}
$$

The training data $\mathbf{x}$ are generated uniformly from a certain region $\widehat{C} \in \mathbb{R}^n$ which can be enlarged in training. For each data point $\mathbf{x}$, one calculates the desired increment ΔV^0 of the Lyapunov function by

$$\Delta V^0(\mathbf{x}) = -\mathbf{x}^T \mathbf{Q}\, \mathbf{x} \tag{89}$$

Now, for the same data point one uses the network approximation $\widehat{\mathbf{g}}$ of the feedback law to calculate the next state $\mathbf{x}^+$, namely

$$\mathbf{y} = \mathbf{h}(\mathbf{x}), \qquad \mathbf{u} = \widehat{\mathbf{g}}(\mathbf{y}; \mathbf{w}), \qquad \mathbf{x}^+ = \mathbf{f}(\mathbf{x}, \mathbf{u}) \tag{90}$$

This enables to calculate the corresponding increment of the Lyapunov function

$$\Delta V(\mathbf{x}, \mathbf{x}^+) = \mathbf{x}^{+T} \mathbf{P}\, \mathbf{x}^+ - \mathbf{x}^T \mathbf{P}\, \mathbf{x} \tag{91}$$

Since the goal is to obtain the Lyapunov function increment ΔV not greater than the desired one ΔV^0, the cost function will take into account only those $\mathbf{x}$ for which $\varepsilon(\mathbf{x}) = \Delta V - \Delta V^0$ is positive, namely

$$J = \frac{1}{2} \sum_{\mathbf{x} \in \mathcal{A}} \varepsilon^2(\mathbf{x}) \tag{92}$$

where $\mathcal{A} = \{\mathbf{x} : \varepsilon(\mathbf{x}) > 0\}$.

Gradient backpropagation for any weight w of the $\widehat{\mathbf{g}}$ network has thus a form

$$\begin{aligned} \frac{dJ}{dw} &= \sum_{\mathbf{x} \in \mathcal{A}} \sum_{j=1}^{q} \frac{dJ}{du_j} \frac{\partial \widehat{g}_j}{\partial w} \\ \frac{dJ}{du_i} &= \sum_{j=1}^{n} \frac{dJ}{dx_j^+} \frac{\partial f_j}{\partial u_i} \\ \frac{dJ}{dx_i^+} &= 2\, \varepsilon\, (\mathbf{P}\mathbf{x}^+)_i \end{aligned} \tag{93}$$

Consequently, (93) can be rewritten for the veight vector as

$$\frac{dJ}{d\mathbf{w}} = 2 \sum_{\mathbf{x} \in \mathcal{A}} \widehat{\mathbf{g}}_{\mathbf{w}}^T\, \mathbf{f}_{\mathbf{u}}^T\, \mathbf{P}\, \mathbf{x}^+\, \varepsilon \tag{94}$$

where $\widehat{\mathbf{g}}_{\mathbf{w}}$ and $\mathbf{f}_{\mathbf{u}}$ are Jacobian matrices. As usual, any gradient method can be used for minimization of J. It is proven in [67] that the resulting closed loop system is asymptotically stable in some open neighborhood of the origin.

5.5.4. Dead-beat controller

Feedback linearization can be applied only to a class of nonlinear systems. A direct stabilization method working in a more general case has been proposed by Levine and

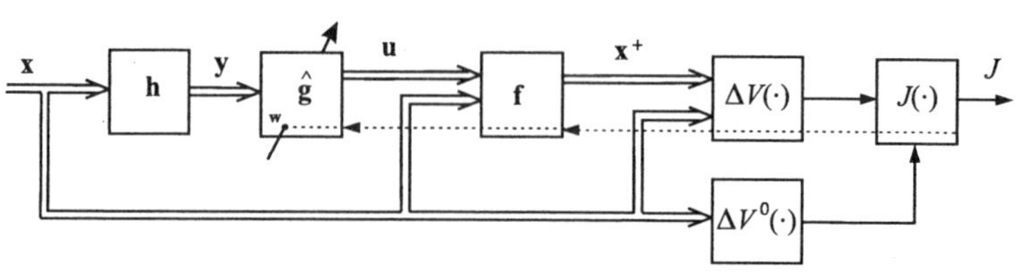

Figure 16: Lyapunov method approach to stabilization.

Narendra [33] for systems

$$\mathbf{x}(k+1) = \mathbf{f}(\mathbf{x}(k), \mathbf{u}(k)) \tag{95}$$

with the equilibrium at the origin and bounded continuously differentiable Lipschitz state transformation function $\mathbf{f}$. The plant is assumed to be known, otherwise the design procedure must start from setting up a neural model of the plant. The method consists in training a neural dead-beat controller $\widehat{g}(\mathbf{x}; \mathbf{w})$ that drives the overall system to the origin in n steps, Fig. 17, if the initial state $\mathbf{x}_0$ belongs to an origin-centered ball $\mathcal{B}_\rho$ of radius $\rho > 0$. The error function takes into account the distance of the state from the origin after n steps, namely

$$J = \begin{cases} \frac{1}{2}\,\|\mathbf{x}(n)\|^2 & \text{if } \|\mathbf{x}(n)\| > \lambda\,\|\mathbf{x}_0\| \\ 0 & \text{otherwise} \end{cases} \tag{96}$$

where λ, initially close to 1, controls a region in which the n-step mapping realized by the system is a contraction mapping. Decrease of λ may speed up the controller.

The system must be run multiple times, with the initial conditions uniform in $\mathcal{B}_\rho$. Parameter ρ may be decreased if learning is not convergent, and increased to make the control time shorter. Controller parameters can be tuned with any gradient method, with the gradient calculated by the error backpropagation.

5.6. Tracking

5.6.1. *Preliminaries*

Suppose a SISO plant output is to follow the *reference signal* $r_y(k)$ which is the output of the *reference model* $\mathbb{S}^R$. We are to find $u(k)$ such that the state $\mathbf{x}(k)$ of the closed-loop system is bounded for all k and

$$|y(k) - r_y(k)| \underset{k\to\infty}{\longrightarrow} = 0$$

for $(\mathbf{x}(0), r_y(0))$ in some neighborhood of the origin. For linear controllable plants, if the reference model $\mathbb{L}^R$ is linear, observable, and has simple eigenvalues, then

$$u(k) = \mathbf{K}\,\mathbf{x}(k) + \mathbf{K}^R\, r_y(k)$$

solves the output tracking problem if and only if all the eigenvalues are different than the zeros of the transfer function of the plant $\mathbb{L}$. This solution can be extended to nonlinear plants $\mathbb{S}$. If the linearized plant $\mathbb{S}_L$ is controllable, and the reference model $\mathbb{L}^R$ is linear, observable and has simple eigenvalues, then the desired control signals $u(k)$ are given by a superposition of a linear function of the state and a nonlinear function of the reference signal, namely

$$u(k) = \mathbf{K}\mathbf{x}(k) + g^R(r_y(k))$$

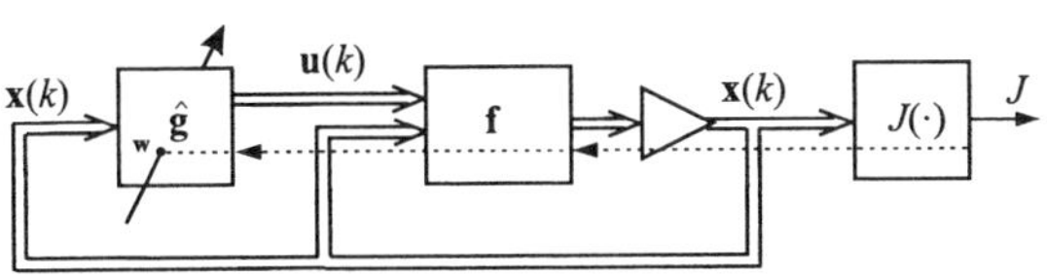

Figure 17: Gradient calculation in a local dead-beat controller.

provided all the eigenvalues are different than the zeros of the transfer function of the linearized plant $\mathbb{S}_L$.

Finally, suppose that the reference model $\mathbb{S}^R$ is nonlinear. Assume that the reference model $\mathbb{S}^R$ is stable and its linearized version $\mathbb{S}^R_L$ has the eigenvalues on the boundary of the unit circle. If $\mathbb{S}$ has well defined relative degree, and $\mathbb{S}_L$ is controllable and satisfies conditions for linear tracking, then the control that realizes the output tracking is a function of the state and the reference signal

$$u(k) = g(\mathbf{x}(k);\ r_y(k)) \tag{97}$$

5.6.2. *Zero dynamics and the state "kick-back"*

Tracking a given signal may not always be physically realizable even for linear systems. The reason is that while the output is forced to follow a given signal, the state may "kick back" and grow unbounded. This behavior is well analyzed for linear systems. Consider first the tracking of the null signal for a linear system $\mathbb{L}$ (40). Given $\mathbf{x}(0)$, a sequence $\{u(k)\}$ can be always chosen that makes $y(k) \equiv 0$. The resulting autonomous system is called the *zero dynamics* $Z(\mathbb{L})$. It is well known that $Z(\mathbb{L})$ is of order the relative degree $rd(\mathbb{L})$. Moreover, for controllable and observable linear systems, the eigenvalues of $Z(\mathbb{L})$ are identical to the zeros of the transfer function of the plant $\mathbb{L}$. Consequently, $\{\mathbf{x}(k)\}$ is a bounded sequence if and only if $\mathbb{L}$ is *minimum-phase*, i.e. if the zeros of the transfer function of $\mathbb{L}$ are asymptotically stable.

Similar results have been obtained for nonlinear systems. For the system

$$y(k+1) = \psi(\mathbf{q}^{-n}y(k),\ \mathbf{q}^{-n+d}u(k-d)) \tag{98}$$

the zero dynamics is given by the solution of

$$\psi\left(\mathbf{0},\ \mathbf{q}^{-n+d}u(k)\right) = 0 \tag{99}$$

where $d = \mathrm{lrd}(\mathbb{S})$.

5.6.3. *Model reference control*

The problem of tracking a setpoint sequence r in such a way that the dynamics of the entire control system is identical to a given stable *reference model* is referred to as the model reference control. Various versions of model reference control are exploited in [65]. We present only a basic simple version discussed in [49]. We consider the plant

$$\begin{aligned} x(k+1) &= \psi(\mathbf{q}^{-n}x(k),\ q^{-d+1}\,\mathbf{q}^{-m}u(k)) \\ y(k) &= x(k) + v(k) \end{aligned} \tag{100}$$

where v models the effect of disturbances and d denotes the relative degree, and $m = n-d+1$. The model (100) can be transformed to the predictor form (72), namely

$$\begin{aligned} x(k+d) &= \overline{\psi}(\mathbf{q}^{-n}x(k),\ \mathbf{q}^{-n}u(k)) \\ y(k) &= x(k) + v(k) \end{aligned} \tag{101}$$

The reference signal r is filtered by a transversal filter

$$r_y(k+d) = \mathbf{a}^T\mathbf{q}^{-n}\,r_y(k+d-1) + \mathbf{b}^T\mathbf{q}^{-n}\,r(k) \tag{102}$$

and the filtered reference signal r_y is to be followed by the plant. For the null static gain, namely if $\sum a_i = -\sum b_i$, the filter does not modify the reference trajectory but imposes the trajectory following dynamics. If there are no disturbances, by (102) and (101) we have

$$r_y(k+d) = \overline{\psi}(\mathbf{q}^{-n}x(k),\ \mathbf{q}^{-n}u(k)) \tag{103}$$

hence if the model is feedback linearizable and the reference signal is bounded, there exists a stable control signal $u(k)$ that make the system follow (103) in the region of interest [40, 33]. In other words, there exists a function g such that

$$u(k) = g(r_y(k+d),\ \mathbf{q}^{-n}x(k),\ \mathbf{q}^{-n+1}u(k-1)) \tag{104}$$

If the plant (101) is unknown and is modeled by a neural network, namely

$$y(k+d) = \widehat{\overline{\psi}}(\mathbf{q}^{-n}y(k),\ \mathbf{q}^{-n}u(k);\ \mathbf{w}) \tag{105}$$

where $\mathbf{w}$ denotes the weight vector, then the feedback rule (104) must be replaced by

$$u(k) = \widehat{g}(r_y(k+d),\ \mathbf{q}^{-n}y(k),\ \mathbf{q}^{-n+1}u(k-1);\ \mathbf{v}) \tag{106}$$

where $\widehat{g}$ is an *inverse network* with weights $\mathbf{v}$, which approximates the inverse of $\widehat{\overline{\psi}}$ with respect to $u(k)$. This setup requires to train both the plant model network $\widehat{\overline{\psi}}$ and the control network $\widehat{g}$. The situation simplifies if the plant is modeled by an affine network model (62), namely

$$y(k+d)\widehat{\overline{\psi}}_0\left(\mathbf{q}^{-n}y(k),\ \mathbf{q}^{-n+1}u(k-1);\ \mathbf{w}_0\right) + \widehat{\overline{\psi}}_1\left(\mathbf{q}^{-n}y(k),\ \mathbf{q}^{-n+1}u(k-1);\ \mathbf{w}_1\right)u(k) \tag{107}$$

In this case, the inverse network $\widehat{g}$ is not needed since the control can be simply calculated as

$$u(k) = \frac{\overline{r}(k+d) - \widehat{\overline{\psi}}_0(\mathbf{q}^{-n}y(k),\ \mathbf{q}^{-n+1}u(k-1);\ \mathbf{w}_0)}{\widehat{\overline{\psi}}_1(\mathbf{q}^{-n}y(k),\ \mathbf{q}^{-n+1}u(k-1);\ \mathbf{w}_1)} \tag{108}$$

Robust adaptive control methods suggest various ways to modify the gradient algorithm to train the networks. Typically, an error threshold is applied that leads to a dead zone update, namely

$$w(k+1) = w(k) - \delta(k+1)\,D(\varepsilon(k+1))\,\frac{d\overline{y}(k+1)}{dw} \tag{109}$$

where

$$D(\varepsilon) = \begin{cases} \varepsilon - d_0 & \text{if } \varepsilon > d_0 \\ 0 & \text{if } |\varepsilon| \le d_0 \\ \varepsilon + d_0 & \text{if } \varepsilon > d_0 \end{cases} \tag{110}$$

It is proven by Chen and Khalil [8] that for any threshold $d_0 > 0$, any set $\mathcal{K}$ around the origin, any required network approximation accuracy ε^*, and any initial state bound, $y(k) - r(k)$ converges to a ball of radius d_0 centered at the origin, provided the zero dynamics is exponentially stable, with quadratic Lyapunov function approximations valid in $\mathcal{K}$, $\mathbf{x}(0) \in \mathcal{K}$, and the initial weight vector sufficiently close to the one that satisfies the approximation accuracy condition on $\mathcal{K}$. Another neural technique for the asymptotic tracking is presented in [9].

5.6.4. *Internal model control*

The tracking method using a a reference model may become unsatisfactory if the plant model accuracy become too low. It is thus useful to monitor the plant model accuracy to be able to adjust the control accordingly. An idea of the internal model control control [49, 23, 29, 13] consists in employing a model of the plant and modifying the reference signal namely

$$r^*(k) = r(k) - (y(k) - \widehat{y}(k)) \tag{111}$$

where $\widehat{y}$ denotes the *internal model* output. Such a design is robust against model inaccuracies and plant disturbances (Fig. 18). To show this design in more details, we use the original plant equations (100), and approximate the plant with a neural network, namely

$$y(k+d) = \widehat{\psi}(\mathbf{q}^{-n}y(k+d-1),\ \mathbf{q}^{-m}u(k);\ \mathbf{w}) \tag{112}$$

where $\mathbf{w}$ denotes the weight vector. The resulting control has the form

$$u(k) = \widehat{g}(r_y(k+d),\ \mathbf{q}^{-n}y(k+d-1),\ \mathbf{q}^{-m+1}u(k-1);\ \mathbf{v}) \tag{113}$$

where $\widehat{g}$ is an *inverse network* with weights $\mathbf{v}$, which approximates the inverse of $\widehat{\psi}$ with respect to $u(k)$. If the plant is modeled by an affine network model (62) then the inverse network $\widehat{g}$ is not needed since the control can be calculated as

$$u(k) = \frac{r_y(k+d) - \widehat{\psi}_0(\mathbf{q}^{-n}y(k+d-1),\ \mathbf{q}^{-m+1}u(k-1);\ \mathbf{w}_0)}{\widehat{\psi}_1(\mathbf{q}^{-n}y(k+d-1),\ \mathbf{q}^{-m+1}u(k-1);\ \mathbf{w}_1)} \tag{114}$$

Note that while the plant model (112) uses less past control values than (105) yet for $d > 1$ the controller (114) requires the proces outputs $y(k+d-1), \ldots, y(k+1)$ unavailable at the moment k. In other words, it is necessary to employ an internal model of the system that predicts the unknown values.

Training of the control network can be better organized if we use predicted signals, namely the $d-1$-step-ahead output predictor $\widehat{y}_p(k) = \widehat{y}(k+d-1)$ and a future value of the reference signal $r_p(k) = \bar{r}(k+d-1)$ (Fig. 19). By (112, 113) we obtain

$$u(k) = \widehat{g}(r_p(k+1),\ \mathbf{q}^{-n}\widehat{y}_p(k),\ \mathbf{q}^{-m+1}u(k-1);\ \mathbf{v}) \tag{115}$$

$$\widehat{y}_p(k+1) = \widehat{\psi}(\mathbf{q}^{-n}\widehat{y}_p(k),\ \mathbf{q}^{-m}u(k);\mathbf{w}) \tag{116}$$

Finally, the reference model (105) expressed in the predicted signals, and with the modified input (111), has the form

$$r_p(k+1) = \mathbf{a}^T\mathbf{q}^{-n}\, r_p(k) + \mathbf{b}^T\mathbf{q}^{-n}\, r^*(k) \tag{117}$$

Properties of the entire control system (Fig. 20) are analyzed in details in [49].

5.6.5. General tracking

The general tracking problem is formulated as a problem of tracking the arbitrary reference signal r. *Asymptotic tracking* consists in finding an analytic function g and a constant N such

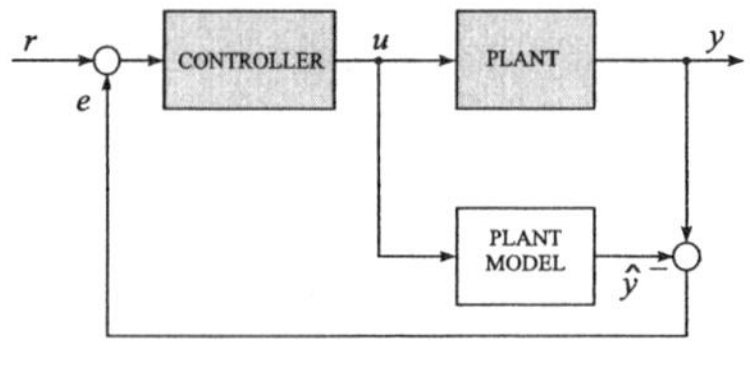

Figure 18: Schematic view of the internal model control.

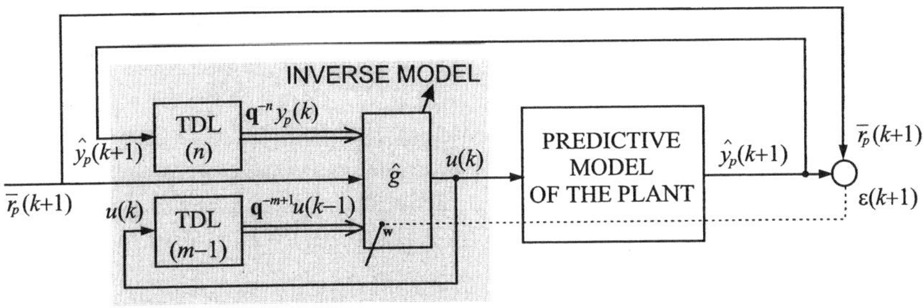

Figure 19: Training of the controller in the internal model control scheme.

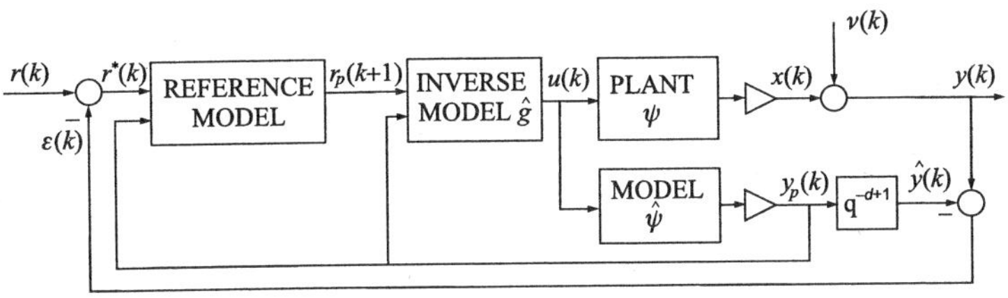

Figure 20: Implementation of internal model control.

that for the control signal

$$u(k) = g(\mathbf{x}(k),\, r(k), \ldots, r(k+N))$$

the resulting closed–loop system is asymptotically stable for $r \equiv 0$ and for every $\mathbf{x}(0)$ sufficiently close to $\mathbf{0}$

$$|y(k) - r(k)| \underset{k\to\infty}{\longrightarrow} 0 \tag{118}$$

For the *exact tracking* it is required that for every $\|\mathbf{x}(0)\|$ sufficiently small

$$|y(k) - r(k)| = 0 \quad \text{for all } k \geq N \tag{119}$$

The input-output tracking problems require to determine the control based on past values of the output rather than the state.

The exact tracking has a solution if and only it $d = \mathrm{lrd}(\mathbb{S})$ is well defined, and the zero dynamics is asymptotically stable. The feedback system tracks the desired signal in d steps, and only $r(k+d)$ is needed ($N = d$), namely (Fig. 21)

$$u(k) = \widehat{g}(\mathbf{q}^{-n}y(k),\, \mathbf{q}^{-n+1}u(k-1),\, r(k+d)) \tag{120}$$

where $\widehat{g}$ is a neural model of g. The asymptotic tracking is possible under the same conditions, but the solution is not unique. Another neural technique for tracking unknown signal is presented in [53].

5.6.6. *Linearization around the desired trajectory*

The tracking method proposed in [1] assumes that the plant has the predictor NARX representation (72) in a region of interest with the relative degree d well defined. The control signal is derived through a linearization of the output-input mapping around the desired trajectory r at each time instant. The resulting control signal has a form

$$u(k) = u(k-1) + \text{sat}_\epsilon\Big(\frac{r(k+d) - y(k+d-1)}{\overline{\psi}_u(k-1)}\Big) \tag{121}$$

where $\overline{\psi}_u(k) = \dfrac{\partial\overline{\psi}(\mathbf{q}^{-n}y(k), \mathbf{q}^{-n}u(k))}{\partial u(k)}$, and sat_ϵ denotes the saturation function, namely

$$\text{sat}_\epsilon(x) = \begin{cases} -\epsilon & \text{if } x < -\epsilon \\ x & \text{if } |x| \le \epsilon \\ \epsilon & \text{if } x > \epsilon \end{cases} \tag{122}$$

It is shown that for sufficiently slow reference trajectories r and $\epsilon > 0$ sufficiently small, the reference signal is asymptotically tracked and the resulting closed loop system is stable. To build the control signal for unknown plants, it is necessary to know both $\overline{\psi}$ and $\overline{\psi}_u$. It is suggested to either set up a neural model of $\overline{\psi}$ and approximate $\overline{\psi}_u$, or set up a neural model of $\overline{\psi}_u$ and approximate $\overline{\psi}$. The networks are trained off-line.

5.7. Optimal control

5.7.1. *Finite horizon problems*

Optimal control problems usually cannot be solved analytically, with the exception of LQ problems (control of linear systems with quadratic cost). Consider an optimal control of a known time-varying system

$$\mathbf{x}(k+1) = \mathbf{f}_k(\mathbf{x}(k), \mathbf{u}(k)) \tag{123}$$

that minimizes a cost index on a finite time period $[0, N]$

$$J = \rho_N(\mathbf{x}(N)) + \sum_{k=0}^{N-1} \rho_k(\mathbf{x}(k), \mathbf{u}(k)) \tag{124}$$

The control law is sought in a feedback-feedforward form, namely

$$\mathbf{u}(k) = \mathbf{g}_k(\mathbf{x}(k), \mathbf{x}(N)), \qquad k = 0, \ldots, N-1 \tag{125}$$

for any $\mathbf{u}(0) \in \mathcal{X}(0)$, $\mathbf{u}(N) \in \mathcal{X}(N)$, where $\mathcal{X}(0)$ and $\mathcal{X}(N)$ are given compact sets.

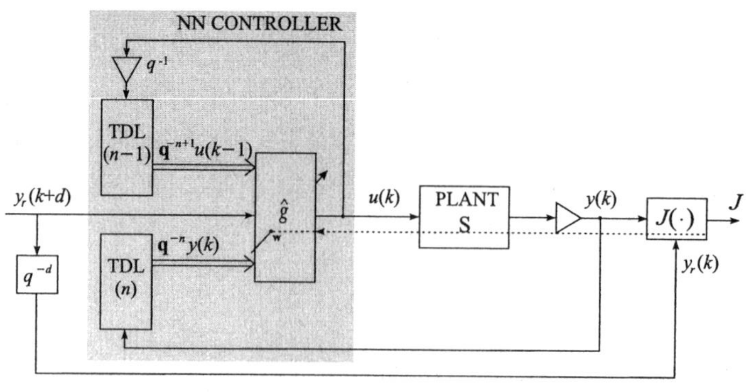

Figure 21: Tracking a general signal.

The above problem can in principle be solved by the dynamic programming. This procedure yet calls for the state space discretization at each decision stage. The control rule (125) additionally requires that the final state be parameterized, what is equivalent to doubling the size of the state space. Inevitably, the user faces here the curse of dimensionality. The solution proposed by Zoppoli and Parizini [66] consists of approximation of the control law by a neural network. Namely,

$$\mathbf{u}(k) = \widehat{\mathbf{g}}(\mathbf{x}(k), \mathbf{x}(N); \mathbf{w}(k)), \quad k = 0, \ldots, N-1 \tag{126}$$

where the weight vectors are defined separately for each time moment. In other words, a separate network is assigned to each time moment. The cost (124) can thus be written as a function of all the weights $\mathbf{w} = (\mathbf{w}(0), \ldots, \mathbf{w}(N-1))$ and $\mathbf{x}(0)$ and $\mathbf{x}(N)$, namely

$$J = J(\mathbf{w};\ \mathbf{x}(0), \mathbf{x}(N)) \tag{127}$$

The weights are adjusted to minimize the expected cost

$$\mathcal{E}J(\mathbf{w};\ \mathbf{x}(0), \mathbf{x}(N) \,|\, \mathbf{w}) \tag{128}$$

where $\mathbf{x}(0)$ and $\mathbf{x}(N)$ are treated as random variables drawn from a uniform distribution on $\mathcal{X}(0) \times \mathcal{X}(N)$. Since it is necessary to calculate the gradient with respect to all the weights, one must backpropagate through all the networks. For any weight $w(k)$ of k-th network we thus have for $k = 0, \ldots, N-1$

$$\begin{aligned}
\frac{dJ}{dw(k)} &= \sum_j \frac{dJ}{du_j(k)} \frac{\partial \widehat{g}_j(k)}{\partial w(k)} \\
\frac{dJ}{du_i(k)} &= \sum_j \frac{dJ}{dx_j(k+1)} \frac{\partial f_j(k)}{\partial u_i(k)} + \frac{\partial \rho_k(k)}{\partial u_i(k)} \\
\frac{dJ}{dx_i(k)} &= \sum_j \frac{dJ}{du_j(k)} \frac{\partial \widehat{g}_j(k)}{\partial x_i(k)} + \sum_j \frac{dJ}{dx_j(k+1)} \frac{\partial f_j(k)}{\partial u_i(k)} + \frac{\partial \rho_k(k)}{\partial x_i(k)}
\end{aligned} \tag{129}$$

and for $k = N$

$$\frac{dJ}{dx_i(N)} = \frac{\partial \rho_N(N)}{\partial x_i(N)} \tag{130}$$

Consequently, we obtain a system of recursive equations to be solved backward in time, for $k = N-1, \ldots, 0$

$$\begin{aligned}
J_{\mathbf{w}}(k) &= \widehat{\mathbf{g}}_{\mathbf{w}}(k)^T J_{\mathbf{u}}(k) \\
J_{\mathbf{u}}(k) &= \mathbf{f}_{\mathbf{u}}(k)\, J_{\mathbf{x}}(k+1) + \rho_{\mathbf{u}}(k) \\
J_{\mathbf{x}}(k) &= \widehat{\mathbf{g}}_{\mathbf{x}}(k)\, J_{\mathbf{u}}(k) + \mathbf{f}_{\mathbf{u}}(k)\, J_{\mathbf{x}}(k+1) + \rho_{\mathbf{x}}(k)
\end{aligned} \tag{131}$$

with the initial conditions at $k = N$, namely $J_{\mathbf{x}}(N) = \rho_{\mathbf{x}}(N)$. Jacobians $J_{\mathbf{w}}(k)$, employed in the weight adjustment procedures, can be calculated also by backpropagation, once the structure of the networks is decided. Note that we used backpropagation in time, and suggested also backpropagation inside the networks. The gradients originally calculated in [66] use forward-propagation in time, and backpropagation only in the networks.

The control rule (125) can be parameterized by additional in-between control points, if the state is to take pre-assigned values at some given time moments. The control rule can also be additionally a function of parameters of the plant model or the cost function. Note yet that while the control rule will optimally respond to those additional parameters, all the additional arguments of the control rule must be know before the control action takes place.

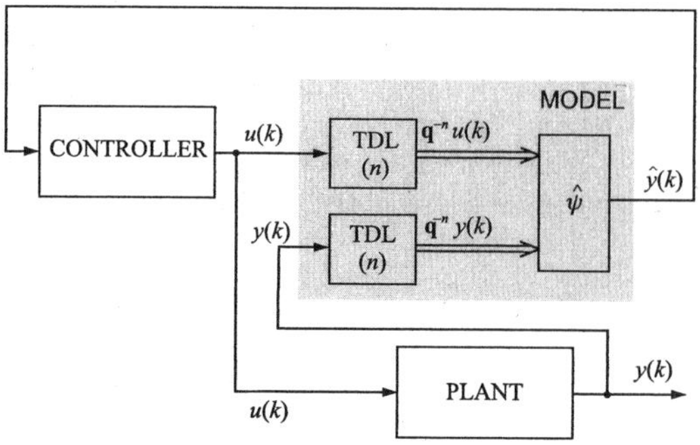

Figure 22: One-step-ahead model predictive control.

The above method can be also applied to infinite horizon problems [66, 47]. Another approaches to the infinite horizon optimal control problem is presented in [24].

5.7.2. *Predictive control*

Predictive control [10, 30, 58] is one of popular control techniques for infinite horizon problems that consists in solving an optimal control problem for a certain finite horizon on the base of a predicted output, applying only the first control out of the entire control sequence, and repeating the procedure at each next time step. We use the predictive control to solve a tracking problem for a SISO system with the unit relative degree

$$y(k+1) = \psi(\mathbf{q}^{-n}y(k), \mathbf{q}^{-n}u(k)) \tag{132}$$

For a given desired signal r the one-step-ahead predictive control $u(k)$ is to be found such that the cost

$$J = (y(k+1) - r(k+1))^2 \tag{133}$$

is minimized subject to (132) and some additional input-output constraints. If ψ is unknown, it can be approximated by a neural model $\widehat{\psi}$ of the form

$$\widehat{y}(k+1) = \widehat{\psi}(\mathbf{q}^{-n}y(k), \mathbf{q}^{-n}u(k); \mathbf{w}) \tag{134}$$

where $\mathbf{w}$ is the weight vector. In [30] it is proposed to take care of the neural model inaccuracies by a modification of the cost (133), namely

$$J = (\widehat{y}(k+1) + \alpha(k) - r(k+1))^2 + \rho|u(k) - u(k-1)| \tag{135}$$

where ρ is a regularizing coefficient and $\alpha(k)$ is an additional uncertainty parameter. The resulting technique consists at each step of solving the extended problem (135) with the input-output constraints to obtain $\overline{u}(k)$, applying the control

$$u(k) = \mu\,\overline{u}(k) + (1-\mu)\,u(k-1)) \tag{136}$$

to the system, and estimating $\alpha(k)$. Conditions for a robustly stable closed-loop tracking control are derived in [30].

5.7.3. *Dual control*

The dual control solves two problems in parallel: first, it controls the plant *with caution*, i.e. taking into account the uncertainty of the models involved, and secondly, it *probes the environment* to reduce the uncertainty and to obtain better estimates of the system parameters. Typical dual controller minimizes a certain cost index in a stochastic environment, e.g.

$$J = \mathcal{E} \sum_{k=1}^{N} q(k) \tag{137}$$

where $q(k)$ is the momentary cost that for tracking problems typically depends on a difference between the reference trajectory $\mathbf{r}$ and the actual one $\mathbf{y}$, e.g.

$$q(k) = \|\mathbf{y}(k) - \mathbf{r}(k)\|^2 \tag{138}$$

While the appropriate Bellman equations can solve the problem in the dynamic programming setup, this is in most cases too time-consuming to be of practical value. Note that

$$\mathcal{E}_{k-1} q(k) = \mathcal{E}_{k-1} \|\widehat{\mathbf{y}}(k|k-1) - \mathbf{r}(k)\|^2 + \mathcal{E}_{k-1} \|\boldsymbol{\varepsilon}(k)\|^2 \tag{139}$$

where $\mathcal{E}_k$ denotes the conditional expected value conditioned on the observations available at the moment k and the *innovation*

$$\boldsymbol{\varepsilon}(k) = \mathbf{y}(k) - \widehat{\mathbf{y}}(k|k-1) \tag{140}$$

is the difference between the actual and the predicted model output. The first term in (139) penalizes a deviation of the predicted plant output from the reference trajectory, and the second term is the cost of inaccuracies of the plant output prediction. An influence of the second (innovation) term on the control, related to a reduction of the model uncertainty, is called the *dual effect*. One of possible sources of prediction errors is the difference between the model and the actual plant. If the model — e.g., a neural model of a nonlinear plant — is substituted in place of the plant, and the control is calculated as if the model was identical to the plant, then the second term in (139) is ignored, and we say that a *heuristic certainty equivalence principle* is applied. If it is of interest to diminish the dual effect, one may modify the cost (138) by *subtracting* a part of the dual cost, namely [12]

$$q(k) = \|\mathbf{y}(k) - \mathbf{r}(k)\|^2 - c_\varepsilon \|\boldsymbol{\varepsilon}(k)\|^2 \tag{141}$$

where $0 \le c_\varepsilon \le 1$. For the maximal $c_\varepsilon = 1$, the dual effect is neglected entirely and the control is based on the heuristic certainty equivalence principle. Drawbacks of the heuristic certainty equivalence, like overshoot and stability problems, can be compensated by performing an off-line training of the plant model to start the control procedure with the already reduced plant uncertainty. Additionally, one may modify the cost (141) by adding the term $c_u\, u^2(k-1)$, $c_u \ge 0$, that penalizes a control cost.

Consider a SISO plant in the affine NARX form (61)

$$y(k+1) = \psi_0(\mathbf{q}^{-n} y(k),\ \mathbf{q}^{-n+1} u(k-1)) + \psi_1(\mathbf{q}^{-n} y(k),\ \mathbf{q}^{-n+1} u(k-1))\, u(k) + e(k) \tag{142}$$

where $\{e\}$ are independent Gaussian $\mathbf{N}_{0,\sigma^2}$ and represent the plant uncertainty. If the plant equations were known then the control at k influences the cost only at the next moment. Assuming that ψ_1 is bounded away from zero, the optimal control can be easily calculated

$$u(k) = \frac{y(k+1) - \psi_0(\mathbf{q}^{-n} y(k), \mathbf{q}^{-n+1} u(k-1))}{\psi_1(\mathbf{q}^{-n} y(k), \mathbf{q}^{-n+1} u(k-1))} \tag{143}$$

If the plant equations are not known, and a model is to be used, the control influences also the estimated model. Suppose we use the model of the form (142), namely

$$y(k+1) = \widehat{\psi}(\mathbf{q}^{-n} y(k),\ \mathbf{q}^{-n+1} u(k-1))^T \begin{bmatrix} 1 \\ u(k) \end{bmatrix} + e(k) \tag{144}$$

where now e represents the neural model uncertainty. If $\widehat{\psi}$ is a (2-output) Gaussian RBF network, we may write

$$\widehat{\psi}(\mathbf{q}^{-n}y(k),\ \mathbf{q}^{-n+1}u(k-1)) = \mathbf{V}\,\eta(k) \tag{145}$$

where $\eta(k) = \eta(\mathbf{q}^{-n}y(k),\ \mathbf{q}^{-n+1}u(k-1))$ is the hidden layer output. Consequently, (144) can be rewritten in a form linear with respect to the output weights

$$y(k+1) = \eta(k)^T\mathbf{V}^T\begin{bmatrix}1\\ u(k)\end{bmatrix} + e(k) = \overline{\eta}^T(k)\,\mathbf{v} + e(k) \tag{146}$$

where $\mathbf{v} = \begin{bmatrix}\mathbf{v}_0\\ \mathbf{v}_1\end{bmatrix}$ is the 'vectorized' weight matrix $\mathbf{V} = \begin{bmatrix}\mathbf{v}_0^T\\ \mathbf{v}_1^T\end{bmatrix}$, and $\overline{\eta}(k) = \begin{bmatrix}\eta(k)\\ \eta(k)\,u(k)\end{bmatrix}$. The output layer weights $\mathbf{v}$ appear linearly in the system model, hence one may use a Kalman filter to update the weights estimators $\widehat{\mathbf{v}}(k)$, namely

$$\begin{aligned}
\mathbf{K}(k) &= \frac{\mathbf{P}(k-1)\,\overline{\eta}(k-1)}{\sigma^2 + \overline{\eta}^T(k-1)\,\mathbf{P}(k-1)\,\overline{\eta}(k-1)}\\
\mathbf{P}(k) &= \left(\mathbf{I} - \mathbf{K}(k)\,\overline{\eta}^T(k-1)\right)\mathbf{P}(k-1)\\
\widehat{\mathbf{v}}(k) &= \widehat{\mathbf{v}}(k-1) + \mathbf{K}(k)\left(y(k) - \overline{\eta}^T(k-1)\,\widehat{\mathbf{v}}(k-1)\right)\\
\widehat{y}(k+1|k) &= \overline{\eta}^T(k)\,\widehat{\mathbf{v}}(k)
\end{aligned} \tag{147}$$

with the initial conditions $\widehat{\mathbf{v}}(0) = 0$, $\mathbf{P}(0) = c_\sigma\mathbf{I}$ where c_σ is a 'large' parameter. While the Kalman filter may lead to intensive computations for large networks, various simplifications of the filter are known.

Well known properties of Kalman filter estimator enable to show that

$$\mathcal{E}_k q(k+1) = (1-c_\varepsilon)\left(\overline{\eta}(k)^T\mathbf{P}(k)\,\overline{\eta}(k) + \sigma^2\right) + c_u\,u^2(k) + \left(\widehat{\mathbf{v}}^T(k)\,\overline{\eta}(k) - r(k+1)\right)^2 \tag{148}$$

This allows for calculation of the optimal cost, namely

$$u(k) = \frac{r(k+1)\,\mathbf{v}_1^T(k)\,\eta(k) - \eta^T(k)\,\mathbf{Q}_1(k)\,\eta(k)}{c_u + \eta(k)^T\mathbf{Q}_2(k)\,\eta(k)} \tag{149}$$

with

$$\begin{aligned}
\mathbf{Q}_1(k) &= \mathbf{v}_0(k)\,\mathbf{v}_1^T(k) + (1-c_\varepsilon)\mathbf{P}_{10}(k)\\
\mathbf{Q}_2(k) &= \mathbf{v}_1(k)\mathbf{v}_1^T(k) + (1-c_\varepsilon)\mathbf{P}_{11}(k)+
\end{aligned} \tag{150}$$

where the partition $\mathbf{P} = \begin{bmatrix}\mathbf{P}_{00} & \mathbf{P}_{01}\\ \mathbf{P}_{10} & \mathbf{P}_{11}\end{bmatrix}$ corresponds to the partition of $\mathbf{v}$. Note that the uncertainty is taken into account through $\mathbf{P}$, and is entirely ignored if $c_\varepsilon = 1$, and maximally attenuated if $c_\varepsilon = 0$. The first case, for $c_u = 0$, is equivalent to the controller based on the heuristic certainty equivalence principle, while the second corresponds to the cautious controller, where the model parameters as treated as the actual plant parameters.

5.8. Reinforcement learning

The term *reinforcement learning* is often used exchangeably with *neuro-dynamic programming*. Ideas of reinforcement, originating in experimental biology and psychology, have been first introduced into heuristic schemes of machine learning, and later incorporated into formal concepts of dynamic programming. Various control ideas proposed by reinforcement learning are now well understood in the context of controlled Markov processes, and current intensive research will hopefully enable to understand the reasons of successes and failures of many other. The reinforcement methods may overcome the curse of dimensionality due to parametric approximations of functions (like the *cost to go* function) which otherwise require an exponential growth of resources with the problem dimension. Moreover, the reinforcement methodology can be applied to only approximately known or unknown plants.

Control methodology coming from biology has a special reason to be included in this discussion of neurally-inspired control methods, even though neural networks are not necessarily built into the reinforcement control schemes. Being bound by the size of this Chapter, we will not elaborate on various reinforcement control methods, but rather show how neural approximations are built into reinforcement schemes. The reader interested in the reinforcement control field is directed to books of Sutton and Barto [55] and Bertsekas and Tsitsiklis [5].

We introduce some basic reinforcement methods for a time invariant nonlinear plant (7) with the state fully observed ($\mathbf{x} = \mathbf{y}$) and with a state feedback control loop, namely

$$\mathbf{x}(k+1) = \mathbf{f}(\mathbf{x}(k), u(k)) \tag{151}$$

$$u(k) = g(\mathbf{x}(k)) \tag{152}$$

The *reinforcement* r, understood as a momentary control cost, is assigned to each state-control pair, namely

$$r(k) = \rho((\mathbf{x}(k), u(k)) \tag{153}$$

While we consider only infinite horizon control problems, we may distinguish a special *termination state* $\mathbf{x}^e$ that stops the control process. The goal of control is to minimize the discounted *cost to go* (called also the secondary utility or strategic utility) defined as

$$R(t) = \sum_{k=0}^{\infty} \alpha^k \, r(t + k+1) \tag{154}$$

where $\alpha \in [0, 1)$ is the *discount rate*. If $\alpha = 0$ then the 'long term' extends only for one moment ahead $R(t) = r(t + 1)$, and the increase of α enlarges the number of time moments "practically" taken into consideration in R. In the limit case $\alpha = 1$ there is no discount.

We generalize the state equations (151) to include state uncertainties, assuming that $\mathbf{f}$ is random. More exactly, we assume that for any initial state and any stationary feedback law g, the resulting sequence of states is a Markov process, and conditional distribution $P_g(\mathbf{x}, u)$ of a "next state" $g(\mathbf{x}, u)$ given the "previous" state $\mathbf{x}$ and control u does not depend on time.

It also fruitful to extend the deterministic control rule (152) to a stochastic rule. One of the reasons of this departure from the deterministic optimal control is to allow for better observations of the environment. Another is to be able to smooth out the control rule in cases where the control space is finite, e.g. for binary control. One may then define a randomized control as a differentiable function a parameter such that, for specific values of the parameter, we obtain the preassigned binary values. As for the state equations, we may at each time extend the feedback law (152) by a random element, and assume that each random element is independent of any other random element, and has identical (time-independent) distribution. We denote the resulting (time-independent) distribution of $g(\mathbf{x})$ conditioned on $\mathbf{x}$ by $P_g(\mathbf{x})$. Note that if the control rule is deterministic than the distribution $P_g(\mathbf{x})$ is concentrated on a single point $\mathbf{x}$, i.e. $P\{g(\mathbf{x}) = \mathbf{x}\} = 1$.

The expected discounted cost for a given control policy represented by a state feedback g for a plant presently at state $\mathbf{x}$

$$J(\mathbf{x}) = \mathcal{E}(R(t) \,|\, \mathbf{x}(t) = \mathbf{x}) \tag{155}$$

is called the (state) *value function*. (Additionally, we define $J(\mathbf{x}^e) = 0$.) The expected discounted cost for a plant presently at state $\mathbf{x}$ that applies action u and furthermore continues with control policy given by g

$$Q(\mathbf{x}, u) = \mathcal{E}(R(t) \,|\, \mathbf{x}(t) = \mathbf{x},\ u(t) = u) \tag{156}$$

is called the *action value* function Q. It is easy to notice that J and Q are related to each other, namely

$$J(\mathbf{x}) = \mathcal{E}_{\mathbf{x}} Q(\mathbf{x}, g(\mathbf{x})) = \int Q(\mathbf{x}, u)\, dP_g(u \,|\, \mathbf{x}) \tag{157}$$

$$Q(\mathbf{x}, u) = \overline{\rho}(\mathbf{x}, u) + \alpha\, \mathcal{E}_{\mathbf{x},u} J(\mathbf{f}(\mathbf{x}, u)) = \overline{\rho}(\mathbf{x}, u) + \alpha \int J(\mathbf{x}')\, dP_{\mathbf{f}}(\mathbf{x}' \,|\, \mathbf{x}, u) \tag{158}$$

where $\overline{\rho}(\mathbf{x}, u) = \mathcal{E}_{\mathbf{x},u}\rho(\mathbf{x}, u)$. Note that J depends directly on the state uncertainty, while Q on the control uncertainty. By the elimination of either Q or J from the above equations, one obtains the *Bellman equation*, namely

$$\begin{aligned} J(\mathbf{x}) &= \mathcal{E}_{\mathbf{x}}\big(\overline{\rho}(\mathbf{x}, g(\mathbf{x})) + \alpha\, J(\mathbf{f}(\mathbf{x}, g(\mathbf{x})))\big) \\ &= \int \Big(\overline{\rho}(\mathbf{x}, u) + \alpha \int J(\mathbf{x}')\, dP_{\mathbf{f}}(\mathbf{x}' \,|\, \mathbf{x}, g(\mathbf{x}))\Big) dP_g(u \,|\, \mathbf{x}) \end{aligned} \tag{159}$$

Similar relation can be written in terms of the action value function. For deterministic feedback rules, (157) simplifies to

$$J(\mathbf{x}) = Q(\mathbf{x}, g(\mathbf{x})) \tag{160}$$

and then the Bellman equation (159) also simplify, namely

$$\begin{aligned} J(\mathbf{x}) &= \overline{\rho}(\mathbf{x}, g(\mathbf{x})) + \alpha\, \mathcal{E}_{\mathbf{x}} J(\mathbf{f}(\mathbf{x}, g(\mathbf{x}))) \\ &= \overline{\rho}(\mathbf{x}, g(\mathbf{x})) + \alpha \int J(\mathbf{x}')\, dP_{\mathbf{f}}(\mathbf{x}' | \mathbf{x}, g(\mathbf{x})) \end{aligned} \tag{161}$$

Under quite general assumptions, the Bellman equations have *unique solutions* [4].

The reinforcement control we discuss is similar to those considered earlier in this Chapter, yet with a special way to calculate the cost of control. The cost is calculated by an element called traditionally the *critic*. The goal of the critic is to convert instantaneous cost r into a long term cost.

5.8.1. HDP/BAC: Heuristic Dynamic Programming with Backpropagated Adaptive Critic

The HDP structure proposed by Werbos [60, 61, 63, 64] uses *adaptive critic* to approximate the cost-to-go in a control scheme, and backpropagates the gradient of the cost-to-go to the controller to approximate the optimal feedback. The adaptive critic consists of an approximator (like a neural network) that estimates the value function with the use of the time difference method. Namely, since

$$d(t) = \rho(\mathbf{x}(t), u(t)) + \alpha\, \widehat{J}(\mathbf{x}(t+1); \mathbf{w}(t)) - \widehat{J}(\mathbf{x}(t); \mathbf{w}(t)) \tag{162}$$

then $(d(t))^2$ may serve as the error to be minimized with respect to the weights. Consequently

$$\mathbf{w}(t+1) = \mathbf{w}(t) + \delta \frac{\partial}{\partial \mathbf{w}(t)} \widehat{J}(\mathbf{x}(t); \mathbf{w}(t))\, d(t) \tag{163}$$

Note that only the weights of the current estimate (at $\mathbf{x}(t)$) are adapted, and the future estimate of the value function together with the current reinforcement serve as the desired value. Consequently, the weights are modified with a one-step delay. Two copies of the critic model are required in calculations, Fig. 23. The first network uses the new value of the state $\mathbf{x}(t+1)$ to calculate the estimate $\widehat{J}(\mathbf{x}(t+1); \mathbf{w}(t))$, and the second network, with identical weights, uses the previous value of the state $\mathbf{x}(t)$ to calculate the estimate $\widehat{J}(\mathbf{x}(t); \mathbf{w}(t))$. This makes it possible to evaluate the time difference (162) and to calculate the gradient of the squared time difference with respect to the weights of *the second network*

$$\mathbf{g}(t) = d(t) \frac{\partial}{\partial \mathbf{w}(t)} J(\mathbf{x}(t); \mathbf{w}(t)) \tag{164}$$

This enables to make the weight vector adjustment step (for instance, using the simple gradient method $\mathbf{w}(t+1) = \mathbf{w}(t) + \delta\, \mathbf{g}(t)$) in both networks. All the elements of the entire HDP control scheme (controller, plant model, critic) may in general be approximated by neural networks, it is yet suggested that the plant model be approximated first. The controller network weights must be approximated in such a way as to minimize the approximated cost-to-go $\widehat{J}$, as calculated by the adaptive critic, in the system

$$\begin{aligned} u(t) &= \widehat{g}(\mathbf{x}(t); \mathbf{v}(t)) \\ \widehat{\mathbf{x}}(t+1) &= \widehat{\mathbf{f}}(\mathbf{x}(t), u(t)) \\ \widehat{J}(t+1) &= \widehat{J}(\widehat{\mathbf{x}}(t+1); \mathbf{w}(t)) \end{aligned} \tag{165}$$

In this order, the backpropagated adaptive critic (BAC) technique can be used [63]. Namely, the derivative $\widehat{J}$ with respect to the weights $\mathbf{v}$ of the control network is calculated by backpropagation through the critic and the model networks to the control network (Fig. 24).

5.8.2. *Dual heuristic programming*

Dual heuristic programming (DHP) is a critic design that uses a different type of critic [60, 63, 64]. Here the critic network approximates the gradient of J with respect to the state $\lambda(\mathbf{x}) = \frac{\partial}{\partial \mathbf{x}} J$. To give a rough idea of this design, we assume smooth differentiability of the necessary functions and obtain by differentiation of (159) with respect to the state

$$\lambda(\mathbf{x}) = \mathcal{E}_{\mathbf{x}}\big(\bar{\rho}_{\mathbf{x}}(\mathbf{x}, \mathbf{u}) + \mathbf{g}_{\mathbf{x}}^T(\mathbf{x})\bar{\rho}_{\mathbf{u}}(\mathbf{x}, \mathbf{u}) + \alpha\,(\mathbf{f}_{\mathbf{x}}^T(\mathbf{x}, \mathbf{u}) + \mathbf{g}_{\mathbf{x}}^T(\mathbf{x})\,\mathbf{f}_{\mathbf{u}}^T(\mathbf{x}, \mathbf{u}))\,\lambda(\mathbf{f}(\mathbf{x}, \mathbf{u}))\big) \tag{166}$$

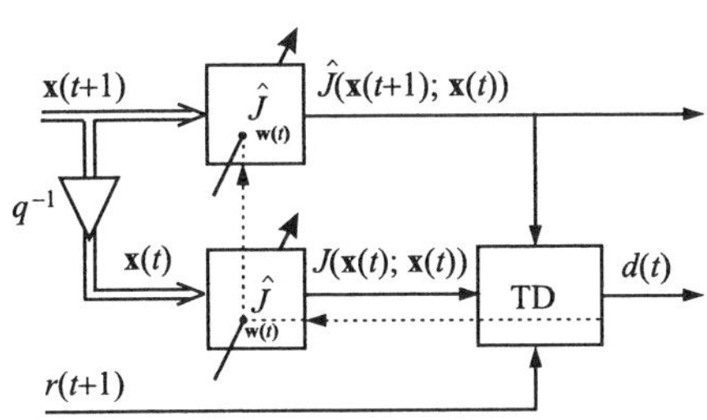

Figure 23: The adaptive critic using the time difference weight adjustment.

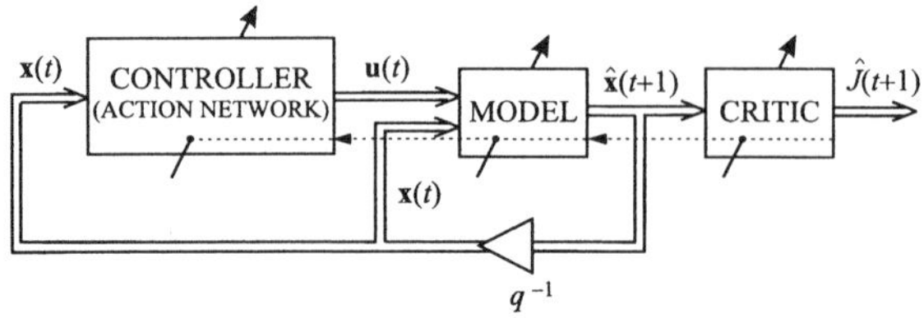

Figure 24: The heuristic dynamic programming control scheme.

where $\overline{\rho}_{\mathbf{x}}$ and $\overline{\rho}_{\mathbf{u}}$ are gradients, $\mathbf{f}_{\mathbf{x}}$, $\mathbf{f}_{\mathbf{u}}$, and $\mathbf{g}_{\mathbf{x}}$ are Jacobian matrices, and $\mathbf{u} = \mathbf{g}(\mathbf{x})$. The above equation is a basis for an adjustment of the weights $\mathbf{w}$ of the estimator $\widehat{\lambda}(\mathbf{x};\mathbf{w})$ to minimize $\frac{1}{2}\|\mathbf{d}(t)\|^2$, where $\mathbf{d}$ is the DHP vector equivalent of the scalar time difference in the HDP design. Here

$$\mathbf{d}(t) = \widehat{\lambda}(\mathbf{x};\mathbf{w}) - \mathbf{a}(t) - \alpha\,\mathbf{A}(t)\,\widehat{\lambda}(\mathbf{x}^+;\mathbf{w}) \tag{167}$$

where

$$\begin{aligned}\mathbf{a}(t) &= \overline{\rho}_{\mathbf{x}}(\mathbf{x},\mathbf{u}) + \mathbf{g}_{\mathbf{x}}^T(\mathbf{x})\,\overline{\rho}_{\mathbf{u}}(\mathbf{x},\mathbf{u})\\ \mathbf{A}(t) &= \mathbf{f}_{\mathbf{x}}^T(\mathbf{x},\mathbf{u}) + \mathbf{g}_{\mathbf{x}}^T(\mathbf{x})\,\mathbf{f}_{\mathbf{u}}^T(\mathbf{x},\mathbf{u})\end{aligned} \tag{168}$$

with $\mathbf{x} = \mathbf{x}(t)$, $\mathbf{x}^+ = \mathbf{x}(t+1)$, and for $\mathbf{u} = \mathbf{g}(\mathbf{x}(t))$ calculated on the base of the plant model. Like for the HDP design, two copies of the critic model are required in calculations. The first network uses the new value of the state $\mathbf{x}(t+1)$ to calculate the estimate of $\lambda(\mathbf{x}(t+1);\mathbf{w}(t))$, and the second network, with identical weights, uses the previous value of the state $\mathbf{x}(t)$ to calculate the estimate $\lambda(\mathbf{x}(t);\mathbf{w}(t))$. This enables to calculate $\mathbf{d}(t)$ and the gradient of $\frac{1}{2}\|\mathbf{d}(t)\|^2$ with respect to the weights of *the second network*

$$\mathbf{g}(t) = \frac{\partial}{\partial \mathbf{w}(t)}\,\lambda(\mathbf{x}(t);\mathbf{w}(t))^T\mathbf{d}(t) \tag{169}$$

The DHP feedback rule is approximated by an action network. Assuming differentiability of (159) with respect to $\mathbf{u}$ one obtains

$$\mathcal{E}_{\mathbf{x}}(\overline{\rho}_{\mathbf{u}}(\mathbf{x},\mathbf{u}) + \alpha\,\mathbf{f}_{\mathbf{u}}^T(\mathbf{x},\mathbf{u})\,\lambda(\mathbf{f}(\mathbf{x},\mathbf{u}))) = \mathbf{0} \tag{170}$$

and the weights of the action network $\mathbf{u} = \mathbf{g}(\mathbf{x};\mathbf{v})$ can be adjusted to minimize the squared norm of

$$\mathbf{c}(t) = \overline{\rho}_{\mathbf{u}}(\mathbf{x},\mathbf{u}) + \alpha\,\mathbf{f}_{\mathbf{u}}^T(\mathbf{x},\mathbf{u})\,\lambda(\mathbf{f}(\mathbf{x},\mathbf{u})) \tag{171}$$

Interesting examples of applications of DHP to difficult control problems, like multiple generator control, and fed-batch fermentor optimization, together with comparisons with other reinforcement control methods including HDP, are presented in [56, 57, 25].

5.9. Concluding remarks

5.9.1. Tuning traditional controllers

With all the "modern" techniques available, the industry still relies on the "old good" PID control. There exists a variety of techniques for tuning the PID controllers, yet they are typically assuming that the plant is a delayed first order linear system. Methods for more complex plants are available but they require that the plant model be first identified.

A method for tuning the PID controller *without* such prior identification is proposed in [17]. A neural network $\widehat{g}(y; \mathbf{w})$ approximates the controller, and is trained to minimize the usual cost $J = \frac{1}{2}\sum_{k=1}^{N} |\varepsilon(k)|^2$ where $\varepsilon(k) = y(k) - r(k)$. We have

$$\frac{dJ}{dw} = \sum_{k=1}^{N} \frac{dJ}{du(k)} \frac{\partial \widehat{g}(k)}{\partial w}$$
$$\frac{dJ}{du(k)} = \varepsilon(k) \frac{\partial h(k)}{\partial u(k)} \tag{172}$$

hence the instantaneous estimate of the gradient $\dfrac{dJ}{d\mathbf{w}}$ is equal to

$$\eta(k)\, \varepsilon(k) \frac{\partial \widehat{g}(k)}{\partial \mathbf{w}} \tag{173}$$

where the Jacobian $\eta(k) = \dfrac{dh(k)}{du(k)}$ just modifies the magnitude of the gradient once its sign is known. In other words, (173) is replaced by

$$\mathrm{sign}(\eta(k))\, \varepsilon(k) \frac{\partial \widehat{g}(k)}{\partial \mathbf{w}} \tag{174}$$

Incidentally, this correspond to the cost function $J = \sum_{k=1}^{N} |\varepsilon(k)|$. After the training, the PID controller parameters are calculated by the least squares method, with the use of the neural controller results. The method gives good results also for noisy and open-loop unstable plants where most of traditional tuning methods fail. Another neural technique for adaptive tuning PID controller is proposed in [22].

5.9.2. *Summary*

The area of adaptive systems took decades to shape, having been modified with the increasing availability of new powerful mathematical and computational tools. One of the newest tools are neural networks. It seems that the *enthusiasm not contaminated with knowledge*, seen by Minsky in early days of neural networks, has converted into enthusiasm supported by knowledge. We also faced a reverse side of the same attitude, namely a *scepticism not contaminated by knowledge*. At present, the methods provided by neural networks have matured and seem to be indispensable in control, system modeling and identification.

With all the theoretical achievements of neural techniques in control, always the simplest controllers that satisfy the demands and constraints will be chosen in applications. And usually, neural controllers are rather complex, and may even carry a stigma of something unusual, having an unpredictable behavior. Moreover, the mechanisms inside the neural controllers are often little understood by practitioners, hence such controllers may be treated as practically unsafe. Consequently, to pave the way to neural controllers in particular applications, traditional controllers must first be proven inadequate. On the other hand, safety issues, often underestimated by control theoreticians, must be of greater concern.

Even in contemporary solutions there is sometimes to much heuristics and too little theory, which is especially needed in novel control solutions. For instance, training of networks off line is currently still preferred since system identification in a closed loop is computationally intensive and the on-line training can make the overall system unstable. Namely, if the local relative degree is not well defined, tracking performance may not be acceptable. Even if it is well defined but the zero dynamics is not stable, the system identification may work but the control may grow unboundedly and the tracking error, first small, may get out of control. It is thus important to understand well certain properties of system to be applied. But here comes another problem: theoretical system properties must be deduced from models, which have different structure than the systems, and only in some sense, like a similarity of output signals, are "close" to the modeled systems. This may be not sufficient to claim that theoretical properties, fulfilled by the object, will be fulfilled by the model. Another theoretical issue that needs more light is the stability of nonlinearly parameterized networks that are trained in dynamic environments. These areas are still open to research.

Acknowledgement

The author is deeply grateful to Wodek Macewicz for making the final drawings and continual help with TEX.

References

[1] O. Adetona, E. Garcia, and L.H. Keel, "A new method for the control of discrete nonlinear dynamic system using neural networks, *IEEE Trans. on Neural Networks*, vol. 11, No. 1, pp. 102–112, Jan. 2000

[2] D. Aeyels, "Generic observability of differentiable systems," *SIAM Journal of Control and Optimization*, vol. 19, pp. 595–603, 1981

[3] A. Barron, "Universal approximation bounds for superposition of a sigmoidal function," *IEEE Trans. on Information Theory*, vol. 3, pp. 930–945, 1993

[4] D.P. Bertsekas, *Dynamic Programming and Optimal Control*, vols. I and II, Athena Scientific, Belmont, Mass. 1995

[5] D.P. Bertsekas and J.N. Tsitsiklis, *Neuro-Dynamic Programming*, Athena Scientific, Belmont, MA, 1996

[6] J.B.D. Cabrera and K.S. Narendra, "Issues in the Application of Neural Networks for Tracking Based on Inverse Control," *IEEE Trans. on Automatic Control*, vol. **44**, No.11, pp. 2007–2027, 1999

[7] F.-C. Chen and C.C. Liu, "Adaptively controlling nonlinear continuous-time systems using multilayer neural networks," *IEEE Trans. on Automatic Control*, Vol. 39, No.6, pp. 1306–1310, 1994

[8] F.-C Chen and H. Khalil, "Adaptive control of a class of nonlinear discrete-time systems using neural networks," *IEEE Trans. on Automatic Control*, vol. 40, No. 5, pp. 791–801, May 1995

[9] Y-C Chu and J. Huang, "A neural-network method for the nonlinear servomechanism problem," *IEEE Trans. on Neural Networks*, vol. 10, No. 6, pp. 1412–1423, Nov. 1999

[10] D.W. Clarke, C. Mohtadi, and P.S. Tuffs, "Generalized predictive control," *Automatica*, vol. 23, pp. 137-160

[11] G. Cybenko, "Approximation by superpositions of a sigmoidal function," *Mathematics of Control, Signals, and Systems*, vol. 2, pp. 303–314, 1989

[12] S. Fabri and V. Kadirkamanathan, "Dual adaptive control of nonlinear stochastic systems using neural networks," *Automatica*, vol. 34, No. 2, pp. 245–253, 1998

[13] D. Flynn, S. McLoone, G.W. Irwin, M.D. Brown, E. Swidenbank, and B.W. Hogg, "Neural control of Turbogenerator Systems," Automatica, vol. 33, No. 11, pp. 1961–1973, 1977

[14] K. Funahashi, "On the approximate realizations of continuous mappings by neural networks," *Neural Networks*, vol. 2, No. 3, pp. 183-192, 1989

[15] G.C. Goodwin, P.J. Ramadge, and P.E. Caines, "Discrete time multivariable adaptive control," *IEEE Trans. on Automatic Control*, vol. 25, pp. 449–456, June 1980

[16] S. He, K. Reif, R. Unbehauen, "A neural approach for control of nonlinear systems with feedback linearization," *-IEEE Trans. on Neural Networks*, vol. 9, No. 6, pp. 1409–1421, Nov. 1998

[17] E.M. Hemerly and C.L. Nascimento Jr., "An NN-based approach for tuning servocontrollers," *Neural Networks*, vol. 12, pp. 513–518, 1999

[18] K. Hornik, "Approximation capabilities of multilayer feedforward neural networks," *Neural Networks*, vol.4, pp. 251–257, 1990

[19] K. Hornik, "Some results on neural networks approximations," *Neural Networks*, vol.6, pp. 1069–1072, 1993

[20] K. Hornik, M. Stinchcombe, and H. White "Multilayer feedforward networks are univeral approximators," *Neural Networks*, vol. 2, No. 5, pp. 359–366, 1989

[21] K. Hornik, M. Stinchcombe, and H. White "Univeral approximation of an unknown mapping and its derivatives using multilayer feedforward networks," *Neural Networks*, vol. 3, No. 5, pp. 551–560, 1990

[22] S.N. Huang, K.K. Tan, and T.H. Lee, "A combined PID/adaptive controller for a class of nonlinear systems," *Automatica*, vol. 37, pp. 611–618, 2001

[23] K.J. Hunt and D. Sbarbaro, "Studies in neural-network-based control" in *Neural Networks for Control and Systems,* K. Warwick, G.W. Irwin, and K.J. Hunt, Eds., Peter Peregrinus Ltd., London, U.K., pp. 94–122, 1992

[24] E. Irigoyen, J.B. Galván, and M.J. Pérez-Ilzarbe, "Neural networks for constrained optimal control of non-linear systems," *Proc. of the 2000 International Joint Conference on Neural Networks IJCNN'00*, Como, Italy, 2000

[25] M.S. Iyer and D.C. Wunsch, II, "Dynamic reoptimization of a fed-batch fermentor using adaptive critic design," *IEEE Trans. on Neural Networks*, vol. 12, No. 6, pp. 1433–1444, Nov. 2001

[26] S. Jagannathan, "Control of a class of nonlinear discrete-time systems using multilayer neural networks," *IEEE Trans. on Neural Networks*, vol. 12, No.5, pp. 1113-1120, Sept. 2001

[27] B. Jakubczyk, "Feedback linearization of discrete-time systems," *Systems Control Letters*, vol. 9, pp. 411–416, 1987

[28] L. Jin, P.N. Nikiforuk, and M.M. Gupta, "Approximation of discrete-time state-space trajectories using dynamic recurrent neural networks, *IEEE Trans. on Automatic Control*, vol. 40, No. 7, pp. 1266–1270, July 1995

[29] J. Kalkuhl, K.J. Hunt, and H. Fritz, "FEM-based neural-network approach to nonlinear modeling with application to longitudinal vehicle dynamics control," *IEEE Trans. on Neural Network*, vol. 10, No. 4, pp, 885–897, July 1999

[30] C. Kambhampati, J.D. Mason, K. Warwick, "A stable one-step-ahead predictive control of non-linear systems," *Automatica*, vol. 36, pp. 485–495

[31] H.G. Lee, A. Araphostathis, and S.I. Marcus, "On the linearization of discrete-time systems," *International Journal of Control*, vol. 45, pp. 1103–1124, 1987

[32] M. Leshno, V. Lin, A. Pinkus, and S. Schocken, "Multilayer feedforward networks with a nonpolynomial activation funtion can approximate any function", *Neural Networks*, vol. 6, No. 6, pp. 861–867, 1993

[33] A.U. Levin and K.S. Narendra, "Control of nonlinear dynamical systems using neural networks controllability and stabilization," *IEEE Trans. on Neural Networks*, Vol. 4, No. 2, 192–206, 1993

[34] A.U. Levin and K.S. Narendra, "Recursive identification using feedforward neural networks," *International Journal of Control*, vol. 61, No. 3, pp. 533–547, 1995

[35] L. Ljung, J. Sjöberg, and H. Hjalmarsson, "On neural network model structures in system identification," in S. Bittanti and G. Picci (Eds.) *Identification, Adaptation, Learning. The Science of Learning Models from Data*, pp. 366–399, Springer-Verlag, Berlin 1996

[36] A.S. Morse, "Global stability of parameter adaptive systems," *IEEE Trans. on Automatic Control*, vol. 25, pp. 433–439, June 1980

[37] S. Mukhopadhyay and K.S. Narendra, "Disturbance rejection in nonlinear systems using neural networks," *IEEE Trans. on Neural Networks*, vol. 4, No. 1, pp. 63–72, Jan 1993

[38] K.S. Narendra "Neural Networks for Control: Theory and Practice," *Proceedings of the IEEE*, vol. **84**, No. 10, pp. 1385–1406, 1996

[39] K.S. Narendra and Y.H. Lin, "Stable direct adaptive control," *IEEE Trans. on Automatic Control*, vol. 25, pp. 456–461, June 1980

[40] K.S. Narendra and S. Mukhopadhyay, "Adaptive control of nonlinear multivariable systems using neural networks," *Neural Networks* vol. 7, No. 5, pp. 737–752, 1994

[41] K.S. Narendra and K. Parthasarathy, "Identification and control of dynamical systems using neural networks," *IEEE Trans. on Neural Networks*, Vol. 1, No. 1, pp. 4–27, 1990

[42] G.W. Ng *Applications of Neural Networks to Adaptive Control of Nonlinear Systems*, Research Studies Press Ltd., Somerset, England, 1997

[43] D.H. Nguyen and B. Widrow, "Neural networks for self-learning control systems," *IEEE Control Systems Magazine*, Vol. 10, pp. 18-23, 1990

[44] A. Pacut, "Symmetry of Backpropagation and Chain Rule," *Proc. of the 2002 International Joint Conference on Neural Networks IJCNN'02*, Honolulu, HA, IEEE Press, Piscataway, NJ, pp. 530–534, 2002.

[45] T. Parizini and R. Zoppoli, "Neural networks for feedback feedforward nonlinear control systems," *IEEE Trans. on Neural Networks*, Vol. 5, No. 3, pp. 436–449, 1994

[46] T. Parisinio and R. Zoppoli, "Neural approximations for multistage optimal control of nonlinear stochastic systems," *IEEE Trans. on Automatic Control*, vol. 41, pp. 889–895, 1996

[47] T. Parisinio and R. Zoppoli, "Neural approximation for infinite-horizon optimal control of nonlinear stochastic systems," *IEEE Trans. on Neural Networks*, vol. 9, No. 6, pp. 1388–1408, Nov. 1998

[48] J. Park and I.W. Sandberg, "Universal approximation using radial-basis function networks," *Neural Computations*, Vol. 3, pp. 246–257

[49] I. Rivals and L. Personnaz, "Nonlinear Internal Model Control Using Neural Networks: Applications to Processes with Delay and Design Issues," *IEEE Trans. on Neural Networks*, vol. 11, No. 1, pp. 80–90, Jan. 2000

[50] D.E. Rummelhart, G.E. Hinton, and R.J. Williams "Learning internal representation by errror propagation," in *Parallel Distributed Processing: Exploration in the Microstructure of Cognition*, D.E. Rummelhart and J.L. McClelland, Eds., vol. 1, Chap. 8, Cambridge, MA, MIT Press, 1986

[51] I.W. Sandberg, "Approximation theorems for discrete-time systems," *IEEE Trans. Circuits and Systems*, vol. 38, No. 5, pp. 564-566, May 1991

[52] R.M. Sanner and J.-J.E. Slotine, "Gaussian networks for direct adaptive control," *IEEE Trans. on Neural Networks*, Vol. 3, No. 6, 837–863, 1992

[53] Q. Song, J. Xiao, and Y.C. Soh, "Robust backpropagation training algorithm for multilayer neural tracking controller," *IEEE Trans. on Neural Networks*, vol. 10, No. 5, pp. 1133–1141, Sept. 99

[54] E.D. Sontag, *Mathematical Control Theory*, Springer-Verlag New York 1990

[55] R.S. Sutton and A.G. Barto *Reinforcement Learning. An Introduction*, MIT Press, Cambridge, MA

[56] G.K. Venayagamoorthy, R.G. Harley, and D.C. Wunsch, "Comparison of a heuristic dynamic programming and a dual heuristic programming based adaptive critic neurocontrollers for a turbogenerator," *Int. Joint Conference on Neural Networks IJCNN'00*, Como, Italy 2000,

[57] G.K. Venayagamoorthy, R.G. Harley, and D.C. Wunsch, "Excitation and turbine neurocontrol with derivative adaptive critics of multiple generators on the power grid," *Int. Joint Conference on Neural Networks IJCNN'01*, Washington, DC, 2001

[58] L.-X. Wang and F. Wan, "Structured neural networks for constrained model predictive control," *Automatica*, vol. 37, No. 8, pp. 1235–1243, 2001

[59] P. Werbos, "Backpropagation: Past and future," *IEEE Int. Conference on Neural Networks, San Diego, California, July 1988*, vol. I, pp. 343–353, 1988

[60] P. Werbos, "A menu of designs for reinforcement learning over time," Ch. 3 in W.T. Miller III, R.S. Suttotn, and P.J. Werbos (Eds.), *Neural Networks for Control*, MIT Press, Cambridge, Mass., pp. 67–95, 1990

[61] P.J. Werbos, "Consistency of HDP applied to a simple reinforcement learning problem", *Neural Networks*, vol. 3, pp. 179–189, March 1990

[62] P. Werbos, *The Roots of Backpropagation: From Ordered Derivatives to Neural Networks and Political Forecasting*, Wiley 1994

[63] P.J. Werbos, "Stable adaptive control using new critic designs," *http://xxx.lanl.gov/html/adap-org/9810001*, 1998

[64] P.J. Werbos "New directions in ACDs: Keys to intelligent control and understanding the brain," *Int. Joint Conf. on Neural Networks IJCNN'00*, Washington, DC, vol. III, pp. 61–67, 2000

[65] B. Widrow and E. Walach, *Adaptive Inverse Control*, Prentice-Hall, Englewood Cliffs, NJ, 1996

[66] R. Zoppoli and T. Parisini, "Neural approximations for finite and infinite-horizon optimal control," Ch. 12 in O. Omidvar and D.L. Elliott (Eds.), *Neural Systems for Control*, Academic Press, San Diego, CA, pp. 317–351, 1997

[67] S-H Yu and A.M. Annaswamy, "Stable neural controllers for nonlinear dynamic systems," *Automatica*, Vol. 34, No. 5, pp. 641–650, 1998

[68] T. Hrycej, *Neurocontrol. Towards an Industry Control Methodology*, Willey, New York 1997

Neural Networks for Instrumentation, Measurement and Related Industrial Applications
S. Ablameyko et al. (Eds.)
IOS Press, 2003

Chapter 6
Neural Networks for Signal Processing in Measurement Analysis and Industrial Applications: the Case of Chaotic Signal Processing

Vladimir GOLOVKO, Yury SAVITSKY, Nikolaj MANIAKOV
Laboratory of Artificial Neural Networks, Brest State Technical University
Moskovskaja str. 267, 224017 Brest, Belarus

Abstract. This chapter discusses the use of neural networks for signal processing. In particular, it focuses on one of the most interesting and innovative areas: the chaotic time series processing. This includes time series analysis, identification of chaotic behavior, forecasting, and dynamic reconstruction. An overview of chaotic signal processing both by conventional and neural network methods is given.

6.1. Introduction

Neural techniques have been successfully applied to many problems in the area of signal processing. Different goals and perspectives can be considered in manipulating data sequences generated by physical processes.

Signal filtering is a classical technique to modify the characteristics of the signal itself. Like in traditional approaches, in the neural approaches the signal is observed through a sampling window sliding in time over the signal itself: whenever the observation window photographs a set of signal samples, filtering or transformation is applied and generates the output view of the incoming signal. Many practical examples have been reported in the literature related to various application areas (e.g., in electronics, electrical engineering, mechanical systems, chemical plants, biomedical systems, radio transmissions).

Noise cancellation in a continuous signal is one of the most interesting applications desirable in a wide variety of practical cases. To reduce the noise we can use a finite-duration impulse response (FIR) filter [5], the transformation from the spatial to the frequency space by means of the Discrete Fourier Transform, the Wavelet Shrinkage method [11], or median filtering [12]. However is not always efficient. The use of the ICA (independent component analysis) neural network for extracting noise-free data has been shown a powerful approach [13]. In the case of Gaussian data the PCA (principal component analysis) neural network was shown efficient [14]; it can also be adopted data compression and reduction.

Prediction and cross-correlation abilities of the neural network can be used to reconstruct signals whenever the noise makes the signal poorly understandable or when the sensor observing the signal is occasionally or temporarily not working properly.

Neural implementation of some classical transformations (e.g., Walsh, Hough) has been also studied to exploit the adaptivity of the neural paradigms in configuring the filter coefficients; harmonic signal analysis by neural networks is another high-level transformation.

Signal processing can also be used to extract relevant information from the input signal, e.g., to detect the occurrence of characteristics waveforms, pulses, spikes, and regularities. Several applications are known in speech and sound processing (e.g., automatic typewriters; phoneme and word recognition; speech understanding; automatic translators; voice and sound compression, equalization and manipulation; voice and sound synthesis). Other industrial applications are related to identification of the operating conditions of machinery, plants, and production processes by observing sensor data, and to data cleaning for system diagnosis.

Overviews of different types of neural networks suited for signal processing as well as overviews of their effective applications can be found in [4-14]. Feedforward neural networks are one of the most used, especially the multilayer perceptron (MLP) and the radial basis function networks (RBF) [7-9]. Both of these network types have been shown to be universal function approximators [9] and, consequently, very appropriate for signal processing applications. Another family suited for dynamic modeling is the recurrent neural network (also called time-delay neural network) that was used, e.g., in nonlinear prediction and modeling, adaptive equalization of communication channel, speech processing and measurement [10].

In many real systems (e.g., compound pendula, dripping faucets, predator-prey ecologies, measle epidemics, oscillating chemical reactions, irregular heart beats, stock market, EEG patterns of brainwave activity, central nervous system, physical systems, social behavior), a chaotic behavior has been observed, i.e., a complex, erratic, extremely input-sensitive behavior which cannot be easily understood. Chaos theory is nowadays widely studied and applied in various areas to describe, characterize, and possibly predict the system behavior when such kind of complexity occurs. Due to the increasing interest in these kinds of models and processing, this chapter focuses therefore on chaotic signal processing.

In the system theory, chaotic systems are deterministic models that can be used to describe random, noisy, unpredictable behaviors that are present in natural systems. The behavior of a chaotic system is governed by simple deterministic nonlinear rules that are iteratively applied to generate the next state from the current state and input values; although these rules do not contain any noise, randomness, or probabilities, their repeated application leads to very complex system behaviors in the long term, that cannot be captured by simple global rules. In this sense, unpredictability "emerges" over time.

The chaotic behavior of a dynamical system can be described either by nonlinear mathematical equations or by experimental data. Unfortunately, often we do not know the nonlinear equations that describe the dynamical system. In general we have only experimental signals from the unknown dynamical system. The problem consists therefore in identifying the chaotic behavior and building a model that captures the important properties of the unknown system by using only the experimental data. In order to determine the main properties of our model, we can use the dynamic invariants (namely: correlation dimension, Lyapunov's exponents, and Kolmogorov's entropy).

A chaotic system has a sensitive dependence on the initial conditions: starting from very close initial conditions a chaotic system may very rapidly moves to different final states.

Another problem concerning chaotic signals is that they are unpredictable on the long term, because an error at the beginning of prediction increases exponentially in time [1,2]. An improvement of the prediction accuracy is therefore fundamental. Besides, this allows also for understanding the observed behavior of a nonlinear system and for reconstructing the space of the system states by taking into account the numerical data measured in the system. This is based on the embedding theorem [3], which guarantees that the full knowledge about the system behavior is contained in the time series of characteristic quantities measured in the system; the complete multivariate phase space can be constructed from these time series. The embedding theorem is characterized by some parameters, namely the embedding dimension and the time delay. The estimation of these parameters provides a maximum predictability of the chaotic time series and can be used to choose the optimal window size (number of input samples) to perform forecasting. Neural approaches have been shown effective in forecasting for chaotic systems: examples and techniques will be described in this chapter.

A further problem concerns the chaotic time series processing by using only observed data. From small data samples it is in fact very difficult to reconstruct the system dynamics and to compute the Lyapunov's spectrum. Also in this case neural networks have been shown more powerful for chaotic time series processing than traditional approaches.

To tackle chaotic signal processing by means of neural paradigms, multilayer perceptron (MLP) and radial basis function networks (RBF) [7-9] as well as time-delay neural networks (TDNN) [10] can be applied both to chaotic signal identification and forecasting. The ICA (independent component analysis) and the PCA (principal component analysis) neural networks are suited for advanced filtering [13,14].

Processing of a chaotic signal can be divided in four stages, as shown in Fig. 1. In the first stage the time series analysis is performed to extract the characteristics of the signal. Then the embedding parameters are evaluated to identify the chaotic behavior. Prediction can be performed on the identified model. Finally the phase space reconstruction can take place or the neural network can be built for optimal forecasting.

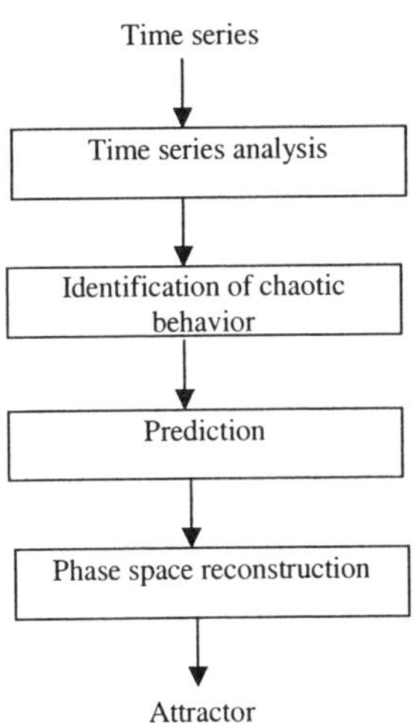

Figure 1: Functional diagram of data processing.

The rest of the chapter is organized as follows. Section 2 reviews the use of multilayer neural networks for signal processing. Section 3 discusses the nonlinear dynamical systems suited for chaotic signal processing and the strange attractor, using Lorenz and Henon data. Section 4 presents different approaches for identification of chaotic behavior. Section 5 describes the time series analysis, namely the computation of the embedding parameters. Section 6 tackles the analytical approaches for computing the Lyapunov's exponents that characterizes the system chaoticity. Section 7 presents the neural network approach to determine the Lyapunov's spectrum, having very low computational complexity and requiring small data sets. Section 8 introduces the neural network approach for chaotic time series forecasting for individual data points. Section 9 discusses the use of neural network for state space reconstruction.

6.2. Multilayer neural networks

In this section the multilayer neural networks are briefly reviewed with respect to their use in signal processing. Namely, multilayer perceptron, radial basis functions, and recurrent neural networks are discussed.

The multilayer perceptron MLP with one hidden layer is given by:

$$y(l) = \sum_{j=1}^{m}\left(v_{jl} F\left(\sum_{i=1}^{n} w_{ij} x_i - T_j \right) - T_l \right) \quad \text{for } l = \{1, p\} \tag{1}$$

where F is the nonlinear function (sigmoid or other nonlinear), m is the number of hidden units, n and p are the numbers of input and output units respectively, v_{jl} and w_{ij} are the weights, T_j are the thresholds.

The radial basis function network RBF is described by:

$$y(l) = \sum_{j=1}^{m}\left(v_{jl} F\left(\sum_{i=1}^{n} (w_{ij} - x_i)^2 \right) - T_l \right) \quad \text{for } l = \{1, p\} \tag{2}$$

where F is the Gaussian function.

These types of neural networks can be viewed as extensions of the classical approaches to model time series, e.g., the linear autoregressive (AR) model. The AR model is:

$$x(t) = \sum_{i=1}^{n} w_i x(t-i) + \varepsilon(t) \tag{3}$$

where w_i are the weights, $\varepsilon(t)$ is the noise term.

The AR model is equivalent to a linear adaptive filter, based on the least-mean square (LMS). This filter can be built by using a single neuron and the LMS algorithm for its training [4]. The use of an AR model for a stationary processes is based on the Wold's decomposition theorem, according which any discrete-time stochastic process can be decomposed into the sum of a generalized linear process and a predictable process, being each of these processes uncorrelated to the other [5]. The AR model was used in a wide range of signal processing applications, encompassing speech, audio, and images.

Unfortunately, in many real-life applications the signal is generated by nonlinear dynamics and may be non-stationary. Such signals are better represented by nonlinear autoregressive (NAR) processes. These models can be defined by:

$$x(t) = F(x(t-1), x(t-2), ..., x(t-n)) + \varepsilon(t) \tag{4}$$

MLP and RBF networks can be effectively used to model NAR processes. These networks can be configured by appropriate algorithms, e.g., backpropagation and its advanced variations, conjugant gradients, and Levenberg-Marquard.

The recurrent neural networks (RNN), also called time-delay neural networks (TDNN), are extensions of the feed-forward neural networks, obtained by introducing time delays on connections [10] as shown in Fig. 2. This approach was widely used in speech recognition, nonlinear prediction, adaptive equalization of communication channels, and plant control. According to the type of feedback loop, we distinguish the Jordan's network, the Elman's network, and the multi-recurrent neural network.

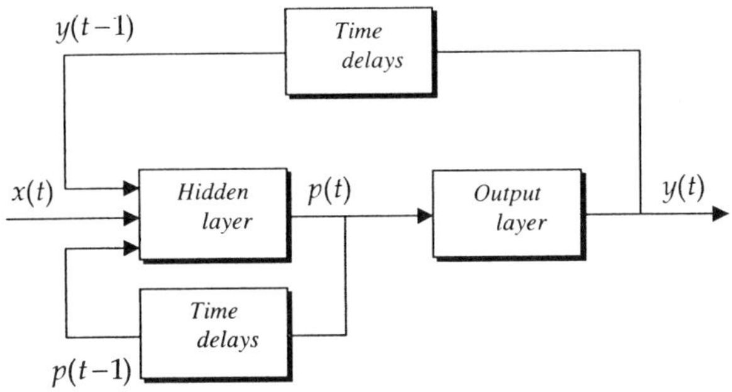

Figure 2: Recurrent neural network

The Jordan's network consists of a multilayer perceptron with one hidden layer and a feedback loop from the output to additional inputs (or context). It computes a nonlinear function of n past sequence elements and q past estimates:

$$y(t) = F(x(t-1), x(t-2), ..., x(t-n), \overline{x}(t-1), \overline{x}(t-2), ..., \overline{x}(t-q)) \tag{5}$$

where $\overline{x}(t)$ is the actual value, and $x(t)$ is the desired value. This model is the nonlinear extension of the ARMA model, i.e., the combination of AR and MA (moving average) components.

The Elman's network has a feedback loop from the hidden layer to additional inputs (or states). This model is described by:

$$\begin{aligned} P(t) &= F(W_1 X(t) + W_2 P(t-1)), \\ Y(t) &= F(W_3 P(t)), \end{aligned} \tag{6}$$

where the matrixes W_1, W_2, W_3 represent three sets of weights: from the input layer to the hidden one, from the hidden layer to the state inputs, and from the hidden layer to the output one.

The multi-recurrent neural network has a feedback both from the hidden and the output layers to the input one. This model is represented by:

$$\begin{aligned} P(t) &= F(W_1 X(t) + W_2 P(t-1) + W_4 Y(t-1)), \\ Y(t) &= F(W_3 P(t)), \end{aligned} \tag{7}$$

where matrix W_4 is set of weights from output layer to context inputs.

The recurrent neural networks may be trained by using of backpropagation algorithm and its more efficient extensions. Another very powerful approach is based on the extended Kalman filter (EKF) [11].

6.3. Dynamical systems

A dynamical system is any object or process for which it is possible to unambiguously define the state at a given time (as the set of characteristic parameters that uniquely identify the system behavior) and the transition function (as the rule that uniquely describes the changes –evolution– of the state in time). The transition function (also called evolution rule) allows for forecasting future states of the dynamical system, starting from a known initial state. A dynamical system may be a mechanical object, a physical system, a chemical substance, a biological entity, a computational process, or any information processing that is performed according with a deterministic algorithm. Description of the evolution rules can be realized in different way, e.g., by differential equations, discrete mapping, graph theory, or Markov series. The selection of the description method may be lead by to the actual mathematical model of the considered dynamical system.

The n-order system can be represent by a set of n ordinary differential equations:

$$\frac{d\bar{x}(t)}{dt} = \Phi(\bar{x}(t), t) \tag{8}$$

where $\bar{x}(t) = [x_1(t), x_2(t), ..., x_n(t)]$ is the vector of the system state and Φ is the vector field. The system is called autonomous if the function Φ is not changing in time, i.e.,

$$\frac{d\bar{x}(t)}{dt} = \Phi(\bar{x}(t)) \tag{9}$$

The system state at any time is defined as a point in the n dimensional space. The vector field maps a manifold to a tangent space. The integral curve (or trajectory) identifies a flow on the manifold. The set of these flow curves are called orbits.

In the case of linear differential equations the trajectories either asymptotically descend in a phase space to the fixed point or are closed orbits when $t \to \infty$. In the case of a nonlinear function Φ under suitable conditions, the behavior is chaotic and the orbits become the complex subset called strange attractor. Some strange attractors have a known mathematical description (e.g., Lorenz's and Rossler's attractors, Mackey-Glass chaotic time series). Other attractors have been experimentally confirmed to be chaotic but there is no known analytical description (e.g., fluid turbulence, Gravity waves, EEG data).

As an example, the attractor of Lorenz system is shown in Fig. 3; it is described by the following three coupled nonlinear differential equations:

$$\begin{cases} \dfrac{dx}{dt} = G(y - x) \\ \dfrac{dy}{dt} = -xz + rx - y \\ \dfrac{dz}{dt} = xy - bz \end{cases} \tag{10}$$

where G=10, r=28, and b=8/3. Lorenz proposed this model for the atmospheric turbulence. An attractor is a subset of the manifold to which an open subset of points (the basin of the attractor) tends to the limit when $t \to \infty$. These are called dissipative systems.

The chaotic flow has a very sensitive dependence on the initial conditions, i.e., points that are initially close each others may exponentially diverge in time. In Fig. 4 two series of a Lorenz system are shown: Series I starts from the initial point [*0, 0.1, 0*], while Series II starts from [*0.001, 0.1, 0*]. A little change in the initial condition leads shortly to different behaviors. This high sensitivity results in unpredictability of the chaotic systems in the long term, since any little inaccuracy is later increased exponentially in time. However, it is important to point out that both of the above series describe the same attractor.

When a dynamical system is described by a first-order differential equation, a chaotic behavior is observed only if the dimension of phase space is greater than 2. However, when the dynamical system is described by difference equation, then the chaotic behavior occurs also in the 2-dimensional space. For the Henon's map:

$$\begin{cases} x_{n+1} = 1 - \alpha x_n^2 + y_n \\ y_{n+1} = \beta x_n \end{cases} \tag{11}$$

where $\alpha = 1.4$ and $\beta = 0.3$, the strange attractor is shown in Fig. 5.

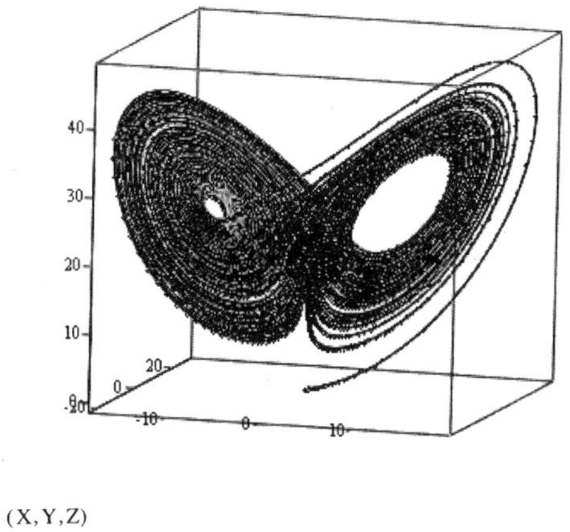

Figure 3: Lorenz's attractor

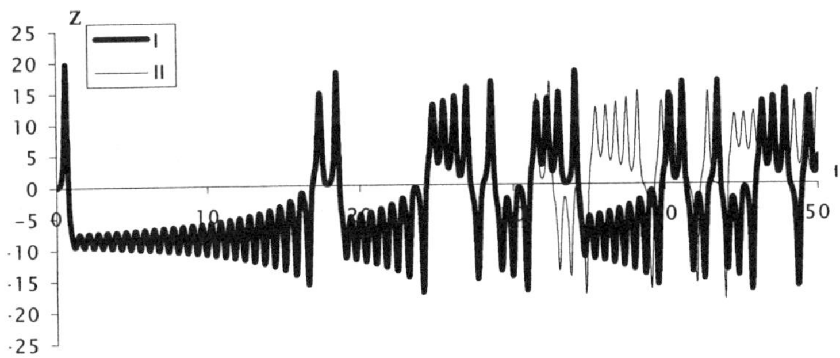

Figure 4: Sensitive dependence on the initial conditions in Lorenz's X-series

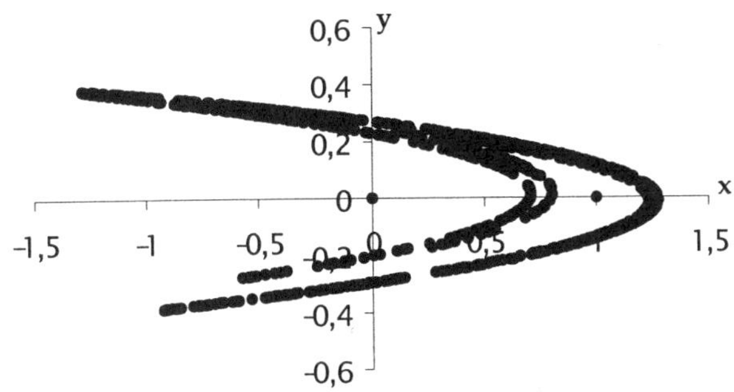

Figure 5: Henon's attractor

As already said, the chaotic behavior can be described either by nonlinear mathematical equations or by experimental data. However, in general only experimental samples of signals produced by the unknown dynamical system are available. The problem consists therefore of identifying the chaotic behavior from these samples and building a model that captures the underlying dynamics of the unknown system. As dynamic invariants correlation dimension, Lyapunov's exponents, and Kolmogorov's entropy can be used.

6.4. How can we verify if the behavior is chaotic?

Chaotic systems include a class of signals that lie between predictable periodic or quasiperiodic signals and totally irregular stochastic signals, which are completely unpredictable. Chaotic processes are deterministic, although they are highly sensible to the initial conditions. Therefore, basic questions in time series analysis are the following: is the process chaotic? How can we distinguish a chaotic process from random (stochastic) or periodic ones? To analyze time series the following methods can be used:

1. the Poincare's section,
2. the power spectrum,
3. the autocorrelation function,
4. the fractal dimension,
5. the Lyapunov's exponents.

One of the easiest ways to identify the chaotic process is to use the Poincare's section. Let's consider a system attractor in the n dimensional phase space and a suited $(n\text{-}1)$ dimensional hyperspace S. The orbits of the dynamical system intersect S in points s_k, where k indicate number of consecutive intersections. The coordinates of these points are transformed into the coordinates system associated to the hyperspace. In such way the mapping $F: s_k \rightarrow s_{k+1}$ is obtained. This mapping is called Poincare's mapping (or stroboscopic mapping). By using this method the n-dimensional dynamical system can be reduced to representation with less dimensions, while preserving the main properties of original system. The surface S should be selected so as to maximize the number of intersections, i.e., to minimize the time intervals between them. On a low dimensional representation it is easier to determine the existence of a chaotic behavior. Unfortunately, this approach is not feasible if the equations are unknown.

The fundamental question is to determine the chaoticity of a one-dimensional signal. For this kind of signal we consider the mapping of the consecutive maximum z_k in the time series and we plot the diagram of z_k versus z_{k+1}. This mapping – inspired by the basic concepts of the Poincare's section – reduces the n-dimensional system into only one dimension. By taking the maximum of a coordinate time series we take a sequence of points in which the temporal derivative of the signal is equal to zero: this identifies a hyperspace. For example, by taking the sequence of the maximum in the Z-series of the Lorenz system (Fig. 6), we plot the hyperbolical paraboloid $bz = xy$. In this way a mapping similar to the stroboscopic mapping is therefore built with respect to the considered surface by taking into account only the sequence of z coordinates in real phase space.

By analyzing the diagram of the maximum sequence some conclusions can be derived about the chaoticity. If there is some regularity the process is deterministic, otherwise the process is random. For example, in the diagram of the consecutive maximum in the Lorenz Z-series shown in Fig. 7 the regularity is clear: the behavior is therefore deterministic.

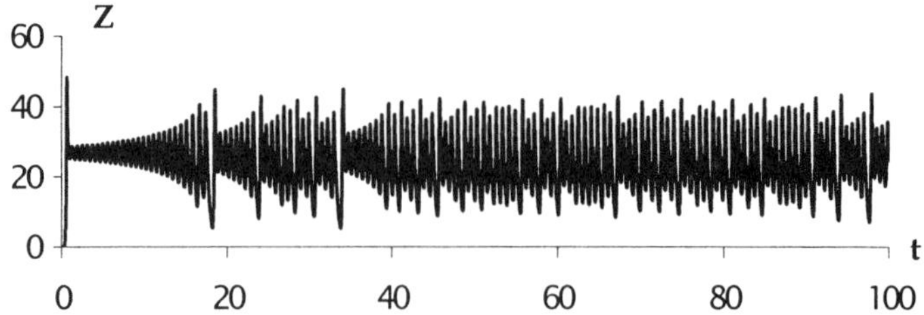

Figure 6: Lorenz's Z-series

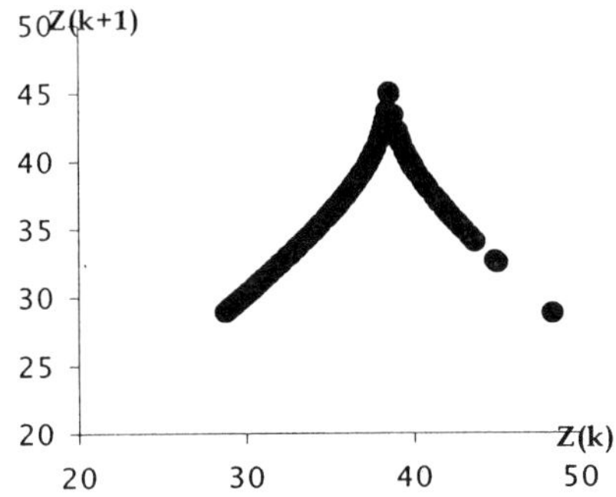

Figure 7: Mapping of the consecutive maximum of the Lorenz's Z-series

Unfortunately, this method is not effective with data affected by noise: for small time derivatives additional extremes can by produced by the perturbations induced by the noise and, consequently, the behavior may become similar to a random process.

Another tools to verify the chaotic behavior is the Fourier transform:

$$x(\varpi) = \lim_{T \to \infty} \int_0^T e^{i\varpi t} x(t)\,dt \tag{12}$$

that transforms the function *x(t)* into the frequency spectrum. The power spectrum is defined as $P(\omega) = |x(\varpi)|^2$. For a periodic oscillation the power spectrum contains a finite number of frequencies. For a chaotic process it is a broad band. It is worth noting that a multi-harmonic power spectrum does not necessarily correspond to a chaotic system. Systems with a high number of degrees of freedom can generate similar power spectrum.

When a system is represented by samples taken at discrete times in a 2^n period (as in the case of time series), we can use the discrete Fourier transform:

$$x^n(t) = \sum_k a_k^n \cdot e^{2\pi ikt/2^n} \tag{13}$$

In Fig. 8 the continuous power spectrum of Henon X-series (for 1024 points) is presented: it allows for identifying the chaotic motion or the multi-harmonic oscillation.

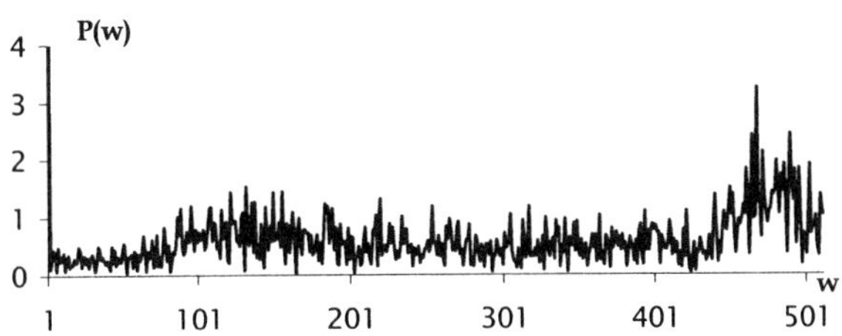

Figure 8: Power spectrum of the Henon's X-series

Another tool to check the process chaoticity is the autocorrelation function, which is defined as follows for continuous and discrete signals, respectively:

$$C(\tau) = \lim_{T \to \infty} \frac{1}{T^2} \int_0^T x(t) \cdot x(t+\tau)dt \tag{14}$$

$$C(\tau) = \lim_{N \to \infty} \frac{1}{N^2} \sum_{t=1}^{N} x(t) \cdot x(t+\tau) \tag{15}$$

In the practice these formulas need to be approximated since only a finite number of point is available. The autocorrelation of a periodical signal produces a periodical function. For chaotic or random signals the autocorrelation function rapidly descend to zero: the autocorrelation function of the Lorenz X-series is shown in Fig. 9.

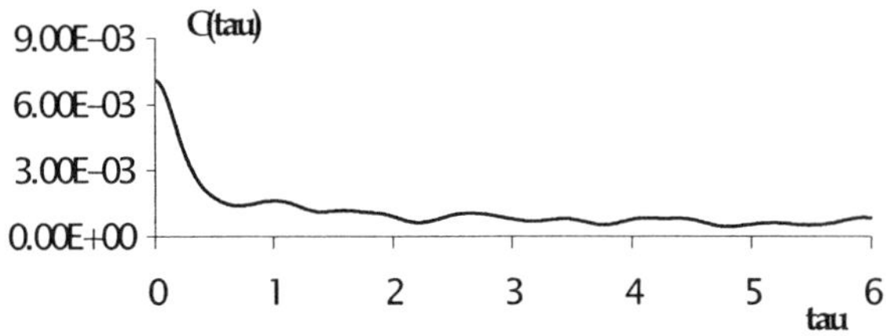

Figure 9: Autocorrelation function of Lorenz's X-series

Another technique to verify the chaotic behavior is the fractal dimension. The attractor of a chaotic process at any time has in fact a fractal dimension. For the one-dimensional observation of the process the correlation dimension D_2 can be evaluated by the algorithm presented in [1]; since this technique requires the use of embedding parameters, it will be discussed in section 5.

The most common and effective test for chaotic behavior verification consists of the Lyapunov's exponent. If the largest Lyapunov's exponent is positive, the process is chaotic; if the sum of all Lyapunov's spectrum is negative the system dissipates and converges to the attractor. The computation both of the largest Lyapunov's exponent and the Lyapunov's spectrum will be discussed in section 6.

6.5. Embedding parameters

A dynamic source of chaotic signals is not fully represented by a one-dimensional observation in the time domain since the chaotic dynamics take place in a phase space having a higher number of dimensions (e.g., for the differential equation it is at least 3). However, the phase space of a chaotic process can be reconstructed from only one time series of observations by using the embedding parameters, as first shown in [2]: the points of time series and their difference (like a derivative) are used as coordinates to build the state space. In [3] the formal proof is given, which is known as the following Time-Delay Embedding Theorem. Let's consider a dynamical system having a solution $(x(t), y(t), \dots, z(t))$ in a d-dimensional phase space. By using only one coordinate $x(t)$, under general conditions it is possible to build such space of lag points $(x(t), x(t+\tau), x(t+2\tau), \dots, x(t+(D-1)\tau))$, that will be a diffeomorphism between itself and the attractor of the dynamical system in the real phase space. The dimension D satisfies $D \geq 2\lfloor d_F \rfloor + 1$, where d_F is the fractal dimension of the attractor and $\lfloor . \rfloor$ is the integer part.

The condition $D \geq 2\lfloor d_F \rfloor + 1$ is sufficient but not necessary for reconstructing the dynamics. Besides, also the above theorem assumes that the observable signal is noiseless. However, in the practice signals are noisy time series. Therefore, the experimental data must be preprocessed in order to minimize the influence of noise on the subsequent analysis. To this purpose a FIR filter or an ICA neural network can be used.

The embedding theorem states that even from a single measured signal it is possible to reconstruct the state space that is equivalent to the unknown dynamical system.

To reconstruct the state space the time delay τ and the embedding dimension D must be evaluated. The procedure for finding a suitable D is called embedding. Unfortunately, the embedding theorem does not provide any guidance in choosing the embedding delay τ.

The time delay τ is the period between the components of the points in the reconstructed phase space. The time delay τ should be chosen so that the coordinates of the vectors constituting the embedding space are independent, in order to obtain a faithful reconstruction of the original phase space. In fact if τ is too large, the dynamics at one time step become disconnected from the dynamics at the next time step; consequently, the components of the vector constituting the embedding space will be uncorrelated. The dimension of the reconstructed attractor will be close to the dimension of the embedding space [15] and the attractor will look very complex. This becomes noticeable in the presence of noise: this case is called irrelevance [16]. If τ is too small, all components of the vector will be nearly the same and the attractor will lie close to the line of identity. Consequently, all points will be indistinguishable: this case is called redundancy. All of these cases lead to bad prediction of the chaotic time series.

There are various methods to evaluate the time delay τ:

1. the autocorrelation function,
2. the average displacement method,
3. the mutual information.

The method based on the autocorrelation function $C(\tau)$ is computationally efficient. This approach uses the first zero (or a point which is very close to zero) of the autocorrelation function. The components of the vectors $x(t)$ and $x(t+\tau)$ are thus uncorrelated. Unfortunately, some functions do not reach their first zero in a short time or even do not reach it at all. To avoid this drawback, Zeng advices to take τ as the time at which $C(\tau)$ first falls to e^{-1}/N^2 (where N is the number of points considered in the time series) [17], while Holzfuss suggests to take τ equal to the time at which the autocorrelation function reaches its first minimum [18]. However, these methods do not usually lead to good results because component uncorrelation does not coincide with independency.

The average displacement method [19] estimates the optimum expansion of the reconstructed attractor from the identity line of the reconstructed phase space. To this purpose the following function is used:

$$S(m,\tau) = \frac{1}{N}\sum_{i=1}^{N}\sqrt{\sum_{j=1}^{m-1}(x(i\tau + j\tau) - x(i\tau))^2} \tag{16}$$

where N is the number of points in the time series, m is the dimension of the embedding space, and τ is the time delay. For a given m $(m=1,2,...)$, τ is varied until a point in which the function $S(m, \tau)$ reaches a plateau is found. For each dimension of the embedding space a time delay can thus be found.

For higher simplicity, the time delay τ is usually chosen by using the method of mutual information [20], derived from the standard information theory [21]. The set of the time series points is divided into m intervals. The suited number m of intervals is computed by using the Starjes formula: $m \approx \log_2 N + 1 \approx 3.32 \ln N + 1$, where N is the number of points in the time series. The length l of each interval is $l=(x_{max} - x_{min})/m$, where x_{max} and x_{min} are the maximum and the minimum values of the time series, respectively. The mutual information function is defined as:

$$I(\tau) = \sum_{i,j} P_{ij}(\tau) \cdot \ln\frac{P_{ij}(\tau)}{P_i \cdot P_j} \tag{17}$$

where P_i is the probability to observe a value of the time series in the i-th interval, and $P_{ij}(\tau)$ is the joint probability that the observed value is located in the i-th interval while the subsequent observation after the time τ falls in the j-th interval. The function $I(\tau)$ characterizes the probability of observing an $x(t+\tau)$ from the observation of $x(t)$. If the mutual information is equal to zero, no information about $x(t+\tau)$ can be extrapolated. This is equivalent to look for independency of the coordinates' vectors $x(t)$ and $x(t+\tau)$. Unfortunately, it is not possible to find a point in which the mutual information function becomes zero: consequently, the time delay is taken equal to the first minimum of this function. The first minimum of the mutual information function of the Lorenz X-series is 0.16 (Fig. 10).

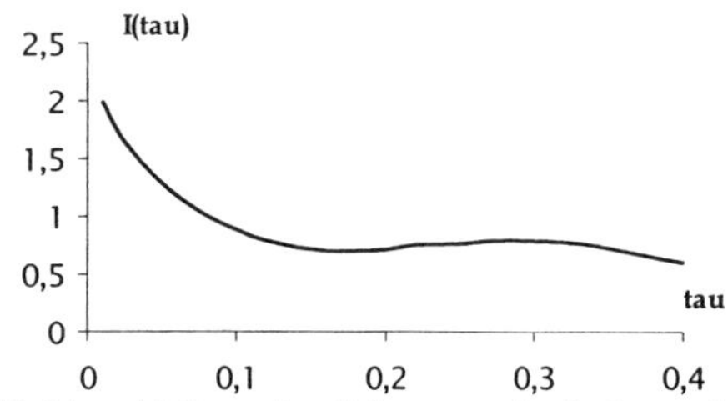

Figure 10: Mutual information $I(\tau)$ versus τ for the Lorenz's X-series

The second fundamental embedding parameter is the dimension D of the reconstructed phase space. Various methods can be used for its evaluation:

1. the singular value decomposition,
2. the Takens' theorem,
3. the false nearest-neighbors method.

The singular value decomposition (or principal component analysis, or Karhunen-Loeve decomposition) is effective for a linear system [22]. For this technique, a large embedding space must be considered. The most relevant eigenvalues of the covariance matrix of the embedding samples are taken into account since they characterize the behavior of the system; the others are discarded. The number of these principal components estimates the embedding dimension. Unfortunately, it does not always work for non-linear systems.

The Takens' theorem states that the attractor can be reconstructed from a one-dimensional observation in a phase space with dimension $D \geq 2\lfloor d_F \rfloor + 1$, where d_F is the fractal dimension of the attractor and $\lfloor . \rfloor$ is the integer part. The computation of the dimension D consists therefore of computing the fractal dimension d_F. The algorithm for computing the correlation dimension D_2 presented in [1] can be used to this purpose.

The correlation dimension D_2 is an invariant measure defined by:

$$D_2 = \lim_{r \to 0} \frac{\ln Cor(r)}{\ln r} \tag{18}$$

where $Cor(r)$ is the probability that a distance shorter than r separates a pair of randomly chosen points [23]. For a point $\bar{x}_1, \bar{x}_2 \ldots \bar{x}_n$ in the phase space, $Cor(r)$ is approximated by:

$$Cor(n,r) = \frac{1}{n(n-1)} \times \{number\ of\ pair\ i \neq j\ such, that \|\bar{x}_i - \bar{x}_j\| < r\} =$$

$$= \frac{1}{n(n-1)} \sum_{i,j=1}^{n} H(r - \|\bar{x}_i - \bar{x}_j\|) \tag{19}$$

where H is the Heaviside function

$$H(x)=\begin{cases}0, & x<0\\ 1, & x\geq 0\end{cases} \tag{20}$$

For $n\to\infty$, $Cor(n,r)\to Cor(r)$.

To estimate D_2, the diagram of $\ln(Cor(n,r))$ versus $\ln(r)$ is plotted for the embedding attractor in the phase space having dimension $n=1,2,\ldots$; for each value n, the slope of the curve when the diagram is approximately linear is evaluated. Let's consider increasing values n of the embedding dimension: the value at which the slope becomes constant is the dimension of the one-dimensional observation. Fig. 11 shows log-log diagram of $Cor(n,r)$ vs. r for the Henon's X-series for n=1..4. Starting from $n=2$ the slope of the straight line is about 1.21; this estimates the correlation dimension for the Henon's attractor. For the Takens' theorem the minimum embedding dimension is $D=2\lfloor d_F\rfloor+1=2\lfloor 1.21\rfloor+1=3$.

For a random process the slope always increases for increasing values of the embedding dimension. This allows distinguish a chaotic process from a random one.

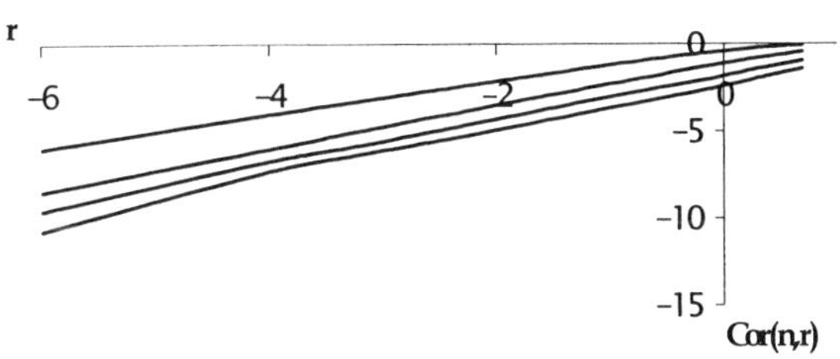

Figure 11: Log-log diagram of *Cor(n,r)* vs. *r* for the Henon's X-series

The most popular method for estimating the embedding dimension is the False Nearest Neighbors method [24]: the basic idea is related to the non self-intersection of the reconstructed attractor. The original attractor in fact lies on a smooth manifold. The self-intersection of the reconstructed attractor proves that it does not lie on a smooth manifold and, thus, the reconstruction was not correct. For the principle of non self-intersection, when the attractor is reconstructed successfully in R^m, then all neighboring points in R^m should be also the neighbors in R^{m+1}. The method verifies the neighbors for successively higher values of the embedding dimension, until only a negligible number of false neighbors is found when the dimension is increased from m to $(m+1)$. Such m is chosen as the smallest value of the embedding dimension that produces a reconstruction without self-intersections [25].

Formally, for each point $\bar{x}(t)=[x(t),x(t+\tau),\ldots,x(t+(m-1)\tau)]$ of the time series the nearest neighbor $\bar{x}(t_n)=[x(t_n),x(t_n+\tau),\ldots,x(t_n+(m-1)\tau)]$ is identified in the reconstructed phase space of dimension m by using the Euclidean metric:

$$R_m(t,\tau)=\left\|\bar{x}(t)-\bar{x}(t_n)\right\|_m=\sqrt{(x(t)-x(t_n))^2+\ldots+(x(t+(m-1)\tau)-x(t_n+(m-1)))^2} \tag{21}$$

By considering the dimension $(m+1)$, the distance between these points $R_{m+1}(t,\tau)$ is computed. Then, it is:

$$F_t=\sqrt{\frac{R_{m+1}^2(t,\tau)-R_m^2(t,\tau)}{R_m^2(t,\tau)}}=\frac{\left|x(t+m\tau)-x(t_n+m\tau)\right|}{\left\|\bar{x}(t)-\bar{x}(t_n)\right\|_m} \tag{22}$$

If F_t is greater than a given heuristic threshold, this point is marked as false nearest neighbor. By computing the percentage of false nearest neighbors in every dimension m=1,2,..., the dimension D having percentage close to zero is identified. This is the embedding dimension. Fig. 12 shows the diagram of the percentage of false nearest neighbors versus the embedding dimension m for the Lorenz's X-series. In this case the time delay τ is 0.16. From this diagram the minimum embedding dimension for the Lorenz's X-series can be evaluated to be equal to 5, where percentage of false nearest neighbors is 0.3%. A more detailed explanation of this method is given in [26] by using the Gamma test [27].

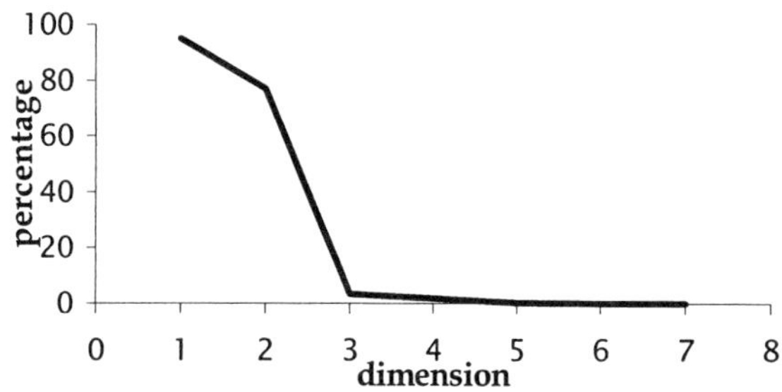

Figure 12: Percentage of false nearest-neighbors points versus embedding dimension m for the Lorenz's X-series

6.6. Lyapunov's exponents

Let's consider a dynamical system described by n differential or difference equations. This system has n Lyapunov's exponents λ_i (i=1,2,...,n), that are globally called Lyapunov's spectrum. The Lyapunov's spectrum describes the system dynamics by defining the evolution of the attractor's trajectories and characterizes the sensitive dependence on the initial conditions. These exponents are the average exponential rates of convergence (divergence) of nearby trajectories in the phase space. The largest Lyapunov's exponent is the statistical measure of the divergence between two orbits starting from slightly different initial conditions. In a chaotic system the largest Lyapunov's exponent is positive.

Let's consider a small sphere at the initial condition in the n-dimensional phase space. Through the time this sphere is transformed into an ellipsoid with n principal axes: the Lyapunov's spectrum measures the exponential growth for the principal axes of the evolving ellipsoid. In fact, let's consider the following Lyapunov's spectrum:

$$\lambda_1 \geq \lambda_2 \geq \ldots \geq \lambda_n \tag{23}$$

and let's order the axis of the ellipsoid by decreasing length; λ_1 corresponds to the longest axis, λ_2 corresponds to the subsequent one, and so on. The Lyapunov's exponent λ_i is defined as:

$$\lambda_i = \lim_{t \to \infty} \frac{1}{t} \cdot \ln \frac{l_i(t)}{l_i(0)} \tag{24}$$

where $l_i(0)$ and $l_i(t)$ are the lengths of i-th axis at the initial time and at a time t, respectively. Therefore every Lyapunov's exponent characterizes the modification of the principal axis of the ellipsoid. In an n-dimensional chaotic system the sum of the n Lyapunov's exponents is negative for dissipative systems. The positive exponents are responsible for the sensitivity to initial conditions. The sum of the positive Lyapunov's exponents is equal to Kolmogorov's entropy.

As already said, the most common test to verify the chaotic behavior consists of checking the highest Lyapunov's exponent: the system is chaotic if such an exponent is positive. When the dynamical system is described by known equations, the highest Lyapunov's exponent can be easily evaluated, e.g., by using the algorithm given in [28].

Let's consider a dynamical system described by the discrete mapping $\bar{x}_{n+1} = F(\bar{x}_n)$, where $\bar{x}$ is the state vector, and n is the index for the discrete time. Starting from an arbitrary point in basin of attraction the mapping is iterated until the obtained point lie on the attractor. This point is $\bar{x}_0$. The nearby point is $\hat{x}_0 = \bar{x}_0 + \tilde{x}_0$, where $\|\tilde{x}_0^0\| = \varepsilon$ ($\|.\|$ denotes the Euclidean metric). By repeating these operations on the interval T the points $\bar{x}_T$ and $\hat{x}_T$ are derived: the distance vector $\tilde{x}_T = \hat{x}_T - \bar{x}_T$, having length $d_1 = \|\tilde{x}_T\|$, measures the distance between these two points. d_1/ε characterizes the variations of the perturbation vector at the time T. Then, the point $\bar{x}_T$ is assumed as the new point $\bar{x}_0$ and a new point $\hat{x}_0$ is taken in the direction of the vector $\tilde{x}_T$ so that $\|\hat{x}_0 - \bar{x}_0\| = \varepsilon$. By repeating these operations the new length d_2 is obtained. After M steps the factor that modifies the amplitude of the perturbation is given by:

$$P = \prod_{k=1}^{M} (d_k/\varepsilon) \tag{25}$$

The highest Lyapunov's exponent can be therefore estimated as:

$$\lambda \cong \frac{1}{MT} \ln P = \frac{1}{MT} \sum_{k=1}^{M} \ln \frac{d_k}{\varepsilon} \tag{26}$$

with M large enough. As a consequence of using a large value for M, the computational complexity becomes high. To limit the computational efforts, the number of iterations should be smaller. To this purpose the variation of the logarithm of the distance d between two nearby point $\bar{x}_0$ and $\hat{x}_0 = \bar{x}_0 + \tilde{x}_0$ is computed in time. By taking in account only the value $d<1$, the straight regression line is identified and its slope can be computed. This estimated slope gives the approximate value of highest Lyapunov's exponent. For example, the highest Lyapunov's exponent for the Henon's system is 0.418, while for the Lorenz's system is 0.906.

Unfortunately, for one-dimensional time series the equations that describe the process are not known. To compute the highest Lyapunov's exponent a different approach must be adopted. First of all, the phase space must be reconstructed from the observation $x(t)$ by using the technique presented above. After having estimated the embedding dimension D and the time delay τ, the lag space $[x(t), x(t+\tau),..., x(t+(D-1)\tau)]$ is built. By taking an arbitrary point in the attractor the nearest point according to the Euclidean metric is identified among the other lag-points. Then the variations of the logarithm of the distance d between these two nearby points are evaluated as discussed above. Finally, the highest Lyapunov's exponent is computed.

The conventional approach to compute λ is as follows:

1. Let's start from two points in the basin of attraction that are separated by the distance d_0. Usually, d_0 is less the 10^{-8}.
2. Execute one iteration for each orbit and compute the new divergence between the corresponding trajectories by using the Euclidean metric. Then evaluate $\ln d_1$.

3. Step 2 is repeated for the n points. $\ln d_2$, $\ln d_3, \ldots,$ and $\ln d_n$ are computed.
4. Plot the diagram of $\ln d$ versus n.
5. By using the least square method the straight regression line is drawn, by taking into account only the points having $\ln d < 0$. The slope of the regression line estimates the highest Lyapunov's exponent.

Estimating λ by using this algorithm is –in general– difficult because the initial divergence d_0 is less than 10^{-8}. This approach can be used on experimental data only when the sequence of data is very long: unfortunately, this is usually very difficult to be achieved in real cases. To overcome this limit, the neural networks can be effectively adopted to estimate the highest Lyapunov's exponent.

Another fundamental problem in chaos theory is the computation of the complete Lyapunov's spectra. Its numerical computation can be performed by means of the algorithm presented in [29]. For its estimation the exponential growth of the principal axes of the ellipsoid must be defined.

Let's consider a dynamical system described by n equations. For example, let be n=3. Let's take any point x_0 in the attractor as initial point. Orthonormal frames $\tilde{x}_0^0, \tilde{y}_0^0, \tilde{z}_0^0$ are used for the initial perturbation vectors. After the time T, the trajectory arrives at the point x_1 and the perturbation vector becomes $\tilde{x}_1, \tilde{y}_1, \tilde{z}_1$. The vectors must be reorthonormalized by using the Gram-Schmidt procedure:

$$\tilde{x}_1^0 = \frac{\tilde{x}_1}{\|\tilde{x}_1\|}$$

$$\tilde{y}_1' = \tilde{y}_1 - (\tilde{y}_1 \cdot \tilde{x}_1^0)\tilde{x}_1^0, \quad \tilde{y}_1^0 = \frac{\tilde{y}_1'}{\|\tilde{y}_1'\|} \tag{27}$$

$$\tilde{z}_1' = \tilde{z}_1 - (\tilde{z}_1 \cdot \tilde{x}_1^0)\tilde{x}_1^0 - (\tilde{z}_1 \cdot \tilde{y}_1^0)\tilde{y}_1^0, \quad \tilde{z}_1^0 = \frac{\tilde{z}_1'}{\|\tilde{z}_1'\|}$$

Then the point x_1 and the perturbation vectors $\tilde{x}_1^0, \tilde{y}_1^0, \tilde{z}_1^0$ are considered. During the next time interval T, the new perturbation vectors $\tilde{x}_2, \tilde{y}_2, \tilde{z}_2$ is obtained. They must be reorthnormalized again. After M steps, the Lyapunov's exponents can be computed as:

$$\lambda_1 = \frac{1}{MT}\sum_{i=1}^{M} \ln\|\tilde{x}_i\|, \quad \lambda_2 = \frac{1}{MT}\sum_{i=1}^{M} \ln\|\tilde{y}_i\|, \quad \lambda_3 = \frac{1}{MT}\sum_{i=1}^{M} \ln\|\tilde{z}_i\| \tag{27}$$

M should be rather large. By using this method the Lyapunov's exponents for the Henon's system are equal to 0.418 and -1.622, while the ones for the Lorenz's system are 0.906, 0 and -14.572.

6.7. A neural network approach to compute the Lyapunov's exponents

The use of neural networks for computing the highest Lyapunov's exponent and the Lyapunov's spectrum was presented in [30]; it relies on the evaluation of the divergence between two orbits at n step ahead by means of an iterative approach.

The neural network for the highest Lyapunov's exponent is a multilayer network with $k \geq D - 1$ input units (where D is the embedding dimension), p hidden units, and one output unit (Fig. 13). This network is trained by means of the sliding window method:

$$x(t+i\tau)=F(x(t+(i-1)\tau), x(t+(i-2)\tau),\ldots, x(t+(i-k)\tau)) \quad \text{for } i = \overline{1,n} \tag{28}$$

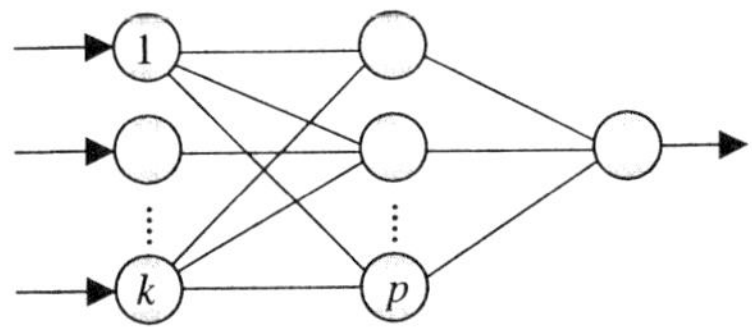

Figure 13: Predicting neural network

Starting from any point of the state space, this neural network finds the nearest –as much as desired– attractor. The highest Lyapunov's exponent by using a small data set can therefore be computed as follows [30]:

1. From the training set a point $[x(t),x(t+\tau),..,x(t+(D\text{-}2)\tau)]$ that lies nearby the attractor is chosen and its trajectory $x(t+(D-1)\tau), x(t+D\tau),...$ is computed by using the multistep prediction.
2. In the reconstructed phase space the nearby point $[x(t),x(t+\tau),..,x(t+(D\text{-}2)\tau)+d_0]$, where $d_0 \approx 10^{-8}$, is selected and its behavior $x'(t+(D-1)\tau), x'(t+D\tau),...$ is predicted by using the neural network.
3. Define $\ln d_i = \ln|x'(t+(D-2+i)\tau) - x(t+(D-2+i)\tau)|$, $i=1,2...$, and mark the points for which $\ln d_i<0$.
4. Plot the diagram $\ln d_i$ versus $i\tau$.
5. Build the regression line for the marked points and compute its slope, which is equal to the highest Lyapunov's exponent.

By using this technique the highest Lyapunov's exponent for the Henon's and the Lorenz's time series are 0.43 and 0.98, respectively. Only the X-series has been used in both cases; the size of the data set was 70 and 100 points, respectively. This result is very close to the actual values computed in the previous section. This method is highly advantageous as computational complexity, accuracy, and small data set are concerned. Figg. 14 and 15 represent the diagram of $\ln d_i$ versus $i\tau$ and the straight regression line for the Henon's and Lorenz's X-series, respectively.

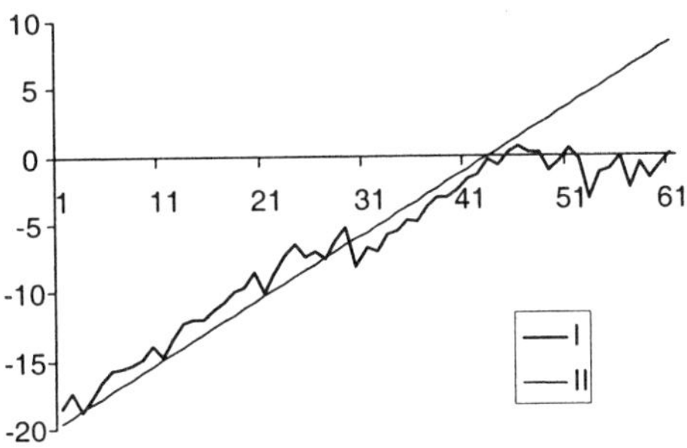

Figure 14: (I) The evolution of the distance between two nearby orbits for the Henon's X-series; (II) the regression line

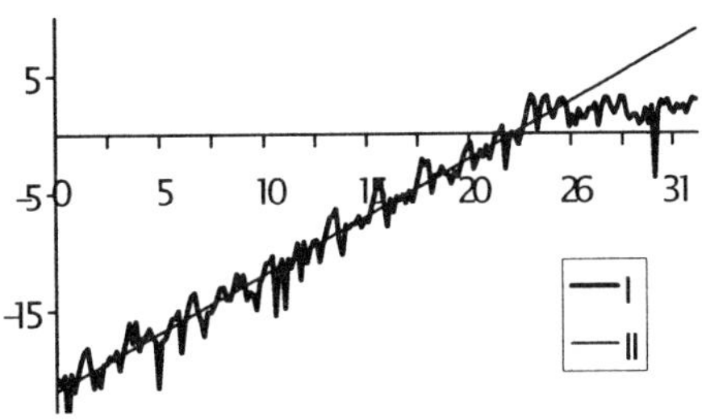

Figure 15: (I) The evolution of the distance between two nearby orbits for the Lorenz's X-series; (II) the regression line

The Lyapunov's spectrum can be computed in a similar way by using an observable time series. Let's consider a dynamical system described by the n-dimensional observable vector $x(t)=[x_1(t),x_2(t),\ldots,x_n(t)]$ and assume that the observations $x_i(t)$ are known. A neural network can be created to forecast the next state of dynamical system from the previous one. This network is a multilayer network with n input units, m hidden units, and n output units (Fig. 16). The output is defined as $x(t+1) = F(x(t))$.

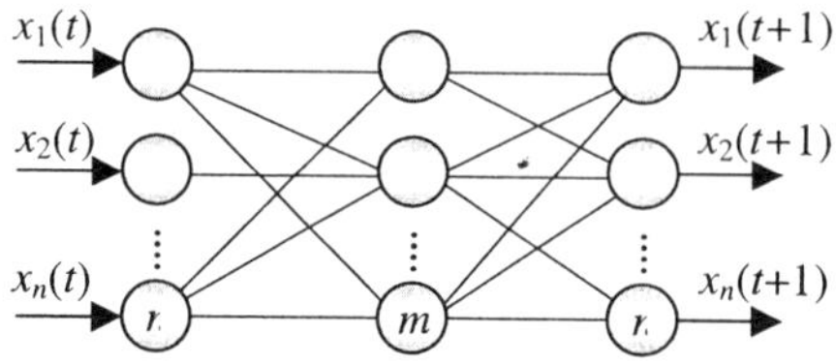

Figure 16: Predicting neural network

Starting from a given initial condition, this network is able to compute the state of the dynamical system at any time, as well as to describe the evolution of the phase trajectory points. At each step the Gram-Schmidt orthogonalization procedure must be used to adjust the output vector. Let $|w_i(t)|$ be the length of the i-th vector at the time t. This length characterizes the value of the vector along the i-th ellipsoid axis. Thus, the i-th Lyapunov's exponent is given by:

$$\lambda_i = \lim_{p\to\infty}\frac{1}{p}\sum_{t=1}^{p}\ln\frac{|w_i(t)|}{|w_i(t-1)|} \tag{29}$$

The correspondent length $|w_i(t)|$ can be evaluated by using a neural network and, consequently, the Lyapunov's exponents can be estimated. The algorithm to compute the complete Lyapunov's spectrum is as follows:

1. Take the initial point $N(0)=[x_1(0),x_2(0),\ldots,x_n(0)]$ from the basin of attraction.
2. Choose a small value $\varepsilon \approx 10^{-8}$ and define the coordinates of next n points as follows:

$$\begin{aligned} &A_1(0)=[x_1(0)+\varepsilon,x_2(t),\ldots,x_n(t)]\\ &A_2(0)=[x_1(0),x_2(t)+\varepsilon,\ldots,x_n(t)]\\ &\ldots\\ &A_n(0)=[x_1(0),x_2(t),\ldots,x_n(t)+\varepsilon]\end{aligned} \tag{30}$$

The following orthogonal vectors are obtained:

$$\begin{aligned} &NA_1(0)=[\varepsilon,0,\ldots,0]\\ &NA_2(0)=[0,\varepsilon,\ldots,0]\\ &\ldots\\ &NA_n(0)=[0,0,\ldots,\varepsilon]\end{aligned} \tag{31}$$

3. Compute the length of each vector $|NA_i(0)|=|w_i(0)|=\varepsilon$, where $i=\overline{1,n}$.
4. At the time $t=0$, use the set of points $N(0)$, $A_1(0)$, $A_2(0)$,…, $A_n(0)$ as the input vector of the neural network. The output produced by the predicting network is the set of the coordinates of the points at the next time $t=t+1$:

$$\begin{aligned} &N(1)=[x_1(1,N),x_2(1,N),\ldots,x_n(1,N)]\\ &A_1(1)=[x_1(1,A_1),x_2(1,A_1),\ldots,x_n(1,A_1)]\\ &A_2(1)=[x_1(1,A_2),x_2(1,A_2),\ldots,x_n(1,A_2)]\\ &\ldots\\ &A_n(1)=[x_1(1,A_n),x_2(1,A_n),\ldots,x_n(1,A_n)],\end{aligned} \tag{32}$$

where $x_j(1,A_j)$ is the j-th coordinate of the point A_j at the time $t=1$. This leads to the next set of vectors:

$$\begin{aligned} &NA_1(1)=w_1(1)=[w_{11},w_{21},\ldots,w_{n1}]\\ &NA_2(1)=w_2(1)=[w_{12},w_{22},\ldots,w_{n2}]\\ &\ldots\\ &NA_n(1)=w_n(1)=[w_{1n},w_{2n},\ldots,w_{nn}]\end{aligned} \tag{33}$$

where w_{ij} is the i-th coordinate of the j-th vector, having defined $w_{ij} = x_i(1, A_j) - x_i(1, N)$.

5. The basis $[w_1(1), w_2(1), \dots, w_n(1)]$ is transformed into the orthonormal frame by using the Gram-Schmidt algorithm, as follows:
   a) The first vector of the orthonormal frame is chosen as:

$$w_1'(1) = \left[\frac{w_{11}}{|w_1(1)|}, \frac{w_{21}}{|w_1(1)|}, \dots, \frac{w_{n1}}{|w_1(1)|}\right] \tag{34}$$

   where $|w_1(1)| = \sqrt{w_{11}^2 + w_{21}^2 + \dots + w_{n1}^2}$.

   b) The subsequent vectors are defined by the following recurrent formulas:

$$\begin{aligned} w_i(1) &= w_i(1) - \sum_{j=1}^{i-1}(w_i^T(1) \cdot w_j'(1)) \cdot w_j'(1) \\ |w_i(1)| &= \sqrt{w_{1i}^2 + w_{2i}^2 + \dots + w_{ni}^2} \\ w_i'(1) &= \left[\frac{w_{1i}}{|w_i(1)|}, \frac{w_{2i}}{|w_i(1)|}, \dots, \frac{w_{ni}}{|w_i(1)|}\right] \end{aligned} \tag{35}$$

   where $i = \overline{2, n}$.

   c) Compute:

$$s_i(1) = \ln \frac{|w_i(1)|}{|w_i(0)|} \tag{36}$$

   where $i = \overline{1, n}$.

   The result is the new set of points:

$$\begin{aligned} N(1) &= [x_1(1, N), x_2(2, N), \dots, x_n(1, N)] \\ A_1(1) &= [\bar{x}_1(1, A_1), \bar{x}_2(2, A_1), \dots, \bar{x}_n(1, A_1)] \\ A_2(1) &= [\bar{x}_1(1, A_2), \bar{x}_2(2, A_2), \dots, \bar{x}_n(1, A_2)] \\ &\dots \\ A_n(1) &= [\bar{x}_1(1, A_n), \bar{x}_2(2, A_n), \dots, \bar{x}_n(1, A_n)], \end{aligned} \tag{37}$$

   where $\bar{x}_j(1, A_j) = w_{ij} + x_i(1, N)$.

6. Repeat from step 3 to step 5 for $t = \overline{1, p}$, where $p \approx 1000$.

7. Define the Lyapunov's spectrum as:

$$\lambda_i = \frac{1}{p} \sum_{t=1}^{p} s_i(t) \tag{38}$$

   where $i = \overline{1, n}$. The following Lyapunov's exponents are therefore obtained:

$$\lambda_1 \geq \lambda_2 \geq \dots \geq \lambda_n \tag{39}$$

By using this approach, the Lyapunov's exponents of the Henon's time series are 0.442 and –1.625 (the actual values are 0.418 and -1.622, respectively). For the Lorenz's time series they are 0.777, 0.003, and –14.472 (the actual values are 0.906, 0, and –14.472, respectively). Figg. 17 and 18 show the dependence of λ_i from p for the Henon's and the Lorenz's time series, respectively.

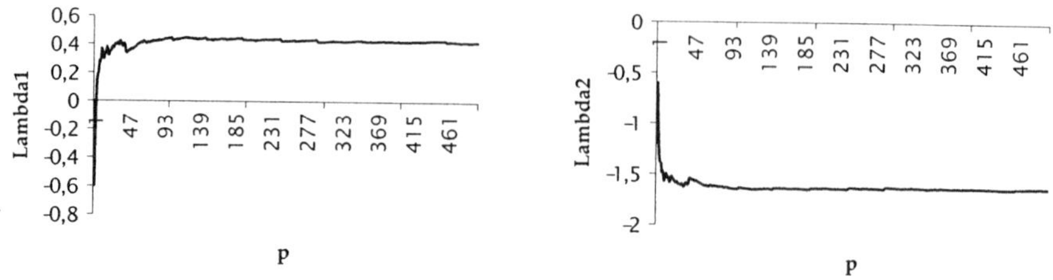

Figure17: Estimation of the Lyapunov's spectrum for the Henon's time series

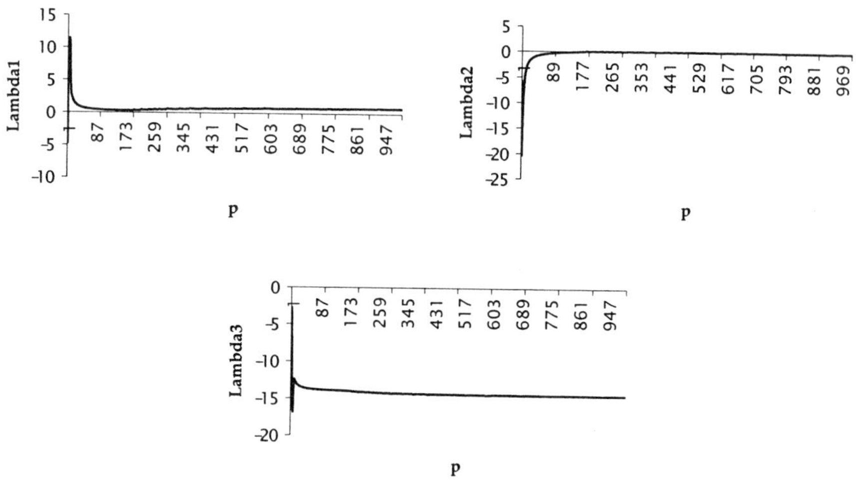

Figure18: Estimation of the Lyapunov's spectrum for the Lorenz's time series

6.8. Prediction of chaotic processes by using neural networks

Prediction of a time series consists of finding the sequence $x(l+1)$, $x(l+2)$... that follows a given sequence $x(1)$, $x(2)$..., $x(l)$. The nonlinear predictive model is formally defined by:

$$x(t) = F(x(t-1), x(t-2), \ldots, x(t-k)) \tag{40}$$

where $t = \overline{k+1, N}$, F is the nonlinear prediction function, and k is the size of the sliding window.

The Multilayer Perceptron (MLP) can be effectively adopted for time series prediction, also for chaotic case. The input layer is composed by at the least $(D\text{-}1)$ units (where D is the embedding dimension), while one output unit delivers the predicted output. The network is trained by using the known data sequence $[x(t), x(t+\tau), \ldots, x(t+(D-2)\tau)]$ to generate the predicted output $x(t+(D-1)\tau)$. This structure of the predicting network derives directly from the meaning of embedding. When the time series has been learnt by ("embedded in") the neural network, in D-dimensional phase space such manifold is obtained that –for every D-1 coordinates of any point– the D-th coordinate is produced and the nearby points in the D-1 dimensions are very close to the D-th coordinate (i.e., the mapping is smooth).

To obtain the maximum predictability the embedding parameters must be defined. Let's consider the Lorenz's and the Henon's attractors as chaotic systems to be modeled. The Lorenz's attractor is defined by the three-coupled differential equations (10); this system is chaotic for G=10, r=28, and b=8/3. Equations (10) can be solved by using a 4-th order Runge-Kutta approach with time step 0.01; Fig. 4 shows the Lorenz's time series (x-axis). The mutual information allows for computing $\tau=0.16$, while the method of the false nearest neighbors evaluates the embedding dimension $D=5$. The window size must be $k \geq D-1=4$. The Henon's attractor is described by the equations (11), where the chaotic behavior occurs for $\alpha=1.4$ and $\beta=0.3$; Fig. 19 shows the Henon's X-series. By using the same reasoning discussed above, the windows size is $k \geq 2$ and $\tau=1$.

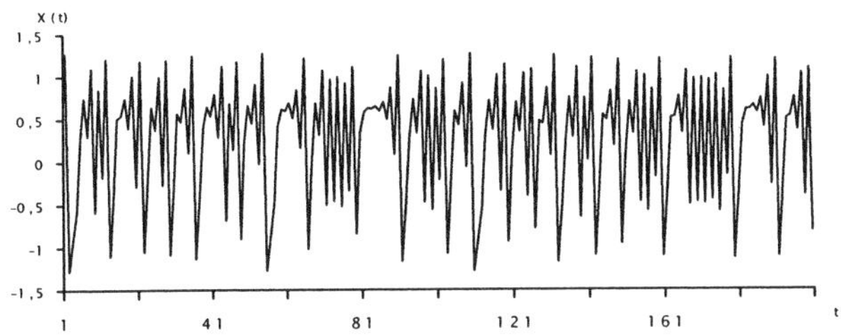

Figure 19: The Henon's X-series (first 200 elements)

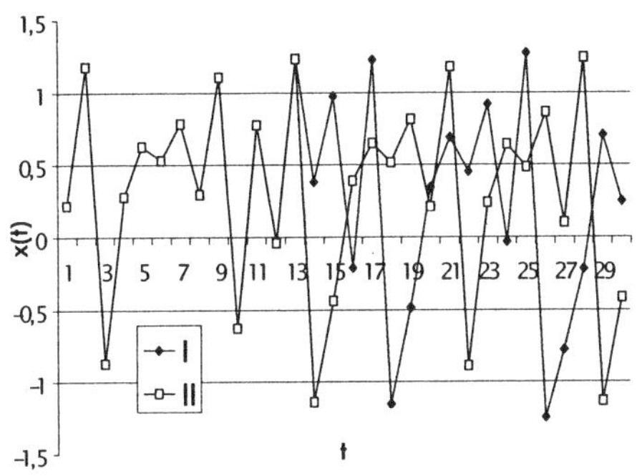

Figure 20: The Henon's process. Prediction results for 30 predicting iterations by using the retraining approach: (I) prediction, (II) original time series

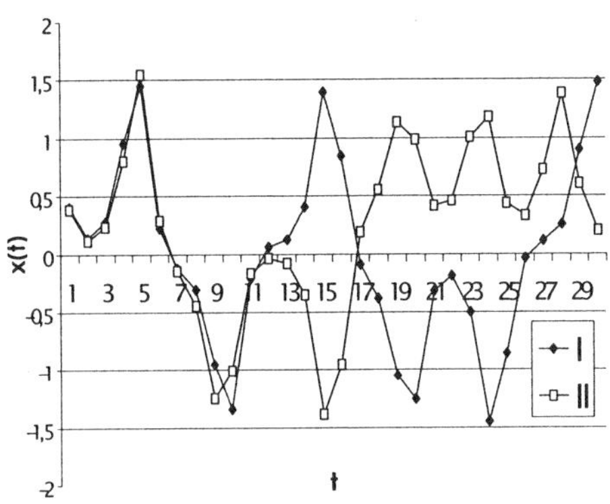

Figure 21: The Lorenz's process. Prediction results for 30 predicting iterations by using retraining approach: (I) prediction, (II) original time series

To perform forecasting at the level of individual points the MLP can be adopted. A neural network with 7 input units, 5 sigmoid hidden units, and 1 linear output unit is verified sufficient to perform this task [30]. Efficient backpropagation is used for training. By using the iterative approach the Henon's and the Lorenz's data series have been predicted for 1500 step ahead; the training set consists of 1500 and 930 patterns for the Henon's and the Lorenz's time series, respectively. Figg. 20 and 21 show the prediction results on 30 steps ahead for the Henon's and the Lorenz's time series, respectively: prediction at the level of the individual data points is unreliable. This unpredictability is one of the main characteristics of a chaotic system.

Prediction can span over a longer time than the individual point. The prediction horizon is the interval of time in which an accurate forecasting is feasible. As said before chaotic data are unpredictable on the long term because the measurement error at the initial condition grows exponentially in time. Since this sensitive dependence is given by a positive value of the highest Lyapunov's exponent, such a value determines the upper prediction limit. It is well known that the sum of all positive Lyapunov's exponents is equal to the Kolmogorov's entropy [31]; consequently, according to the chaos theory, the prediction horizon is [31]:

$$T \approx \frac{1}{K} \cdot \ln\left(\frac{1}{d_0}\right) \tag{41}$$

where $K = \sum_i \lambda_i$ is the Kolmogorov's entropy, $\lambda_i > 0$, and d_0 is the initial prediction error.

According to equation (41), accurate prediction can be achieved only in the range T. Therefore, after having trained the neural network the prediction horizon for the given initial point can be computed. Prediction will be performed with such a horizon to ensure accuracy.

To increase the prediction horizon a suited retraining of the neural network can be performed. Let's assume that the neural network was trained by using the data set $X=\{x(1),x(2),..,x(N)\}$. Prediction will be accurate only for T points ahead: $x(N+1),x(N+2),\ldots,x(N+T)$. The new training set for retraining is $X'=\{x(1),x(2),..,x(N+T)\}$: this allows for extending the prediction horizon. The effectiveness of this approach has been tested for the Henon's and the Lorenz's time series. Tables 1 and 2 show the results achieved with the iterative and the retraining approaches for the Henon's time series. MSE1 and MSE2 are the mean square error for the predicted points $x(N+1),x(N+2)$, $x(N+3)$, $x(N+4)$ and $x(N+5)$, $x(N+6)$, $x(N+7)$, $x(N+8)$, respectively; MSE is the total mean square error and NIT is the number of the training iteration. Tables 3 and 4 show similar results for the Lorenz's time series. The retraining approach usually achieves a better prediction accuracy than the iterative approach and is effectively able to extend the prediction horizon.

6.9. State space reconstruction

Let's finally consider the reconstruction of the state space for a chaotic process by using neural networks, in the presence of a small training data set. Figg. 3 and 5 show the original Lorenz's and Henon's attractors, respectively.

A multilayer perceptron with 7 input units, 5 hidden units, and 1 output unit has been used. The training set consists of 100 and 200 patterns for the Henon's and the Lorenz's time series, respectively. With this neural network, after 3000 training iteration, the mean square errors for the Henon's and the Lorenz's time series are 0.00033 and 0.0008, respectively. Based on the iterative approach the Henon's and the Lorenz's data have been

Table 1: Iterative approach for training the predictive neural network for the Henon's series

Approach	NIT	Size of training set	MSE	T	MSE1	MSE2
Iterative approach	308	950	$3 \cdot 10^{-4}$	4	0.0002227	0.0311980
Retraining approach	276	954	$3 \cdot 10^{-4}$	4	0.0000332	0.0080427

Table 2: Retraining approach for training the predictive neural network for the Henon's series

Approach	Actual value	Desired value	Absolute error
Iterative approach	0.365621	0.363170	0.002451
	0.992627	1.002511	0.009884
	-0.274204	-0.298088	0.023884
	1.191078	1.176354	0.014724
	-1.101723	-1.026758	0.074965
	-0.363043	-0.123019	0.240024
	0.512435	0.670785	0.158350
	0.524174	0.333160	0.191014
Retraining approach	0.364677	0.363170	0.001507
	1.001295	1.002511	0.001216
	-0.288775	-0.298088	0.009313
	1.182933	1.176354	0.006579
	-1.046040	-1.026758	0.019282
	-0.247162	-0.123019	0.124143
	0.592083	0.670785	0.078702
	0.434126	0.333160	0.100966

Table 3: Iterative approach for training the predictive neural network for the Lorenz's series

Approach	NIT	Size of training set	MSE	T	MSE1	MSE2
Iterative approach	1000	800	0.001357	5	0.0053618	0.1628954
Retraining approach	578	805	0.0014	5	0.0011142	0.0698684

Table 4: Retraining approach for training the predictive neural network for the Lorenza's series

Approach	Actual value	Desired value	Absolute error
Iterative approach	-0.155480	-0.163600	0.008120
	-0.556713	-0.617800	0.061087
	-1.573766	-1.633100	0.059334
	-0.536221	-0.439700	0.096521
	0.085535	0.186400	0.100865
	0.237657	0.520500	0.282843
	0.719185	1.254000	0.534815
	1.509935	0.938200	0.571735
	0.461715	0.245600	0.216115
	-0.042810	0.230800	0.273610
Retraining approach	-0.169124	-0.163600	0.005524
	-0.613167	-0.617800	0.004633
	-1.598149	-1.633100	0.034951
	-0.430258	-0.439700	0.009442
	0.121533	0.186400	0.064867
	0.317614	0.520500	0.202886
	0.940051	1.254000	0.313949
	1.336355	0.938200	0.398155
	0.301510	0.245600	0.055910
	0.011798	0.230800	0.219002

predicted for 1500 step ahead. The predicted Lorenz's and Henon's attractors are shown in Figg. 22 and 23: the neural network is able to capture the underlying properties of the chaotic behavior and, therefore, can be used for an accurate reconstruction of the state space and an accurate prediction of the system behavior.

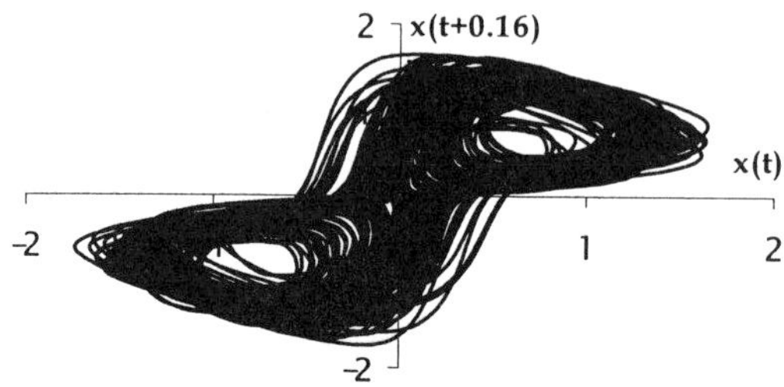

Figure 22: The predicted Henon's attractor: it was built on 1500 predicting iterations in the embedding space

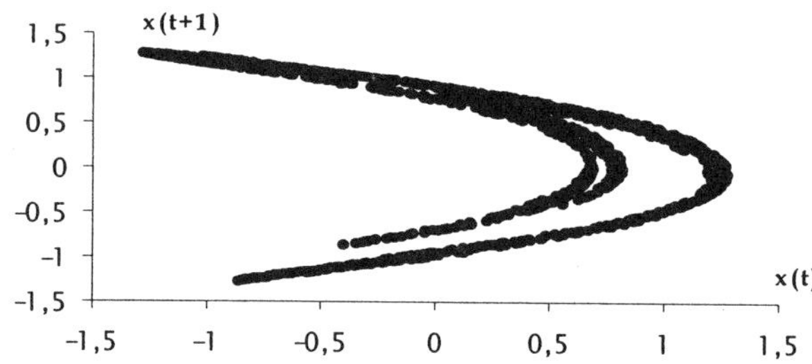

Figure 23: The predicted Henon's attractor: it was built on 1500 predicting iterations in the embedding space

Let's finally summarize the overall approach to time series processing by using only observable data. The global purpose of this approach is to identify the chaotic behavior, predict the time series at level of the individual points, and reconstruct the system dynamics. The time series of observations is represented by $\mathbf{X}(t)=(X_1(t), X_2(t),\ldots, X_n(t))$ – or shortly $\mathbf{X}(t)=X_i(t)$ – with $t=\overline{1,p}$. The time series processing approach is as follows:

1. Select any data from a single observable $X_i(t)$, $t=\overline{1,p}$.
2. Compute the embedding delay τ and take the time series by using this embedding delay.
3. Compute the minimum embedding dimension D.
4. Build the multilayer perceptron having $k \geq D-1$ input units, l hidden units, and one output unit.
5. Prepare the training data:
   $\mathbf{X}(t)=(X_i(t), X_i(t+1),\ldots, X_i(t+k-1))$
   $Y(t)=X_i(t+k)$,
   where $\mathbf{X}(t)$ is the input sequence and $Y(t)$ is desire output, for $t=\overline{1,p}$.
6. Train the neural network by using an efficient version of the backpropagation algorithm.
7. Compute the highest Lyapunov's exponent by using the neural network and identify the chaotic behavior of the nonlinear system.
8. If the n observable time series are known, where $n=\frac{D-1}{2}+1$, the Lyapunov's spectrum can be computed.

9. Forecast the data $X_i(t)$ for the subsequent iterations.
10. Reconstruct the system dynamics.

This algorithm has a low computational complexity with respect to the approaches available in the literature and can be effectively used even with a small set of training data.

6.10. Conclusion

In this chapter the fundamental aspects of chaotic time series processing have been addressed, namely determination of the embedding parameters, the Lyapunov's spectrum, forecasting of chaotic data at the level both of the individual data points and the emergent structure. Both conventional and neural network approaches have been analyzed for chaotic signal processing. In various domains neural networks have been shown powerful tools with respect to conventional techniques. The neural approaches allow for evaluating the Lyapunov's spectrum and for reconstructing the state space accurately and efficiently only by using the observed data. Besides, the largest Lyapunov's exponent and the Lyapunov's spectrum can be computed by neural networks even on small data sets; this allows both for reducing the computationally complexity and for limit the observation time.

References

[1] P. Grassberger and I. Procaccia, Measuring the strangeness of strange attractors, Physica D 9,1983
[2] N.H. Packard, J.P. Crutchfield, J.D. Farmer and R.S. Shaw, Geometry from a Time Series, Physical Review Letters 45, 1980, pp.712-716.
[3] F. Takens, Detecting strange attractors in turbulence, Lecture Notes in Mathematics, Vol. 898, Springer-Verlag, Berlin, 1980, pp. 366-381; and in Dynamical System in Turbulence, Warlock, 1980, eds. D. Rand and L.S. Young.
[4] S. Haykin, Signal processing: Where physics and mathematics neet, IEEE Signal Processing Magazine, vol.18, pp.6-7, July 2001.
[5] S. Haykin, Adaptive filter theory, 4th Edition, Prentice-Hall, 2001.
[6] S. Haykin, Neural Networks: A comprehensive foundation, Second edition, Prentice-Hall, 1999.
[7] CybenKo G.: Approximation by Superpositions of a Sigmoidal Function, Math Control Signals Syst, 2, pp.303-314, 1989.
[8] Hertz J.A., Palmer R.G., Krogh A.S., Introduction to the theory of neural computation, Addison-Wesley, Redwood City, 1991.
[9] Hornik K., Stinchcombe M., White H., Multi-layer feedforward networks are universal approximators, Neural Networks, 2 pp.359-366, 1989.
[10] Waibel A., Consonant Recognition by Modular Construction of Large Phonetic Time-delay Neural Networks, in Touretsky D.: Advances in Neural Information Processing System, Moggzn Kaufmann, Los Altos, CA, pp. 215-223, 1989.
[11] Donoho D.L., Johnstone I.M., Kerkyacharian C., Ricard D., Wavelet shrinkage: asymptopia? Journal of the Royal Statictical Society, Series B, 57, pp.301-337, 1995.
[12] Gonzalez R., Wintz P., Digital image processing, Reading, MA: Addison-Wesley, 1987.
[13] A. Hyvarinen, E. Oja, Independent component analysis: algorithms and applications, Neural Networks, vol.13, pp.411-430, 2000.
[14] Oja E., Neural networks, principal components and subspaces, International Journal of Neural Systems, 1, pp.61-68, 1989.
[15] A.M. Albano, J. Muench, C. Schwartz, A.I. Mees and P.E. Rapp, Syngular-Value Decomposition and the Grassberger-Procaccia Algorithm, Physical Review A 38, 1988, pp. 3017-3026.
[16] M. Casdagli, S. Eubank, J.D. Farmer and J. Gibson, State space reconstruction in present of noise, Physica D 51, 1992, pp. 52-98.
[17] X. Zeng, R. Eykholt and R.A. Pielke, Estimating the Lyapunov-Exponent Spectrum from shot Time Series of Low Precision, Physical Review Letter 66, 1991, pp. 3229-3232.

[18] J. Holzfuss and G. Mayer-Kress, An approach to error estimation in the applications of dimensional algorithms, in Dimensions and Entropies in Chaotic Systems, editor G. Mayer-Kress, Springer-Verlag, New York, 1986, pp. 114-122.

[19] M.T. Rosenstein, J.J. Colins, C.J. De Luca, Reconstruction expansion as a geometry-based framework for choosing proper delay time, Physica D 73, 1994, pp. 82-98.

[20] A.M. Fraser and H.L. Swinney, Independent coordinates for strange attractor from mutual information, Physical Review A 33, 1986, pp. 1134-1140.

[21] C.E. Shannon and W. Weawer, The mathematical theory of information, University Press, Urbana Ill.

[22] H.D.I. Abarbanel, R. Brown, J. Sidorovich and L. Tsimring, The analysis of observed chaotic data in physical systems, Reviews of Modern Physics, Vol. 65, •4, 1993, pp. 1331-1392.

[23] R. Castro, T. Sauer, Correlation dimension of attractor through interspike intervals, Physical Review E 55, 1997.

[24] M.B. Kennel, R. Brown and H.D.I. Abarbanel, Determining embedding dimension for phase-space reconstruction using a geometrical construction, Physical Review A 45, 1992, pp. 3403-3411.

[25] D. Kugiumtzis, State Space Reconstruction Parameters in the Analysis of Chaotic Time Series – the Role of the Time Window Length, 1996.

[26] M. Otani and A.J. Jones, Automated embedding and the creep phenomenon in chaotic time series, 2000.

[27] A. Stefansson, N. Koncar and A.J. Jones, A note on the Gamma test, Neural Computing and Aplications 5, 1997, pp. 387-393.

[28] G. Benettin, L. Galgani, J.-M. Strelcyn, Kolmogorov entropy and numerical experiments, Physical Review A 14, 1976, pp. 2338-2345.

[29] G. Benettin, L. Galgani, A. Giorgilli, J.-M. Strelcyn, Lyapunov characteristic exponents for smooth dynamical systems and for Hamiltonian systems: A method for computing all of them. P. I: Theory. P. II: Numerical applications, Meccanica, Vol. 15, 1980, pp. 9-30.

[30] V. Golovko, Y. Savitsky, N. Maniakov and V.Rubanov, Some Aspects of Chaotic Time Series Analysis, Proceedings of the 2nd International Conference on Neural Networks and Artificial Intelligence, October 2-5, 2001, Minsk, Belarus, pp. 66-69.

[31] H. Schuster. Deterministic chaos. An introduction. Physic-Verlag, Weinhheim, 1984, p.240.

Neural Networks for Instrumentation, Measurement and Related Industrial Applications
S. Ablameyko et al. (Eds.)
IOS Press, 2003

Chapter 7
Neural Networks for Image Analysis and Processing in Measurements, Instrumentation and Related Industrial Applications

George C. GIAKOS
Department of Electrical and Computer Engineering, The University of Akron
Akron, OH 44325-3904, USA

Kiran NATARAJ, Ninad PATNEKAR
Department of Biomedical Engineering, The University of Akron
Akron, OH 44325-0302, USA

Abstract. During the last decade, a significant progress in both the theoretical aspects and the applications of neural networks on the image analysis, and processing, has been made. In this paper, basic neural network algorithms as applied to the imaging process as well their applications in different areas of technology, are presented, discussed, and analyzed. Novel ideas towards the optimization of the design parameters of digital imaging sensors utilizing neural networks are presented.

7.1. Introduction

Digital imaging is a process aimed to recognize objects of interest in an image by utilizing electronic sensors and advanced computing techniques with the aim to improve image quality parameters [1-6]. It contains intrinsic difficulties due to the fact that image formation is basically a many-to-one-mapping, i.e., characterization of 3-d objects can be deduced from either a single image or multiple images.

Several problems associated with low-contrast images, blurred images, noisy images, image conversion to digital form, transmission, handling, manipulation, and storage of large-volume images, led to the development of efficient image processing and recognition algorithms. Digital imaging or computer vision involves image processing and pattern recognition techniques [1-6]. Image processing techniques deal with image enhancement, manipulation, and analysis of images. The advantages of digital imaging are shown in Table 1.

Table 1: Advantages of Digital Imaging

Accurate data acquisition
Better combination of spatial and contrast resolution
No degradation with time or copying
Compact storage/easy retrieval
Data correction/manipulation/enhancement
Fast accurate image transmission

Digital image processing methods arise from two principal application areas:
a) improvement of image content for human interpretation and processing, and
b) processing of scene data for machine perception.

Some of their image processing methods include:
i) digitization and compression
ii) enhancement, restoration, and reconstruction, and
iii) matching, description, and recognition.

On the other hand, pattern recognition deals with object identification from observed pattern and images. In the last few years, significant advances have been made in pattern recognition, through the use of several new types of computer architectures that utilize very large-scale integrated circuits (VLSI) and solid state memories with a variety of parallel high-speed computers, optical and opto-digital computers, as well as a variety of neural network architectures and implementations. Artificial neural networks have shown great strength in solving problems that are not governed by rules, or in which traditional techniques have failed or proved inadequate. The inherent parallel architecture and the fault tolerant nature of the ANN is maximally utilized to address problems in variety of application areas relation to the imaging field [10,11]. Artificial neural networks find their application in pattern recognition (classification, clustering, feature selection), texture analysis, segmentation, image compression, color representation and several other aspects of image processing [2-13], with applications in medical imaging, remote sensing, aerospace, radars, and military applications [14-65].

7.2. Digital imaging systems

Digital systems with increased contrast sensitivity capabilities and large dynamic range, are highly desirable [1].

By defining contrast as the perceptible difference between the object of interest and background, the contrast sensitivity of an imaging system is the measure of its ability to provide the perceptible difference. It can be an operator dependent or independent parameter. In this study, the observer independent contrast sensitivity was measured. Also, it is very important that a detector system is capable to record a wide range of signals coming off the object. The dynamic range provides quantitative measure of detector's system ability to image objects with widely varying attenuating structures. It is defined as the ratio of the maximum signal to the minimum observable image signal. Mathematically,

$$DR = S_{max} / \Delta S_{min} \quad (1)$$

where DR is the dynamic range, S_{max} is the maximum signal from the detector before saturation or non-linearity occurs and ΔS_{min} is the minimum detectable signal above the noise threshold. Several digital imaging techniques have been developed for a large gamma of applications, such as aerospace, surveillance, sub terrestrial, marine imaging, and medical imaging applications.

Applications range from imaging systems in the visible and infrared through x-rays, MRI, ultrasound, sonar, and radar applications, as shown in Table 2.

Table 2: Digital Imaging Modalities

Radar imaging and surveillance
Microwave imaging
Optical 2-d and 3-d imaging (tomography)
x-ray digital imaging
Computed tomography (CT)
Nuclear imaging (SPECT, PET)
Magnetic resonance imaging (MRI)
Ultrasound imaging

Several electronic sensors can be utilized in the design of digital imaging systems, such as:

- Radiation detectors (soft x-rays, x-rays, gamma rays)
- Synthetic Aperture Radars (SAR) (microwaves, lightwaves)
- Electromagnetic sensors (RF sensors, microwave sensors, MRI coils)
- Optical sensors (PIN photodiodes, avalanche photodiodes, fiberoptical scintillating crystal plates coupled to photomultipliers/photodiodes, CCD cameras, C-MOS, operating in the UV, visible, near infrared and infrared
- Ultrasound sensors (piezoelectric sensors)
- Hybrid sensors (combination of more than one detector media, such as gas/solid).

The application of the imaging sensors are summarized in Table 3.

Table 3: Imaging Sensors Applications

AREAS	**APPLICATIONS**
MILITARY	Reconnaissance Target acquisition Fire control Navigation
CIVIL	Law Enforcement Fire fighting Borger patrol
MEDICAL ENVIRONMENTAL	Digital radiography (mammography, chest, dental, electronic portal imaging) Computed Tomography (CT) Nuclear Medicine (SPECT, PET) Ultrasound, MRI
INDUSTRIAL	Maintanance, Manufacturing, Non-Destructive Testing
AEROSPACE	Aircraft engine inspection, structural inspection, space imaging

7.3. Image system design parameters and modeling

System modeling is the mathematical formalism that includes physical parameters, geometrical parameters, system characteristics, observer experience, monitor parameters, and a variety of miscellaneous factors. For instance, referring to an electro-optical imaging system for target recognition, the perceived image quality can be affected by a number of parameters. These parameters are shown on Table 4., although its length underscores the complexity of target acquisition.

Table 4: Image Quality Contributors

IMAGE QUALITY CONTRIBUTORS	PARAMETERS
PHYSICAL PARAMETERS	Optical beam profile and quality, detector composition, detection efficiency (quantum efficiency, conversion efficiency, collection efficiency)
GEOMETRICAL PARAMETERS	Source-to-detector distance and solid angle, object and source magnification
SYSTEM PARAMETERS	Spatial resolution, contrast resolution, sensitivity, dynamic range, noise
OBSERVER EXPERIENCE	Training, fatique, workload
ATMOSPHERIC TRANSMITTANCE	Haze, fog, rain, dust
MONITOR PARAMETERS	Luminance, Contrast, resolution
SCENE CONTENT	Target characteristics, background characteristics, motion, clutter
MISCELLANEOUS	Ambient illumination, vibration, noise, psychological parameters

No single model can be accounted for all the factors listed. Using a model to predict performance for scenarios where the model is not validated can lead to inaccurate predictions. Often several techniques are used and the results are combined. For instance Russo and Ramponi [82] proposed robust fuzzy methods for multisensor data fusion. Similarly, physiologically motivated pulse coupled neural network (PCNN)-based image fusion modeling can be used to fuse the results of several object detection techniques, with applications in mammography and automatic target recognition [77].

7.4. Multisensor image classification

Applications of ANN's towards the classification of multisensor data have been reported in several works [75,76]. Multisensor image classification relies on the use of structured neural networks to the supervised classification of multisensor images. This technique can be applied in cases where different sensors are used to extract information from the same image, with applications in remote sensing, medical diagnosis, visual inspection and monitoring of industrial products, robotics and others. Main problems encountered by conventional multisensor classification techniques consist of the difficulty to create an integral multivariate statistical model for different sensors as well as of the absence of compensatory mechanisms to automatically weight sensors according to their reliability.

These problems can be easily overcome by utilizing ANN's, since ANN's they do not require a-priori knowledge of statistical data distribution, as well as they take into consideration the reliability of each sensor. A multi-input single-output 'tree-like-networks (TLNs), aimed to overcome the difficulties related to the architecture definition, and opacity, have been proposed [77]. The neural network architecture is shown in Fig. 1.

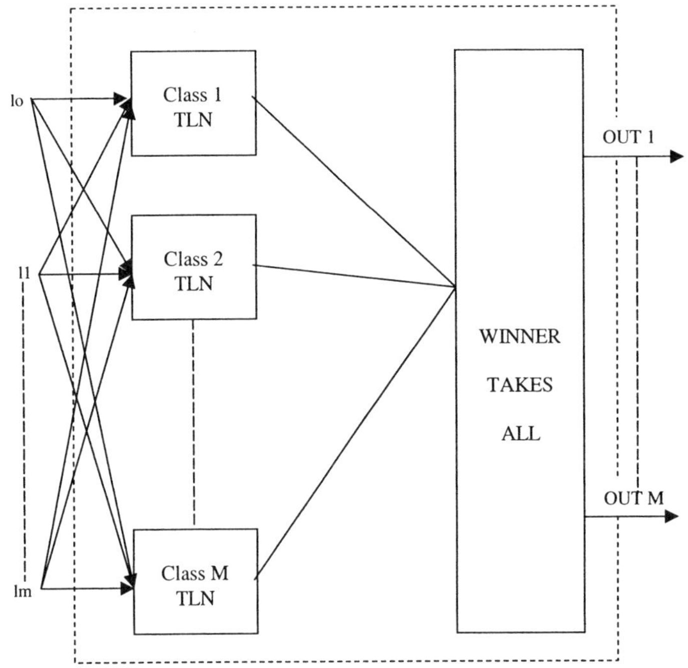

Figure 1: TLN is dedicated to each class of data; the final classification is provided by a Winner-Takes-All block [77].

Based on the above, a novel neural architecture of a multisensor classification problem, have been proposed [77]. This neural architecture geometry is shown in Fig. 2. In this neural architecture, for each class, a TLN with two hidden levels have been proposed. The first hidden layer consists of a committee of neurons, the first-level committee, to check the constraints on data. The results of such checks are managed by the output neuron of the subnet, which resembles a "vote taking unit (VTU). The output neurons of the sensor-related subnets resemble the members of a second-level-committee, each member of which is an expert in the analysis of the data from a single sensor element. Again, the output unit of the TLN is regarded as the VTU of this committee, combining the judgements provided by the sensor-related committees.

7.5. Pattern recognition and classification

Pattern recognition is one of the most difficult problems in image processing especially in very noisy conditions. Arsenault et al. in 1988 have developed a technique to improve the performance of ANN in pattern recognition and classification. The superior performance is achieved by introducing an invariant into the network by changing the interconnection between layers of the network, or by means of some pre-processing of the input data.

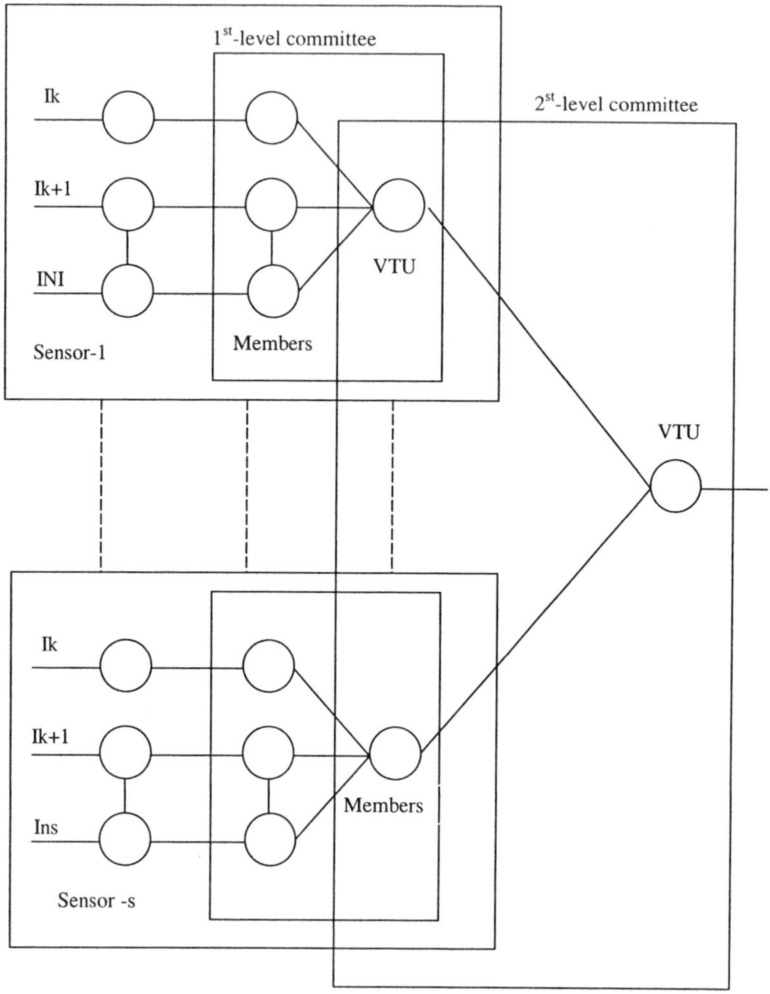

Figure 2: Block diagram of Tree-like Networks applied for multisensor classification problems [77].

They have shown the robustness of this approach when highly degraded partial images rapidly converged to the closest stored image. However this research has not addressed the issue of shift and rotational variance. They conclude that methods involving data preprocessing is the most viable option.

Several researchers have developed high performance image classification systems based on ensemble of neural networks [8-14]. Most of the research has shown that the ensemble of neural networks work best when the neural networks forming the ensemble make different errors. Giacinto et al. [9] have improved on these models by using an automated design to arrive at the best ensemble of neural networks for pattern classification. Their method not only showed the effectiveness of their approach in image classification but also provided a systematic method in choosing neural. The Kohonen network (Fig. 3) provides advantage over classical pattern recognition techniques because it utilizes the parallel architecture of a neural network and provides a graphical organization of pattern relationship.

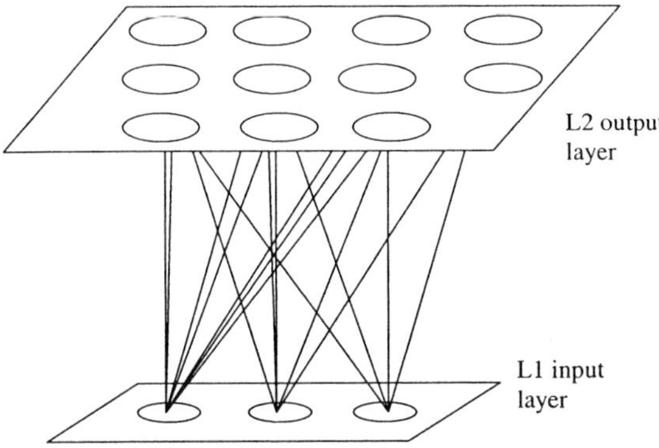

Figure 3: A two-layer network. (Kohonen learning).

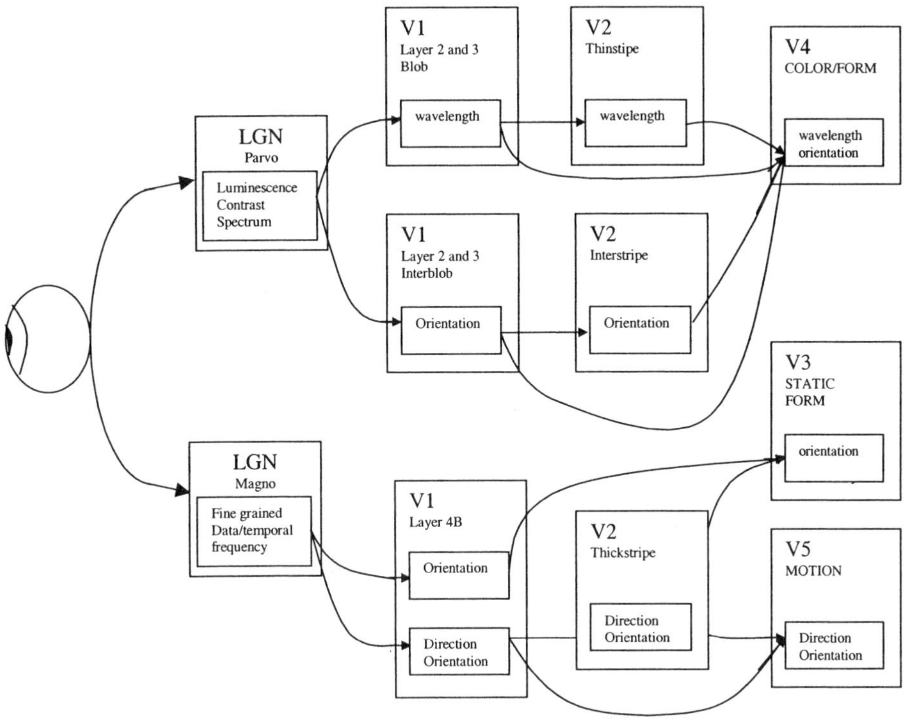

Figure 4: Forward information flow of the visual system model [78].

Physiologically motivated pulse coupled neural network (PCNN)-based image fusion modeling can be used to fuse the results of several object detection techniques to enhance object detection accuracy [78]. PCNN can be used to segment and fuse target features information extracted through image processing techniques such as wavelets, fuzzy-logic morphological, and others. Application of the PCNN techniques have been demonstrated on mammograms and Forward Looking Infrared Radar (FLIR) images. This information fusion is performed by using primate vision processing principles which are utilized to design a pulse coupled neural network (PCNN)-based image fusion network. The block-diagram of the visual system model is shown in Fig. 4 [78]. It can be seen that the biological foundation for the fusion network is modeled by two basic hierarchical pathways, the parvocellular pathway and the magnocellular pathway. The former pathway processes color information, while, the later processes form and motion. The entry point of an image is retina, while the area marked LGN models the biological lateral geniculate nucleus. The areas of the model labeled with the letter V model specific areas in the human visual cortex, while the numbers indicate specialty areas which process selective information such as color, form, or motion. Overall, this model exceeds the accuracy obtained by individual filtering methods.

7.6. Image shape and texture analysis

Many studies in the area of image processing are devoted to shape and texture analysis [15,16], [18,19], Ferrari et al. [15], used both shape and texture features from original regions of interest from images to classify early breast cancer, which are associated with microcalcifications. They implemented different topologies of ANN and used the receiver operating characteristic approach to analyze the performance of the ANN. The percentage of correct diagnosis, either benign or malignant, was over 85%.

An adaptive neural network model [74] for distinguishing line and edge detection from texture presentation, for both biological and machine vision applications, is shown in Fig. 5. The model provides different representations of a retinal image in a way that line or edges are distinguished from textures. Specifically, an hierarchy of adaptive Artificial Neural Network (ANN) modules, the so called Entropy Driven Neural Network (EDANN) modules, is introduced for performing two essential different tasks, namely, line and edge detection, and texture segregation. The texture segregation pathway is defined by the EDANN1-, EDANN2, and EDANN3 modules, while, the EDDAN1+ and the EDANN4 modules define the line-and edge detection pathway.

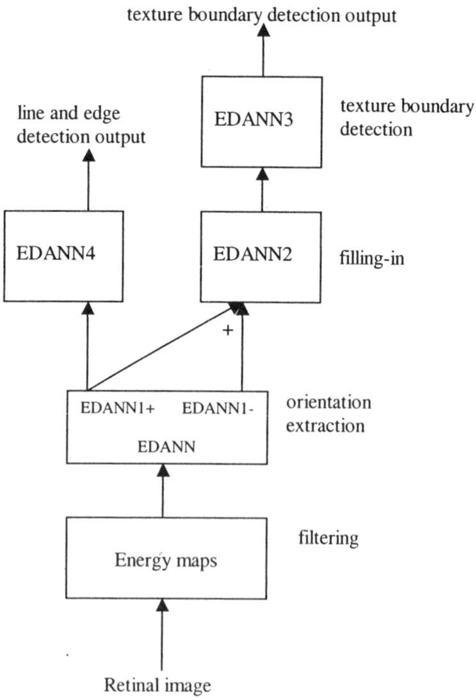

Figure 5: Simplified block-diagram of the model.

7.7. Image compression

Image compression has always been a relevant issue in the field of image processing (Fig.6). Possible applications include:

- image archival and retrieval (medical imaging)
- image transmission (teleconferencing, broadcast television, high definition television)
- dealing with imaging problems (pattern recognition).

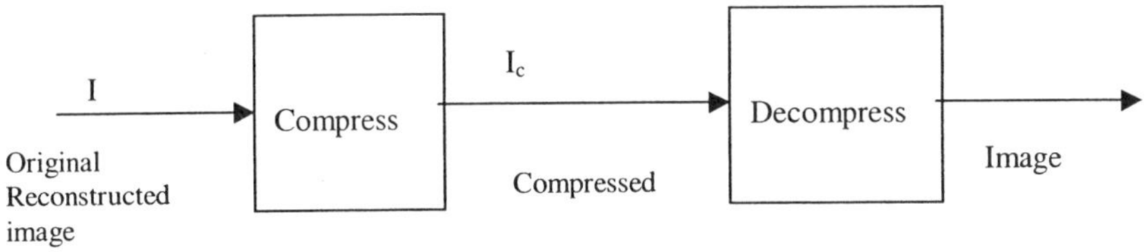

Figure 6: General image compression block diagram.

A number of neural networks based approaches have been developed in order to compress the images, with little loss of information [53-64]. In general, *nonlinear* and *linear* neural networks have been utilized for image compression. They are based on a 1- or 2-layer perceptron, in which the first perform the compression and the second, the reconstruction (Fig. 7).

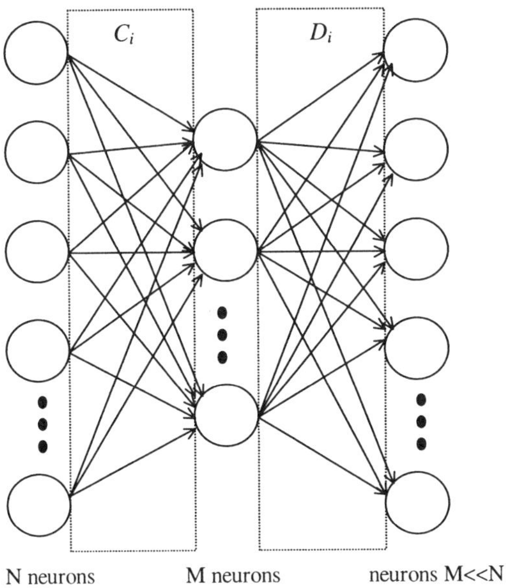

Figure 7: A Neural Network compression/decompression pair.

Panagiotidis et al. [64] have used a neural network approach for lossy compression of medical images (Fig. 8). They differentially code regions of interest in contrast to the rest of image areas to achieve high compression ratios. Specifically, the authors have developed an efficient coding and compression scheme, which takes into consideration the difference in visual importance between areas of the same image, by coding with maximum precision regions of interest (ROI), while performing a lossy reconstruction of the low-interest areas. A diagram of the hierarchical network used to classify the difference in visual importance between areas, is shown in Fig. 9.

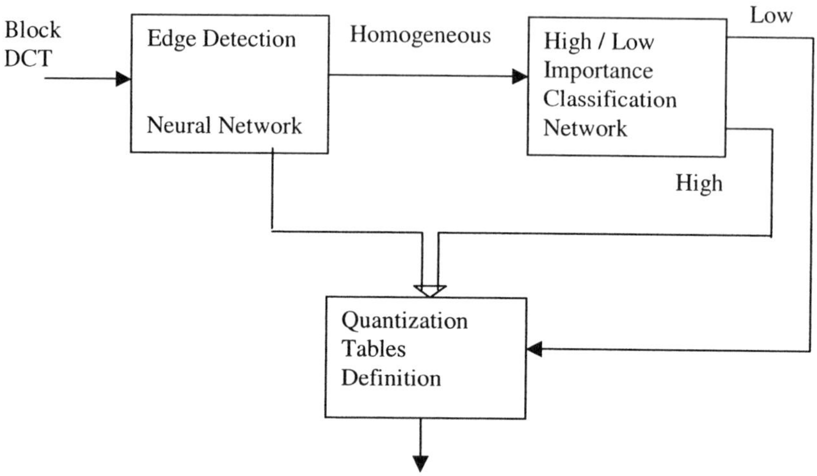

Figure 8: Proposed neural network architecture [64].

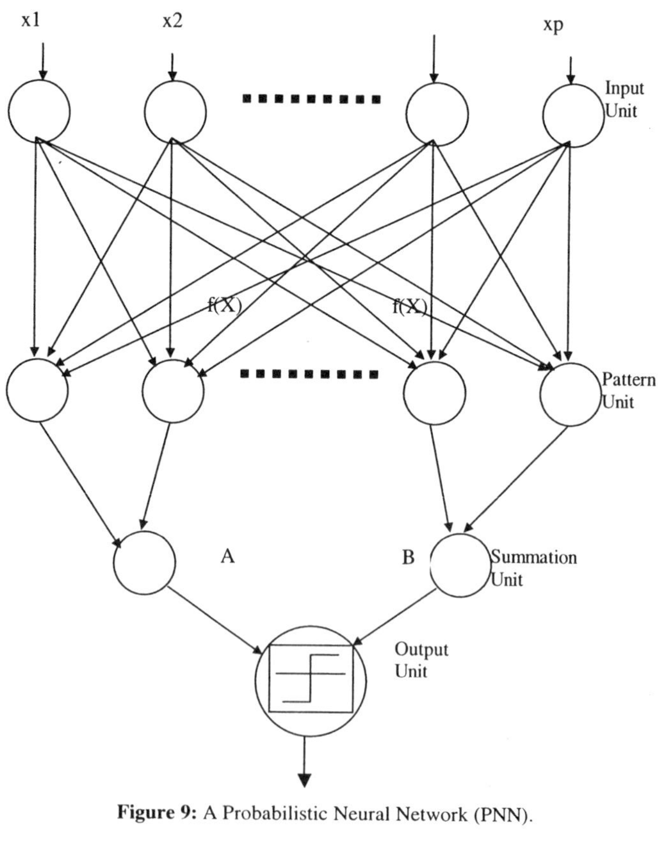

Figure 9: A Probabilistic Neural Network (PNN).

7.8. Nonlinear neural networks for image compression

The perceptron is trained via the backpropagation algorithm, which has been discussed earlier, using a set of images and setting the desired output equal to the input image. According to this algorithm, each branch weight w_{ij} from node i to node j is modified according to a term δj which is proportional to the error between the desired and the actual output of the node:

$$w_{ij}(t+1)=w_{ij}(t)+\eta\delta_j(t)x_i(t) \tag{2}$$

where $x_i(t)$ is the input at the branch i and η is the gain factor. Including a momentum term, Eq. 6 becomes:

$$w_{ij}(t+1)=w_{ij}(t)+\eta\delta_j(t)x_i(t) +\mu(wij(t)-wij(t-1)) \tag{3}$$

where $0<\mu<1$.

The convergence speed is critically dependent on the gain parameter η and the momentum μ. Fixed μ, the value of η is decreased during learning according the speed of convergence. The learning is eventually stopped when no further improvement is obtained in the performance of the NN and η has reached a predefined minimum.

This solution allows a fast convergence during the first part of the learning, and successive accurate approaching to the minimum.

7.9. Linear neural networks for image compression

A 2-layer perceptron can be used, the same as in the previous section, but no nonlinearity is present at the nodes output.

The original images are fed into the input layer and the principal components of the set of images are obtained at the output layer, so that a basis which corresponds to the Karhunen-Loeve Transform (KLT) is determined.

Interestingly enough, given a set of images, the most powerful linear technique is the KLT Transform. In this case, a basis for the linear space mapped by the images is found, in which the basis vectors are ordered according to their importance, so the energy preserved in the remaining coefficients is minimized (the base is restricted as in the case of the image compression problems).

7.10. Image segmentation

Image segmentation provides a means for evaluating the association of a particular pixel to an object of interest within an image. Image segmentation aids in analysis of shape of objects and edges. By segment we imply the labeling of the image at every voxel with the correct anatomical descriptor.

Some applications are:

- magnetic resonance,
- computed tomography,
- surgical planning,
- radiation therapy.

Artificial neural networks have been used as a tool for image segmentation in the field of echocardiography [20,22,24], showed that segmented images preserved better the heart structure at the cost of higher fragmentation of the image. They showed that segmented images had sufficient details of the anatomy of the heart to allow medical diagnosis. Ahmed and Farag, 1997, using neural networks have shown that neural networks yield accurate results by better extraction of the 3D anatomical structures of the brain [21]. Also, they claim that their technique could be adapted to real-time application of image analysis. Other researchers have used neural networks as an effective tool for image segmentation [24-26] with emphasis on MRI.

7.11. Image restoration

Image restoration addresses the problem of retrieving the source image form its degraded version. Considerable amount of research has focused on image restoration [46-52]. Perry and Guan [47] have used ANN model for image reconstruction with an apriori edge information to recover the details and reduce ringing artifact of subband-coded image. Their approach is particularly suitable for high contrast images and also has a great potential for implementation in real time. Qian and Clarke [52] have developed a novel wavelet-based neural network with fuzzy-logic adaptivity for image restoration. Their objective was to restore degraded images due to photon scattering and collimator photon penetration that are common when using a gamma camera. They showed that their approach is efficient in restoring the degraded image and also more efficient by a factor of 4-6 compared to an order statistic neural network hybrid model. The restored images were smoother, with less ringing artifacts and better defined source boundaries. Also, their model was stable under poor signal to noise ratio and low-count statistics. In addition, an adaptive neural network filter for removal of impulse noise in digital images has been reported. It provides a detailed statistical analysis of their approach in contrast with the traditional median-type filters for removal of impulse noise. Their results demonstrate their ability to detect the positions of noisy pixels and also that their approach outperforms the traditional median-type filters.

7.12. Applications

7.12.1 Military applications

Image processing coupled with ANN find usefulness in determining aircraft orientation, tracking (localization), and target recognition [41-43]. Rogers et al. [42] have explored the use of ANN for automatic target recognition (ATR) and have shown it to be an interesting and useful alternate processing strategy. Agarwal and Chaudhuri [41] obtained a set of spatial moments to characterize the different views of the aircraft corresponding to the feature space representation of the aircraft. The feature space is partitioned into feature vectors and these vectors are used to train several multi-layer perceptrons (MLP) to develop functional relations to obtain the target orientation. They show that training of several MLPs provide a better analysis of aircraft orientation when compared to a single MLP trained across the entire feature space. Liu et al [65] have used two-layered ANN for extracting hydrographic objects from satellite images. They have shown that the neural network approach preserves boundaries and edges with high accuracy with while greater suppression of noise within each region.

Super-resolution techniques are aimed to obtain an image with a resolution higher than that allowed by the imaging sensor, with applications in areas such as surveillance and automatic target recognition. In a two-step procedure, a super-resolved image is obtained through the convolution of a low-resolution test image with an established family of kernels [79]. The proposed architecture for super-resolving images using a family of kernels, is shown in Fig. 10:

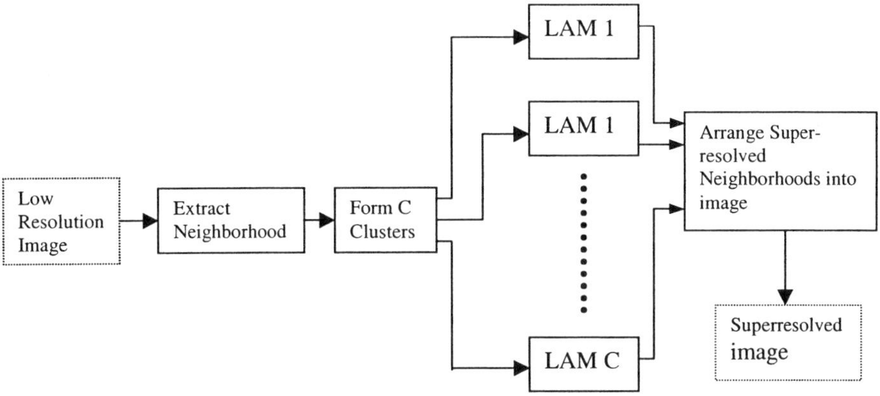

Figure 10: Super-resolution architecture based on local correlations [79].

The low-resolution image neighborhoods are partitioned into a finite number of clusters, where the neighborhoods within each cluster exhibit similarities. Then, a set of kernels, implemented as linear associative memories (LAM's) can be developed which optimally transform each clustered neighborhood into its corresponding neighborhood [79].

After the low-resolution images is synthesized the training the super-resolution architecture proceeds according to Fig. 11:

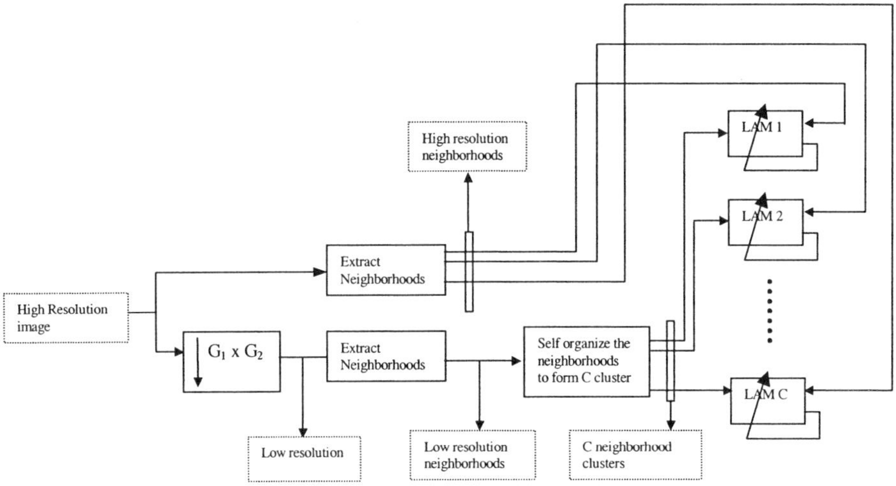

Figure 11: Training procedure for the super-resolution architecture [79].

7.12.2 Remote sensing

Remote sensing relies to the interaction of electromagnetic radiation with matter. In remote sensing, fuzzy neural networks have been used for a variety of applications such as military reconnaissance, flood estimation, crop prediction, mineral detection, and oil exploration [2]. Active systems such as synthetic aperture radar (SAR) can penetrate clouds that block the view of passive systems, such as multispectral and panchromatic sensors.

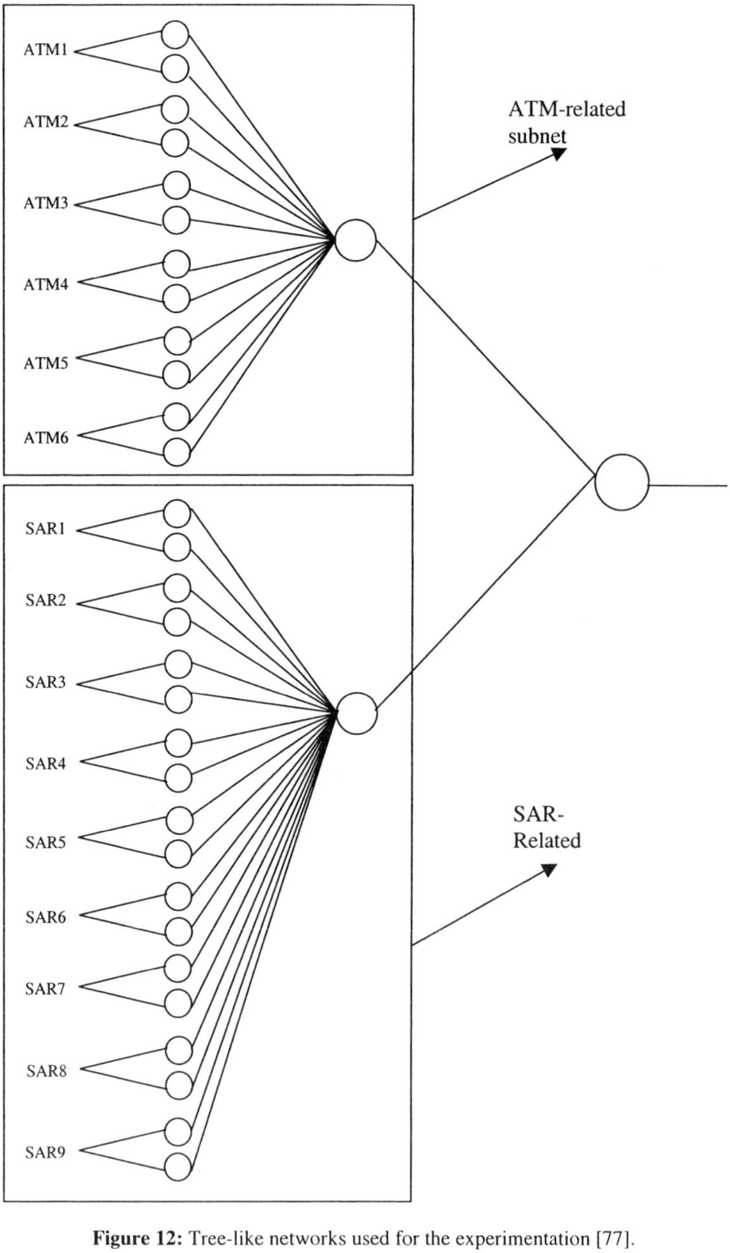

Figure 12: Tree-like networks used for the experimentation [77].

Similarly, is important to extract the features from Doppler echo information of moving target indication (MTI) radar and to recognize radar moving target by the statistical method of pattern recognition [6]. Imaging parameters of interest:

- spatial resolution,
- spectral resolution.
- Combination of neural an statistical algorithms for supervised classification, have been utilized effectively [2,6,9].

Based on the multisensor image classification by structured neural network principles [77], presented in section 7.4, a tree-like network used to analyze and process data obtained through a multisensor remote-sensing imager is shown in Fig 12. The multisensor remote-sensing imager consists of a Daedalus 1268 Airborn Thematic Mapper (ATM) scanner, together to a multiband, fully polarimetric, NASA/JPL imaging synthetic aperture radar (SAR). The imager system and the accompanying network architecture has been use to analyzed imges related to the agricultural fields. Specifically, the selected imaging pixels were representing five different agricultural fields. For each feature, a feature vector was computed by utilizing the intensity values in six ATM bands, and nine features were extracted from the SAR images.

7.12.3 Nuclear magnetic resonance spectroscopy

Nuclear magnetic resonance (NMR) spectroscopy is used as a non-invasive tool for tissue biochemistry and diagnosis of tissue abnormalities be it focal lesions or tumors [2], [25-40].

Artificial neural network approach has been used as an effective tool in NMR spectral characterization. Specifically, important steps in analyzing MRI and CT is segmentation, i.e., pixels are labeled with terms denoting types of tissue.

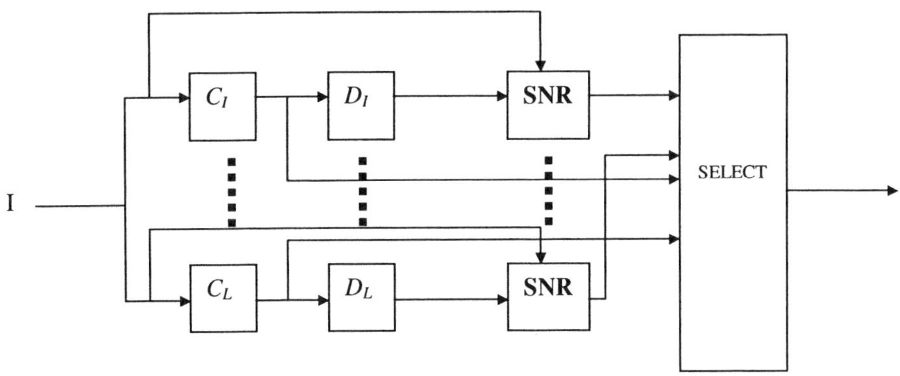

Figure 13: Block diagram the adaptive recurrent neural network processor.

By means of the adaptive recurrent neural network processor, shown in Fig. 13, detailed topographical properties and symmetries in MRI can be studied.

The accurate and reproducible interpretation of an MRI remains an extremely time consuming and costly task. MRI scans allows measurements of three tissue –specific parameters:

- the spin-spin relaxation time (T2)
- the spin-lattice relaxation tissue (T1) and,
- the proton density.

Each pixel is represented by 3-d vector.

Several research groups have used ANN's to differentiate between benign and malignant tissue [29-35], specifically:

- El-Deredy and Branston [36], classified sites of high toxicity from high resolution urine spectra;
- Anthony et al. [34], classified thyroid neoplasms [35];
- classification of high and low grade gliomas [37],
- quantification lipoprotein lipids [38,39], and classify muscle disease [40].

7.12.4 Mammography

Based on the discussion of section 7.5, PCNN fusion architecture used to fuse breast cancer is presented in Fig. 14:

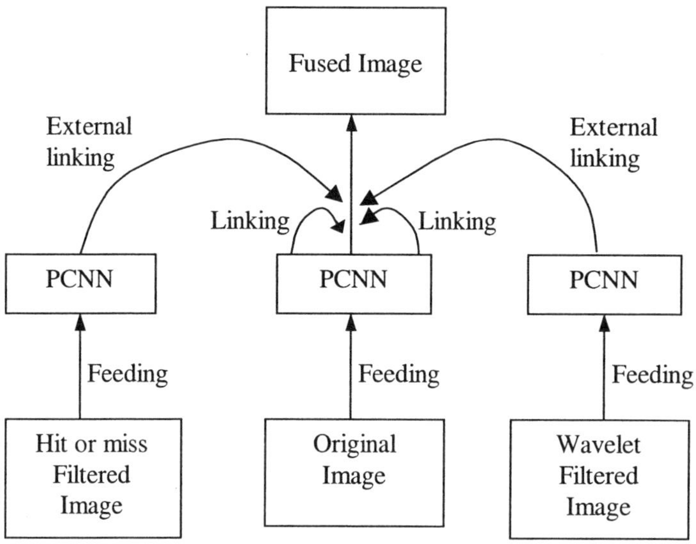

Figure 14: PCNN fusion architecture used to fuse breast cancer and FLIR images [78].

Object detection is performed by means of PCNN fusion networks that take an orginal and several unfiltered versions of a gray scale image and outputs of a single image in which the desired objects are the brightest and then easily detected. Each PCNN has one neuron per input image pixel, while the pulse rate of each neuron in the center PCNN is used as a brightness value for the pixels in the output image.

7.13. Future research directions

Flat-panel digital detectors are being developed for radiological modalities such as radiography and fluoroscopy [66-73]. These systems comprise large area pixel arrays which use matrix addressing to read out charges resulting from x-ray absorption in the detector medium. There are two methods for making flat panel image sensors. In one method, the indirect method [1], a phosphor converter absorbs the incident x-rays and emits visible light which is converted by an a-Si:H p-I-n photodiode to an electronic image. The signal is read out by utilizing a thin film transistor (TFT) readout array. Alternatively, various diode switching modes can be serve as electronic readout. However, the diode readout exhibits a strong nonlinearity and large charge injection. Overall, the indirect method is inefficient and can lead to increased image noise, particularly when signals are low. The other approach, the direct method [1] uses a photoconductive layer to absorb x-rays and collect the ionization charge which is subsequently read-out by an active matrix array. Lead iodide (PbI_2), cadmium zinc telluride (CdZnTe) [67,68], and amorphous selenium, (a-Se) are good candidates. The direct method has a higher intrinsic resolution compared to the indirect method because it avoids the x-ray to light conversion stage. However, poor transport characteristics, associated with the slow motion of ions and the presence of impurities in CdZnTe detectors, can compromise the otherwise excellent detector performance.

Future directions of NN research in digital radiography or more generally in digital electronic sensor design, should be include the optimization of detector parameters [73], such as:

- collection efficiency
- space charge
- charge-carrier trapping-detrapping
- electric field non uniformity
- detector medium aging or impurities
- electron-hole recombination
- radiation scattering
- multipath detection-parallax effects.

In a first step, the design of digital sensors would be optimized by means of NN algorithms, trained to classify extract and classify intrinsic detector signal parameters such as amplitude, rise time and fall time, transit time, signal dispersion and distortion, and signal-to-noise ratio (SNR) characteristics (Fig. 15). As a result, enhanced image quality, by removing nonlinearities, noise, and multipath detection effects would be achieved [73].

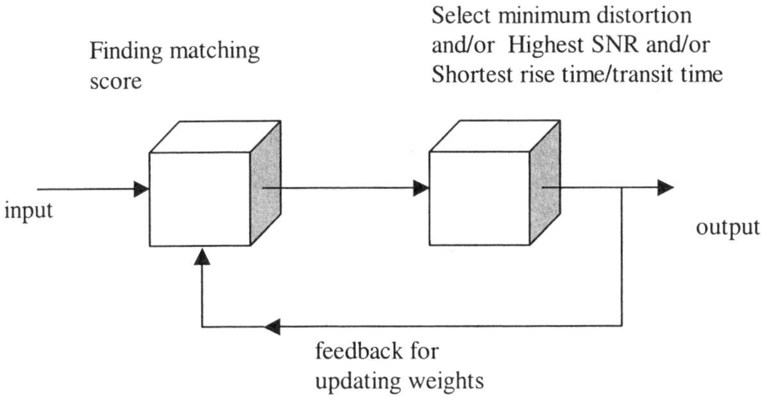

Figure 15: Neural network classifier for digital sensor design optimization.

In addition, novel architectures of oscillatory neural networks using phase-locked loops (PLL's) are currently being explored for pattern recognition [80,81]. The PLL and the associated neural network architecture, is shown in Fig 16. Its major advantage is that PLL circuit technology is well developed and understood. The PLL based neural network architecture stores and retrieves complex oscillatory patterns as synchronized states with appropriate phase relations between the neurons. Overall oscillatory neural networks possess all the neurocomputational properties of standard Hopfield networks, except that the memorized patterns are not equilibria but synchronized oscillatory states in which neurons fire periodically, establishing a relationship between their phases.

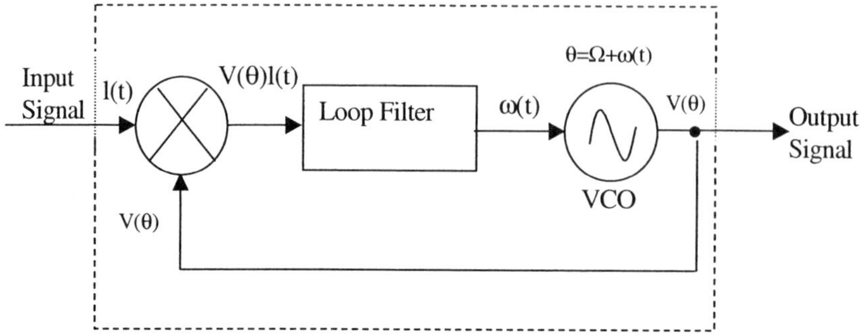

Phase-Locked Loop.

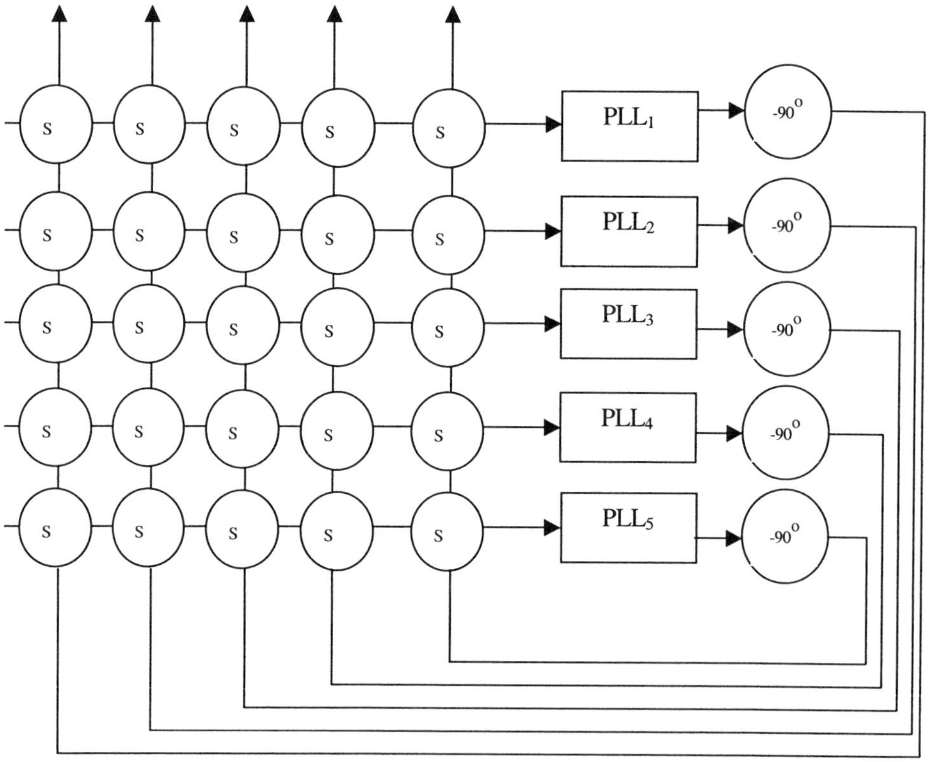

PLL Neural Network

Figure 16: Conceptual Architecture of the PLL neural Network [80,81].

References

[1] G.C. Giakos, "Key Paradigms of Emerging Imaging Sensor Technologies", IEEE Transactions on Instrumentation and Measurement, vol. 40, No. 6, pp. 1-9, December 1998, (invited paper).
[2] A. D. Kulkarni, "Computer Vision and Fuzzy-Neural Systems", Prentice Hall, 2001.
[3] A. D. Kulkarni, "Artificial Neural Networks for Image Understanding", ITP, 1994
[4] R. Ritter, and J. N. Wilson, "Computer Vision Algorithms in Image Algebra", CRC, 2001.
[5] L. M. Fu, "Neural Networks in Computer Intelligence", McGraw-Hill, 1994.
[6] T. Suzuki, H. Ogura, and S. Fujimura, "Noise and Clutter Rejection in Radars and Imaging Sensors", Proc. Of the Second International Symposium on Noise and Clutter Rejection in Radars, IEICE, 1990.
[7] F. Russo, "Evolutionary Neural Fuzzy Systems for Data Filtering", IEEE Instrumentation and Measurements Technology Conference Proceedings, pp. 826-831, 1998.
[8] R. Battiti, and A.M. Colla, Democracy in neural nets: voting schemes for classification, Neural Networoks v. 7, pp. 691-707, 1994
[9] G. Giacinto, and F. Roli, Ensembles of neural networks for soft classification of remote sensing images, Proceedings of the European Symposium on Intelligent Techniques, Bari, Italy, pp. 166-170, 1997
[10] G. Giacinto, F. Roli, and L. Bruzzone, Combination of neural an statistical algorithms for supervised classification of remote-sensing images, Pattern Recognition Letters v. 21, n. 5, pp. 385-397, 2000
[11] T.K. Ho, J.J. Hull, and S.N. Srihari, Decision combination in multiple classifier systems, IEEE Transactions on Pattern Analysis and Machine Intelligence n. 18, pp. 66-75, 1994
[12] Y.S. Huang, K. Liu, and C.Y. Suen, A method of combining multiple experts for the recognition of unconstrained handwritten numerals, IEEE Transactions on Pattern Analysis and Machine Intelligence, n. 17, pp. 90-94, 1995
[13] J. Kittler, M. Hatef, R.P.W. Duin, and J. Matas, On combining Classifiers, IEEE Transactions on Pattern Analysis and Machine Intelligence, n. 20, pp. 226-239, 1998
[14] L. Xu, A. Krzyzak, and C.Y. Suen, Methods for combining multiple classifiers and their applications to handwriting recognition, IEEE Transactions on Systems, Man, and Cybernetics, n. 22, pp. 418-435, 1992
[15] R.J. Ferrari, A.C.P.L.F. de Carvalho, P.M. Azevedo Marques. A.F. Frere, Computerized classification of breast lesions: shape and texture analysis using artificial neural network Image processing and its application, Conference publication, n. 465, pp. 517-521, 1999.
[16] L. Shen, R.M. Rangayyan and J.E.L. Desautels, Application of shape analysis to mammographic calcifications, IEEE Transactions on Medical Imaging n. 13, pp. 263-274, 1994
[17] W.G. Wee, M. Moskowitz, W.C. Chang, Y.C. Ting, and S. Pemmeraju, Evaluation of mammograhic calcifications using a computer program, Radiology, n. 110, pp. 717-720, 1975
[18] H.P. Chan, K. Doi, S. Galhotra, C.J. Vyborny, H. MacMahon, and P.M. Jokich, Image feature analysis and compute-aided diagnosis in digital radiography. I. Automated detection of microcalcifications in mammography, Medical Physiology, n. 14, pp. 538-548, 1987
[19] R.M. Haralick, K. Shanmugam, I. Dinstein, Texture features for image classification, IEEE Transactions on Systems, Man, and Cybernetics, n. 3, pp. 610-621, 1973
[20] L. Piccoli, A. Dahmer, J. Scharcanski, and P.O.A. Navaux, Fetal echocardiographic image segmentation using neural networks, Image processing and its application, Conference publication, n. 465, pp. 507-511, 1999.
[21] M.N. Ahmed, and A.A. Farag, Two-stage neural network for volume segmentation of medical images, IEEE Transactions on medical Imaging, pp. 1373-1378, 1997.
[22] M. Sussner, T. Budil, and G Porenta, Segmentation and edge-detection of echocardiograms using artificial neuronal networks, EANN.
[23] M. Belohlavek, A. Manduca, T. Behrenbeck, J.B. Seward, and F. Greenleaf Image analysis using modified self-organizing maps: Automated delineation of the left ventricular cavity boundary in serial echocardiograms, VBC, n. 1131, 247-252, 1996
[24] S. Haring. M. Viergever, and K. Kok, A multiscale approach to image segmentation using kohonen networks, Proceedings IPMI, Berlin, pp. 212-224, 1993.
[25] S.C. Amartur, and Y. Takefuji, Optimization on neural netwoks for the segmentation of MRI images, IEEE Transactions on Medical Imaging, v 11, n. 2, pp. 215-220, 1992
[26] X.Li, S. Bhide, and M.R. Kabuka, Labeling of MRI brain images using Boolean neural network, IEEE Transactions on Medical Imaging, v. 15, pp. 628-638, 1996.
[27] M.N. Ahmed and A.A. Farag, 3D segmentation and labeling of CT brain images using self organizing kohonen network to quantify TBI recovery, Proceedings from the IEEE Engineering in Medicine and Biology Society (EMBS) conference, Amsterdam 1996.
[28] D.G. Gadian, "NMR and its Application to Living Systems" Oxford Science Publication, Oxford, 1995
[29] M.L. Aston and P. Wilding, Application of neural networks to the interpretation of laboratory data in cancer-diagnosis. Clinical Chemistry, n. 38, pp. 34-38, 1992

[30] S.L. Howells, R.J. Maxwell, A.C. Peet, and J.R. Griffiths, An investigation of tumour 1H nuclear magnetic resonance spectra by the application of chemometric tenchniques, Mag. Reson. Med, n. 28, pp. 214-236, 1992.
[31] N.M. Branstom, R.J. Maxwell, and S.L. Howells, Generalization performance using backpropogation algorithms applied to patterns derived from tumour ^{1}H-NMR spectra, Journal of Microcomputer applications, n. 16, pp. 113-123, 1993
[32] S.L. Howells, R.J. Maxwell, F.A. Howe, A.C. Peet, and J.R. Griffiths, Pattern recognition of ^{31}P magnetic resonance spectroscopy tumour spectra obtained in vivo. NMR in Biomedicine, n.6, pp. 237-241, 1993
[33] P.J.G. Lisboa, and A.R. Mehriehnavi, Sensitivity methods for variable selection using the MLP, Proceedings International Workshop on Neural Networks for Identification, Control, Robotics and Signal Processing, pp.330-338, 1996
[34] M.L. Anthony, V.S. Rose, J.K. Nicholson, and J.C. Lindon Classification of toxin-induced changes in 1H NMR spectra of urine using artificial neural network, Journal of Pharmaceutical Biomedical Annals, n. 12, pp. 205-211, 1995
[35] R.L. Somorjai, A.E. Nikulin, N. Pizzi, D. Jackson, G. Scarth, B. Dolenko, H. Gordon, P. Russell, C.L. Lean, L. Delbridge, C.E. Mountford and I.C.P. Smith, Computerized consensus diagnosis: A classification strategy for the robust analysis of MR spectra. I. Application to 1H spectra of thyroid neoplasms, Magnentic Resonance Med, n. 33, pp. 257-263, 1995
[36] W. El-Deredy, and N.M. Branston, Identification of relevant features of ^{1}H MR tumour spectra using neural networks, Proc. IEEE Int Conf on Artificial neural networks, pp. 454-459, 1995
[37] N.M. Branston, W. El-Deredy, A.A. Sankar, J. Darling, S.R. Williams, and D.G.T. Thomas, Neural network analysis of 1H-NMR spectra identifies metabolites differentiating between high and low grade astrocytomas in vitro, J. Neuro-Oncology, n28, pp. 83, 1996
[38] Y. Hiltunen, E. Heiniemi, and M Ala Korpela, Lipoprotein lipid quantification by neural network analysis of 1HNMR spectra from human plasma, J. Mag Reson Series B, n. 106, pp. 191-194, 1995
[39] M. Ala Korpela, Y. Hiltunen, and J.D. Bell, Quantification of biomedical NMR data using artificial neural network analysis: Lipoprotein lipid profiles from 1H NMR data of human plasma, NMR Biomed, n. 8, pp. 235-244, 1995
[40] S. Kari, N.J. Olsen, and J.H. Park, Evaluation of muscle disease using artificial neural network analysis of 31P MR spectroscopy data, Mag. Res. Med, n. 34, pp. 664-672, 1995.
[41] S. Agarwal, and S. Chaudhuri, Determination of aircraft orientation for a vision-based system using artificial neural networks, Journal of Mathematical Imaging and Vision, n. 8, pp. 255-269, 1998.
[42] S.K. Rogers, J.M. Colombi, C.E. Martin, J.C. Gainy, K.H. Fielding, T.J. Burns, D.W. Ruck, M. Kabrisky, and M. Oxley, Neural networks for automatic target recognition Neural Networks, n. 7/8, v. 8, pp.1153-1184, 1995.
[43] S. Shams, Neural network optimization for multi-target multi-sensor passive tracking, Proceeding of the IEEE, Special issue on Engineering Application of Artificial Neural Networks, v. 84, n. 10, pp.1442-1458, 1996
[44] A.K. Katsaggelos, and R.M. Mersereau, A regularized iterative image restoration algorithm, IEEE Transactions on Signal Processing v. 39, n. 4, pp. 914-929, 1991
[45] P. Bao, and D. Wang, An edge-preserving image reconstruction using neural network, Journal of Mathematical Imaging and Vision, v. 14, pp. 117-130, 2001
[46] J. Paik, and A. Katsaggelos, Image restoration using a modified Hopfield network, IEEE Transactions on Image Processing, v. 1, n. 1, pp. 49-63, 1992
[47] S. Perry, and L. Guan, Neural network restoration of images suffering space-variant distortion, Electronics Letters, v. 31, n. 16, pp. 1358-1359, 1995
[48] S.W. Perry, and L. Guan, A statistics-based weight assignment in a hopfield neural network for adaptive image restoration, IEEE, pp. 922-927, 1998
[49] Y. Yang, N.P. Galatsanos, and A.K. Katsaggelos, Regularized reconstruction to reduce blocking artifacts of block discrete cosine transform compressed images, IEEE Transactions on Circuits and Systems for Video Technology, v. 3, n. 6, pp. 421-432, 1993
[50] Y. Zhou, R. Chellappa, A. Vaid, and B. Jenkins, Image restoration using neural network, IEEE Transactions on Acoustics speech, Signal Processing, v. 36, n. 7, pp. 1141-1151, 1988
[51] W. Qian, and L.P. Clarke, Wavelet-based neural network with fuzzy-logic adaptivity for nuclear image restoration, Proceedings of the IEEE, v.84, n. 10, pp. 1458-1473, 1996.
[52] A.N. Netravali, and J.O. Limb, Picture coding: A review, Proceeding of IEEE, v. 68, pp. 366-406, 1980
[53] A.K. Jain, Image data compression: A review, Proceedings of IEEE, v. 69, pp. 349-389, 1981
[54] N.S. Jayant, and P Noll, Digital coding of waveforms, Englewood Cliffs, NJ, Prentice-Hall 1984
[55] A.N. Netravali, and B.G. Haskell, Digital pictures: Representation and Compression, New York: Plenum 1988

[56] A. Gersho, and R.M. Gray, "Vector Quantization and Signal Compression", Norwell, MA: Kluwer 1992
[57] N. Jayant, J. Johnston, and R Safranek, Signal compression based on models of human perception, Proceedings of IEEE, v. 81, pp. 1385-1421, 1993
[58] R.D. Dony, and S. Haykin, Neural network approaches to image compression, Proceedings of IEEE, v. 83, n. 2, pp. 288-303, 1995
[59] L.E. Russo, and E.C. Real, Image compression using an outer product neural network, Proceedings of IEEE Int. Conf. Acoust. Speech and Signal Process, pp. II 377-389, 1992
[60] A. Namphol, M. Arozullah, and S. Chin, Higher order data compression with neural networks, Proc Int Joint Conf on neural Networks, pp, I 55-59, 1991
[61] R. Kohno, M. Arai, and H. Imai, Image compression using a neural network with learning capability of variable function of a neural unit, SPIE v 1360, Visual Commun and Image Proc, pp. 69-75, 1990
[62] D. Anthony, E. Hines, D. Taylor, and J. Barhām, A study of data compression using neural network and principal component analysis, Colloquium on Biomedical Applications of Digital Signal Processing, pp. 1-5, 1989
[63] G.L. Sicuranzi, G. Ramponi, and S. Marsi, Artificial neural network for image compression, Electronic letters, v. 26, pp. 477-479, 1990
[64] N. G. Panagiotidis, D. Kalogeras, S.D. Kollias, and A. Stafylopatis, Neural network-assisted effective lossy compression of medical images, Proceedings of IEEE, v.84, n. 10, pp. 1474-1487, 1996
[65] X. Liu, D. Wang, and J.R. Ramirez, Extracting hydrographic objects from satellite images using a two layered neural network, IEEE, pp. 897-902, 1998
[66] C.E. Cann et.al., "Quantification of Calcium in Solitary Pulmonary Nodules Using Single-and Dual Energy CT", Radiology, vol. 145, pp. 493, 1982.
[67] G.C. Giakos, A. Dasgupta, S. Suryanarayanan, S. Chowdhury, R. Guntupalli, S. Vedantham, B. Pillai, and A. Passalaqua, "Sensitometric Response of CdZnTe Detectors for Chest Radiography", IEEE Transactions on Instrumentation and Measurement, vol. 47, no. 1, pp.252-255, 1998.
[68] G.C. Giakos, S. Vedantham, S. Chowdhury, Jibril Odogba, A. Dasgupta, S. Vedantham, D.B. Sheffer, R. Nemer, R. Guntupalli, S. Suryanarayanan, V. Lozada, R.J. Endorf, and A. Passalaqua, "Study of Detection Efficiency of CdZnTe Detectors for Digital Radiography", IEEE Transactions on Instrumentation and Measurement, vol. 47, no. 1, pp. 244-251, 1998.
[69] G.C. Giakos, and S. Chowdhury, "Multimedia Imaging Detectors Operating on Gas-Solid State Ionization Principles", IEEE Transactions on Instrumentation and Measurement, vol. 40, No. 5, pp. 1-9, October 1998.
[70] G.C. Giakos, US Patent, 6,207,958, "Multimedia Detectors for Medical Imaging", March 23, 2001.
[71] G.C. Giakos, US Patent 6, 069, 362, on "Multidensity and Multi-atomic Number Detector Media for Applications", May 30, 2000.
[72] G.C. Giakos, European Patent 99918933.5-2213, on "Multidensity and Multi-atomic Number Detector Media for Applications", December 28, 2000.
[73] G.C. Giakos, NATO Advanced Research Institute, Lecture Series, NIMIA 2001, Crema, Italy, 9-20 October 2001.
[74] M.M. Van Hulle, T. Tollenaere, and G.A. Orban, "An Adaptive Neural Network Model for Distinguishing Line-and Edge Detection from Texture Segregation", International Joint Conference on Neural Networks, Singapore, 18-21 November, pp. 1409-1414, 1991.
[75] O.K. and D. Hong, "Parallel, Self-Organizing, Hierarchical Neural Networks", IEEE Transactions on Neural Networks, vol. 1., No. 2, pp. 167-178, 1990.
[76] H. Bishcof, W. Schneider, and A.J. Pinz, "Multispectral Classification of LandSat-images using Neural Networks", IEEE Transactions on Geoscience and Remote Sensing, vol. 30, no. 3., pp. 482-490, 1992.
[77] F. Roli, S.B. Serpico, and G. Vernazza, "Multisensor Image Classification by Structured Neural Networks", IEEE Trans. On Geoscience and Remote Sensing, vol. 28, no. 4, pp. 310-320, 1993.
[78} R. P. Broussard, S.K. Rogers, M.E. Oxley, and G.L. Tarr, "Physiologicaly Motivated Image Fusion for Object Detection using a Pulse Coupled Neural Network", IEEE Transactions on Neural Networks, vol. 10., No. 3., pp. 554-562, 1999
[79] F.M. Candocia, and J.C. Principe, "Super-Resolution of Images Based on Local Correlations", IEEE Transactions on Neural Networksw, vol. 10., no. 2., pp. 372-380, 1999.
[80] T. Aoyagi, "Network of Neural Oscillators for Retrieving Phase Information", Phys. Rev. Lett., Vol. 74., pp. 4075-4078, 1995.
[81] F. C. Hoppensteadt, and E. M. Izhikevich, "Pattern Recognition via Synchronization in Phase-Locked Loop Neural Networks", IEEE Transactions on Neural Networks, vol. 11, No. 3, 2000.
[82] F. Russo, and G. Ramponi, "Fuzzy methods for Multisensor Data Fusion", IEEE Transactions on Instrumentation and Measurements", vol. 43, n.2, pp. 288-294, 1994.

Neural Networks for Instrumentation, Measurement and Related Industrial Applications
S. Ablameyko et al. (Eds.)
IOS Press, 2003

Chapter 8
Neural Networks for Machine Condition Monitoring and Fault Diagnosis

Robert X. Gao
Department of Mechanical and Industrial Engineering, University of Massachusetts Amherst, MA 01003, USA

Abstract. This chapter introduces several fundamental aspects of neural networks and their applications in the industry, in particular for machine condition monitoring and fault diagnosis. Several research highlights in bearing condition monitoring and health assessment using neural networks are presented

8.1. Need for Machine Condition Monitoring

Growing demand for high quality and low cost production has increased the need for automated manufacturing systems with effective monitoring and control capabilities [1-2]. As a critical component, sensor-based machine condition monitoring and fault diagnosis has been gaining increasing attention from the research community worldwide [3-4]. The goal of machine condition monitoring is to obtain real-time working status of the machines and use the information 1) to identify potential machine faults and failure before they occur, thus reducing unexpected and costly machine downtime and ensure the highest possible productivity, and, 2) to more accurately control the quality of products, which is closely related to the working condition of the machines. The information gathered from the monitoring sensors ultimately provides insight into the manufacturing process itself, enabling effective high-level decision-making for quality production at a lower cost.

Unexpected machine breakdowns can cause significant economical losses due to the material damage and lost production time. A solution to this problem is to constantly monitor the working status of the machine, alert the machine operators of any incipient dangers, and shut down the machine before catastrophic failures occur. The growing competitiveness worldwide has further increased the importance of condition-based machine monitoring and fault diagnosis. It has been estimated that up to 70 % of the operating costs can be taken by maintenance if proper maintenance procedures are not followed [5]. Economic concerns such as replacement part costs, maintenance-scheduling, and production logistics are essential in deciding a suitable maintenance strategy. As rotating machinery is widely present in many manufacturing systems as well as in air and ground transportation, it is of critical importance to avoid catastrophic failures in such systems, as they may endanger human lives. In the railroad industry, it has been reported that almost fifty train derailments occur each year in the US due to bearing burn-offs [6]. Thus, in addition to economical reasons, machine condition monitoring has the potential impact in maintaining operation safety and reliability.

Two major issues concerning machine condition monitoring are machine fault diagnosis and prognosis. Diagnosis refers to the determination of the current "health" status or working condition of the machine being monitored, whereas prognosis refers to the prediction of the remaining service life in the machine. Reliable diagnosis and prognosis techniques not only reduce the risks of unexpected machine breakdowns, but also help in prolonging machine life. Due to these reasons, the current trend in the maintenance industry is increasingly shifted towards condition-based, preventative, and proactive maintenance.

8.1.1 State of Knowledge

In the machine tool industry, condition-based monitoring has been manifested through the monitoring of the overall machine system (e.g. total energy consumption), the specific tools (wear or lubrication status), the work piece (quality parameters), and the machining processes (e.g. chip formation or temperature variation). The fault condition of a machine is judged by symptoms and signs, which are generally related to the operation parameters. The variation in time of these parameters is an indicator of the fault progression and can be used to forecast the future trend of its development, as well as serving as the basis for generating alarm signals. Among the various symptoms used, machine vibration has long been used as a practical fault indicator [7-8]. Most machinery equipment consists of bearings, gears, motor, shafts, and other rotating elements, and vibration caused by the presence of structural faults in these components provides a source of information of the machine health condition, since the vibration profile of the machine would change as the fault develops. Such a change could be reflected by an increase in the vibration level of characteristic frequencies. The fundamental issues in condition monitoring include: 1) identification of the fault pattern, and 2) quantification of the fault development. The physical variables that can be measured for the vibration analysis include displacement, velocity, or acceleration. It is important to specify the frequencies at which the vibration levels become critical for the type of machinery being monitored. The measured data set, which is representative of a particular fault, is extracted for features by suitable signal processing techniques.

Historically, the identification of a faulty machine or machine components was made by comparing the sound emitted by the machine to that from a "healthy" machine in good working condition [9]. But this approach lacks objectivity, is vulnerable to ambient noise and is subject to human errors [10]. Other methods used have included the acoustic emission (AE) signals, which is associated with the transient elastic waves generated by sudden release of strain energy. Such energy release is basically due to stress concentrations, which can be caused by the presence of structural defects such as cracks. Applications of sub-surface defect diagnosis using AE techniques have been reported in [11-12]. General difficulties with AE-based measurement involve quantification of the relatively low AE signal magnitudes, and noise contamination from other machine structures [13]. AE techniques have been applied for tool breakage detection [3]. Surveys have also revealed extensive use of AE sensors coupled with force sensors for tool wear monitoring. Furthermore, temperature measurement has been used as an indirect technique in conjunction with vibration analysis for tool condition monitoring. The advantage of using temperature is that it is not related to structural defects as closely as the tribological conditions do [14]. In addition, lubrication debris has also been considered a reasonably good indicator of bearing wear [15]. However, since it is generally time-consuming to collect and analyze the debris, such a technique is not suited for on-line applications.

The major components of a condition-based monitoring system include the machinery, condition-monitoring sensors, signal processors, fault classifiers, machine models, and the monitoring output. Errors and uncertainties in fault classification can lead to false alarms, which motivates research for better, more robust and reliable condition monitoring systems.

8.1.2 Recent Trend in Research

Different types of sensors have been used to monitor different aspects of the machine environment [16]. Machine fault diagnosis is a challenging topic given the fact that signals resulting from structural faults are generally weak at the incipient stage and thus often submerged in ambient noise and structural vibrations. Traditionally, vibration sensors such as accelerometers were placed on the machine housing, often far away from the component to be monitored. The long signal transmission path between the monitoring sensor and the component to be monitored leads to a poor signal-to-noise ratio. In such cases, the sensor would pick up vibration signals from everything along the way, and defect-induced vibration signals would suffer from attenuation as they propagated to the sensor. Efforts have been made to place the sensor as closely as possible to the machine component to be monitored, e.g. through structural integration into a rolling bearing inside a machine [17-19]. Such an embedded sensing approach has the potential to greatly enhance the effectiveness of the machine condition monitoring [20].

Besides signal detection, an equally important issue in machine condition monitoring is signal processing. Traditional techniques for signal processing fall under the categories of time-domain and frequency-domain analysis. In the time domain, statistical parameters of vibration signals such as root mean square [4], peak values [21], kurtosis [22], and crest factor [7] have been used. Spectral techniques have been widely applied in the past decades, such as Windowed Fourier Transform [23], power cepstrum analysis [24], and Wigner-Ville distribution [25]. Since such techniques are generally limited to the analysis of stationary signals and thus not suited for non-transient signal analysis [26], recent development has focused on wavelet transform that is a time-scale domain technique and well suited for detecting and analyzing machine faults that are transient in nature [26].

The application of neural networks for machine condition monitoring has been demonstrated by various researchers [27-29]. The development is rooted in the need for automated and adaptive condition monitoring techniques that can "learn" from and adapt to the changing environment where data are being analyzed. Traditional time domain techniques such as statistical analysis suffer from interference or noise contamination. Peak values of defect signals may vary with the change in operating speed, load, or temperature [30], making threshold setting inaccurate or inappropriate. The existence of multiple faults can make fault identification highly complex, especially at the incipient stage when the effects are "fuzzy". Hence, introducing a neural network that mimics the ability of a biological neuron in the human brains to learn from and adapt to the changing environment provides a viable solution, especially when no exact physics-based mathematical models of the machine system are available [29]. The application of neural networks to machine condition monitoring has been shown in applications such as pattern classification for image processing [31], sensor network analysis [3], or user context identification [32]. Once a neural network has been "trained" for a particular task, it can identify situations that were "unknown" to it before. A critical issue is how to train a neural network effectively and efficiently. For machine condition monitoring, this has to do in the first place with the choice of parameters to be selected that describe the condition of the machine. Too many parameters will increase the complexity of the network design and increase the computational load, whereas too few parameters may not provide an accurate description of the system for the neural network to rely on [33].

Different statistical approaches have been proposed for machine condition monitoring [34-35]. The major challenge is for a condition monitoring technique to be able to differentiate changes in the signals measured that are due to machine defects from those that are due to the changing operating conditions. A statistical method proposed was based on the identification of different operating conditions that give rise to significantly different statistics [35]. Subsequently, the statistics of vibration data for various defects were determined and the combination of the two sets was used to serve as the reference base for models to test other segments of data. Statistical modeling methodology such as Hidden Markov Model (HMM) [34] has been found to be well suited for the classification of operating parameters and defects.

8.2. Condition Monitoring of Rolling Bearings

8.2.1 Significance

Rolling element bearings have been used in virtually every machine system. Many of their applications are critically important and require that the machines be maintained at highly reliable condition to avoid unexpected, premature machine breakdowns. Defects arise in bearings during their usage because of adverse operating conditions, faulty installation, or material fatigue. Adverse operating conditions may be caused by overloading, insufficient or over-lubrication, or contamination in the rolling contact zone. At any point in time, only a portion of the rolling elements is within the load zone, and high stress occur periodically below the loaded surface. These stresses may cause microscopic cracks, which gradually appear on the raceway surface after an extended period of use. Fragments of the raceway then break away when rolling elements pass over these cracks, causing spalling or flaking [36], which is a common mode of failure in bearings. The spall area increases with time and can be identified by increased level of vibrations of the bearing. The debris generated in the defect development process contaminates the lubricant, diminishes its effect, and causes localized overloading [37].

Unexpected, premature bearing failure can be disastrous, especially if related to transportation vehicles such as an airplane or a passenger train [38-39]. It is desired to enable on-line bearing condition monitoring so that no time lag would exist between the data collection, diagnosis and maintenance actions. In a motor reliability study, it was found that bearing problems accounted for over 40 % of all machine failures [40]. It has also been found that a majority of bearings fail before they attain their service life, and only about a third die from "old age" due to surface fatigue [41]. To investigate the real reasons and find out better ways of preventing bearing failures have drawn considerable interest in the research community and industry in recent years.

Every time when a rolling element hits a structural defect in the raceway, a series of vibration pulses will be generated. Depending on the specific location of the defect (e.g. on the inner or outer raceway, or on the rolling element itself), the family of the pulses will contain characteristic frequencies specific to the bearing geometry and operation condition (e.g. rotating speed). The highest pulse amplitude will be generated within the load zone of the bearing. The difficulty in bearing fault detection stems from interference due to structural vibrations generated by other parts of the machine system. A bearing diagnostic tool needs to be designed robust enough to differentiate various vibration signals, in order to effectively classify faults without generating false alarms. Understanding of the bearing defect characteristics is critical to the proper design of bearing diagnostic tools.

8.2.2 Bearing Failure Modes

Due to the rotational nature of bearing operations, bearing failures are associated with characteristic defect frequencies that are related to the speed of the bearing, the location where the defect appears, and the bearing geometry [42]. Many of the defect frequencies can be determined analytically, as shown in [43]. For example, if a point defect is located in the outer race of the bearing, a frequency component of *BPFO* (ball pass frequency for outer race) can be identified as:

$$BPFO = \frac{N_i}{2}(1 - \frac{D}{d_m}\cos\alpha)Z \quad (1)$$

where N_i is the rotational speed of the inner raceway in Hz, d_m is the diameter of the pitch circle of the rolling balls, D is the ball diameter, α is the contact angle and Z is the number of balls in the bearing. Such characteristic frequencies play an important role in bearing fault diagnosis and prognosis, especially when using spectral techniques. They also can be used as input parameters for a diagnostic neural network [44].

8.2.3 Research Challenge

Research on bearing prognosis focuses on the prediction of a bearing's remaining life. Prognosis is a logical step forward from fault diagnosis. However, it has been found that reliably predicting the remaining service life of a bearing based on what has been diagnosed can be highly challenging, due to the uncertainty involved. As the vibrations produced by a surface defect in the bearing are periodic in nature, the defect characteristic frequencies are often used in conjunction with other time-domain parameters (e.g. RMS or peak values) for diagnosis and prognosis purposes. To ensure reliable analysis, the defect frequencies need to be distinct and separable from the rest of the signals.

Bearing defects can be broadly classified as distributed and localized. The lack of roundness and uneven ball diameter are examples of distributed defects, whereas spalls or corrosion spots are typical localized defects. Difficulty in bearing diagnosis arises when frequency components from multiple defects overlap in the spectrum, mixing up with the harmonics and interference. In particular, the frequency spectrum of the vibration from a bearing with multiple defects may appear similar to the spectrum from a bearing with a single defect, causing signal "masking", as is illustrated in Figure 1, where *S(f)* is the vibration amplitude, $\Delta\varphi_d$ is the angular separation of two inner raceway faults in degrees, and f_i is the inner raceway defect frequency [45]. Thus, designing a bearing diagnostic tool that can learn from the signal variations due to fault "growth" presents a research challenge as well as an opportunity for enhanced bearing condition monitoring.

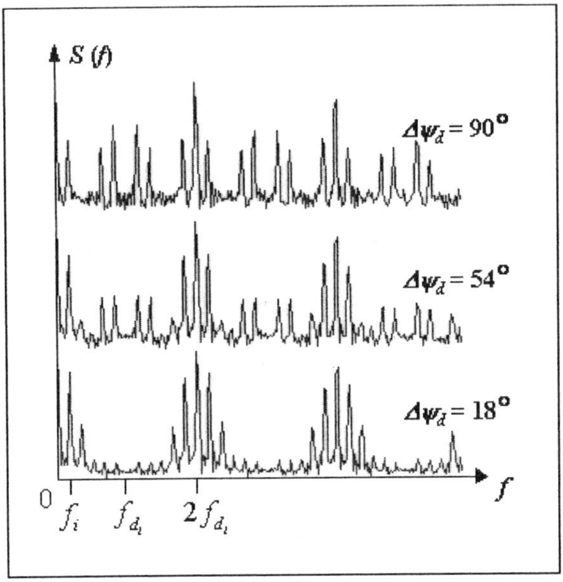

Figure 1: Signal masking in a ball bearing

8.3. Neural Networks in Manufacturing

The degree of success of an effective machine fault diagnostic and prognostic system is influenced by diverse factors: selection of the physical parameters to be monitored, the choice of sensors and their placement, and the algorithms used for data processing are just a few examples. The basic function of a diagnostic algorithm is to extract fault features and subsequently assess the nature of the fault. The latter is basically a classification problem.

The use of artificial neural networks has been motivated by the recognition of the fact that the computation methodology of the human brain is very different from a digital computer. The human brain accomplishes perceptual recognition tasks (such as recognizing a familiar face in an unfamiliar scene) with astonishing accuracy and in much less time than it would take a modern computer. The brain has a complex neuro-structure that enables it to build its own rules over a period of time, commonly referred to as "experience". It is the experience that helps the nerve system to adapt to a new environment. Neural networks are designed to model the method by which human brains accomplish a certain task. Some features of the neural networks that have led to their widespread use include:

1) Ability of generalization: a neural network can "learn" by adjusting the parameters such that certain input signals correspond to a desired response. Such a "training" process is a continuous process until no significant adjustment is required.
2) Online adaptability: a neural network trained to work in a specific environment can be retrained to account for changes in the operating conditions. Such a feature is valuable for prognosis in machine condition monitoring. Even though the initial training results may not be accurate, its performance would improve with time as more samples are provided.
3) Robustness: this refers to the fact that degradation in the performance of a neural network due to a faulty component would be minimal comparing to other techniques, because the parallel structure of the network. This intrinsic feature of neural networks is of considerable value for real-world machine condition monitoring applications.

The drive towards reliability, safety, and optimum utilization of machines by the industry has put the spotlight on early machine fault detection (diagnosis) and warning (prognosis) systems. Because of the complexity and non-linearity involved, such systems lend themselves well to the use of neural networks, benefiting from the networks' online learning and adaptive abilities. Early fault detection and warning provide “lead” time to machine operators for maintenance, parts replacement, and better production scheduling. A reliable diagnostic and prognostic system further improves the cost effectiveness of the plant by ensuring that a machine part is replaced only when it has reached the end of its utility and not before. Over the past decades, neural networks have been applied to improve process monitoring (e.g. for cooling condition monitoring in steel rolling), production optimization (e.g. temperature, pressure, and flow rate monitoring for optimized debutanization), or product quality control (e.g. feature recognition of defective products) [3].

8.3.1 Tool Wear Estimation

On-line tool wear estimation provides valuable input to better understanding of the machining process. Tool wear, and in particular flank wear, affects the surface finish of the product being machined. Flank wear is considered an effective indicator of the extent of tool wear and is defined by the height of the flank wear land (h_w). In many applications, a cutting tool may start wearing out within half an hour. Hence, a suitable estimation methodology should be able to estimate the values of the flank wear between the limiting values (e.g. up to 0.018 inches) within this time span.

A neural network estimation for flank wear has been demonstrated by [46], using a recurrent neural network. Experiments were designed for five cutting speeds and five feeds, at a constant depth of cut on a heavy-duty lathe. Three sensors were used to measure 1) cutting, feed, and thrust forces, 2) vibrations along the main and feed directions, and 3) acoustic emission of the tool. The network estimated the current flank wear using a time lagged predicted value and six other inputs as shown in Figure 2. The measured signals were transformed into the wavelet domain and three wavelet coefficients were used as part of the input vector to the network. A fresh tool edge was used for cutting during each experimental run. Signals were collected every minute and a microscope was used to measure the flank wear. The network was trained using these observed values and was tested using 150 patterns. The overall estimation error was below 0.0011 inch, which was better than the pre-defined limit of 10 % of the total range. This study showed that a simple and robust recurrent network architecture was capable of estimating continuous flank wear. Besides, it illustrated its potential in the failure and degradation estimation of other machining processes.

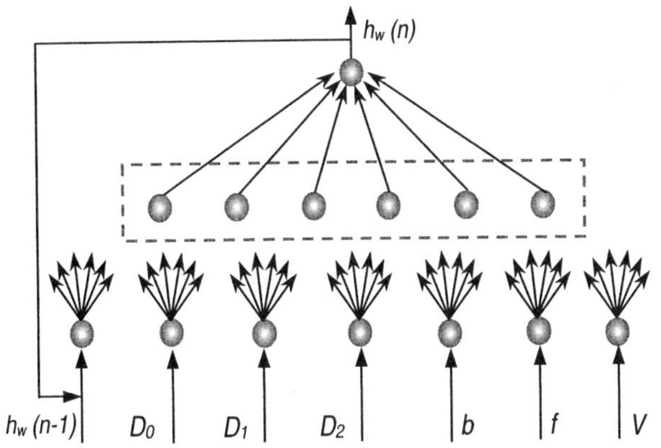

Input parameters:	
V:	cutting speed
f:	feed
b:	depth of cut
D_0:	capacity dimension
D_1:	information dimension
D_2:	relation dimension
$h_w(n-1)$:	predicted flank wear
Output:	
$h_w(n)$:	Current prediction of flank wear

Figure 2: Flank wear estimation using a neural network

8.3.2 Remaining Life Prognosis

The mere determination of the existence of a defect is not sufficient for the purpose of breakdown avoidance. Once a fault is detected, it is desirable to predict how long the machine will still be able to run, without causing catastrophic failure. Determination of the warning levels must ensure optimal maintenance scheduling. Often, the vibration levels measured are used as the basis for setting up the warning thresholds. However, the application of such general guidelines may fail as machine operating conditions depend on the specific operating environment. Furthermore, machines of identical models may not display identical behavior, and fault characteristics may differ substantially. To accommodate the influence of the varying environment on the warning threshold levels, the threshold set-up itself needs to be integrated into an adaptive scheme.

As illustrated in Figure 3(A), vibration characteristics of a bearing undergo a noticeable change at point A, after the defect initiation. It would be advantageous to estimate the remaining life of the bearing starting from this point onward. The maintenance scheduling for the machine could be based on this estimate instead of on a preset threshold value for a vibration level. Such a maintenance scheme would be preferred as it would maximize the service life of the bearing. Neural networks have been found to be suited for such applications. The use of a feed-forward neural network for machine prognosis has been demonstrated in [47]. The prediction of a parameter one time step into the future (K_t) was based on the use of values of a vibration parameter from the past time steps, which served as input to the network (K_{t-1}, K_{t-2},..., K_{t-n}), as shown in Figure 3(B). For predicting a discrete number of time steps in the future, the time-lagged values of the predictions were used as input parameters. Hence, the values for K_{t-1}, K_{t-2}..., K_{t-n} were predicted values for the output but time lagged by the appropriate number of unit delay parameter D. Investigations of remaining life prognosis using a recurrent neural network have also been reported, where the advantage of such a network over other prognosis schemes was illustrated [44].

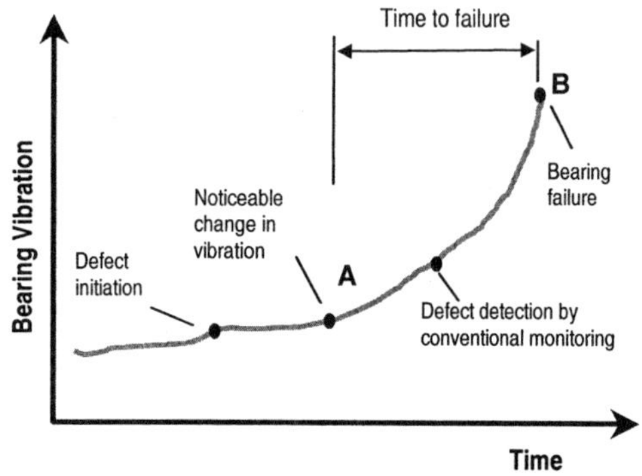

a) Illustration of time to failure

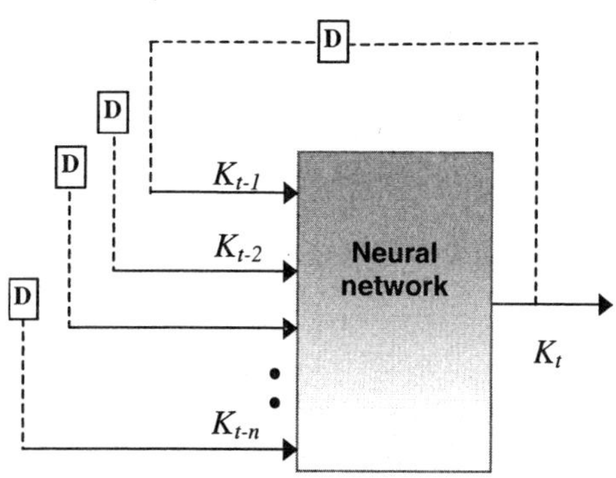

b) A neural network with time-lagged feedback

Figure 3: Prognosis of bearing remaining life using a neural network

8.3.3 Tool Monitoring

Multiple sensors have been used for tool conditioning monitoring where the measurement of different parameters was required for the evaluation of tool condition [3]. The challenge in a multiple sensor system is the reduction of data flow from numerous sensors to extract reliable features for network learning and decision-making. Studies on the feature selection for a neural network for multi-spindle drilling operations have been presented in [48-49]. The objective was to identify wear and failure of individual drills out of an ensemble of ten drills. The measurement vector (input data) consisted of outputs from the spindle and feed motor current sensors, vibration sensors, and AE sensors at pre-determined positions. The neural network was found to be better suited than statistical analysis and genetic algorithms for the drill wear monitoring task.

In another application of neural networks using multiple system inputs, the learning abilities of a back propagation network for turning operations were studied [50]. The input variables included feed rate, cutting depth and cutting speed and their effect on the output variables (cutting force, power, temperature and surface finish) was studied. The network was used to estimate the material removal rate subject to the operating conditions. A feed forward network was used for the purpose, and it was shown that the network could effectively learn with the desired level of accuracy. An "incremental" scheme, as illustrated in Figure 4, was studied in which the network learned and synthesized simultaneously. For the three inputs, corresponding output values measured by sensors are fed to train the network. The weights of the network were then adjusted and the network was considered partially trained. Subsequently, the system predicts an optimal input condition based on the constraints or performance indices. This "incremental" learning was continued until the predicted input has reached a level such that the error between the output recorded by the sensors and the outputs of the neural networks was within the predetermined limits.

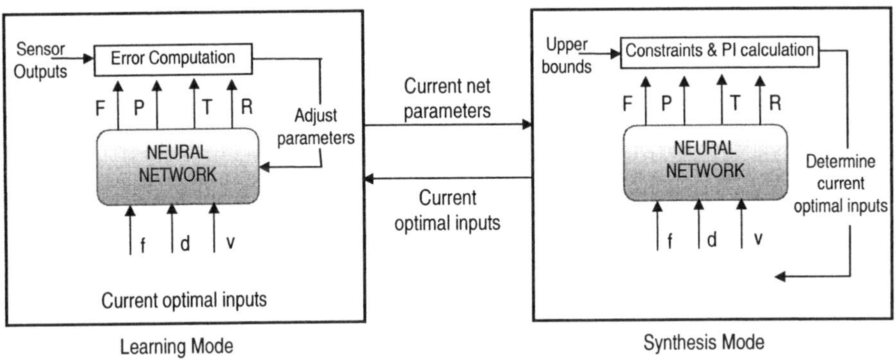

Figure 4: Incremental scheme applied in a neural network for tool condition monitoring

8.4. Neural Networks for Bearing Fault Diagnosis

Researchers in the past have identified various parameters in both the time and frequency domains, which can be used for the condition monitoring of rolling element bearings. These parameters can also be used as input to a neural network to diagnose faults and predict the future working condition of the bearing. In the work conducted in [51-52], it was proposed that the neural network be trained such that the output of the network provides an indicator of the severity of the defect. This output can then be used in conjunction with a prognosis model to predict the remaining life of a bearing.

A mechanical test bed was designed and manufactured to conduct bearing experiments. The experimental results provided input to the design and configuration of a suitable neural network, which was then used to provide an accurate description of the bearing condition in an on-line fashion. A hydraulic system was used to apply loads to the test bearing. A photographic view of the bearing test bed is given in Figure 5.

A miniaturized piezo-sensor was placed in the load zone of the bearing, which is characterized by:

$$q(\psi) = \begin{cases} q_{\max}\left[1 - \frac{1}{2\varepsilon}(1-\cos\psi)\right]^n, for -\psi_l > \psi > \psi_l \\ 0, elsewhere \end{cases} \quad (2)$$

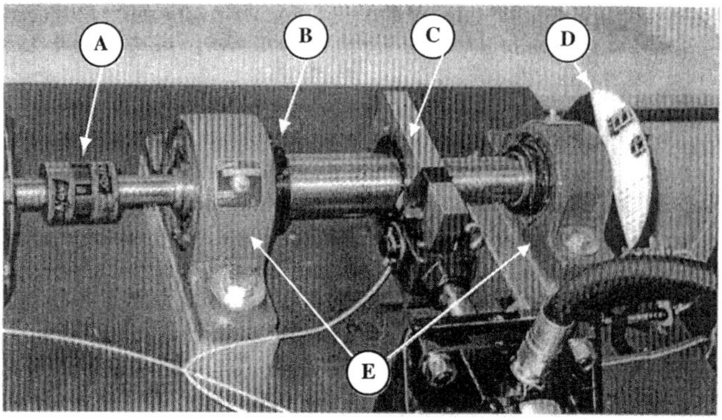

A: Flexible coupling
B: Eccentric ring
C: Test bearing housing
D: Speed measurement
E: Support bearings

Figure 5: A bearing test bed

where $q_{\max}$ represents the maximum load, n is dependent on the type of bearings involved, ψ is the angle of contact, and ε is the load distribution factor [43]. To simulate defect growth in the bearing, holes of different sizes were drilled on the bearing races, with the smallest hole being 0.34 mm in diameter. The experiments were conducted by measuring vibration signals from the bearing and correlating the results of the spectral analysis to the specific bearing speed (rpm) and loads, for each hole size (defect). To validate the reproducibility of the data analysis, each data point was sampled three times. The bearing speed was varied from 300 rpm to 900 rpm. The upper limit of the load applied to the bearing was determined from the design specification sheet, which 300 psi when converted to the setting on the hydraulic system.

8.4.1 Network Input Feature Construction

In order to reliably diagnose faults in a bearing, it is critical to select feature(s) that can quantitatively describe the condition of the bearing vibrations, and use these features as inputs to the diagnosing neural network. Since diagnosis essentially involves pattern recognition, the goal of the neural network is to recognize the pattern of the relevant fault features. Realistically, the presence of noise in the vibration spectrum and the fact that a feature may represent a multitude of failure criteria complicates the problem. Furthermore, the number of features to be used as the input to the neural network also affects the final performance: too many input features will result in high computational load and slow response, whereas too few features may not provide an accurate representation of the defect. Ultimately, parameters that do not contribute to the diagnosis of faults should be rejected.

An algorithm has been proposed in [33] to extract an optimal parameter (feature) set from a candidate set. The two main criteria used for determining if a parameter should be included in the set or not are the *sensitivity* and *consistency* of the parameter. The sensitivity S_{ij} of a parameter is used to evaluate its classificatory ability (or contribution to the optimal set of features), and is defined as:

$$S_{ij} = \left| \frac{\partial y_i}{\partial x_i} \right| \tag{3}$$

where x_i represents the parameter, y_i the condition of the machinery being monitored (e.g. the "health" of a bearing), and j refers to the signal pattern. Using the classificatory result, the output set of a back propagation network was trained by a learning algorithm. Feature selection was viewed as a special case of feature extraction, where the mapping between the feature parameter x and the classificatory result y was considered to be a linear mapping.

For the study conducted in [51], all the parameters used for the bearing vibration analysis were considered likely candidates for the feature set to a neural network. The parameters considered in the time domain included average amplitude values, Root Mean Square values, velocity, displacement, skew, kurtosis, and crest factor. The parameters considered in the frequency domain included Ball Spin Frequency (BSF), Ball Pass Frequency in Outer Race (BPFO), Ball Pass Frequency in Inner Race (BPFI), and the energy dissipated in the bearing, which is given by the area under the spectral curves. The reason to consider all these parameters as likely candidates for the feature sets was to identify the best suited parameters in a systematic and comprehensive way.

In another study, four vibration signals were identified and considered for the input feature construction of a neural network [52]. These include: 1) vibration due to outer-raceway defects with the frequency f_{BPFO}, 2) vibration due to inner raceway defects of frequency f_{BPFI}, 3) vibration due to ball rotation along the raceway, with the basic frequency of f_{BPFO}, and 4) vibration due to misalignment and/or unbalance with the frequencies of $2f_r$ and f_r, respectively (with f_r being the shaft speed). To enhance the feature extraction ability of the system for incipient defects, a combined wavelet and Fourier analysis were used to extract the features of defect vibrations. The four features constructed for the neural network included:

x_1: RMS of the first four harmonic peaks of the outer-raceway defect vibration, extracted from a combined wavelet-Fourier analysis:

$$x_1 = \frac{\sqrt{\sum_{i=1}^{4} P(f_{iBPFO})^2 / 4}}{\sqrt{\frac{1}{5f_{BPFO}} \int_0^{5f_{BPFO}} P(f)^2 df}} \tag{4}$$

x_2: RMS of the first four harmonic peaks of the inner-raceway defect signal, extracted from a combined wavelet-Fourier analysis:

$$x_2 = \frac{\sqrt{\sum_{i=1}^{4} P(f_{iBPFI})^2 / 4}}{\sqrt{\frac{1}{5f_{BPFI}} \int_0^{5f_{BPFI}} P(f)^2 df}} \tag{5}$$

x_3: RMS of the two peaks of unbalance vibration ($F(f_u)$) and misalignment vibration ($F(f_m)$) in the spectrum ($F(f)$) of Fourier analysis:

$$x_3 = \sqrt{\frac{F(f_u)^2 + F(f_m)^2}{2}} \tag{6}$$

x_4: RMS of the four harmonic peaks in the spectrum ($F(f_{iBPFO})$, i=1~4) of Fourier analysis:

$$x_4 = \sqrt{\frac{\sum_{i=1}^{4} F(f_{iBPFO})^2}{4}} \tag{7}$$

8.4.2 Network Configuration and Implementation

Different types of neural networks have been used for bearing fault diagnosis, e.g. self-organizing maps [53], adaptive resonance theory networks [54], Bayesian networks [55] and back propagation network [56-57]. To evaluate the performance of a neural network for fault diagnosis, a combination of various parameters needs to be considered. These include the activation functions and a suitable learning rate. For the experiment conducted in [51], a feed forward network was used, as the analysis was based on a given defect size. The severity of the defect was the output of the neural network. In this study, networks of different configurations (different input and hidden layer sizes) were trained with the data set produced by the experiments. The objective was to arrive at a combination of input parameters for a neural network of certain size that can estimate the defect severity with the least error.

Complexity can be built into a neural network by adding hidden layers between the input and output layers. Such hidden layers help in modeling the non-linear behavior of the system. However, adding hidden layers also increases the computational load for the network. The size of the neural network should be carefully chosen so that it is large enough to absorb all the information and yet small enough so that it can be easily trained.

In a comparison study between three different auto-regressive modeling techniques [29], a back propagation neural network was found to be the most appropriate. The other two models that were compared were the Box-Jenkins models and non-linear radial basis models. In these techniques, the model provided a prediction of a vibration signal parameter based on the regression of its previous values. A general auto-regressive function has the form:

$$\hat{y}(t) = f(y(t-1), y(t-2), ..., y(t-n)) \tag{8}$$

Hence, previous outputs are used to calculate the present vibration signal parameter by means of regression. The error was defined as the difference between the actual and the predicted value:

$$e(t) = y(t) - \hat{y}(t) \tag{9}$$

An auto-regressive predictor exists for each class of faults to be recognized. These model sets are grouped together to observe the vibration signal of the bearing tested. Each model set predicts the current vibration level based on the history. The objective of the model was to minimize the error. The signal-to-noise ratio is used as an averaging process to quantify and compare the three models that are investigated. The aim was the robust recognition of the faults by the minimization of prediction errors using the least-squares algorithm.

Neural networks have also been used in conjunction with wavelet transforms [28], although the analysis was done for a simple combination of defects only. In essence, the wavelet transform is similar to a localized (or Windowed) Fourier transform except that the transform is conducted in the time-scale domain instead in the frequency domain. Various families of wavelets exist, which are specified by their coefficients. A time-signal $x(t)$ can be decomposed into a summation of wavelets. This transformed signal can then be used as a preprocessor to a neural network, which is then trained to identify defects in a bearing. The reported study has shown that the convergence of the network output was faster than using other techniques.

The study in [51] has utilized a wide range of possible combinations for the architecture design of a neural network. Recent advances in computing power have made the calculations for such a large number of combinations possible. The process of selecting the best network architecture was started with one hidden layer, and the best ten input node combinations were isolated.

8.4.2.1 *Bearing Defect Severity*

To identify the defect in a bearing with a quantifier, a neural network was trained in [52] to output a numerical value for bearing defect. This value can be then used by a prognosis model to predict the remaining life of the bearing. It was assumed that the progression of the defect severity in a bearing follows an exponential function (Figure 6), before reaching a predetermined limit. The defect severity was related to the critical defect size, which was used as the normalization basis to characterize the present defect severity.

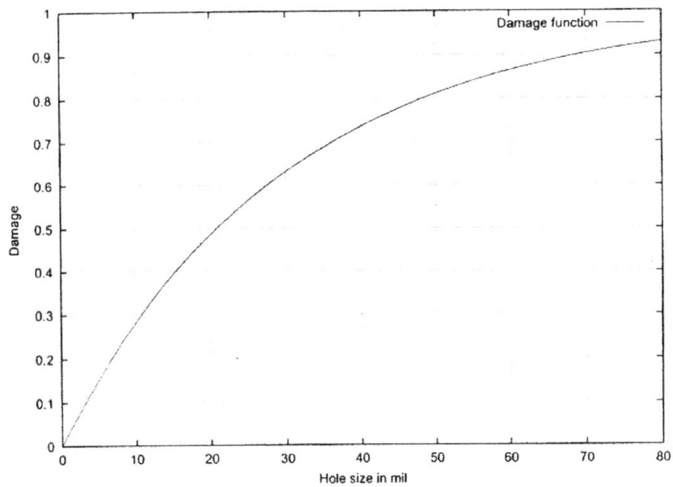

Figure 6: Bearing defect severity progression

Using this approach the neural network was trained with initial conditions, and the output was the defect severity given by:

$$d_i = 1 - e^{-\delta_i / A_{OP}} \tag{10}$$

where δ_i is the defect diameter and A_{OP} is the critical defect diameter. When $\delta_i = A_{OP}$, the defect severity d could be calculated to be 0.63, which was used as the alarm threshold. For a value of $d < 0.63$, the operation of the bearing was classified as "safe". A danger threshold was defined for $\delta_i = 2A_{OP}$, which gives a defect severity of 0.86. The bearing condition was classified as "danger" for values of d between 0.63 and 0.86. If the value is greater than this, the bearing is said to have "failed". For multiple defects, the individual indices were multiplied and the overall defect severity of the bearing was quantified by:

$$d_i = 1 - (1 - d_1)(1 - d_2).......(1 - d_k) \tag{11}$$

where $d_1, d_2, ..., d_k$ are the individual defect severity pertaining to each defect. The health index of the bearing was then defined as:

$$h = 1 - d \tag{12}$$

8.4.2.2 *Bearing Condition Assessment*

In the work conducted in [51], a one-hidden-layer network was analyzed. Twelve parameters were considered as inputs to the neural network for the experiment. A software code was written which allowed the variation of number of nodes in the hidden layer from one to seven. This resulted in 28,665 combinations to be analyzed. Out of the total number of combinations, the objective was to determine the best combination, which gave the least error. The network was trained using the back-propagation algorithm. The number of epochs was set to 2000 because no changes in the mean squared error were seen after this value.

The study concluded that the parameter "energy" was present in all of the "best" performing networks. The 'best' networks were chosen with respect to the least mean squared error for the overall network, as shown in Table 1. The entries in the first column represent the number of input nodes followed by the number of hidden and output nodes. The error was seen to be the least for 40 hidden nodes. The error increased irrespective of whether the number of nodes are increased or decreased from this value.

Table 1: Best performing networks

Nodes	Parameters					Mean Square Error ($x10^{-3}$)
5-30-1	Energy	BPFO	BPFI	BPFO2	BPFI2	2.2
5-35-1	Energy	BPFO	BPFI	BPFO3	BPFI3	2.2
5-40-1	Energy	BPFO	BPFI	BPFO4	BPFI4	2.1

Energy was found to be a feature in over 90 % of the top 500 combinations, followed by the BPFI and BPFO as the second most important factors. In addition, the first harmonics for the ball passing frequency for both inner (BPFI2) and outer raceways (BPFO2), and kurtosis were found to play a major role. The best network without the energy parameter consisted of crest factor, BPFO and BPFO2. It had an error of $2.5x10^{-3}$, which was 14% higher than the error for the best network. The occurrence of the BPFO factor can be explained by the fact that the defect was on the outer raceway initially. Examining the occurrence of parameters in the top 100 combinations, it was found that RMS value, RPM, load and crest factor were not very effective in identifying bearing defects (Table 2).

Table 2: Parameter occurrence in top 100 combinations

Parameter	Occurrence (%)
Energy	99
BPFO	84
BPFI	81
BPFI2	57
Kurtosis	56
BPFO2	55
Max. Speed	55
Max. Displacement	54
Crest factor	2
RPM	0
RMS value	0
Load	0

The occurrence of crest factor appeared to be random. Based on the occurrence of these parameters in the best combinations, a revised combination could be chosen so that the total numbers of parameters used would be much less and only the relevant parameters are emphasized for better quality results.

No single neural network based on one unique set of operating parameters was found to be completely successful in diagnosing faults in the test bearing under all operating conditions. To solve this problem, the entire operating spectrum was divided into sixteen regions, each of which containing a specific combination of load and speed values at which experiments were conducted. Subsequently, sixteen different neural networks were designed and applied to these regions. This approach enables a more adaptive, condition-specific solution to be provided to the system being monitored. The division of the adaptive areas and the use of separate neural networks to form a layered analysis structure are illustrated in Figure 7.

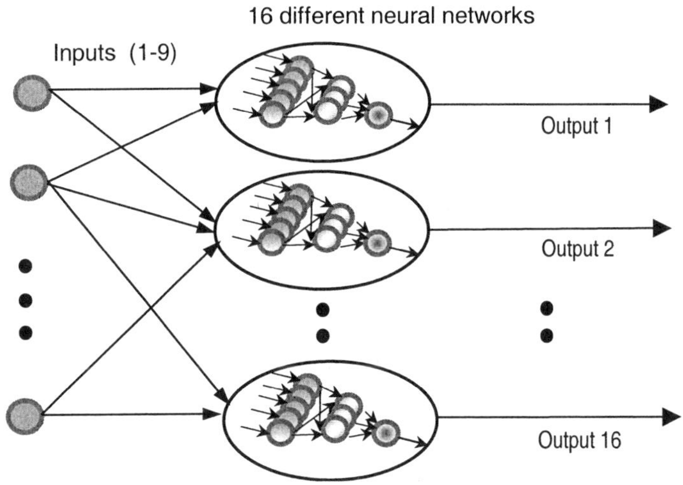

Figure 7: Layered analysis using multiple neural networks

The division of the operation spectrum into sixteen regions is shown in Figure 8. Analysis was made for each region, using all the parameters available as described in the previous section. Then the nine most often occurring input parameters were analyzed for the least error. The gray shaded pattern in Figure 8 denotes the importance of the respective parameters, with dark gray areas illustrating the "best" solution provided by the parameter for the specified region, and the light gray areas showing their performance as the "second best" solution.

The pattern revealed the relative importance of various parameters under different operating conditions. For example, both BPFI and BPFO appear to be essential parameters for high bearing speeds. This can be explained by the high energy content of the signals involved at high speeds that makes these two parameters distinctive. The pattern also confirmed previous analysis using one neural network that energy is a critical parameter for most of the operation conditions. The crest factor and kurtosis have shown effective coverage for relatively low operation speeds, and the speed and displacement appeared to be good indicators under higher load conditions.

To better understand the importance trend, research is being conducted to evaluate the combined effect of multiple parameters simultaneously for each region. Furthermore, a "cluster" analysis will be performed on larger regions consisting of the present individual regions.

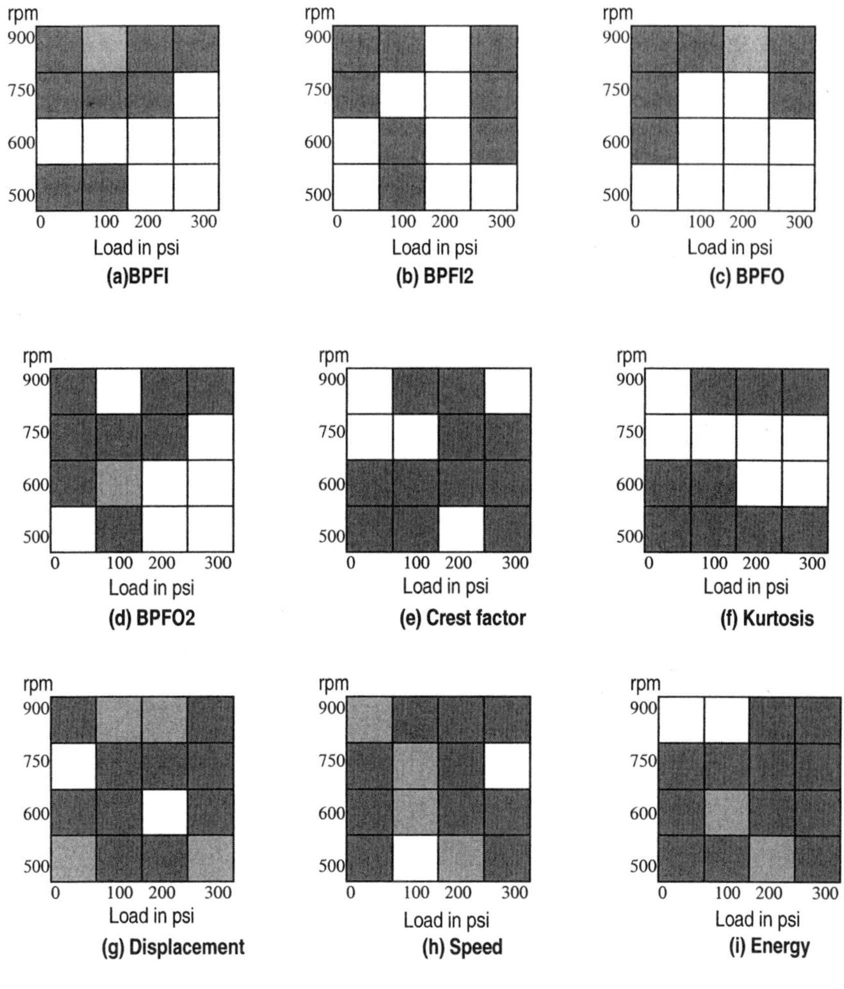

Figure 8: Importance of various parameters as input to a bearing-monitoring neural network

In the work reported in [51], two separate neural networks were built to evaluate two different types of defects on the inner and outer raceways. The architecture of the network was determined based on experimentation using various combinations of hidden layer nodes. Two sets of input features $\{x_1, x_2, x_3, x_4\}$ were obtained for the defects, using the Eqs. (4) - (7). The defect severity output information for these two networks was multiplied to give the overall health of the bearing as shown in Figure 9.

A total of 960 feature vectors were constructed from the outer and inner raceway analysis. Three bearings with a point defect in the form of a 0.25 mm and 3 mm hole in the inner or outer raceway or a combination of both were tested. Two thirds of the feature vectors were used as training data and the rest for checking purpose. For the inner raceway defect evaluation, the error converged to 0.013 after 2,267 epochs (Figure 10). To test the performance of the network, the checking data was used to classify the input data from the bearing faults under different load, speed and temperature conditions. It was observed that the error in the defect severity of the network was within 0.1 (Figure 11). With an error limit of 0.15/2 for classification, it was concluded that the network has achieved a success rate of 99%.

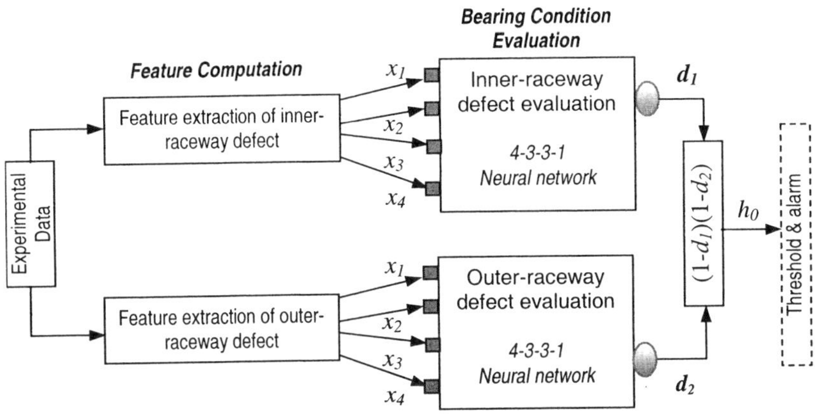

Figure 9: Bearing health evaluation using neural network

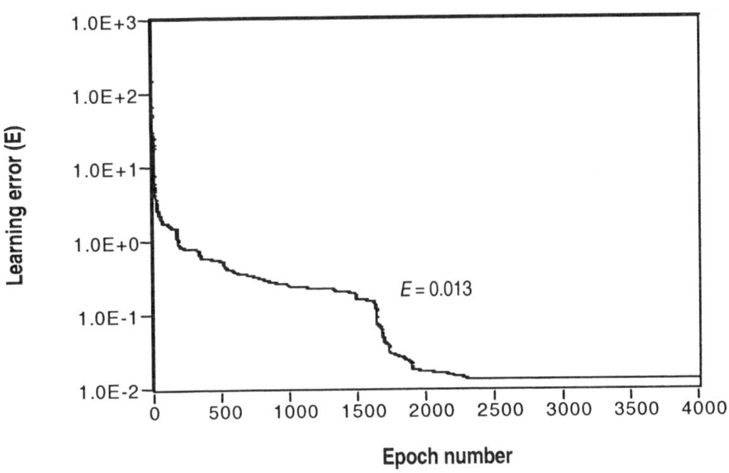

Figure 10: Learning error curve for inner raceway defect

8.4.3 Bearing Life Prediction

Generally, bearing life prediction is based on analyzing the trends of related parameters with time to predict the future state of the bearing condition. These trends are generally non-linear in nature, making prognosis a difficult task. Studies to monitor defect propagation have not been entirely conclusive. For example, the progression rate of a spall can be better determined if the surface texture is exactly known, which however is not given in most cases [58]. A mathematical model has been developed in [51], whose output represents the defect size. This was subsequently used as an input to a prognosis model, which predict the crack growth rate as:

$$\frac{da}{dN} = C_0 (\Delta K)^n \quad (13)$$

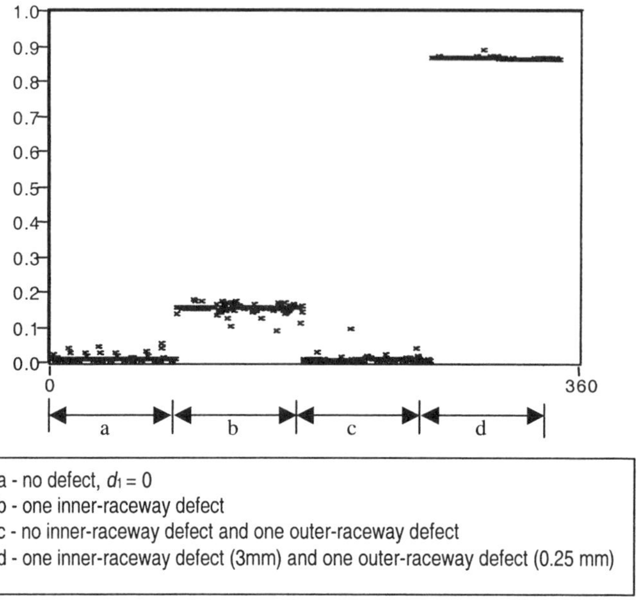

Figure 11: Checking data result for the trained neural network

where a is the crack length, N is the number of cycles, C_0 is a material constant and ΔK is the stress intensity factor. Assuming that the stress constant remains unchanged for the life of the bearing, the constants C_0 and n can be determined based on the experimental data points, and subsequently, the formula can be used to predict the crack growth. Based on the growth rate found, a neural network was used to determine the time constant for the prognosis model by analyzing how the size of a defect has grown in time.

The remaining life of a bearing is defined as the number of cycles or hours at which the bearing runs under a certain combination of speed and load, before failure is initiated. In reality, the remaining life of a bearing depends is influenced by other conditions such as the assembly, temperature, quality of lubrication, etc. To account for the various scenarios, different bearing life models have been proposed [47] that describe the relationship between the bearing condition and these parameters as a linear, exponential, or polynomial functions. The four curves in Figure 12 represent such functions, with $\psi(t)$ representing the rate of bearing deterioration with respect to time t.

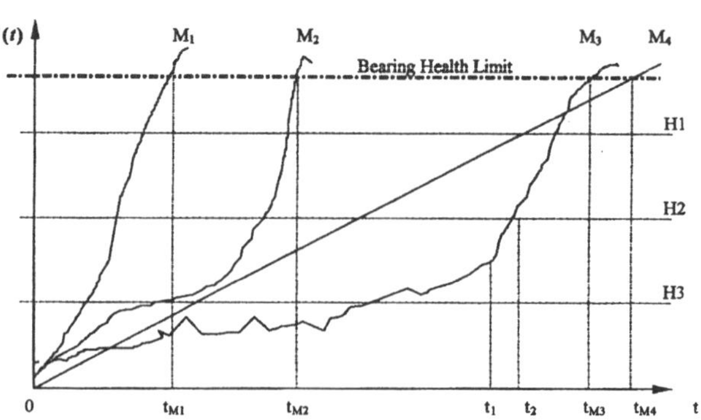

Figure 12: Simulated trend of bearing deterioration

The input vector to a neural network $\overline{X} = [x_1, x_2, ..., x_n]$ may contain measurement data from various physical sensors, e.g. load, temperature, displacement, or acoustic emission. In the vector, n is the number of variables, which is equal to the number of input neurons in the network. To avoid large pivots in the neural network calculations, the constituent elements of the input vector can be normalized such that $x_i \in [0,1]$. If a back-propagation neural network with one hidden layer is used, the output function of the neural network can be written as:

$$\hat{\phi}_{it} = f(\phi_{it-1}, \phi_{it-2}, ..., \phi_{it-p}) \tag{14}$$

where $\hat{\phi}_{it}$ is the predicted output function at time t for the variable x_i, and $\phi_{it-1}, \phi_{it-2}, ...\phi_{it-p}$ are the values for the variable x_i measured from time steps *(t-1)* to *(t-p)* respectively:

$$\hat{\phi}_{it} = \sum_{n=1}^{N} w'_n f\left(\sum_{j=1}^{p} w_{nj}\phi_{it=j} + b_m\right) \tag{15}$$

Here, the weights of the interconnections between the input layer and the hidden layer (w_{nj}) and those between the hidden layer and the output layer (w'_n) are fixed, before the neural network is trained using the experimental data $\hat{\phi}_i = (\phi_{i1}, \phi_{i2}, ..., \phi_{iN})$. Once the training is completed, the neural network is subjected to data gathered from the time steps *(t-1)* to *(t-p)*, in order to obtain the failure trend for the particular bearing being monitored.

Given that the crack propagation may not be fully described by a idealized crack geometry and size, and realistic crack parameters would only be available when measured on a disassembled bearing, it was suggested that an adaptive prognostic scheme be used [59-60]. The resulting prediction was then compared with the actual condition of the bearings being monitored, and recursive iteration was implemented to improve the model performance. Through time-domain integration, the defect size can be expressed as:

$$\ln D = \alpha + \beta(t + t_0) \tag{16}$$

where t_o is the time when the smallest defect area *(D_o)* occurs, α and β are constants depending on the material. These parameters were first estimated, given the fact that they may vary with the progression of damage. A recursive least squares algorithm was used to update their values, based on the vibration and acoustic emission measurements conducted on a defective bearing. The resulting defect propagation model was then coupled with the defect diagnostic model to adaptively predict the remaining life of the bearing.

8.5. Conclusions

Extensive research over the past decade has turned neural networks into an indispensable tool for solving a wide range of problems in both scientific labs and on the factory floor. In the specific areas of machine condition monitoring, fault diagnosis, and remaining service life prognosis, neural networks will play an increasingly important role, and its ability will be continually enhanced through other innovative and complimentary technologies. Research is continuing in the author's group, with the ultimate goal to develop effective and efficient bearing condition monitoring and diagnostic techniques that can be applied to solving real-world problems.

Acknowledgment

Research described in this paper was sponsored by the US National Science Foundation under CAREER award #DMI-9624353. Support from the SKF corporation is appreciated. The author is grateful to the valuable contribution and assistance from his former and present graduate students Dr. C. Wang, Dr. B. Holm-Hansen, M. Kaczorowski, and A. Malhi.

References

[1] G. Byrne, D. Dornfeld, I. Inasaki, G. Ketteler, W. Konig and R. Teti, "Tool conditioning monitoring-The status of research and industrial application", *Annals of the CIRP*, Vol. 44, No. 2, pp. 541-567, 1995.

[2] K. Ng, "Overview of machine diagnostics and prognostics", *Symposium on Quantitative Nondestructive Evaluation, ASME IMECE Conference*, Dallas TX, November, 1997.

[3] P. Keller, R. Kouzes and L. Kangas, "Neural network based sensor systems for manufacturing applications", *Advanced Information Systems and Technology Conference*, Williamsburg, VA, PNL-SA-23252, 28-30 March, 1994.

[4] S. Billington, Y. Li, T. Kurfress, S. Liang and S. Danyluk "Roller bearing defect detection with multiple sensors", *Proceedings of the 1997 ASME International Mechanical Engineering Congress and Exposition –Tribology Division,* Vol. 7, pp. 31-36, 1997.

[5] P. Tse and D. Wang, "A hybrid neural network based machine condition forecaster and classifier by using multiple vibration parameters", *IEEE International Congress on Neural Networks*, Vol. 4, pp. 2096-2100, 1996.

[6] J. Kline and J. Bilodeau, "Acoustic wayside identification of freight car roller bearing defects", *Proc. of ASME/IEEE Joint Railroad Conference*, Vol. 6, pp. 79-81, 1998.

[7] S. Braun and B. Datner, "Analysis of roller/ball bearing vibrations", *ASME Journal of Mechanical Design*, Vol. 101, pp. 118-124, 1979.

[8] D. Dyer and R. Stewart, "Detection of rolling element bearing damage by statistical vibration analysis", *ASME Journal of Mechanical Design,* Vol. 100, pp. 229-235, 1978.

[9] J. Breggren, "Diagnosing faults in rolling element bearings: Part 1", *Vibrations*, Vol.4, No. 1, pp. 5-13, 1988.

[10] T. Igarashi and S. Yabe, "Studies on the vibration and sound of defective rolling bearings", *Bulletin of JSME*, Vol. 26, No. 220, pp. 1791-1798, 1983.

[11] N. Tandon and B. Nakra, "Defect detection in rolling element bearings by acoustic emission method", *Journal of Acoustic Emission*, Vol. 9, No. 1, pp. 25-28, 1990.

[12] C. Tan, "Application of acoustic emission to the detection of bearing failures", *Proc. of the Engineers of Australia Tribology Conference*, Brisbane, pp. 110-114, Dec. 3-5 1990.

[13] K. Mori, N. Kasashima, T. Yoshioka and Y. Ueno, "Prediction of spalling on a ball bearing by applying the discrete wavelet transform to vibration signals", *Wear*, Vol. 195. No. 1-2, pp. 162-168, 1996.

[14] A. Gibson and L. Stein, "Reduced order finite element modeling of thermally induced bearing loads in machine tool spindles", *Proc. of ASME*, DSC Vol. 67, pp. 845-852, 1999.

[15] K. Goddard and B. MacIsaac, "Use of oil borne debris as a failure criterion for rolling element bearings", *Lubrication Engineering*, Vol. 51, No. 6, pp. 481-487, 1995.

[16] T. Moriwaki, Presentation at working group meeting, *Proc. of First Workshop on Tool Condition Monitoring-CIRP,* Paris, January 1993.

[17] B. Holm-Hansen and R. Gao, "Vibration analysis of a sensor-integrated ball bearing", *ASME Journal of Vibration and Acoustics*, Vol. 122, pp. 384-392, 2000.

[18] R. Gao and P. Phalakshan, "Design consideration for a sensor integrated roller bearing", *Proc. ASME International Mechanical Engineering Conference and Exposition, Symposium on Rail Transportation*, RTD-Vol. 10, pp.81-86, 1995.

[19] B. Holm-Hansen and R. Gao, "Smart bearing utilizing embedded sensors: design considerations", *Proc. SPIE 4th International Symposium on Smart Structures and Materials,* Paper No. 3041-51, San Diego, CA, pp. 602-610, 1997.

[20] C. Wang and R. Gao, "Sensor module for integrated bearing condition monitoring", *Proc. ASME – Dynamics Systems and Control Division*, Vol. 67, pp. 721-728, 1999.

[21] N. Tandon, "A comparison of some vibration parameters for the condition monitoring of rolling element bearings", *Journal of the International Measurement Confederation*, Vol. 12, No. 3, pp. 285-289, 1994.

[22] R. Heng and M. Nor, "Statistical analysis of sound and vibration signals for monitoring rolling element bearing condition", *Applied Acoustics*, Vol. 53, No. 1-3, pp. 211-226, 1998.

[23] W. Staszewski and G. Tomlinson, "Application of the moving window procedure in spur gear", *COMEDEM-93*, Bristol, England, July 21-23, 1993.
[24] R. Randall, "Cepstrum analysis and gearbox fault diagnosis", *Bruel and Kjaer Application Note*, pp. 233-280, 1982.
[25] P. McFadden and W. Wang, "Time frequency domain analysis of vibration signals for machinery diagnostics: introduction to Wigner-Ville distribution", *Technical Report, Department of Engineering Science, Oxford University*, Report No. OUEL 1859/90, 1990.
[26] P. McFadden, "Application of wavelet transform to early detection of gear failure by vibration analysis", *Proc. International Conference of Condition Monitoring*, University College of Swansea, Wales, 1994.
[27] I. Alguindigue, A. Loskiewicz-Buczak and R. Uhrig, "Monitoring and diagnosis of rolling element bearings using artificial neural networks", *IEEE Transactions on Industrial Electronics*, April, Vol. 40, No. 2, pp. 209-217, 1993.
[28] B. Paya, M. Badi and I. Esat, "Artificial neural network based fault diagnostics of rotating machinery using wavelet transforms as a preprocessor", *Mechanical Systems and Signal Processing*, Vol. 11 (5), pp. 751-765, 1997.
[29] D. Baillie and J. Mathew, "A comparison of autoregressive modeling techniques for fault diagnosis of rolling element bearings", *Mechanical Systems and Signal Processing*, Vol. 10, pp. 1-17, 1996.
[30] J. Shiroishi, Y. Li, S. Liang, T. Kurfess and S. Danyluk, "Bearing condition diagnostics via vibration and acoustics emission measurements", *Mechanical Systems and Signal Processing*, 11(5), pp. 693-705, 1997.
[31] G. Krell, A. Herzog and B. Michaelis, "An artificial neural network for real time image restoration", *Proc. IEEE Instrumentation and Measurement Technology Conference* IMTC'96, Brussels, Belgium, pp. 833-838, 1996.
[32] K. Van Laerhoven, K. Aidoo and S. Lowette, "Real-time analysis of data from many sensors with neural networks", *Proc. of the 4th International Symposium on Wearable Computers*, ISWC, Zurich, Switzerland, IEEE Press, 2001.
[33] Y. Shao, K. Nezu, K. Chen and X. Pu, "Feature extraction of machinery diagnosis using neural networks", *IEEE International Congress on Neural Networks*, Vol. 1, pp. 459-464, 1995.
[34] C. Bunks and D. McCarthy, "Conditon-based maintenance of machines using hidden markov models", *Mechanical Systems and Signal Processing*, Vol. 14(4), pp. 597-612, 2000.
[35] T. Tallian, "A data fitted bearing life prediction model", *Tribology Transactions,* Volume 39, pp. 249-258, 1996.
[36] P. Eschmann, L. Hasbargen and K. Weigand, "Ball and roller bearings: their theory, design and application", *K. G. Heyden and Co. Ltd.*, London, 1958.
[37] M. Hartnett, "Analysis of contact stresses in rolling element bearings", *ASME Journal of Lubrication Technology*, Vol. 101, No. 1, pp. 105-109, 1979.
[38] A. Duquette, "FAA orders inspections of GE90 engines installed on Boeing 777 aircraft", *FAA News*, APA 63-97, 1997.
[39] A. Duquette, "FAA/Industry to improve engine inspections", *FAA Press release*, APA 63-97, 1997.
[40] R. Schoen, T. Habetler, F. Kamran and R. Bartheld, "Motor bearing damage detection using stator current monitoring", *IEEE Transactions on Industry Applications*, Vol. 31, No. 6, pp. 1274-1279, 1995.
[41] J. Berry, "How to track rolling element bearing health with vibration signature analysis", *Sound and Vibration*, Vol. 25, No. 11, pp. 24-35, 1991.
[42] A. Barkov and N. Barkova, "Condition assessment and life prediction of rolling element bearings", *Sound and Vibration,* www.vibrotek.com/articles/sv95/part1/index.htm, June and September, 1995.
[43] T. Harris, "Rolling bearing analysis", 3rd. Ed., Wiley, New York, 1991.
[44] P. Tse and D. Atherton, "Prediction of machine deterioration using vibration based fault trends and recurrent neural networks", *Journal of Vibration and Acoustics,* Vol. 121, pp. 355-362, 1999.
[45] B. Holm-Hansen, "Development of a self-diagnostic rolling element bearing", *PhD Dissertation,* University of Massachusetts, Amherst, MA, September, 1999.
[46] S. Bukkapatnam, S. Kumara and A. Lakhtakia, "Fractal estimation of flank wear in turning", *ASME Journal of Dynamic Systems, Measurement and Control,* Vol. 122, pp. 89-94, 2000.
[47] Y. Shao and K. Nezu, "Prognosis of remaining bearing life using neural networks", *Proceedings of Institution of Mechanical Engineer – Journal of Systems and Control Engineering,* Vol. 214 (3), pp.217-230, 2000.
[48] A. Sokolowski, M. Rehse and D. Dornfeld, "Feature selection in tool wear monitoring using fuzzy logic and genetic algorithms", *LMA Research Reports*, University of California at Berkeley, pp. 91-97, 1993.
[49] M. Rehse, "In process tool wear monitoring of multi spindle drilling using multi sensor system", *Diplomarbeit, LMA/University of California at Berkeley and WZL/RWTH Aachen*, 1993.

[50] S. Rangwala and D. Dornfeld, “”Learning and optimization of machining operations using computing abilities of neural networks”, *IEEE Transactions Systems, Man and Cybernetics*, Vol. 19, No. 2, pp. 299-314, 1989.
[51] M. Kaczorowski, “A neural network approach for ball bearing life prognosis”, *Project Report, Mechanical and Industrial Engineering Department*, University of Massachusetts, May, 2001.
[52] C. Wang, “Embedded Sensing for Online Bearing Condition Monitoring and Diagnosis”, *PhD Dissertation*, University of Massachusetts, Amherst, MA, May, 2001.
[53] S. Zhang, R. Ganesan, and G. Xistris, “Self-organizing neural networks for automated machinery monitoring systems”, *Mechanical Systems and Signal Processing*, Vol. 10(5), pp. 517-532, 1996.
[54] N. Roehl, C. Pedreira, and H. Teles de Azevedo, “Fuzzy ART neural network approach for incipient fault detection and isolation in rotating machines”, *IEEE International Conference on Neural Networks*, Vol. 1, pp. 538-542, 1995.
[55] G. Betta and A. Pietrosanto, “Instrument fault detection and isolation: State of the art and new research trends”, *IEEE Transactions on Instrumentation and Measurement*, Vol. 49, No. 1, pp. 100-106, 2000.
[56] C. Rodriguez, S. Rementeria, J. Martin, A. Lafuente, J. Muguerza and J. Perez, “A modular neural network approach to fault diagnosis”, *IEEE Transactions on Neural Networks*, Vol. 7, No. 2, pp. 326-339, 1996.
[57] Z. Chen and J. Maun, “An artificial neural network based real-time fault locator for transmission lines”, *Proc. IEEE International Conference on Neural Networks*, Vol. 1, pp. 63-68, 1997.
[58] M. Hoeprich, “Rolling element bearing fatigue damage propagation”, *ASME Journal of Tribology*, Vol. 114, pp. 328-333, 1992.
[59] Y. Li, S. Billington, C. Zhang, T. Kurfress, S. Danyluk and S. Liang, “Adaptive prognostics for rolling element bearing condition”, *Mechanical Systems and Signal Processing*, Vol. 13(1), pp. 103-113, 1999.
[60] Y. Li, S. Billington, C. Zhang, T. Kurfress, S. Danyluk and S. Liang, “Dynamic prognostic prediction of defect propagation on rolling element bearings”, *Tribology Transactions*, Volume 42, pp. 385-392, 1999.

Neural Networks for Instrumentation, Measurement and Related Industrial Applications
S. Ablameyko et al. (Eds.)
IOS Press, 2003

Chapter 9
Neural Networks for Measurement and Instrumentation in Robotics

Mel SIEGEL
The Robotics Institute, School of Computer Science, Carnegie Mellon University
Pittsburgh, PA 15213, USA

Abstract. The chapter begins with a historical review of the parallel conceptualization of neural networks and intelligent machines. Neural networks were actually created as brain models for the perceptual, cognitive, and actuation systems of future robots. We then develop the title topic, largely via examples. First we present a case that illustrates the architectural issues that we developed abstractly in the introduction. The particular application involves image understanding for robot navigation on a surface. Next we present a broad sample of the intersection between neural networks and robotics via thirteen distinct projects, each briefly summarized, illustrated, and referenced; each ends with a summary of issues, problems, and techniques that are raised or clarified by the example. In the last part we present detailed examinations of two cases. The first case involves image understanding for detection and characterization of aircraft surface flaws. The second case involves interpretation and fusion of signals from solids state chemical sensors. The flaw detection case effectively illustrates a situation wherein either neural network or fuzzy logic technology is potentially applicable, but in practice one or the other works better for specific types of flaws; we speculate that the difference is related to the contrasting nature of the cognitive skills required to accomplish the two tasks. The chemical sensor case similarly contrasts classification and quantitation applications of neural networks; both capabilities are required for different aspects of the practical problem. Both general and case-specific literatures are briefly reviewed at the end of the introduction; a complete list of references, including URL pointers to on-line papers or abstracts, is provided at the end of the chapter.

9.1. Instrumentation and measurement systems for robotics: issues, problems, and techniques

9.1.1 Historical review

The first connection between neural networks and robotics can be dated to the first discussion of what we would today call neural networks. Rosenblatt, in the seminal "Principles of Neurodynamics" [1], stated that the aim of his work on "perceptrons" was to build mathematical models of how brain-like systems might be organized based on available biological evidence. His perspective corresponded exactly with the modern "sense, think, act" – to which I would add "communicate" – paradigm for robotic systems, with a brain model intimately based on inputs from sensors, outputs to actuators, and active learning about the environment. This early close connection to robotics was supplanted, in the 1980s, by a more abstract focus on systems that "learn" arbitrary transfer functions by iterative fitting of general function parameters.

So, despite later backsliding toward abstraction, the earliest efforts – from the mid-1950s through the mid-1960s – were firmly grounded in an explicit robotic model. A hardware implementation of the "perceptron" architecture had a small (~16x16) photocell array simulating a binary retina, neural network nodes realized by relays that responded to the sum of several input currents, inter-node weights realized by motor-driven rheostats, and an iterative training regimen that included positive and negative feedback for "reward" and "punishment". These hardware implementations could learn, e.g., block letters with arbitrary x-y translations on the retina, but generally not rotations, partial letters, or other transformations and degradations that we would today regard as essential tests of an ability to generalize and abstract. Figure 1 illustrates the "Mark I Perceptron".

Figure 1: Mark I Perceptron.

Early neural network terminology was actually much closer to modern robotic terminology than is modern neural network terminology. The bland abstract modern terms "input units", "hidden units", and "output units" were originally "sensory units" (or "S-units"), "associative units" (or "A-units"), and "response units" (or "R-units"), terms that require practically no explanation to modern practitioners of robotics. The early model is illustrated in Figure 2.

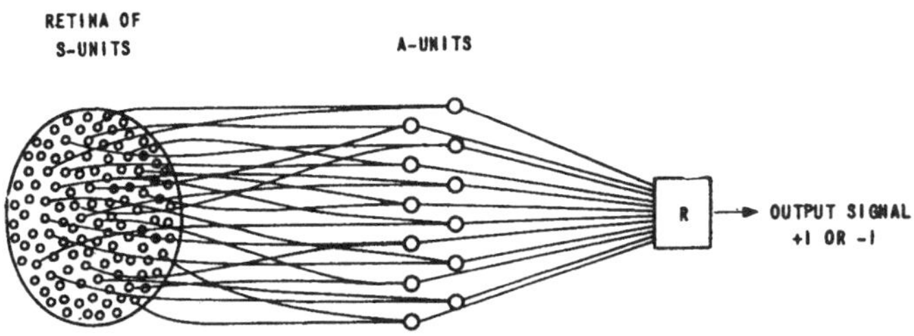

Figure 2: Sensory, associative, and response units in an early representation of a neural network ("perceptron architecture").

This model is clearly seen to anticipate – by about 25 years – the modern "sense/think/act" defining paradigm – of robotics. It was explicitly designed to fit within a biologically motivated model of an adaptive control loop. The same model describes modern robotic control architectures, as illustrated in Figure 3.

It is important to note that, the many similarities between this early work and modern neural network implementations notwithstanding, in the late 1950s and early 1960s when this work was done, it was generally presumed that node inputs and outputs would be binary (on/off), whereas in modern implementations a continuum of "analog" values is generally allowed. This is particularly important from the quantitative sensing, measurement, instrumentation and control perspectives, where continuous outputs are usually desired.

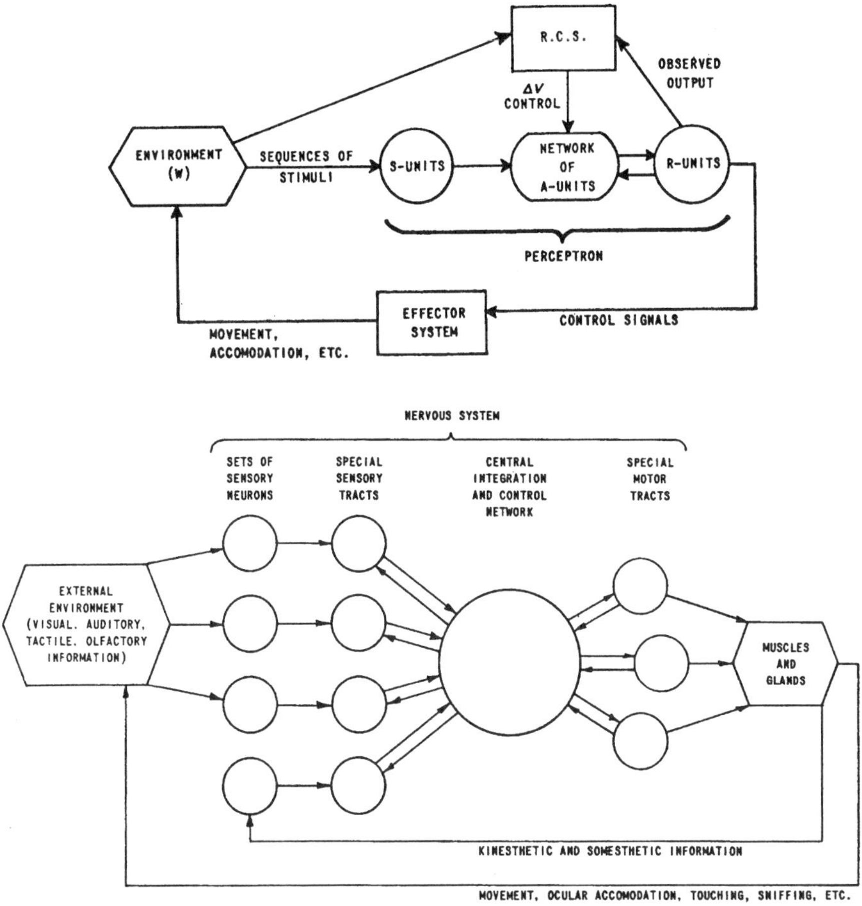

Figure 3: (top) Model of "perceptron" in an adaptive control loop, (bottom) its equivalent in terms of corresponding biological structures and functions.

It is interesting to examination the motivation, aside from the desire to understand biological systems via their modeling, for this computational approach, and also to contrast it with modern motivations. Today neural nets are typically employed to synthesize input-output functions in situations where complexity precludes an explicit analytical model, but the context is conducive to learning from a sufficiently broad set of examples. The original arguments, formulated at a time when digital computers were far less capable and far less reliable than today's, emphasized robustness more than the tractability of the problem. It was then thought that it is advantageous for a numerical computer to fail catastrophically, "with a bang not a whimper", so as to call attention to the failure, minimizing the possibility that a subtle error will be generated and overlooked. A catastrophic failure would also be easier to localize and repair than a subtle failure. The "holographic" memory of a neural network was seen primarily as more robust than digital computing: if well designed, a neural network based decision system ought to be able to continue generating reasonable – albeit imperfect – outputs even if something like one-third of the nodes and connections are randomly destroyed. The modern reality, in contrast, is that digital devices can be and are designed to detect and correct errors, and to transparently insert redundant "spare parts" in case of failure of primary components, whereas in practice if not in theory, neural net sorts of implementations can prove more-or-less unexplainably brittle.

As a kind of historical footnote, similar ideas re-appeared in the early-1970s, possibly independently, in the control context, in the form of the CMAC "cerebellar model articulation controller" of David Marr, perhaps best known today for the Marr-Poggio model of stereo vision, e.g., [16], and articulated by Albus in 1975 [17,18].
The history of the evolution from binary to "analog" outputs is also interesting. Initially, S-, A-, and R-units were imagined as providing only binary outputs, e.g., +1 and -1; continuum values could, of course, be obtained by summing binary values with continuum link weights. The thresholding function was taken to be the unit step Heaviside function, which, because of the infinity in its derivative, is difficult to incorporate in analytical models of system behavior. Thus in the 1980s the step threshold was replaced by sigmoidal functions, as in Figure 4, not for reasons relating to measurement and control issues, but rather because their bell-shaped derivative functions were easier to handle in the behavior models. The appearance of continuous outputs at the R-units, although primarily a side effect of the modeling effort, was nevertheless of profound importance to the measurement and control community.

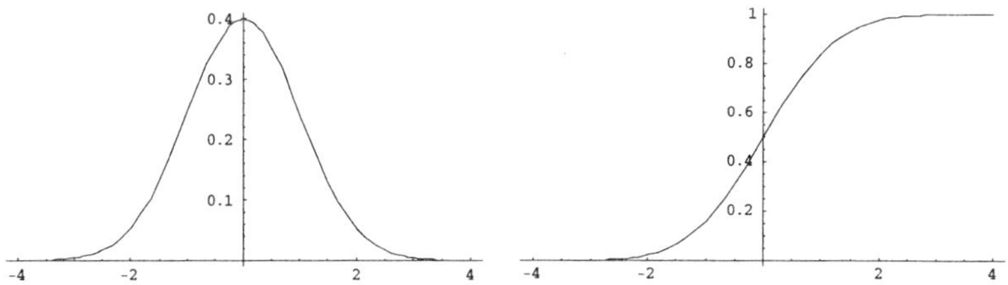

Figure 4: Importance of the emergence of sigmoidal threshold functions. The integral of any "bell shaped curve" is a sigmoidal ("S"-like) curve. The "error function", the integral of the Gaussian function, is well known, but is generally not suitable because its value, an integral under the Gaussian, can be computed only numerically. A popular sigmoidal threshold function in the neural network field is $(1 + \mathrm{Exp}[-x/x_0])^{-1}$, the integral of $\mathrm{Exp}[-x/x_0]/(x_0(1+\mathrm{Exp}[-x/x_0])^2)$, as both the threshold function and its derivative are straightforward and not too expensive to evaluate numerically. The appearance of continuum outputs brought neural networks into the world of sensing and measurements.

9.1.2 Signals, connections, and responses

Continuing to follow Rosenblatt's development, a *signal* is defined as "any measurable variable, such as a voltage, current, light intensity, or chemical concentration, typically characterized by its amplitude, time, and location". A signal generating unit, or S-unit, is then a "physical element, or device, capable of emitting a signal". Note that with this definition the S-unit concept is more-or-less the fusion of current concepts of the sensor or transducer per se, signal conditioning, signal preprocessing, and the input node of the neural network. Note also that in this framework the concept of signal is not limited to the sensor-to-input node subsystem, but that the internal communications among neural network nodes also constitute signals.

Consistent with this broad definition of a signal, a *connection,* is then defined as "any channel, e.g., a wire or nerve fiber, by which a signal emitted by one signal generating unit (the origin) may be transmitted to another (the terminus)". A connection is characterized by a transmission function that relates the amplitude of the signal received at the terminus unit as a function of the amplitude and time of the signal transmitted by the origin unit. A *signal transmission network* is then a system of signal generating units linked by connections.

Sensor units, or S-units, are defined as transducers that respond to "physical energy, e.g., light, sound, pressure, heat, radio signals, etc., by emitting a signal that is some function of the input energy", and a *simple S-unit* is defined as an S-unit that generates a binary output, say +1 if its input signal exceeds a threshold, and 0 otherwise. Although somewhat restrictive from the perspective of the sensing and measurement scientist, i.e., sensors that respond fundamentally to environmental parameters other than deposited energy are well known, allowing the response to be "some function of the input energy" surely encompasses all the actual possibilities. In any case, the firm grounding of S-units, or in modern usage *input units*, to the transduction of information, carried by energy, between the environment and the measurement system, is refreshingly concrete in comparison with modern abstract formulations of neural network fundamentals.

Association-units, or A-units, are "signal generating units, typically logical decision elements, having input and output connections". These clearly correspond exactly to the "hidden units" of modern neural network theory. A *simple A-unit* is defined as a logical decision element that generates a binary output signal, say +1 if the algebraic sum of its input signals exceeds a threshold and 0 otherwise. The term *active* is employed to designate an A-unit that is activated, i.e., whose output state is +1.

Response-units, or R-units, are defined as "signal generating units having input connections, and emitting signals that are transmitted outside the network, i.e., to the environment or external system". These clearly correspond exactly to the "output units" of modern neural network theory. A *simple R-unit* is defined as an R-unit with that generates a binary output signal, say +1 if the algebraic sum of its input signals is strictly positive, -1 if the algebraic sum of its input signals is strictly negative, and either zero or indeterminate or perhaps oscillatory if the algebraic sum of its input signals is zero.

With these definitions – and equivalent mathematical notation – Rosenblatt went on to define *perceptron* and the *simple perceptron* in a way that most current readers will recognize as corresponding to the basic modern definition of a neural network. The perceptron is defined as "a network of S-, A-, and R-units with a variable interaction matrix *V* (formally defined previously) that depends on the sequence of past activity states of the network". Concretely, the definition of a simple perceptron say it is a perceptron in which "(i) there is only one R-unit, with a connection from every A-unit; (ii) connections are only from S-units of A-units and from A-units of S-units; (iii) the weights of the S-unit to A-unit connections do not change with time; (iv) transmission time between units is constant; (v) the output signal of any unit is a function of the algebraic sum of its input signals". This definition is easily seen to correspond very closely to the modern definition of a three layer fully connected neural network with one output node and no interlayer coupling; the main difference is that the general modern neural network definition would not manifestly require the S-to-A coupling to be fixed in time. Note, however, that "time" in this context refers to running time, not training epoch – indeed, training has not yet been mentioned – and in modern typical practice no weights would be changed during runtime unless there were an explicit hybrid run-train strategy.

Reinforcement, what we would now call *learning*, enters via the definition of the *reinforcement system*, "a set of rules by which the interaction matrix (or memory state) of a perceptron may be altered through time", and the *reinforcement control system*, a "mechanism external to a perceptron that is capable of altering the interaction matrix of the perceptron in accordance with the rules of a specified reinforcement system". Implicit in the latter definition, of course, is that the strategy is something sensible, like "increase weights that contribute to correct response and decrease (or increase negatively) weights that contribute to incorrect response.

Finally, Rosenblatt defines an *experimental system*: "a system consisting of a perceptron, a stimulus world, and a reinforcement control system; the reinforcement control system may be an automatic regulating device, e.g., a thermostat, or a human operator, capable of responding to the responses of the perceptron and the stimuli in the environment by applying the appropriate reinforcement rules, altering the memory state of the perceptron". In other current terminology, this is a *robot*.

By the early 1960s, theorems had been stated and proved to the effect that solutions, i.e., weight matrices, exist that map specified kinds of input spaces into specified kinds of output spaces, and that these weight matrices can be found in finite time by iterative procedures, i.e. "training". However no practical implementation strategy was found until, in the mid-1980s, the rediscovery of the "back propagation (of error)" algorithm made actual implementation practical.

9.1.3 Example of a neural net application in robotics: how to make a machine vision system see lines of rivets on an aircraft skin

In the following section we will review a variety of applications so as to convey something of the scope of neural network technology in robotics. For the sake of completeness before ending this introductory section, we will briefly survey one of the applications that we will cover in increasing detail in section 2 and 3.

The problem relates to navigation of a mobile robot that traverses an aircraft's skin (using suction cups to adhere to the sides and belly) looking for cracks, corrosion, mechanical damage, and other flaws [19]. The part of this problem of interest now is not the inspection sensing technology per se, but rather the proprioceptive ("self-awareness") technology that the robot needs in order to traverse the skin surface in a systematic and knowledgeable way. Aircraft features are normally described in an embedded coordinate system based on enumerating the circumferential and longitudinal "lines of rivets" that attach the skin to the airframe skeleton. The problem for us is that "lines of rivets" are an abstraction constructed by the human eye-brain system: in reality there are no lines, there are only rivets that our eye-brain abstracts into lines. Our machine vision task is then to develop an algorithm that can reliably find "lines of rivets" in video imagery of aircraft skin. The problem is difficult in the vision technology domain as well as in the computational algorithm domain: the contrast of metal rivets in a metal skin is very low, and the difficulty is exacerbated by specular reflections. Figure 5 shows an exemplary low resolution, low contrast image with five rivets "in a line", plus one rivet below the line.

Our approach is to train a neural network operator to recognize the "rivetness" quality of a square window on the image. Training is under human supervision. The output of the neural network "rivetness" operator is illustrated in Figure 6. This is a 15x15 pixel input network whose output is a measure of the similarity of the pixels under the current window to the rivet-containing windows in the training set. Contrast of metallic rivets against metallic skin is greatly enhanced by this operator.

Figures 7 and 8 illustrate the remaining steps. The latter shows the result of applying a conventional edge-finding algorithm to the image in the former; contrast is further enhanced, i.e., the fuzziness of the "rivetness" image is removed. The combined result of the last two steps is shown in Figure 8. First, region filling and binarization completely and accurately isolate the rivets. Then a robust line-fitting algorithm draws the "line of rivets". The robust algorithm is needed to reject the outlier rivet below the line: if it were not rejected, the line obtained would not make human sense, nor would it be practically useful.

In summary, in a typical application the neural net is *one step* in a pipeline of algorithms; each step is typically simple and more-or-less standard; the "magic" is in the choice and order of the steps. In this example, we began with noisy, low resolution, low contrast image data, and employed steps that:

- accented features of interest for the navigation problem, i.e., "rivetness", using a neural network operator;
- sharpened features of interest using a standard edge-finding operator;
- enhanced features of interest using standard region-filling and thresholding;
- applied a "robust line fitting" algorithm to find the rivet line in the image, free of perturbation by outliers.

Figure 5: Low resolution, low contrast image illustrating difficulty of finding rivets and "lines of rivets" on aircraft skin.

Figure 6: Output of the neural network "rivetness" operator. Note dramatic improvement in contrast. Rivet-like regions are larger than the actual rivets by about half the operator window size.

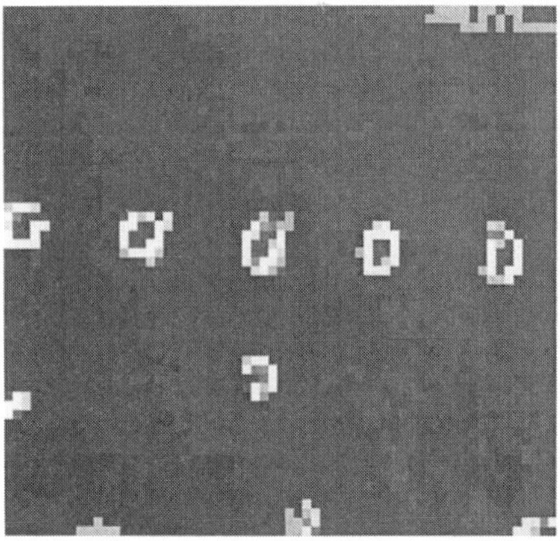

Figure 7: Output of a conventional edge-finding algorithm.

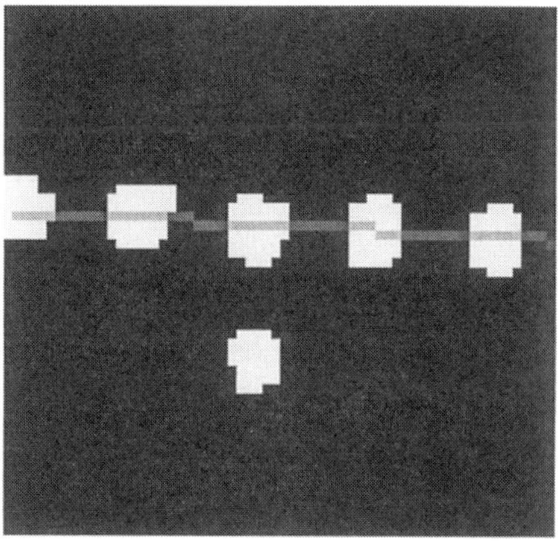

Figure 8: Rivets isolated by region filling and binarization, followed by application of a robust line-fitting algorithm.

9.1.4 Overview of the literature

The References section at the end of the chapter lists a relatively small number of articles and books in four categories: (1) general references that provide additional detail and alternative perspectives about the basic facts and principles under discussion, (2) items, mostly books, that address the general title subject of "neural networks" AND "robots", and (3) items, mostly books, that address the specific title subject of "neural networks" AND "robots" AND "industrial applications", and (4) references to books, articles, etc., cited in the text, especially in connection with illustrative applications. The intention, particularly in (1), (2), and (3), is not to be comprehensive in a formal scholarly sense, but rather straightforwardly to provide the reader with useful and accessible sources of additional practical information.

In the "general references" category, [1] highly is recommended; the section *Historical Review* is largely drawn from this book. [2] on the one hand completed the work described in [1], and on the other hand, by its pessimism, for a decade nearly closed off research in field. The other general references, some to purely web-based resources, may or may not appeal to particular readers, depending on their individual preferences and perspectives.

9.1.5 Summary

To summarize:

- Neural network technology grew out of early thinking about perceptive active "creatures" that can learn about their environments.
- The resulting paradigm was later recognized to be a useful practical technology for creating functions that fit, interpolate, and perhaps extrapolate data ("generalization")
- A neural net that is one link in a control loop is often the intellectual/instrumentation signal-to-understanding translation element

Figure 9 pictorially represents this summary in the form of an architecture for a closed-loop system with sensing, understanding, and acting elements.

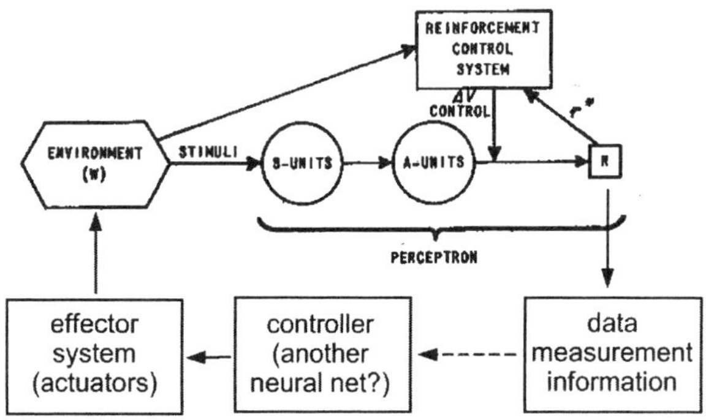

Figure 9: Architectural model for neural network for measurement and control in robotic applications. The bracketed portion labeled PERCEPTRON is a neural network. Its S-unit (sensory, input) layer receives stimuli from the ENVIRONMENT, and can influence the environment via its R-unit (response, output) activity. The REINFORCEMENT CONTROL SYSTEM monitors the ENVIRONMENT and the RESPONSE, and corrects (•V CONTROL) the connection weights to bring the actual response into closer accord with the desired response. To close the control loop and achieve some practical action of, e.g., a robot, the R-unit output is interpreted in the block labeled DATA/MEASUREMENT/INFORMATION. This block's output provides data need by a MOTION CONTROL SYSTEM (which may itself be a neural network, e.g., model of robot system dynamics) to effect useful action in the ENVIRONMENT. The MOTION CONTROL SYSTEM output provides power and information to the EFFECTOR SYSTEM (actuators, robots). The control loop is closed when the EFFECTOR system's output modifies the environment.

9.1.6 Some questions

We end this section with some questions for the reader to ponder on the theme "why use a neural network?"

- Is the neural network a model of nature or a pragmatic solution to, e.g., nonlinear sensing and control problems?
- Under what circumstances can the connection between input and output data be found better in a single step than by iteration?

- What are the consequences of the fact that, typically, the neural network has many more degrees of freedom (parameters) than the physical system it models?
- How does the neural network's "holographic" memory aid (or detract from) system robustness?
- Once the net is trained, should you expect to be able to look inside it and understand why, in terms of the physical system it models, it works the way it does? If yes, then does not the true utility of the neural network approach lie in the training phase, i.e., the discovery of the input-output function of the physical system, after which, in the running phase, the neural network can be discarded in favor of a concise algebraic and Boolean restatement of what the network has learned?

9.2. Neural network techniques for instrumentation, measurement systems, and robotic applications: theory, design, and practical issues

In this section we briefly review a wide-ranging sample of neural network applications within the broad context of robotics. The specific applications, drawn primarily from the activities at my home institution, are:

- Road Driving Vehicle Controller [20]
- Off-Road Driving Controller [21]
- Hand Tremor and Error Correction [22]
- Drowsy Driver Detection [23]
- Robotic Inspection of Aircraft Skin [24]
- Estimation of Stability Regions [25]
- Robot Models for Motion Planning [26]
- Numerical Solutions [27]
- Learning Human Control Strategies [28]
- Detecting Pedestrians in City Traffic [29]
- Chinese Character Recognition [30]
- Face Recognition [31]
- Gesture-Based Communication [32]

The aim of this selection is to give the reader the flavor of neural network application in robotics via many brief summaries that in the aggregate span great breadth. In contrast, section 3 will examine two applications – both from the author's laboratory – in detail.

9.2.1 Road driving vehicle controller

This application [20] involves a neural network implementation of a vehicle controller for driving on roads and highways. As illustrated in Figure 10, it uses a three layer multi-output perceptron examining the video stream from a camera; each cameral pixel corresponds to an input (or S-) unit. There are five hidden (or A-) units, and 32 output (or R-) units corresponding to 32 potential steering directions. Learning employs an "evolutionary" approach vs. the back-propagation algorithm; this approach results in higher training cost, but the resulting performance is empirically better. Application domain specific error metrics are developed and employed to increase the effectiveness of the training process. Apropos of the last question posed at the end of section 1, the paper looks into the trained network in an attempt to understand *what* is actually being learned.

Issues, problems, and techniques of this application are summarized as follows:

- The task is a relatively simple one (to drive in lane), but the environment is extremely complex (road or highway with traffic, distractions, imperfect lane markings, etc.); in this sort of scenario, what is actually being learned, and what is its relevance to the application task?

- The controller response to observed heading error is essentially linear; then why not use a neural net *sensor* but a conventional *controller?*
- Steering direction is determined by computing the centroid of ~30 analog outputs; what is the advantage of this approach over an output with a single bipolar analog output proportional to the desired steering angle?

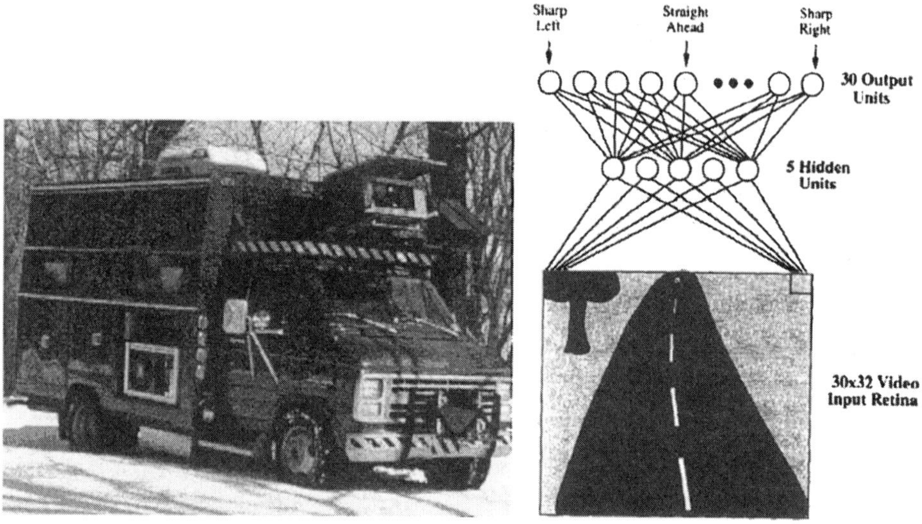

Figure 10: ALVINN: (left) the vehicle, (right) image input to neural network whose outputs indicate the steering direction needed to follow the road.

9.2.2 Off-road driving vehicle controller

As illustrated by the previous application, for on-road driving *one* sensing modality is enough, e.g., computer vision based detection of lane-markings. In contrast, off-road driving requires the fusion of *multiple* modalities, e.g., vision AND range AND texture. The modular neural network architecture developed in the course of this work [21] explicitly facilitates sensor fusion via the separate learning of separate aspects. Although this work predates the current interest in "context aware computing", it in fact fits well within this paradigm.

The MAMMOTH modular neural network architecture, illustrated in Figure 11, employs separate, separately trained neural networks to derive steering direction information from by analysis of data from red, green, and blue channels of a CCD camera and, and from a laser rangefinder that detects primarily off-road obstacles in the vehicle's path. The hidden (A-) unit layers of the CCD steering and laser rangefinder steering networks are then combined, with additional training, to generate a steering direction that represents the fusion of the two sensing modalities.

Issues, problems, and techniques of this application are summarized as follows:

- What is the advantage of fusing first like (homogeneous) sensors, then unlike (heterogeneous) fusions of like sensors?
- Does this architecture potentially hamper discovering correlations, e.g., a correlation that might exist between blue CCD channel AND range?
- How to measure robustness? For example, what is the relative loss of performance if "one third of the wires" are lost in one module vs. in all modules?

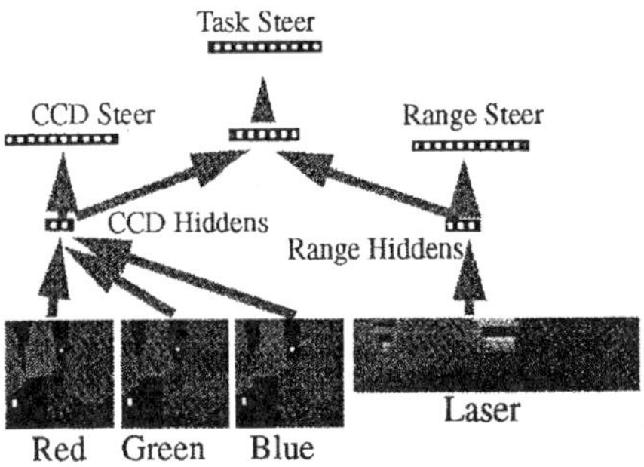

Figure 11: MAMMOTH modular neural network architecture for trained fusion of steering directions obtained from independently trained image based and rangefinder based sensing modalities.

9.2.3 Hand tremor and error correction

This application [22] is in the area of medical robotics, specifically robotic aids to microsurgery. Vitreoretinal (eye) surgery is of particular interest because of its extreme delicacy and the extreme consequences of surgical inaccuracy. The hypothesis of the research is that a sense-think-act electromechanical system inserted between the surgeon's hand and the patient can sense and compensate for hand tremor and certain errorful motions, while faithfully transmitting the surgeon's intent to the surgical site. The prototype apparatus, Figure 12, uses three accelerometers and three rate gyros to detect motion of the tool in the surgeon's hand. Three piezoelectric actuators move the knife contrary to tremor and erroneous motion. Tremor is compensated by an electromechanical filtering algorithm. Error is compensated by a trained neural network whose input is a measurement of the actual trajectory and whose output is the desired trajectory. Preliminary experiments indicate an overall error reduction of about 44%.

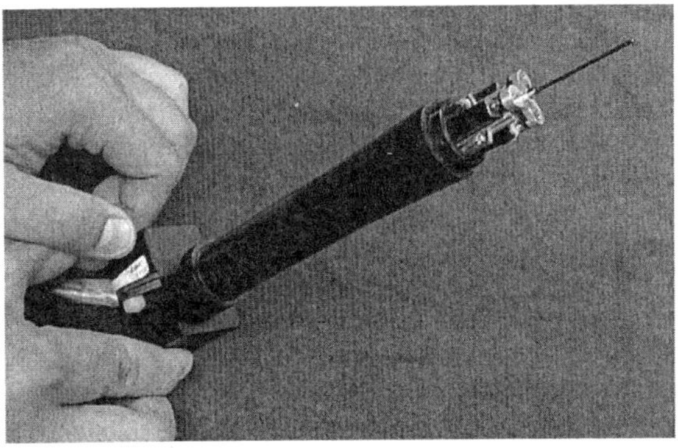

Figure 12: Tremor and error correcting tool; protective end cap has been removed to make actuators visible.

Issues, problems, and techniques related to this application may be summarized as follows:

- It is potentially difficult to distinguish tremor-related motion from error-related motion.
- How will the system distinguish surgeon error from surgeon intent?
- Is it necessary to re-train the neural network for each surgeon? Does it have to be done before each surgery, or is training fast enough that it could be done during the first few minutes of "set up"?
- How is it possible to assure stability of closed-loop control system in all application scenarios?

9.2.4 Drowsy driver detection

"PERCLOS" is a standard measure of driver drowsiness related to observation of slow eyelid closure, percentage of time the eye is closed, and percentage of eye area covered by the eyelid. Other – currently non-standard – measures of driver drowsiness relate directly to driver performance as measured primarily by lane keeping, steering wheel movements, and lateral acceleration. The object of this effort [23] is to correlate the PERCLOS measure with these direct measures. Since automated measurement of PERCLOS – using video and image understanding – is difficult, expensive, and may be regarded by the driver as intrusive, obtaining an indirect measure of PERCLOS via direct measure of driver performance would be valuable. The neural network solution that was developed successfully achieves this correlation.

Issues, problems, and techniques related to this application are summarized as follows:

- Since the fundamental issue is driver performance – with which the indirect PERCLOS measure is known to correlate – why, in the long run, is it useful to correlate the direct measures with PERCLOS vs. simply adopting the direct measures?
- Is it necessary to train for individual drivers?
- If yes, will the approach be rendered impractical by the requirement to install a PERCLOS detector in order to train the performance-based detector?

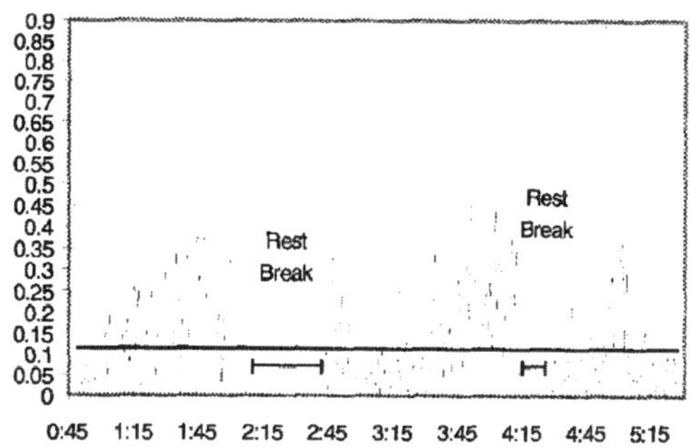

Figure 13: PERCLOS measure as a function of time-of-night and recentness of driver rest periods.

9.2.5 Robotic inspection of aircraft skin

At the end of section 1 we presented the example of a neural network approach to a proprioceptive (self-awareness) application, the navigation of a mobile robot used for inspection of aircraft skin. In this work, neural network techniques – as well as fuzzy logic techniques – are also used for the inspection task *per se*. Several robot types were investigated, each optimized for a particular inspection modality, the main ones being an eddy current probe technique and a visual technique. We focus now on the visual technique [24]. First, a teleoperated mobile robot collects stereoscopic imagery under dynamic lighting conditions that replicate the inspection protocol used by human visual inspectors. The resulting images are decomposed in a wavelet expansion, and the expansion coefficients grouped into feature vectors. A neural network technique classifies feature vectors representative of skin regions of interest (primarily around rivets) into classes such as "healthy", "cracked", and "corroded". Subsequent investigation showed that, in comparison with a fuzzy logic implementation of the classifier, the neural network classifier was better for finding corrosion and the fuzzy logic classifier was better for cracks. This is discussed in detail in section 3.

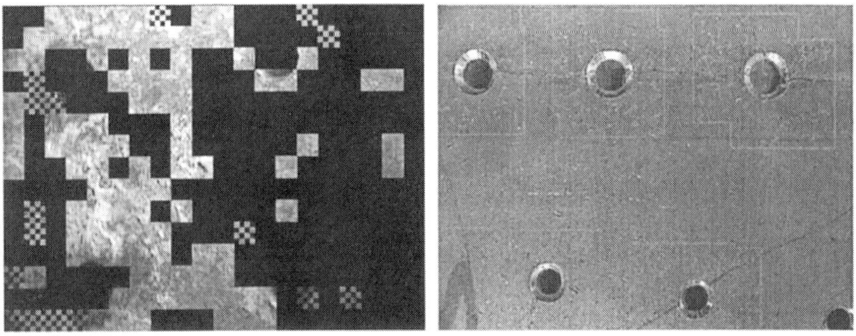

Figure 14: Regions with corrosion (left) and cracks (right) identified by neural network classification of wavelet feature vectors.

Issues, problems, and techniques related to this application may be summarized as follows:

- How will it be possible to verify agreement between the results of automated inspection and human inspection following government-mandated protocols?
- The preprocessing provided by the wavelet decomposition is clearly important to achieving efficient neural net classification – versus, e.g., presenting the whole image to a neural network – but how is it possible to verify that the preprocessing does not filter out valuable clues to the presence of defects?
- Given the range of possible defects – and the flexibility of the human visual and judgment systems in identifying them -- how is it practically possible to obtain an adequate training set, with an appropriate mix of defect and normal examples?
- Is it possible to decide a priori whether a neural network or a fuzzy logic classifier is better matched to a particular classification task? (See section 3)

9.2.6 Estimation of stability regions

The problem is the estimation of stability regions of autonomous nonlinear systems [25], e.g., robots. The approach is to use empirical stability data to train a multi-layer neural network – versus the usual differential equation model based analytical approach. The methodology developed quantitatively characterizes regions of the control space with stability estimates and their confidence intervals.

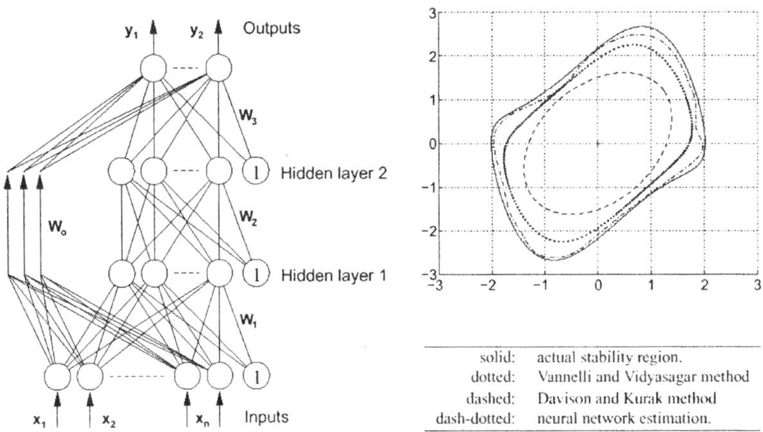

Figure 15: (left) Multi-layer neural network for estimation of stability regions in control space, and (right) comparison of actual stability region, two conventional estimation models, and neural network estimate.

Issues, problems, and techniques related to this application may be summarized as follows:

- What is the difference – besides terminology (or "spin") – between neural net and other parameter-based approximation methods?
- This solution uses a multi-layer (i.e., two or more hidden layer) solution. Is there a systematic way of designing minimal architectures that can represent reality?
- Similarly, how can we decide when, how, and why to use and architecture that admits or requires connections between non-adjacent layers?

9.2.7 Robot models for motion planning

This example involves an application superficially similar to the previous one: modeling of motion planning for a robot with multiple degrees of freedom having nonlinear interactions. However the issue in this case is not stability but path optimality [26]. Optimal motion planning algorithms are well developed for electric motor drive robots, but they do not port well to hydraulic robots. In the domain of interest, excavation and construction, optimality translates directly into economics. The solution employs multiple neural networks to model individual actuator response functions; the system model runs at about 75 times real-time, allowing the evaluation of multiple alternatives in anticipation in advance of commanding any actual motion.

Issues, problems, and techniques related to this application are summarized as follows:

- Issues common to modular neural networks, as discussed above.
- Although nonlinear, the actuator system range is well constrained both mechanically and in terms of total available power and power available to individual actuators, suggesting there may be an alternative analytical solution base.
- A ubiquitous human-machine interaction problem is apparent: automating control of complex multi-actuated systems with non-intuitive human interfaces.

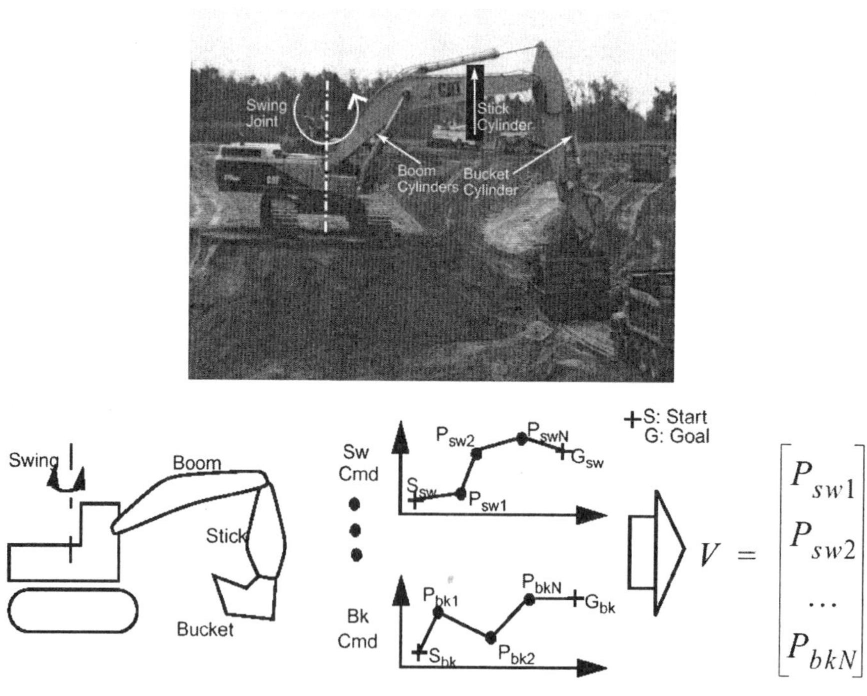

Figure 16: (top) Hydraulic robot excavator, and (bottom) model.

9.2.8 Numerical solutions

This example addresses a robotic application of a neural network as a "function approximator" [27]. The neural network is used to approximate the solution to the Hamilton-Jacobi-Bellman (HJB) equation for the "car on a hill" problem, a two dimensional highly nonlinear control problem. This is an interesting and unusual example of authors actually reporting an application in which the neural network approach proves to be of questionable utility: the high density of general solutions near the specific minimum-error solution makes the outcome unreliable.

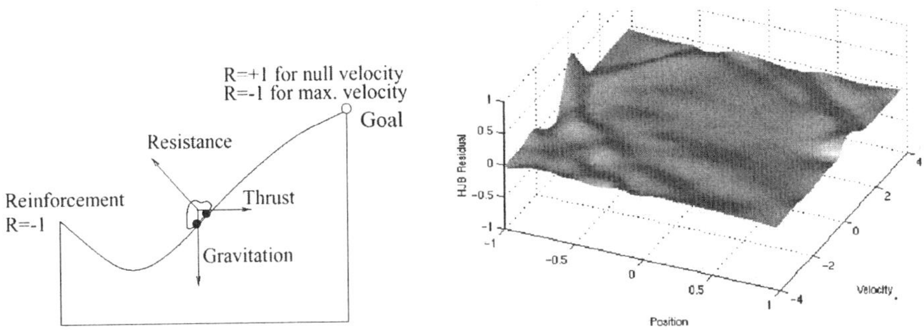

Figure 17: (left) Illustration of the "car-on-the-hill" problem, and (right) neural network approximation to the control surface.

Issues, problems, and techniques related to this application may be summarized as follows:

- Issues are similar to those raised in other applications in which the neural network technique is used to create a function-like connection between parameters and data.
- How does the result obtained compare, in actual structure and by various performance measures, to numerical solution of the differential equations?

9.2.9 Learning human control strategies

The aim of this application is to learn how humans control a complex nonlinear manipulator, and thereby to be able to incorporate human strategies in an automatic controller [28]. A useful technology must incorporate validation of actual controller performance for comparison with human performance and alternative control strategies. As a practical matter, it proves appropriate to employ different learning strategies and models for discrete and continuous time human actions. Measures of similarity and difference between learned (neural network) and acquired (human) strategies are developed and incorporated.

Issues, problems, and techniques related to this application are summarized as follows:

- Rationalization of mechanics and control: need for a general abstract model of manipulator based on degrees of freedom, ranges, sensitivities, etc.
- The high level model is matched to anticipated tasks, but the implementation's controls are not. A valid engineering implementation may need to incorporate explicit – versus implicitly human intuitive models – based on component strengths, economic considerations, etc.
- Should the emphasis then be on a (neural net?) "translator" between human (virtual) and machine (actual) actuator controls?
- Does the system react gracefully to unexpected circumstances and events?

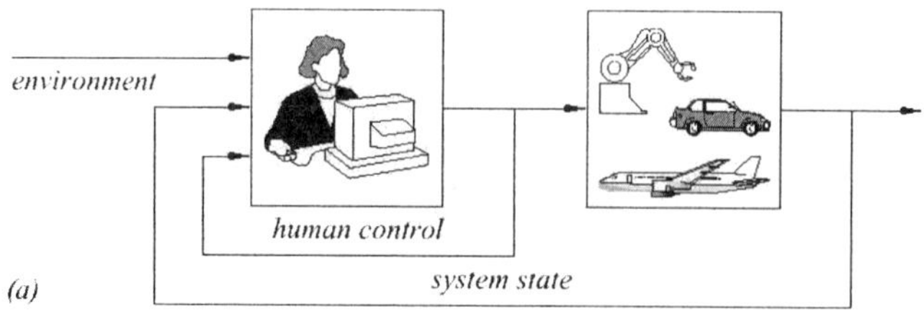

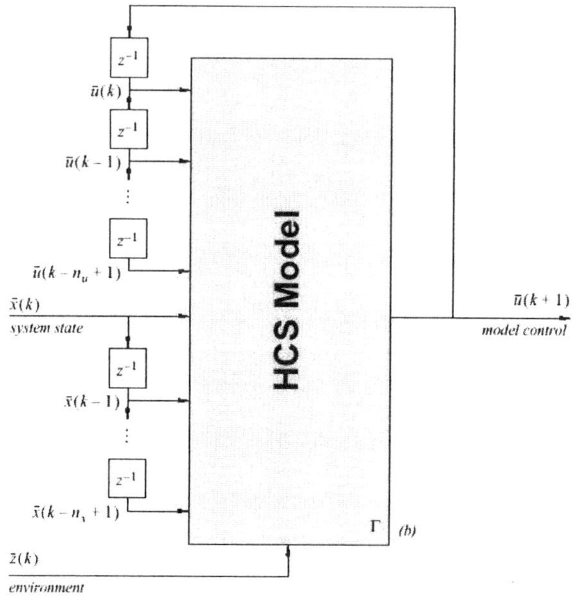

Figure 18: Human experience-based control. (a) Monitoring and capture of human control strategies. (b) Architecture of Human Control System (HCS) controller.

9.2.10 Detecting pedestrians in city traffic

In this application a stereoscopic machine vision system and neural network based image analysis is used to detect moving and stationary pedestrians in urban traffic [29]. First, the perspective and motion (both camera and scene) based stereo extract objects from the background. Then a neural network examines the objects and identifies pedestrians in various poses, sizes, dress, states of occlusion, etc. The neural network uses 30x65 input layer, 5 hidden units, 1 analog output unit, and a decision threshold designed to trade-off detection against false alarm rates. Real-time application appears to be feasible even in crowded urban environments.

Issues, problems, and techniques related to this application are summarized as follows:

- The neural network is actually the easy part; the "magic" is in the preprocessor that isolates the objects that are potentially pedestrians.
- An intensity gradient image technique is used to reduce pedestrians to silhouettes without overhead of an explicit thresholding step.
- Can the "magic", i.e., segmenting the raw image stream into objects, be automated, e.g., by a neural network approach?

Figure 19: Finding pedestrians in city traffic. (left) Stereo based extraction of objects in the scene. (right) Neural network based identification of pedestrians in various poses, states of motion, etc.

9.2.11 Chinese character recognition

The problem is recognition of ~40,000 Chinese characters in 3 or 4 fonts with random distortion of individual characters [30]. The approach adopted is a "probabilistic neural network" recognizer. The methodology is to model the probability distribution of the variants; to avoid storing all the variants, the recorded distributions are used to generate the variations on-the-fly.

Issues, problems, and techniques related to this application may be summarized as follows:

- The functionality of a trained system depends on having a content-complete and statistically realistic training set.
- A distortion model provides a shortcut to collecting a comprehensive training set; you might also want a model for mapping training set statistics to actual population statistics.
- The essential technology needed for success of this sort of application is to have a model for translating the available training set into a realistic training set; could training be short-circuited by applying known statistics during training?

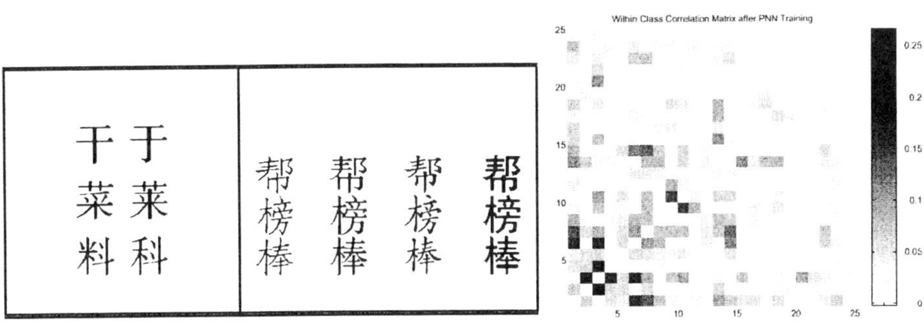

Figure 20: Chinese character recognition.
(left) Examples of similar looking but different characters in one font, and identical characters in different fonts. (right) Within-class correlation matrix after probabalistic neural net training.

9.2.12 Face recognition

The task is to recognize both permanent features (eyebrows, mouth) and transient features (deepening of furrows, pursing of lips) in human facial expression [31]. A modular neural network approach is adopted: separate neural networks are constructed to analyze upper facial expressions (eyes, eyebrows, checks) and lower facial expressions (wrinkles, lips), then these are fused to characterize the overall expression (happy, angry, afraid, etc.). The paper cited focuses particularly on the details of the upper face module; this neural network recognizes seven "upper face action units" that are parametric components of a vector space that is classified by the upper face neural network.

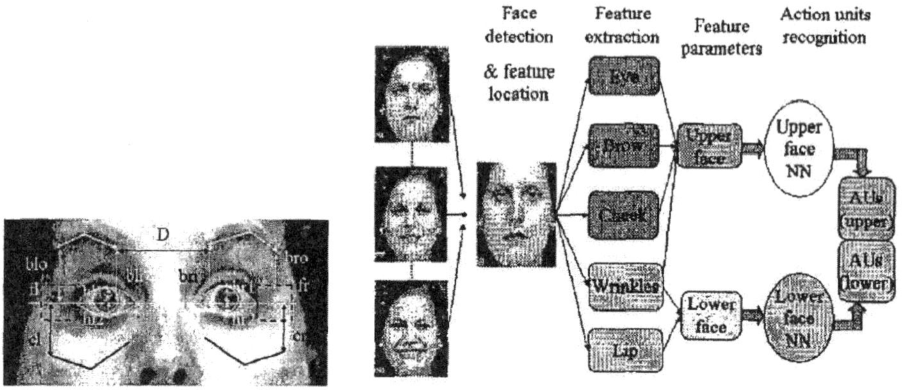

Figure 21: Face recognition application. (left) Specification of upper face features. (right) Modular neural network approach for upper face recognition, lower face recognition, and fusion of the two.

Issues, problems, and techniques related to this application may be summarized as follows:

- Are there still issues related to the completeness of the parameterization? There are many different ways to parameterize faces (etc.); do faces (etc.) with similar parameters look similar to human observers?
- Are there still issues related to the suitability of the parameterization? Are the parameters (close to) "orthogonal" with respect to, e.g., human perception?
- Is it necessary also to include dynamics, e.g., to achieve natural-looking speech, laughing, sneezing, etc?

9.2.13 Gesture-based communication

The goal of this project is to effect communication with "service robots" via natural and/or defined human gestures [32]. The approach is a neural net recognition and interpretation of the human's static pose, dynamic gestures, etc. Issues that need to be addressed to achieve robust performance in real-world environments include lighting intensity and color tracking of the human "employer". The system was demonstrated in a trash clean-up task.

Issues, problems, and techniques related to this application are summarized as follows:

- Natural gestures have different meanings in different cultures; invented gestures put the burden on the person vs. on the machine, thus negating the "natural interaction" paradigm.
- How will the system distinguish a "gesture" from just randomly passing through a "gesture state"?
- Like ALVINN [Figure 10], this implementation uses multiple output units to encode a single scalar value (e.g., direction); this is pragmatically effective, but *why*, e.g., versus a single continuum output proportional to steering direction, is not intuitively or quantitatively obvious.

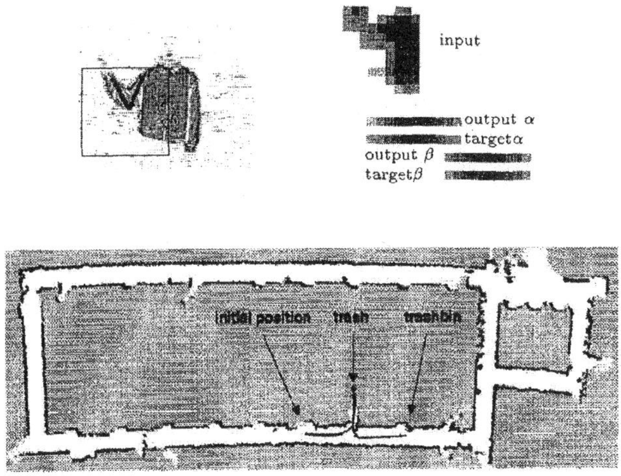

Figure 22: Gesture and meaning. (top) Neural network based pose analysis. (bottom) Map of the robot's operational range.

9.2.14 Summary

To summarize:
- Robotics is a lot more than robots:
    - Few "robotics" people ever see an anthropomorphic robot.
    - "Robotic applications" are just applications.
- Neural nets in instruments carried by robots are just neural nets in instruments.
    - Robot navigation, manipulation, etc., rarely require an instrument-like, instrument-grade internal representation.

9.3. Case studies: neural networks for instrumentation and measurement systems in robotic applications in research and industry

In this section we look in detail at two case studies applications of neural networks for instrumentation and measurement in robotics:
- Robotic Enhanced Visual Inspection of Aircraft Skin [24,33]
- Odor Detection and Classification Using Arrays of Relatively Non-Specific Sensors [34,35].

Both applications are drawn from parts of projects that were done in the author's lab, the first primarily with graduate student Priyan Gunatilake and other collaborators, and the second with graduate student Huadong Wu and other collaborators.

9.3.1 Robotic enhanced visual inspection of aircraft skin

We touched on the robotic inspection of aircraft application in both section 1, where we examined a vision-based robot navigation algorithm based on finding "lines-of-rivets" on the aircraft skin (Figure 8 and reference [19]), and in section 2, where we briefly introduced the topic of flaw inspection, particularly for cracks and corrosion (Figure 14 and reference [24]). In this case study we will look at the latter application in more detail. Readers interested in a complete description, including comparison with alternative approaches and complete contextual material on aircraft inspection practice and problems, should see [33].

Figure 23: (left) Hangar environment for robotic inspection of aircraft. (right) Current practice, inspectors in safety-harnesses on aircraft crown.

9.3.1.1 Why use robots for aircraft inspection?

Arguments that have been advanced in favor of robotic inspection of aircraft, especially in contrast to the current practice of human visual inspection, include:

- assurance of complete coverage of the programmed path;
- guaranteed achievement of a uniform level of concentration;
- correctness:
    - assurance that the instrument is set up correctly;
    - assurance that the deployment protocol is accepted and intended one;
- recordability:
    - the automated instrument remembers every reading perfectly;
    - with systematic navigation, any sensor can generate C-scans;
    - retrospective interpretation of data becomes feasible;
- but other reasons, such as:
    - get the man off the airplane;
    - scan fast;
    - scan now, look later;

  for a variety of economic, cultural, and legal reasons seem less important in retrospect than they did initially.

9.3.1.2 Aircraft inspection robot designs

Figure 24 illustrates two aircraft skin crawling robots, Autocrawler, a powerful suction cup based robot developed by Henry R. Seemann and CIMP, developed in the author's laboratory. CIMP, the Crown Inspection Mobile Platform, has the main advantage that it does not use suction cups. This is an advantage because suction cups require an umbilicus to supply high-pressure air (the suction cup vacuum is produced by air-powered "ejectors"), and when a robot has an umbilicus, all the developers' effort goes into overcoming its clumsiness. Of course, lacking suction cups, CIMP's motion is limited to the aircraft crown, where gravity helps rather than hinders. This means that, in contrast to every other known aircraft skin inspection robot, CIMP delivers useful data.

Figure 25 shows a close up view of CIMP's sensor pod, typical stereoscopic image pairs collected by its video system, and the human interface, including a radio control unit for navigation and sensor system control and a stereoscopic video system for monitoring and remote inspection.

Figure 24: Typical crawler: CIMP.

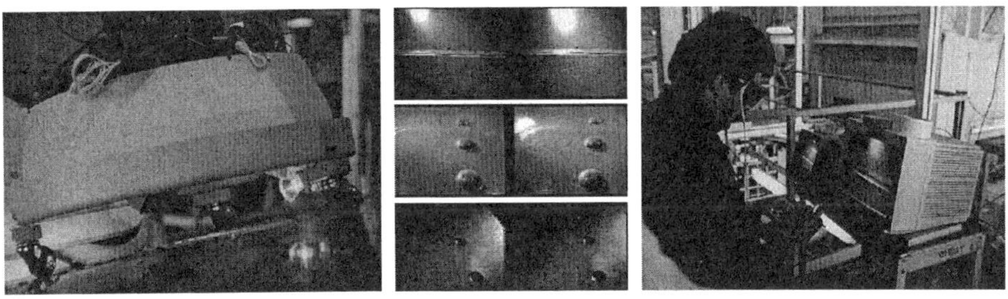

Figure 25: CIMP: (left) Sensor pod containing camera, diffuse illumination, dynamic spot illumination, (middle) stereoscopic image pairs of lap joint (top), button head rivet line (middle), and sample from defect library (bottom), and (right) inspector at stereoscopic workstation.

9.3.1.3 Real-time and off-line inspection

In real-time, CIMP is a remote inspection tool for a human operator. Off-line, we have developed algorithms to automate the image interpretation, particularly with respect to finding cracks and corrosion damage. Figure 26 illustrates typical input to and output from the crack detection pipeline, and Figure 27 illustrates typical input to and output from the corrosion detection pipeline.

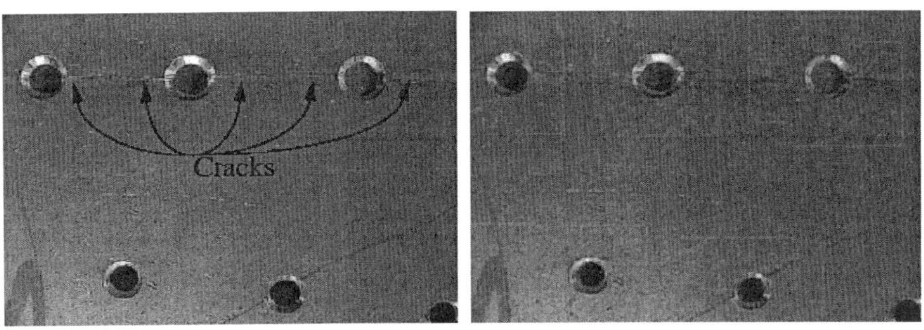

Figure 26: Crack detection. (left) raw image with cracks indicated, and (right) processed image with regions-of-interest isolated around rivets, crack-line-regions identified (green in the original), cracks found and marked with measure of high confidence (red in the original) and moderate confidence (blue in the original).

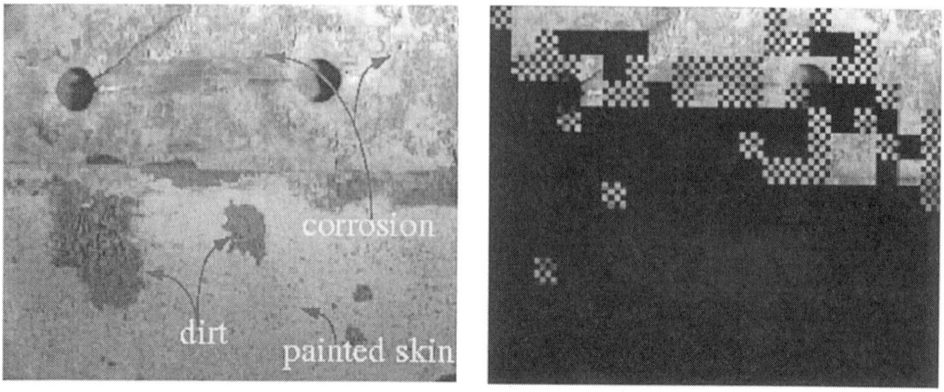

Figure 27: Corrosion detection. (left) raw image with regions of actual corrosion, surface dirt, and painted skin marked, and (right) corroded regions identified with high confidence (gray level image) and with moderate confidence (checkerboard gray level and black).

9.3.1.4 Crack and corrosion detection pipelines

Both crack and corrosion detection proceed via an image processing and interpretation pipeline that is illustrated, for both modalities, by Figure 28. In both cases the algorithm begins with isolation of regions of interest – generally square windows around rivets – followed by a multiresolution wavelet decomposition, feature extraction to populate a feature vector, classification of the feature vector as, e.g., normal, representative with high certainty of a crack or corrosion, or possibly representative of a crack or corrosion, to be decided later, e.g., by human intervention. The two pipelines differ in detail in the implementation of the multiresolution decomposition, the content of the feature vector, and the implementation of the neural network used for classification of the feature vectors. In both cases, a fuzzy logic classifier was implemented as an alternative to the neural network classifier. The neural network classifier was found to work better for corrosion, and the fuzzy logic classifier was found to work better for cracks. We speculate that this the case because corrosion detection and identification is a relatively low level texture recognition problem more amenable to neural network simulation, whereas crack detection and identification is a higher level semantic reasoning process more amenable to a fuzzy logic, i.e., rule based solution.

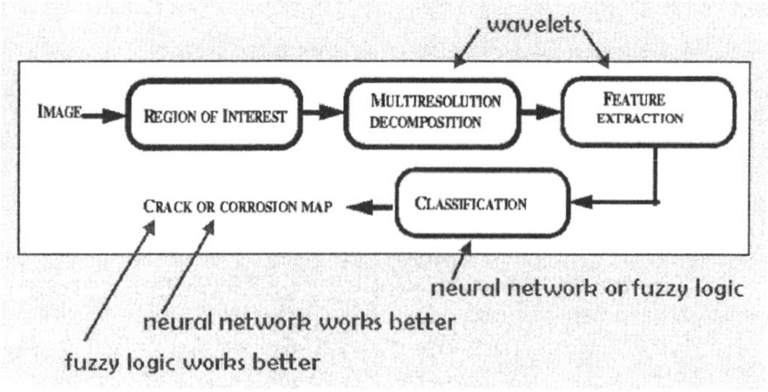

Figure 28: Crack and corrosion detection processing pipelines.

9.3.1.5 Corrosion detection pipelines

The wavelet decomposition for corrosion, illustrated in Figure 29, characterizes each 32x32 pixel block in the image according to features of the luminance (Y) and chrominance (I and Q) channels describing its intensity and color. For each pixel block, the decomposition generates a 14-element feature vector: 10 intensities ("energies") from the Y-image, and 4 energy ratios from the I- and Q- images.

The classification module is a 3-layer neural network whose inputs are the14 components of the feature vector. The best performing architecture converged on 40 hidden units. As stated, three output states of two binary output units were recognized: no corrosion (state [0,1]), corrosion with high certainty (state [1,0]), and possible corrosion (state [0,0] or [1,1]). Training involved 3200 hand-classified feature vectors and 2000 training epochs. The resulting system, tested on 800 test vectors that were not in the training set, yielded a probability of detection (PoD) of corrosion of 94%.

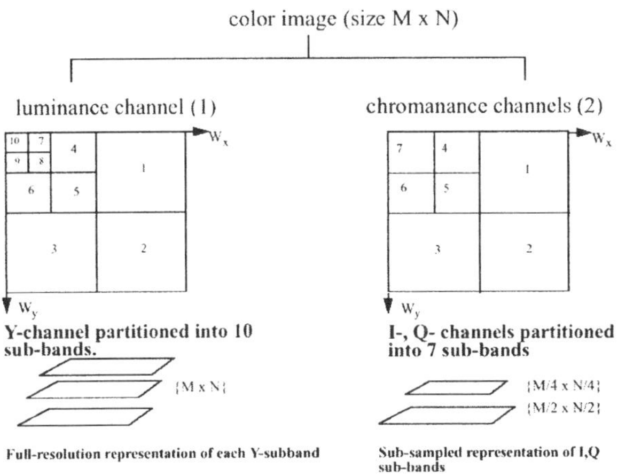

Figure 29: Wavelet decomposition for corrosion detection. The feature vector uses components from the luminance and chrominance channels as illustrated.

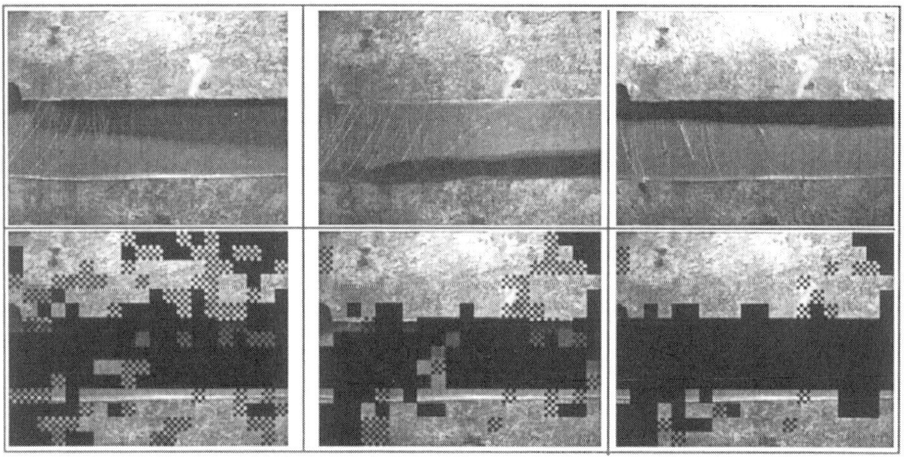

Figure 30: Extension to multiple lighting alternatives. (top) three lighting alternatives; (bottom left and middle) outputs under corresponding to lighting conditions; (bottom right) block-by-block selection of highest confidence of three alternatives.

A small follow-up effort to extend the analysis to finding the optimum fusion of several classifications is illustrated in Figure 30. Consistent with the human inspectors' practice of examining the aircraft skin under multiple lighting conditions, we proceeded to (i) examine multiple images with different lighting direction and directionality; (ii) define confidence in terms of absolute difference between output and threshold; (iii) output is mosaic of individual block classifications with highest confidence over the set of images covering each block. Inspection of the figure illustrates the substantial improvement in detection and removal of ambiguity obtained by this fusion technique.

9.3.1.6 Crack detection pipelines

Although crack detection and classification worked reasonably well using a neural network scheme that paralleled the scheme outlined above for corrosion detection and classification, a rule-based scheme implemented in a fuzzy logic framework worked substantially better. For comparison, in this section we will thus outline the key features of the fuzzy logic implementation. We will also attempt to discern *why* one of these problems seems to be more amenable to a neural network solution, the other to a fuzzy logic, i.e., rule-based solution.

First, crack-line features in the image were identified by a standard edge-finding algorithm approach. Edges were then characterized by a five-component feature vector:

- *edge length:* the number of pixels in the edge;
- *propagation depth:* the number of scales in which the edge is seen;
- *edge shape:* the RMS difference between the edge pixels and a robust straight line fit to the edge pixels;
- *edge type:* normal or ridge edge type (see Figure 31);
- *differential intensity:* a measure of line quality in which scratches yield negative number and cracks yield a 1positive number.

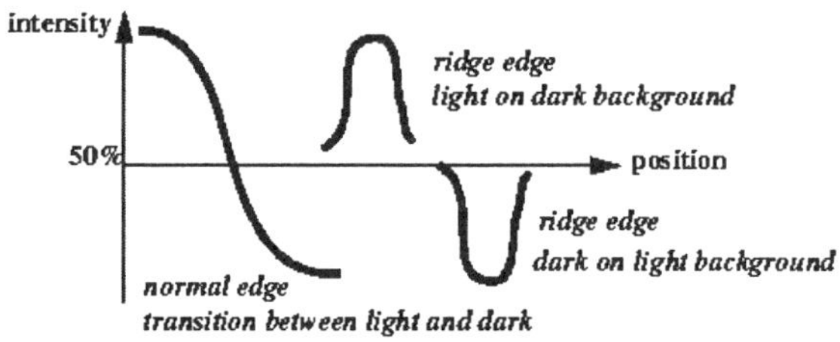

Figure 31: Crack feature vector components.

Discussions with visual inspectors of aircraft discerned many rules that they routinely apply to distinguish among various line-like features on aircraft skins. Step-like features, e.g., between painted and unpainted regions, are clearly neither scratches nor cracks, and are easily eliminated both visually and algorithmically. Ridge-like features may be light on a dark background or dark on a light background; in general the former are scratches and the latter are scratches, but this cannot be guaranteed, since the appearance of a scratch may change with both lighting angle and viewing angle. However a true crack is almost invariably dark. The inspectors' rules may be summarized in this slightly simplified form:

- if edge is dark and edge type is ridge then edge is crack;
- if edge is dark and edge shape is line then edge is crack;
- if edge is dark and edge length is short or medium then edge is crack;
- if edge is dark and edge propagation depth is low then edge is crack.

These rules are encoded as fuzzy logic membership functions as illustrated in Figure 32. The figure also illustrates the meaning of "light and dark ridge-type edges".

So we may now ask *why* fuzzy logic works better for cracks whereas neural networks work better for corrosion? We don't know, but we feel we can offer some reasonable speculation, and, based on this experience, some higher level guidance about what kind of problems are most amenable to which techniques. It seems that corrosion is detected by a relatively low level two-dimensional pattern matching process with little reasoning involved:

- <this feature vector> is located in <a particular subspace> of the space of feature vectors that has been segmented into regions corresponding to <corrosion>, <no corrosion>, <possible corrosion>.

In contrast, crack-like features are best classified as being cracks, scratches, etc., via a relatively higher-level semantic reasoning process:

- ... if <feature appearance> then <feature nature>...

involving the invocation of a set of rules that are conveniently implemented mechanically via a fuzzy logic formulation.

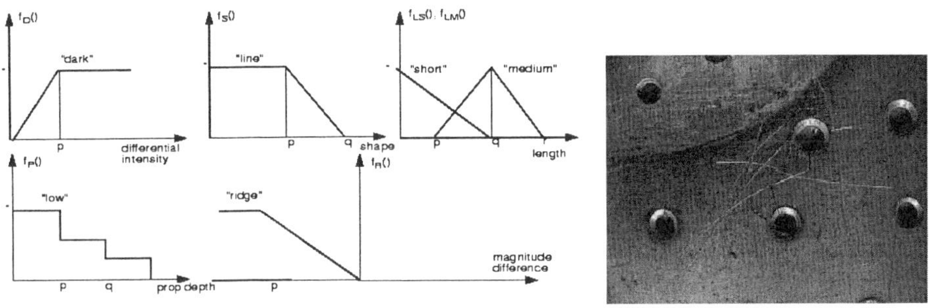

Figure 32: Fuzzy logic, i.e., rule-based alternative to neural network classifier. (left) membership functions; (right) illustration of "light and dark ridge-type edges".

9.3.1.7 State-of-the-art of robotic inspection and flaw detection

The state-of-the-art of robotic inspection and flaw detection may be summarized as follows:

- All major subsystems have been demonstrated:
  - mobility, e.g., robotic crawlers move and navigate on the aircraft;
  - manipulation, e.g., eddy current scanning, dynamic lighting;
  - measurement, e.g., probabilities of specific flaws;
  - monitoring, e.g., workstations for teleoperation and inspection.
- CIMP delivered useful data to on-the- job inspectors in actual environment;
- ANDI demonstrated vision-based alignment and sensor scanning;
- Algorithms have been demonstrated for detection of:
  - cracks: fuzzy logic works better than neural networks;
  - corrosion: neural networks work better than fuzzy logic.

The theory and technology are thus manifestly ready for commercialization.

9.3.2 Odor detection and classification using arrays of relatively non-specific sensors

Chemical sensing systems are required for a variety of applications, including household safety, e.g., sensing for gas leaks, automotive efficiency, e.g., monitoring and controlling air-fuel mixture, industrial production, e.g., semiconductor dopant stream monitoring, health care, e.g., monitoring for tell-tale body odors [34], and military/security applications, e.g., explosives detection and identification. Among the enormous variety of chemically responsive sensors and instruments available, we are particularly interested in metal oxide semiconductor (MOS) chemically sensitive resistors. These "Taguchi sensors" [35,36] are in widespread use in many applications, especially in Japan, where sensing for residential gas leaks is mandatory.

Tin is commonly the metal employed. Its oxide, SnO_2, is a ceramic-like insulator. But if the oxide is slightly reduced, to $SnO_{2\text{-}\varepsilon}$ (where ε is small) then the slight excess of metal, i.e., free electrons, makes it an n-type semiconductor. Adding oxygen in the surrounding gas phase environment causes ε to decrease, thus causing the material's resistivity to increase, whereas removing oxygen – or adding a reducing (fuel) gas – causes ε to increase, thus causing the material's resistivity to decrease. Empirically the resistance of a MOS sensor pretty well obeys the relationship $R = R_0\ ([O_2]/(1+K_X[X])^{\beta}$ where R_0 is a baseline resistance, $[O_2]$ is the concentration of oxygen in the environment, $[X]$ is the concentration of a reducing gas contaminant in the environment, K_X is the rate constant for reaction between X and O_2, and β is a constant of order unity that depends on the particular sensor.

The good news is that that MOS sensors are inexpensive, rugged, and – for appropriate sample types – exquisitely sensitive. The bad news is that there is no way for one of these sensors to distinguish between a small concentration of environmental contaminant X for which K_X is relatively large and a large concentration of environmental contaminant Y for which K_Y is relatively small. That is, their sensitivity is potentially high, but they have no selectivity.

Fortunately there is an elegant solution: the detailed sensitivities to various environmental contaminants can be modified substantially – albeit usually only empirically – by changing the operating temperature, by adding trace quantities of various metallic catalysts, or both. If we have two contaminants, X and Y, and two sensors, A and B, each sensitive to X and Y but with somewhat different sensitivities, then from the responses of A and B together we can calculate the individual concentrations [X] and [Y]. Similarly, from N sensors each of which has a distinct pattern of response to N contaminants we can obtain enough information to calculate all N concentrations.

Figure 33 illustrates a typical type of SnO_2 sensor sensitivity dependence on target chemical species – ethanol, methanol, and heptane – for two sensor temperatures. Notice the shorter recovery time of the hotter sensor, as expected.

Since the relationship $R = R_0\ ([O_2]/(1+K_X[X])^{\beta}$ is nonlinear – and since K_X, the sensitivity to X, often depends on the concentration of moisture or another contaminant Y – in practice the concentrations of multiple simultaneously present components are rarely easy to actually back out. These difficulties present us with at least three opportunities for neural network solution:

- identifying the model parameters (b, K_X) that describe response to individual contaminants as a function of concentration and temperature;
- calibrating multi-sensor systems in the face of cross sensitivity, i.e., the sensitivity to X depends on the concentration of Y;
- learning the responses particular sensors and sensor arrays show to new types of environmental contaminants, chemical warfare threats, odors symptomatic of health problems, etc., without any requirement to redesign hardware or modify the architecture of existing software.

Figure 34 illustrates, on the left, an assortment of Taguchi-type sensors. They are all "homemade" [35] except for the commercial sensor in the middle column, last row (this is one sensor with the protective cap removed). The one commercial device is a single sensor, but all the homemade ones are in one way or another integrated arrays of multiple sensors. The enlargement on the right shows one of these: the three different color shades in the horizontal rows indicate that each row has been prepared with a different noble metal catalyst. The dark vertical stripe at the left is a restive heater; there is thus a temperature gradient decreasing from left to right across the device. By appropriate selection of contacts, 25 different resistances can be measured, each characteristic of a particular temperature and catalyst.

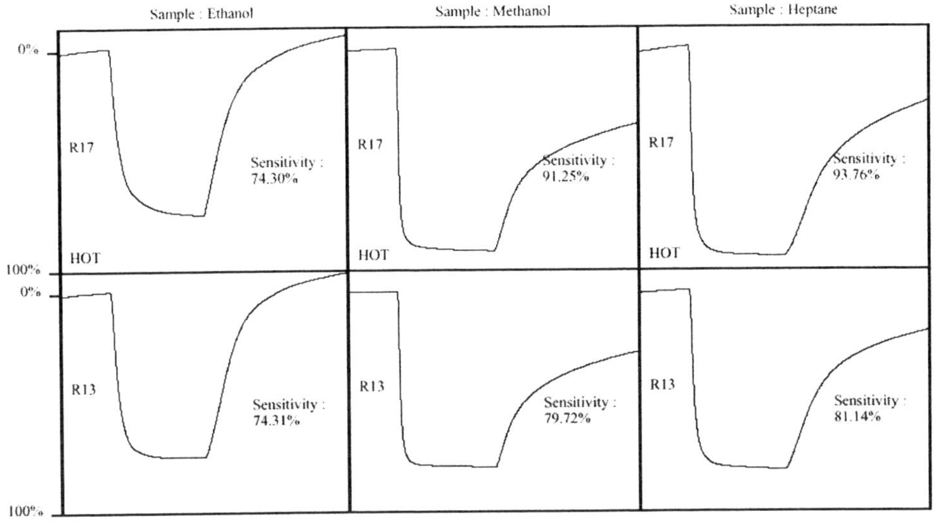

Figure 33: Sensitivity to transient samples of ethanol, methanol, and heptane of two chemically sensitive resistors, R17 and R13, essentially identical but R17 is at a higher temperature. Horizontal axis is time, vertical axis is percent change in resistance from baseline.

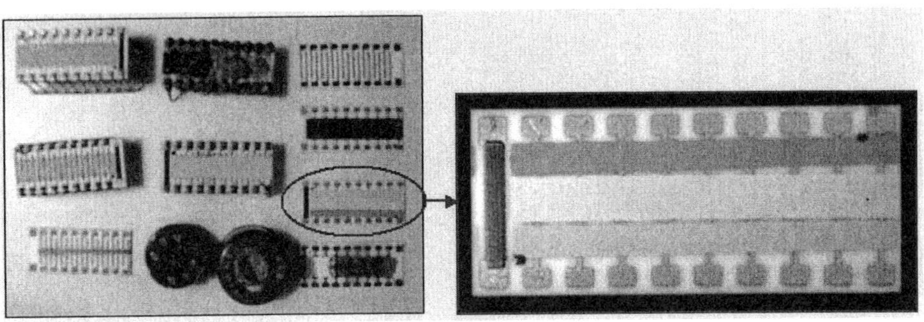

Figure 34: Integrated chemical sensing systems.

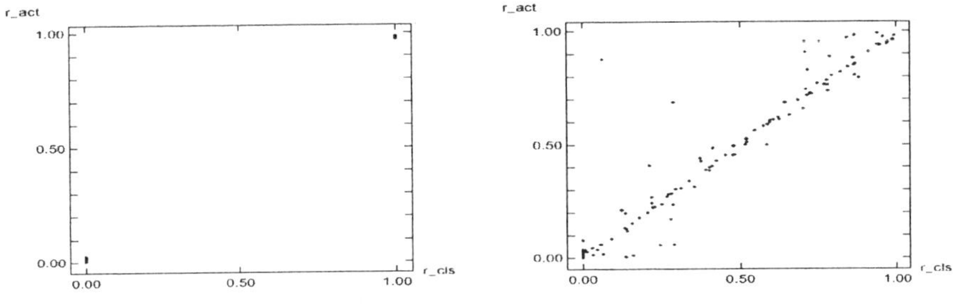

Figure 35: Classification and quantitation: (left) classification – output is one of two components (dots in lower left and upper right corners); (right) quantitation: output is fractional concentration of two components.

Applications of neural networks to classification and quantitation of data from sensor arrays is illustrated in Figure 35. On the left, we see the output of a neural network that was trained on single components and exercised on single components, e.g., ethanol and methanol. All the run-time data are concentrated in the lower left and upper right corners, indicating classification behavior with near-discrete outputs near 0 and 1. On the right we see the output of a neural network that was trained on random binary mixtures and exercised on random binary mixtures. All the run-time data are concentrated around the diagonal, indicating well-calibrated quantitation behavior.

9.3.3 Summary

We examined in detail two application case studies in which neural networks were used in practical measurement and control problems broadly in the field of robotics. The first application, in the field of aircraft inspection, involved image understanding for the presence of corrosion and cracks in a well defined and well understood context. The second application, in the field of chemical sensing, was more diffuse, in that it needs to consider a wider range of potential field applications, and a wide variety of requirements whose endpoints are identified as "classification" – what is it? – and "quantitation" – how much of it is there? In reality, few applications are really so black-and-white.

A capsule summary and statement of conclusions is:

- How best to capture and automate a human classification and decision-making capability may depend strongly on whether the task is primarily "left brain", i.e., quantitative or "right brain", i.e., qualitative.
  - For a quality-based decision, e.g., texture-based detection of corrosion, a neural net solution seems more effective.
  - For a quantity-based decision, e.g., discrimination of cracks from scratches, a fuzzy logic solution seems more effective.
- Neural networks are pragmatically useful for capturing and interpolating complex nonlinear response surfaces, e.g., with the sort of cross-sensitivities exhibited by chemically sensitive resistors.

References

[1] Rosenblatt F, Principles of Neurodynamics: Perceptrons and the Theory of Brain Mechanisms. 1961, Washington DC: Spartan Press.

[2] Minsky M, Steps Toward Artificial Intelligence. Proceedings of the IRE, 1960. 49: p. 8-30. Available on-line at http://www.ai.mit.edu/people/minsky/papers/steps.html

[3] Galkin I, "Crash Introduction to Artificial Neural Networks," 2001, http://ulcar.uml.edu/~iag/CS/Intro-to-ANN.html

[4] Hertz J, A Krogh, and R G Palmer, Introduction to the theory of neural computation, vol. I: Addison-Wesley, 1991. (Santa Fe Institute Series in the Sciences of Complexity)

[5] Lewis F L, "Neural Network Control of Robot Manipulators," in IEEE Expert Intelligent Systems & Their Applications, 1996.

[6] Dorst L, Lambalgen M v, and Voorbraak F, Reasoning with uncertainty in robotics: international workshop, RUR95, Amsterdam, The Netherlands, December 4-6, 1995; Springer (1966).

[7] Hebert M, C E Thorpe and A Stentz, Intelligent unmanned ground vehicles: autonomous navigation research at Carnegie Mellon, Kluwer (1997).

[8] Lewis FL, Jagannathan S and Yesildirek A, Neural network control of robot manipulators and nonlinear systems, Taylor & Francis (1999).

[9] Omidvar O and P v d Smagt, Neural systems for robotics, Academic (1997).

[10] Pomerleau D A, Neural network perception for mobile robot guidance, Kluwer (1993).

[11] Wilson E, Experiments in neural-network control of a free-flying space robot, NASA NTIS (1993).

[12] Zalzala A M S and A S Morris, Neural networks for robotic control: theory and applications, Ellis Horwood (1996).

[13] Fogelman Soulie F and P Gallinari, Industrial Applications of Neural Networks, 1998. (From ICANN'95 conference of the European Neural Network Society.)

[14] Neural Network Applications in Manufacturing (compiled primarily by Stefan Korn, Glasgow Caledonian University) http://www.emsl.pnl.gov:2080/proj/neuron/bib/manufacturing.html
[15] NN Reference - Robotics (books, classic papers, etc) http://www.nd.com/nnreference/nnref-robotics.htm
[16] Marr D and T Poggio (1976). Cooperative computation of stereo disparity. Science, 194:283--287.
[17] Albus J and J M Evans Jr, sidebar in "Robot Systems", Scientific American, February 1976.
[18] Albus J, "A New Approach to Manipulator Control: The Cerebellar Model Articulation Controller (CMAC)," Journal of Dynamic Systems, Measurement and Control, American Soc. of Mechanical Engineers, Sep 1975.
[19] Davis I and M Siegel, "Vision Algorithms for Guiding the Automated NonDestructive Inspector of Aging Aircraft Skins", presented at SPIE Conference on Aging Infrastructures, San Diego CA, 1993.
[20] Baluja S, Evolution of an artificial neural network based autonomous land vehicle controller, http://www.ri.cmu.edu/pubs/pub_3832.html and P Batavia, D Pomerleau and C Thorpe, Applying Advanced Learning Algorithms to ALVINN, 1996, Robotics Institute, Carnegie Mellon University, http://www.ri.cmu.edu/pubs/pub_423.html
[21] Davis I and A Stentz, Sensor fusion for autonomous outdoor navigation using neural networks, Proceedings 1995 IEEE/RSJ International Conference On Intelligent Robotic Systems (IROS '95) 1995, http://www.ri.cmu.edu/pubs/pub_3619.html and http://www.ri.cmu.edu/pub_files/pub2/davis_ian_1995_2/davis_ian_1995_2.pdf
[22] Ang W-T, C Riviere and P Khosla. An Active Hand-held Instrument for Enhanced Microsurgical Accuracy, Third International Conference on Medical Image Computing and Computer-Assisted Intervention, 2000, http://www.ri.cmu.edu/pubs/pub_3511.html
[23] Grace R, V E Byrne, D M Bierman, J M Legrand, D Gricourt, B K Davis, J J Staszewski and B A Carnahan, Drowsy Driver Detection System for Heavy Vehicles, 17th Digital Avionics Systems Conference, 2001, http://www.ri.cmu.edu/pubs/pub_3644.html
[24] Gunatilake P and M Siegel, "Remote Enhanced Visual Inspection of Aircraft by a Mobile Robot," in 1998 iMTC Conference, 1998, pp. 49 - 58. http://www.ri.cmu.edu/pubs/pub_1316.html
[25] Ferreira E and B Krogh, Training Guidelines for Neural Networks to Estimate Stability Regions, Proceedings of 1999 American Control Conference, 1999 June, v4 pp.2829 - 2833. http://www.ri.cmu.edu/pubs/pub_3064.html
[26] Murali K and J Bares, Constructing fast hydraulic robot models for optimal motion planning, Field and Service Robotics Conference (FSR '99), 1999 August). http://www.ri.cmu.edu/pubs/pub_2932.html
[27] Munos R, L Baird, and A Moore, "Gradient Descent Approaches to Neural-Net-Based Solutions of the Hamilton-Jacobi-Bellman Equation," in International Joint Conference on Neural Networks.1999. http://www.ri.cmu.edu/pubs/pub_2623.html
[28] Nechyba M, "Learning and Validation of Human Control Strategies" (thesis), Robotics Institute Carnegie Mellon University, 1998. http://www.ri.cmu.edu/pubs/pub_478.html
[29] Liang Z and C Thorpe, "Stereo and Neural Network-based Pedestrian Detection," presented at Int'l Conf. on Intelligent Transportation Systems, 1999. http://www.ri.cmu.edu/pubs/pub_3317.html
[30] Romero R, D Touretzky, and R H Thibadeau, "Optical Chinese Character Recognition using Probabilistic Neural Networks", 1996. http://www.ri.cmu.edu/pubs/pub_2962.html
[31] Tian Y-L, T Kanade, and J Cohn, "Recognizing upper face action units for facial expression analysis," IEEE Conference on Computer Vision and Pattern Recognition (CVPR '00), 2000. http://www.ri.cmu.edu/pubs/pub_3625.html
[32] Waldherr S, S Thrun, and R Romero, "A neural-network based approach for recognition of pose and motion gestures on a mobile robot," 5th Brazilian Symposium on Neural Networks, 1998, pp. 79 -84. http://www.ri.cmu.edu/pubs/pub_3589.html
[33] Siegel M, P Gunatilake, and G W Podnar, "Robotic Assistants for Aircraft Inspectors," in IEEE Instrumentation and Measurements (I&M) Magazine, vol. 1: IEEE Instrumentation and Measurements Society, 1998, pp. 16-30.
[34] Wu H-D and M Siegel, "Odor-Based Incontinence Sensor," in IEEE Instrumentation and Measurement Technology Conference (IMTC'2000). Baltimore MD: IEEE Instrumentation and Measurement Society, 2000.
[35] Siegel M, "Olfaction, Metal Oxide Semiconductor Gas Sensors, and Neural Nets," in Traditional and Non-Traditional Sensors for Robotics (NATO Advanced Workshop, Maratea Italy), vol. F63, T. Henderson, ed., Berlin Germany: Springer-Verlag, 1990, pp. 143-157
[36] Taguchi N, US Patent 3 695 848, 1972.

Neural Networks for Instrumentation, Measurement and Related Industrial Applications
S. Ablameyko et al. (Eds.)
IOS Press, 2003

Chapter 10
Neural Networks for Measurement and Instrumentation in Laser Processing

Cesare ALIPPI
Department of Electronics and Information, Politecnico di Milano
piazza L. da Vinci 32, 20133 Milano, Italy

Anthony BLOM
Centre For Technology - Mass Products & Technology, Royal Philips Electronics NV
P.O. Box 218, 5600 MD, Eindhoven, The Netherlands

Abstract. Laser processing is in general a complex process, requiring a lot of knowledge and experience for introducing and maintaining it in industry. This "expert knowledge threshold" obstructs the acceptance of laser technology for new applications. Introduction of process monitoring techniques in combination with sophisticated data analysis tools and artificial intelligence has opened new options to add self-tuning capabilities and closed loop feedback control to laser processing equipment. Some very interesting work has been done in recent years by using soft computing techniques to reach a new level of equipment performance in the field of laser material processing. Advances have been obtained for different types of laser processes, ranging from heavy industry seam welding in shipyard building down to automotive, laser cutting of metal sheets and micro spot welding in the electronics industry. Multi sensor process monitoring systems have been evaluated and their (multi dimensional) outputs related to the process performance through soft computing techniques. Sets of fast sensors are the basic elements to monitor the process from which signal features are extracted and processed by composite traditional/neural-based techniques to perform automatic classification of welded and cut parts. The article presents a comprehensive presentation of the laser processing technology, starting from the basic physics of the process up to a set of industrial applications covering a large range of applications solved by the interaction of traditional processing techniques and neural networks ones.

10.1. Introduction

Although laser processing is an accepted technology in industry for several years, the activity is still surrounded with highly educated process engineers for maintaining process performance and introducing new applications. To solve this problem, most of the self-respecting laser equipment suppliers have an application laboratory to carry out dedicated application development for their customers.

In order to make laser technology easier accepted in industry, there is a drive to introduce self-tuning characteristics to the laser processing equipment, making the system more robust to changing parameters in the process. Introduction of feedback techniques based on information from the evolving process is necessary to achieve this goal. Some form of process monitoring has to be introduced and the process signals have to be analysed and related to the quality of the process. It is at this point where the strength of sophisticated soft computing technologies is essential. The main problem here is that the quality of the process operation cannot be measured directly with a straightforward measurement, as is done with traditional feedback loops. Instead, the wished information has to be derived from indirect measurements done on the process. Therefore, multi sensor systems and/or sensor arrays (camera's) are envisaged to monitor the evolution over time of the entities involved in the laser process.

Soft computing routines are indispensable to process the recorded data for identifying the significant signal properties and finding the relations between the process and the sensor signals since laser processes feature a relatively high degree of stochastic variation in the sensor signals due to the partly chaotic behaviour of the actual fusion process. This puts even higher demands on the signal processing techniques to achieve a certain confidence level of the extracted information. Having the laser process operational, it becomes interesting to know whether the processed artefact is good or not.

This quality analysis –most of times associated with a classifier development– is the natural playground for Neural Network structures or similar techniques. Of course, accuracy of the final solution to the application is a main goal to be pursued but not the unique one. In fact, fast calculation routines are essential to prevent the process from running into out of control conditions or, at a higher level, satisfy real time requirement. The accuracy/constraints trade-off can be reached by exploring the solution space of the application and investigating different solutions integrating traditional processing techniques and parameterised ones.

The structure of the paper is as follows. Section 2 provides an introduction of the basic physics and laser sources associated with laser processing. An overview of the most relevant laser-based applications is given in section 3. Section 4 focuses on the design of a composite traditional/neural network-based system solving the quality analysis problem. Aspects related to candidate solution generation, training, validation, features extraction and selection are addressed in detail. Finally, section 5 provides three applications related to laser processing (seam welding, laser cutting and laser spot welding) in which the authors have taken active part in designing the systems and developing a composite solution. Such applications have been part of two European Union projects: the Brite-Euram project "MAIL" (Multi sensor Assisted Intelligent Laser processing) and the IMS project "SLAPS" (Self tuning user independent LAser Processing unitS).

10.2. Equipment and instrumentation in industrial laser processing

Laser material processing is a thermal treatment of the material. The energy flow is coming from a very intense light source within a very limited wavelength range. This limited wavelength range is obtained from the stimulated emission of light from a cavity, i.e., an optical oscillator. The most important features of the light from these laser sources is that it can be focussed to very small spot sizes, enabling very precise and local heating of the work piece. Moreover, light can be manipulated very comfortably by using scanner mirrors. Fast systems can be created in this way, as the dynamic behaviour of the scanning system is the main limiting factor. Because there is no physical contact between energy source and the work piece, there is a lot of design freedom in the machinery. Moreover, the contactless treatment is of high importance for the ever-increasing miniaturisation in modern industry. One of the features of the focussed laser beam is that it enables deep processing, which opened the way to laser drilling, laser cutting and heavy industry laser welding.

10.2.1 Laser sources

A laser source is an optical resonator in which a certain amount of energy is kind of bouncing between two mirrors as a light wave. The light is emitted by a medium between the mirrors which determines the wavelength of the light (colour) because it is related to a specific energy jump of the electrons of the excited medium. The medium is excited by means of an external light source. The electrons of the excited atoms can fall back to the lower level spontaneously or stimulated by the external excitation source as explained by A. Einstein in 1915. The special thing about the stimulated emission is that these emissions have the same wavelength, phase and polarisation as the source it was excited by.

From the time that the theoretical proof was given that laser could exist (1915), it took about 45 years before one was actually build into operation [1].

Nowadays, there are quite a number of different laser sources; only those types, which are used for the processes to be discussed, will shortly be described here.

10.2.1.1 CO_2 laser

The CO_2 laser was one of the first types to be developed and used for industrial applications. The laser is of the molecular gas types, with a mixture of gases: He (65-80%), N_2 (15-22%) and CO_2 (5-13%). Only the CO_2 gas is responsible for the laser radiation due to the positive fact that Nitrogen can be excited rather easily. This is done by means of a gas discharge in the gas mixture exciting the nitrogen into a level which coincides with the excitation level of the carbon-dioxide molecules. Energy is transferred from the N_2 atoms to the CO_2 atoms with He acting as a catalyst.

The main advantage of this laser type is the very high efficiency of the laser, being around 5-15%. It also has a very good beam quality. Due to the large wavelength of about 10 μm, the diffraction behaviour is courser compared to what we are used to in the visible wavelength range: very small spot sizes are thus not possible with this laser type.

10.2.1.2 Nd:Yag laser

Nd:YAG lasers are solid state ion laser based on the excitation of a Neodymium (≈1%) doped Yttrium-Aluminium Granate crystal. The crystal is pumped with an optical source, which can be a tungsten halogen lamp, a krypton arc lamp or a solid-state laser diode array (AlGaAs). The pumping bands are in the region of 800 nm, after which several laser lines exist (the 1064 line is the most important one). An often-used arrangement is an elliptical cylinder filled with water for cooling the system. The Nd:YAG crystal rod is placed in one focus line of the cylinder, while the pumping (flash)lamp is placed in the other.

The lasers can operate either in continuous wave mode (CW) or in pulsed mode, either via switching of the pumping lamps or using a Q-switch (switching the damping of the optical resonator). The emission will not start as long as the damping remains high. The pumped optical energy will remain in the Nd:YAG rod. Immediately after switching the Q, the accumulated energy will come available via stimulated emission in the form of a laser pulse.

10.2.2 General laser processing aspects

For all applications in laser processing there are some general rules related to the interaction between laser radiation and the work piece material to be processed [2,3].

10.2.2.1 Absorption, reflection, transmission

Radiation onto a surface will partly be absorbed by the material, partly reflected and partly pass through the material. The actual interaction between laser beam and material is taking place in a very thin upper layer of the work piece. Heat conductivity has to take care of the distribution of the energy through the structure.

10.2.2.2 Temperature dependency of absorption and diffusion

Since the specific resistance is temperature dependent, the absorption will also change with the temperature. Metals show a positive temperature coefficient for the specific resistance, which leads to an increasing absorption of laser radiation with increasing temperature. A step-like change of the specific resistance is often observed around the phase change from solid to liquid and can create problems in processing some materials (like copper). Apart from the changing absorption coefficient, also the heat conductivity changes with temperature. Depending on the type of material, this change can be either positive or negative.

10.2.2.3 Plasma formation

At high energy densities, (>10 W/m2), plasma may be formed, which absorbs the incoming laser beam for a certain part. The laser process at the surface of the work piece will thus be obstructed for a short period, because the plasma formation will stop as soon as the obstruction reaches a certain level. A kind of oscillating process behaviour will result in this way. Absorption of laser energy by the plasma depends very much on the wavelength of the laser, which is the reason why this effect is not observed for all laser processing applications.

10.2.2.4 Keyhole formation

Figure 1 shows the different process phases. A strong recoil pressure will be built up with surface temperatures well above the evaporation temperature (2). This 'local high pressure regime' will push away the molten material, leading to an increasing absorption due to the bowl shaped surface (3). The increased absorption will stimulate further heating and thus increase evaporation, leading to the formation of a hole in the surface. The hole will act as a kind of 'black hole' or 'wave guide', which traps the laser beam for almost 100% and guides its energy to the bottom through multiple reflections along the edges of the hole. The process has now entered the drilling phase (4). For some processes this is a desired operating condition (drilling, cutting, deep welding), for others it is highly undesirable (Structuring, annealing, bending, heat conduction welding).

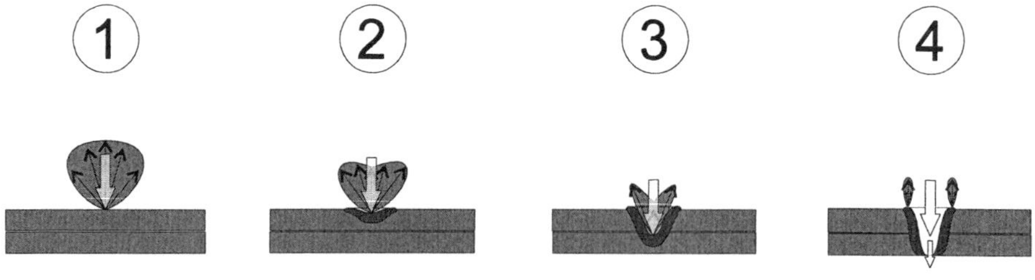

Figure 1: Laser processing phases; Heating (1), Melting (2), Fusion (3), Full penetration (4)

10.3. Principal laser-based applications

10.3.1 Laser cutting

Laser cutting is used in industry all over the world as an accepted technology. Basically the process can be divided into two phases: First a hole has to be made in case a cutting contour does not start at the edge of the work piece, a process normally indicated as 'piercing'. After that, either the processing head with beam delivery optics or the work piece has to be moved to let the laser beam remove material along the traversing path. Both phases will have their specific process conditions. Figure 2 shows a simple representation of the process.

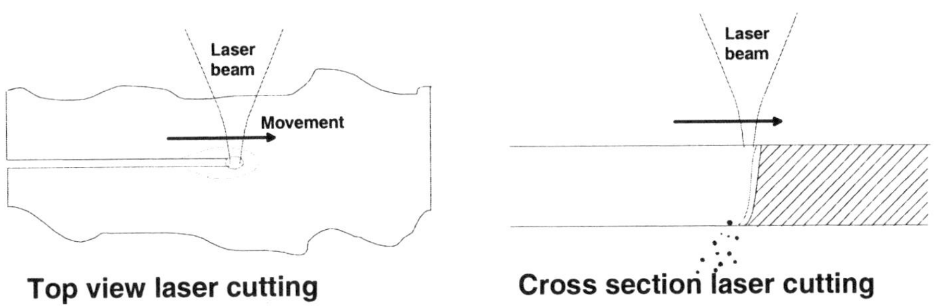

Figure 2: Basic laser cutting process

Laser cutting heads contain the focussing optics and a nozzle, which provides the processing gas. The laser energy melts the material, while the processing gas blows out the molten metal from the gap. Often a reactive gas (O_2) is used, in which case the reaction provides extra energy for the cutting process.

Most machines are meant for processing steel or steel alloys from about 1 mm up to 10 mm or even thicker. CO_2 lasers are mostly used for these types machines because of their high power output and high efficiency.

10.3.1.1 Most important process disturbances

There are many process parameters, which have to be set for a certain process. The most important ones are: processing gas flow, cutting speed, laser power and focus position.

Modern machines are equipped with automatic focussing techniques, a technology, which measures the distance between processing head and the work piece and maintains it at a specific fixed value for that machine: this would normally not create problems.

Operators are always in a hurry and tend to obtain the highest possible cutting speed in order to shorten the process time. In case the cutting speed gets so high that the processing gas is not able to remove the material, the cutting process looses efficiency very fast. In such a case the laser beam 'runs out of the cut'. Modern machines detect the threatening danger of this situation by detecting the amount of plasma between work piece and nozzle. When excessive plasma level is detected, the processing speed will be decreased for good performing cutting. When the cutting speed gets in a critical high zone, the material removal becomes unstable, which results in the forming of burrs and metal pearls on the lower edge of the work piece and along the cutting sides. Although the cutting (separation) is still achieved, the result can be unacceptable. Selecting a safe cutting speed is the alternative, which means that the most economic cutting speed is not used.

Experts who are working with laser cutting machines have noticed that there is a relation between the pattern of the sparks coming from the cut at the lower side of the work piece and the quality of the cut. Although it seems pretty logical to look at the spark pattern, the relation between cutting quality and spark pattern is not that simple. Besides changing with work piece geometry, it also changes significantly with different materials.

The challenge is to find the relationship between the quality of the cutting process and the behaviour of the pattern of sparks.

10.3.1.2 Process monitoring

The distance between work piece and processing head is measured using a non-contact capacitive or in-contact inductive or resistive detection technique. A straightforward control technique is implemented to drive the focus servo loop for optimum focus position. Important for the proper operation of the capacitive sensing technique is that the amount of plasma between work piece and processing head remains low, because it can have dramatic effect on the impedance between nozzle tip and work piece. Plasma monitoring can be used to identify the 'running out of the beam' in case the processing speed is too high for the given process conditions. Immediate change of the cutting speed or laser power is the remedy to proceed. Maintaining the process in such a condition that it is well away from an unsafe or critical situation results in a good cutting quality while remaining at the highest possible processing speed, would be the best. When it is possible to find a clear relation between the sparks pattern and the cutting quality, this would be a good tool for classification of the process quality as well as an option to control the process for optimum performance. A standard CCD camera can be used for this purpose, in combination with a frame grabber board for capturing and storing the images on a mass storage medium.

10.3.1.3 Automatic classification and options for control

Automatic control of the height of the cutting head above the surface of the work piece is already state of the art technique. Recording of the plasma behaviour and optical emission during the piercing and cutting processes is one important source of information about the behaviour of the process and the related work piece quality. Analysing the 'spreading of sparks' in relation to the quality of cutting is a very promising technique, both as far as automatic classification of processed work pieces is concerned as well as for control of the process conditions. Cutting speed and/or laser power are the most obvious parameters to be controlled in this case.

10.3.2 Laser seam welding

Laser seam welding is a technique which is used over a wide range of industrial activities. It ranges from fine seam welding of battery casings, pacemaker casings via seam welding of automobile body parts, automotive engine- and transmission parts up to seam welding of subassemblies for container vessels.

An often-used weld geometry is the but-joint, in which case the two parts that have to be joined are placed next to each other in the same plane. Another geometry frequently used when processing metal sheets is the overlap fillet weld or lap joint. One metal sheet is placed over the other in this case, while welding at the edge of the top plate. Also the T-joint is often used, which means that a plate is positioned (almost) perpendicular to a second sheet and welded in both corners between these plates.

For seam welding, the local processing area is moved along the line where both work piece parts meet. The most used laser systems for seam welding are CO_2 lasers (heavy industry and automotive) and continuous Nd:YAG lasers (low power seam welding). Also seam welding by overlapping spot welds, using a pulsed Nd:YAG laser is applied in industry. What makes laser welding so special is the ability to obtain a deep processing depth due to the keyhole effect. This is very different from arc welding, which is the biggest competitor on welding. Here the heat is mainly generated in the sub surface of the work piece parts, where the largest portion of the current flows. With the keyhole in action and the processing area moved along the seam, new material will be melted at the 'front' of the keyhole, while material will cool down and solidify in the 'trail' of the keyhole. In this way, the actual fusion takes place in the trail of the keyhole (see figure 3).

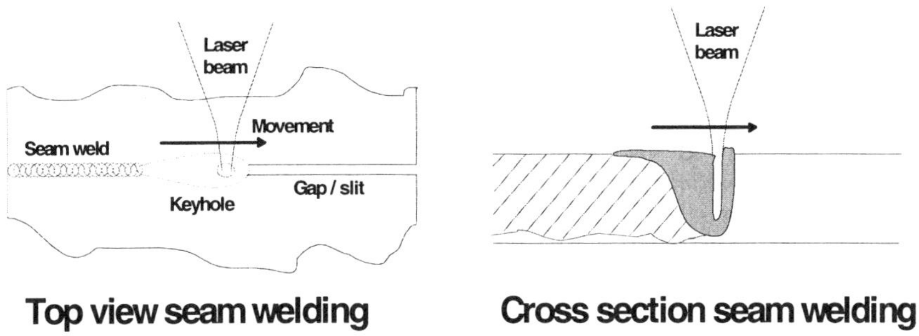

Figure 3: Laser seam welding

10.3.2.1 Most important process disturbances

Although the keyhole operation of laser welding is nice from the welding point of view, the problem on the process side is that it is not simple to keep the keyhole process in a stable operating area, without vapour bubbles ending up in the solidified material.

The most important process disturbances are:
- Unstable keyhole operation, leading to pores
- Too large gap between parts, giving no or a bad fusion
- Focus position, seam tracking, work piece parts alignment

Related to the above process disturbances, the key quality parameters for seam welding are:
- Penetration depth of the fusion area
- No pores
- Proper alignment of the parts
- No more then a certain percentage of weld defects (no or bad fusion).

10.3.2.2 Process monitoring

Most of the monitoring systems used today are based on the detection of the optical emission from the keyhole area. Single sensor systems look for deviations from the nominal operating process. The major drawback of this technique is that the system is based on the integral process emission from the keyhole. It can detect that a welding process is not performing normally, but the cause for this performance decrease cannot be recognised. Other systems have made some distinction in the source of radiation and monitor separately the emission from the weld pool surface (temperature) the plume above the surface (plume emission) and the reflected laser power from the welding area (absorption). This brings more detailed information from the welding area, which can be used to pin point the cause for a certain defective operation of the process.

More sophisticated process monitoring techniques are being developed at this moment, revealing information about the thermal distribution of energy through the work piece structure. Either line array cameras or 2-D array cameras are used for this technology. The recently introduced CMOS camera's are of interest here for their large dynamic response. They can view the high intensity of the actual keyhole as well as the low level (near) infrared emission of the trail of the seam. Although the advantages of imaging technology are there, the implementation in industrial set-ups is not always easy and certainly needs more sophisticated processing.

10.3.2.3 Automatic classification and options for control

Classification of seam welds is nowadays often done on bases of the optical emission from the keyhole area, by observing the behaviour of this emission over time. Deviations from the nominal value exceeding pre-set values are identified as defective seam welds.

As mentioned in the previous chapter, control actions can only be implemented if the cause of the process deviations can be traced down to a certain (set of) process parameters, which have to be changed for better performance. The new (heat) imaging technique which is coming up for seam weld process monitoring will need image analysis techniques to extract the information about the performance of the process. Developments are in full progress now on this topic.

10.3.3 Laser spot welding

Laser (micro) spot welding is a joining technology, which is frequently used for miniature welds on small products. The typical characteristic of this joining technology is that the laser beam remains focussed on the same spot while processing. The processing times are short, in the order of 1 – 20 ms. The laser power during the short time is still considerable, ranging from a few hundred Watts for thin stainless steel up to several kilowatts for copper parts. Pulsed Nd:YAG lasers are mostly used for this type of joining technology

With the beam stationary on the same spot, the process runs very fast from the heating phase into melting of the metal and soon after that to keyhole operation. The short process time gives a low thermal loading of the work piece, which is one of the most important features of this joining technology. The process runs rather stable on stainless steel products due to the physical behaviour of stainless steel. For other metals the spot welding behaviour can be much less stable. Copper for instance, is a material having a low absorption coefficient for 1064 nm light (about 5% at room temperature), while the heat conductivity is also very high. It is difficult to get the energy in, and when it is in, it is distributed very fast through the structure: the surface temperature will only increase slowly. With increasing temperature however, the absorption increases while the heat conductivity decreases: energy will be accepted easier while it is diffusing slower through the structure. This leads to an avalanche kind of process behaviour. Going into the key-hole type of process phase gives another absorption increase, which means a change in process behaviour. The only option which state of the art technology offers now is to use a very carefully chosen pulse shape: the laser power changes over time during the laser pulse.

10.3.3.1 Most important process disturbances

The spot welding processes for stainless steel run very well with a stable process window. The quality of the cutting and forming tools, leaving burrs and scratches on the parts and/or not proper closing of folded metal sheets onto each other are the main process disturbances.

Pollution of the optics during operation can be a serious problem when no proper actions, like preventive maintenance/cleaning, is implemented in manufacturing.

Variations in absorption coefficient and heat conduction (gap between parts) are important factors in laser processing of copper.

10.3.3.2 Process monitoring

The whole process of micro spot welding is based on the absorption of the laser energy and the distribution of this energy over the work piece geometry over time. A set of sensors is used to monitor the performance of the process. The use of multi sensor process monitoring is important here because the short spot weld process hardly comes into a stationary situation: The heating-, melting-, fusion and cooling phase all have a significant influence on the process result. Physical phenomena related to all these process phases have to be monitored and evaluated.

Laser input power and reflected laser power are monitored to evaluate the in-coupling of the laser energy. The infra-red emission from the weld spot is used to detect the behaviour of the surface temperature via the T4 relation between temperature and emitted power. The effect of plume emission, related to the evaporation of metal, is detected via the optical emission from this plume.

The physical properties of a metal, like electrical resistance and magnetic permeability, changes with temperature. This is the basis for using eddy current detection techniques to monitor the penetration of the melt pool through a structure of metals.

It is well known among experienced laser equipment maintenance people, that it can be heard by ear from the process, whether it runs properly or not, at least for certain types of process conditions like proper focussing. Based on this information, also the acoustic emission in the frequency range between 50 Hz and 20 kHz is detected, using a small microphone. The image of the spot welded surface can tell a lot about the quality of the weld by its appearance. Basic information like spot size, weld symmetry and presence of spatters are important from the quality point of view and can reveal extra information about the source of errors.

10.3.3.3 Automatic classification and options for control

Since several years, investigation is being done to find techniques which are able to classify the welded products automatically through the evaluation of the recorded process signals during the spot welding process and the image of the realised spot weld.

Adaptive control techniques can be used to cope with more or less slowly varying process parameters like defocusing (thermal drift), laser power at the work piece (pollution), absorption (material lot), slowly increasing gap between the parts (wear of tools), etc. Some process conditions can change from weld to weld, like for instance the gap between the parts, the absorption coefficient due to variations in surface conditions. Real-time feedback control of the laser spot welding process within each process time is the only option to cope with this range of process condition variations.

The state of the art technique at present for spot welding of difficult materials like copper and aluminium is to change the laser power during the process according to a fixed pre-determined pattern. For copper welding, the power should be very high at the beginning in order to get the process running, while it must be decreased rapidly as soon as the melting phase is starting. Research activities are now being aimed at the development of adaptive control strategies to have the system tune automatically to the most optimal pulse shape, based on the evaluation of the process signals.

A real time control loop on top of this adaptive loop is needed to handle the instantly acting process disturbances and keeping the process stable during the spot weld.

10.4. A composite system design in laser material processing applications

10.4.1 The need for a composite system in laser processing applications

Design of a laser-based application requires, as a preliminary step, the identification of the computational modules composing it. At this high level of the design flow the solution of the application is generally described as a set of interacting functional modules, each of which is characterized by a suitable algorithm. Each module of the computational chain characterizes and describes the processing to be performed by the addressed processing component.

At this abstraction level, we can identify two types of modules: the ones for which the computation is associated with a well defined and specified algorithm and those whose computation can be described by suitably parameterized unspecified elements. A FFT transform, a butterworth low-pass filter acting at a given frequency, a fixed manipulation of data are examples of the former class; a low-pass filter with an unknown ideal cutting frequency, a physical model of a process with unknown parameters and a neural network, are examples of the latter. The main difference between the two types of modules is that parameterized models represent a family of models in their unspecified parameters: a model is obtained by fixing the parameters. Before integrating parameterized models in the final application a parameter configuration (or training) phase is needed which tunes the parameters according to the information content present in a set of data generally given in terms of *(input,output)* pairs.

Parameterized modules are quite common elements in a computational chain for many laser-based applications. There are two types of parameterized models: equation-based models and model-free models. Equation-based models are characterized by a known mathematical description of the system to be approximated and only some parameters need to be identified. Examples are filters in which the cutting frequency must be tuned directly on the specific application or pre-processing modules extracting features from a given signal with a threshold identified on the application data so as to optimize a certain given goal function. In the model-free case no a priori information is available regarding the structure of the module solving part of the application. As such, the computation associated with the module must be identified by following suitable system identification procedures [4]. In this large family of modules we find ARX, ARMAX, OE, and all linear models as well as those related to static and recurrent neural networks [5].

In several applications, model-free modules are envisaged also when the physical-based equations ruling a process are given but the description is too complex for the application needs or it is computationally unacceptable (e.g., we have to compute complex differential equations). In such cases, model-free models are envisaged to simplify the process description and, indirectly, solve an accuracy/constraints tradeoff for the application.

In several cases, the solution to a complex application cannot be effectively developed by considering only "traditional" or model-free models and a composition of the two is needed. Complex *composite systems* can be derived, which combine the capabilities of soft-computing techniques of neural networks type with those associated with more traditional processing ones.

It has been experimentally shown [6] that a composite system can solve the application by providing additional freedom to the design phase and, hence, it eases the integration of several application requirements at a very high abstraction level. Among traditional application requirements we find *accuracy,* defined as a measure of the performance of the application/module. Model/system accuracy is estimated according to a suitable loss function (e.g., the Mean Squared Error) and surely represents the most relevant constraint for the application. Nevertheless, accuracy is not, in general, the unique requirement to be pursued in solving a dedicated application. *Computational and algorithm complexity* (addressing the computational load required/tolerated by the envisaged module), *robustness* (ability to tolerate classes of perturbations affecting the computational flow) just to name the few, are additional constraints which must be taken into account to derive the best embedded-solution for the particular application.

A constrained environment is particularly common in laser-based applications since we have to guarantee a real-time execution and a limited on-board memory for control/quality analysis (computational and algorithmic complexity) and finite precision representations for sensorial information and/or interim variables involved in the embedded processing (robustness). The high-level design of composite systems can be interpreted as a "codesign" activity between traditional modules and parameterised ones where, in general, a trial and error approach is considered to configure a suitable composite solution for a given application. Since a composite system can provide significant benefits in solving an application characterised by strong constraints, we suggest developing and testing a small set of composite solution whenever the use of a pure traditional or parameterised model is not acceptable. The different activities which must be accomplished to generate effective composite systems can be summarised in the following six steps.

10.4.1.1 Module decomposition step: generation of a set of candidate composite systems

Starting from a high level module-oriented description of the computational flow we have to generate a set of feasible composite systems and, during the candidate system generation, integrate the application constraints. At the end of this phase we obtain a set of different solutions for the application in which the parameterised models have not yet been trained. After parameter configuration, based on accuracy and constraints' satisfaction, the best solution will be identified. While traditional modules are somehow fixed, we can only act on parameterised modules to generate a set of interesting new candidates for the composite system.

As suggested in the recurrent neural network literature [5,7] it is interesting to consider topologies in which the parameterised module is replicated according to the series/parallel philosophy. In the series decomposition a parameterised model is substituted with two parameterised models, the slave receiving the outputs of the master as well as its inputs. In the parallel decomposition the module is substituted with two parallel modules, which receive the same inputs, process them with different algorithms and provide the outputs to subsequent modules.

In generating a composite system we can consider an iterative procedure which, by starting from the generic module M, partitions the same in series or parallel as depicted in figure 4. Another operator can be considered which clones/moves unspecified modules along the algorithm connections of the composite system followed by a suitable module collapsing. For each sub-module we do not specify, at this level, the nature of its specific computation. In the decomposition we have that the generic module M is decomposed either in series or parallel into two sub-modules M, each of which can be either a model M or a terminal Simple Module –SM–. Examples of simple modules are the best linear model obtained by training the module, an equation-based module or a model-free one.

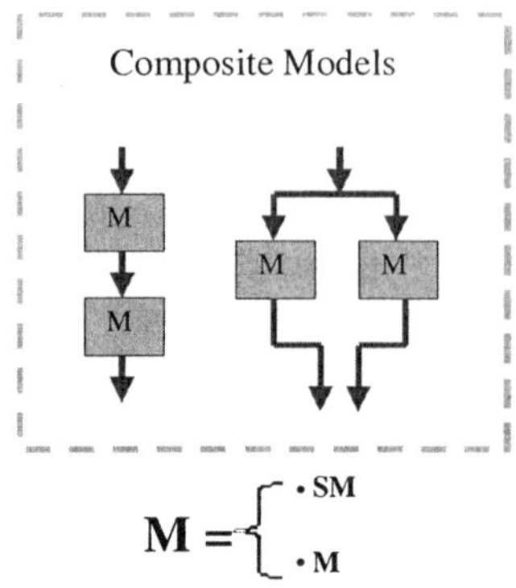

Figure 4: Model of computation for Composite models

In real applications it is common to iterate the system partitioning procedure only for a couple of iterations since more complex situations do not provide in general significant improvements (the approximation ability of the complex composite system becomes equivalent to a simpler one). An example of decomposition is given in figure 5a where we denoted by T a traditional, specified, module which acts most of times, as a feature extraction element executing a traditional computation. Figure 5b shows the same composite system where the parallel modules moved before the T one and collapsed into a single module M. Of course, in carrying out these operators the obtained composite module must be feasible.

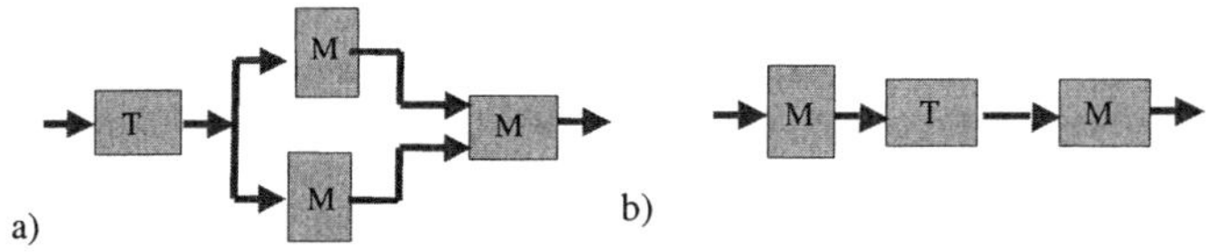

Figure 5: a) A composite system example; b) the composite system after a moving and collapsing operations

10.4.1.2 Model family selection

The second step to be accomplished accounts for associating a specific model family to the unspecified model-free models, i.e., associate a value to the parameters of modules M. We can envision linear or non-linear families, feed-forward or recurrent neural networks depending on the nature of the application. The pool of model families we can think of are those inherited directly from the system identification theory [4] or from the neural network literature [7]. More in general, it will be a mix of the two.

For instance, if we know a priori that the application module refers to a classification problem we could consider Radial Basis Function or Feed Forward Neural Networks while the feature extraction procedures are carried out by traditional algorithms.

With respect to the particular decomposition of figure 5 we could envision for T the feature extraction module, while associated with the parallel modules, the best linear module obtained by identifying the original system with the best linear family and the best non linear one. The right-most module M would act as a compensation module by processing the partial information already extracted from the previous ones and completing them with a training phase.

10.4.1.3 Features extraction

A features extraction step is required by most of model-free model families. Conversely, when we are envisaging equation-based models we do not need in general a feature extraction phase since the relevant features are immediately evident from the mathematical structure of the model. As such, we focus the attention on model-free models. Identification of the appropriate features which must fed the model-free model plays a key role in solving the application. In general, a set of features is extracted from the available data and represents the minimal but relevant information present in the signals.

Features extraction allows for a compact representation of the relevant information and influence the nature of the module since

- the use of redundant information impacts on the input topology (model complexity),
- redundant information reduce/impair the effectiveness of the tuning algorithm (think of the excitability matrix in linear system identification).

Given the limited size of experimental data set, a further data reduction step is mandatory in order to prevent the "curse of dimensionality" problem. The data reduction step differs from feature extraction as it follows a solution-centric rather than problem-centric approach. Among the most effective ones we identify the Principal Component, Independent Component, Spectral and Covariance-based Analyses, [8,9].

The unique drawback associated with feature extraction is the computational burden requested to extract the features. In fact, in some cases, the feature extraction step is quite a time consuming phase which largely accounts for the whole system/module computation. Moreover, in most of cases, it is extremely difficult to identify the best features for a specific application. This observation is much more evident in laser-based applications where only little information is available about the physics of the ongoing process.

As a general guideline, we should extract all those features that have a physical meaning (e.g., the power of the whole signal/part) or represent some important aspect of the measured process (e.g., maximum and minimum values, turning and stationarity points and, for turning points the gradient, etc). In some other cases, we extract features with a spectral analysis (Cepstral coefficients [10], energy in sub-bands) or a wavelets decomposition [11].

When noise is present in the application and affects the signals some features might become either difficult to be identified or not robust enough (e.g., stationarity points). In such cases, the application designer has to exploit all his technical background to identify relevant-easy to be generated- features.

10.4.1.4 Input/output pair generation

In principle, training the unspecified modules composing the system can be carried out in a unique solution by configuring contemporarily all system parameters. Nevertheless, the computational burden (which significantly scales with the number of parameters for quasi-Newton training procedures) and the increased problem associated with local minima make this solution practically ineffective in many applications. The parameters' configuration phase should therefore be carried out incrementally, module by module. This approach requires that each module is defined in terms of its (input, output) pairs and not by means of the ones available at the system output: a propagation of the input/output examples to the module output must be therefore taken into account. The input/output pair generation step aims at propagating the system input examples to the module inputs and back-propagate the associated system outputs to the module output. While inputs can be easily propagated up to the first unspecified module, we cannot guarantee that the same operation can be carried out to characterise its output (functional inversion for the computation between the module under configuration and the system output is required and not always possible).

10.4.1.5 Parameters tuning

In the training phase we can identify three possibilities:

1. tune the modules for which the I/O system examples are available or can be propagated at the input and output of the module under training;
2. when step 1 is not feasible propagate the inputs up to the module. Then, tune the module by removing the connections with other unspecified modules and consider that the outputs of the module are those of the system;
3. execute a global tuning of the system for optimising all trained parameters.

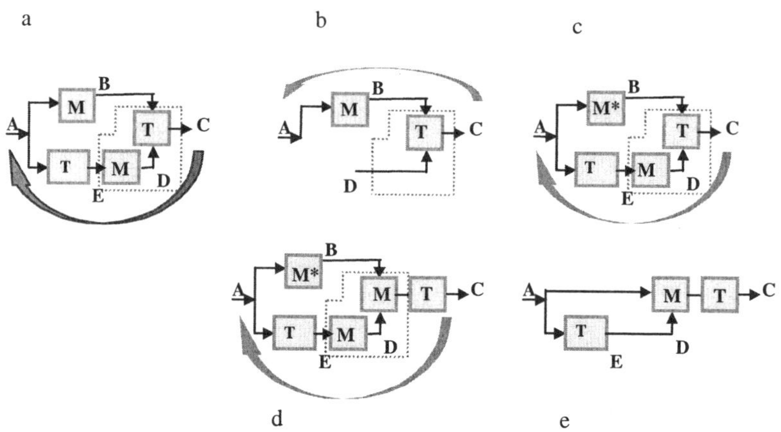

Figure 6: The Input/Output pairs propagation step

We present the three possibilities by referring to figure 6a which shows a composite system composed of two unspecified modules (M) and two traditional ones (T). The training phase requires a careful inspection of the structure of the system to carry out a module by module training. For instance, we could first consider training of module M_{AB}. Since outputs cannot be back-propagated at point B and M_{CB} is a traditional module we can solve the problem by developing the best module M_{AB} on the basis of the available information. In this case, we can assume that the traditional module T_{CBD} receives null values for D. With this assumption we can train module M_{AB} by considering a training function acting on the A-C system level (figure 6b). We denote the training module as M*. It should be noted that M* represents the best model obtainable constrained by the fact that the outputs at point B were not available. We have now to train module M_{ED}. In reality we have to possibilities: the first one (figure 6c) configures module M_{ED} by applying the training function at the A-C level, the second expands the module M with a series decomposition so as to introduce an additional module M (figure 6d) which acts as a compensation module. With a non-linear Neural Network based compensation module we can "correct" the errors introduced at lower levels. At this point, training can be carried out for the unspecified modules M. Of course, different composite system could have been considered depending on the particular training solution the designer is pursuing. The designer should test different reasonable solutions by applying, where necessary, a partition of the modules and select, at the end, the best one. It is interesting to note that the original composite system of figure 6d can degenerate and we could consider the final solution to the embedded system given in figure 6e. This model reduction can happen by keeping in mind that training a module requires availability of input and output training pairs at its output and by applying the partitioning and collapsing operators. Of course, system reduction depends on the particular families considered for module M and by remembering that several neural network families are universal function approximators. Based on this example the reader can understand why composite system partitioning applied to the original solution (figure 6a) can lead to simpler and computationally less demanding solutions (figure 6e). During the training phase one should consider the most adequate parameter tuning algorithm. On complex applications one should prefer the use of Quasi-Newton derived algorithms instead of pure gradient-based simple procedures such as back-propagation since pure gradient descent algorithms become quite ineffective around the minimum of the training function. Among the most efficient Quasi-Newton training algorithms we encounter the BFGS, the DFP, the Levenberg-Marquardt along with their recurrent variants. For a review of the different training algorithms please refer to [12]. While BFGS is surely the most effective training algorithm, it is also particularly time consuming. The Levenberg-Marquardt algorithm is a nice compromise in these cases since it is quite effective still requiring a reasonable computational burden.

10.4.1.6 Modules and system validation

Validation of the modules composing the systems, and by extending the approach the whole system itself, can be accomplished with several validation techniques [7,9].

Surely, the easiest one is Cross Validation –CV– which partitions the N data set into two subsets, the first one to be used for training the module, the second to validate it. For ease of presentation, we apply the analysis to a classification problem. The accuracy performance of the classifier (e.g., the number of correct classification evaluated on the validation set composed of N_v samples) is simply $\hat{\varepsilon} = \frac{N_{v,OK}}{N}$ where $N_{v,OK}$ represents the number of correct classifications in the validation set. It is undoubt that cross-validation provides an unbiased estimate for the validation accuracy of the module. Nevertheless, cross-validation suffers from a main disadvantage: the estimate confidence depends on the available set and, if the number of validation pairs N_v is limited so it is the confidence associated with results. In addition, cross validation is in contrast with a leading statistical philosophy: saving data for validating the model reduces the data available for training and, hence, the model is less accurate [7,9]. K-fold cross validation techniques can be considered when there is a limited number of data and the complexity of the training elements is not too high.

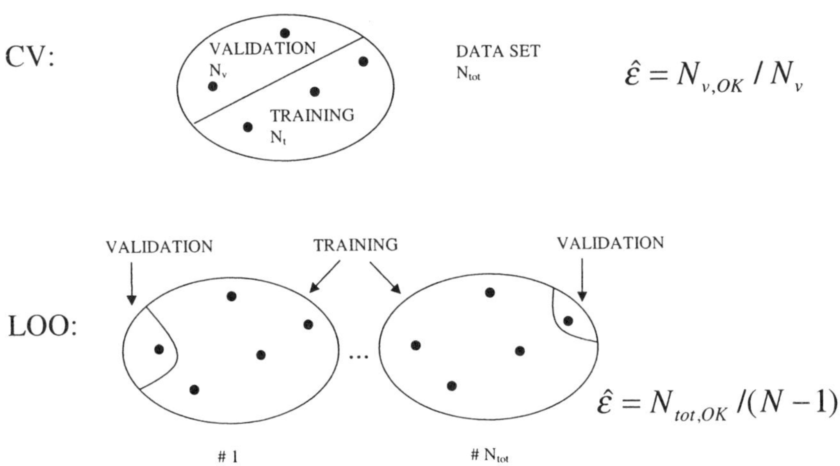

Figure 7: Cross validation and Leave One Out

Following this last comment we end up with different validation criteria which suggest to consider most of available data to be used for training and just few -if any- for validation. FPE, NIC, GPE criteria and Leave One Out –LOO- follow this principle [7,9]. LOO is an interesting validation criterion and constitutes the bases for the feature selection core presented in section 4.2. With LOO, given N samples we have to develop N classifiers, each of which trained over a N-1 samples sub-set and validated over the last untrained pattern. The procedure now iterates for all the spare patterns and the performance estimate is simply the ratio between the number of correctly classified patterns and the total number of patterns minus one, i.e., $\hat{\varepsilon} = \frac{N_{tot,OK}}{N_{tot} - 1}$. The difference between cross-validation and LOO is presented in figure 7. The presence of a limited data set poses an additional problem related to the confidence of the validation index. When we assert that validation performance is x% we have to remind that the validation index is a random variable depending on the particular realisation of the data: different data would have generated a different validation performance. A confidence degree must then be introduced to grant, at least in probability, what we are asserting.

For classification applications, the ones envisaged in our laser test-beds, we can assume in primis that the generic trained classifier coincides with the best Bayes's one. In such a case, depending on the number of data N, and the validation accuracy $\hat{\varepsilon}$, with a confidence of 95% [7] we have the situation depicted in figure 8. The entry point is $\hat{\varepsilon}$ which intersects the two curves associated with a given N and we read the interval to which the real validation performance error belongs at least with probability 0.95. Since we are assuming that the considered classifier is optimal the approach provides the best possible solution. Nevertheless, since we cannot guarantee that our classifier is the optimal one we can state that, in the best case, our classifier will be characterised by the given performance interval.

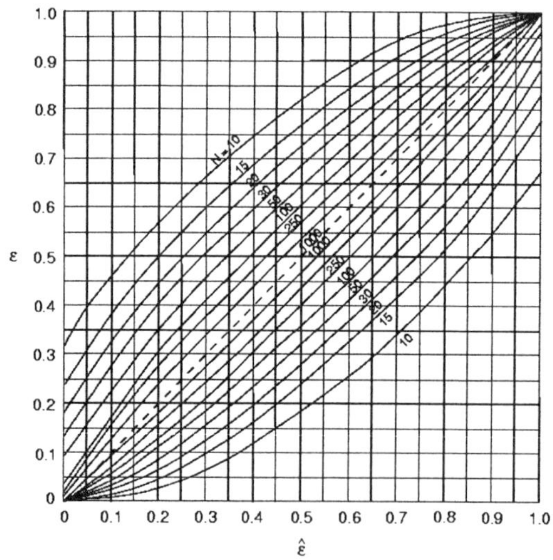

Figure 8: The estimated accuracy and the accuracy interval

10.4.2 *The KNN classifiers*

The K Nearest Neighbours KNN classifier [7] is a statistical classifier where a pattern is classified according to the majority of the K nearest training patterns close to it.

The main features of the classifiers are that

- The KNN classifier consistently approximates the optimal Bayes classifier;
- Probability distributions are locally estimated based on each training point;
- KNN does not need a true training phase

The KNN classifier is a table-based classifier where all the N available training samples are stored in the table, e.g. as tuples ($feat1_j$, $feat2_j$, ... , $featf_j$; $class_j$), j=1...N.

When a pattern is presented to the classifier in the format (feat1, feat2, ... , featf) the distance to the new pattern according to some distance measure (e.g., Euclidean or Manhattan norm) is evaluated.

The set S of the K training samples which score the least values for the distances are selected and the majority class of the training samples provides the classification output for the one under test.

It has been experimentally discovered that odd K values normally yield better performances than even values and that when the Euclidean norm is considered the classifier performance improves with a preprocessing stage leading to a zero mean and unit standard deviation inputs.

10.4.3 Features selection

As we have pointed out features extraction represents a main issue for developing an accurate model-free module but it is also a critical aspect since it is very hard to identify relevant features for the given process. What happens is that the designer identifies and selects, from each sensorial data, as many features as possible. The choice is based on physical properties associated with the feature, min and max values, variances, deviations from some interesting conditions, etc.

Moreover, we could approach the features extraction problem from a different perspective. If there exists at least a relevant feature associated with a sensorial signal it means that a relevant feature is also associated with a relevant sensor. Even if this observation is quite obvious it has a striking implication on laser-based applications where little is known about a generic laser process and we do not know in advance which sensors will be useful for the envisaged application.

The identification of the sensors to be placed around the optical head is ruled by two opposite design guidelines: keeping the experimental set-up as simple as possible (which requires a minimal number of sensors) and obtaining a sensorial view of the ongoing process (which, conversely, would suggest to use all available sensors).

Since scarce a priori information is available in general for a generic laser based process, it is difficult to identify a priori the sensors whose signals convey the relevant information allowing for the application solution. Therefore, it is quite a common strategy to consider a large set of sensors during the first prototypal configuration for the optical head and deciding, later on, the ones really relevant to the specific application and that will also be considered in the operational phase.

Because of the duality sensor/features relevance we can say that a sensor is surely not relevant if the features extracted from the associated signal do not provide a real information content gain with respect to the other ones. Of course, we could rank the relevance of different features/sensors by also taking into account the cost of the sensors, its averaged life etc. This multi-objective optimisation goal is out of our analysis but it can be suitably integrated within. We focus therefore the attention on the feature/sensor aspect.

If possible, all the meaningful acoustic, thermal, visual and electromagnetic phenomena from the ongoing laser process to be monitored should be considered and as many features as possible extracted. Examples of sensors are temperature sensors (inspecting the radiation at different frequency), on-axis and off-axis reflected radiation monitors, sonic and ultrasonic sensors, CCD cameras, eddy current sensors and plasma radiation ones.

The final choice for the sensors to be considered derives, of course, from the background experience of the team involved in the set-up, available information and hints from the related literature, economical issues and last, but not least, dimension of the optical head. In many laser-applications, the laser head must be placed in a spatial constrained environment and the sensors on it make it difficult the moving of the same (wire problem, weight, robustness of the sensors once subject to strong forces due to accelerations).

A methodology based on a sensitivity (features relevance) analysis encompassing KNN classifiers has been developed to solve the feature extraction aspect. The basic idea supporting the methodology is that a feature is relevant to a classification task if it provides additional contribute to performance improvement. Unfortunately, the feature extraction problem is NP-hard in the sense that all possible classifiers receiving all the possible groups of features must be envisaged. Moreover, for each classifier we have to consider a training phase which, by itself, is a time consuming approach. A methodology can be derived based on KNN classifiers which solves the features extraction problem with a Poly-time complexity in the number of features.

The heuristics make an approximation for the different actors for the features extraction problem by assuming that the KNN classifier coincides with the best Bayes classifier (i.e., the analysis is optimistic). The assumption is supported by the fact that the KNN classifier is a consistent estimate of the Bayes's one (when the number of data tends to infinity the performance provided by the two coincides). The relevant advantage of a KNN w.r.t. other consistent classifiers (e.g., feedforward and Radial Basis Function NNs) is that it does not require a computationally intensive training phase. In fact, it is simple to generate a KNN from a set of training data. To validate the effective performance of the obtained classifier we considered a LOO validation technique at 95% of confidence. We can therefore state that the performance of the classifier is reliable with high probability. This procedure should be iterated for all the possible classifiers receiving all possible combinations of features. A solution to this a problem is given by the following algorithm:

1: U = set of all the features
2: Build all the S_i subsets of U containing N features
3: For each S_i estimate the LOO performance of all the KNN classifiers
with S_i as inputs
4: Select those S_i which yield a performance above a threshold;
if only one S_i is selected goto 5
else build their union U and goto 3
5: Greedily grow S_i with the other features one by one,
until no further performance improvement is scored
6: Select the best performing classifier

The classifier maximising the LOO performance is the best one for the particular problem. The interesting related effect is that the feature it receives are the most relevant ones to solve the envisioned application and the sensors generating such signals should be considered in the experimental set-up.

10.5. Applications

10.5.1 Laser cutting of steel/stainless steel

The Laser cutting of steel/stainless steel for a class of materials is a complex process, yet an interesting application for its industrial and economical impact.

In the application, carried out in collaboration with TRUMPF GmbH, we observed that by monitoring the evolution of the sparks jet, which is generated during cutting, we can extract those information needed for quality analysis.

During the cutting process, non-optimal situations can occur which impair the quality of the produced artefact. The two most relevant ones are:

- a discontinuous cut (there are segments of uncut material);
- pearls of metal (i.e., melted material which deposits and solidifies on the cut edges).

Three examples of sparks' jets retrieved during the cutting process from the bottom side of the cut artefact are given in figure 9. Sparks jets vary both in intensity and shape and, in some extreme cases, the main jet separates in two parts. The rightmost scene refers to a pearl of metal situation; pearls are visible in the figure as hot spots of melted material which deposit on the lower edges of the cut.

Figure 9: Three examples of sparks' jets

In this first application we apply in detail the whole methodology by focusing, in the subsequent applications, on main results.

The first step of the methodology addresses the generation of a set of candidate composite systems for the application starting from a simple high level design of the solution. To this end, we note that the pearls of metal situation is completely different from the other cases since here the sparks jet somehow degenerates. As such, we consider two distinct solutions, one dealing with the identification of the pearls and the other with the continuous/discontinuous cut.

In the pearls of metal case a pattern-matching filter tailored to the size/nature of the pearls becomes a straightforward high level solution; the filter solves the specific problem by classifying a sub-image as pearls free or affected. Since the filter's coefficients and structure are unknown we have to consider a model-free module to be suitably identified.

Conversely, identification of discontinuous cuts is a more complex problem and requires, a priori, identification of a set of features. Features must be related to the structure of the sparks jet (e.g., some angles characterising the aperture of the jet) augmented with external features such as cutting speed, type and pressure of gas used and thickness of the material to be processed. It is reasonable to consider traditional modules for extracting the internal features while an unspecified module acting as a classifier will process the features to characterise the local quality of the cut.

The high level structure of the composite system is given in figure 10. Of course, other composite systems could be generated from the first one by considering parallel and series decomposition of the M modules as well as moving and collapsing operators. In particular, we verified that a single composite system of T-M nature (Traditional following by a parameterised model) can be considered to solve the problem. In this case the M module receives also features related to the presence of pearls of material. Unfortunately, such composite system, even if less computationally intensive, is characterised by poorer performance.

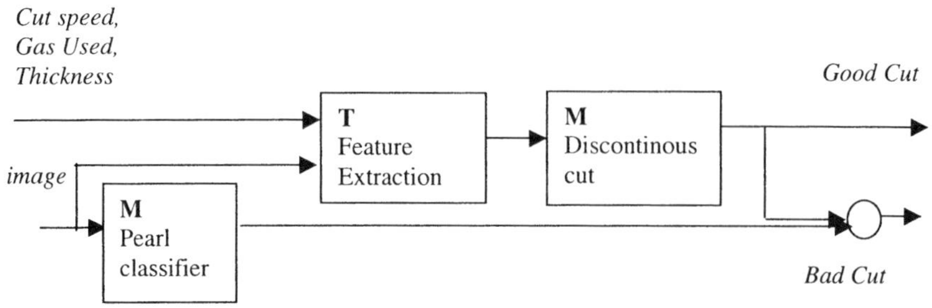

Figure 10: The chosen composite system

The second step to be accomplished refers to model family selection for the model-free modules. We considered feed-forward classifiers since they have been proven to be universal function approximators. The specific neural computation e.g., sigmoidal- based or RBF is not relevant at this step.

The third phase requires to generate a set of relevant features for the specific application. Since features must characterise the nature of the sparks' jet we considered the set of angles outlined in figure 11. In particular, the potentially interesting angles are the inclination angle α of the core of the sparks jet, the aperture angle β of the core of the jet and the angle γ characterising the opening of the whole jet. Please note that at this abstraction level we do not know which features will be relevant to the process.

Identification of the features-angles is everything but an easy task since the sparks jet is rather noise-affected (several sparks are outside the main core): this observation has an immediate impact on the computational load and the complexity of the solution.

In particular, the main difficulty is associated with the identification of the origin of the sparks, which represents the reference point for angle determination. The presence of a significant noise in the image and the non perfect linearity of the sparks trajectory once ejected make particularly complex the identification of such reference point.

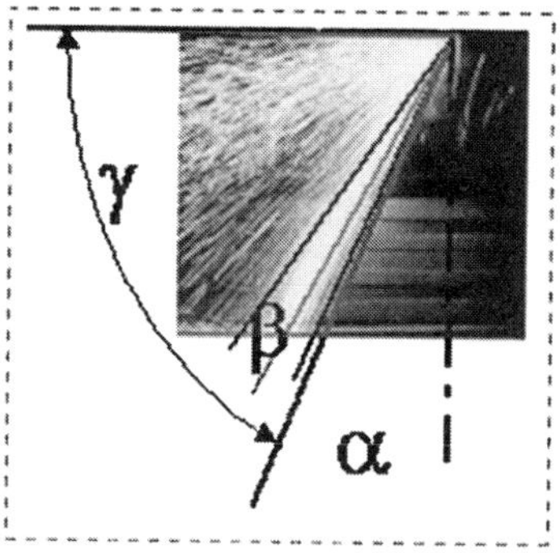

Figure 11: the internal features extracted from the sparks jet

The high level steps leading to the identification of the reference point can be summarised as follows:

- Preliminary identification of the reference point. The critical information is the horizontal co-ordinate which can be estimated by identifying a "first significant increment" of the luminous intensity of the spark's core, along the vertical direction;

- Application of the Radon Transform to compute the direction of the principal axis of the sparks jet. The minimum value assumed by the variance of the projections indicates the main jet's axis;
- intersecting the horizontal line and the principal axis;
- applying a Least Mean Square Technique;
- translate the principal axis to the jet starting point and obtain the α angle.

The β and γ angles can be then estimated with an additional processing of the image. In particular, the steps to be accomplished require

- Median filtering
- Image binarization
- Cumulate the intensity in rows
- Find left/right edges of the sparks jet
- Apply a linear regression on the left and right sides by imposing that angles must pass trough the vertex.

Once the features have been extracted and input/output pairs generated, the next step requires training the classifiers. The chosen training algorithm was the Levenberg-Marquardt applied to a Mean Square Error training function.

10.5.1.1 Pearls classifier

The neural topology is composed of a simple network receiving a 15x18 pixel image, it is characterised by two hidden layers with 12 and 6 hidden neurons respectively, and provides the indication pearls/no_pearls. We considered a two layered neural network since two layers can solve a complex application with a lower number of hidden units. The neural network has been trained on a set of images containing pearls and non pearls situations (some training examples are given in figure 12). In a way, the neural network behaves as a non-linear pattern-matching filter which scans the image looking for potential pearls of material. Once pearls are identified the associated cut at the instant of time the image was retrieved by the camera is classified as bad. Conversely, we cannot guarantee that the cut is error prone when the classification is no_pearls since other sources of bad classification can be present.

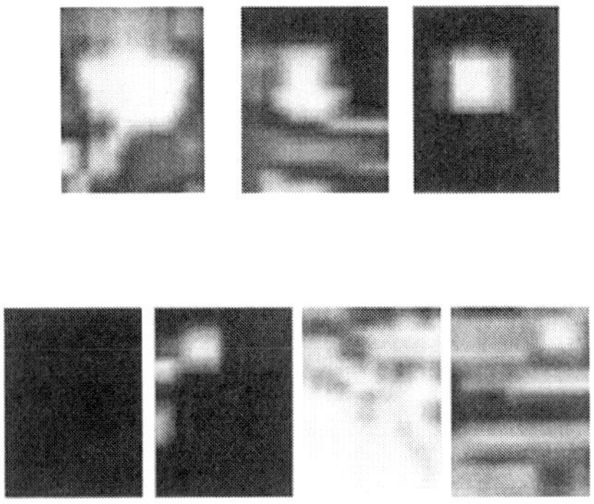

Figure 12: a) pearls; b) no pearls

The neural classifier was always able to identify the presence of pearls without errors.

10.5.1.2 The quality-of-cutting classifier

When there are no pearls we can identify 10 different classes which differ in the type of metal, thickness and gas used. Without going into details, which are outside the goals of the paper, we developed a dedicated classifier for each class. This solution, in contrast with the one suggesting a single classifier able to solve the whole problem, has two main advantages:

1) it allows for better performance (features are selected according to the effective needs of the problem);
2) The computation required by each classifier reduces since the complexity of the dedicated classifier is significantly smaller than the complex one.

Table 1: Results for two classes

Application Structure	Validation Error	Features considered
Mild steel,	46.7%	Pressure, cutting speed
6mm thickness, O_2	0%	Pressure, cutting speed, α,β
Stainless steel	6.1%	Pressure, cutting speed
3mm thickness, O_2	1.1%	Pressure, cutting speed, α,β

Before training the classifiers we run the features selection algorithm for each class and we identified the most suitable features for each of them. Interesting enough, some classes need solely the external features to solve the specific applications while other classes significantly improved by also considering angles. As an example we consider two classes with structure, features and results as given in table 1. We realise that an adequate choice for the composite system and features is fundamental to solve the application.

By considering the α and β angles the performance of the classifiers improve. Results have been estimated over a large data set and, as such, the validation error is a consistent estimate of the effective accuracy of the classifiers.

10.5.2 Laser seam welding of gears

In general, the quality analysis of a seam welding process is assessed by an offline inspection of each welded component carried out with ultrasonic or X-ray devices. A different approach envisages an on-line quality analysis which is implemented directly during the welding process. By following this principle we address the laser welding quality analysis with a composite system that detects defects on-line directly during the welding phase. The industrial process under monitoring refers to the laser welding of automotive components carried out at the CRF-FIAT laboratories. The specific test bed is a steel gear, a critical part in the gearbox for a passenger vehicle obtained by joining the two rings composing the gear with a CO_2 laser.

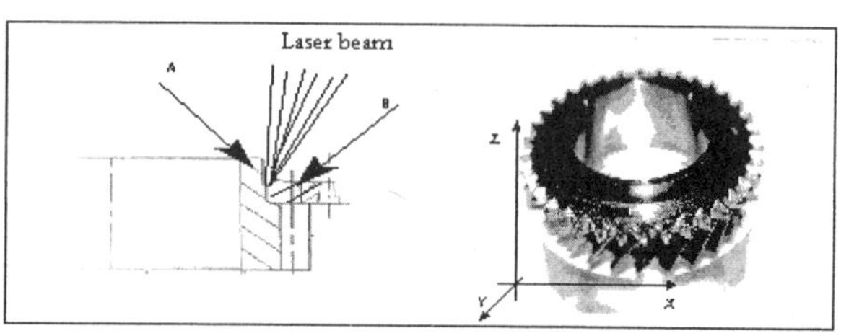

Figure 13: The gear and the welding area

Small power changes once the keyhole has been formed can cause remarkable changes in the weld results while the presence of non-metallic contaminants may produce spatters and porosity in the welded region. In the considered application we wish to identify errors associated with

- Porosity (spontaneous and caused by misalignment or power lack);
- Decrease in laser power level (up to 10% of the nominal value)
- Mounting errors (the two pieces to be welded are misaligned)

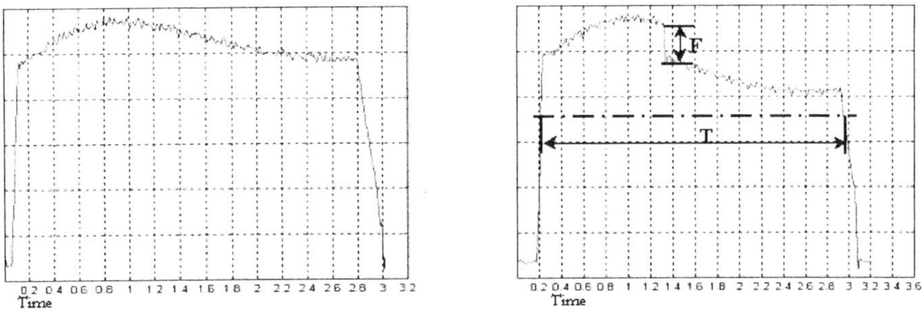

Figure 14: laser power signal. a) normal situation; b) power lack

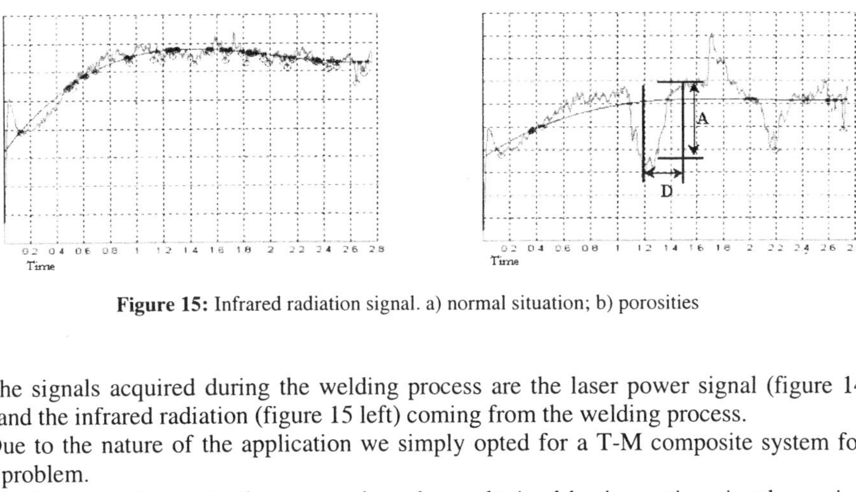

Figure 15: Infrared radiation signal. a) normal situation; b) porosities

The signals acquired during the welding process are the laser power signal (figure 14 left) and the infrared radiation (figure 15 left) coming from the welding process.

Due to the nature of the application we simply opted for a T-M composite system for each problem.

The features relevant to the process have been obtained by inspecting signals coming both from correct and anomalous operations.

We discovered that the laser power signal possesses enough information to detect power decrease or power lack. Conversely, the signal from the photodiode is suitable for carrying out the quality analysis for porosity formation, detection and individuation of misalignment errors.

In particular, and referring to figure 14b, we see that a power decrease is visible. As features, we extracted the power decrease (F) and the time duration (T) associated with the part of the power signal above its mean value.

To identify the features associated with the infrared radiation we applied a low-pass filter to remove high frequency components in the signal and a cubic interpolation of the signal or reference signal.

The features to be extracted, and interesting to the porosity formation, are now the deviations from the reference signal, i.e., the time duration (A) and the amplitude (D) of the main deviations. The feature selection phase validated the choice for the features.

The misalignment of the parts to be butt-welded can be identified by processing the infrared signal. A characteristic signal measured in presence of a misalignment is given in figure 16.

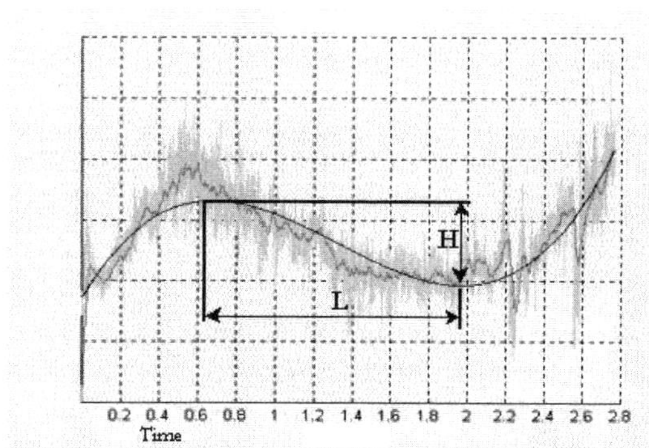

Figure 16: Infrared radiation signal. Misalignment.

We extracted as relevant features, the index H and L which represent the amplitude between the two stationarity points and the corresponding time interval, respectively. Such features have been extracted on the cubic interpolation to reduce the computational burden.

The final classifier has been trained to solve each class of errors based on a set of good-no_good welding experiments.

To compare performance in classification for this test-bed we considered both a one hidden layer feed-forward neural classifier and the KNN one. Results are given in table 2 where FF-NN have been validated with Cross-validation while the KNN with the Leave-One-Out validation technique.

Since the application is characterised by a significantly small number of samples, we introduced the accuracy intervals as suggested by figure 8 (confidence level of 0.95).

Table 2: KNN and FF-NN classification performance in the seam-welding of gears

	Classifier	**Training samples**	**CV /LOO Samples**	**Validation Error**	**Accuracy interval**	**Notes**
Power decrease	KNN	69	68	0%	•0-8%	
	FF-NN	48	21	0%	•0-8%	4 hidden units
Mountin g error	KNN	55	54	1.8%	•0-10%	
	FF-NN	39	16	0%	•0-8%	2 hidden units
Porosity presence	KNN	215	214	0.35%	•0-4%	
	FF-NN	199	86	0%	•0-4%	4 hidden units

We can see that the best neural classifier has a maximal complexity of 4 neurons, noticeably lower once compared to the complexity of the corresponding KNN classifier which requires to compare the actual pattern with each training one. We note that the feed-forward Neural networks always provide a 0% of validation error.

10.5.3 Automatic classification of laser spot welded electron gun parts

Micro spot welding is being used at the production site of electron gun parts for many years. The advantages of low thermal and mechanical loading of the product are the main issues for using this joining technology. The production plant of Philips electronics in Sittard, has over 100 lasers in use to assemble the parts for the electron guns and the final assembly itself, which has about 120 laser spot welds on each finished product. Several types of spot welds are used in this production facility, of which the overlap penetration and the overlap fillet weld are the most important. Figure 17 shows a schematic overview of the electron gun, generating the electrons, focussing them to a narrow beam and accelerating the electrons for their travel to the screen.

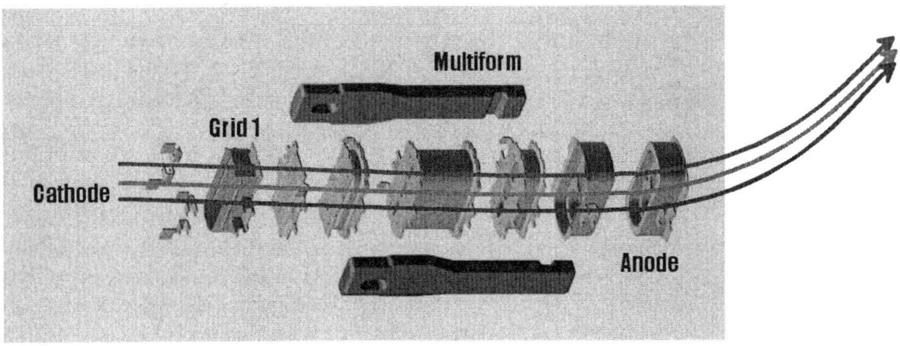

Figure 17: Overview of an electron gun assembly

Quality assurance is nowadays done by means of picking samples at random and verifying their quality. This takes a precious time and is certainly not a 100% check of all produced products. The quest for zero defect delivery is growing, increasing the demand for automatic 100% check of all produced parts.

The general opinion among the production managers at the electron gun components factory, is that the process runs well enough without any control technique implemented. Well-engineered equipment with pure feed-forward controlled laser processing is working satisfactory. Producing some defective parts is not a big loss as long as it stays with these parts. If a defective part is being used during the assembly of the electron gun ending up in a complete cathode ray tube, the situation will be quite different. Testing of the sub-components of the tube is complicated, as the tube has to be closed and pumped to vacuum before functional testing can take place. This indicates the need for 100% good parts in the delivered lot of pre-assembled parts to the end-assembly department. A properly functioning check of the produced parts is essential. Product quality checking is done at this moment by taking samples at random at certain intervals. If bad products are identified, the whole production lot produced between that time and the last check with good result will be taken out and regarded as defective products. This method needs costly manual inspection and leads to a certain amount of good products ending up in a badly classified lot, meaning loss of production.

Since several years, investigation is being done to find techniques, which are able to classify the welded products automatically through the evaluation of the recorded process signals during the spot welding process. This case study describes some of the major results obtained over the recent years on this topic, both with traditional process monitoring techniques as well as with sophisticated Neural Network based automatic classifiers.

The goal of the activities was to develop an automatic classification tool, recognising defective welded products on-line, based on the evaluation of measured process phenomena during the welding process. The reliability of the classifier should be high:

- A few percent good products in the lot of products classified as bad is acceptable.
- Only a few ppm of bad products in the lot of products classified as good is accepted.

Training of the automatic classifier should be as simple as possible, enabling easy implementation in production environment.

Defining the quality of a laser spot welded joint requires more then a simple description. Several characteristics of the joint have to be taken into account to describe the quality.

Although the electron gun parts as such are mechanically static products, the mechanical demands toward the product parts are important due to high thermal loads on the products (cyclic temperature stressing). The spot welds for the electron gun parts must meet a set of demands to be acceptable:

- Good penetration depth, identified by recognising a certain de-colouring of the material on the bottom side of the work piece.
- Good alignment of the joined parts, the gap between the parts should not be too large.
- No spatters of steel particles in the vicinity of the weld.

Because of the variety of parameters to be taken into account, it is not enough to evaluate these parameters on basis of only one sensor. A set of sensors is selected as bases for the evaluation of the quality parameters.

10.5.3.1 Multi sensor process monitoring

The micro spot welding process can be divided into three successive process phases: Heating, melting and fusion and cooling. The work piece surface temperature is increased from room temperature up to melting temperature during the heating phase. The used laser beam power and the absorption coefficient of the work piece material are the most dominant parameters, which influence the evolving process here. The input laser power and part of the reflected laser power is detected to have information about these parameters. The surface temperature, the amount of metal evaporation and the penetration depth are important factors during the melting and fusion phase. The infra red emission from the weld spot, the optical emission from the plume and the change of induced eddy currents are detected to monitor these process parameters. Surface temperature is also an important parameter during the cooling phase.

It is of essential importance to note that there are several combinations of process parameters, which will give a quite different process behaviour but will lead to good welding quality in these cases. This means that good spot welding quality is not uniquely related to a specific narrow bounded process parameter combination. It is possible to select another combination of process parameters (for instance using a longer process time with lower laser power for having less evaporation of metal), will lead to different process signals, while maintaining the welding quality. This makes it even more important to use a broad set of sensors for the process-monitoring task.

The set of signals used for the final test of automatic classification was:

1. Laser input power
2. On-axis reflected laser power(back-reflected into the aperture of the welding set-up)
3. Off-axis reflected laser power(diffuse reflected laser power)

4. Plume emission
5. Variation of the angular orientation of the plume w.r.t. the surface
6. Surface temperature (logarithmically amplified visible emission, Silicon sensor)
7. Surface temperature (logarithmically amplified i.r. emission, Germanium sensor)
8. Sonic acoustic emission (microphone)

10.5.3.2 Data reduction and feature extraction

For efficient data analysis, it is necessary to reduce the amount of data. Feature extraction in an effective way to achieve this. Specific signal features have been defined, using a priori knowledge about the behaviour of the signals and the related process. This has lead to a list of 34 signal features for the whole set of 8 sensor signals. It showed that the most important signal features were directly related to process parameters or process phases. Figure 18 gives an example of some signals and features extracted from these signals.

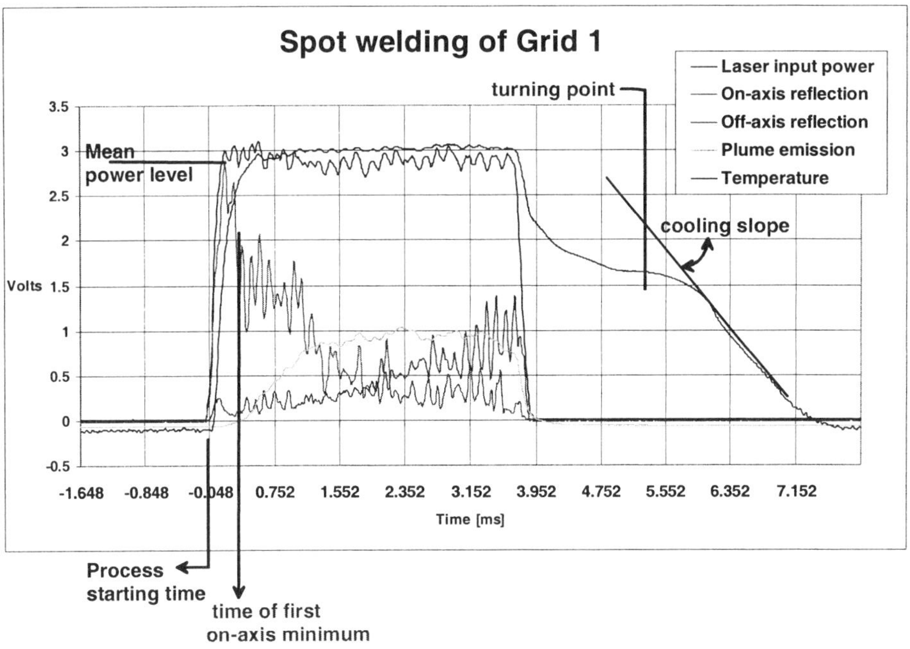

Figure 18: Example of some signals and features extracted from these signals

The general approach for the classification problem is to extract features from the process signals and to compare this set of features with sets of features of welds who's quality levels are known. Figure 19 shows the approach via a schematic overview of the used functional blocks.

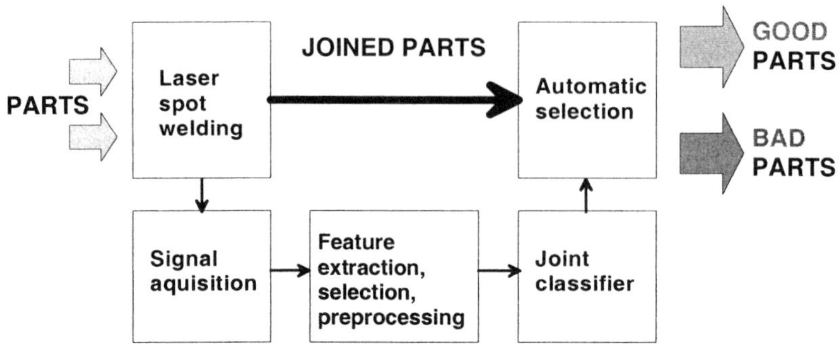

Figure 19: Approach to automatic classification of the quality of micro spot welding

10.5.3.3. Designing the classifiers

Two types of classifiers have been evaluated during the first evaluation phase. The first work focussed the attention on a neural network with a variable number of input neurons, one for each feature used. One hidden layer was used with various numbers of neurons and one output neuron was used, giving the estimated welding quality. Training of this type of classifier requires the optimisation of the used set of features and number of neurons in the hidden layer, and at the same time the optimisation of the weighing factors of all neurons. It needs no long theoretical treatment to understand that this operation is a complicated and time-consuming action.

The performance of the Nearest Neighbour classifier (KNN classifier) was tested at second instance, using either one or two neighbours (1NN and 2NN). This type of classifier performed almost at the same level as the neural network, but has the advantage that it requires no complicated training. In the case of the 2NN classifier, the feature patterns to be classified are compared to the two most near neighbouring reference patterns. The fact that undecided situations can occur now, can be used to implement a kind of 'on site training' by demanding the experts decision in case of one 'Good' neighbour and one 'bad' neighbour. The new 'expert identified feature pattern' is added to the reference pattern. One of the most important drawbacks for this strategy is that this 'on site training' requires a very consequent reasoning of the 'expert' over time. Using several experts working in shifts has shown to lead to continuously changing classification boundaries.

As we have see, the nice thing about the KNN classifier is that it needs basically no actual training session, the identification of a certain set of reference patterns with known classification levels is all what is needed. Specifically with respect to ease of implementation of automatic classifier in industrial applications, this was recognised as a very important factor; acceptability is an important issue for introduction of new technology in industry. For this reason, the KNN classifier was selected for the automatic classification of micro laser spot welds.

Throwing in as much information into a neural network or KNN classifier as possible is certainly not the way to get reliable results. Just as the human brain is getting confused when confronted with too much information, which is even partly not significant for the given problem, so will artificial intelligence. Optimal performance with respect to classification accuracy will be achieved by a sub-set of the most significant features. Finding this optimum sub-set is an important step in the design of an automatic classifier.

Training the classifier is in the first place in need of reference data. A large series of spot welding experiments have been done to gather process data. Experiments have been done under various combinations of process parameters. Process parameters have been varied over the range we expect to face in industry.

The complete set of features extracted from the data files in combination with the off-line classification give us the reference patterns for the process. This completes the 'training' process for the KNN classifier.

Testing of the classifier is done on basis of the 625 available experiment data sets with known classification. A number of steps have to be made to test the performance of the classifier, which can be divided into three different parts:

1. Loading of the original recorded 'MAIL' data file
2. Extraction all features for all data files
3. Selecting the appropriate features (based on the feature selection results)
4. Normalisation of the features (to unity variance and zero mean)
5. Splitting of the data set into a part used for training and for testing
6. Reading the results from the manual classification (excel file)
7. Invoking the classifier to classify the 'test-set'
8. Verification of the performance of the classifier by comparing its output with that of the manual classification.

A general conclusion from the work in 'MAIL', is that the results are encouraging but not reliable enough yet for industrial implementation.

The results on our classifier testing showed a level of 98 % correct classifications and 2 % incorrect classified cases for the 1NN classifier. The 2NN classifier showed a performance level of 95.5% correct classifications and 1% incorrect classifications. In 3.5% of the cases the classification did not decide. Within the 1% incorrect classifications were also 'Bad' welds which had been classified as 'Good', a situation we would like not to happen. Of course, since the number of data is finite a 6-8% accuracy interval must be considered and centred around the nominal accuracies obtained.

References

[1] A. E. Siegman, Lasers, Oxford University Press, 1986

[2] W. M. Steen, Laser material processing, Springer-Verlag, London, 1991

[3] D. Bäuerle, Laser processing and diagnostics, Springer-Verlag, Berlin, 1984

[4] L.Ljung, System identification: theory for the user, Prentice Hall, 1987

[5] K.S. Narendra, K.Parthasarathy, Gradient methods for optimization of dynamical system containing neural networks. IEEE TNN, vol 1, no. 1, 4-27, 1990

[6] C. Alippi, S. Ferrari, V. Piuri, M. Sami, F. Scotti: "New trends in intelligent system design for embedded and measurement application, IEEE- I&M Magazine, Vol. 2, No. 2, June 1999

[7] M.H.Hassoun, Fundametals of Artificial Neural Networks, The MIT press, 1995

[8] A.Hyvarinen. Survey on Independent Component Analysis, Neural Computing Surveys, Vol. 2, 1999

[9] K.Fukunaga. Introduction to statistical pattern recognition. Academic Press, 1972

[10] S.Furui, Cepstral analysis technique for automatic speech verification, IEEE Transactions on Acoustics, Speech and Signal Processing, Vol. 29, No. 2, April 1981

[11] G.Strang, T.Nguyen , Wavelet and Filter Banks, Wellesley-Cambridge Press, 1996

[12] L.Ljung, J.Sjoberg, H.Hjalmarsson, On neural Network Model Structures in System Identification, NATO-ASI, Identification, Adaptation, Learning, Springer, 1996

Neural Networks for Instrumentation, Measurement and Related Industrial Applications
S. Ablameyko et al. (Eds.)
IOS Press, 2003

Chapter 11
Neural Networks for Measurements and Instrumentation in Electrical Applications

Salvatore BAGLIO
Dipartimento di Ingegneria Elettrica Elettronica e Sistemistica, University of Catania
V.le A. Doria 6, Catania, 95125 Italy

Abstract. This chapter gives an overview of the use of soft computing methodologies in measurement systems for electrical quantities, although the presented approaches can be extended to deal also with other quantities whenever these quantities are first converted into electrical ones. The basic electrical properties of materials (e.g., resistivity and permittivity) and the methods for their measurement are introduced. Then, a brief discussion on the soft computing methodologies that can be used for measurement systems will be performed. Finally, some real applications of soft computing technologies in measurement systems for industrial applications are presented.

11.1. Instrumentation and measurement systems in electrical, dielectrical, and power applications

Due to the large number of measurement issues and applications in the areas of electrical, dielectrical, and power measurements, this chapter addresses only on some aspects that are common to all problems in measurement of electrical and dielectrical quantities. Most of the instruments and measurement procedures considered in this chapter are in fact related to the electrical properties of the measured object, e.g., to resistivity, permittivity, and permeability. Consequently, this chapter focuses on measurement of the very basic electrical properties, since these constitute the foundation for a very wide spectrum of industrial applications. First of all, an overview of the basic electrical quantities is given and, then, some traditional methodologies and instruments are introduced to allow for a comparison with soft computing solutions. More details can be found, e.g., in [1-4].

11.1.1 Electrical conductivity and resistivity

Resistivity of is one of the main electric characteristics of materials. Wires, bars, and sheet are in fact often used as electrical conductors. To observe and quantify external phenomena through measurement procedures, it is fundamental to understand how resistivity (or conductivity) depends on the various physical quantities by means of a model.

The electrical resistivity ρ of a given material describes how much the material opposes the current flow. Resistivity is measured in "ohm • meter" [Ωm]. A change in resistivity will result in a variation of the current flowing through the materials at a fixed voltage difference. The study of the parameters that may induce changes in the resistivity and the approaches to measure these changes are very important from a measurement point of view. This leads in fact to relate the changes to the physical phenomena inducing them and, in turn, to find ways to indirectly measure these phenomena.

An analytical model that relates the electrical resistivity to all physical quantities influencing it can be derived from the simple system shown in Fig. 1. The bar is made of an isotropic and homogeneous material; its length, width, and height are l, w, h, respectively. The voltage difference V is applied across its length and the current I flowing in the bar is measured.

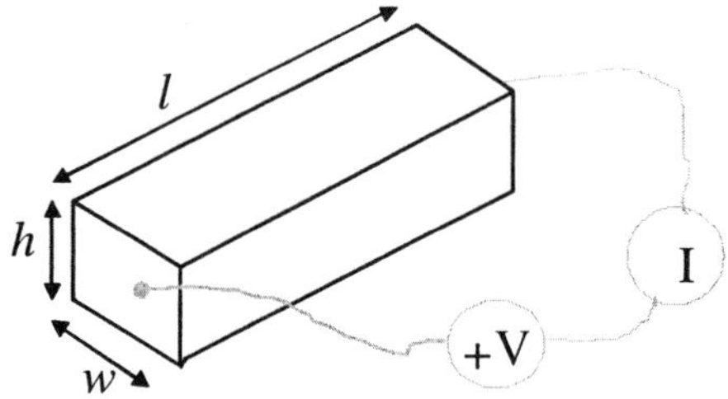

Figure 1: The measurement system for resistivity

In the bar of isotropic and homogeneous material the electric field E produced by the voltage V is:

$$E = \frac{V}{l} \quad [V/m] \tag{1}$$

Being the bar section area $A=hw$, the current density J is:

$$J = \frac{I}{A} \quad [A/m^2] \tag{2}$$

The relation between the current density and the electric field leads to the resistivity definition given above:

$$E = \rho J \tag{3}$$

Therefore, it is:

$$V = \frac{I\rho \ l}{A} \tag{4}$$

The resistance of the bar is therefore defined by including not only its electrical properties but also its geometrical dimensions. The resistance, measured in Ohm [Ω], is:

$$R \equiv \frac{\rho \ l}{A} \tag{5}$$

In general, the resistance R depends on the size and the shape of the object, while resistivity ρ depends only on properties of the object material.

Finally, the proportionality between the voltage applied across the conductor bar and the resulting current flowing in the bar itself is stated by the well-known Ohm law:

$$I = \frac{V}{R} \tag{6}$$

The relationship between voltage and current is very different in semiconductor materials, although the electric field and the current density are still locally proportional.

At a microscopic level, it is:

$$\rho = \frac{m}{ne^{2}\tau} \tag{7}$$

where m is the mass of the electron, n is the number of charge carriers, τ is the average time between two collisions of the free carrier with the stationary atoms of the material, and e is the electron charge. Equation 7 can be useful to understand, for example, the behavior of thermal sensors based on the change of resistivity. The resistivity of metals usually increases with temperature since τ decreases, while the resistivity of semiconductors usually decreases with temperature since n increases.

Measuring the resistivity (or the resistance) is not always easy: in general, it is in fact rather difficult to make good electrical contacts in order to get good measures. In the "two-point" measurement scheme shown in Fig. 1, contact resistances may easily lead to meaningless measurements.

A well-known method to measure the resistivity (the "four-point technique") is based on separate voltmetric and amperometric measures, performed by using two separate circuits (Fig. 2). The separate voltmetric circuit allows for neglecting the effects of the contact resistance in the evaluation of the resistivity. In fact, if the input impedance of the voltmeter is large enough, a very small current flows through the voltmetric circuit and, thus the voltage drop across its contact resistances can be neglected. The high currents in the amperometric circuit generate undesired effects as in the two-point technique: however, in the "four-point" approach, the contact resistances are located outside the region of voltmetric measurement and, consequently, do not affect the voltage reading.

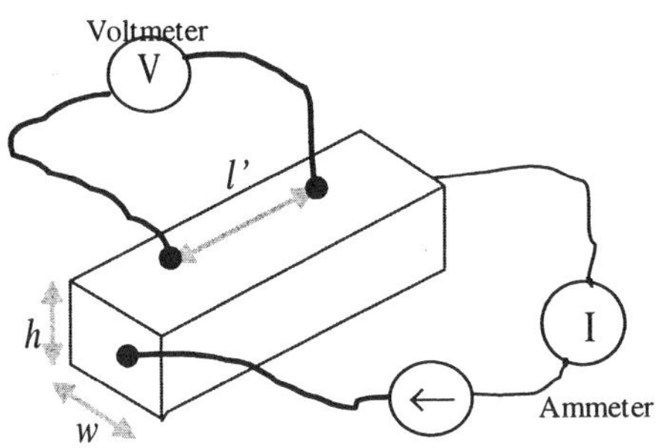

Figure 2: Four point technique for resistivity estimation

Resistivity is obtained from the voltage and the current readings:

$$\rho = \frac{V\ w\ h}{I\ l'} \tag{8}$$

This relationship holds when the physical dimensions of the objects are large enough with respect to the measurement area. Excessive currents should be avoided, although high voltage readings are desirable to increase the reading accuracy, since heating can affect the measure.

11.1.2 Permittivity measurements

Dielectric materials have relatively few free charge carriers: most of the charge carriers are in fact bonded and cannot participate to conduction. Therefore dielectric materials have high resistivities, typically of the order of 10^{15}-10^{18} [Ωm].

However, an external electric field can displace the bonded charges. Atoms or molecules form electric dipoles that tend to oppose to the applied electric field. A dielectric material that exhibits nonzero distribution of these charge separation are called *polarized.* The volume density of the polarization $\vec{P}$ describes the volume density of the dipoles.

For a linear, isotropic material, the polarization density is related to the applied field $\vec{E}$:

$$\vec{P} = \varepsilon_0 \chi_e \vec{E} \tag{9}$$

where ε_0=8.854 10^{-12} [F m^{-1}] is the permittivity of vacuum, and χ_e is called the electric susceptibility of the material.

The electric flux, or displacement, $\vec{D}$ is defined as:

$$\vec{D} = \varepsilon_0 \vec{E} + \vec{P} = \varepsilon_0 (1 + \chi_e) \vec{E} = \varepsilon_0 \varepsilon_r \vec{E} \tag{10}$$

where $\varepsilon = \varepsilon_0 \varepsilon_r$ is the permittivity of the material, and ε_r is its relative permittivity (or dielectric constant).

A material whose characteristics depend on frequency is called *dispersive*. For time-harmonic fields (e.g., $e^{j\omega t}$), the generalized Ampere law is, in the phasor form:

$$\nabla \times \vec{H} = \vec{J}^e + \vec{J} + jw\vec{D} \tag{11}$$

where H is the magnetic field intensity [A/m], J^e is the source current density [A/m^2], J is the conduction current density [A/m^2], and $jw\vec{D}$ represents the displacement current density. J^e will be zero for a source-free region.

Being $\vec{J} = \sigma \ \vec{E}$, where σ is the conductivity of the materials [S/m], it is:

$$\nabla \times \vec{H} = \vec{J}^e + \sigma \ \vec{E} + jw\varepsilon \ \vec{E} \tag{12}$$

Conduction current represents the loss of power. In dielectric materials there is another source of loss. When a time-harmonic electric field is applied, the dipoles flip back and forth continuously. Since the charge carriers have finite mass, the field must perform work to move them and, moreover, they might not respond instantaneously. The polarization vector will lag behind the applied electric field.

$$\nabla \times \vec{H} = \vec{J}^e + \sigma \ \vec{E} + w\kappa'' \ \vec{E} + jw\varepsilon \ \vec{E} = \vec{J}^e + jw\left(\varepsilon \ - j\frac{\sigma \ + w\kappa''}{w}\right)\vec{E} = \vec{J}^e + jw\varepsilon^* \vec{E} \tag{13}$$

The *complex relative permittivity* of a material is defined by:

$$\varepsilon_r^* = \frac{\varepsilon^*}{\varepsilon_0} = \frac{1}{\varepsilon_0}\left(\varepsilon \ - j\frac{\sigma \ + w\kappa''}{w}\right) = \varepsilon_r' - j\varepsilon_r'' \tag{14}$$

The dispersion characteristics of a large class of materials can be represented by the empirical equation (Cole-Cole):

$$\varepsilon_r^* = \varepsilon_\infty + \frac{\varepsilon_s - \varepsilon_\infty}{1 + (jw\tau)^{1-\alpha}} \tag{15}$$

where ε_∞ and ε_s are the relative permittivity at infinite and zero frequencies, respectively and τ is the characteristic relaxation time in seconds. For α=0 Eq. 15 is the Debye equation.

The above parameters significantly change both with material and frequency. From the measurement point of view, these changes are useful to realize capacitive sensors, for example to estimate the nature of a material. As an example, Tables 1 and 2 report the dispersion parameter and the complex permittivity for some frequencies and some materials.

Table 1: Dispersion at room temperature

	ε_∞	ε_S	α	τ [ps]
water	5	78	0	8.0789
ethanol	4.2	24	0	127.8545
acetone	1.9	21.2	0	3.3423

Table 2: Complex permittivity at room temperature

	60 Hz	*1 MHz*	*10 GHz*
nylon	3.60-j 0.06	3.14-j 0.07	2.80-j 0.03
polyethylene	2.26-j 0.0005	2.26-j 0.0005	2.26-j 0.0011
glass	6.78-j 0.11	6.73-j 0.06	6.64-j 0.31

A parallel plate capacitor can be used to determine the complex permittivity of a dielectric sheet. For a separation d between plates of area A in vacuum, the capacitance is:

$$C_0 = \varepsilon_0 \frac{A}{d} \tag{16}$$

In the case of guard electrodes (Fig. 3), often used to reduce fringe effects, the smaller plate must be considered to evaluate C_0.

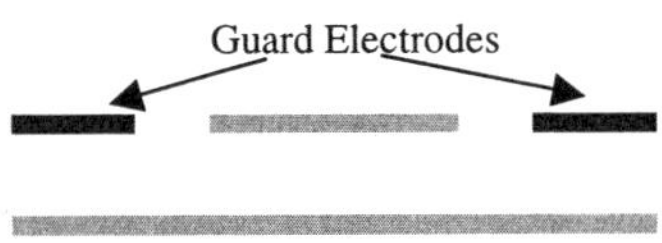

Figure 3: Guard electrodes configuration for a parallel plate capacitive sensor

By using the Debye model (α=0) the equivalent circuit is shown in Fig. 4.

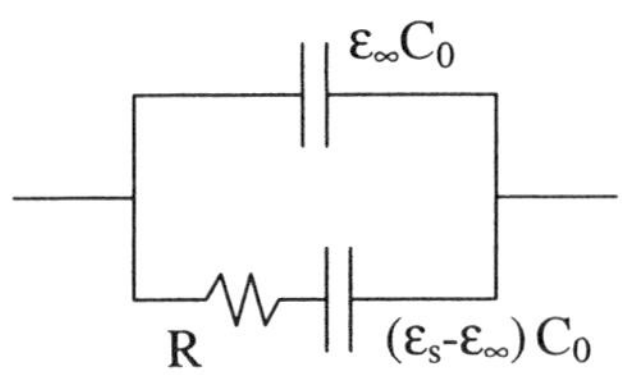

Figure 4: Equivalent circuit for a capacitive sensor

If a step voltage V is applied to the dipole, the current I is:

$$I = \varepsilon_0 C_0 V \delta\ (t) + \frac{VC_0(\varepsilon_0 - \varepsilon_\infty)}{\tau} exp\left(-\frac{t}{\tau}\right) \tag{17}$$
$$\tau = RC_0(\varepsilon_0 - \varepsilon_\infty)$$

The first term represents the charging current of the upper capacitor: this current is not measured. The second term is the charging current of the lower branch of the equivalent circuit. The time constant τ can be determined and the resistance R can be estimated by extrapolating the curve for t =0.

11.1.3 Permeability measurements

A magnetic field interacts with any material that is immersed in the field itself. The magnetic field is usually visualized by means of "flux lines" (or "lines of force"): when these flux lines encounter any material, they are reduced or increased by the interaction between the magnetic field and the material. The original magnetic field is modified (amplified or attenuated) in the body of the material as a result of this interaction.

The magnetic permeability of a material describes the intensity of this interaction, i.e., the degree to which a material can be magnetized. Materials have different degrees of magnetization:

- ferromagnetic materials are highly magnetizable materials that strengthen the magnetic field (e.g., iron or nickel),
- paramagnetic materials are weakly magnetizable materials that increase the magnetic field only marginally (e.g., Al),
- diamagnetic materials are "negative magnetizable materials" since slightly weaken the applied magnetic field (e.g., Cu, rare gases).

When a magnetic field **H** [A/m] is externally applied to an object, the field magnetizes the object to a degree **M** ([Wb/m^2]) while passing through the body of the object. The combined effect of the applied magnetic field and the object magnetization produces a total flux density **B**, called magnetic induction (measured in Wb/m^2, or Tesla T).

$$B = \mu_0 H + M \tag{18}$$

where μ_0 is the permeability of vacuum ($4\pi\ 10^{-7}$ Wb A^{-1} m^{-1}).

The absolute permeability μ of a magnetized body is defined as the induction produced by the applied magnetic field:

$$\mu = \frac{B}{H} \tag{19}$$

The relative permeability is:

$$\mu_r = \frac{\mu}{\mu_0} \tag{20}$$

In any atom the electrons orbit and spin, thus behaving like very tiny current loops. As for any moving charged particle, a magnetic momentum is associated with each electron. Diamagnetism occurs when the total momentum obtained by adding the contributions of all electrons is null. The magnetic field applied to a diamagnetic material induces can induce a momentum in the material that opposes the applied field.

In a paramagnetic material the total momentum generated by all electrons of an atom is not null. When a magnetic field is applied, the weak diamagnetic response is dominated by the atom tendency to align its own momentum with the direction of the applied field.

Diamagnetic and paramagnetic substances are characterized by their magnetic susceptibility κ [Wb A^{-1} m^{-1}]

$$\mu_r = 1 + \frac{M}{\mu_0 H} = 1 + \frac{\kappa}{\mu_0} \tag{21}$$

Ferromagnetic materials are a subclass of the paramagnetic materials. However, they are less affected by the thermal energy than the paramagnetic materials because the individual atomic momenta of a ferromagnet are coupled in a rigid parallelism, even in the absence of an applied field. A demagnetized ferromagnet contains several magnetic domains. All individual atomic momenta within a domain are parallel and, consequently, the domain has a total nonzero magnetization. The direction of this magnetization is generally opposing to the ones of its neighboring domains: the global momentum of the whole material is therefore zero. In the presence of an applied magnetic field, the domains whose momentum is about oriented in the direction of the applied field grow at the expense of the other domains, thus increasing the total field in the material.

11.1.4 Conditioning circuits for resistive sensors

Resistive sensors are devices whose resistivity depends from an external physical quantity that has to be measured. From the measure of the resistance and by knowing the function relating the resistance to the desired physical quantity, the measure of such a quantity can be derived.

The resistance can be measured through a voltage measurement by means of a suited conditioning circuit: the Wheatstone bridge (Fig. 5). This is a direct measurement methodology where an unknown resistance is compared with reference resistors through some regulating elements.

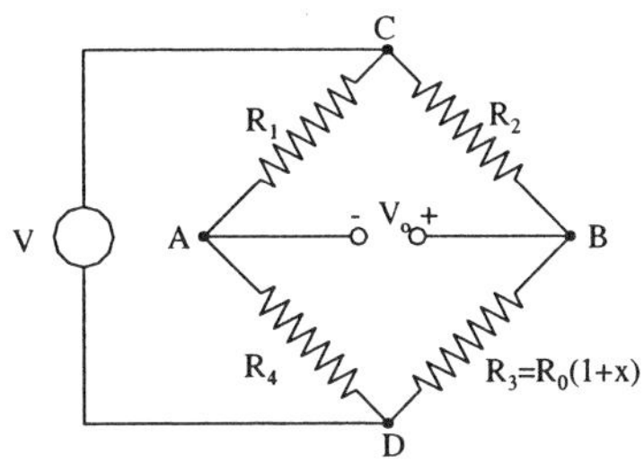

Figure 5: Wheatstone bridge circuit for resistive sensors conditioning

In Fig. 5, when V_o=0 the following relationship among the resistors holds:

$$R_3 = \frac{R_2}{R_1} R_4 \tag{22}$$

The unknown resistance R_3 (the unknown relative resistance change x with respect the fixed value R_0) is directly derived from R_4 through the scaling factor R_2/R_1.

If the unknown resistance has to be continuously monitored in time to observe its variations (and, consequently, the variations of the physical phenomena inducing the resistivity changes), verifying the bridge balance condition (V_o=0) could become a severe problem.

In these cases a deflection methodology can be adopted. The output voltage can be expressed as a function of x as follows:

$$V_o = V\frac{kx}{(k+1)(k+1+x)} \qquad k = \frac{R_1}{R_4} = \frac{R_2}{R_0} \tag{23}$$

Although the output function is nonlinear with respect to x, it can be approximated to a linear function when $x<<k+1$. However, if the sensitivity S is taken into account, k cannot be made arbitrarily large. As shown in Eq. 24, a tradeoff must be found between linearity and sensitivity:

$$S = \frac{V_o}{xR_0} = \frac{V}{xR_0}\frac{kx}{(k+1)(k+1+x)} = \frac{1}{R_0}\frac{kV}{(k+1)(k+1+x)} \tag{24}$$

$$S_{max} \rightarrow k^2 = x+1$$

Linearity can be improved by using different conditioning circuits. An intrinsically linear circuit is shown in Fig. 6; its output voltage is:

$$Vo = -V\frac{x}{2} \tag{25}$$

In the linearity region of the operational amplifier, this conditioning circuit is linear with x, without any restriction on its amplitude.

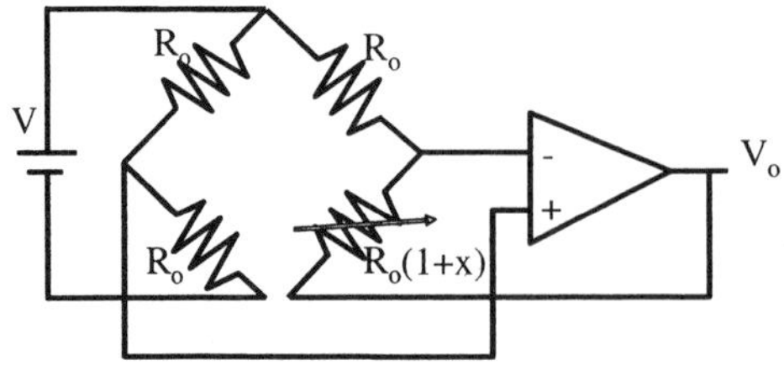

Figure 6: Intrinsically linear resistance for the voltage conversion circuit

11.1.5 Conditioning circuits for reactive sensors

Similarly to the resistive case, a widely used methodology for conditioning the output of a reactive sensor and measuring its impendence is based on the bridge circuit for direct comparison between unknown and reference impedances. The general scheme is shown in Fig. 7.

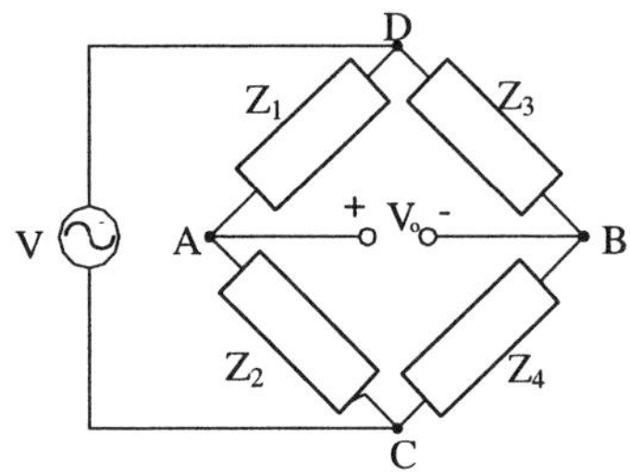

Figure 7: Scheme of the AC bridge for signal conditioning for reactive sensors

For this circuit the following general relationships hold:

$$\dot{V}_{AB} = \dot{V}_{AC} - \dot{V}_{BC}$$
$$\dot{V}_{AB} = \dot{V}\left(\frac{\dot{Z}_2}{\dot{Z}_1 + \dot{Z}_2} - \frac{\dot{Z}_4}{\dot{Z}_3 + \dot{Z}_4}\right) \tag{26}$$

At the equilibrium, the following relationships hold among the moduli and the phases of the four impedances:

$$V_{AB} = 0 \quad \Rightarrow \quad \begin{cases} \dot{Z}_1\dot{Z}_4 = \dot{Z}_2\dot{Z}_3 \\ \varphi_1 + \varphi_4 = \varphi_2 + \varphi_3 \end{cases} \tag{27}$$

Two of the four elements are usually fixed and used as scaling factor, to evaluate the unknown impedance the remaining one can be then varied until the equilibrium condition on the output voltage is reached. At this point the conditions reported in Eq.27 hold and the unknown impedance can be estimated. As an example, taking Z_1 as unknown, in the following two among the possible alternatives are considered:

$$\frac{\dot{Z}_3}{\dot{Z}_4} = k \;\Rightarrow\; (R_1 + jX_1) = k(R_2 + jX_2) \Rightarrow \begin{cases} R_1 = kR_2 \\ X_1 = kX_2 \end{cases}$$

$$\frac{\dot{Z}_3}{\dot{Z}_4} = jk \;\Rightarrow\; (R_1 + jX_1) = jk(R_2 + jX_2) \Rightarrow \begin{cases} R_1 = -kX_2 \\ X_1 = kR_2 \end{cases} \tag{28}$$

11.2. Soft computing methodologies for intelligent measurement systems

Soft computing methodologies and technologies have been developed to exploit the tolerance for imprecision and uncertainty in the description of problems and solutions to achieve tractability, robustness, and low cost. In this section, the main features of these paradigms that are relevant to the implementation of intelligent measurement systems are briefly reviewed, with specific reference to neural networks, fuzzy systems and hybrid solutions.

11.2.1 Neural networks

Neural networks have been widely presented in the literature and in the previous chapters of this book. Some general references are given in Chapter 1.

The basic characteristic that is relevant to realize measurement systems for electrical and dielectrical quantities is the fundamental property of being universal approximators, under very general conditions. As said in the previous section, measuring a physical quantity can often by reduced to

- measuring the resistance (or the impedance) at the output of a sensor sensible to variations in this electrical parameter due to variations of the physical quantity to be measured, and
- transforming this measured value back to the corresponding measure of the desired physical quantity.

This last operation is achieved by applying a suited function, which in general is non-linear. This function can be well approximated be a neural network by exploiting its universal approximation ability. Multilayered perceptrons have been shown effective in the literature to achieve this goal, with various shapes of activation functions (e.g., step, linear, logistic, and Gaussian functions).

11.2.2 Fuzzy systems

Fuzzy logic theory allows for dealing with uncertainty of several types:

- in stochastic uncertainty an event occurs with a given probability,
- in lexical or linguistic uncertainty, description of an object or concept is imprecise,
- in informational uncertainty, uncertainty is caused by missing or incomplete information.

Fuzzy logic (e.g., see [5-7] for more details) can be introduced, e.g., by referring to the example shown in Fig. 8. In the classical ("crisp") logic an element x either belongs to set A or not. If a membership function $\mu(x)$ is defined, it is:

$$\mu(x) \in \{0,1\} \tag{29}$$

In the fuzzy environment a membership function is allowed to assume any value (degree of membership) in the real interval [0,1].

Fuzzy sets can have any suitable shape and are defined on a Universe of Discourse that considers the variable itself. On fuzzy sets a suited mathematical theory has been developed: several operations can be performed, e.g., sum, product, and other Boolean functions.

Linguistic variables are defined by fuzzy descriptions, each providing the membership degrees to a fuzzy set defined in the Universe of Discourse U. Fig. 9 shows an example concerning the definition of temperature.

Fuzzy rules allow for representing dependencies, by means of if-then rules like:

if <antecedent> then <consequence>

For example:

if <u>*temperature*</u> *is* A_T *and* <u>*pressure*</u> *is* C_P *then* <u>*heating*</u> *is* B_H

where *temperature*, *pressure*, and *heating* are linguistic variables; A_T, C_P, and B_H are linguistic values derived from the fuzzy sets defined on the universes of discourse of the variables.

Systems are described by the set of fuzzy rules (fuzzy rulebase). Fuzzy inferences are necessary to determine the actual output for a given input. In Fig. 10 the fuzzy rule base for a hypothetic temperature control system is reported.

The rulebase inference consists of several steps. First of all, the degree of membership for each term of an input variable is determined. Then, the *degree of fulfillment* for the entire antecedent is computed by using a "fuzzy AND". Finally, the degree of membership of the antecedent is applied to the consequent of the rule by using a suited rule (t-norm), namely the *min* or the *prod* operators. These steps are summarized in Fig. 11.

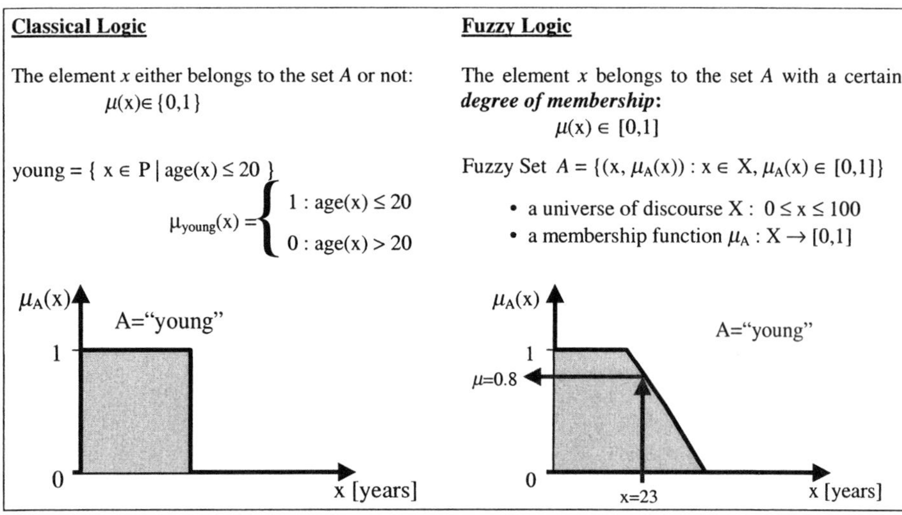

Figure 8: Example of the working principle of fuzzy logic

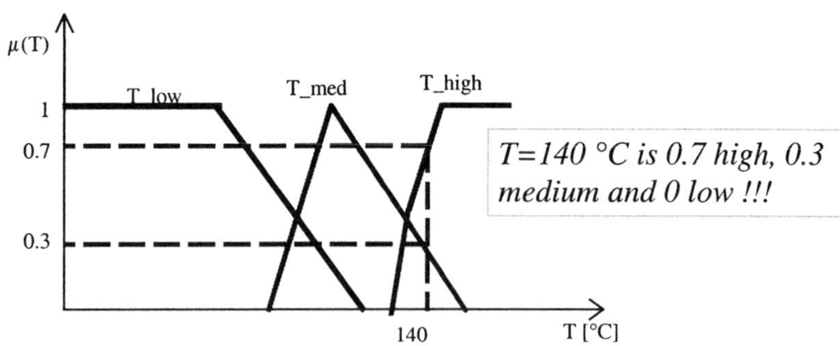

Figure 9: Definition of the linguistic variable "temperature"

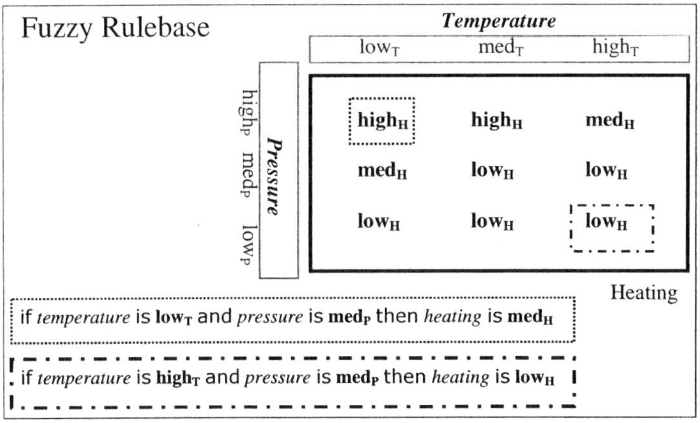

Figure 10: Fuzzy rulebase for a temperature control system

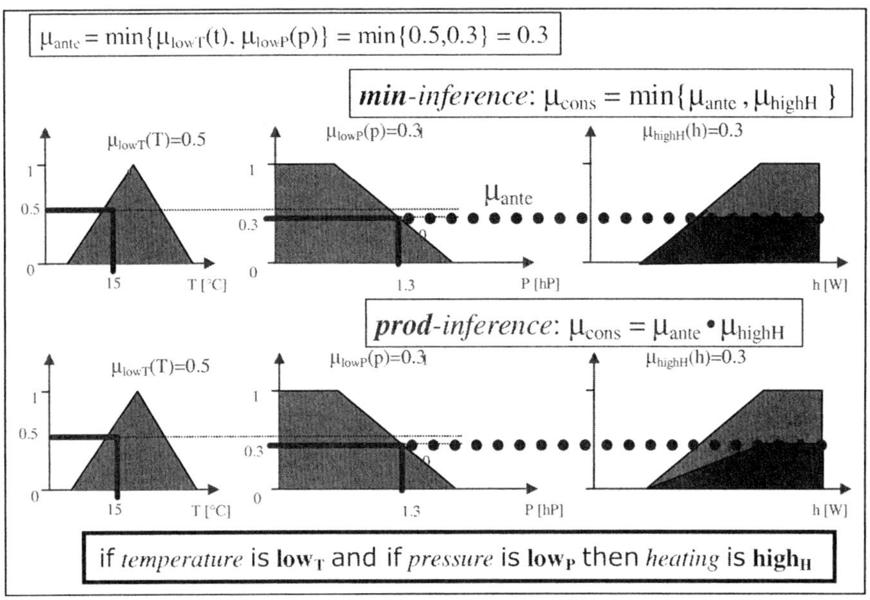

Figure 11: Examples of fuzzy inferences

The final step is defuzzification. Consequents are aggregated by using the max-operator to implement union. Then, a crisp output value h_{COG} is derived from the output membership function. This last operation is performed by using, for example, the method of the center of gravity (see Fig. 12):

$$h_{COG} = \frac{\sum_i \mu_i A_i C_i}{\sum_i \mu_i A_i} \tag{30}$$

where, for each fuzzy set i, μ_i is the degree of membership, A_i is the area, and C_i is the center of gravity.

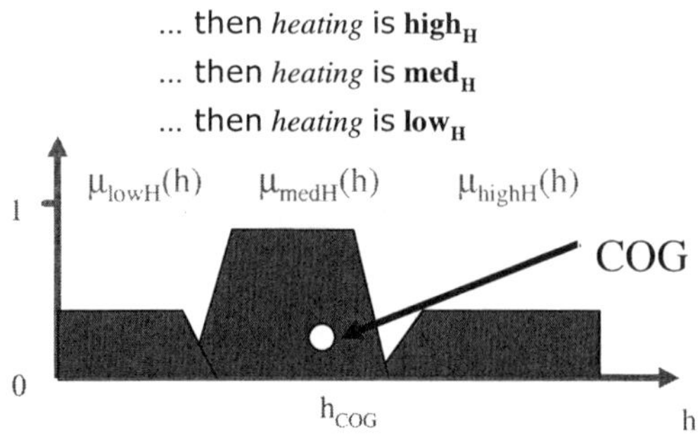

Figure 12: Defuzzification

Different rules can be defined according to the consequent form. The *Mamdani rule* produces fuzzy sets (as in the example shown in Fig. 12). In the *Takagi-Sugeno-Kang (TSK)-rule* the outputs are functions $f(x_i)$ (e.g., *if* X_1 *is* A_1 *and* X_2 *is* A_2 .... X_n *is* A_n *then* $Y=f(x_1,x_2,..x_n)$).

A fuzzy algorithm is therefore defined by using a mixed approach that merges operator experience (empirical knowledge) with map learning (learning from set of experimental data). This allows for achieving a much higher flexibility with respect to the neural networks in merging empirical knowledge with experimental data.

A fuzzy algorithm can be summarized in the following steps:

- choose the input variables, i.e., measured quantities that are directly related to the actual measurand,
- choose the membership functions and their shape for antecedents,
- choose the consequent membership function or the output rules functions,
- tune the consequent values from a set of measured examples,
- adjust the rulebase by adding some rules derived from the experience.

11.2.3 Neuro-fuzzy networks

Neuro-fuzzy networks are architectures similar to neural networks that are suited to implement an optimized fuzzy system. They typically consist of a five-layer structure; an example related to the case of two input quantities is shown in Fig. 13. The membership function parameters in layer 1 and the consequents in layer 4 are determined by using a learning algorithm. Layers 2, 3, and 5 are fixed and perform fuzzy inferences. Membership function shape is chosen in advance (e.g., the Gaussian function, characterized by center and variance).

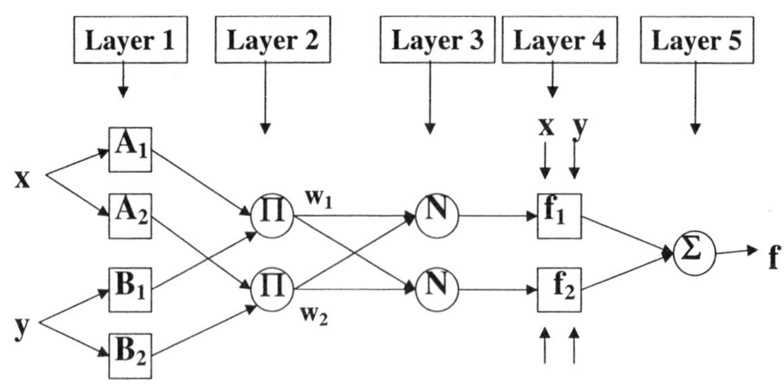

Figure 13: A two-input neuro-fuzzy network

Layer 1:
- Every node i is an adaptive node,
- $O_{1,i}$ is the membership grade of a fuzzy set A (A_1, A_2, B_1, B_2); it specifies the degree to which the given input satisfies the corresponding attribute A.
- The parameter set that characterizes each membership function for the fuzzy set are referred to as premise parameters.

$$O_{1,i} = \mu_{A_i}(x) \qquad i = 1,2$$
$$O_{1,i} = \mu_{B_{i-2}}(y) \qquad i = 3,4 \tag{31}$$

Layer 2
- Every node is a fixed node that represents the fire strength of each rule (AND, T-norm):

$$O_{2,i} = w_i = \mu_{A_i}(x)\mu_{B_i}(y) \quad i = 1,2 \tag{32}$$

Layer 3
- The outputs are called normalized firing strengths.
- Every node is a fixed node that computes the ratio between the i-th rule's firing strength and the sum of all rules' firing strengths:

$$O_{3,i} = \overline{w}_i = \frac{w_i}{w_1 + w_2} \qquad i = 1,2 \tag{33}$$

Layer 4
- The parameter set is called consequent parameters.
- Every node is an adaptive node with function:

$$O_{4,i} = \overline{w}_i f_i = \overline{w}_i^{\,2}(p_i x + q_i y + r_i) \tag{34}$$

Layer 5
- The node is a fixed node that computes the overall output as the summation of all incoming signals:

$$O_{5,1} = \sum_i \overline{w}_i f_i = \frac{\sum_i w_i f_i}{\sum_i w_i} \tag{35}$$

This kind of network is equivalent to a first-order Sugeno fuzzy model. An example is shown in Fig. 14.

Two input: ***x*** **and** ***y***
Typical rule structure:
Rule 1: ***If*** **x is A_1** ***and*** **y is B_1** ***then*** **$f_1 = p_1x + q_1y + r_1$**
Rule 1: ***If*** **x is A_2** ***and*** **y is B_2** ***then*** **$f_2 = p_2x + q_2y + r_2$**

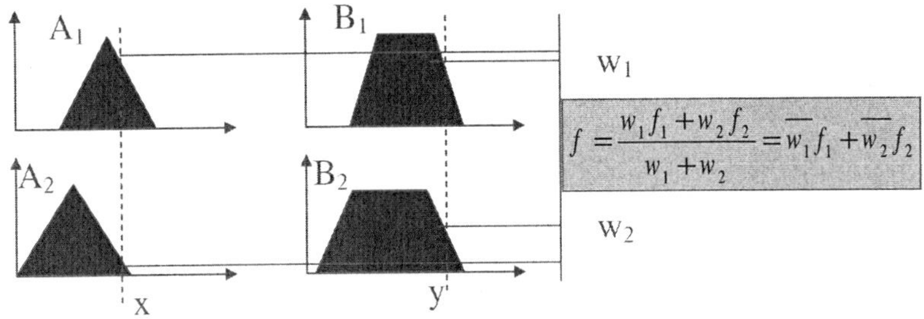

Figure 14: Two-input, first-order Sugeno fuzzy model

11.2.4 Neural measurement systems and soft sensors

In measurement systems for electrical quantities, soft computing methodologies are useful from different points of view. In particular, they have been used to identify models of complex measurement instruments and to merge information coming from different sensors (multisensor data fusion).

Neural networks and fuzzy systems are universal approximators. Therefore they can be effectively used to create system models and, in particular, to represent the non-linear complex function that transform the electrical outputs of a set of sensors into the value of the desired physical quantity, as discussed in the previous section.

For more information about the function approximation ability of neural networks, refer to the previous chapters (especially, to chapter 4).

The function approximation ability of fuzzy systems derives from the configurability of their parameters. Let's consider a system to be modeled by means of a fuzzy approach, as summarized in Fig. 15: let *u(k)* and *y(k)* be the sampled input and output signals, respectively.

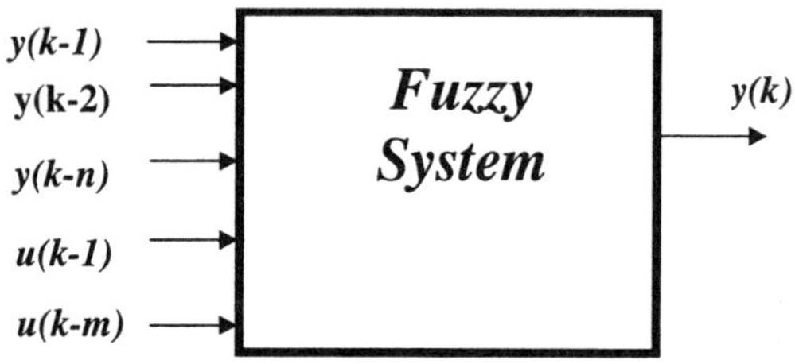

$$R_j : IF\left(y(k-1)\ IS\ A_1^j\right) AND \left(y(k-2)\ IS\ A_2^j\right) AND \ldots AND \left(u(k-m)\ IS\ A_{n+m}^j\right) THEN\ y(k) = y_j$$

Figure 15: Fuzzy system modeling

Once the membership function both of the input variables *u(k)* and *y(k)* of the fuzzy model and their regressions (i.e., the previous values to be considered to describe the system dynamics) have been defined, the antecedent of each rule is completely specified for each input. The unknowns to be determined for system identification are the rules' output values y^*_j ($j=1,,.,R$, where R is the number of the fuzzy rules R_j that are used to represent the system model). For each set x of the input values, the output Y^* of the fuzzy system (i.e., the fuzzy model output) is a linear combination of the rule outputs:

$$Y^* = f(x) = \sum_{j=1}^{R} p_j(x) y_j^* \tag{36}$$

where p_j is the activation level of the j-th rule.

Let's take M sets of measurements (with $M>R$) that describe the system behavior accurately and completely (as it is done for any other modeling technique). The unknown parameters of the fuzzy model must be tuned so that the fuzzy model simulate the system behavior, i.e., the output of the fuzzy model Y^* should optimally fit the actual system output y. The following system of M equations in R unknowns can be written:

$$\mathbf{Y} = \mathbf{P}\ \mathbf{C} \tag{37}$$

where $\mathbf{C}_{\mathbf{Rx1}}$ is the vector of the unknown fuzzy rule outputs, $\mathbf{P}_{\mathbf{MxR}}$ is the matrix of the activation levels and $\mathbf{Y}_{\mathbf{Mx1}}$ is the vector of measurements. This system can be solved with a least square approach:

$$\mathbf{C} = \left(\mathbf{P}^T\mathbf{P}\right)^{-1}\mathbf{P}^T\mathbf{Y} \tag{38}$$

thus completing the fuzzy model.

As any model, also a fuzzy model needs to be validated by using a set of data that has not been used for configuration. In the case of nonlinear systems, the validation data set should include examples of all system behaviors considered in the learning data set, although examples must be different from the one used for learning. The statistical properties of the output error must be analyzed to certify the quality of the identified model: the error should in fact have a Gaussian distribution.

Soft sensors are therefore models of actual sensors that have been realized by using soft computing methodologies. These measuring systems are useful for substituting or cooperating with the real sensors.

11.3. Industrial applications of soft sensors and neural measurement systems

In this section some applications of soft computing methodologies to industrial cases involving electrical measurements are presented. The basic goal is to show the effectiveness of this approach to realize highly efficient sensors and measurement systems. Efficiency is mainly related to opportunity of using simple sensors that do not need sophisticated and expensive analog signal conditioning circuits, while derivation of the desired information from the measurement signals is left to the generalization abilities of neural and neuro-fuzzy systems. Additional information and examples are available in [8-12].

11.3.1 Neural measurement systems for electrical motor modeling

Asynchronous machines are very interesting both from an academic point of view and for the industry since they have many applications. Unfortunately, these systems are very complex, non-linear, and difficult to model and control.

Control strategies based on the flux are difficult to be used since direct and accurate flux measurement is not feasible. A model of this machine and a device to observe the flux (e.g., a soft flux sensor) is therefore needed. Neural networks can be effectively adopted to build a NARMAX (Nonlinear Autoregressive Moving Average with Exogenous Input) model of the asynchronous machines and to design nonlinear flux observers (for system modeling and control see chapters 4 and 5, [13]).

In the literature a fifth-order *d-q* model is shown suited to represent the behavior of the asynchronous machine. In the state space form the machine equations are:

$$
\begin{aligned}
\frac{d\psi_{qr}}{dt} &= \frac{-\omega_b R_r}{X_r}\psi_{qr} - (\omega_e - \omega_r)\psi_{dr} + \frac{\omega_b R_r X_m}{X_r} i_{qs} \\
\frac{d\psi_{dr}}{dt} &= (\omega_e - \omega_r)\psi_{dr} - \frac{\omega_b R_r}{X_r}\psi_{dr} + \frac{\omega_b R_r X_m}{X_r} i_{ds} \\
\frac{d\omega_r}{dt} &= -\frac{3\overline{p}^2}{2J\omega_b^2}\frac{X_m}{X_r} i_{ds}\psi_{qr}\omega_b + \frac{3p^2}{2J\omega_b^2}\frac{X_m}{X_r} i_{qs}\psi_{dr}\omega_b - \frac{\overline{p}}{J}T_L \\
\frac{di_{qs}}{dt} &= \frac{X_m}{X_r}\frac{\omega_b R_r}{X_r X_k}\psi_{qr} - \frac{X_m}{X_r X_k}\omega_r\psi_{dr} - \frac{\omega_b}{X_k}\left(R_s + \frac{X_m}{X_r}\frac{R_r}{X_r}\right)i_{qs} - \omega_e i_{ds} + \frac{\omega_b}{X_k}V_{qs} \\
\frac{di_{ds}}{dt} &= \frac{X_m}{X_r X_k}\omega_r\psi_{qr} + \frac{X_m}{X_r}\frac{\omega_b R_r}{X_r X_k}\psi_{dr} - \frac{\omega_b}{X_k}\left(R_s + \frac{X_m}{X_r}\frac{R_r}{X_r}\right)i_{ds} + \omega_e i_{qs} + \frac{\omega_b}{X_k}V_{qs}
\end{aligned}
\tag{39}
$$

where ψ_{dr} and ψ_{qr} are the rotor fluxes; ω_r *and* ω_b are the rotor and the base electrical angular velocity, respectively; ω_e is the electrical supply frequency; T_L is the load torque; J is the system inertia; R_r is the rotor resistance referred to the stator; X_s, X_m, and X_r are the stator self, mutual, and rotor reactance referred to the stator, respectively; p is the number of pair poles; $u=[V_{qs}, \omega_e, T_L]$ is the input vector; $x=[\psi_{dr}, \psi_{qr}, \omega_r, i_{qs}, i_{ds}]$ is the state vector; and $y=[\omega_r, i_{qs}, i_{ds}]$ is the output vector. Besides, it is:

$$X_k = X_s - \frac{X_m^2}{X_r} \quad X_F = \frac{X_m}{X_r} \tag{40}$$

A neural network approach was successfully experimented in [8] to create a NARMAX model by learning through examples. A multilayer perceptron with a single hidden layer and with feedback from the network outputs was chosen. Since the desired system model is a fifth-order dynamical one, five previous samples of both input and output signals must be considered.

To reduce the configuration time, one separate neural network for each one of the three output signals has been adopted.

For each network, the number n_i of input units is therefore 30; since a single-step prediction is required, the number n_o of output units is 1; the number n_h of hidden units is 6 and was experimentally determined as the smallest value that gives suitable accuracy and learning convergence.

To obtain a meaningful nonlinear model, the input signals for training the networks by means of the backpropagation have been chosen so as to describe the working conditions in a large area centered in the following working point:

$$\begin{aligned} w_e &= 314.0 \quad [rad/s] \\ T_L &= 30.0 \quad [N \cdot m] \\ V_{qs} &= \sqrt{\frac{3}{2}} \cdot 380 \ [V] \end{aligned} \tag{41}$$

A white noise signal with maximum value equal to twice the working point was adopted to produce the learning signals.

For validation two set of data have been used: signals not considered during learning, and output signals obtained with zero input but nonzero initial conditions. This second operating condition was not explicitly included in the learning set. It must be highlighted as, during validation and autonomous operation, the outputs of the neural networks are fed back to provide the signals for the subsequent iterations.

In Fig. 16 the validation results of the output i_{ds} are shown for these two operating conditions, for the case of three separate networks corresponding to the three separate outputs with 6 hidden units. The model describes adequately the system behavior with the white noise input since the maximum error is less than 10% (Fig. 16a); however, the adopted neural model has not sufficient generalization abilities since the error with nonzero initial conditions (Fig. 16b) is too large.

By pruning the hidden layer was optimized and reduced to 3 units, thus removing unnecessary degrees of freedom that were not properly configured by learning: validation showed now a much better model behavior also in the second operating condition (Fig. 17).

Neural networks have also been used to realize a nonlinear flux observer that estimates the flux from indirect measurements [8].

To estimate the flux ψ_{dr} the input vector to be presented to the neural network is:

$$[w_e(k-1), T_L(k-1), V_{qs}(k-1), w_r(k-1), i_{qs}(k-1), i_{ds}(k-1), \Psi_{dr}(k-1), \Psi_{qr}(k-1)] \tag{42}$$

while the output vector becomes $[\Psi_{dr}(k)]$. The neural network suited to model each component (ψ_{dr} and ψ_{qr}) of the flux observer is therefore a multilayered structure, with 8 inputs, 7 hidden units, and 1 output neuron. In the presence of measurement noise and parameters variations, the learning set must include sufficient examples to adequately cover these operating conditions. Validation results are shown in Fig. 18.

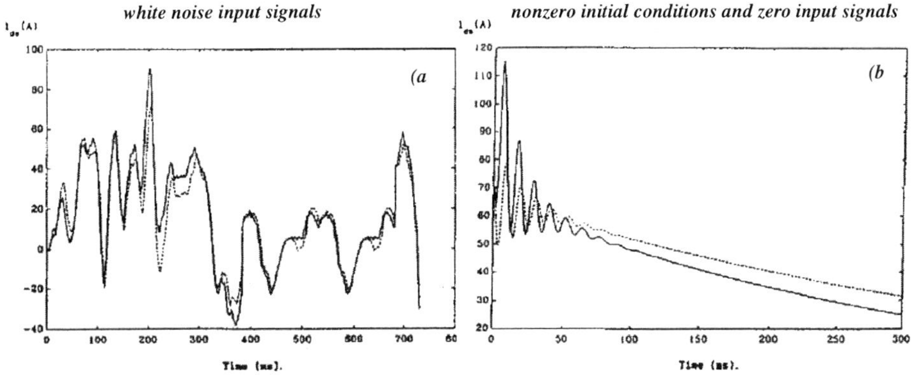

Figure 16: Neural model validation for the output i_{ds}, with 6 hidden neurons and autonomous evolution: (a) white noise input, (b) nonzero initial conditions and zero input (continuous line: system output; dashed line: model output).

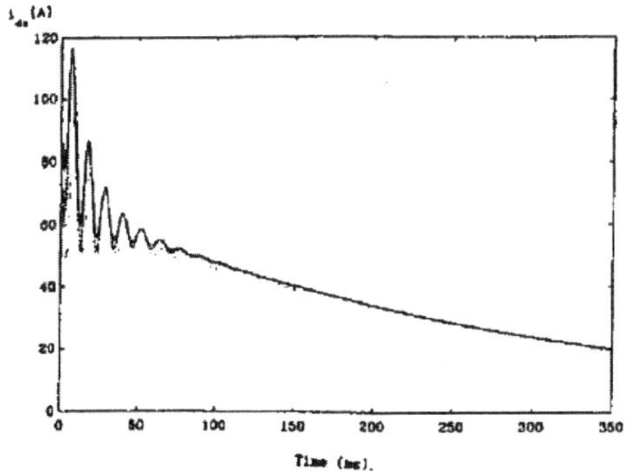

Figure 17: Validation for the neural model with 3 hidden neuron in autonomous evolution (continuous line: system output; dashed line: model output)

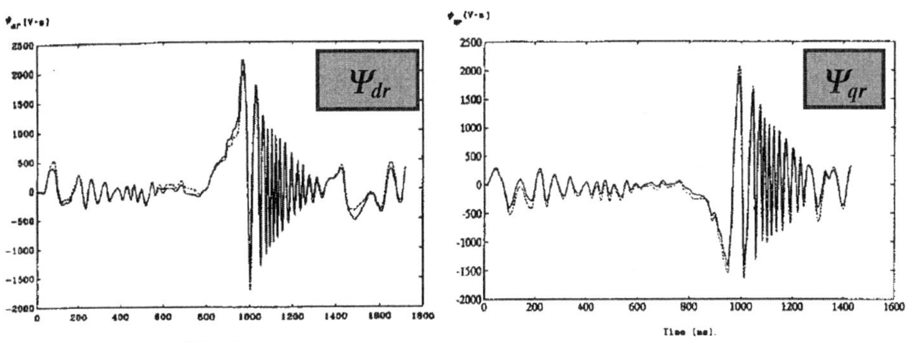

Figure 18: Validation of the neural-based flux observer (continuous line: system output; dashed line: model output).

11.3.2 Neural models of integrated power electronic devices

This application deals with the development of neural models for integrated power bipolar-junction transistors (BJTs) in electronic ignition circuits [9].

Simulation is one of the main steps in microelectronic circuits design. Accuracy, effectiveness, and efficiency of simulation strongly depend from the availability of accurate device models. In many cases models are based on a fixed structure derived from the theory, whose parameters have been identified by using set of experimental data. Unfortunately, theory is sometimes not sufficiently developed yet to capture all details of the real devices and thus more accurate models need to be created from sampled data. An example is the vertical power bipolar junction transistor.

Power bipolar transistors are usually organized in a four-layer vertical structure with alternate doping in the layers. This architecture allows for maximizing the area crossed by the current and, therefore, for minimizing the forward resistance of the component. This structure has a very different behavior with respect to the low-power devices, both in the *i-v* characteristics and in the switching operations. In particular, the width of the quasi-saturation region is quite large in power devices due to the width of the collector drift region whose low doping factor and charge storage effect influence the switching time.

The Gummel-Poon model is usually adopted to describe BJTs. This model takes into account several phenomena (e.g., the Early effect), while the charge control approach allows for describing transient behaviors.

The Gummel-Poon parameters are usually determined with a curve fitting approach based on experimental data. However, this model does not adequately describe several effects in power BJTs, especially in the quasi-saturation region.

Soft computing can be used to create a better model for this class of power electronic components. The ultimate goal is to create a description suited for a conventional circuit simulator like SPICE®. This will allow for performing numerical simulations of more complex systems that include power BJTs, e.g., the industrial devices like those produced by STMicroelectronics (for this reason, the following numerical simulations have been performed by using the STSpice® simulator).

The measured collector current I_C and the output signal $I_C=f(V_{CE},IB)$ produced by a classical numerical simulator with the Gummel-Poon model are shown in Fig. 19. Creating a completely new model with a smaller error only from the sampled data suited to be included in the circuit simulator may lead to a computationally-expensive model. The adopted solution preserves the well-assessed theoretical knowledge contained in the Gummel-Poon model and focuses on the compensation of its error with respect to the measured data. This compensation consists of a controlled current source, $I_{Comp}=g(V_{CE},I_B)$, that is added to the classical Gummel-Poon model as shown in Fig. 20.

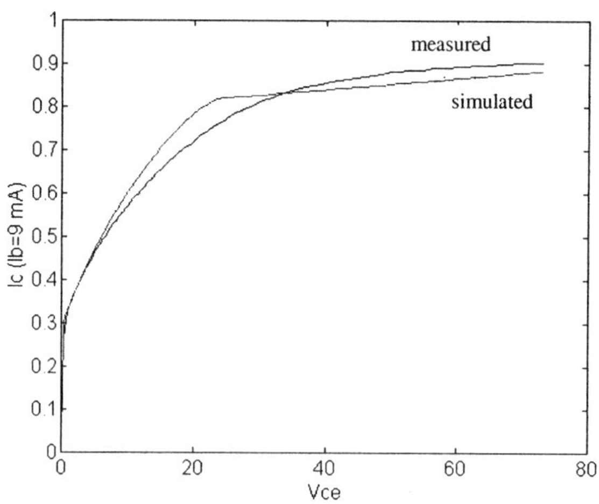

Figure 19: The measured and the Gummel-Poon simulated output current for power BJTs.

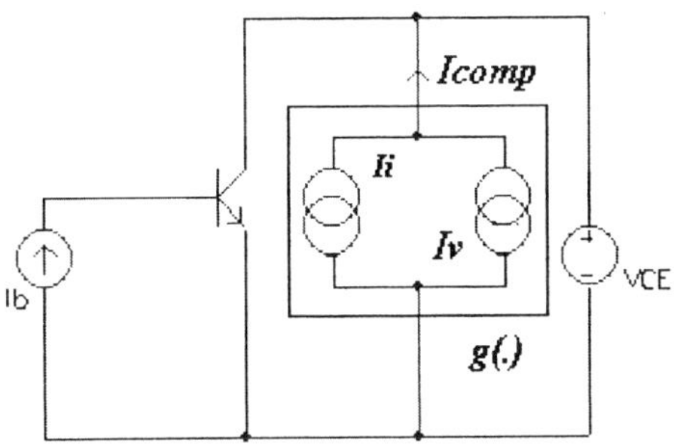

Figure 20: The compensation scheme for increasing the accuracy of the Gummel-Poon model for power BJTs.

Two approaches were considered to obtain a model for I_{Comp}: polynomial and neural models. Although having several limitations, polynomial models can be implemented in the SPICE simulator in a straightforward way. Neural models may have higher flexibility and accuracy, although may have higher computational complexity; experiments have shown good results by using multilayer perceptrons with one 5-unit hidden layer. In Fig. 21 the measured data and the different models are shown: the advantage of using the compensated model (i.e., the compensating controlled current generator) is relevant.

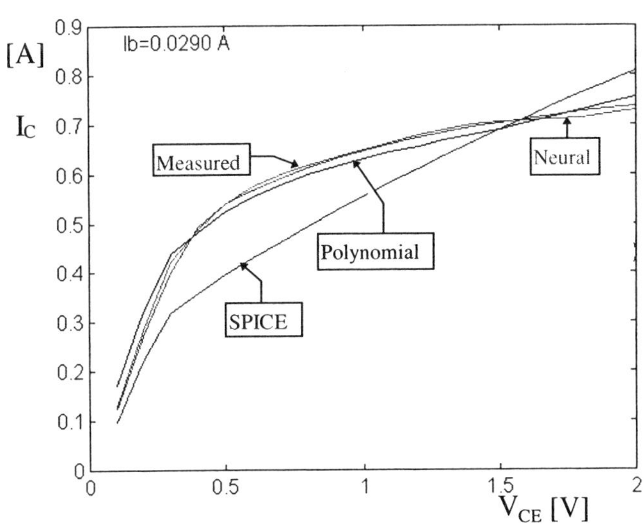

Figure 21: Output characteristics of an industrial power BJTs. Comparison among the measured data and the various models.

The importance of using more accurate models becomes even more evident when they are used to simulate complex devices that include the modeled component. A first example is the simulation of a Darlington transistor: the output characteristics of this device obtained with the various BJT models are shown in Fig. 22.

Another –much more complex– example that includes the power transistor model is the industrial electronic ignition device developed in the STMicroelectronics laboratories. The measured output voltage applied to the inductor is shown in Fig. 23a: the much higher accuracy of the neural-enhanced model with respect to the classical Gummel-Poon model can be observed in Fig. 23b.

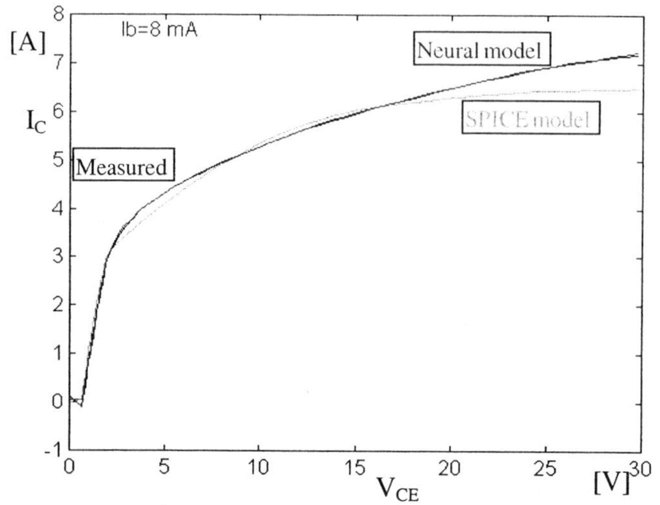

Figure 22: Output characteristics of an industrial Darlington transistor based on the various BJT models.

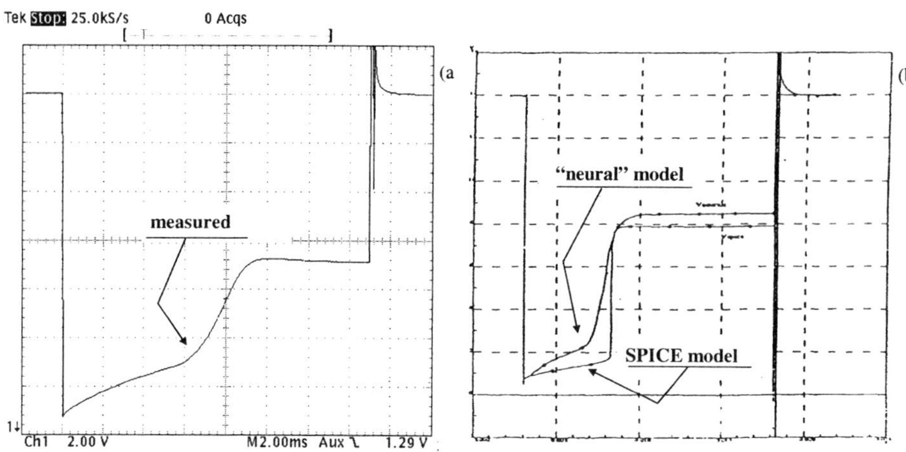

Figure 23: The voltage applied to the output inductor in the STMicroelectronics electronic ignition circuit: (a) the measured voltage, and (b) the simulation results by using the classical SPICE model and the neural-enhanced model for the power transistors.

11.3.3 Soft sensors for hot-wire flow measurements

Soft sensors for flow measurements have great importance in many industrial applications. Neuro-fuzzy networks have been here used in industrial applications for the indirect measurement of air velocity in cooking hoods.

A flow measurement system was developed for flow control in suction hoods, by exploiting the hot-wire principle [10,12] and by compensating the interfering effects of flow temperature by means of a differential technique.

Hot-wire flow measurements are based both on the convective heat extraction performed by a flowing fluid from a heated wire, and on the value of material resistivity related to the temperature. In the simplest case a wire, carrying a constant current, is exposed to the flow. The wire temperature increases until the heat produced by the Joule effect is balanced by the convective heat loss.

The wire temperature influences the wire resistivity (e.g., resistivity generally increases with temperature in electrical conductors).

When a thermal equilibrium condition is reached, the flow velocity can be related to a resistance measurement. At the equilibrium condition, the energy balance gives:

$$I^2 R_w = h A\left(T_w - T_f\right) \tag{43}$$

where I is the electrical current in the wire, R_w is the wire resistance, T_w is the wire temperature, T_f is the fluid temperature, h is the heat transfer coefficient of the wire film, and A is the heat transfer surface. The h coefficient is given by the King's law:

$$h = C_0 + C_1\sqrt{v} \tag{44}$$

where C_0 and C_1 are suited coefficients, and v is the flow velocity. In Fig. 24 experimental measurements from the hot-wire sensor are shown for constant flow temperature: the voltage is proportional to the resistance since a constant current is driven into the sensor.
It must be noted as the reading increases with the flow velocity when the sensor temperature lowers, this is due to the fact that a semiconductor resistor has been used here as hot-wire sensor.

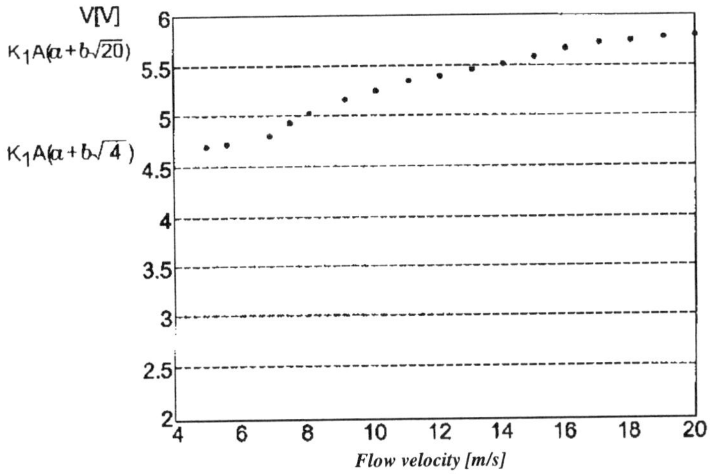

Figure 24: Voltage across the sensor vs. fluid velocity.

A resistance measurement allows therefore for estimating the flow velocity. However, the wire resistance depends also on the flow temperature (see Eq. 43). Compensation of this interfering effect is needed. The scheme of the measurement system is shown in Fig. 25: two Negative Temperature Coefficient (NTC) resistive sensors (thermistors) are used. The main sensor NTC2 is located to sense the fluid velocity: its output thus depends both on the fluid velocity and the fluid temperature. The other resistive sensor NTC1 is located in a "static" environment so that it is sensible only to the fluid temperature and does not experience convective heat loss.

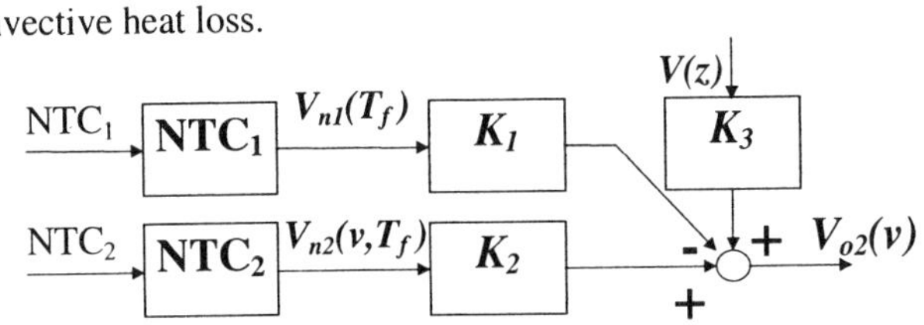

Figure 25: Hot-wire flow measurement system with flow temperature compensation.

The analog signal condition circuit for this measurement system based on conventional approaches is shown in Fig. 26. The output voltage is:

$$V_{02} = K_2 V_{n2} - K_1 V_{n1} - K_3 V_z \tag{45}$$

where:

$$K_1 = \frac{R_4}{R_3} + \frac{R_4 R_{10} R_{11}}{R_3 R_8 (R_9 + R_{10})},$$

$$K_2 = \frac{R_6 R_{10}}{(R_5 + R_6)(R_9 + R_{10})} + \frac{R_4 R_6}{R_3 (R_5 + R_6)} + \frac{R_6 R_{10} R_{11}}{R_8 (R_5 + R_6)(R_9 + R_{10})} + \frac{R_4 R_6 R_{10} R_{11}}{R_3 R_8 (R_5 + R_6)(R_9 + R_{10})},$$

$$K_3 = \frac{R_{10} R_{11}}{R_8 (R_9 + R_{10})}.$$

The term $K_3 V_z$ in Eq. 45 is used to set the working point of the output voltage. The effectiveness of the flow temperature compensation system is shown in Fig. 27.

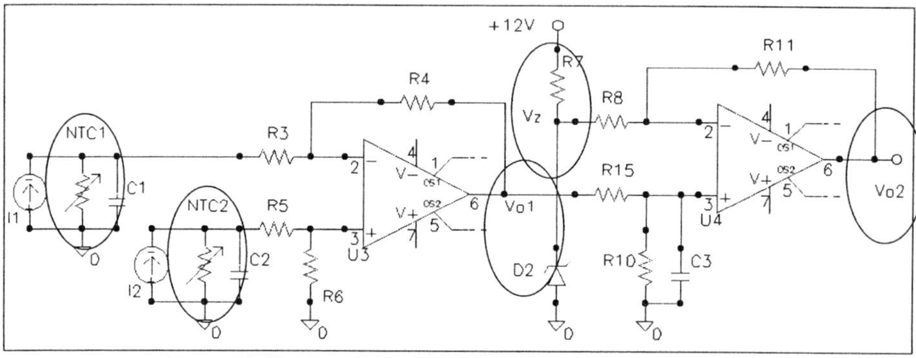

Figure 26: Signal conditioning circuit for hot-wire flow measurement

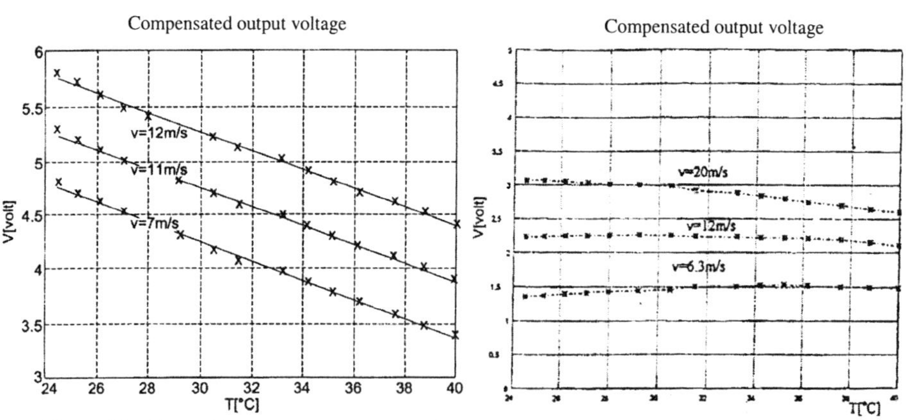

Figure 27: Effect of thermal compensation on the output signal of the flow measurement system.

The output voltage of the measurement system is finally shown if Fig. 28. Experimental data were fitted by using a polynomial model:

$$Y = aX^2 + bX + c \tag{46}$$

whose coefficients were estimated to be $a = -0.0053\ Vs^2/m^2$, $b = 0.245\ V$, and $c = 0.102\ V$.

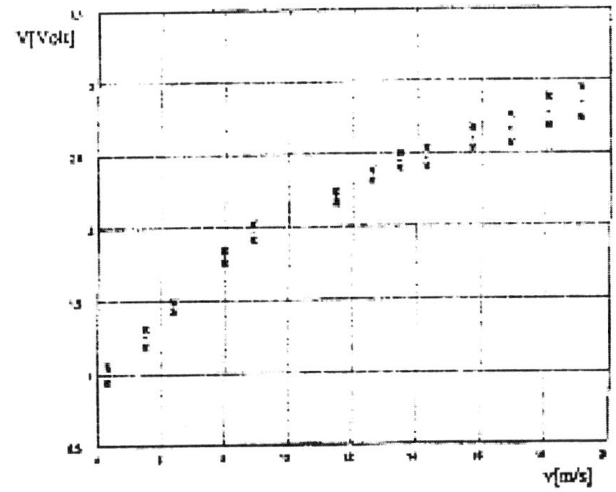

Figure 28: Output voltage vs. flow velocity
for the analog thermally-compensated hot-wire measurement system.

Instead of using sophisticated analog signal conditioning circuits, soft computing can be exploited to create a soft sensor that reads directly the primary sensor outputs and computes the output voltage as a function only of the flow velocity, without any dependence from the flow temperature.

The input signals are the voltages across the two thermistors NTC1 and NTC2. Sixteen fuzzy sets were associated to each of the input voltages. The global set of fuzzy rules and, hence, the number of output fuzzy sets has been determined through the fuzzy identification method summarized in section 12.2.3; the system consists of 121 rules.

In Fig. 29 the output of the soft sensor is compared to the readings of a reference flow meter. Although the fuzzy measurement system still makes use of the hot-wire approach, the required components are simple and no sophisticated analog electronics is needed for signal conditioning.

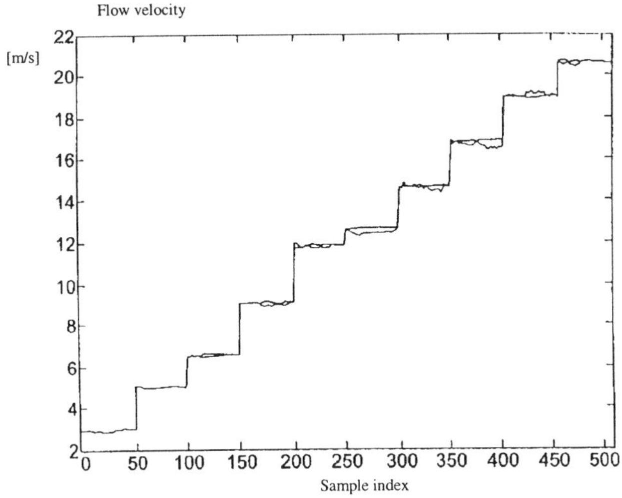

Figure 29: Estimation of the flow velocity by using the soft sensor based on fuzzy systems (uneven line), compared to the output of a reference flow meter.

References

[1] P.T. Moseley, A. J. Crocker, Sensor Materials, IOP Publishing 1996
[2] R. Pallas-Areny, J.G. Webster, Sensors and Signal Conditioning, John Wiley & sons, 1991
[3] The Measurement Instrumentation and Sensors Handbook, J. G. Webster Editor, IEEE Press 1999
[4] E. O. Doebelin, Measurement Systems: Application and Design, McGraw-Hill, 1990
[5] C.H. Chen, Fuzzy Logic and Neural Network Handbook, McGraw-Hill, 1995
[6] C.T. Lin, C.S.G. Lee, Neural Fuzzy Systems, Prentice-Hall, 1996
[7] J.S.R. Jang, C.T. Sun, E. Mizutani, Neuro-Fuzzy and Soft computing, Prentice-Hall, 1997
[8] P. Arena, L. Fortuna, A. Gallo, S. Graziani, G. Muscato, "Induction motor modeling using multi-layer perceptrons", IEICE Trans. Fundamentals, vol.E76 A, no.5, 1993
[9] S. Baglio, S. Graziani, M. Marletta, G. Privitera, D. Tagliavia, "Identification of neural models for power BJTs in industrial electronic ignition circuits", Proc. 30th ISATA, Florence, Italy, June 1997
[10] S. Baglio, F. Di Marco, S. Graziani, F. Milazzo, N. Pitrone, "A Neuro-Fuzzy Approach for the Characterization of Hot-Wire Flow Measurement Systems", Proc. IMEKO 1997, Tampere, Finland, 1997
[11] B. Andò, S. Baglio, A. Cucuccio, S. Graziani, A. La Terra, "A smart sensor for pressure measurement", Proc. IEEE IMTC97, Ottawa, Canada, May 1997
[12] S. Baglio, F. Di Marco, S. Graziani, M. Lo Presti, "Fluid flowmeter based on a neuro-fuzzy approach", US PATENT 6.119.529, September 2000
[13] D.T.Pham, X.Liu, Neural Networks for Identification, Prediction and Control. London: Springer-Verlag, 1995

Neural Networks for Instrumentation, Measurement and Related Industrial Applications
S. Ablameyko et al. (Eds.)
IOS Press, 2003

Chapter 12
Neural Networks for Measurement and Instrumentation in Virtual Environments

Emil M. PETRIU
School of Information Technology and Engineering, University of Ottawa
800 King Edward, Ottawa, Ontario, Canada, K1N 6N5

Abstract. Neural Networks (NNs), which are able to learn nonlinear behaviors from a limited set of measurement data, can provide efficient modeling solutions for many virtual reality applications. Due to their continuous memory behavior, NNs are able to provide instantaneously an estimation of the output value for input values that were not part of the initial training set. Hardware NNs consisting of a collection of simple neuron circuits provide the massive computational parallelism allowing for higher speed real-time models. A virtual prototyping environment for Electronic Design Automation (EDA) and a NN model for the 3D electromagnetic field are discussed in a representative case study.

12.1. Introduction

Virtual Reality (VR) is a computer based mirror of the physically reality. Synthetic and sensor-based, computer representations of 3D objects, sounds and other physical reality manifestations are integrated in a multi-media *Virtual Environment* (VE), or *virtual world*, residing inside the computer. Virtual environments are dynamic representations where objects and phenomena are animated/programmed by scripts, by simulations of the laws of physics, or driven interactively directly by human operators and other real world objects and phenomena, Fig. 1.

The original VR concept has evolved finding practical applications in a variety of domains such as the industrial design, multimedia communications, telerobotics, medicine, and entertainment.

Distributed Virtual Environments (DVEs) run on several computers connected over a network allowing people to interact and collaborate in real time, sharing the same virtual worlds. Collaborative DVEs require a broad range of networking, database, graphics, world modeling, real-time processing and user interface capabilities, [1].

Virtualized Reality™ *Environment* (VRE), [2], is a generalization of the essentially synthetic VE concept. While still being a computer based world model, the VRE is a conformal representation of the mirrored real world based on sensor information about the real world objects and phenomena. *Augmented Reality* (AR) allows humans to combine their intrinsic reactive-behavior with higher-order world model representations of the immersive VRE systems. A *Human-Computer Interface* (HCI) should be able to couple the human operator and the VRE as transparently as possible. VRE allow for *no-penalty training* of the personnel in a variety industrial, transportation, military, and medical applications.

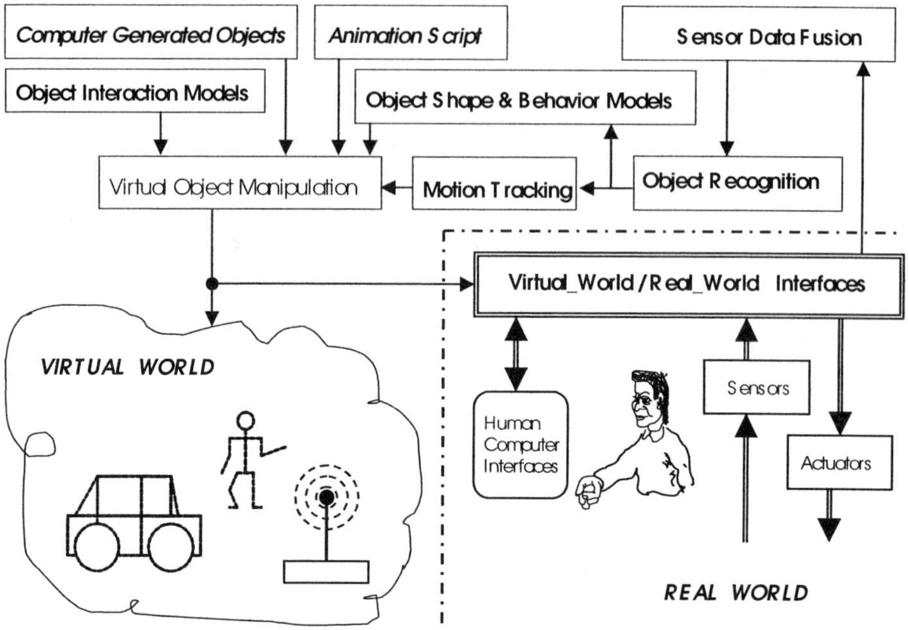

Figure 1: Synthetic and sensor-based computer representations of natural objects and phenomena are integrated in a dynamic multi-media *Virtual Environment.*

There are many applications such as remote sensing and telerobotics for hazardous environments requiring complex monitoring and intervention, which cannot be fully automated. A proper control of these operations cannot be accomplished without some AR telepresence capability allowing the human operator to experience the feeling that he/she is virtually immersed in the working environment. In such cases, human operators and intelligent sensing and actuator systems are working together as *symbionts*, Fig. 2, each contributing the best of their specific abilities, [3,4].

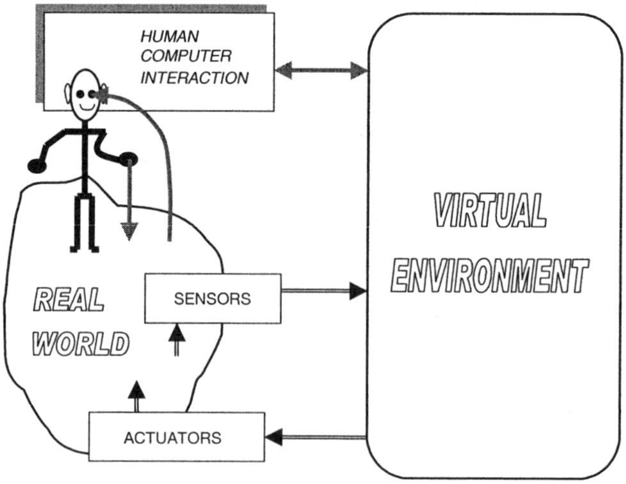

Figure 2: Human-Computer-Real_World interaction in the augmented virtual reality.

VR methods are also successfully used in the *concurrent engineering* design. The traditional approach to the product development is based on a two-step process consisting of a *Computer Aided Design* (CAD) phase followed by a physical prototype-testing phase. The limitations of this approach are getting worse as the design paradigm shifts from a sequential domain-by-domain optimization to a multi-domain concurrent design exercise. VR methods allow simulating the behavior of complex systems for a wide variety of initial conditions, excitations and systems configurations - often in a much shorter time than would be required to physically build and test a prototype experimentally. *Virtual Prototyping Environment* (VPE) design methods could be used to conduct interactive what-if experiments on a multi-domain virtual workbench. This results in shorter product development process than the classical approach, which requires for a series of physical prototypes to be built and tested.

12.2. Modeling natural objects, processes, and behaviors for real-time virtual environment applications

VREs and VPEs depend on the ability to develop and handle conformable (i.e., very close to the reality) models of the real world objects and phenomena. The *quality and the degree of the approximation* of these models can be determined only by validation against experimental measurements. The convenience of a model is determined by its ability to allow for extensive parametric studies, in which independent model parameters can be modified over a specified range in order to gain a global understanding of the response.

Advanced computation techniques are needed to reduce the execution time of the models used in interactive VPE applications when analysis is coupled with optimization, which may require hundreds of iterations.

Model development problems are compounded by the fact that the physical systems often manifest behaviors that cannot be completely modeled by well-defined analytic techniques. Non-analytical representations obtained by experimental measurements have to be used to complete the description of these systems.

Most of the object models used in virtual environments are discrete. The objects are represented by a finite set of 3D sample points, or by a finite set of parametric curves, stored as *Look Up Tables* (LUTs). The fidelity of these discrete models is proportional with the cardinal of the finite set of samples or parametric curves. The size of the corresponding LUTs is not a matter of concern thanks to the relatively low cost of today's RAM circuits. However, the main drawback of these discrete models is the need for a supplementary time to calculate by interpolation the parameters of each point that is not a sample point. This will increase the response time of the models, which in turn will affect the real-time performance of the interactive virtual environment.

Higher efficiency models could be implemented using NNs that can learn nonlinear behaviors from a limited set of measurement data, [5,6]. Despite the fact that the training set is finite, the resulting *NN model has a continuous behavior* similar to that of an analog computer model. An analog computer *solves the* linear or nonlinear differential and/or integral equations representing mathematical model of a given physical process. The coefficients of these equations must be exactly known as they are used to program the coefficient-potentiometers of the analog computer's OpAmps. The analog computer doesn't follow a sequential computation procedure. All its computing elements perform simultaneously and continuously. Because of the difficulties inherent in analog differentiation, the equation is rearranged so that it can be solved by integration rather than differentiation, [7]. A Neural Network does not require a prior mathematical model. A learning algorithm is used to adjust, sequentially by trail and error during the learning phase, the synaptic-weights of the neurons. Like the analog computer, the NN does not follow a sequential computation, all its neuron performing simultaneously and continuously. The neurons are also integrative-type processing elements.

The NN may take a relatively long time to learn the behavior of the system to be modeled, but this is not critical as it is done off-line. On the other hand, the recall phase, which is what actually counts in this type of interactive applications, is done in real-time.

Due to their continuous memory, NNs are able to provide instantaneously an estimation of the output value for input values that were not part of the initial training set. Hardware NNs consisting of a collection of simple neuron circuits provide the massive computational parallelism allowing for even higher speed real-time models.

The following chapter discusses *Neural Network* (NN) techniques for real-time modeling and pattern recognition in VRE and VPE applications.

12.3. Hardware NN architectures for real-time modeling applications

Random-pulse data representation was proposed by von Neuman in 1956 as a cybernetic model explaining how algebraic operations with analog variables can be performed by simple logical gates, [8]. Due to the simplicity of its circuitry, this data representation was used to build low cost instrumentation during the 60s, when the digital IC technology was still relatively expensive, [9-11]. There is a renewed interest in random-pulse data systems as their high functional packing density makes them quite suitable for the VLSI implementation of neural networks, [12-14].

Random-pulse data are produced by adding a uniformly distributed dither to an analog input signal V and then passing the result through a 1-bit quantizer. As variables are represented by the statistical averages of random pulse streams, the resulting data processing system has a better tolerance to noise than the classical deterministic systems. The digital technology used to implement these *random-pulse machines,* [15], offers a number of advantages over the analog technology: modular and flexible design, higher internal noise immunity, simpler I/O interfaces. An important drawback is the relatively long time needed to get an acceptable accuracy for these statistical averages. However, the effects of this drawback can be mitigated by using a generalized multi-bit dithered quantization, [16,17].

Generalized random data representations are produced by *multi-bit analog/random-data conversion,* or dithered quantization, Fig. 3. The analog input V, supposed to have a relatively low variation rate, is mixed with an analog dither signal R uniformly distributed within a quantization interval, i.e between $+\Delta/2$ and $-\Delta/2$. The resulting analog signal VR is quantified with a b-bit resolution and then sampled by a clock CLK to produce the random sequence VRP of b-bit data.

The ideal statistical average over an infinite number of samples of the random-data sequence VRP is:

$$\begin{aligned} E[VRP] &= (k\text{-}1)\cdot p[(k\text{-}1.5)\Delta < VR < (k\text{-}0.5)\Delta] + k\cdot p[(k\text{-}0.5)\Delta < VR < (k\text{+}0.5)\Delta] \\ &= (k\text{-}1)\cdot\beta + k\cdot(1\text{-}\beta) = k\text{-}\bullet\beta \end{aligned} \quad (1)$$

The estimation accuracy of the recovered value for V depends on the quantization resolution Δ, the finite number of samples that are averaged, and on the statistical properties of the dither R.

Because of the computational and functional similarity of a neuron and a correlator, we found useful to consider the relative speed performance figures for correlators with different quantization levels given in Table 1, [17].

For instance, a basic 2-level (1-bit) random-pulse correlator will be 72.23 times slower than an ideal analog correlator calculating with the same accuracy the correlation function of two statistically independent Gaussian noise signals with amplitudes restricted within $\pm 3\sigma$. A 3-level (2-bit) correlator will be 5.75 times, and a 4-level (2-bit) correlator will be 2.75 times, slower than the analog correlator.

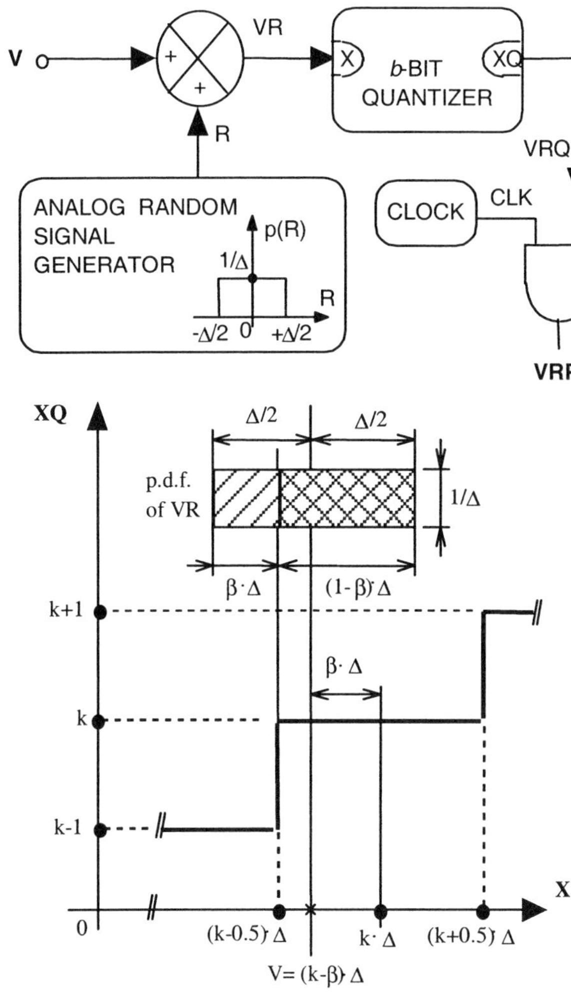

Figure 3: Multi-bit analog/random-data conversion.

Table 1: Relative speed performance for correlators with different quantization levels.

Quantization levels	Relative mean square error
2	72.23
3	5.75
4	2.75
...	...
8	1.23
...	...
analog	1

Based on these relative performance figures we have opted for a NN architecture using a 3-level generalized random-data representation, produced by a dithered 2-bit dead-zone quantizer. This gives, in our opinion, a good compromise between the processing speed and the circuit complexity, [18-20].

Random-data/analog conversion allows to estimate the deterministic component V of the random-data sequence as an average V^*_N over the finite set of *N* random-data $\{VRP_i \mid i=1,2,...N\}$. This can be done using a *moving average* algorithm, [21,22]:

$$V^*_N = \frac{1}{N}\sum_{i=1}^{N} VRP_i = \frac{1}{N}\left(\sum_{i=1}^{N-1} VRP_i + VRP_N\right)$$
$$V^*_N = V^*_{N-1} + \frac{VRP_N - VRP_0}{N} \qquad (2)$$

While the classical averaging requires the addition of N data, this iterative algorithm requires only an addition and a subtraction. The price for this simplification is the need for a shift register storing the whole set of the most recent N random data. Fig. 4 shows the mean square error of V^*_N, calculated over 256 samples, as function of the size of the moving average window in the case of the 1-bit and respectively 2-bit quantization.

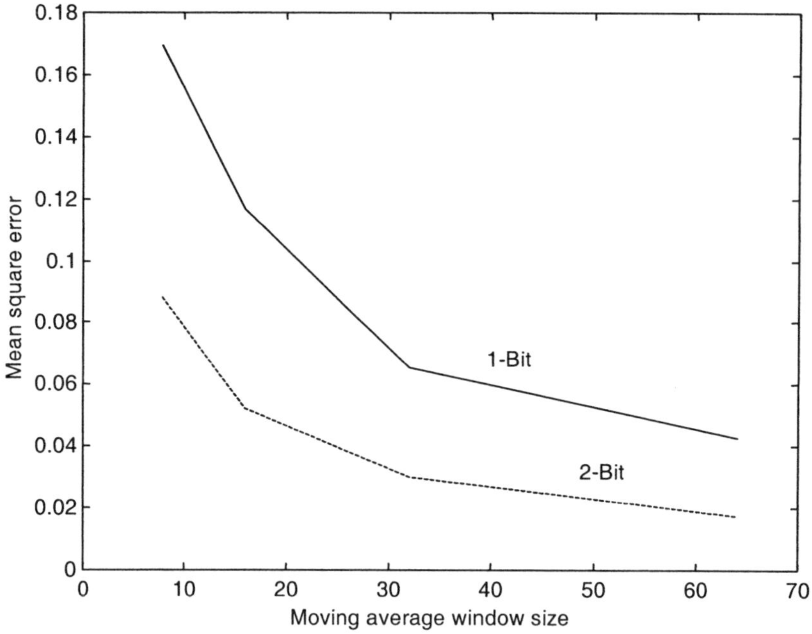

Figure 4: Mean square errors of the moving average algorithm function of the size of the window.

The analog/random-data and random-data/digital conversions are illustrated in Fig. 5 showing a step-like analog signal x2 is converted to a sequence of random-pulses x2RQ which is then reconverted as a moving average over N=16 random-pulses to produce the analog estimation MAVx2RQ.

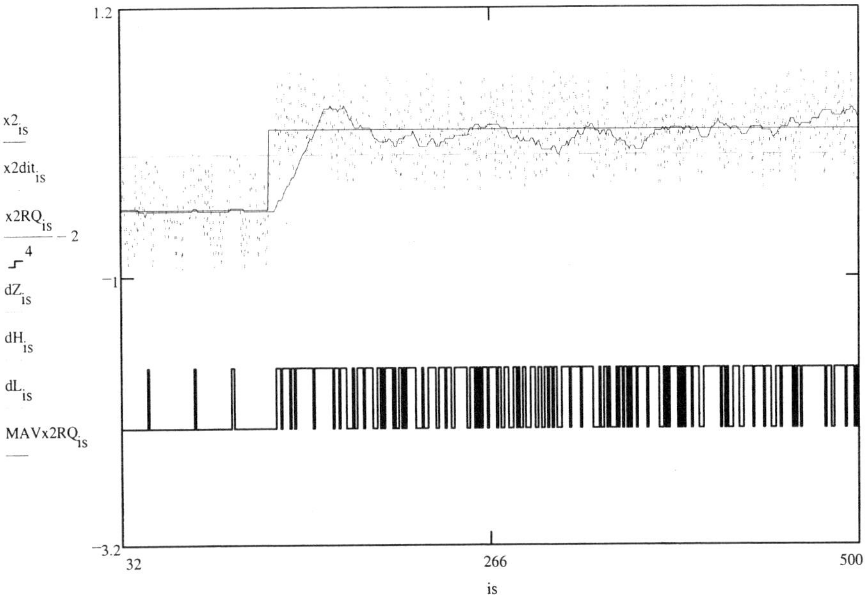

Figure 5: Simulations illustrating the *analog/random-data* and *random-data/digital* conversions.

One of the most attractive features of the random-data representation is that simple logical operations with individual pulses allow arithmetic operations with the analog variable represented by their respective random-pulse sequences to be carried out, [15]. This feature is still present in the case of low bit random-data representations.

The *arithmetic addition* of m signals $\{x_i \mid i=1,2,...,m\}$represented by their b-bit random-data $\{X_i \mid i=1,2,...,m\}$ is be carried out, as shown in Fig. 6, by time multiplexing the randomly decimated incoming random-data streams. The decimation is controlled by uniformly distributed random signals $\{S_i \mid i=1,2,...,m\}$ with $p(S_i)= 1/m$. This random sampling removes unwanted correlations between sequences with similar patterns, [10]. The random-data output sequence $Z = (X_1+...+X_m)/m$ represents the resulting sum signal $Z = X_1 +...+ X_m$

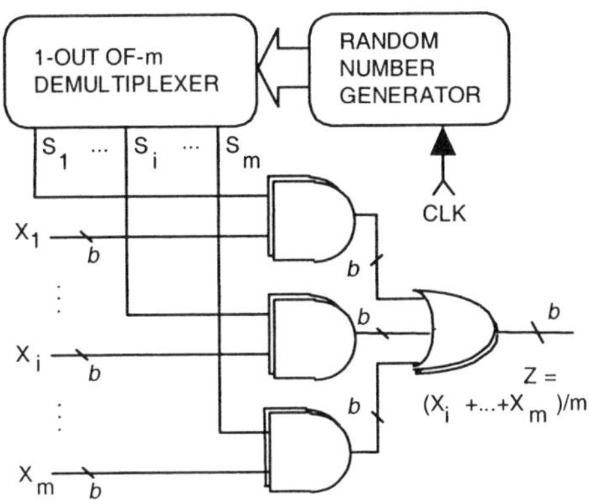

Figure 6: Circuit performing the arithmetic addition of *m* signals represented by the b-bit random-data streams $X_1, X_2,..., X_m$

We will consider further the case of 3-level unbiased random-data produced by a dithered 2-bit dead-zone quantizer. The truth table for the *multiplication* of two signed 2-bit random-data, $Z = X * Y$ is:

Y		**0**	**1**	**-1**
		00	*01*	*10*
0	*00*	**0** *00*	**0** *00*	**0** *00*
1	*01*	**0** *00*	**1** *01*	**-1** *10*
-1	*10*	**0** *00*	**-1** *10*	**1** *01*

Fig. 7 shows the resulting logic circuit for this 3-level 2-bit random data multiplier.

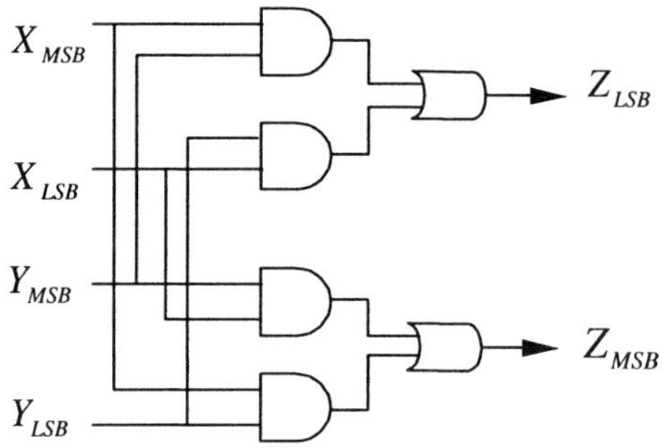

Figure 7: Two-bit random-data multiplier.

12.3.1 Neural-network architecture using generalized random-data representation

We have developed a NN hardware architecture based on the described 3-level 2-bit random data processing. Each synapse multiplies an incoming random data streams X_i, where i=1,2,...,m, by a synaptic-stored weight w_{ij} , which is adjusted during the learning phase. The positive–valued weights are considered *excitatory* and those with negative values are considered *inhibitory*. The neuron-body adds up the $DT_{ij} = X_i * w_{ij}$ signals from all the incoming post-synaptic channels, Fig. 8. The results of this addition are then integrated by a moving average random–data/digital converter. Since the neuron output will be used as a synaptic input to other neurons, a final *digital/random–data converter* stage is used to restore the randomness of Y_j.

Using this 2-bit random-data neuron structure we implemented an auto-associative memory for pattern recognition applications, Fig. 9, which can learn input-pattern/target $\{P_q, t_q\}$ associations:

$$\{P_1, t_1\},\ \{P_2, t_2\},\ \cdots\ \{P_Q, t_Q\} \tag{3}$$

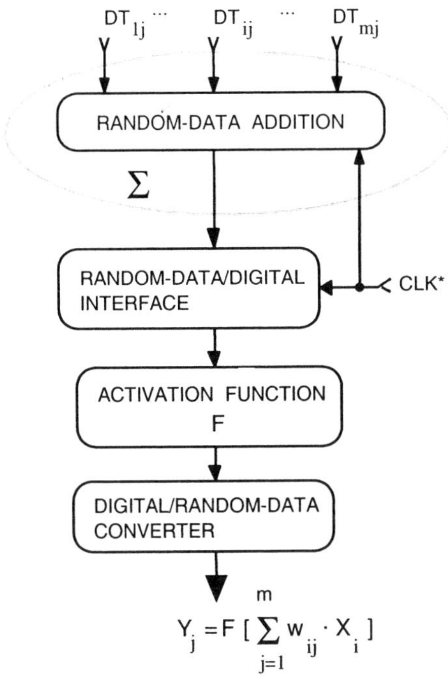

Figure 8: Random-data implementation of the neuron body.

The NN is able to recognize any of the initially taught associations. If it receives an input $P=P_q$ then it produces an output $a=t_q$, for $q = 1,2,...,Q$. It can also recognize patterns corrupted by noise: i.e if the input is changed $P=P_q+\delta$ the output will still be $a=t_q$.

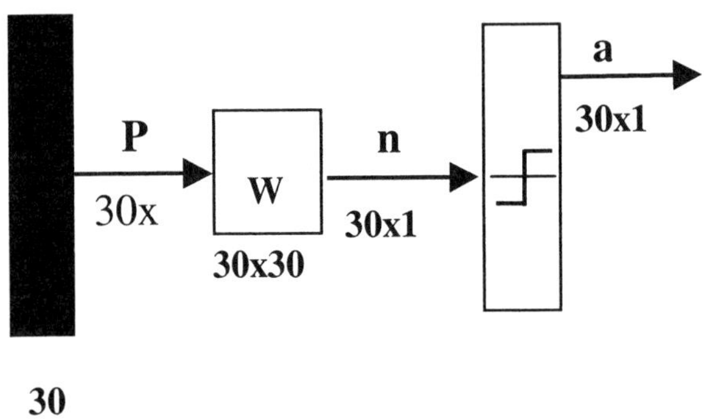

Figure 9: Auto-associative memory NN architecture.

Fig. 10 shows as an example three training patterns, which represent the digits {0,1,2} displayed as a 6x5 grid. Each white square is represented by a "-1", and each black square is represented by a "1". To create the input vectors, we scan each 6x5 grid one column at a time. The weight matrix in this case is $W = P_1P_1^T + P_2P_2^T + P_3P_3^T$.

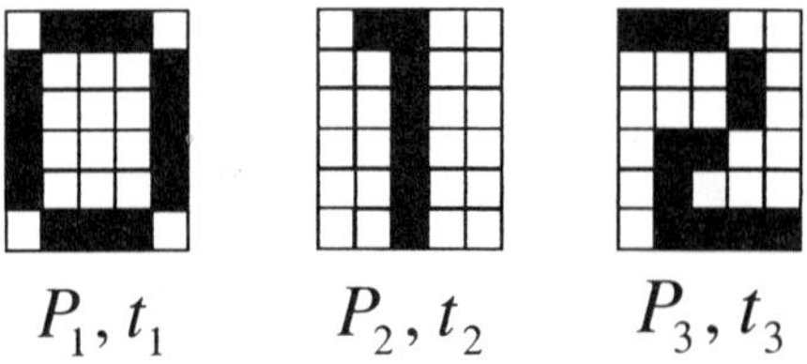

Figure 10: Training set for the auto-associative NN.

In addition to recognizing all the patterns of the initial training set, the auto-associative NN is also able to deal with up to 30% noise-corrupted patterns as illustrated in Fig. 11.

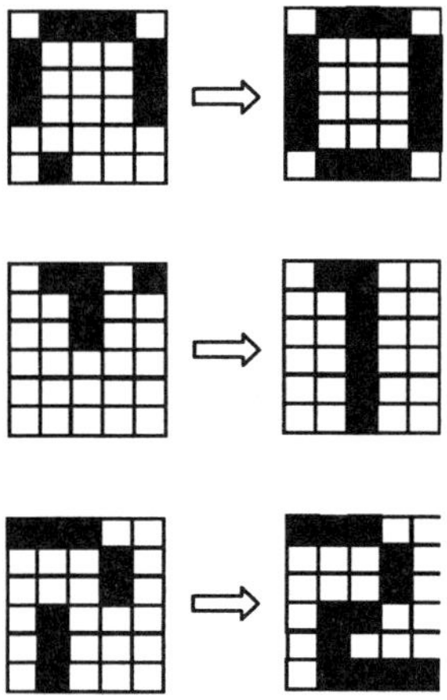

Figure 11: Recovery of 30% occluded patterns by the auto-associative NN.

12.4. Case study: NN modeling of electromagnetic radiation for virtual prototyping environments

The experimental VPE for *Electronic Design Automation* (EDA) developed at the University of Ottawa, [23,24], provides the following interactive object specification and manipulation functions:

(i) updating geometric, electrical and material specifications of circuit components, as illustrated in Fig. 12;

(ii) 3D manipulation of the position, shape, and size of the circuit components and layout.

(iii) accounting for 3D EM and thermal field effects in different regions of the complex electronic circuit.

The VPE scenes are composed of multiple 3D objects: printed circuit boards (PCBs), electronic components, and connectors, Fig. 13. Any object in the VPE is characterized by its 3D geometric shape, material property and *safety-envelopes* defining the 3D geometric space points where the intensity of a given field radiated by that object becomes smaller than a user-specified threshold value. Each type of field (EM, thermal, etc.) will have its own safety-envelope, whereas the geometric safety-envelope is the object shape itself.

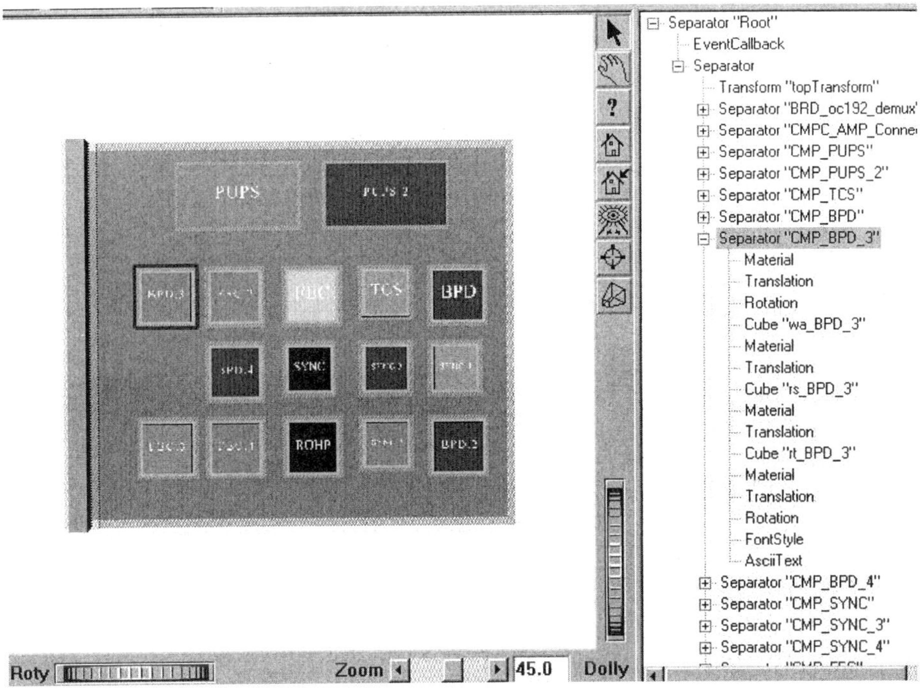

Figure 12: Editing component properties in VPE.

Figure 13: 3D scene with a complex circuit assembly.

Electronic components are placed on a PCB where they are interconnected according to functional CAD specifications and to design constraints taking in consideration the EM interference between the PCB layout components. However, this design phase does not take in consideration the interference due to the EM and thermal fields radiated by the integrated circuits and other electronic components. These problems are identified and ironed out during the prototyping phase, which may take more *what-if* iterations until an acceptable circuit placement and connection routing solution is found. Traditionally this phase involves building and testing a series of physical prototypes, which may take considerable time.

Such a multi-domain virtual workbench allows conducting more expediently, in a concurrent engineering manner, *what-if* circuit-placement experiments. The VPE is able to detect the collisions between the safety-envelope of the circuit currently manipulated by the manipulator dragger and the safety-envelopes of other objects in the scene. When a collision is detected, the manipulated circuit returns to its last position before the collision.

Virtual prototyping allows a designer to test the prototype's behavior under a wide variety of initial conditions, excitations and systems configurations. This results in shorter product development process than the classical approach, which requires for a series of physical prototypes to be built and tested, Fig. 14.

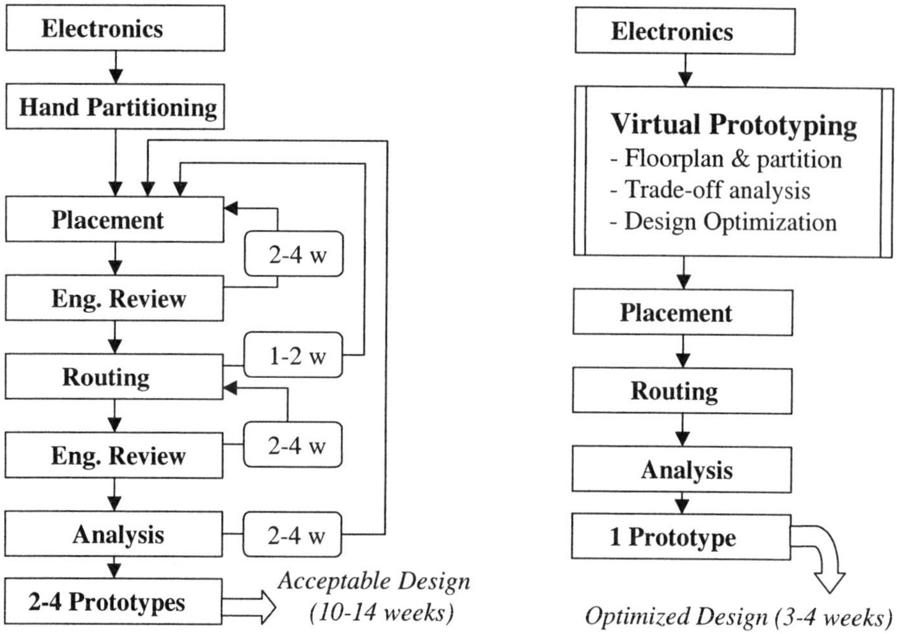

Figure 14: Product design cycles for the traditional and respectively virtual prototyping.

A key requirement for any VPE is the development of conformable models for all the physical objects and phenomena involved in that experiment. Neural networks, which can incorporate both analytical representations and descriptions captured by experimental measurements, provide convenient real-time models for the EM fields radiated by a variety of electronic components.

12.4.1 Neural Network modeling of EM fields

As a representative case, we consider the NN model of the 3D EM field radiated by a dielectric-ring resonator antenna, Fig. 15, with a ring radius *a* and a ring height *d* both with values from 4 to 8 mm in steps of 1 mm, and the dielectric constant of the ring ε_r with values from 20 to 50 in steps of 1, [25].

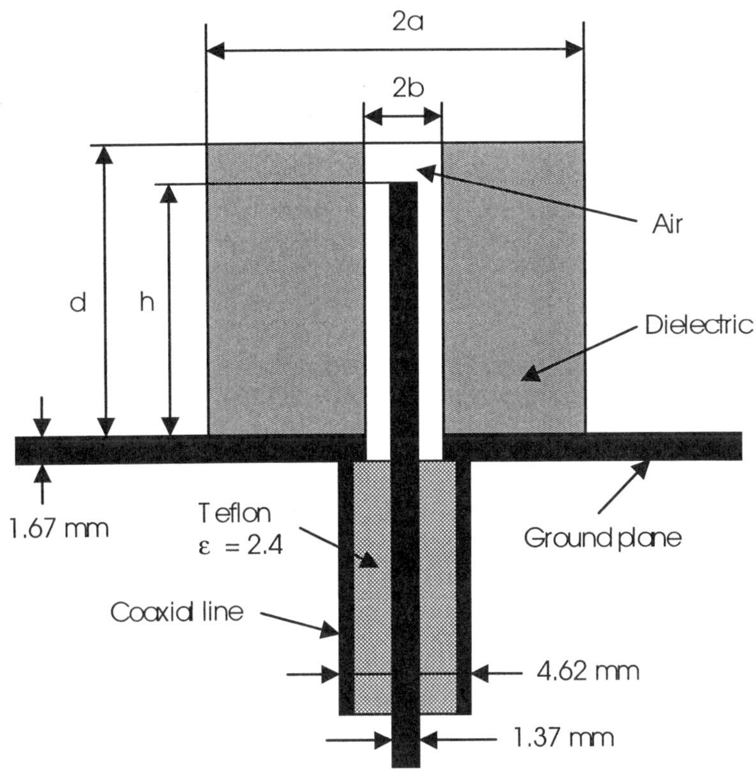

Figure 15: The dielectric ring resonator antenna.

The backpropagation NN using the Levenberg –Marquard algorithm consists of two input neurons, two hidden layers having 5 neurons with hyperbolic tangent activation function on each layer, and one output linear neuron.

The training data set, Fig. 16, was obtained analytically by calculating far-field values in 3D space and frequency from near-field data using the finite element method combined with the method of integral absorbing boundary conditions, [26]. Each geometrical configuration was solved using the *Finite Element Method* (FEM) for each of the 31 dielectric constants and for 1400 frequency steps from 2 to 16 GHz. The 200 epochs training took 55 s on a SPARC 10 workstation.

The resulting NN model, shown in Fig. 17, has a continuous (analog memory) behavior allowing it to render EM field values with a higher sampling resolution than that of the initial training data set. It took only 0.5 s on the same SPARC 10 workstation to render 5,000 points of the 3D EM field model.

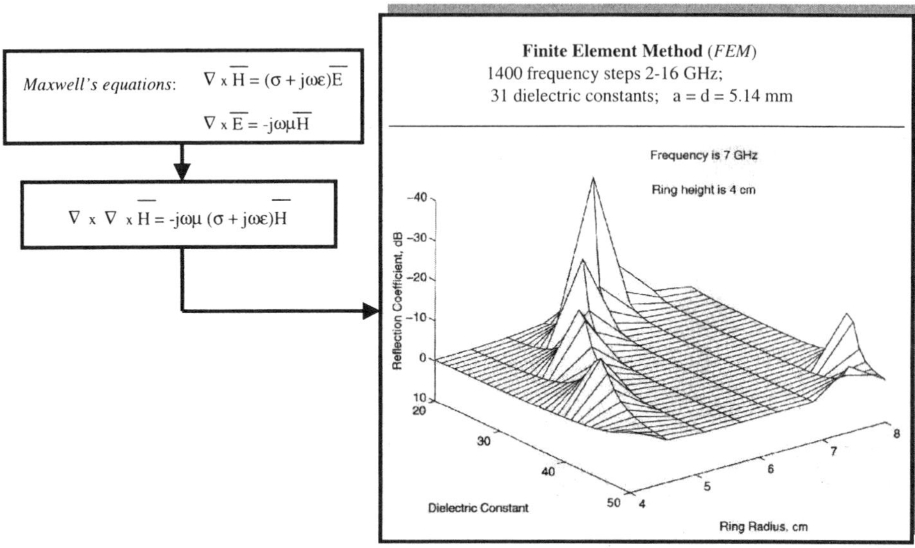

Figure 16: The training data are obtained as analytically by calculating far-field values from near-field data using the finite element method.

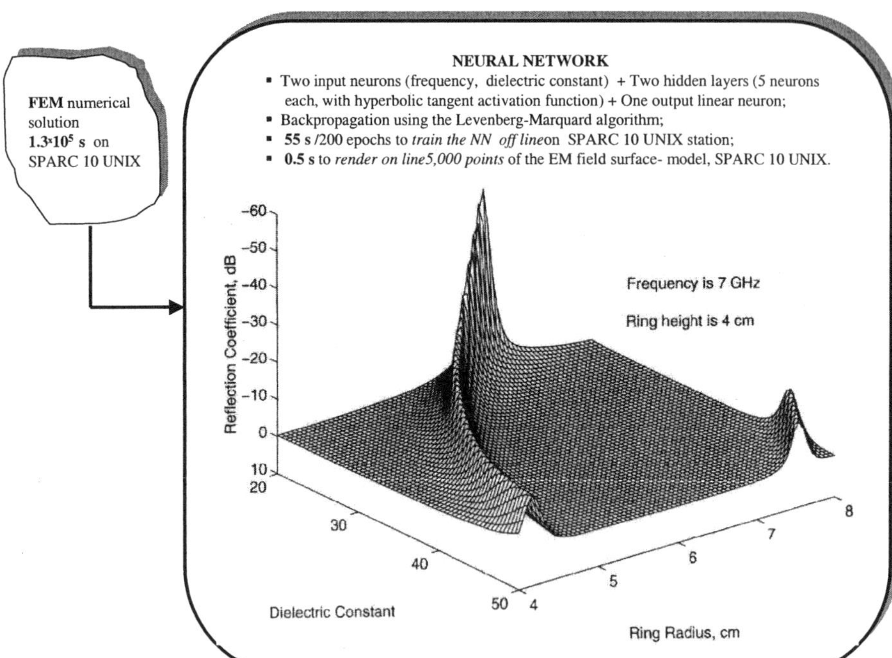

Figure 17: NN model of the 3D EM field radiated by the dielectric-ring resonator antenna.

12.4.2 Model Validation

While the VPE idea is gaining wider acceptance, it also becomes apparent the need for calibration techniques able to validate the conformance with reality of the models incorporated in these new prototyping tools.

Better experimental test-beds and validation methodologies are needed to check the performance of the computer models against the ultimate standard, which is the physical reality. Some of the challenges to be faced are:

(i) the development of an experimental setup which should allow the desired manipulation of multi-domain (geometric, mechanical, electric, thermal, material, etc) design parameters;

(ii) the identification and measurement of multi-domain phenomena which are considered to be behavioral characteristics for a given circuit design;

(iii) finding the minimum set of experimental setups, cause-effect analytical/correlation methods, and calibration methodologies that provides a guaranty by interpolation (within acceptable error margins) the performance of the VPE computer models over wide ranges of multi-domain design parameters.

The analysis in homogeneous space simplifies greatly the problem of calculating *Far field* (FF) EM values from *Near Field* (NF) measurements, [26]. The radiating *Device Under Test* (DUT) is modeled as an array of short dipoles sitting on top of a table. The equation to solve for the electromagnetic fields is Helmholtz' wave equation:

$$\nabla^2 \vec{H} + k^2 \vec{H} = 0 \tag{4}$$

in a homogeneous volume V bounded on one side by a surface where the magnetic field values of H are known through measurements and on the other side by the ground plane.

An explicit solution allowing to evaluate the magnetic field H anywhere in the volume V from its field values and its derivatives on a surface S_1 as proposed in [27]:

$$H(r') = \frac{1}{4\pi} \int_{S_1} \left[G(r,r') \frac{\partial H(r)}{\partial n} - H(r) \frac{\partial G(r,r')}{\partial n} \right] dS_1 \tag{5}$$

where S_1 is the closed surface on which measurements are made, n is the normal to S_1, and $G(r,r')$ is the free space Green's function.

This algorithm is independent of the type of radiation. While it shares some sources of error with other transform algorithms, the integral transform employed here is more immune to aliasing errors than the FFT-based algorithms. Another advantage over conventional FFT transforms is that the far-field results are available everywhere and not only at discrete points.

The EM field measurement system, [28], is shown in Fig. 18. It consists of a turning table with a highly conducting grounded surface on which the DUT is resting. The EM field probe can be positioned anywhere on a 90° arc of circle above the turning table.

A special interface was developed for the control of the probe positioning and the collection of the measurement data via a spectrum analyzer. The turning table and the probe can be positioned as desired by steering them with position-servoed cables driven by motors placed outside an anechoic enclosure. The probe positioning system and the steering cables are made out of non-magnetic and non-conductive material in order to minimize disturbance of the DUT's fields. EM field measurements are taken on both hemispherical surfaces, providing data for the interpolative calculation of the derivative's variation on the surface S_1. The surfaces are closed with their symmetric image halves. This is possible due to the presence of the ground plane.

The actual angular positions of the table and that of the probe are measured using a video camera placed outside the enclosure. The azimuth angle j is recovered by encoding the periphery of the turning table with the terms of a 63-bit pseudorandom binary sequence, [29]. This arrangement allows to completely identify the 3D position parameters of the EM probe while it scans the NF around the DUT.

Figure 18: Experimental setup for measuring the 3D EM near-field signature.

12.5. Conclusions

Virtual environment technology has found applications in a variety of domains such as the industrial design, multimedia communications, telerobotics, medicine, and entertainment.

Virtualized Reality™ environments, which provide more conformal representations of the mirrored physical world objects and phenomena, are valuable experimental tools for many industrial applications. Virtual environment efficiency depends on the ability to develop and handle conformable models of the physical objects and phenomena. As real world objects and phenomena more often than not manifest behaviors that cannot be completely modeled by analytic techniques, there is a need for non-analytical models driven by experimental measurements. Neural networks, which are able to learn nonlinear behaviors from a limited set of measurement data, can provide efficient modeling solutions for many virtualized reality applications.

Due to their continuous, analog-like, behavior, NNs are able to provide instantaneously an estimation of the output value for input values that were not part of the initial training set. Hardware NNs consisting of a collection of simple neuron circuits provide the massive computational parallelism allowing for even higher speed real-time models.

As a representative case of the *Virtualized Reality*™ technology, the virtual prototyping environments for EDA allow developers to interactively test complex electronic systems by running concurrently *what-if* multi-domain (mechanical, electrical, thermal, etc) experiments. For many an electromagnetic radiation problem it is not possible to derive an analytic solution. In this case, the only practical solution would be to use NN models trained by experimental measurement data. It is worthwhile to note that even when analytic solutions could be derived, the NN models still have better real time performance than classical numerical EM field methods.

As the performance of the NN models can be decided only by a validation against experimental measurements, there is need for a concerted effort to characterize and catalogue the EM radiated field signatures of all the integrated circuits and electronic components used for EDA.

Many real-world objects are characterized by a multitude of parameters of different nature. In order to capture this complexity, future efforts are need in order to develop composite models integrating 3D geometry, radiated fields, and other material properties. This could achieved by using a multi-sensor fusion system that integrates a variety of sensors covering all four phases in the perception process: far-away, near-to, touching, and manipulation.

Acknowledgment

This work was funded in part by NSERC, the Natural Sciences and Engineering Research Council of Canada, and CITO - Communications and Information Technology Ontario. The author gratefully acknowledges the contributions and assistance provided over the years by his collaborators Hassan Ali , Igor Ratner, Marius Cordea, Lichen Zhao, Arto Chubukjian, and Jie Mao.

References

[1] R.C. Waters and J.W. Barrus, "The Rise of Shared Virtual Environments," *IEEE Spectrum*, Vol.34, No. 3, pp. 18-25, March 1997.
[2] T. Kanade, *Virtualized Reality™*, http://www.cs.cmu.edu/~virtualized-reality/, Robotics Institute, Carnegie Mellon University, Pittsburgh, PA, USA.
[3] R.W. Picard, "Human-Computer Coupling," *Proc. IEEE*, Vol.86, No.8, pp. 1803-1807, Aug. 1998.
[4] E.M. Petriu and T.E. Whalen, "Computer-Controlled Human Operators," *IEEE Instrum. Meas. Mag.*, Vol. 5, No. 1, pp. 35 -38, 2002.
[5] C. Alippi and V. Piuri, "Neural Methodology for Prediction and Identification of Non-linear Dynamic Systems," in *Instrumentation and Measurement Technology and Applications*, (E.M. Petriu, Ed.), pp. 477-485, IEEE Technology Update Series, 1998.
[6] C. Citterio, A. Pelagotti, V. Piuri, and L. Roca, "Function Approximation – A Fast-Convergence Neural Approach Based on Spectral Analysis, *IEEE Tr. Neural Networks*, Vol. 10, No. 4, pp. 725-740, July 1999.
[7] A.S. Jackson, *Analog Computation*, McGraw-Hill Book Co., 1960.
[8] J. von Neuman, "Probabilistic logics and the synthesis of reliable organisms from unreliable components," in *Automata Studies*, (C.E. Shannon, Ed.), Princeton, NJ, Princeton University press, 1956
[9] B.P.T. Veltman and H. Kwakernaak, "Theorie und Technik der Polaritatkorrelation fur die dynamische Analyse niederfrequenter Signale und Systeme," *Regelungstechnik*, vol. 9, pp. 357-364, Sept. 1961.
[10] B.R. Gaines, "Stochastic computer thrives on noise," *Electronics*, pp.72-79, July 1967.
[11] "*SEM - Electronic Correlator*," NORMA Messtechnik Tech. Doc., PM 4707E.
[12] A. Hamilton, A.F. Murray, D.J. Baxter, S. Churcher, H.M. Reekie, and L. Tarasenko, "Integrated pulse stream neural networks: results, issues, and pointers," *IEEE Trans. Neural Networks*, vol. 3, no. 3, pp. 385-393, May 1992.
[13] M. van Daalen, T. Kosel, P. Jeavons, and J. Shawe-Taylor, "Emergent activation functions from a stochastic bit-stream neuron," *Electron Lett.*, vol. 30, no. 4, pp. 331-333, Feb. 1994.
[14] E. Petriu, K. Watanabe, T. Yeap, "Applications of Random-Pulse Machine Concept to Neural Network Design," *IEEE Trans. Instrum. Meas.*, Vol. 45, No.2, pp.665-669, 1996.

[15] S.T. Ribeiro, "Random-pulse machines," *IEEE Trans. Electron. Comp.*, vol. EC-16, no. 3, pp. 261-276, June 1967.

[16] F. Castanie, "Signal processing by random reference quantizing," *Signal Processing*, vol. 1, no. 1, pp. 27-43, 1979.

[17] K-.Y. Chang and D. Moore, "Modified digital correlator and its estimation errors," *IEEE Trans. Inf. Theory*, vol. IT-16, no. 6, pp. 699-706, 1970.

[18] E. Petriu, "Contributions to the improvement of correlator performance," Dr. Eng. Thesis, Polytechnic Institute of Timisoara, Romania, (in Romanian), 1978.

[19] E. Pop, *E.M. Petriu*, "Influence of Reference Domain Instability Upon the Precision of Random Reference Quantizer with Uniformly Distributed Auxiliary Source," *Signal Processing* (EURASIP), North Holland, Vol. 5, pp.87-96, 1983.

[20] L. Zhao, "Random Pulse Artificial Neural Network Architecture," M.A.Sc. Thesis, OCIECE, University of Ottawa, Canada, 1998.

[21] A.J. Miller, A.W. Brown, and P. Mars, "Moving-average output interface for digital stochastic computers," *Electron Lett.*, vol. 10, no. 20, pp. 419-420, Oct. 1974.

[22] A.J. Miller and P. Mars, "Optimal estimation of digital stochastic sequences," *Int. J. Syst. Sci.*, vol. 8, no. 6, pp. 683-696, 1977.

[23] E.M. Petriu, M. Cordea, and D.C. Petriu, "Virtual Prototyping Tools for Electronic Design Automation," *IEEE Instrum. Meas. Mag.*, Vol. 2, No. 2, pp. 28-31, 1999.

[24] E.M. Petriu, M. Cordea, D.C. Petriu, Lou McNamee, "Modelling Issues in Virtual Prototyping Environments," *Proc. VIMS'99, IEEE Workshop on Virtual and Intelligent Measurement Systems*, pp. 1-5, Venice, Italy, May 1999.

[25] I. Ratner, H.O. Ali, and E. Petriu, "Neural Network Simulation of a Dielectric Ring Resonator Antenna," *J. Systems Architecture*, vol. 44, pp. 569-581, 1998.

[26] R. Laroussi and G.I. Costache, "Far-Field Predictions from Near-Field Measurements," *IEEE Tr. Electromagnetic Compatibility*, Vol. 36, No.3, pp. 189-195, 1994.

[27] A.J. Poggio, and E.K. Miller, "Integral equation solutions of three dimensional scattering problems", in *Computer Techniques for Electro-magnetics*, Mittra R., ed., Pergamon Press, Oxford, 1973.

[28] A. Roczniak, E. Petriu, and G.I. Costache, "3-D Electromagnetic Field Modeling Based on Near Field Measurements," *Proc. IMTC/96, IEEE Instrum. Meas. Technol. Conf.*, pp.1124-1127, Brussels, Belgium, 1996.

[29] E. Petriu, W.S. McMath, S.K. Yeung, N. Trif, and T. Bieseman "Two-Dimensional Position Recovery for a Free-Ranging Automated Guided Vehicle," *IEEE Trans. Instrum. Meas.*, Vol. 42, No. 3, pp. 701-706, 1993.

Neural Networks for Instrumentation, Measurement and Related Industrial Applications
S. Ablameyko et al. (Eds.)
IOS Press, 2003

Chapter 13
Neural Networks in the Medical Field

Marco PARVIS, Alberto VALLAN
Dipartimento di Elettronica, Politecnico di Torino
Corso Duca degli Abruzzi 24, 10129 Torino, Italy

Abstract. This chapter, after an overview of the most important applications where the neural networks play an important role in the medical diagnosis, discusses a possible approach which can be used to tackle with both the uncertainty presence and the reduced number of available training examples. A set of examples drawn from the medical field is then presented.

13.1. Introduction

This chapter is basically divided into two main sections which are related to the role of neural networks in the medical field and to the prediction of the output uncertainty of medical instruments that embed neural networks.

13.2. Role of neural networks in the medical field

Purpose of this section is to investigate where and how neural networks are used in the medical field. The section in divided into three subsections devoted to the instrumentation for diagnosis purposes, to decision making instruments, and to the available databases, which represent an invaluable tool for the validation of algorithms employed in the medical field.

13.2.1 Neural networks in medical instrumentation for diagnosis purposes

Although several different kind of instruments have been developed, it is usually possible to identify within each instrument a common structure similar to the one shown in fig. 1. The quantity we are interested in, the measurand, is a physical, chemical or a biological quantity and represents the input of the instrument. The instrument converts the input quantity into a numerical value that can be employed either by the physicians, in order to perform a diagnosis, or by other instruments, in order to perform a more complex processing, for example to extract more meaningful features or even, as it will be described later, to automatically perform the diagnosis.

The figure shows several blocks, which are required for a correct instrument operation, but three of them play a fundamental role as they are on the input/output path: the sensors, the signal conditioning and conversion and the signal processing.

Neural networks are rarely employed both in the sensor and in the AD Conversion sections, since these sections are inherently analogue and realized with conventional devices [1], while it is not uncommon to find neural networks in the signal processing section.

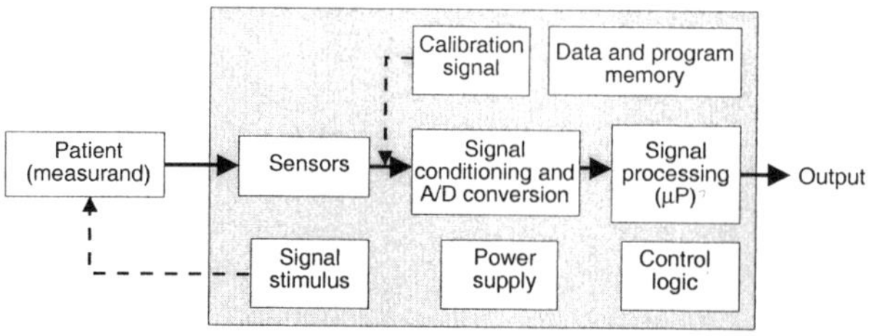

Figure 1: Block diagram of a generic medical instrument.

Table 1: Examples of neural network applications in medical instruments

Kind of network	Application
Standard MLP	ECG signal compression [2] Image equalization for radiography [3]
Time-delay neural networks	Noise cancellation in magnetic resonance imaging [4] Detection of real-time ischemia episodes [5] Non-linear adaptive filtering of stimulus artifact [6]
FIR MLP	EEG signal classification [7]
Fuzzy min-max NN with overlapping hyperbox	Tissue classification in echocardiograms [8]
Recurrent Neural Network	ST-T change detection [9] Filtering of adult and fetal ECG [10]
Local Linear Map	Topological analysis of lymphocytes [11]
Self-organizing map	EMG signal classification [12] ECG beat classification [13]
neuro-processor based	White cell blood identification [14] Image filtering [15]

A noticeably exception to this scheme is represented by the so called *smart sensors* (see chapter 4) where neural networks can be used for linearization or for data-fusion purposes, but such smart devices can be thought as examples of complete though simplified instruments and will not be described here.

Neural networks can be used in several ways and it is almost impossible to list all the different uses. Table 1 shows, as an example, some of the most common uses, clustered for network topology. As one can see, most examples deal with either signal filtering or classification issues.

The wide use of neural networks for filtering applications can be explained remembering that most of the signals that are encountered in the medical field have particular characteristics, which make the filter design not easy:

- the signal to noise ratio (SNR) can be very poor;
- the spectral content greatly depend on the patient and is often time-dependent;
- the useful spectral band is often overlapped with the noise band;
- unwanted signals, such as mains interferences and electromyographyc signals, are often present;
- sometimes artefact signals are present, that can be correlated with the signal we are interested in;

Furthermore, because of the non-linear behavior of the "human system", the noise is often non-gaussian and non-additive and this adds other constraints to the filter choice and leads to situations that can take advantage of the neural network features.

In fact, neural networks can describe non linear phenomena and can be designed to implement adaptive filters that tune they parameters by means of the network learning algorithms.

An interesting and clarifying example can be found in [16] where a neural-network-based QRS detector is described. The identification of the QRS complex (see fig. 5 in the next section) is often employed as a reference point to extract the ST segment and is also mandatory for many others ECG analysis [17]. Traditional techniques for QRS identification employ a band-pass filter in order to improve the signal to noise ratio and then identify the signal peak. These simple techniques work well only in the presence of moderate noise. Unfortunately the acquired ECG signals are very low (a few millivolt) and sometimes are severely corrupted from several others unwanted signals, such as muscle signals, mains interference (50 Hz or 60 Hz) and electrical noise. Furthermore the QRS spectral content is time-varying and often signal and disturbance spectra are overlapped, so that the traditional filtering techniques would risk to corrupt the signal.

In order to overcome these problems, the QRS detector proposed in [16] employs a non-linear adaptive matched filters. Adaptive filters work well in the presence of non-stationary signals because they adapt themselves during the signal changes, and the filter non-linearity are useful when the input signals are generated from a non-linear system, such as the human body.

The detector structure is shown in Fig. 2(a). The ECG signal is employed as a trigger signal for a QRS template generator. Both the ECG and the template signals are filtered with the same adaptive filter, whose structure, shown in fig. 2(b), is the same of a typical predictive filter [18]. In this case the predictive filter employs the Time-Delay Neural Network shown in fig. 2(c) that acts as non-linear filter. Aim of the filters is to remove the noise components which are correlated with the signal component. The filter outputs are matched together through a matched filter and eventually the signal peak is detected by means of a threshold checking technique. The network weights are updated by means of a gradient-search based algorithm.

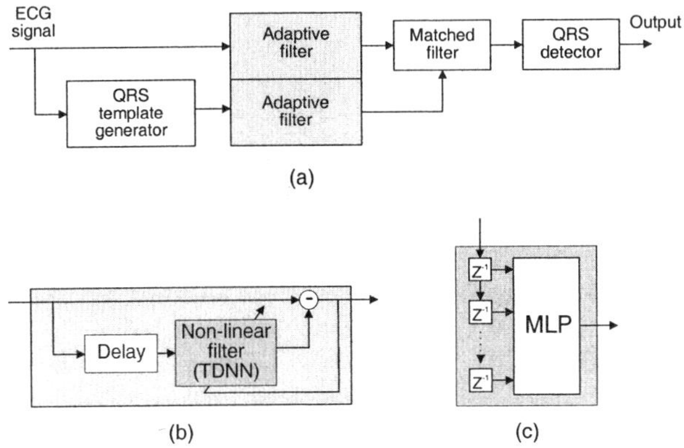

Figure 2: (a) The QRS detector based on neural networks. (b) The adaptive filter structure. (c) The Time-Delay Neural Network employed as non-linear filter.

Table 2: QRS detection results obtained by means of linear and non-linear algorithms.

Filter type	Failed detection rate with noisy signals
Neural network based adaptive filter	2.3%
Linear adaptive filter	4.4%
Band-pass filter	12.5%

This system has been tested by using different records of the MIT/BIH database [19] and its performance has been compared with other 'traditional' filtering methods.

As expected, adaptive non-linear filters work better that linear filters and a noticeable reduction of erroneous detections is obtained.

Fast applications of filtering techniques are another field where neural networks are successfully employed. General purpose processors and Digital Signal Processors (DSPs) are often inadequate when large medical images have to be processed in real-time. Specific processors, designed to implement neural structures, can be employed for these time-consuming applications. The so called 'neuro-processors' [15] or 'ZISC' (Zero Instruction Set Computer) [20] are nowadays available on the market at a cost which is comparable to a top-class DSP. Such processors are based on a massive parallel architecture and are able to implement neural-based algorithm faster than DSPs, even thought their flexibility is still limited.

13.2.2 Neural networks in decision making instruments

Decision making instruments are devices designed to help the physician in the diagnosis activity. From an engineering point of view, the diagnosis activity can be thought as an indirect evaluation of a patient disease. The core of the diagnosis system, shown in 3, is the decision making instrument that 'classifies' the patient disease on the basis of several patient-related quantities. The figure highlights that such quantities can be obtained in two different ways: through the measurement of physical, chemical and biological quantities, and through subjective evaluations gathered by interviewing the patient about his/her history and symptoms.

Neural networks can be employed in the measurement instruments, as described in the previous section, and in the decision making instrument.

Two main problems have to be solved in order to develop an automatic diagnosis systems: the subjective evaluations have to be converted into a numerical format, since neural networks requires numerical values, and the decision algorithms have to be formalized in order to be implemented by the instrument software.

The coding of medical data not yet expressed in a numerical format can be a not easy task because these information are often expressed in a linguistic format. One should note that neural network based algorithms are able to adapt themselves to the input values so that a non-optimal choice of the input data encoding almost always affects only the learning time. However, even though it is impossible to provide universal coding rules, some basic guidelines can be remembered depending on the input quantity types:

binary information such as sex, smoker/non smoker, are easily coded with a binary variable; e.g. sex = 1 male, 0 female;

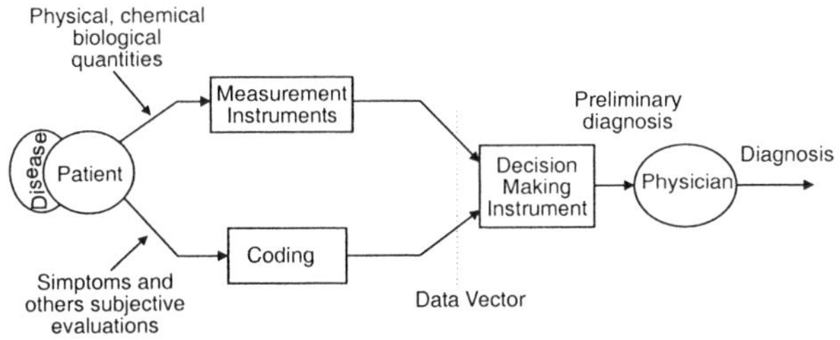

Figure 3: A diagnosis system based on a decision making instrument.

orderable categorical data can be coded by means of a single multi-value variable; e.g. disease evolution = 0 worse, 1 steady, 2 better;

non-orderable categorical data could also be tackled by a multi-value variable, but it is better to employ one binary variable for each categorical data since this eases the data interpretation; as an example, if a diagnosis can be related to the presence of either a symptom A or a symptom B or both, the encoding could conveniently be obtained by means of two binary variables: symptom A= 1 yes, 0 no; symptom B= 1 yes, 0 no.

Both measured and encoded data compose the data vector that has to be processed by the decision making instrument according to a structure similar to the one shown in fig. 4.

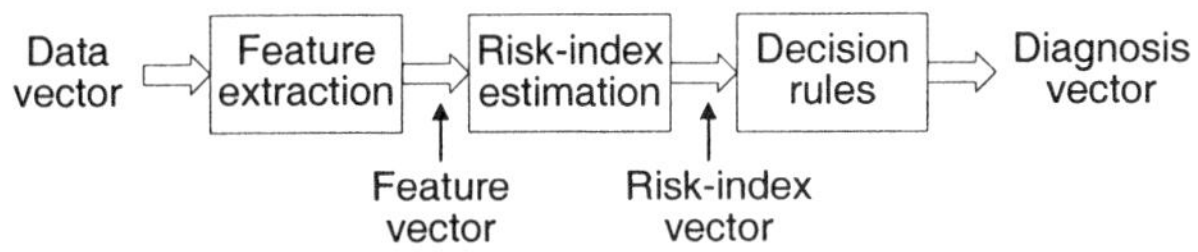

Figure 4: The structure of a decision making instrument based on neural network.

The decision process can be logically split into three parts.

The feature extraction stage is used to extract the information useful for the diagnosis from the input data thus reducing the amount of information sent to the second stage. The risk-index estimation stage combines the features to compute a set of risk indexes associated to the investigated pathologies, eventually the decision stage analyzes the different risk indexes to obtain the final diagnosis.

Neural networks can be employed in all the three stages even though most feature extraction algorithms are conventional. Such algorithms are closely related to the medical application and to the structure of the input data (signals, images, ...). Among the different algorithms the most commonly employed refer to the computation of morphological characteristics, of spectral and time-frequency content [17, 21] and to the classification of signals into predefined classes.

The feature vector is then sent to the risk-index estimation stage whose aim is to classify the patient disease. Neural networks are here extensively employed because they do not require to write the mathematical model, which connect symptoms and disease. The network is usually trained to recognize a predefined set of classes, which correspond to the suspected diseases, plus two special classes: unrecognized disease and no disease. The network output is

Table 3: Examples of neural network applications for diagnosis purposes.

Kind of network	Application
Standard MLP	System for diagnosing and treating hypertension [22] Early detection of ovarian cancer [23] Prediction of respiratory disorder in new-born babies [24]
Fuzzy Neural Network	Non-invasive detection of Coronary Artery Disease [25]
Fourier-transform Neural Network	Real-time discrimination of ventricular tachyarrhythmia [17]
Wavelet MLP	Coronary artery disease classification [26]
Radial Basis Networks	Predictive control for insulin delivery [27]
Kohonen maps	Analysis of trabecular bone structure [28]
Modular Neural Networks	Detection of breast cancer nuclei [29]
Probabilistic Neural Networks	Breast cancer classification using mammogram and history data [30]

a vector of values that represents the estimation of the risk-indexes associated to the different diseases.

Eventually the risk-index vector is sent to the decision rules block. Aim of this stage is to choose, by means of suitable rules, the correct diagnosis on the base of the risk-index values. Several rules can be employed such as: winner take all, rules based on thresholds and rules based on boolean operations. One should note that sometimes this stage is missing either because it is inherently provided by the topology of network employed in the risk-index stage or because it is not needed or not desired. This happens when either physicians prefer to take the final decision on the basis of the actual risk index values or when the required output is a not binary value as in the case of a drug dosage [27].

Table 3 lists some applications of neural network clustered on the base of the network topology.

Let we end also this section with an example that shows how a neural network based analyzer can be employed to completely automatize the diagnosis procedure of ischemic events.

The cardiac muscle produces electrical signals that propagates through the patient body. These signals can be measured by means of commercial electrocardiographs (ECG) that are able to simultaneously acquire up to 12 signals. These instruments are able to store either several short or few longer signals (Holter instruments typically acquire only two signals but for up to 24 hours).

Fig. 5 shows an ideal ECG trace. The signal level is of few millivolts while the period RR is related the the patient activity and is of about 1 s at rest.

The analysis of the ECG traces is useful to infer the heart functionality; e.g. the geometrical characteristics of ST segment (see fig. 5) are strictly related to the presence of ischemic events and other coronary artery diseases.

Since the analysis of real traces, as those shown in right side of fig. 5, is a long and time consuming operation, modern instruments [31, 32] are often designed to perform an automatic classification and interpretation of the ECG signals.

Several automatic algorithms have been investigated, both conventional and neural. The example reported here describes a neural approach, proposed by Maglaveras and others [5], that is designed for the interpretation of ECG signals in order to detect ischemic episodes. The proposed system, shown in fig. 6, has the typical structure of the generic decision making instrument previously described. The system firstly extracts the features that are related to the investigated pathology from the input signals. In this case, ischemia appears in the ECG as a

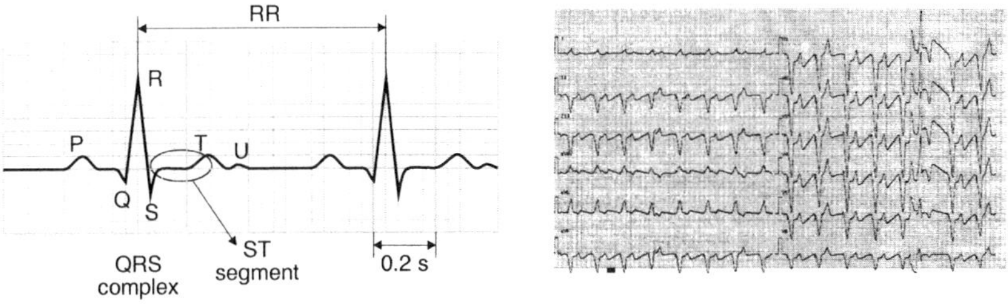

Figure 5: Ideal (left) and real (right) electrocardiographic traces.

Table 4: Comparative results of the neural network based ischemic detector. Sensitivity and predictivity are defined making reference to four values: *TP=True Positive, TN=True Negative, FP=False Positive* and *FN=False Negative.*

	Sensitivity $\frac{TP}{TP+FN}$	Predictivity $\frac{TP}{TP+FP}$
NN-based algorithm	89%	78%
Others algorithms [33]	84%	87%

change in the ST segment morphology. The feature extraction algorithm therefore is designed to identify the ST and to compare it against a template that has been previously obtained from the same patient when no ischemic events were present. The difference with respect to the template is considered to be the feature to be forwarded the risk-index estimation stage. The input vector for the risk estimation stage is therefore composed of 20 samples representing the difference between template and actual signal during the ST interval.

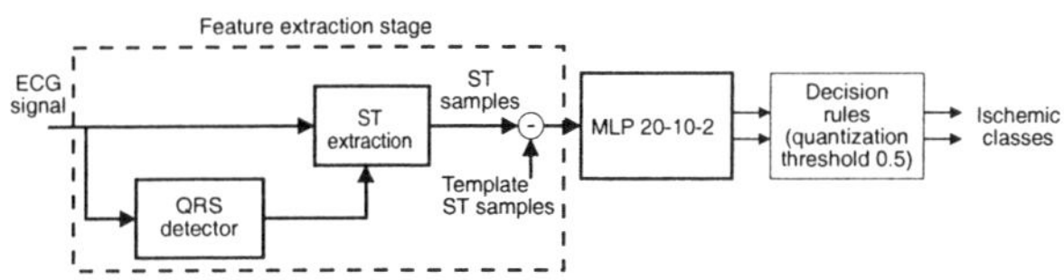

Figure 6: Ischemic detector able to provide a linguistic justification of the diagnosis.

The network in the risk-index stage has to manage time series so that a Time-Delay Neural Network, see fig. 2(c), is employed. The network core is a tree layer MLP with 20 inputs, 2 outputs and 10 sigmoidal neurons in the hidden layer. A back propagation algorithm with an adaptive learning rate is employed during the learning phase and the network is trained to recognize four classes: *normal ST*, *depressed ST*, *elevated ST* and *unclassifiable ST*. Training and test sets were composed of 120 patterns (50% normal, 25% had ST depression and 25% ST elevation) and were extracted from the European ST-T database. .

Table 4 shows a comparison of the network performance with respect to other systems. It is easy to see that the network obtains results similar to the other solutions both in sensitivity and predictivity, with the advantage that it does not require the physician to identify the input/output model. In addition, it is faster than other methods, so it is suitable to be employed in real-time detector systems.

This type of approach is effective, but the system does not provide any explanations of the reasons of its result, so physicians lack the possibility to understand the reasons of the diagnosis. Others approaches have been developed in order to provide a medical description of the reasons of the network result. As an example, a mixed fuzzy/neural approach has been employed to provide a linguistic description of the diagnosis [34]. Non-neural decision techniques can be also employed in order to obtain an explanation of diagnosis reasons. The rule based techniques [35] are self-explanatory, but require an accurate description of the 'human model', description that is not always available. Some hybrid techniques, which mix neural and non-neural approaches, can be also employed. As an example, ProstAsure [36], which is an early detector of prostate cancer based on neural network, employs some rules which are based on the assessed medical knowledge in order to improve the learning efficiency [37].

13.2.3 Medical data-sets

The training phase is one of the most critical steps during the development of any neural network based system. In this phase the network designers have to choose a suitable learning algorithm and have to provide a reliable set of examples, the so called *training set*. Once the network has been trained a second set of examples, the *test set* is required in order to test the network performance.

Sometimes, in order to avoid the overfitting phenomena, special techniques, such as the early stopping algorithm, are employed during the learning phase. In this case the training of the network is performed by means of the training set, but, periodically, the learning process is stopped and a cost function (e.g. the mean squared error) is computed on the validation set. According to the early stopping algorithm the network is trained until the cost function reaches the minimum value [38].

These techniques require a third set of example to be employed. A meaningful training, validation, and test of a network thus require a large amount of examples. Unfortunately real examples are not easy to obtain in the medical field: each record in a data-set requires a patient and data have to be manually processed by an expert physician. Furthermore, a pool of experts is often required to analyze the examples in order to get the correct diagnosis. Fortunately many medical problems are world-wide diffused so some researchers have decided to share own data with others researchers. Several collections of medical data are nowadays available that cover the most diffuse medical problems. Here is a list of some data-sets that are freely downloadable from the internet.

Proben1 [39] is an archive that contains 15 benchmark problems and set of benchmarking rules which can be used to compare algorithms. The benchmarks cover medical and non-medical fields and are related to classification and function approximation problems. *Proben1* provides data-set already subdivided into three classes: training set, validation set and test set. The benchmarks cover several medical topics: diagnosis of breast cancer, diagnosis of diabetes, detection of intron/exon boundaries in DNA sequences, prediction of heart disease and diagnosis of thyroid hyper or hypo-function.

Proben1 also provides specific benchmarks to be used as reference values when testing the performance of different networks. For each reference result the following information are provided: input/output values, normalization rules, nominal attribute coding, missing attribute values, training algorithm and termination criteria, cost (or error) function, network topology, classification method, activation functions and weight initialization.

PhysioBank [40] is a collection of database sites and software. The archive contains contains multi-parameter data-set, ECGs, EEGs, images and other medical data. An important database that is accessible from *PhysioBank* is the European ST-T database that contains 90 records composed of two-channel ECG signals digitized at 250 Hz. Each record lasts 2 hours and contains at least one ischemic episode. The episodes are marked by expert cardiologists.

Wisconsin Datasets [41] contains multi-parametric and image data-set useful both for the diagnosis and the prognostic of breast cancer.

The University of South Florida database [42] contains more than two thousands mammography images for breast cancer diagnosis that are grouped, depending on the medical diagnosis, into 43 classes. In addition it contains software, which can be used to extract and process images.

13.3. Prediction of the output uncertainty of a neural network

When a neural network is directly involved in the measurement process at least two questions arise. The first is related to the way the uncertainties of the input values propagate to the outputs, i.e. how one can estimate the uncertainty that affects the network outputs as a consequence of the uncertainties which affect the network inputs.

The second question is related to the network training phase. Neural networks behave according to what they have learned from the examples used during the training phase, but the information about the uncertainty that affects such examples is usually not made available to the network. This can lead to either an incorrect training or, at least, a non-optimal training.

This section discusses a possible approach to tackle both these problems. The approach is suitable for most "memory-less" network topologies that use a supervised training.

13.3.1 Neural networks and measurements

Neural networks are nowadays widely employed in the medical field as well as in industrial and in research environments. Their use is continuously spreading and today applications are available that embed different flavors of neural networks in complex measurement systems even though the network role in the *measurement affair* is not always clear.

As an example of network use, we can focus on the medical field and recall three main uses that appear to have rather different properties. Neural networks can be employed to:

- discriminate among different pathologies
- determine medical parameters which show the evidence of a pathology
- select the most appropriate therapy

Are all these uses of neural networks really measurements?

According to the classical definition, the measurement of a quantity is the determination of a number, which represents the ratio between the measured quantity value and a recognized standard. In a trivial example: we measure the length of a rod by comparing it against a ruler that has been calibrated against the accepted *standard* that materializes the length of *one meter*.

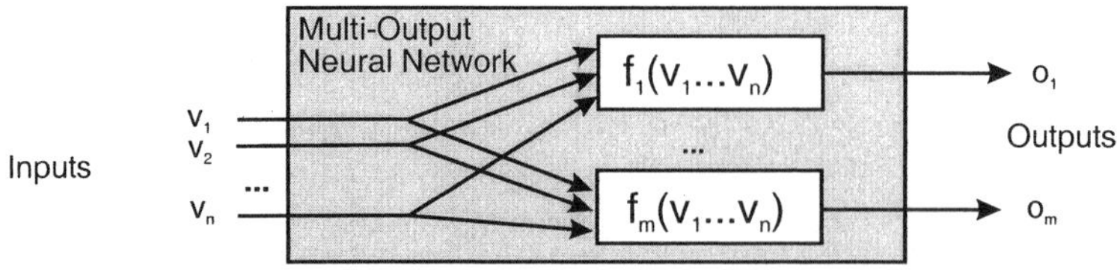

Figure 7: Metrological model of a static neural network.

Neural networks behave rather differently with respect to this paradigm so that an obvious question arises: how can a neural network produce a measurement?

The answer can be found by recalling that most measurements are *indirect*, i.e. they are obtained by using a suitable model to combine several *direct* measurements, i.e. by combining measurements that are obtained by means of instruments.

To fix the ideas let us consider the velocity measurement. The mean velocity of a vehicle, which is defined as the ratio of the distance s covered by the vehicle and the time t it takes to cover such a distance, can be obtained by measuring the time and the distance and combining them by means of a suitable model. The model is of course:

$$v = \frac{s}{t} \tag{1}$$

and we use it to obtain the measurement of the velocity m_v by means of the measurements of space m_s and time m_t:

$$m_v = \frac{m_s}{m_t} \tag{2}$$

From the input-output point of view, a static, memory-less, neural network, i.e. a network where the outputs depend on the actual inputs but not on the input history, can be depicted as in fig. 7.

According to this scheme, a generic multi-output neural network is a device which receives several quantities $v_1, \cdots, v_n$ as inputs and computes the outputs $o_1, \cdots, o_m$ by means of a set of defined equations $f_1, \cdots, f_m$:

$$o_i = f_i(v_1, ...v_n) \qquad i = 1, \cdots, m \tag{3}$$

where f_i is the relationship, tuned during the training phase, that describes the neural network behavior regarding the ith output.

Therefore the neural network actually combines several inputs, i.e. several measurements, to determine an *output*, and can thus be thought as a device that produce *indirect measurements*.

However when we perform a *conventional* indirect measurement we employ a system for which:

- we *a-priori* know the combination rule the indirect measurement system has to realize, i.e. we exactly knows the relationship between the direct measurements we employ and the indirect measurement we wish to obtain.

- we work referring to an accepted standard, i.e. the indirect measurement we are looking for has its own standard and, in principle, could be measured directly. The combination rule we use is actually the one (and usually the only one) that allows us to obtain the same result we could obtain by directly measuring the required quantity.

On the other hand, when we perform a *network based* indirect measurement:

- we do not explicitly know the actual combination rule, since it is embedded inside the network;
- we train the network with *examples* (or leave the network free to adapt, if an unsupervised training is employed).

Therefore two interesting questions arise:

- How can we ensure the network learns the *correct* combination rule?
- How can we ensure the result is the same we could obtain by directly measuring the required quantity?

In addition, there is the possibility that we use the network to compute a quantity which is not already defined, i.e. that *cannot* be defined with respect to any accepted standard or combination of accepted standards. This network use opens some interesting questions regarding the meaning, under the metrological point of view, of the *newly defined* quantity: the analysis of these questions is beyond the scope of this discussion and is omitted here.

Therefore, summarizing these aspects, we have to face two scenarios:

1. **Non-defining network** The network is employed to obtain a measurement of an already defined quantity: the network is used to avoid writing the model; we face a *model error* due to the imprecise matching of the network behavior with respect to the correct model. As an example we can focus the attention on a network that is used to locate the position of a specific pattern in a noisy signal. The use of the network is simpler than writing an extraction model and implementing it, but we cannot be sure the time stamp we obtain really represent the actual pattern position. We can refer to this problem as the presence of a *model* error.

2. **Defining network** The network is used to obtain a quantity that is not yet defined and therefore cannot be measured directly: the network *defines* the new quantity, i.e. the network *becomes the standard* for measuring that quantity. In this case we do not have model errors, but what is the new quantity? How can we combine it with other *conventional* measurements? As an example we can focus the attention on a network designed to estimate the *prettiness* of a human being. The network inputs could be height, weight, and other dimensions; the training could be performed on a *prettiness score* obtained by some other human beings. The network output is of course an estimation of the *prettiness score* given the dimensions of any human beings. We do not have any model errors, but the standard defined by the network might not be universally accepted ...

Apart from the model error, two other uncertainty sources should be considered (as in every measurement system!): uncertainties that affect the network inputs and *propagate* to the network output and uncertainties connected to the existence of physical quantities, which affect the measured quantity, but are neither measured nor controlled (also known as *influence quantities*). Table 5 summarizes the uncertainty causes discussed so far.

There are two additional minor problems connected to the uncertainties that require some words of explanation:

Table 5: Uncertainty causes in neural networks

Cause	Effect	Processing
Uncertainty on the input quantities	The uncertainty propagates to the output according to the input *importance*	?
Model uncertainty	The network does not describe the actual input-output relationship	?
Other uncertainties	Reflect the effect of the influence quantities	Must be know in advance ("a-priori" information)

1. The input problem. When we speak of *indirect measurements* we refer to a scenario where the inputs are measurements, i.e quantities whose values can be defined with respect to an accepted standard (length, time, ...), but sometimes in the medical field we encounter quantities which belong to enumerated sets (i.e. smoker/non-smoker). This aspect has already been discussed in the previous section and requires different solutions depending on the type of variable, but a problem still remains: what is the uncertainty of these *special* quantities?

2. The output problem. We train the network with *examples* for which we know the target (i.e. we have measured it...), but how can we deal with the uncertainty connected to the target? The normal solution is a no-solution: this uncertainty enters into the model error.

We have now to discuss the problem of the input/output uncertainty propagation and how to take the model related uncertainty into account.

13.3.2 Input Uncertainty Propagation

The output uncertainty that is a consequence of the input uncertainties, can be evaluated by using the well known propagation rules, either by means of the standard uncertainties, as suggested in the ISO guide [43], or by looking for the maximum expected output deviation. The latter solution was the most common way of dealing with the uncertainties in the past and was referred to as the *deterministic* approach; as a contrast, the ISO suggested new approach can be referred to as the *statistical* one.

Both approaches relies on the possibility of linearizing the input/output relationship around the actual output value:

$$o_i \approx f_i\left(v_{10}, v_{20}, ...v_{n0}\right) + \sum_{j=1}^{n} \left.\frac{\partial f_i}{\partial v_j}\right|_{v_{10}, v_{20}, ...v_{n0}} \delta v_j \tag{4}$$

where o_i is the ith output, $v_{10}...v_{n0}$ are the n values that correspond to the actual measured values so that $f_i\left(v_{10}, v_{20}, ...v_{n0}\right)$ is the *nominal* value of o_i, and δv_j are the changes of the inputs respect to the measured values.

By using this equation it is therefore possible to preview any output change δv_j corresponding to any combination of input changes:

$$\delta o_i \approx \sum_{j=1}^{n} \left.\frac{\partial f_i}{\partial v_j}\right|_{v_{10},v_{20},\ldots v_{n0}} \delta v_j \quad (5)$$

The output change is therefore obtained as a weighted summation of the input changes where the weights are represented by the partial derivatives and are often referred to as *sensitivity factors* or *sensitivity coefficients*.

Deterministic model The deterministic point of view tries to determine the maximum output change that corresponds to the worse combination of input changes. In mathematical terms this corresponds to a summation of absolute values:

$$\delta o_i = \sum_{j=1}^{n} \left|\frac{\partial f_i}{\partial v_j}\right|_{v_{10},v_{20},\ldots v_{n0}} \delta v_j \quad (6)$$

Statistical model If the *statistical* model is employed as suggested by the ISO guide, the uncertainties affecting the input quantities are managed as random variables and are characterized in terms of their standard deviation and their combination follows the well known rules of the random processes:

$$u^2(o_i) = \sum_{j=1}^{n} \left(\frac{\partial f_i}{\partial v_j}\right)^2 u(v_j)^2 + 2\sum_{j=1}^{n-1}\sum_{k=j+1}^{n} \frac{\partial f}{\partial v_j}\frac{\partial f}{\partial v_k} u(v_j)u(v_k)\rho_{v_j v_k} \quad (7)$$

where $u(o_i)$ is the expected output standard deviation, $u(v_j)$ are the standard deviations of the input signals, $\rho_{v_j v_k}$ is the correlation coefficient between the jth input and the kth input. The subscripts that remember that all the derivatives are computed in the nominal input point are omitted for clarity.

Of course, in the absence of correlation among the different inputs i.e. when $\rho_{v_j v_k} = 0 \forall j, k$, eqn. 7 simply becomes:

$$u^2(o_i) = \sum_{j=1}^{n} \left(\frac{\partial f_i}{\partial v_j}\right)^2 u(v_j)^2 \quad (8)$$

One should note that both equations involve input uncertainties and derivatives of the network function, but there is no need to compute such derivatives in an analytical way and a numerical approach can be usefully employed.

Before ending this section it could be interesting to investigate how to move from the deterministic *old* way of dealing with the uncertainties to the *new* statistical approach. Of course a general solution is not available, but a simple conversion can be obtained if one knows the shape of the input density function *p()*, or if such a function can be reasonably hypothesized. In this case it is possible to compute analytically the variance, and thus the standard deviation, as:

$$u^2(v_i) = \int_{-\delta(v_i)}^{\delta(v_i)} p(v_i)(v_i - v_{i0})^2 dv_i \quad (9)$$

Table 6: Uncertainty causes in neural networks.

Cause	Effect	Processing
Uncertainty of the input quantities	The uncertainty propagates to the output according to their sensitivity factors	Compute the output uncertainty by combining the input uncertainties
Model uncertainty	The network does not describe the actual input-output relationship	Take the maximum difference between the network output and the actual value as uncertainty indicator. A partition of the output-space can be employed if different regions exist
Other uncertainties	Reflect the effect of the influence quantities	Must be know in advance ("a-priori" information)

where $\delta(v_i)$ is the maximum expected uncertainty. As an example, if the uniform distribution is supposed, eqn. 9 leads to:

$$u(v_i) = \frac{\delta v_i}{\sqrt{3}} \tag{10}$$

13.3.3 Model Uncertainty

Dealing with model uncertainty is not so easy...If we knew the exact model we could estimate the effect of simplifying it, but if we already had such a model we would employ it! In addition, in the neural network world, we do not *know* the model the network is realizing. However we perform a test phase on a set with *known* results and we can observe how the network describes the expected values. The model uncertainty can be estimated from the errors that are not explained by the uncertainty related to the inputs.

Table 5 can be now updated to reflect the discussion of these last section and to obtain a complete summary as explained in Table 6.

13.3.4 Uncertainty Combination

The three uncertainty causes contribute to the overall measurement uncertainty so we need a way to combine the uncertainty contributions and to obtain a single uncertainty indicator.

The estimation is easy when the deterministic model is used, since the worst uncertainty, combination is a simple summation:

$$\Delta o_i = \delta o_i + \delta m_i + \delta n m_i \tag{11}$$

where Δo_i is the expected output maximum deviation; δo_i is the term that takes the input effect into account (see eqn. 6); δm_i is the deviation due to the model error and $\delta n m_i$ is the deviation connected to the other non model-related effects i.e. to the influence quantities.

The uncertainty combination when the ISO model is employed is more difficult and questionable. The ISO approach combines the different uncertainty causes in terms of standard deviation, but both the model error and the other uncertainties exploit a deterministic effect. If the statistical uncertainty model has to be used anyway, the cumulative standard deviation corresponding to the three uncertainty causes can be conservatively computed as:

$$u_c(o_i)^2 = u(o_i)^2 + \delta m_i^2 + \delta nm_i^2 \tag{12}$$

where $u_c(o_i)$ is the expected cumulative standard deviation; $u(o_i)$ is the terms that take the input effect into account (obtained either from eqn. 7 or from eqn. 8); δm_i is the deviation due to the model error and δnm_i is the deviation connected to the other effects.

One should note that the value obtained from eqn. 12 corresponds to a distribution that has a not null mean and thus an interpretation of the uncertainty in terms of probability is rather difficult.

13.3.5 Taking the uncertainties into account during the training phase

During a supervised training phase some parameters that define the network behavior, such as weights and biases in a Multi Layer Perceptron (MLP), are modified in order to force the network to produce the requested outputs.

The training effectiveness depends on the availability of a training set that contains at least one example of the most important occurrences the network is expected to encounter. Unfortunately, this constraint is not sufficient in the presence of a non negligible uncertainty on the input values.

Several examples of different measurements corresponding to the same nominal condition are required in order to force the network to take the uncertainty presence into account. In the absence of such examples, the network tends to learn a specific combination of uncertainties and lacks part of its generalization ability.

Unfortunately, in most practical situations, the training set dimension is limited and often very few examples that correspond to the same nominal condition are available. In addition, a direct method of embedding the uncertainty values in the training phase when the input set is not wide enough is not yet available.

Many approaches have been proposed to reduce the problems connected to a small training set that is also affected by noise. Some authors implemented constraints on the weights or similar approaches during the training phase [44, 45]. Other authors tackled the problem by adding noise to the training set [46].

This last approach can easily be extended to take the uncertainty presence on the inputs into account.

When using this approach, the training process is carried out employing a modified stream of inputs, which is obtained by manipulating the original one. The goal is to provide groups of examples that highlight the uncertainty presence for all the most important situations.

Each group can be obtained by generating several replicas of the original example. Each replica is obtained by corrupting the original input values with different combinations of the expected uncertainties.

There is no definite rule to choose the required number of replicas. One possibility would be that of mapping all the combinations that can be obtained by adding and subtracting the expected uncertainties to each input. This would produce, for each example, a group of 2^N new examples for a network that has N inputs. The training set therefore could become unacceptably large if N is greater than three-four. In this case the required number of replicas can be determined by means of a trial-and-error process where the network is trained by adding replicas until its behavior does not change significantly.

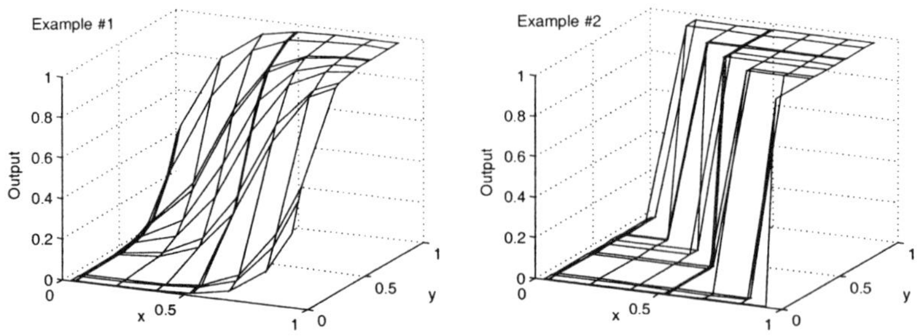

Figure 8: Two examples of training sets.

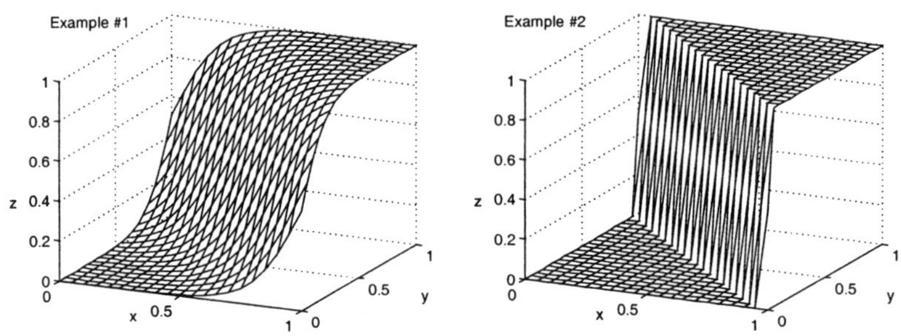

Figure 9: The (unknown) output surfaces of the two examples.

One should note that the proposed method can be extended to the entire training set simply by concatenating replicas of the entire training set. This approach can be convenient when the training set has a limited dimension or when the analysis of such a training set, in order to cluster the examples that refer to similar conditions, is difficult or impossible.

The impact of training with the modified set depends on the network response type and is remarkable if the network has regions in which a steep output change is required. In such a case the uncertainty presence can produce dramatic output changes that reflect in an overall poor behavior, as explained in the two examples of the following section.

13.3.6 Two examples

Two examples have been designed to be easily shown and to highlight the previously discussed topics i.e. the effect of the *conventional* and *enhanced* training, and the computation of the output uncertainty.

Both examples deal with a network with two inputs and one output so that the input/output relationship can be shown on a 3D plot. The input and output spaces are confined in the range $[0, 1]$. The examples use training sets composed of 120 examples based on randomly selected points (uniform distribution) in the $[0, 1]$x$[0, 1]$ square; the points are supposed to be affected by an uncertainty (uniform distribution) whose maximum amplitude is 0.05 that corresponds to 5% of the input range.

The aspect of the two training sets is shown in fig. 8. The two training sets look quite strange, but in reality they have been produced by employing a rather simple equation and the strange aspect is a consequence of the uncertainty presence.

The hypothesized indirect measurements refers to a bidimensional function $z = f(x, y)$ which is defined as:

$$z = \frac{1}{1 + e^{-k(x+y-1)}} \tag{13}$$

This function has been chosen for the examples since it has two major advantages. Firstly it can easily be approximated even though a simple single-neuron MLPs is employed since the equation is one of the functions that is commonly used to implement the neuron activation.

Secondly the function sharpness can easily be controlled by means of the parameter k. This permits an easy investigation of the effect of the function steepness on the network behavior with respect to the input uncertainties.

The first example regards the approximation of a "smooth" function, which is obtained by setting $k = 10$, while the second one regards an example of a very "steep" function, which is obtained by setting $k = 1000$.

Of course in a real situation we should not know the equation at the time of training and we should not know the actual aspect of the output surface, but it is interesting to see what the network should approximate. Fig. 9 shows the two surfaces and highlights the great difference in the steepness of the two transitions.

The network behavior and the effect of the uncertainty presence on both the training and the expected output uncertainty is dramatically different for the two examples.

The *smooth* surface is *easy* to describe: fig. 10 shows the outputs obtained within the training set by employing either the conventional or enhanced training.

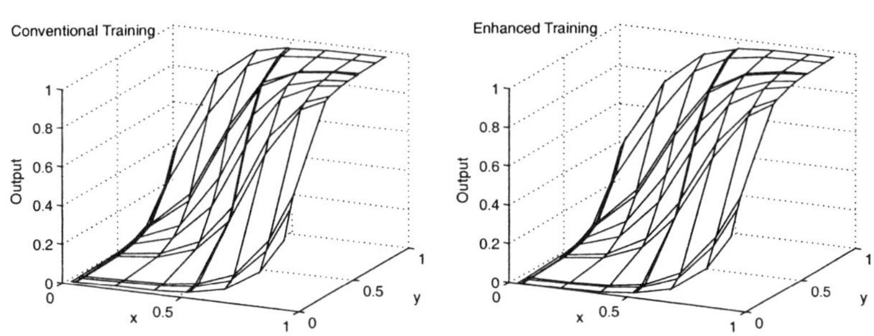

Figure 10: Results of conventional and enhanced training for the case of $k = 10$.

This pictures are important since they are the only results available at the time of training and the quality of the approximation within the training set is often taken as an indicator to decide how many neurons to employ in the hidden layer and when to stop the training process. As one can see, the uncertainty presence does not impair the training since the effect of the uncertainty is to slightly shift the output value. Feeding the network with *equivalent* values, as we do during the training with the enhanced training set, does not require a significant change in the network parameters and we expect the networks generated by the two different training to behave approximately in the same way.

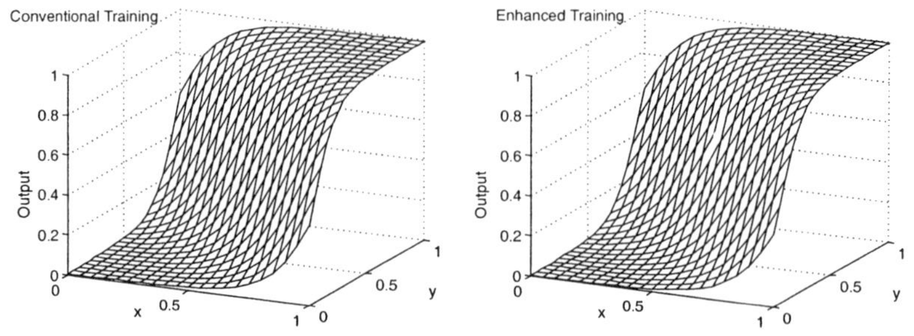

Figure 11: Output surface obtained after conventional and enhanced training in the case of $k = 10$. The two surfaces look rather similar.

Once the network is trained we can easily observe the output surface and preview the effect of the input uncertainties.

Fig. 11 shows the aspect of the output surface obtained by training the network either in the conventional way or with the enhanced approach. It is easy to observe that the two surfaces are rather similar, as expected, and therefore that the enhanced training has a negligible effect on the final result.

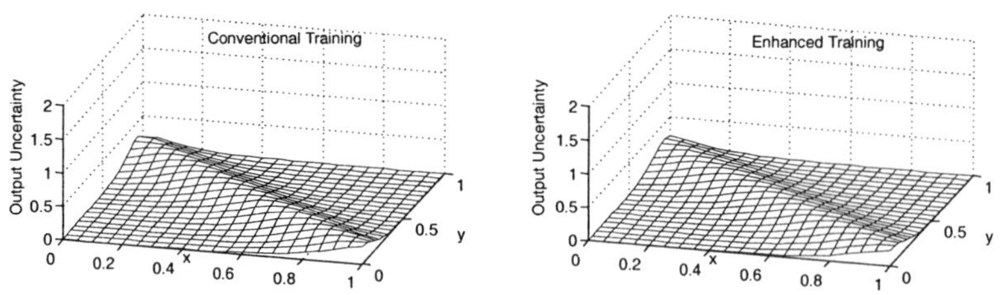

Figure 12: Sensitivity of network output with respect to the inputs for the case $k = 10$. The sensitivities are similar, regardless of the used training.

In order to compute the output uncertainty by employing either eqn. 6 or one of the 7 or 8, we need the derivatives with respect to the inputs. Such derivatives can be easily computed by means of a numerical approach and their aspect is shown in fig. 12.

The test of the network performance during its use can be obtained by feeding the network with new randomly generated examples. Fig. 13 shows a set of 100 examples, ordered by the output value to increase the plot readability. The black asterisks represent the *expected* (true) values, the gray hollow circles the network output values, and the lines the standard deviations (i.e. the expected uncertainties) of the network outputs. It is easy to see that both the conventional and the enhanced training lead to output estimations that contain the corrected value and, in addition, the two trainings lead to quite similar plots.

The same procedure can be followed when the *steep* network is used. Fig. 14 is the counterpart of fig. 10 and shows the output surfaces obtained by training the network with conventional and enhanced training for $k = 1000$.

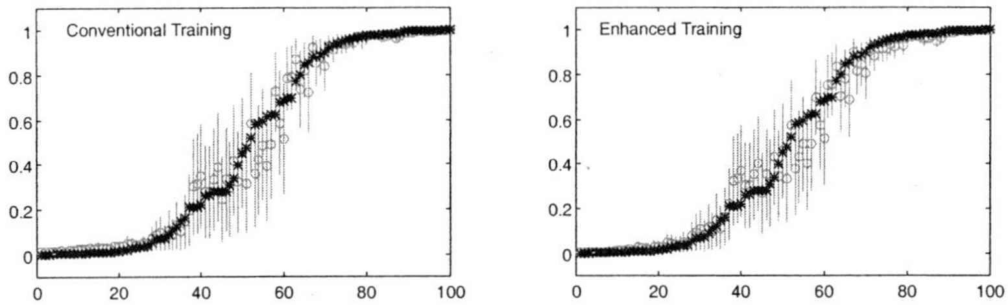

Figure 13: Network behavior with new randomly generated data for the case $k = 10$. The examples are ordered by value to improve the trace readability.

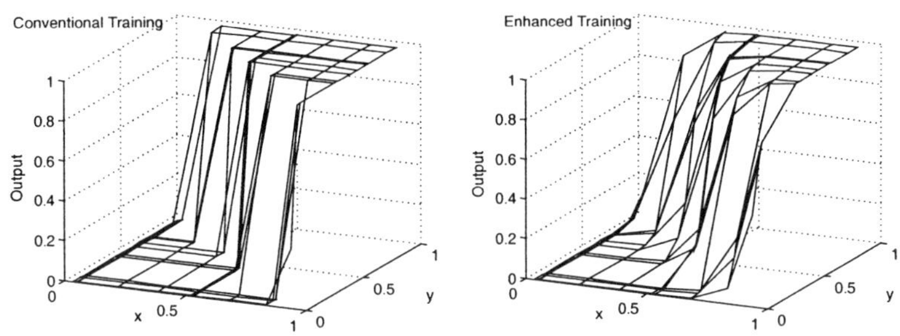

Figure 14: Output surfaces obtained by training the network with either the conventional or enhanced approach for the case of $k = 1000$. The surfaces are rather different in this case.

The two trainings behave quite differently and the first impression is that the *conventional* training leads to a better approximation of the training set, while the enhanced training leads to a result that is less similar to the original one.

In other words, the conventional training leads to a network that try to *correctly* describe the examples, while the enhanced training produces a smoother surface that does not completely fit the examples. The *equivalent* though different examples of the enhanced training set tell the network to interpolate in order to find an *average* value suitable for producing a *reasonable* result regardless of the actual uncertainty combination. The enhanced trained network therefore should be more useful in predicting the correct output (and uncertainty) during its use even though less suitable to describe the training set. We expect the two networks to behave quite differently and the output surfaces, fig. 15, confirms this impression.

Fig. 16 shows the output sensitivity with respect to the input values and highlights how the conventional training has very high peaks of sensitivity near the transition point. The enhanced training produces a smoother surface and therefore a lower sensitivity to small changes of the input values. These different sensitivities turn out in quite different behaviors during the network use, as highlighted in fig. 17. Here it is easy to see how the enhanced training produces a lower overall uncertainty near the transition point even though all the predicted values contain the correct value.

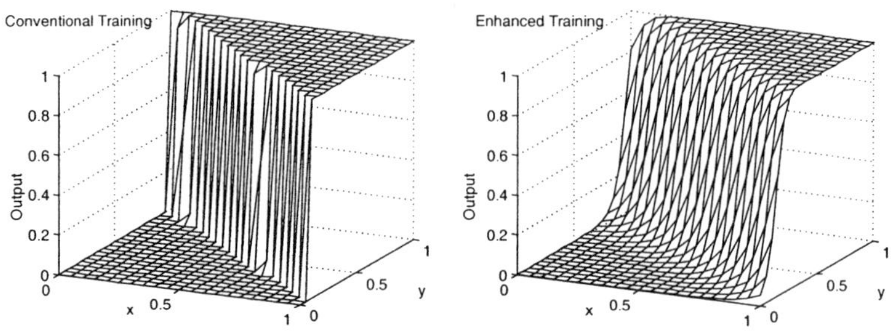

Figure 15: Output surface obtained after conventional and enhanced training in the case of $k = 1000$.

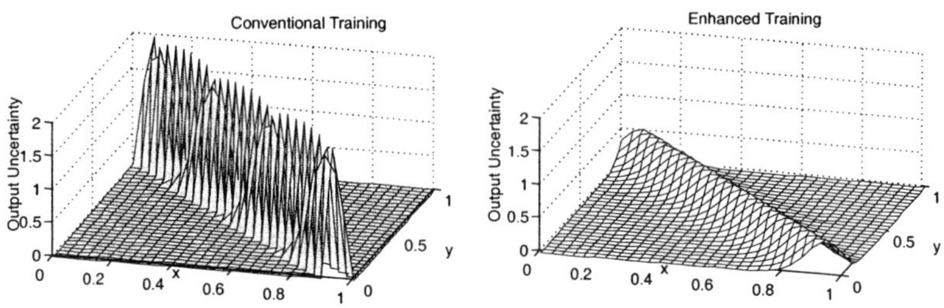

Figure 16: Sensitivity of network output with respect to the inputs for the case $k = 1000$.

13.3.7 Summary

At this point it is possible to summarize the topics discussed so far:

- Neural networks can be used in the medical field to produce indirect measurements, provided that we do not encounter the problem of the *non conventional* inputs (i.e. of input quantities for which the uncertainty cannot be clearly stated). We can employ the neural network in two ways:
  - **Non-defining networks**: the quantity we *want* is already defined and could be measured directly, but the network is easier to use and we do not need to write down the measurement model.
  - **Defining networks**: the quantity we *want* is not defined in other ways and the network *defines* it (once it has been trained). A new training defines a new quantity.
- We must take the uncertainty presence into account, regardless of the type of network we employ. A prediction of the output uncertainty can easily be obtained, provided that: the input uncertainties are known and we can compute the derivatives of the input/output relationship. Both the *deterministic* and *statistical* models can be employed.
- The uncertainty presence should be taken into account at the training level to help the network to *weight* the inputs according to their uncertainties.

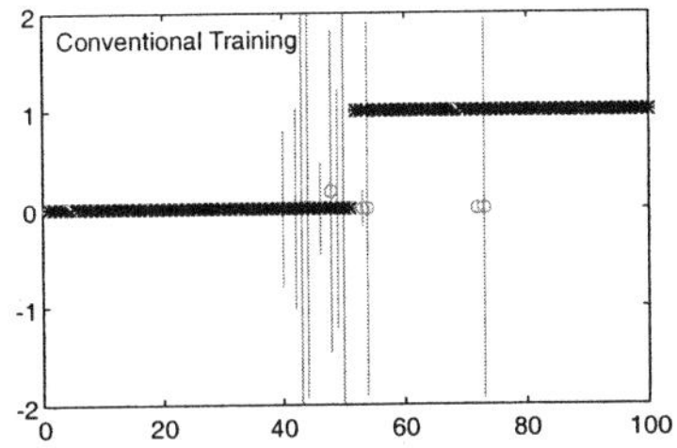

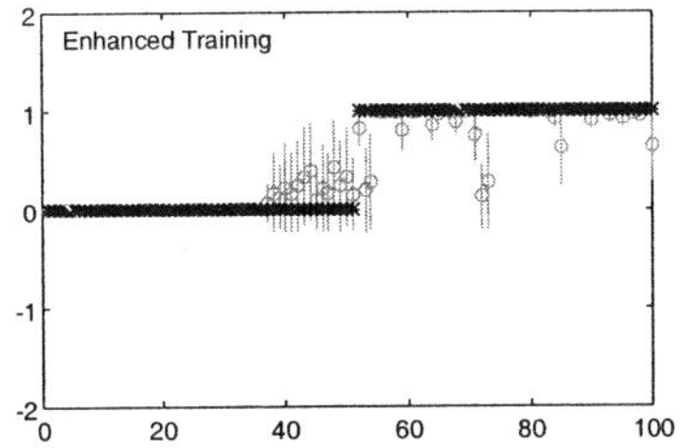

Figure 17: Network behavior with new randomly generate data for the case $k = 1000$. The examples are ordered by value to improve the trace readability.

- If the training set is very large, it contains enough information to allow the network to train correctly and nothing else is required.
- If the training set is small and does not contain enough information about the uncertainties, we can force the network to take the uncertainty presence into account by *creating* an enlarged training set. The enlarged training set can be generated by creating several replicas of the examples each one corrupted by different combinations of the input uncertainties.

In addition to these points we can remind the problem of the output uncertainty of the examples belonging to the training set, which affects the training and can produce an additional *model error* and two other subjects that are inherently connected to any neural network use, but that become important in the medical field due to the limited dimension of the training sets: the *unbalanced* training set issue and the *oversized network* issue.

As far as the first issue is concerned we have to observe that the training algorithm tries to minimize the cumulative error for all the examples. If the training set is mostly composed of a specific kind of examples, the network will adjust to describe such examples at the expense of the others. This is always true, but is especially important in the medical field where small training sets are used and healthy volunteers are easier to find (and measure...) than severely impaired patients. More details on this issue can be found in several papers such as [47].

The second issue is more subtle and connected to the network design approach which is synthesized by the sentence *If the network does not describe the training set... increase the number of neurons!* This approach can be dangerous in the medical field again due to the limited dimension of the training sets.

Let us consider an example based on an MLP with N inputs, M neurons in the hidden layer and one output. The MLP will have: $N \times M$ weights, plus M biases for the connection between inputs and the hidden layer and M weights plus one bias for the connection between the hidden layer and the output i.e. $(M + 2) \times N + 1$ *parameters* to be *identified* during the training. As an example we can discuss a relatively small MLP with 4 inputs 5 neurons in the hidden layer that contains 29 parameters to identify: how many examples do we need to have a *satisfactory* identification (and not a net that describes the examples perfectly instead of approximating the population)?

13.4. Examples of applications of neural networks to the medical field

This section contains two examples of neural network use in the medical field. The first example deals with a single-output network designed for the estimation of the postoperative risk index after lung resection. This example is useful to verify the effect of the uncertainties during the training and the effect of the enhanced training approach.

The second example is a classifier that is designed to differentiate the Airway Diseases by means of Functional Non-Invasive Tests and is useful to highlight the powerful interaction between neural and conventional approaches and to compare the conventional solutions and the neural ones.

Both examples use *conventional* inputs i.e. input quantities that are obtained from measurements acquired using conventional instruments and for which we know the input uncertainty The output is of an *enumerated* type (yes/no or A,B,C type). The output uncertainty of the examples both during training and validation is small and is neglected in the processing.

13.4.1 Example #1: Evaluation of a postoperative risk-index after lung resection

The scenario of this example is the treatment of patients affected by lung cancer. Lung cancer is on the increase and elderly and pulmonary-compromised patients are often candidates for surgical procedures. Unfortunately, these surgical procedures are useful, but always risky. Any way of forecasting the risk of loosing the patient, as a consequence of the surgical procedures, could be very important to avoid useless procedures. More details on this example can be found in [48, 49].

Of course several clinical tests are routinely carried out to forecast post operative risks, but no single test has yet been found to be accurate in the prediction. Better predictions could be expected by combining the results of tests performed both at rest and under working conditions, but no analytical rule that can be used to combine the items of information yet exists.

The test set of this example is small and is composed of 84 patients who underwent a surgical procedure. About 20 different clinical parameters were measured (before the surgical procedure) in all patients (age, weight, sex, ... plus several clinical parameters)

Before starting the network training some preliminary tests to find out the most relevant clinical parameters were carried out trying to select only a few parameters to speed-up the training and giving preference to non-invasively obtained parameters. This operation led to two parameters: the FEV1 (Forced Expired air Volume in one second), determined at rest (% of the predicted value), and the GET (Gas Exchange Threshold) determined under working conditions.

Input data were scaled in the range of 0 to 1 according to their expected range and a network topology composed of an MLP with two neurons in the hidden layer was selected. The data set was divided into two groups: 21 patients were used for the network training and 63 for the network validation.

The training set was generated by using the first 21 patients for whom the ratio of outcome (severe complications vs. no complications) reflects the expected population ratio.

The network was trained in the conventional way to produce an output of 1 in the presence of high risk and 0 otherwise. The network was than tested on the overall data set by putting a threshold at risk index=0.5. In these conditions it gives 81 correct predictions and 3 wrong

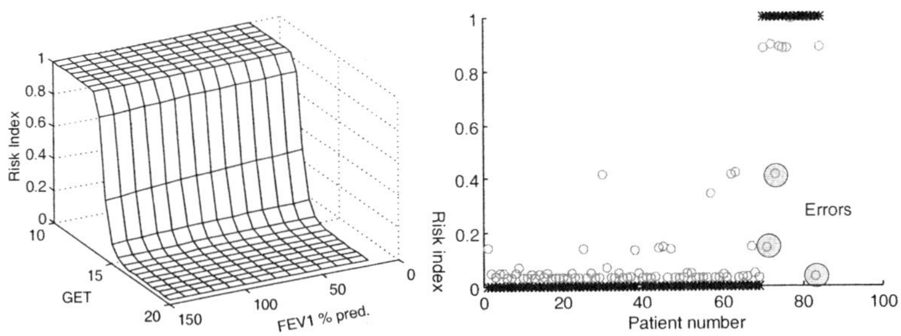

Figure 18: Output surface with conventional training and network performance within test set.

predictions. One of the wrong predictions is connected to an Acute Respiratory Distress Syndrome (ADRS), that is a not predictable event, so that in reality only two errors should be taken into account. Fig. 18 shows the network result and the output surface as a function of the input values.

The overall behavior is rather good, but the training set is *binary*, so the network tends to train for a binary behavior; this means that the input/output relationship is unknown, but the examples suggest to the net that the relation is very steep as shown in fig. 18. As a consequence, even small differences in the measured values can completely change the prediction. This is unnatural: there is only a small band where the forecast is doubtful.

The uncertainties of the input values can be estimated according to American Thoracic Society (ATS) recommendations : $\delta GET = 5\%$ of the expected range, $\delta FEV1 = 2\%$ of the expected range uncertainties estimated as maximum values (*deterministic approach*) for inter-operator measurements and with different instruments. Lower values are expected for intra-operator estimations.

The expected uncertainties could lead to a maximum of 21 false predictions, in the worst case, when applied to the previously trained network. We should take the uncertainty presence into account by using a modified training set to teach the network to take the uncertainty presence into account computing the output uncertainty introducing the concept of *doubtful* prediction.

The training set is too small to embed the information regarding the uncertainty value, but we can create a new enlarged training set by replicating the actual examples while changing them according to the expected uncertainty level. As explained in the previous section, there is not a defined rule to decide how large the added uncertainty has to be.

The larger the uncertainty is, the smoother the surface becomes; fig. 19 shows the result of the conventional training plus two examples obtained with $\pm 60\%$ and $\pm 120\%$ of the expected maximum uncertainties. The training obtained with $\pm 60\%$ has been considered in the following.

It is now possible to compute the uncertainty of the risk index by employing eqn. 8 since the two measurements can be assumed uncorrelated (they are obtained using different instruments under different conditions and with different operators). The input uncertainty is given as the maximum deviation and we can assume a rectangular distribution so that we can use eqn. 10. Fig. 20 shows the results obtained by the conventional and enhanced training.

The physician has now a whole range of risk-values and information regarding the reliability of the prediction. A comparison with the *raw* results can be made by dividing the patients into three categories namely low risk, doubtful, and high risk. The criterion to

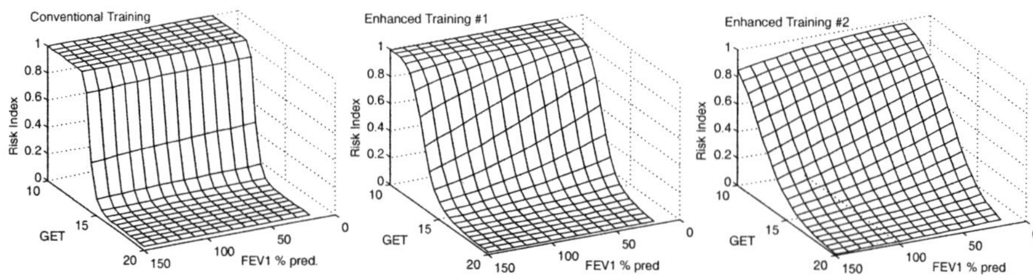

Figure 19: Comparison of the surfaces obtained with the conventional and enhanced training. Two examples of enhanced training with different uncertainties.

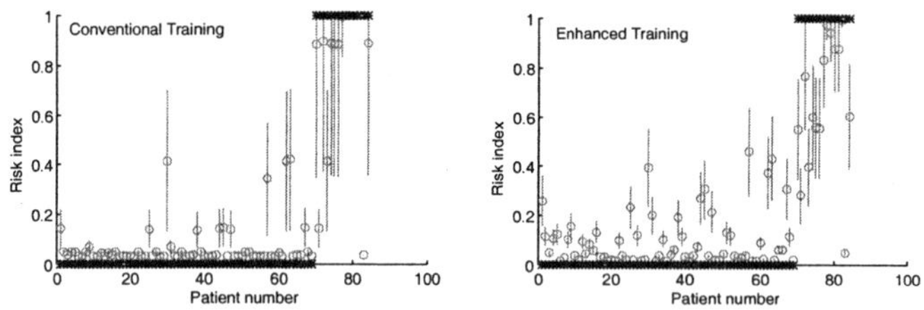

Figure 20: Network output with conventional and enhanced training.

flag the patients as doubtful is somehow arbitrary and has to be chosen as a trade off between the number of tolerated errors and the number of unclassified patients. This issue will be more extensively discussed in the second example; in this case a patient is classified as high risk if the network output minus its uncertainty is above 0.5, low risk if the network output plus its uncertainty is below 0.5, and doubtful otherwise.

By employing this choice the network gives 71 correct predictions (instead of the 81 of the simple data analysis), 2 wrong predictions (instead of 3) and flags 10 patients as doubtful. One should note that the reduction in the number of prediction errors is remarkable: since one of the patient died due to Acute Respiratory Distress Syndrome, which is a not predictable event, the surgically connected *problems* reduce from two to one (at the expense of 10 unclassified patients).

A more complete validation of the network behavior and a complete discussion about the correct criterion to flag a patient as doubtful would require to test the network with new medical cases. Unfortunately, the probability that a patient flagged *high risk* should encounter severe problems is very high and therefore ethical reasons would suggest avoiding interventions on these patients (this is the purpose of the network!). It is not likely there will be other examples of high risk patients who undergo an operation. This means that the training cannot be substantially improved and the validation will mainly be *one way* (i.e. low risk or doubtful patients who are operated and encounter severe problems).

As a final comment to this example we could ask ourself: is all the work with the neural networks worthwhile in this application? The answer is open: after all we have only two inputs and their combination is something like a weighted mean; we could obtain similar prediction results using a *conventional* statistical approach. In addition, the final patient classification into the three categories has been made in an arbitrary way: the statistical approach could have been used instead.

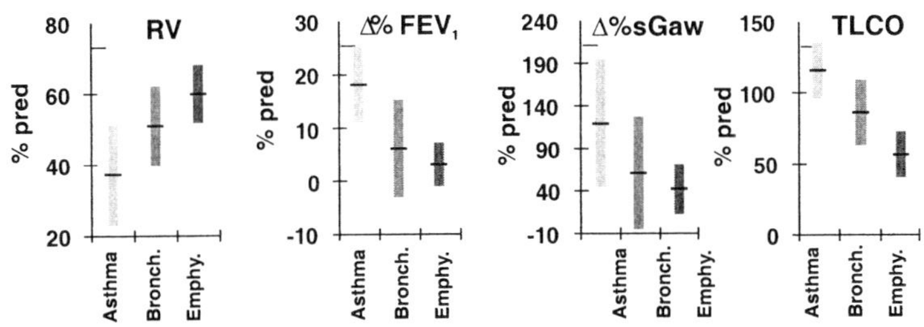

Figure 21: Mean and standard deviation of the four parameters within the three groups.

13.4.2 Example #2: Classification of pulmonary diseases employing non-invasive tests

This second example deals with a classification problem, i.e. with another great class of medical problems often tackled with neural networks. The example deal with the classification of pulmonary diseases between: Asthma, Bronchitis and Emphysema. This is still an open problem since several functional non-invasive tests has been proposed to perform this classification, but none has proved to be completely reliable.

This work is therefore aimed at discovering a way of processing the results of different tests in order to obtain an Asthma, Bronchitis or Emphysema *pathology evidence index*. More details on this example can be found in [50].

The example has been developed working on a population of 158 patients with diagnosis carried out according to the American Thoracic Society: 37 suffering from asthma, 79 suffering from bronchitis, and 42 suffering from emphysema. Patient's data were collected in three different periods with different systems: 96 cases in 1997 and early 1998, 15 cases in early 1999, and 47 cases in late 1999.

Four clinical tests were chosen as predictive of the actual pathology: two related to general lung parameters: (Residual lung Volume RV and Transfer Lung factor for Carbon monOxide $TLCO$) and two related to the change of respiratory parameters before and after bronchodilator (Forced Expired Volume in 1 s $\Delta\%FEV_1$ and specific airway conductance $\Delta\%sGaw$). Test results are expressed in percentage of their predicted values.

Fig. 21 shows mean and standard deviation of the four parameters within the three groups. It is easy to see that a correlation exists between parameters and pathology even though the standard deviations are rather high.

This is a typical classification problem we can tackle either by employing a Bayesian statistical approach i.e. the so called *linear discriminant score* [51], in which we assign to each output a *score* the exams refer to a specific pathology or by means of some kind of neural networks.

Eqn. 14 shows the structure of the linear discriminant score where d_A, d_B, d_E are the three scores, $a_{1A}...a_{4E}$ are 12 parameters that weight the four exams and c_A, c_B, c_E are three penalty coefficients.

$$
\begin{aligned}
d_A &= a_{1A}x_{RV} + a_{2A}x_{FEV} + a_{3A}x_{sGaw} + a_{4A}x_{TLCO} - c_A \\
d_B &= a_{1B}x_{RV} + a_{2B}x_{FEV} + a_{3B}x_{sGaw} + a_{4B}x_{TLCO} - c_B \\
d_E &= a_{1E}x_{RV} + a_{2E}x_{FEV} + a_{3E}x_{sGaw} + a_{4E}x_{TLCO} - c_E
\end{aligned}
\tag{14}
$$

The discriminant score requires therefore to identify a total of 15 parameters. Eqn. 14 can be rewritten in matrix form:

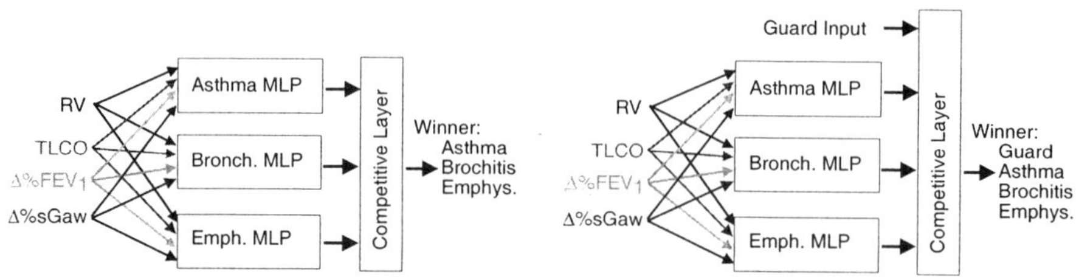

Figure 22: The neural network approach based on three MLPs plus a competitive layer. On the right the enhanced version with the guard neuron.

$$\mathbf{d} = \mathbf{Ax} - \mathbf{c} \tag{15}$$

where:

$$\mathbf{d} = \begin{bmatrix} d_A \\ d_B \\ d_E \end{bmatrix}; \mathbf{A} = \begin{bmatrix} a_{1A} & a_{2A} & a_{3A} & a_{4A} \\ a_{1B} & a_{2B} & a_{3B} & a_{4B} \\ a_{1E} & a_{2E} & a_{3E} & a_{4E} \end{bmatrix}; \mathbf{x} = \begin{bmatrix} x_{RV} \\ x_{FEV} \\ x_{sGaw} \\ x_{TLCO} \end{bmatrix}; \mathbf{c} = \begin{bmatrix} c_A \\ c_B \\ c_E \end{bmatrix} \tag{16}$$

The identification of $\mathbf{A}$ and $\mathbf{c}$ can be obtained by computing the pooled covariance matrix S of the data, the mean value of each test $\mathbf{x_k}$ and the vector $\mathbf{q}$ of the frequencies of each pathology:

$$\begin{aligned} \mathbf{A} &= (\overline{\mathbf{x_k}}'\mathbf{S}^{-1}) \\ \mathbf{c} &= -\tfrac{1}{2}\overline{\mathbf{x_k}}'\mathbf{S}^{-1}\mathbf{x_k} + \ln(\mathbf{q}) \end{aligned} \tag{17}$$

The neural network approach can use a Multi Layer Perceptron (MPL) architecture. We can conceive at least three possibilities:

a) One single-output triple-level-output MPL.

b) One single-level triple-output MLP.

c) Three single-level, single-output MLPs (each MLP trained to identify one of the three pathologies)

The solution with three MLPs allows simpler networks to be employed with 2 or 3 neurons in the hidden layer for each network. This in turn reduces dramatically the number of network parameters of each network and greatly speeds up the training. Each network is trained to produce an output in the range of 0 to 1 (no identification to complete identification). The three outputs have to be combined together to obtain the required classification. The neural network equivalent of the linear discriminant score is the use of a *competitive layer* i.e. a *winner takes all* approach as shown in fig. 22.

In order to compare the performance of the linear discriminant score with respect to the neural network, the patients were divided into a training set composed of 55 patients (13 asthma, 29 bronchitis, 13 emphysema) and a test set composed of 103 patients (24 asthma, 50 bronchitis, 29 emphysema). The training set was used to compute $\mathbf{A}$ and $\mathbf{c}$, for the discriminant score approach, and to train the neural network.

The selection of the patients to be included in the training set was manually performed by a physician who chose among the patients of the first group. The manual selection is required because there are several different *flavours* of each pathology. If we had a very large training set we would be sure of having all the important aspects included in the training set, but with a small training set we must be sure to include at least one example of each *flavour* in the training set.

Once the MLPs are trained with the enhanced training approach described in the previous section, the neural system fails only 8 times (15%) within the training and 23 times (22%) within the test set.

The linear discriminant score system is able to identify 43 patients within the training set with 12 errors (22%) and 70 patients within the test set with 33 errors (32%).

The combination MLPs+Cl therefore performs better than the linear discriminant approach even though we still have several errors. This behavior is intrinsically connected with the CL use: the CL always produces a winner, even though no network is really activated, therefore it is reasonable that most errors can be avoided by discarding too weak winners. This behavior can be obtained by employing a modified Competitive Layer as shown in the right hand side of fig. 22.

Of course the problem becomes the choice of the *correct* guard level. Using a high guard level permits one to avoid most of the errors, but at the expense of several unclassified patients. Using a low guard level reduces the unclassified patients, but also the guard effectiveness; the choice is a trade-off between the two requirements and can be obtained by observing the guard effect on the training set as shown in fig. 23.

The guard neuron use allows one to highlight doubtful or unclassified cases avoiding gross errors, but we still lack a *classification reliability* indicator. This indicator can be obtained by employing a further *post processing* that takes the input uncertainty presence into account. Firstly the three outputs are combined together to highlight the evidence of one pathology with respect to the other two thus computing an *evidence index* e_k:

$$\begin{array}{l} e_k = n_k \prod_{j \neq k} (1 - n_j) \\ k, j = \langle asthma, bronchitis, emphysema \rangle \end{array} \tag{18}$$

where k and j are the pathology indexes which use a modulo-three algebra (i.e if $k = emphysema$ then $k + 1 = asthma$) and n_k and n_j are the correspondent network outputs.

The uncertainty of the evidence indexes can then be computed as:

$$u_c^2(e_i) = \sum_{j=asthma}^{emphysema} s_{ij}^2 u^2(p_j) \tag{19}$$

where: $u_c(e_i)$ is the combined standard uncertainty of ith evidence index, i.e. the expected standard deviation of ith evidence index; $u(p_j)$ is the standard uncertainty of the jth clinical test, and s_{ij} are the sensitivity coefficients of the ith evidence index with respect to the jth clinical test.

The evidence indexes and their uncertainties can eventually be used to define whether the pathology is *clear* or *doubtful*.

Again several criteria can be used to flag a patient as doubtful such as the actual value of the Evidence Index and its uncertainty or the difference between the two highest indexes. The criteria selection is arbitrary, though not critical and the previewed performance of each criteria can be compared by plotting the number of errors vs the number of missed diagnoses within the training set. Fig. 23 shows the results obtained by the simple guard neuron and two different criteria based on the evidence indexes. It is easy to see that the evidence indexes behave better than the guard neuron and that the results of the different criteria are rather similar.

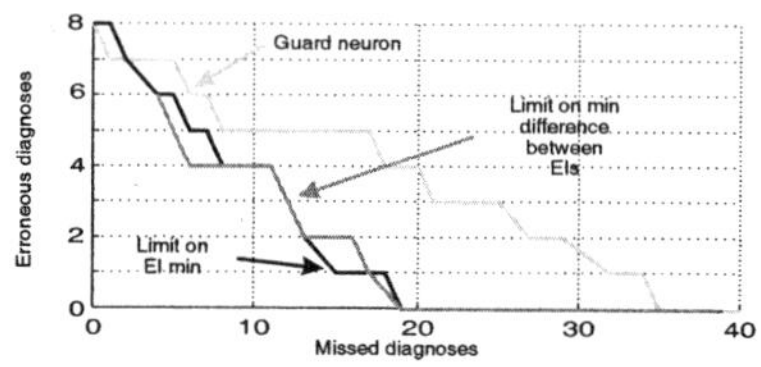

Figure 23: Trade-off between errors and missed diagnoses for the guard neuron and different criteria on the evidence indexes.

At this time, since all the tunings have been done, it is possible to compare the different approaches within the test set. Fig. 24 shows the number of errors and missing diagnoses for the guard-based neural network, with different guard levels, in comparison with the linear discriminant score. The fig. 25 shows the performance of the evidence index approach with different thresholds. The two figures show that the evidence index system behaves better than the others not only in the training set, but in the test set too.

As we did in the previous example we could ask ourself if the neural network introduction is worthwhile. Actually, the neural network approach *seems* easier to implement than the *conventional* statistical approach and *seems* to work better. However we employed only linear statistics, a non-linear statistical approach would probably produce results that are close to the MLP.

The neural network with the guard neuron *seems* to be much better than the *conventional* statistical approach, but we surely could obtain similar results by further manipulating the triplet of discriminant scores, thus introducing the doubtful class into the statistical approach.

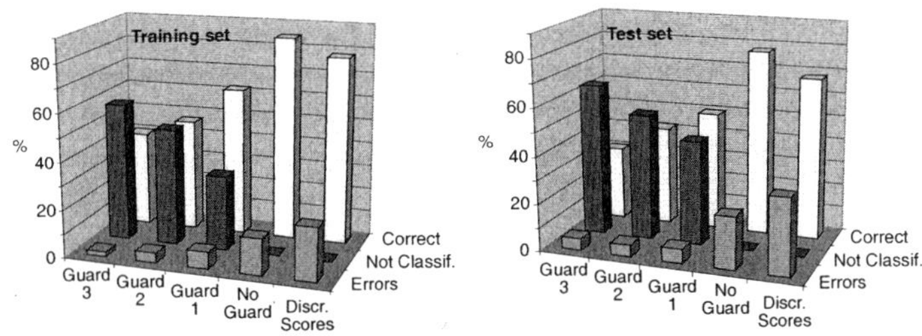

Figure 24: Performance comparison of linear discriminant score and MLP+Cl+ guard neuron.

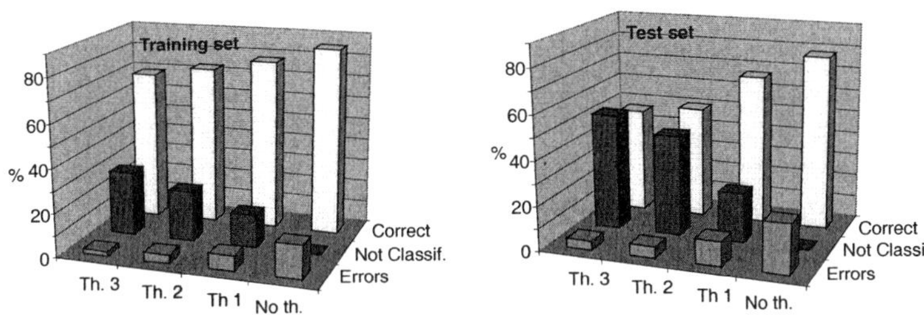

Figure 25: Performance comparison of the evidence index method with different thresholds.

References

[1] *Medical instrumentation, application and design*, Webster editor, Jonh Wiley and Sons Inc., 1995.

[2] Y. Nagasaka A. Iwata and N. Suzumura, "Data compression of the ecg using neural network for digital Holter monitor" *IEEE Engineering in Medicine and Biology Magazine*, vol. 9, no. 3, pp. 53–57, Sept. 1990.

[3] Ick-Tae Kang Ju-Won Lee Han-Wook Lee, Jong-Hoe Lee and Gun-Ki Lee, "A study on lung nodule detection using neural networks" in *Proceedings of the IEEE Region 10 Conference*, vol. 2, pp. 1150–1153.

[4] Tzi-Dar Chiueh C.K. Chen and Jyh-Horng Chen, "Active cancellation system of acoustic noise in MR imaging" *IEEE Trans. on Biomedical Engineering*, vol. 46, no. 2, pp. 186–191, Feb. 1999.

[5] C. Pappas N. Maglaveras, T. Stamkopoulos and M. Gerassimos Strintzis, "An adaptive backpropagation neural network for real-time ischemia episodes detection: development and performance analysis using the european ST-T database" *IEEE Trans. on Biomedical Engineering*, vol. 45, no. 7, pp. 805–813, July 1998.

[6] B. Hudgins R. Grieve, P.A. Parker and K. Englehart, "Nonlinear adaptive filtering of stimulus artifact" *IEEE Trans. on Biomedical Engineering*, vol. 47, no. 3, pp. 389–395, March 2000.

[7] E. Haselsteiner and G. Pfurtscheller, "Using time-dependent neural networks for EEG classification" *IEEE Trans. on Rehabilitation Engineering*, vol. 8, no. 4, pp. 457–463, Dec. 2000.

[8] P. Simpson T. Brotherton, T. Pollard and A. DeMaria, "Classifying tissue and structure in echocardiograms" *IEEE Engineering in Medicine and Biology Magazine*, vol. 13, no. 5, pp. 754–760, Nov.-Dec. 1994.

[9] R. Silipo and C. Marchesi, "Neural techniques for ST-T change detection" *Computer in Cardiology*, pp. 677–680, 1996.

[10] S. Selvan and R. Srinivasan, "A novel adaptive filtering technique for the processing of abdominal fetal electrocardiogram using neural network" in *Adaptive Systems for Signal Processing, Communications, and Control Symposium 2000*, pp. 289–292.

[11] H.J. Ritter T. W. Nattkemper and W. Schubert, "A neural classifier enabling high-throughput topological analysis of lymphocytes in tissue sections" *IEEE Trans. on Information Technology in Biomedicine*, vol. 5, no. 2, pp. 138–149, June 2001.

[12] C.I. Christodoulou and C.S. Pattichis, "Unsupervised pattern recognition for the classification of EMG signals" *IEEE Trans. on Biomedical Engineering*, vol. 46, no. 2, pp. 169–178, Feb. 1999.

[13] J.F. Sobh M.R. Risk and J.O. Saul, "Beat detection and classification of ECG using self organizing maps" in *Proceedings of the 19th Annual International Conference of the IEEE*, vol. 1, pp. 89–91.

[14] The IBM Microelectronics - Essonnes Component Development Laboratory - White cell blood identification, http://www-5.ibm.com/fr/cdlab/zblcell.html

[15] T. Koder W. Eppler T. Fischer, H. Gemmeke and R. Stotzka, "Neural chip Sand/1 for real time pattern recognition" *IEEE trans. on Nuclear Science*, vol. 45, pp. 1819–1823, Aug. 1998.

[16] Y.H. Hu Q. Xue and W.J. Tompkins, "Neural-network-based adaptive matched filtering for QRS detection" *IEEE Trans. on Biomedical Engineering*, vol. 39, no. 4, pp. 317–329, April 1992.

[17] H. Nakajima K. Minami and T. Toyoshima, "Real-time discrimination of ventricular tachyarrhythmia with Fourier-Transform neural network" *IEEE Trans. on Biomedical Engineering*, vol. 45, no. 2, pp. 179–185, Feb. 1999.

[18] Simon Haykin, *Adaptive Filter Theory*, Prentice-Hall International Edition, 1991.

[19] Massachusetts Inst.Technol., Database Distribution, http://ecg.mit.edu/

[20] Silicon Recognition, http://www.silirec.com/

[21] H. Dickhaus and H. Heinrich, "Identification of high risk patients in cardiology by Wavelet networks" in *Engineering in Medicine and Biology Society, 1996.*, vol. 3, pp. 923–924.

[22] G. Coppini R. Poli S. Cagnoni R. Livi and G. Valli, "A neural network expert system for diagnosing and treating hypertension" *Computer*, vol. 24, no. 3, pp. 64–71, March 1991.

[23] Hong Zhang Zhen Zhang and R.C. Bast Jr., "An application of artificial neural networks in ovarian cancer early detection" in *Proceedings of the IEEE-INNS-ENNS International Joint Conference onNeural Networks, 2000*, vol. 4, pp. 107–112.

[24] J. Dripps E. Braithwaite and A.F. Murray, "Prediction of onset of respiratory disorder in neonates" vol. 4, pp. 2203–2207.

[25] W. Welkowitz Y.M. Akay, M. Akay and J. Kostis, "Noninvasive detection of coronary artery disease" *IEEE Engineering in Medicine and Biology Magazine*, vol. 13, no. 5, pp. 761–764, Nov.-Dec. 1994.

[26] E.J. Tkacz and P. Kostka, "An application of Wavelet neural network for classification of patients with coronary artery disease based on hrv analysis" in *Proceedings of the 22nd Annual International Conference of the IEEE Engineering in Medicine and Biology Society, 2000*, vol. 2, pp. 1391–1393.

[27] Z. Trajanoski and P. Wach, "Neural predictive controller for insulin delivery using the subcutaneous route" *IEEE Trans. on Biomedical Engineering*, vol. 45, no. 9, pp. 1122–1134, Sept. 1998.

[28] P.E. Undrill J.S. Gregory, R.M. Junold and R.M. Aspen, "Analysis of trabecular bone structure using Fourier Transforms and neural networks" *IEEE Transactions on Information Technology in Biomedicine*, vol. 3, no. 4, pp. 289–294, Dec. 1999.

[29] Schnorrenberg F. Tsapatsoulis N. C.S. Pattichis C.N. Schizus S. Kollias M. Vassiliou A. Adamou and K. Kyriacou, "Improved detection of breast cancer nuclei using modular neural networks" *IEEE Engineering in Medicine and Biology Magazine*, vol. 19, no. 1, pp. 48–63, Jan.-Feb. 2000.

[30] J.Y. Lo W.H. Land Jr., T. Masters and D.W. McKee, "Application of evolutionary computation and neural network hybrids for breast cancer classification using mammogram and history data" in *Proceedings of the 2001 Congress on Evolutionary Computation, 2001*, vol. 2, pp. 1147–1154.

[31] C.Net2000+, Cardionetics, http://www.cardionetics.com

[32] Holter 2010 Plus, Holter Software for Windows, Philips, http://www3.medical.philips.com/

[33] A. Taddei F. Jager, G.B. Moody and R.G. Mark, "Performance measures for algorithms to detect transient ischemic ST segment changes" in *Computers in Cardiology 1991, Proceedings.*, pp. 369–372.

[34] F. Pincinoli P. Bozola G. Bortolan, C. Combi and C. Brohet, "A hybrid neuro-fuzzy system for ECG classification of myocardial infarction" 1996, pp. 241–244.

[35] Donna L. Hudson and Maurice E. Cohen, *Neural Network and Artificial Intelligence for Biomedical Engineering*, IEEE Press Series in Biomedical Engineering, 2000.

[36] Horul Global HealtNet Inc. 7370 Hodgson Memorial Dr., Suite F3, Savannah, GA, 31406.

[37] Emmanuel C. Ifeachor Paulo J.G. Lisboa and Piotr S. Szczepaniak, *Artificial Neural Network in Biomedicine*, Springer, 1999.

[38] Simon Haykin, *Neural Network, a comprehensive foundation*, Prentice Hall, 1999.

[39] Lutz Prechelt, "PROBEN1 — A set of benchmarks and benchmarking rules for neural network training algorithms" Tech. Rep. 21/94, Fakultät für Informatik, Universität Karlsruhe, D-76128 Karlsruhe, Germany, 1994, Anonymous FTP: /pub/papers/techreports/1994/1994-21.ps.Z on ftp.ira.uka.de.

[40] PhysioNet, MIT Room E25-505A, 77 Massachusetts Avenue, Cambridge, MA 02139 USA, http://www.physionet.org/

[41] Wisconsin Breast Cancer Database, collected by Dr. William H. Wolberg, University of Wisconsin Hospitals, Madison, ftp://ftp.cs.wisc.edu/math-prog/cpo-dataset/machine learn/

[42] University of South Florida, DDSM: Digital Database for Screening Mammography, http://marathon.csee.usf.edu/Mammography/Database.html

[43] ENV 13005 ISO, *Guide to the Expression of Uncertainty in Measurement*, 1999.

[44] A. F. Murray and P. J. Edwards, "Enhanced mlp performance and fault tolerance resulting from weight noise during training" *IEEE Trans. on NN*, vol. 5, no. 3, pp. 792–802, Sept 1994.

[45] J. S. N. Jean and J. Wang, "Weight smoothing to improve network generalisation" *IEEE Trans. on NN*, vol. 5, no. 5, pp. 752–763, Sept 1994.

[46] L. Holmstrom and P. Koistinen, "Using additive noise in back-propagation training" *IEEE Trans. on NN*, vol. 3, no. 1, pp. 24–38, Jan 1992.

[47] C. K. Mohan R. Anand, K. G. Mehrotra and S. Ranka, "An improved algorithm for neural network classification of imbalanced training sets" *IEEE Trans. on NN*, vol. 4, no. 6, pp. 962–969, Nov 1993.

[48] M. Parvis C. Gulotta and R. Torchio, "Evaluation of a postoperative risk index after lung resection by means of a neural network" in *Proceedings of the XIV IMEKO World Congress*, vol. 7, pp. 210–215.

[49] R. Torchio M. Parvis, C. Gulotta, "Evaluation of surgical risks by means of neural networks in the presence of uncertainties" *Measurement*, vol. 23, no. 3, pp. 171–178, Apr 1998.

[50] R. Torchio M. Parvis, C. Gulotta, "Mixed neural-conventional processing to differentiate airway diseases by means of functional non-invasive tests" *IEEE Trans. on IM*, vol. 50, no. 2, pp. 819–824, June 2000.

[51] A. A. Afifi and S. P. Azen, *Statistical Analysis, a computer oriented approach*, Academic Press, Inc., 1979.

Index

D

E

F

G

H

I

J

K

L

M

N

O

P

R

S

T

U

V

W

Z

Author Index